A City Possessed

A CITY POSSESSED

The Christchurch Civic Crèche Case

LYNLEY HOOD

OTAGO UNIVERSITY PRESS
Te Whare Tā o Te Wānanga o Ōtākou

First published in 2001 by Longacre Press, Dunedin
Republished in 2019 by Otago University Press, Dunedin
Te Whare Tā o Te Wānanga o Ōtākou
Level 1, 398 Cumberland Street
Dunedin, New Zealand
university.press@otago.ac.nz
www.otago.ac.nz/press

© Lynley Hood

Lynley Hood asserts her moral right to be identified as the author of this work.

ISBN 978-1-98-853185-4

A catalogue record for this book is available from the National Library of New Zealand. This book is copyright. Except for the purpose of fair review, no part may be stored or transmitted in any form or by any means, electronic or mechanical, including recording or storage in any information retrieval system, without permission in writing from the publishers. No reproduction may be made, whether by photocopying or by any other means, unless a licence has been obtained from the publisher.

Author photograph: Victor Billot

Printed in New Zealand by printing.com, Wellington

*To freedom of speech,
to the author's moral right to the integrity of the work
and to Sandra Moran and John Tizard*

Contents

PUBLISHER'S NOTE 9
AUTHOR'S NOTE 13
CHRONOLOGY 15
ABBREVIATIONS 17
PROLOGUE 19

1. WHAT'S THE PROBLEM? 23

2. SEX, SEXISM AND THE NEW DEMONOLOGY 38
    2.i The Strands of the Seventies 39
    2.ii The Knotted Web of the Eighties 48

3. CRIMEN EXCEPTUM 69
    3.i The Rise of the Sexual Abuse Specialist 70
    3.ii *Crimen Exceptum* 88

4. CHRISTCHURCH POSSESSED 106
    4.i The Place 106
    4.ii The Fever 110
    4.iii The Epidemic 120
    4.iv The Ongoing Malaise 139

5. AND A LITTLE CHILD SHALL MISLEAD THEM 151
    5.i Enter the Devil 151
    5.ii A Model for Early Childhood Education 166
    5.iii Peter Ellis 180
    5.iv The First Allegation 195

6. A COMPLAINT HAS BEEN MADE 208
    6.i The Scapegoat 208
    6.ii The Meeting Was Somewhat Volatile 223
    6.iii Reinstatement Is Not an Option 234
    6.iv The Police Investigation Has Been Reactivated 244

7. PARENTS IN TERROR OF ABUSE DISCOVERY 267
    7.i There Seemed to be No Logic to It 267
    7.ii Peter Was as Good as Hung 283

8. The Whole Crèche Thing Has Blown Up 300
    8.i Anyone Who Has Concerns Should Get in Touch 300
    8.ii A Sustained Campaign of State-Funded Contamination of the Evidence 322
    8.iii Concerns of Abuse by Other Crèche Staff (Totally Confidential) 338

9. They Were All Under Suspicion 353
    9.i It Was Like a Police State Thing Closing In 353
    9.ii Four Child Care Workers Arrested 366

10. Depositions 383

11. Pre-trial Manoeuvres 402

12. The Trial 421
    12.i The Beginning 421
    12.ii The End 449

13. The Aftermath 470
    13.i The Tide Turns 470
    13.ii The Women's Costs Application 473
    13.iii The Nigel Hampton QC Appeal 476
    13.iv The Graham Panckhurst QC Appeal 478
    13.v Graham Panckhurst QC Considers his Options 490
    13.vi *Davidson and Others* v. *Christchurch City Council* 494
    13.vii More Calls for an Inquiry 504
    13.viii The Christchurch City Council Appeals the Employment Court Decision 509

14. The Royal Prerogative of Mercy 514
    14.i The Safety Net 514
    14.ii Testing the Safety Net 517

15. Doing Justice 523
    15.i. New Evidence 523
    15.ii The Judith Ablett-Kerr QC Appeal 528

16. 'It is a Case that Simply Will Not Go Away' 534

References 547
Index 575

Publisher's Note

A CITY POSSESSED: The Christchurch Civic Creche Case by Lynley Hood was first published in hardback by Longacre Press in Dunedin in 2001. It went on to win the Montana Medal for Non-Fiction at the 2002 Montana New Zealand Book Awards.

By then Peter Ellis had completed seven years of his 10-year sentence for child sexual abuse and had been released. All his appeal efforts to that date and since have failed and in 2019, aged 61 and diagnosed with terminal cancer, he still carries the weight of his conviction.

On 31 July 2019 he was granted leave for a final appeal to the Supreme Court. The hearing is set down for mid-November 2019.

This edition of *A City Possessed*, in paperback and ebook, is an *unrevised* reprint of the original book. Small parts of the text (such as the description of Christchurch, written before the earthquakes of 2010–11 and the horrific events of 15 March 2019) are now out of date, but have been retained as important elements of the context of the times in which the events occurred. The essence of Hood's extensive research and detailed accounts of the events that unfolded remain relevant today.

We hope republication will enable members of the public unfamiliar with the case to acquaint themselves with the detail of a case that is, almost 20 years on, once again before the courts.

A sample of reviews of the original publication:

> **Chris Bourke** *North & South*
> Lynley Hood has left no stone unturned in her 672-page examination of the Civic Creche saga, *A City Possessed, that took her seven years to write. The title reflects the conclusion she draws: that a 'moral panic' took place within elements of Christchurch society, driven by madcap political fashions, homophobia or old-fashioned Puritanism.*

Sarah Farquhar *NZ Herald*
A City Possessed *is scholarly in tone but is a gripping and accessible read ... Indeed this is a book that is likely to be referred to by lawyers, historians, sociologists, social workers, child health professionals, psychiatrists and, I hope, educational administrators for years to come.*

Michael Corballis *New Zealand Listener*
This courageous book ... is a detailed, step-by-step account of what happened in the Christchurch Civic Creche case. Lynley Hood has set this sorry affair in the context of the wave of hysteria over ritual child abuse that swept the Western world in the 1980s and early 1990s, and examined some of the historical precedents.

Lisa Brown *Journal Australia & NZ Psychiatry*
Whether or not you agree with author Lynley Hood's views on the falseness of the allegations is not the point of reading this book, the book effectively raises questions that anyone in the area of child sexual abuse will find interesting and challenging.

Ian Freckelton *New Zealand Lawyer*
... a landmark work ... It is well written, excellently edited and professionally presented. It walks the difficult line between a scholarly work and a book that is engaging and accessible. Ultimately, it does so successfully, entertaining, provoking and chronicling an extraordinary legal and social saga which is deserving of the kind of in-depth treatment given ...

Barry Colman *National Business Review*
I think there's a really huge disquiet among New Zealanders everywhere about what happened in that trial. We have got a deep sense of unease about the entire episode. [This] book has been an absolute revelation in this whole affair.

Anthony Frith *Varsity*
Anyone who has reached their own conclusions about Ellis's guilt without reading Hood's extraordinarily well researched and argued A City Possessed *should bite their tongue and hold their pride until they have read it.*

Dr Jim Hefford *New Zealand GP*
Her book is a devastating indictment of the virtual reality rituals of the courtroom, and of significant sections of the counsellors and doctors involved in the sexual abuse field.

Gavin McLean *Otago Daily Times*
This is an important, engrossing and highly disturbing book. Whether you believe Peter Ellis's innocence or not – and I am inclined to – it is worth reading and discussing for the wider issues that emerge. At a time when educators and parents are lamenting the poor performance of boys in schools, any ideological and legal barriers to males entering the caring and teaching professions should be examined closely.

Michael Morrissey *Investigate*
Lynley Hood, an accomplished biographer, has focused her considerable talents on the highly controversial Peter Ellis case. This is a remarkably thorough book which may succeed in prompting an eventual clearance of Ellis's name – a vindication which many believe is overdue.

Greg Newbold *The Best*
Having untangled and examined the numerous threads that make up the Peter Ellis story, Lynley Hood had to weave them into a comprehensible and readable format. The result is nothing less than outstanding; an encyclopaedic work of professorial quality. Hood's treatment is a compelling authority; an opus so deep, detailed, insightful and comprehensive that nobody could now be said to have an informed opinion about the case without having read her book.

Katherine Rich *The Star*
When I picked up Lynley Hood's book A City Possessed *I worried that I wouldn't have the time or the inclination to finish it. I shouldn't have worried. The book is unputdownable.*

Jim Tucker *Daily News*
It takes great courage to step outside mainstream thought and suggest it is not OK to distort the law, condone over-zealous counselling and police work, and cause collateral damage in a quest to rid the country of child molesters. This is what Hood, a 58-year-old Dunedin scientist, writer and grandmother, has done in this book.

Mike Behrens Q.C. *Manawatu Standard*
This is not bandwagon stuff. Hood makes her points clinically and with the authority of an historian who has left no source unturned. Her approach is to state a position and then take lots and lots of words to explain why that is so. It is a technique that works to produce a sickness in the gut ... A City Possessed is a remarkable and notable work. It is full of erudition and sarky wit and is in a style that can strip paint.

Author's Note

MOST OF THE DOCUMENTS on which the Civic Crèche case is based were made public in the course of successive criminal and employment court proceedings. I obtained additional information under the Official Information Act and from interviews with the people involved. To protect the confidentiality of individuals who do not want their identities revealed, my research has been placed under seal for a hundred years. For the same reason I must thank the people who contributed to this book collectively rather than individually. However, this in no way diminishes my gratitude.

Researching and writing this book often felt like the literary equivalent of a solo crossing of Antarctica. From time to time generous individuals emerged from the mist, provided me with emotional, intellectual and spiritual sustenance, and pointed me in the right direction for the journey ahead. A handful of people with expertise in a range of disciplines read my rough drafts and pulled me up whenever they felt I was unfair, unclear or wrong. But they never tried to stop me being controversial or politically incorrect. To everyone who helped along the way – you know who you are – a thousand thanks.

I have used the real names of the individuals and organisations who appear in the book in a significant official capacity (lawyers, police officers and others involved in the justice system, members of the helping professions, members of Parliament, journalists, public servants, local body and union employees, and so on).

The complainant families in the crèche case, and the childcare workers who were not arrested, had their identities suppressed by court order. These people, and the other private individuals and families who became enmeshed in the events of this book, appear under pseudonyms. To help readers keep track of all these people, several identification systems have been used.

I have given families *not* involved in the crèche case single-letter surnames. Crèche families have pseudonyms based on the names of trees. To further assist readers, I have given all the members of any given family the same surname, even if in real life – as was often the case with crèche families – members of the same family had different surnames. For example, the family responsible for the first complaint in the crèche case appears in this book as Geoffrey Magnolia (son), Ms Magnolia (mother), Mr Magnolia (father), Aunt Magnolia (aunt), Grandma Magnolia (grandmother) and Grandpa Magnolia (grandfather).

In this book, each child involved in the crèche case court proceedings has a different surname. In real life, some complainant children were siblings, but a court order prevents the identification of sibling relationships. As a result, I have had to clone some complainant parents (i.e. even though the parents of complainant child X, and the parents of complainant child Y, appear in this book under different surnames, in real life both children may have the same set of parents).

As an additional *aide-memoire*, I have given crèche staff who were not arrested first-name pseudonyms beginning with 'S' (such as Sandi or Susannah), and gay or bisexual men caught up in the police search for a paedophile/child pornography ring first-name pseudonyms beginning with 'B' (such as Brian and Bruce). First-name pseudonyms for children have been allocated more or less at random.

From its inception until the present day, the Christchurch Civic Crèche case has been sustained by rumours – some true, some false, some a mixture of both. Addressing every constantly evolving rumour would be a pointless and never-ending task. Readers who wish to test the validity of rumours not addressed in this book should weigh them against the verifiable facts of the case, and draw their own conclusion.

Without the generosity of my endlessly supportive family and friends this project would never have been completed. The $9000 grant provided by the Arts Council of New Zealand (now Creative New Zealand) is also gratefully acknowledged.

Lynley Hood
DUNEDIN 2001

Christchurch Civic Crèche Case Chronology

1991

20 November	First complaint in crèche case.
21 November	Ellis suspended.
25–29 November	Education Review Office inspection of crèche.
2 December	First mass meeting for crèche parents.
20 December	Crèche investigation closed.

1992

23 January	Ellis dismissed.
30 January	First formal disclosure.
19 February	Crèche investigation reopened.
27 February	First formal disclosure resulting in a conviction. Formal interviews continue all year.
20 March	News of investigation breaks in media.
30 March	Ellis arrested.
31 March	Ellis's first court appearance. Second mass meeting for crèche parents.
6 August	Formal disclosure of 'circle incident'.
12 August	'Phase II' police inquiry established.
3 September	Crèche closed.
1 October	Four women crèche workers arrested (Davidson, Keys, Buckingham, Gillespie).
2 November	Depositions hearing begins.

1993

11 February	Depositions hearing ends.
5 March	Gillespie discharged.
6 April	Davidson, Keys and Buckingham discharged.
26 April	Ellis trial begins.
5 June	Ellis trial ends.
22 June	Ellis sentenced.
July	Government rejects calls for commission of inquiry.
15 December	Women crèche workers' application for costs declined.

1994
14 February	First Ellis appeal aborted (N. Hampton QC).
25–28 July	First Ellis appeal begins (G. Panckhurst QC).
5 August	Ellis appeal ends.
8 September	Appeal judgment delivered.

1995
22 February	Ellis applies for legal aid to Privy Council.
27 Feb–8 March	Crèche staff Employment Court case.
15 March	Ellis Privy Council legal aid application declined.
16 March	Crèche staff Employment Court interim judgment.
7 April	Crèche staff Employment Court supplementary judgment.
8 June	Government rejects calls for commission of inquiry.

1996
21–22 August	Crèche staff Employment Court appeal.
26 September	Crèche staff Employment Court appeal verdict.

1997
2 December	First Ellis petition for prerogative of mercy (Ablett-Kerr QC).

1998
February	Ellis refuses, and is refused, parole.
4 May	Ellis case referred to Court of Appeal.
18 November	Second Ellis petition for prerogative of mercy.

1999
January	Second Ellis petition referred to Sir Thomas Thorp.
February	Ellis refuses, and is refused, parole.
13 May	Ellis case referred to Court of Appeal.
5–9 July	Second Ellis appeal.
14 October	Second appeal judgment delivered.
18 October	Third Ellis petition for prerogative of mercy.

2000
2 February	Ellis completes sentence.
10 March	Eichelbaum Inquiry established.

2001
13 March	Eichelbaum Report released. Government rejects calls for pardon and commission of inquiry.

Abbreviations

ACC	Accident Compensation Commission/Corporation
CFGC	Child and Family Guidance Centre
COSA	Casualties of Sexual Allegations
CPT	Child Protection Team
CYPF	Children, Young Persons, and Their Families Act/Bill
CYPS	Children and Young Persons Service
DLSS	District Legal Services Subcommittee
DSAC	Doctors for Sexual Abuse Care
DSW	Department of Social Welfare
ERA	End Ritual Abuse (Incorporated)
ERO	Education Review Office
FVPCC	Family Violence Prevention Coordinating Committee
MMU	Medical Misadventure Unit (of ACC)
NZCA	New Zealand Childcare Association
PAIN	Parents Against Injustice
PTSD	Post Traumatic Stress Disorder
QC	Queen's Counsel
RAG	Ritual Action Group
SCU	Sensitive Claims Unit (of ACC)
START	Sexual Abuse Therapy and Rehabilitation Team (Incorporated)
THAW	The Health Alternatives for Women
TVNZ	Television New Zealand
YWCA	Young Women's Christian Association

Prologue

READERS OF A BOOK on the vexed topic of child sexual abuse are bound to have some questions about the author, so I shall begin by stating that I am a 58-year-old, heterosexual, politically liberal atheist (or to put it another way, I believe that our gods and demons are of our own making). I regard diversity as the spice of life, and favour rubbing along with those whose beliefs and practices differ from my own in a spirit of tolerance, good humour and compromise over attempting to live by (or, worse still, trying to force others to live by) any ideological dogma – be it political, social, economic, religious or whatever.

I have been married to the same man for more than 30 years. Like most women who raised children in the 1970s I gave up my career (in medical research) for full-time mothering during the preschool years of our three children. I read extensively and was active in several organisations involved with parenting and childcare. During my nine years as a La Leche League counsellor, I attended many counselling training programmes. I was also a research associate of the Dunedin Child Development Study.

As preschoolers, our children led busy social lives, playing with the children of friends, attending informal playgroups and, later, joining our local Playcentre. I recall from those years a great deal of infant and toddler nudity, and many conversations about the fascination that small children have with sex organs, bodily functions and how babies are made. There was also much discussion about the behaviour and development of individual children, but I cannot recall any variations in the norm being attributed to sexual abuse.

To the best of my knowledge none of my closest friends or relatives have complained of, or been accused of, sexual abuse. However, particularly during my work on this book, I have come to know many people in both categories, and many more who regard their unhappy sexual experiences as too fraught with ambiguities for any such classification. The person I know best who was emotionally, physically and possibly also sexually abused as a child was the subject of my first biography: New Zealand writer and educationalist Sylvia Ashton-Warner.[1]

From Ashton-Warner I learnt that sexual abuse is but one form of childhood trauma, and that the causes and effects of all such traumas are complex and intertwined. I also learnt that fantasy and reality can be easily confused, and that even the most concrete words may express ideas that are more symbolic than real. Above all, I learnt that beneath the rational/logical level on which we live our daily lives flow the deep and swirling currents that Ashton-Warner called 'the dark forces of the undermind that determine our actions'.

An additional lesson, which I learnt from comparing the verifiable facts of Ashton-Warner's life with the stories told by people who knew her, was that memories are often unintentionally shaped and coloured by current beliefs, and that even the most perceptive and level-headed individuals may be mistaken in their recall of past events.

My present interest in child abuse in general, and in the Christchurch Civic Crèche case in particular, was not provoked by Sylvia Ashton-Warner, but by my more recent research into the life and death of New Zealand's most famous dead childcare worker, Minnie Dean – the only woman hanged by law in New Zealand.[2]

At the time of the Dean case a wildly contagious public anxiety about the evils of 'baby farming' was sweeping the Western world. In an effort to understand that anxiety I extended my research to the witch-hunts of the 16th and 17th centuries. Since that research will be referred to in this book, it is important to note that the term 'witch-hunt' will not be used here in the modern informal sense – in which it refers to people conspiring to bring down specific individuals – but as a descriptive term for a particular historical event and as an example of a distinctive community phenomenon that may occur at other times and places throughout history.

As a descriptive term, 'witch-hunt' is appropriate: witch-hunting was a constant peculiarity of 16th and 17th century witch prosecuting. Suspects were never obvious, they had to be found and identified; the existence of the special occupation of 'witch finder' indicates this.

To readers who regard witchcraft as an imaginary phenomenon, the prospect of comparing 16th and 17th century attitudes to witchcraft to late-20th-century attitudes to child sexual abuse may seem offensive. After all, child sexual abuse is a real problem. But at a community level, witchcraft too was real. Most of the individuals prosecuted as witches were sharp-tongued older women who offered spells, curses and potions for everything from love sickness to the plague. Sometimes – accidently or deliberately, by poisoning or by psychology – they did more harm than good. Witches were powerful and dangerous, and they made their neighbours understandably anxious.

But though witchcraft at a community level was real, the same cannot be said of the witchcraft sought by witch finders. These misogynists claimed that witchcraft was alarmingly common and a great threat to society. When they found no physical evidence to support their claims, they made another, more extravagant claim: they said that witches belonged to satanic cults of such secrecy and power that their members could indulge in large-scale depravity without leaving a trace.

As an example of a phenomenon that may occur at other times and places throughout history, the great witch-hunts represented the fusion of three separate but related sociological disturbances: a moral panic, an epidemic of mass psychogenic illness and an outbreak of scapegoating.

The first type of disturbance, a moral panic, was described by Stanley Cohen in his classic study *Folk Devils and Moral Panics* this way:

> Societies appear to be subject, every now and then, to periods of moral panic. A condition, episode, person or group of persons emerges to become defined as a threat to societal values and interests; its nature is presented in a stylised and stereotypical fashion by the mass media; the moral barricades are manned by editors, bishops, politicians and other right-thinking people; socially accredited experts pronounce their diagnoses and solutions; ways of coping are evolved or (more often) resorted to ... Sometimes the object of the panic is quite novel and at other times it is something which has been in existence long enough, but suddenly appears in the limelight. Sometimes the panic passes over and is forgotten, except in folklore and collective memory; at other times it has more serious and long-lasting repercussions and might produce such changes as those in legal and social policy or even in the way society conceives itself.[3]

The second type of disturbance, an epidemic of mass psychogenic illness, is an outbreak of an ailment that displays no clinical or laboratory abnormalities and has no scientifically proven cause. Its symptoms reflect the anxieties of the groups in which it proliferates. African schoolgirls blame their outbreaks of uncontrollable crying and laughter on the spirits of dead ancestors; Western schoolgirls blame their outbreaks of nausea and fainting on food poisoning and gas leaks. The victims of mass psychogenic illnesses are predominantly young women, but any age group and both sexes may be affected. In a form of the disorder known as mass psychogenic illness by proxy, one group (usually parents) attributes an imaginary illness to another group (usually children).[4]

The animistic thinking that underpins the third type of disturbance, scapegoating, was described by Sir James Frazer in his extraordinary 12-volume study of the history and anthropology of magic, religion and culture, *The Golden Bough*, this way:

> Because it is possible to shift a load of wood, stones, or what not from our own back to the back of another, the primitive fancies that it is equally possible to shift the burden of his pains and sorrows to another, who will suffer them in his stead. Upon this idea he acts, and the result is an endless number of very unamiable devices for palming off on someone else the trouble which a man shrinks from bearing himself.[5]

With the rise of scientific anthropology, Frazer's idiosyncratic work has come to be regarded as a relic from 'the Covent Garden school of mythology' (an allusion to London's fruit market), but, despite such reservations, his account of ritualised scapegoating remains the most extensive study of the topic undertaken, and his findings – that culturally sanctioned procedures for the symbolic expulsion of evil by means of a scapegoat can be found in most societies throughout human history – have never been seriously challenged.

It is in relation to these definitions, and from a scholarly interest in comparative social history, that the term 'witch-hunt' is used in this book.

> Previously I never thought of doubting that there were many witches in the world; now, however, when I examine the public record, I find myself believing that there are hardly any.
>
> – Friedrich von Spee, *Cautio Criminalis*
> *[Precautions for Prosecutors]*, 1631

> Why do people all over the world, and at all times, want marvels that defy all verifiable fact? And are the marvels brought into being by their desire, or is their desire an assurance rising from some deep knowledge, not to be directly experienced and questioned, that the marvellous is indeed an aspect of the real? ... All I had managed ... was a certainty that faith was a psychological reality, and that where it was not invited to fasten itself on things unseen, it invaded and raised bloody hell with things seen.
>
> – Robertson Davies, *Fifth Business*, 1970

> She said that it started with a wee story but it then got bigger.
>
> – Report on complainant child's retraction,
> Christchurch Civic Crèche case, 1994

CHAPTER 1

What's the Problem?

A POPULAR VANITY in our seemingly advanced society is that past evils took place in dark, uncivilised times, and the forward march of technology has been matched, step by step, with comparable advances in human wisdom. Unfortunately, the history of human folly shows that life is not that simple. That superstition, ignorance and gullibility are modern everyday realities was brought home to me forcefully in the course of my research into the life and death of the Winton baby farmer, Minnie Dean.

Though more than 100 years have passed since her death, Minnie Dean remains Southland's best-known citizen. When I visited the Deep South in search of memories and memorabilia, I was rewarded with a barrage of bizarre and gruesome stories. I was told that she killed babies with hat pins and knitting needles and rusty nails, and that she stuck pins into dolls. I was told that her victims were thrown into waterways, chopped up and fed to pigs or buried along country roadsides with clumps of a wildflower– known in Southland as 'Minnie Dean' – planted on top. Stories were legion about her train journeys, her hanging and her burial ('nothing will grow on her grave').

I came to realise that if I concentrated exclusively on the verifiable facts of the case I would be in danger of missing something important. Not only were most of the Minnie Dean stories demonstrably untrue, they had about them a whiff of folklore and superstition. Yet these were not tall tales recounted by ancient crones in backblocks villages. These stories were presented to me as fact by police officers, lawyers, journalists, farmers, doctors, social workers, housewives and teachers. All around me intelligent, well-educated people kept telling and retelling these stories, and equally intelligent people kept believing them.

Anyone familiar with children's literature will recognise in the Minnie Dean stories echoes of folktales that have been told at all times and all places around the globe. The surface details change with time and place, but the core motifs stay constant. Folktales are about death, injury, kidnapping, sex, tragedy and scandal.

Child abuse is a major folktale theme. In countless spine-chilling stories children are eaten by animals, murdered by stepmothers, cooked by witches and abandoned by uncaring parents.

As Jan Brunvand has shown in *The Vanishing Hitchhiker*, the creation and transmission of folklore is alive and well among modern city-dwellers. Present-day folktales, known as urban legends, are embroidered with details of time, place and source to add veracity. Despite the best efforts of researchers, urban legends nearly always turn out to be unverifiable. But people believe them, and the stories people believe hold an important place in their world view, whether they are actually true or not.[1]

Here are two urban legends on the age-old themes of child abuse and neglect. Story #1: At a given time and place a hippie babysitter got high on drugs. Then she popped a turkey in the oven, cooked it to perfection and ate it all up. And she never noticed that she hadn't cooked and eaten a turkey. She'd cooked and eaten the baby. Story #2: One day a young couple went on holiday before the babysitter arrived. The sitter was late; if they'd waited any longer they would have missed the plane. So they left the baby sitting happily in his highchair. Three weeks later they returned to find the baby still in his highchair. Dead from starvation.

What is it about these blood-curdling stories? Why are they so eternally and universally popular? According to folklorists, at a personal level such tales reflect our fears and gratify our desire to understand the bizarre and the frightening, the embarrassing and the dangerous. Their roots creep and twist deep into the human psyche – down through the foundations of adult rationality, down through the insecurities and guilts of ourselves as parents – to touch that most elemental human fear: that grandmother will turn into a wolf, that the giant will eat Jack, that the stepmother will poison Snow White – that, in the helpless vulnerability of our infancy, mother will turn murderer.[2]

At an interpersonal level, folktales reinforce our stereotypes and validate our ideals and institutions. They encourage us to be vigilant in the care of our children. They promote neighbourliness and censure anti-social behaviour. They help us identify the people we should avoid, and the people we should fear. In untroubled times, folktales channel community fears and maintain social cohesion. But in troubled times, when people are anxious and in need of a scapegoat, a potent brew of folktales – one that may have been simmering away harmlessly for years – can boil over into a 'moral panic'.[3]

So it was in Europe during the great witch-hunts, when an everyday fear of witches became contaminated by an ancient, recurring legend about a powerful secret cult that engaged in cannibalistic infanticide and depraved sexual orgies. Then the whole poisonous brew spilled over into successive waves of mass persecution until no old woman was safe.

In the popular imagination the great witch-hunts are associated with the Middle Ages, that 1000-year span of history when ignorance, superstition and gullibility blanketed Europe. But in the Middle Ages the idea of persecuting a witch, if not unthinkable, was certainly foolhardy. Like trying to persecute a saint or a fairy, it could hardly hope to succeed.[4]

After the Middle Ages, a great revival of art, literature and learning swept Europe. Gutenberg invented the printing press. Columbus discovered the new world. Michelangelo created his masterpieces and Shakespeare wrote his plays. Among scholars, awe in the face of nature's mysteries was replaced by empirical investigation. Galileo revolutionised astronomy. Newton discovered the laws of gravity. Harvey discovered the circulation of the blood. And during the Renaissance the witch-hunts grew and flourished.

Solitary, sharp-tongued older women were first to the stake, followed by a range of other female misfits. Then, as tales of large-scale witches' assemblies ('sabbats') inflamed the panic and the accused were tortured into naming accomplices, a few men and many women previously believed to be of good character were drawn into the maelstrom.

To the villagers who accused them, witches were responsible for the everyday misfortunes that provoke people into searching for causes and culprits. But to the prosecuting authorities, they were members of a powerful subversive force controlled by Satan. Many scholars believed that witches made pacts with the Devil and flew to nocturnal sabbats where they sacrificed babies, ate human flesh and engaged in obscene rituals. (These claims were not invented for, nor restricted to, witches. Throughout history, people have used accusations of infanticide, cannibalism and sexual orgies to dehumanise the fellow mortals they hate and wish to destroy. Karl Jung called this repertoire of images 'the archetype' of the enemy.)

During the 16th and 17th centuries the witch-panic spread in episodic bursts throughout the civilised world. In Scotland, between 1590 and 1680, around 1500 witches were burned at the stake. In England (where torture to extract confessions and the names of associates was not officially sanctioned) the total was barely 1000. In Germany the figure approached 100,000.[5]

That successive waves of sadism, terror and righteous indignation swept Europe in what could otherwise be described as an intellectual climate of rationality and enlightenment has proved difficult for many scholars to acknowledge. Most general histories fail to mention the witch-hunts. The event has been excised from church histories.[6] It is only from the work of specialist historians that we can learn of the phenomenon. Hugh Trevor-Roper reported that, by the 16th century, the need to eliminate witches was clear to people of all shades of religious and political opinion. 'The more learned a man was in the traditional scholarship of the time, the more likely he was to support the witch-doctors [witch-hunters],' he wrote. Trevor-Roper described Jean Bodin, author of *De la Démonomanie des Sorciers* as:

> Bodin the Aristotle, the Monresquieu of the sixteenth century, the prophet of comparative history, of political theory, of the philosophy of law, of the quantitative theory of money, and of so much else, who yet, in 1580, wrote a book which, more than any other, reanimated the witch-fires throughout Europe.

Montague Summers wrote of

> the voluminous and highly technical work of the Inquisitors and demonologists, holy and reverend divines, doctors *utriusque iuris*, hardheaded, slow, and sober lawyers – learned men, scholars of philosophic mind, the most honorable names in the universities of Europe, in the forefront of literature, science, politics and culture ...[7]

The late 19th century 'baby farmer' panic was similar in quality, if not in quantity and duration, to the witch-panic of earlier times. From the 1860s, newspapers throughout the Western world featured sensational accounts of evil women who murdered infants for money. However, when one examines these cases in a cooler light, suspicion arises that the majority were not wilful murderers but poor women struggling to do their best with what they had.

In New Zealand, Minnie Dean's arrest came hard on the heels of sensational cases that took baby farmers to the gallows in Australia, and brought outrage towards baby farmers in this country to a crescendo. On 12 August 1895 Minnie Dean was carried to the scaffold on a wave of moral panic.[8]

• • •

Over lunch at a biography conference in Australia in 1990 I regaled my companions with Minnie Dean stories.

'The same stories – about evil women doing unspeakable things to innocent children – were told about baby farmers around the world,' I said. 'And they're just like the stories that people told about witches during the Renaissance.'

'And they're just like the Lindy Chamberlain stories,' commented a listener.

'And just like the article in the latest *GH*,' said another.

The *Good Housekeeping* article concerned a young American woman named Kelly Michaels, who took the temperature of a child (using a strip on the child's forehead) at the daycare centre where she worked. Four days later the child mentioned this to his mother. His mother thought he'd had his temperature taken rectally and reported the incident to her doctor – who referred her to the child protection agency, who passed her on to the child abuse unit, who contacted the prosecutor's office, who initiated an investigation. During the first day of intensive interviews none of the

51 children in the centre told any investigator that he or she had been abused by Kelly Michaels or anyone else. But Michaels was arrested, and, after six more weeks of interviewing, the prosecutors had built a case. They claimed that each day during her seven months at the centre Kelly Michaels had raped and assaulted children with knives, forks, wooden spoons and Lego blocks. They said she had done this unnoticed by other teachers, school administrators, parents or visitors to the school. They claimed that Michaels had, unnoticed and on a daily basis, licked peanut butter off children's genitals, played the piano nude and made children drink her urine and eat her faeces. Yet while all this was supposed to be happening none of the children had said a word to anyone about it. It seemed like a crime beyond belief, but in 1988 Kelly Michaels was convicted and sentenced to 47 years in prison.[9]

After the biography conference, occasional stories about bizarre cases of sexual abuse in childcare centres around the world, and frequent stories of less spectacular prosecutions in New Zealand, reached me through the media. But it was only when New Zealand's biggest child sexual abuse case hit the headlines that I began to wonder: what on earth is going on? Has child sexual abuse really reached epidemic proportions, or has Western society been seized by another moral panic?

• • •

Here, in outline, are the undisputed facts of the case. On 20 November 1991 one of the most extensive and expensive police investigations in New Zealand history was set in motion when the parent of a child attending the Christchurch Civic Child Care Centre (commonly known as the Christchurch Civic Crèche) stated her suspicion that 'Peter [Ellis] may have been involved in inappropriate sexual behaviour with or around our son.' In the course of the investigation either 116, 118, 127 or 132 children (depending on whose figures you accept) were interviewed by sexual abuse specialists from the Department of Social Welfare.

At the preliminary court hearing, which began on 2 November 1992, Peter Hugh McGregor Ellis, the only male childcare worker at the centre, faced 45 charges of indecencies involving 20 children. A further 15 charges involving five children were laid, jointly with Ellis, against four of his women colleagues: supervisor Gaye Davidson and childcare workers Marie Keys, Janice Buckingham and Deborah Gillespie.

Ellis was alleged to have inserted his fingers, his penis, needles, sticks and food into the vaginas, mouths and anuses of children in his care. He was accused of urinating on them and making them drink his urine and eat his faeces. Gillespie was alleged to have inserted her finger in a child's vagina, and undressed and engaged in sexual intercourse with Ellis in the crèche toilets. Davidson, Keys and Buckingham were accused, together with Ellis, of participating in 'the circle incident', an occasion at which, it was claimed, children had sticks inserted in their anuses and were made to kick each other's genitals and perform other indecencies. The offences were said to have taken place between May 1986 and February 1992.

On 11 February 1993, at the end of the 11-week preliminary court hearing, all five accused were committed for trial. But by the time the case reached the High Court on 26 April the women had been discharged; Ellis alone remained, facing 28 charges involving 13 children. Fourteen of the offences were alleged to have taken place at the crèche. The rest were said to have taken place at 'an unknown address' (10), at a child's home (two), at a house where Ellis once boarded (one) and elsewhere in the building in which the crèche was housed (one). Three charges involving two children were dismissed during the trial. On 6 June 1993, after 24 days of evidence, two days of summing up and three days of deliberation, the jury of nine women and three men found Ellis guilty on three counts of sexual violation, eight counts of indecent assault and five counts of performing, or inducing children to perform, indecent acts. There were no adult eyewitnesses. There was no physical evidence. The verdicts were based on the testimony of seven young children (whose ages ranged from six to nine years). Three weeks later Justice Williamson sentenced Ellis to 10 years in prison. 'The jury disbelieved you,' he said. 'They believed the children, and I agree with that assessment.'

Beyond this bare summary, most details of the case are disputed. Despite often bitter disagreements, everyone involved, in one way or another, believed the children. Some believed the children when they said that nothing had happened, some believed them when they described possible, if somewhat improbable, episodes of abuse, and others believed them when they recounted stories of arcane rituals involving infanticide and cannibalism. The latter group posted this notice on the internet 'Believe the Children Conviction List':

> Children who attended the Christchurch Civic Crèche described bizarre sexual abuse with reference to frightening rituals. The children allege they were removed from the day care facility and transported to other locations, including a cemetery and a Masonic lodge, where they were abused by adults dressed in black and white and wearing masks. In addition to their reports of being used for pornographic purposes, the children described being abused within a circle; chanting and participating in mock marriages; being tied up and confined to cages and boxes buried beneath the ground; being penetrated with needles and sticks; witnessing the torture and killing of animals; being drugged; being forced to hurt other children; having blood poured over their heads; and consuming what they believed was human flesh.

Fourteen months later, in July 1994, a child whom the prosecution had described as 'compelling and believable' at the trial, retracted her allegations. She said she had lied about indecent touching and forced contact with Ellis's penis because she thought that was what her mother had wanted her to say.[10] The Court of Appeal quashed the three convictions relating to that child, but upheld the remaining 13 convictions and left Ellis's sentence unchanged. Ellis continued to maintain his innocence.

The Court of Appeal verdict did nothing to stem the doubts that had swirled around the case since its inception. Investigators believed that up to 300 children had been abused by Ellis. But how could anyone have regularly abused even the seven children that he was convicted of abusing, over a five-and-a-quarter-year period, without anyone noticing? More than 70 families used the crèche on a weekly basis. On average 28 children attended the preschool section and 12 were cared for in the nursery. The rosters worked by the 11 staff ensured staff/children ratios of one to four for the babies and toddlers, and one to eight for the preschoolers. Parents came and went unpredictably. Student teachers were often present. Yet, while all this abuse was supposed to be happening, no adults reported anything suspicious, and no children complained to anyone about it.[11]

But the children said it did happen. During 1992 more than 20 children disclosed to their parents and Social Welfare investigators that they had been sexually abused by crèche staff months, or even years, earlier. Why would they say they had been abused if they had not? Why would the investigators believe them if their stories were not credible? Why would their parents label them as sexually abused children, and subject them to investigations, therapy and criminal proceedings if they had not been abused?

• • •

A few weeks after Ellis's conviction I wrote to a number of people involved in the case, and went to Christchurch to meet them. For the most part they seemed sensible, level-headed folk, but I wasn't sure about Detective Colin Eade. His reply to my letter was handwritten on small sheets of lined paper. It was not, by any stretch of the imagination, an official letter. He wrote that he was closely involved in the case but did not want his superiors to know he had contacted me.

When we met he outlined his credentials: after 14 years in the force he was appointed to the Child Abuse Unit in June 1990; he had attended seminars on child sexual abuse and pornography. He described the development of the case. First came the complaint from a crèche parent. Then came more than two months of informal questioning, formal interviews and sexual abuse therapy for increasing numbers of crèche children. Then came the disclosure that led to the first charge against Ellis. The child responsible was not enrolled in the crèche, but she often called in with a parent to collect her younger siblings. Detective Eade stressed the significance of this revelation:

When we realised that Ellis had abused a child who was never at the crèche for more than a few minutes at a time, and right under her mother's nose, we knew we were onto something far more serious, and far more widespread, than we had ever imagined.

The 'far more serious and far more widespread' phenomenon Eade had in mind was a child-sex ring, comprising the crèche staff and many other people as well, which was in turn part of a worldwide network of pornographers. It was, he confided, his life's ambition to track the villains down. So far, all he had to go on were the stories told by former crèche children, but Eade was undeterred. The offenders were very clever, he explained. Friends, relatives, colleagues and acquaintances of the accused might be passing themselves off as law abiding citizens, but he knew better. Consider the newspaper reporter who had expressed cautious scepticism about the children's testimony (at this point Eade lowered his voice and narrowed his eyes) – 'I have my theories about him,' he said.

Then there was the matter of the dog. Apparently Ellis had named one of his dogs 'Eadie', after the detective who had pursued him relentlessly. Eade has his theories about that too. 'Peter was supposed to have loved animals,' he intoned. 'But he was supposed to have loved children too – and we know what he did to them.'

By this stage in the conversation the hairs on the back of my neck were standing on end. Detective Eade's single-minded line of argument, and the conspiracy beliefs that underpinned it, were chillingly reminiscent of the arguments and beliefs I had read about in demonology manuals of the 16th and 17th centuries. But, before I became too concerned about Detective Eade, I needed to determine just how widely his views were shared and what influence, if any, he had on the development of the case. And I needed to determine what evidence, if any, lay behind his claims.

First, I read the available background information. Then I sought face-to-face interviews with the key players. I approached the professionals directly, and the accused individuals through their lawyers. The identities of the complainant parents were suppressed by court order, and though it did not take long to discover who they were, I felt it would be an invasion of privacy to contact them directly. However, at Detective Eade's urging, I telephoned the parent who initiated the investigation. She declined to be interviewed. Also, at the first Court of Appeal hearing on the Ellis case, I introduced myself to a key complainant parent. She said she would talk to me only if I agreed that Ellis was 'the most heinous criminal in New Zealand history'. I said I preferred to keep an open mind. She declined to be interviewed. Later, on several occasions, acquaintances of the complainant parents approached them on my behalf. Most declined to be interviewed.

Through the media in 1995 and early 1996 I invited people on both sides of the case to contact me. I stressed that I would respect the confidentiality of anyone who did not want their identity revealed. I repeated the invitation at a talk I gave in Christchurch in August 1995.

As a result, I received several letters and phone calls. Some people provided information, others just expressed an opinion. One correspondent wrote of her 30-year friendship with accused crèche worker Marie Keys:

> A more kinder, caring and utterly honest person would be hard to find. This whole case is just so stupid and unfair, that I ask you, beg you, please delve into the background of the 'first accusing parent' and her subsequent accusations of others, also the investigating police officer. Peter Ellis is innocent.

An unsigned letter stated:

> I suppose you are another 'bleeding heart' type who has neither thought nor pity for the victims of this vile person Ellis. My contention has always been that the person on Christchurch Council who employed him should also have been charged. He was a known homosexual and was also into other crime. He should never have been allowed near children. The four women charged (and later dismissed) were also of dubious reputation, one a self-confessed lesbian, two others living in de-facto relationships. Please spare a thought for the little children robbed of their innocence. I, for one, am sure of Ellis's guilt. And hope he stays to serve his sentence.

Another wrote:

> Although I have not met Ellis and don't know anyone involved personally, I do still sometimes lie awake at night worrying about the injustice of it all. I often think of writing a list of unanswered concerns, and nailing it to the door of the high court like Martin Luther did. However, the high court doors are probably glass and aluminium.

Following my January 1996 call for information, I received a letter from Peter Ellis, whom I had visited a few weeks earlier in the forbidding West Wing of Paparua Prison. After more than two years in prison, the man I met still fitted the description in his pre-sentence report:

> ... an outgoing, uninhibited, unconventional person given to putting plenty of enthusiasm and energy into his work and social activities, sometimes to the point of being risque and outrageous, thus opening himself up to being compromised or being seen to exercise poor judgment. It appears, however, that he was able to temper the more effervescent side of his nature by being caring, sensitive and understanding in such a way that both adults and children were attracted to him.

By nature, Ellis was a disturber of the social order. Like the cantankerous crones persecuted as witches in the 16th and 17th centuries, he was the sort of person the community would make an example of when it wished to delineate the boundaries of acceptable eccentricity (though, interestingly, despite his mincing gait, his long hair, his eyeliner and his extravagantly long fingernails, and despite being a convicted child molester, none of the shaven-headed, tattooed thugs that surrounded him in prison had laid a finger on him).

Though my visit was purely social, I took the opportunity to ask him a pressing question. 'Peter,' I said, 'why did you call your dog Eadie?' He replied that, in an effort to lighten a dark situation, he had named all six puppies in a litter after policemen involved in the case. Eadie was a little bitch.

At the time of my visit, Ellis was campaigning for improvement in the conditions for prisoners who, prior to recent changes in the health system, had been cared for within the psychiatric service. Shortly after my visit he was transferred abruptly from high-security Paparua to medium-security Rolleston Prison. His January 1996 letter came accompanied by a satirical newspaper column about subliminal messages in the media and a drawing of a man's head on a red background. His letter read:

> So with trembling fingers Ms Hood holds in her hands one of a flood of letters in response to her request for people to spill all about the Civic Crèche case – just who has written this little number she asks herself??? Alas it is only the 'accused' whose mother is still having to distance herself from her son's terrible spelling, a constant source of embarrassment to her – and to think Mrs Ellis was a school teacher (as is the 'accused's non-involved parent!!). I would like to point out I took some time choosing the drawing that accompanies this letter, firstly to make sure there was no subliminal message hidden in the drawing (Peter Ellis is innocent) and secondly I wanted to make sure that one cannot fold this drawing to make anything that may be deemed obscene (Peter Ellis is innocent). I suppose red is an angry colour and no doubt the man depicted has a furtive look about him – but hey, I'm no psychologist or colour therapist, so I'd actually say the drawing is a not-very-good likeness of one Bob Marley. I thought you might like this article from *The Press*, it rather says it all. Since Gepetto came under fire for manipulating the puppet Pinnochio (though I think the 'politically correct' missed the point and Pinnochio was really a rent boy manipulating an old man) I have been on a personal crusade to have Shari Lewis removed from our screens. I was therefore most pleased to see that I am not the only person in this world of ours that is concerned about where dear Shari is putting her hand! (Ms Magnolia is a witch). I am currently in dialogue with TV2 about the damage that Jason Gunn is doing on prime time children's television – after all, I ask you, should a grown man have his 'Thingee' displayed so often on television!! I also have major concerns about Postman Pat, after all, he is sticking things (Ms Dogwood is a cow) in other people's slots!!

> Hello there Lynley, tiz I, Peter, exiled from Paparua to the back of beyond – here I sit in a little motel-type unit at Rolleston Prison. There are many gains from the move, such as so called 'freedom' and plenty of spare time on one's hands. However I lost all my friends, most I will never be able to see ever again as they are doing 15 years jail. What has become of me, eh? My friends who are very, very precious to me are actually murderers, yet they are people that hurt just like the rest of the world and I do miss them. I won my

battle at Paparua, but paid the price. At least I know that conditions in the West Wing have improved. I just wish I was there to make sure they stay that way and that they got everything else they should. Well I hope you had a good Christmas break and all your celebrations went well. I hope you and yours are all well and in good health. I shall continue on my gay way and be cheerful, looking for silver in the clouds. Love, Peter

I also interviewed a crèche parent who had withdrawn her daughter from the case, and several parents whose children had not disclosed abuse. Some interpreted the nondisclosure as proof that abuse had taken place, others interpreted it as proof that it had not.

From some complainant families my publicity drew only hostility and rejection. I found their feelings understandable. They were deeply hurt and stressed, and intensely protective of their children. In commenting on the case, I had made no secret of my interest in witch-hunting and mass hysteria, but had emphasised that such issues were separate from the guilt or innocence of the people involved. I had repeatedly stated my intention to thoroughly research both sides of the story, and to write about it as fairly, accurately and sensitively as I could. But if some complainant families wanted to keep their distance, that was all right with me.

What wasn't all right with me was their insistence that I had made no effort to contact them and had no intention of doing so. That claim appeared in the August 1995 *End Ritual Abuse Newsletter*:

> Did you know that Dunedin writer Lynley Hood is writing a book on the Civic Crèche case? Hood claims that she is writing the book from a fair, balanced and factual perspective with no hidden agenda (Christchurch talk 3.8.95). Strangely, she has no intention of interviewing any complainant parents, just non-complainant ones who believe that Ellis is innocent. Hood claims to be neutral and fair in her writing with no pre-empted opinion. Sorry, that's bullshit. She has supported Ellis from the beginning of her intention to write a book. It's a bit like how the mainstream media work. Let's write a story, let's put it out to the public. Doesn't matter if they twist the factual information to suit and fit around their pre-empted, opinionated story, doesn't matter if they reabuse victims and their families, in fact it doesn't seem to matter how wrong they get it, or how sensational they make it. We bet some of the healthy, honest and reputable journalists will be cringing to be associated with the shabby and dishonest ones.

The same accusation appeared in a letter I received from Colin Eade. I had intended to renew my contact with Eade but I couldn't find him. He had left the police and was no longer at his old address. Then, in the wake of my January 1996 call for information, I received his letter:

> I note that you never attempted to contact either myself or the Police during your 'investigation'. I am not aware of any parent or child from the 'prosecution' side who has spoken to you and in fact it appears that you only intend to write your book from the

perspective likely to be the most sensational. It is probably too much to ask that you give a balanced and fair account in your book as a result of your 'investigation'. However that isn't likely to sell books is it? The children abused at the crèche certainly deserve more than to have the orchestrated attack on their credibility continue in your book. If you have never spoken to them your book can't be balanced. I will be watching and reading with interest.

The following year Colin Eade wrote to me again, repeating his earlier accusations, adding a few more, and concluding: 'If you think for a minute anything you say in the book will affect myself or any of the enquiry team you are wrong. We've heard it all before and we know what we did had to be done and that it was right.'

Another letter, from the grandmother of a complainant child, reiterated the claim that I had no interest in hearing from complainant families (even though she had been present at my 1995 Christchurch talk, when I had invited them to contact me). She also said that even if I did want to talk to them, they did not want to talk to me.

Despite the attacks, I managed to interview a range of people involved in all aspects of the case. I gave everyone a form letter that laid out my 'ground rules' concerning confidentiality and related issues and made it clear that I was treating everyone I interviewed the same way. The letter also stated that I did not want to interview any of the children. In the course of my research I had been impressed by the persistence with which interviewers had sought disclosures from the children. In the course of an interview lasting over an hour, an interviewer asked one of the children how Peter was naughty 23 times, how he was naughty in the toilets 14 times and how he was naughty and mean 38 times. Even if the children could have contributed to my research, I had no wish to add to their stress.

• • •

I began this project with some experience of writing on controversial issues. Sylvia Ashton-Warner was a saint and martyr to her admirers and a fraud and poseur to her detractors. To some people Minnie Dean was a good woman 'done wrong'; to others she was a hellhag who murdered for money. But the crèche case was by far the most controversial issue I had ever encountered. At times it seemed like the entire nation was deeply and passionately divided between believers (whose conviction that terrible things had happened at the crèche was unshakable) and sceptics (who found the evidence unconvincing).

As I had done with Ashton-Warner and Dean, I pursued every lead and tested every hypothesis in the course of my research. Then I set out to write a book that steered a steady course through the shoals and tempests of the controversy, illuminating the context along the way and providing a balanced picture of the apparently conflicting, but presumably equally valid, points of view.

Much of the controversy revolved around the relative credibility of the accusers and the accused. But, since everyone I spoke to presented their views with sincerity and conviction, I concluded that anyone who honestly believed whatever it was they had chosen to believe would appear credible, regardless of the factual basis for that belief.

Having realised that I could not depend on the credibility of my informants to lead me to the truth, I went on to consider the evidence. And when I considered the evidence, I had to reconsider my approach. The problem was that the more closely I studied the case, the more the evidence of wrongdoing (on the part of the accused) evaporated, and the more the evidence of innocence (on the part of the accused) and prejudice and delusion (on the part of the accusers) accumulated. Try as I might I could not dismiss the suspicion that justice had not been done in the crèche case. In my experience, attempts by authors to camouflage their partisan views as jargon, or to hide them behind research, are doomed to failure; their convictions always end up leaking into the text, thereby sowing suspicion and uncertainty among readers about the author's true motives. To avoid any such uncertainty I want to make my position clear from the outset: this is not an 'everyone's-point-of-view-is-valid-by-their-own-lights' sort of book; this, as I see it, is a story of right and wrong; and in this story those who believe that terrible things happened at the crèche are wrong.

When I began this project, the key question underpinning my research was this: to what extent were the staff of the Christchurch Civic Child Care Centre involved in child sexual abuse? I expected to find the answer within the scope of the case. I expected, sooner or later, to uncover some real-life happenings on which, rightly or wrongly, the allegations of criminality were based. But, in my years of dredging through the mire in which this story has foundered, I found no evidence of illegality by anyone accused in this case. Instead, I found convincing evidence that more than 100 Christchurch children had been subject to unpleasant and psychologically hazardous procedures for no good reason, and that a group of capable and caring adults with no inclinations towards sexual misconduct with children had had their lives ruined as a result. This disquieting outcome drew my focus from the crèche to the forces that had brought about its downfall. By the time I came to write this book the key question I faced was this: how on earth did the complainant families, the child protection services, the police, the justice system and the government get it so wrong? My quest for answers took me far beyond the case itself. This project, which began as an investigation into a single criminal case, escalated into a study of the last 30 years of New Zealand social history, and of much more besides.

• • •

In the course of my research I was confronted by many subtle and not-so-subtle attempts to discourage me from proceeding. The arguments, primarily from social workers and therapists, went like this: child sexual abuse is far more serious and far more widespread than most people realise; it is extremely difficult to detect; only a minority of perpetrators are ever convicted; false accusations are extremely rare and false convictions are rarer still; it doesn't matter if the evidence is inconclusive because the cost of leaving this terrible crime unpunished is far greater than the cost of mistakenly punishing people who may be innocent; anyone who questions these statements is aiding and abetting sexual abuse and putting innocent children at risk.

At the core of these arguments are questions that must be addressed: just how widespread is child sexual abuse, and just how serious are the consequences? (Or, to put it another way: what exactly does the research say, and what exactly does it mean?)

Such questions invite us to search for answers by the cool, clear light of science, but we should not forget that, in the field of child sexual abuse, each word separately ('child', 'sexual', 'abuse') conceals beneath its icy tip a treacherous mass of destabilising emotions, and the three words combined have the power to wreck the most carefully planned scientific journeys. According to philosopher Ian Hacking, child sexual abuse researchers have steered the craft of science into strange uncharted seas:

> When the family falls apart, when parents abuse their children, when incest obsesses the media, when one people tries to destroy another, we are concerned with defects of the soul. But we have learned how to replace the soul with knowledge, with science. Hence spiritual battles are fought, not on the explicit ground of the soul, but on the terrain of memory, where we suppose that there is such a thing as knowledge to be had.[12]

By 'soul' Hacking is referring to 'the strange mix of aspects of a person that may be, at some time, imagined as inner':

> Philosophers of my stripe speak of the soul not to suggest something eternal, but to invoke character, reflective choice, self-understanding, values that include honesty to others and oneself, several types of freedom and responsibility. Love, passion, envy, tedium, regret and quiet contentment are the stuff of the soul.

The notion that the soul itself is a hostage in this drama may help explain the grip that child sexual abuse holds on the public imagination. But, as scientific battles go, it is not the only one to be fought in murky waters. Indeed, there are lessons to be learnt from the undercurrents that flowed, and continue to flow, through some of the more mundane scientific controversies of our age.

In an ideal world, scientific research would be conducted, and results disseminated, for the purpose of increasing the sum of human knowledge. But we do not live in an ideal world. In *How to Lie with Statistics*, Darrell Huff notes that the language of statistics, so appealing to our fact-minded culture, and so essential to the conduct and reporting of scientific research, is routinely employed to sensationalise, inflate, confuse and oversimplify the world around us.[13] We know that in commerce and politics vested interests use research data to win arguments or gain economic advantage. When 'independent experts' tell us that cigarette smoking is safe, we question their backgrounds, their motives, their funding, their research methods and their interpretations of the data. Given that child sexual abuse is a much more emotionally charged topic than cigarette smoking, it would be prudent to ask the same questions of experts in that field.

CHAPTER 2

Sex, Sexism and the New Demonology

WHEN AN INFLUENZA epidemic strikes, the warnings of experts confirm what we know already: there's a lot of it about. But to the average layperson, the current child sexual abuse epidemic is a mystery. Experts say it is widespread, but even with the benefit of that knowledge most of us recognise it only rarely in our midst. Our plight is one with which laypeople of the 16th and 17th centuries would sympathise.

Detailed analyses of the great witch-hunts in Scotland and Germany reveal that they were not spontaneous movements of the people to which the authorities felt obliged to respond. Witch-hunting crises were preceded by official expressions of anxiety about the prevalence of witchcraft and the dangers it posed. Through the promotion of witch-fear, ambitious rulers consolidated their power by feeding the flames of panic; priests and clerics enhanced their authority by demonstrating a new-found expertise in the diagnosis of witchcraft. Laypeople were often sceptical of the experts' more extravagant claims and many tracts critical of the witch-hunts were published. However, most people accepted that witchcraft was a great danger to society, and because they accepted the general truth of the theory they could not effectively challenge its more learned interpreters. Besides, those who did question the authorities were often denounced as witches themselves.[1]

During the height of the witch-panic, as increasing numbers of ordinary women (and a few men) were sent to the stake, all but the most outspoken critics fell silent and many discontented common folk seized the opportunity to make frivolous and vindictive accusations against people they disliked without fear of repercussions. The history of the late-20th-century sexual abuse scare shows a similar pattern.

It began in the 1970s, when a clamour of competing social movements, each with its own agenda and its own moral entrepreneurs, vied for public and political attention. Then, in the early '80s, three major social streams – feminism, religious conservatism and the child protection movement – joined forces under the banner of combatting child sexual abuse. The resulting coalition surged through the '80s and beyond, gathering size and power along the way, sweeping over, around or away most of the obstacles in its path. To understand how that coalition was formed, we need to revisit the 1970s.

• • •

In this review, special attention will be paid to the moral entrepreneurs of the times and the beliefs they promoted. While it is true that social movements are nothing without their followers, for the most part followers simply follow. They believe – or go along with – whatever the rest of the group believes. Constructing a theoretical foundation for those beliefs is left primarily to the group's leaders. Leaders also define objectives, determine the means of achieving them, and promote the group's beliefs to the wider community. Compared to followers, leaders tend to be more intense in their ambitions, more certain of their convictions and more willing to make sacrifices for the cause. Followers may not fully support the beliefs and actions of their leaders, and members of the wider community may be frankly sceptical. But, when confronted with the impassioned rhetoric of energetic, committed and persistent moral entrepreneurs, most people appreciate the price of peace in their personal lives and, with varying degrees of willingness, they are prepared to pay it.

This emphasis on the leader's role is not intended to let followers off the hook. It is a little simplistic but not untrue to suggest that throughout history charismatic zealots have taken out their personal problems on the world when given half a chance. When such leaders acquire power in a democracy, those who follow without question, and those who fail to voice their questions, must be as responsible for any resulting injustices as the single-minded and zealous leaders themselves.

2.i: The Strands of the Seventies

Throughout the Western world the primary goal of 1970s feminism was to free women from male oppression (and especially from the oppression of white, middle-class men). The agenda ranged from the evolutionary (equal pay, quality childcare, safe contraception, liberalised abortion and the abolition of sex-role stereotypes), to the revolutionary (female separatism, the abolition of the patriarchal family and the overthrow of patriarchal society). To evolutionary feminists the problem was sexism; to revolutionary feminists the problem was men.[2]

The first New Zealand women's liberation groups were formed in 1970. In the following years consciousness-raising groups, study groups and activist groups sprang up nationwide. Media coverage, though often patronising and hostile, was extensive. The public was left in no doubt: women were on the move.[3]

As the decade progressed many feminist groups became established national organisations.[4] Rape crisis centres, women's refuges and women's studies courses proliferated. In 1972, 200 women attended the National Women's Liberation Conference in Wellington. United Women's Conventions, held in other cities in 1973, 1975, 1977 and 1979, drew over 1000 participants each.

The New Zealand government was not immune to women's concerns. During the '70s the Equal Pay Act, the Matrimonial Property Act and the Human Rights Act (all of which outlawed discrimination against women) were passed. The Domestic Purposes Benefit (for the support of solo parents) was introduced, a state-run accident compensation scheme that covered non-earners was launched and the state-run national superannuation scheme was revised to give greater independence to married women.

Initially, women's liberation was for all women, and for men as well. *Broadsheet* magazine, which first appeared in 1972, was always primarily by, for and about women, but during its first few years articles by men appeared regularly. 'Don't put men down,' wrote a correspondent. 'Ask them to join the fight.'[5] Conservative women, and a scattering of men, rubbed shoulders with feminists at early United Women's Conventions. A representative of the Catholic Women's League told the first United Women's Convention: 'The true way to happiness is to make Christ our guide and our friend.' The men present were said to be 'largely unobtrusive and reasonably supportive'.

As the '70s progressed, women at the cutting edge of feminism became increasingly radicalised and United Women's Conventions became increasingly disunited. By the end of the decade the inclusiveness had vanished. Conservative women turned their backs on the movement, women who saw themselves as moderates distanced themselves from women they saw as extremists, and feminists at the core of the movement dissipated much of their energy on in-group upheavals over sexual politics, race and social class.[6]

A cornerstone of the radicalisation of the women's movement was the feminist analysis of rape. In October 1975 *Broadsheet* readers were told: '… rape is part of a normal pattern of male behaviour. Males in this society are conditioned from birth to be sexual aggressors while females are conditioned to be passive and submissive – perfect victims … Every male is a potential rapist.'[7]

The statement 'every male is a potential rapist' (which soon became the graffiti slogan 'All men are rapists') fits the definition of a stereotype in Gordon Allport's *The Nature of Prejudice*: 'Whether favourable or unfavourable, a stereotype is an exaggerated belief associated with a category. Its function is to justify (rationalize) our conduct in relation to that category.'[8]

Category formation is an inevitable part of human existence. The business of life goes on with less effort if we stick with our own kind. The problem comes when loyalty to a category (the in-group – commonly united by nationality, race, ethnicity, gender or sexual orientation) leads to hostility to other categories (out-groups). The process is not inevitable; loyalty to New Zealand does not automatically mean hostility to China. It's the negative stereotypes that cause the trouble.

Writing in the 1950s, Allport observed that negative stereotypes, which may or may not originate in a kernel of truth, are used to justify hate-prejudice against Jews (who were believed to be clever, deceitful, over-ambitious and sly), Negroes (who were believed to be lecherous, lazy, filthy and aggressive), and women (who were believed to be hysterical, vain, irrational and intellectually deficient). A category not specifically considered by Allport is homosexuals (believed to be sick, degenerate, sex-mad, corrupters of youth). Allport noted that most stereotypes reflect the human tendency to attribute to others the weaknesses we most despise in ourselves.

Another major figure of Allport's era was psychologist Theodor Adorno, who identified a cluster of character traits in prejudiced people which, taken together, constituted 'the authoritarian personality' (though recent studies suggest that authoritarianism is not so much a personality type as a reflection of the values and norms of the subgroups to which prejudiced people belong). In addition to their high levels of prejudice (which they tend to turn with equal vehemence on Jews, Catholics, homosexuals, communists and splinter-groups within their own movements), authoritarian people are rigidly moralistic, intolerant of ambiguity and deviance, and obsessively interested in other people's sex lives. They feel threatened by powerful external forces and are much given to conspiracy theories.[9]

Allport suggested that what prejudiced people do in relation to groups they dislike may not be directly related to what they think or feel about them, but most negative attitudes eventually express themselves in some sort of action. Historically, outbreaks of persecution of homosexuals, or members of national, racial or ethnic out-groups, are relatively common, but 400 years have passed since the last outbreak of gross persecution on the basis of gender in Western cultures.

While historians continue to debate the political, economic and social antecedents of the great witch-hunts, most scholars agree that the publication of the *Malleus Malificarum* in 1486 was the spark that ignited the most sustained outbreak of misogyny in human history. Through the demonisation of women, the priests who authored that celebrated encyclopaedia of witchcraft created a scapegoat for the discontents of their age and a justification for the persecutions that followed.[10] Their claim – 'All witchcraft is caused by carnal lust which is in women insatiable' – is an example of stereotyping by gender that bears a remarkable resemblance to the contemporary feminist slogan 'All men are rapists'. Also, like the witch-hunters' demonisation of women, the feminists' demonisation of men had far-reaching consequences.

One consequence was the beatification of women. If men were evil and bad, women were virtuous and good. Karl Jung would have explained it this way: there is good and bad in everyone, but, when radical feminists blamed men for all the evil in the world they split their essential selves. Then, having disowned the bad, all they had left for their own self-images was unadulterated good.

With the demonisation of men, the distinction made by women's liberationists between 'men we like' and 'male chauvinist pigs' was abolished. All men were predatory bastards. They ceased to appear in the pages of *Broadsheet*, they were no longer welcome at feminist events, and their responsibility for the oppression of women was subject to further detailed analysis.

The outcome was a 'political critique of the institution and ideology of heterosexuality as a cornerstone of male supremacy' that portrayed sexual violence as 'a constant threat and reminder of the power of men over women', and 'an ultimate expression of female oppression in a patriarchal society'.[11]

The ramifications of this analysis extended from the political to the personal. In the early '70s, feminist leaders protested that they were not bra-burning, man-hating lesbians, and declared that what some women did with other women in the privacy of their own bedrooms was their own business. Then, under the influence of radical feminist theory, what women did in their own bedrooms, and with whom, became issues of central importance. As the decade progressed, and committed feminists analysed their relationships in terms of male supremacy and female oppression, many turned the slogan 'Feminism is the theory – lesbianism is the practice' into a personal reality.[12]

American Charlotte Bunch (who, five years earlier, had been Charlotte Bunch-Weeks, married and heterosexual) visited New Zealand for the second United Women's Convention in 1975, and discussed her lesbianism in an interview with *Broadsheet*:

> ... the best way for a woman to understand herself ... is through a lesbian identity. Until society changes its attitudes, to say you are celibate identifies you with heterosexuality. I have good friends who are heterosexual ... but it is hard to understand since I find lesbianism so much more liberating for a woman.[13]

In *Broadsheet*, many New Zealand women shared their reasons for becoming lesbians. While the opportunity to acknowledge a sexual or romantic preference, escape an unhappy marriage, overcome loneliness, rebel against a rigid upbringing or indulge in sexual experimentation were often contributing factors, to some feminists the ascetic idealism espoused by Charlotte Bunch was the primary attraction. Like nuns in an age of faith, they depicted their lesbianism as a vocational choice that freed them to work for the greater good, unfettered by the distractions, temptations and obligations of a relationship with the opposite sex. From their vantage point on the moral high ground, they pitied their heterosexual sisters. In the popular radical feminist book of the '70s *Lesbian Nation*, Jill Johnston wrote: 'All women are lesbians, except those who don't know it.'

Throughout the '70s a major target of radical feminist criticism was the patriarchal family. In *Broadsheet*, the child-rearing book most frequently cited was Shulamith Firestone's *The Dialectic of Sex*. Like her sister theorists, Firestone regarded sexual oppression as a cornerstone of political oppression, and the patriarchal family as the cornerstone of the patriarchal society. Her solution was radical in the extreme: she called for the abolition of the family. In practice, this feminist utopia proved elusive. Though most feminist mothers interviewed by *Broadsheet* had thrown off the theoretical oppression of the patriarchal family, all they had replaced it with was the practical oppression of solo motherhood.

On the outskirts of feminism, women who had accepted the traditional role of wife and mother without question reconsidered their options. But when they reflected on the changing attitudes of men towards childcare, housework and family decision-making, and weighed the theory of patriarchal oppression against the practical advantages of raising children in a two-parent family, most mainstream women concluded that having a long-term relationship with the father of their children was the best option.

Meanwhile, at the core of feminism, the cauldron of debate congealed into dogma. No one dared ask why the Goddess had made heterosexual intercourse a necessary and pleasurable aspect of human reproduction, no one dared suggest there were decent men in the world for whom the label 'rapist' was as ridiculous as it was insulting, and no one dared express a preference for the early-'70s 'strong, successful, self-reliant' feminist over the late-'70s 'weak and oppressed victim'. As Sandra Coney noted in a 1978 *Broadsheet* column, anyone who questioned the new feminist orthodoxy (or any of its more-oppressed-than-thou factions) laid herself open to invective, rejection and accusations of complicity in 'the anti-woman backlash'.[14]

By the end of the '70s, disillusioned heterosexuals were abandoning the women's liberation movement in droves, leaving lesbian radicals (and a few heterosexual radicals) in control of the feminist high ground. Women who would have been regarded as extremists in the early '70s (by their own unreconstructed selves as well as by the rest of society) became, in the '80s, the core theorists and spokespeople of the movement. Among their number were two energetic, intelligent women who took the feminist analysis of rape from the political to the personal, and on to the professional. Both began the '70s as heterosexual wives and mothers and ended it as lesbian-feminist psychologists. They were Hilary Haines and Miriam Jackson.

Haines and Jackson encountered women's liberation at Auckland University in the early '70s. They joined feminist consciousness-raising groups, became members of the *Broadsheet* collective, and reoriented their sexuality and ended their marriages during their student years. Jackson also fought one of her first political campaigns. 'I drew graphs showing that we were turning people away from the [university] crèche,' she recalled in 1987. 'They were quite distorted graphs, but successful politically in terms of getting an extension on the crèche.'[15] Using distorted statistics for political ends would bring Jackson further success in the years ahead.

Miriam Jackson, with five children of her own, laid the groundwork for her later expertise in child sexual abuse by working with rapists and their victims as a Justice Department psychologist. She also studied overseas research, conducted surveys, gave lectures and wrote articles. Anger was her driving force. 'This anger gave me the energy to gather up society's dirty washing (male violence against women) and hang it out for the people to see and do something about,' she wrote in 1982.[16]

• • •

To feminist activists, rape statistics were an area where radical ideals and everyday reality clashed head on. Despite a vigorous 'believe the victim' campaign and the establishment of rape crisis centres nationwide, rape continued to constitute less than 0.5 percent of recorded crime in New Zealand.[17] Also, despite all the rhetoric about white, middle-class men being the chief perpetrators and beneficiaries of patriarchal privilege through rape and the threat of rape, those convicted of rape were usually poor men from racial minorities. In the light of this outcome, the theorists who argued that all men were rapists, and the rape crisis workers whose services lacked the anticipated demand, were faced with a dilemma: they could admit that their extravagant claims about the prevalence of rape and the identity of the rapists were suspect, or they could redefine the problem and repackage the statistics to produce the results they wanted. In the decade ahead, many enterprising feminists chose the latter option.

• • •

In most respects the antithesis of '70s feminism was '70s religious conservatism. Conservatives favoured a God-fearing society in which men ruled the world and women knew their place. They were opposed to abortion, homosexuality, pornography, sex education, extra-marital sex and working mothers. All that authoritarian conservatives appeared to have in common with authoritarian feminists was an intense interest in what people did in the privacy of their own bedrooms and a tight-lipped disappointment with the creator for making heterosexual intercourse necessary for the continuation of the species. During the permissive '60s the protests of religious conservatives were trampled underfoot in the headlong communal rush to enjoy the fruits of the sexual revolution. But during the '70s, conservatives returned to the public arena with a vengeance.[18]

Patricia Bartlett, ex-nun and indefatigable anti-pornography activist, founded the Society for the Promotion of Community Standards in 1970, and went on to picket, petition, survey, review, debate and lobby with unrelenting vigour but little success for the next 25 years. Another conservative movement of the '70s, the Society for the Protection of the Unborn Child, persuaded parliament to tighten the laws on legalised abortion. But, despite this success, religious conservatism ended the decade still struggling to be taken seriously in the face of ongoing criticism from civil libertarians over issues of censorship, and ridicule from the general public for its busybody prurience.

• • •

The most spectacularly successful social force of the 1970s, the child protection movement, began early in the previous decade. In a 1962 paper, Denver paediatrician Henry Kempe coined the term 'the battered-child syndrome' to remind doctors that not all childhood injuries were accidental. Kempe claimed that this 'unrecognised trauma' was 'a frequent cause of permanent injury or death', and 'one of the most serious concerns facing society'.[19]

Henry Kempe was a man of vision, determination and charisma. Between the publication of his ground-breaking paper in 1962 and the first edition of *The Battered Child* in 1967, he persuaded all 50 American states to pass child abuse reporting laws. The following year, two articles in scholarly journals cast doubt on his alarmist claims but failed to slow his momentum. Following the first article (which reported that only a minority of physically ill-treated children showed frank symptoms of battered-child syndrome), Kempe expanded his frontiers and renamed his territory 'child abuse'. The second scholarly article (which concluded that sensational reports had greatly exaggerated the importance of the problem) appears to have been ignored.[20]

In the second edition of *The Battered Child* (1974) Kempe noted that reports of suspected child abuse in New York City had escalated from 400 in 1966 to 10,000 in 1972. 'Adequate demographic data which provide up-to-date evidence of the true incidence of significant child abuse in the United States is not available,' he added.

It should not have been insurmountably difficult for Henry Kempe to conduct his own prevalence survey. After all, it was the visible, and therefore presumably measurable, evidence of bleeding, bruising, broken bones and death that had enabled him to bring the problem to public attention in the first place. Perhaps he was discouraged by the official figures for childhood deaths due to violence in the United States, which, despite the escalating reporting rate, had stayed constant at 1000 per year in 1969, 1970 and 1971. In a population of 250 million, 1000 deaths per year is not a headline-grabbing figure. It is not a figure likely to inspire decision-makers to allocate more resources to child protection. In fact the constancy of the figure could lead politicians to wonder whether the extra resources allocated thus far were serving any useful purpose.

But while the prevalence of non-accidental childhood injuries in the United States remained uninvestigated, New Zealand Department of Social Welfare researchers analysed information on all cases of suspected or alleged child abuse brought to the attention of the Child Welfare Division of the Department in 1967. Inevitably, some cases would have been concealed, some would have been handled by other agencies, and some would not have been recognised. But, given New Zealand's relatively homogenous population of 2.75 million, the results were probably as reliable as any that could have been obtained anywhere in the world. The researchers concluded:

> ... child abuse is not a problem of major social importance in New Zealand. During the survey year fewer than 3 children in every 10,000 in the 0–16 age group came to the attention of the Child Welfare Division for incidents in which there was evidence of abuse. Even for the high risk (under 1 year old) group the incidence was only 4.5 per 10,000 children. Further, the bulk of incidents ... involved only relatively minor injuries, and of the 255 abused children only 44 were hospitalised as a consequence of abuse. By way of comparison, in the same year 2,401 children in the 0–14 age group were admitted to hospital suffering from the effects of road accidents and a further 2,131 from accidental poisonings in the home.[21]

This finding may have been good news for New Zealand children. But scientific reality is one thing and social reality is something else again, and the social reality was that child abuse was an idea whose time had come.

• • •

In the 19th century, Victorian reformers blamed what they called 'cruelty to children' on the poverty and ignorance of the lower classes, and favoured removing needy children to orphanages and industrial schools. But during the first half of the 20th century, as reformers realised that even the poorest families could do a better job of raising their own children than institutions, society became less inclined to police needy families, and more inclined to support them. And so the occupation of social worker was born.

In the 1960s Henry Kempe put a new spin on the old problem by suggesting that child abuse was a medical and law-enforcement issue, and that children could be mistreated by individuals from any walk of life.[22] Through this approach Kempe created a new research frontier where medical, psychiatric and statistical knowledge could be found and put to use. Almost overnight, he raised the status of people who worked with ill-treated children to undreamt-of heights and new recruits flocked to meet the challenge.

Using arguments couched in the language of civil rights, Kempe campaigned for statutory changes allowing social workers to remove 'at risk' children from their families. His claim – that the rights of children to be protected from abuse outweighed the rights of parents to raise their offspring as they saw fit – encouraged social workers to regard parents as selfish oppressors, and professionals as selfless carers.[23] Though it was no more than linguistic legerdemain, Kempe's claim set the pendulum of child protection swinging away from supporting needy families and back towards policing them.

Also, by presenting child abuse as an illness and a crime, Kempe kept the social issues that normally divide liberals and conservatives off the political agenda. Vice-President Mondale promoted Kempe's Child Abuse Prevention and Treatment Act with slogans like 'This is a political problem, not a poverty problem', and 'Not even Richard Nixon is in favour of child abuse!' In 1974 'the Mondale Act' (which provided federal child-protection funds only to states with mandatory child abuse reporting laws) was passed almost unanimously.[24] The same year the National Centre on Child Abuse and Neglect was established, with an annual budget of $19 million.

Having conquered the United States, Henry Kempe went on to conquer the world. In 1976 the First International Congress on Child Abuse and Neglect was held within the facilities of the World Health Organization in Geneva.

A mood of heady excitement pervaded the congress. 'There has been an explosion of professional and public interest,' a delegate reported. 'The battered child has moved from the back pages of professional journals to the front pages of mass-circulation newspapers. Daily, there are additional news articles, television and radio programmes and community meetings, not to mention professional conferences, on the subject.'[25]

'This could be the start of something big,' observed another delegate.

The momentum continued with the establishment of the journal *Child Abuse and Neglect* in 1977. But, by the time of the second International Congress in London in 1978, change was in the wind.

Along with the successes (more abuse reports, more funding, more media attention) had come problems. From 1976, US statistics were collected annually by the American Humane Association. These showed that the astronomical rise in suspected child abuse cases was accompanied by an equally astronomical rise in false allegations.[26] Yet, throughout the period, the number of children who died at the hands of caregivers each year stayed virtually constant. These points did not go unnoticed by the media. Some articles damned child protection workers for tearing innocent families apart, others damned them for leaving guilty families intact.

By the late '70s the child protection movement was also drawing the wrath of feminists and religious conservatives. Feminists took exception to the claim that most physical child abuse was perpetrated by women (and, all too often, by poor women from racial minorities); while religious conservatives took exception to the movement's wish to deny parents their divine right to hit their own children.

2.ii: The Knotted Web of the Eighties

So there they were, approaching the end of the decade, three separate social movements – feminism, religious conservatism and the child protection movement – each seething with mutual hostility, frustrated ambitions and unrealised potential, and each about to discover an exciting new cause: child sexual abuse.

The upsurge of interest in child sexual abuse had its origins in feminist scholarship. Nothing annoyed '70s feminists more than having their arguments dismissed as the work of hysterical women. Hysterical!? they protested. Who says we're hysterical? The answer was: Sigmund Freud.

When they re-examined the work of Freud, feminist scholars discovered that, between 1895 and 1897, the father of modern psychoanalysis believed that sexual abuse in early childhood was the root cause of the mental disorders he observed in his adult patients. Then, in 1897, he changed his mind. In *An Autobiographical Study* (1925) he wrote:

> Under the influence of the technical procedure which I used at that time, the majority of my patients reproduced from their childhood scenes in which they were sexually seduced by some grownup person. With female patients the part of seducer was almost always assigned to their father. I believed these stories ... however, I was at last obliged to recognize that these scenes of seduction had never taken place, and that they were only fantasies which my patients had made up or which I myself had perhaps forced on them.[1]

By claiming that Freud had got it right the first time, feminist scholars were able to discount the notion that women were inherently hysterical, reinforce the notion that men were inherently depraved and extend the theory of male oppression to include, along with the victimisation of women, the victimisation of children.

The bracketing of women-and-children as victims of male sexual violence brought three great benefits to feminism. First, because children were seen as innocent, vulnerable and dependent, women could be seen that way too (this perception allowed women to demand, and receive, special treatment rather than equality). Second, it supplied the rape crisis movement, which was initially concerned only with contemporary rape cases, with a major new category of clients: adults and children who had been sexually assaulted some time in the past. Third, it created a window of opportunity through which the label 'rapist' could be flung at all the white middle-class men who had breezed through the '70s largely untouched by feminist anger.

During the '80s, retrospective cases came to dominate the rape crisis movement. According to a Statistics New Zealand report, by 1993, 90 percent of new contacts made by groups dealing with sexual assaults were related to incidents that had occurred years earlier.[2] Compared to contemporary rape allegations, these historical allegations were much more likely to involve white middle-class victims and white middle-class perpetrators. Also, because any physical evidence would have long since disappeared, the alleged victims had to be taken at their word. These factors gave the modest contemporary rape statistics a great boost, and, when added to previously unrecognised cases covered by the late-'70s feminist redefinition of rape (which included wolf-whistles, sexual humour, underwear advertisements and consensual sex) and when combined with extravagant estimates of the levels of unreported rape, the resulting statistics made the claim 'all men are rapists' much easier to argue.

The feminist reinterpretation of Freud burst into the public arena in a May 1977 cover story in *MS* magazine, 'Incest: Child abuse begins at home', and the child protection movement wasted no time in joining the crusade. In 1978 Henry Kempe told delegates to the second International Congress on Child Abuse and Neglect in London: 'The frequency of incest is very large and the reported number is now fully equal to that of physical abuse at our centre.'[3]

As a result of Kempe's change of focus, the energies of child protection workers were diverted from blaming women (for physical abuse) to blaming men (for sexual abuse), and feminist hostility to his cause was transformed into feminist support. Also, because the problem was extremely difficult to diagnose – and the diagnosis, once made, was extremely difficult to refute – this change of focus provided the embattled child protection movement with a new and powerful area of arcane expertise. Without the presence or absence of bruising, bleeding or broken bones to prove or disprove the allegations, sceptics had little choice but to accept the opinions of specially trained child protection workers.

In his address to the 1978 congress, Kempe claimed that every country 'goes through a specific sequence of developmental stages in addressing the problem of child abuse'. These were: denial (that physical or sexual abuse exists to a significant extent); recognition of lurid physical abuse; recognition of less severe physical abuse; recognition of emotional abuse and neglect; and recognition of sexual abuse and incest. Kempe presented no evidence to support his analysis, but it was couched in the language of universal truth and scientific authority, and his followers accepted it without question.

In reality, Kempe's claim that denial is the first stage in a predictable sequence of societal responses to child abuse is historically baseless. A search through *New Zealand Truth* (a populist tabloid that has reported court cases in salacious detail for more than 90 years) shows that, in New Zealand at least, a vigorous concern for, and prosecution of, physical and sexual maltreatment of children existed long before Henry Kempe persuaded respectable newspapers and magazines to publicise the problem. Also, as accounts of the public response to 'battered-child syndrome' show, Kempe's ground-breaking paper was greeted not with denial, but with prompt and enthusiastic support.

As it happened, among those present to hear Kempe's address to the 1978 congress were two people who would go on to become leading New Zealand sexual abuse experts. They were paediatrician Dr David Geddis, medical director of The Royal New Zealand Society for the Health of Women and Children (the Plunket Society), and child psychiatrist Dr Karen Zelas, director of the Christchurch Child Health Clinic (and, in 1993, expert witness for the prosecution in the Christchurch Civic Crèche case).[4]

In September 1979, psychologist Miriam Jackson brought the child sexual abuse issue to a wider audience with a questionnaire in the *New Zealand Woman's Weekly* headed: 'Can you help? Your answers to this questionnaire will aid research into a shocking social ill – the sexual abuse of children.'[5] The questionnaire was designed for sexual abuse victims who had suffered deep and lasting trauma. There were no questions for readers who had not been abused, or for readers who had been abused but had got over it.

At the time, 220,000 copies of the *Woman's Weekly* were sold each week.[6] In statistical terms, those predominantly female purchasers made up the sample. It was a large sample by any standards. But, insofar as it excluded the one million New Zealand women who did not buy the *Woman's Weekly*, it was an unrepresentative one.

Of the 220,000 questionnaires distributed, only 315 were returned[7] – a response rate of 0.14 percent. But the possibility that a small response to a biased questionnaire distributed to an unrepresentative sample of New Zealand women would yield meaningless results did not deter Miriam Jackson. As her writings at the time indicated, she held strong views about the prevalence and effects of sexual abuse, and it was those views that mattered.

In fact, so keen was Jackson to publicise her views that she burst into print four months before the results of her questionnaire had been analysed.[8] 'IS SHE SAFE

WITH HER FATHER? INCEST – THE LAST TABOO' screamed the cover of the November 1979 *Broadsheet*. The article began with one woman's harrowing account of childhood incest. Then, on the basis of that story, Jackson went on to generalise and theorise. The father in the article, whom *Truth* readers would have regarded as a disgusting pervert, was to Jackson a normal man, engaging in normal male behaviour: 'Incest is *the* example of the extent to which male domination in the patriarchal family can go ... While the fear of rape controls all women, incest is the method of social control that works in the home.'[9]

Four months later, using figures that purported to be accurate to the second decimal place ('Nearly half– 44.77 percent– were victimised by relatives and nearly a quarter of the women by fathers or stepfathers'), Jackson presented her findings in the *Woman's Weekly*.[10] She claimed that 'the incidence of child molestation and rape – particularly incest – is more widespread than had been thought', and 'small girls are at most risk from friends [and] family'. In a follow-up article in *Broadsheet* she added: 'The men were nearly always white (90 percent) and usually married.' She also endorsed the advice of a respondent concerning 'the need for parents to protect their children and keep them away from adult males'.

At that time, Jackson's findings had little impact on the prevailing view that fathers were, on the whole, benign figures; protectors, providers and loving dads who cuddled, bathed and toileted their children as an everyday part of family life, but her toxic message of sexual anxiety and distrust towards men was promoted vigorously throughout the '80s. By the end of the decade her agonising question ('Is she safe with her father?') and her misanthropic answer (children should be kept away from adult males) had soaked deep into the fabric of New Zealand society.

Jackson's campaign received a major boost in 1981 when her *Woman's Weekly* survey results appeared in book form. *The Sexual Abuse of Children* – authored under Jackson's new name, Miriam Saphira – was published with assistance from the Mental Health Foundation (the organisation for which Hilary Haines was research officer). The book's aim was 'to break the silence and dispel the myths surrounding sexual abuse'.[11]

The book opened with a list of 'myths' and 'facts' about child sexual abuse. First up: The claim that 'It does not happen' is a 'common myth' (a statement reminiscent of the epigram on the title page of the *Malleus Malificarum*: 'to disbelieve in witchcraft is the greatest of heresies'). This is a red herring. The debate is not about whether sexual abuse happens. The debate is about the prevalence of sexual abuse and the damage it causes. In the course of my research I have encountered no one, in print or in person, who believes that sexual abuse does not happen.

Fifteen hundred copies of Saphira's book were given to the Department of Social Welfare, and the author embarked on a Mental Health Foundation-sponsored lecture tour of New Zealand. Her main message was: 'One out of four girls will be molested before she turns eighteen.' Within a few years Saphira's 'one in four' claim became widely accepted as a reliable estimate of the prevalence of sexual abuse in New Zealand.

That figure did not come from Jackson/Saphira's own research. Though she had no hesitation in turning her unscientific results into meaningless statistics, Miriam Saphira must have realised that claiming a molestation rate of 100 percent (on the basis that all her returned questionnaires came from women who had been molested) would have seriously compromised her credibility.

Saphira's 'one in four' figure actually came from a selective reading of the work of Dr Alfred Kinsey,[12] the first sex researcher to apply modern statistical methods to questions of who does what, when, and with whom. Saphira's source, *Sexual Behaviour in the Human Female* (1953), was based on the histories of more than 4000 white, American, female volunteers. Debate over the reliability of Kinsey's statistics has filled many books, and their applicability to other populations has been widely questioned, but Kinsey's study remains the most extensive investigation of human sexual behaviour ever undertaken.[13]

Back in 1937, when Indiana University introduced a course on sex education and marriage, Dr Kinsey, respected entomologist, and husband and father of irreproachable personal conservatism, was selected to be the teacher. He knew little about human sexual behaviour, so he went to the library to learn more. He soon discovered that no one else knew much either, so he decided that if he were to teach the facts he would first have to gather them. Beginning in 1938 and continuing until his death in 1956, Kinsey and his team interviewed 17,500 white adults – from every state in the union and from a range of educational, religious and socio-economic backgrounds – about their sexual histories.[14]

Kinsey found that nearly one woman in four (24 percent) reported at least one (and usually only one) sexual contact before adolescence with a male of at least 15 years of age and at least five years older than she was. Sexual contact was defined as contact with a male 'who appeared to be making sexual advances or who had made sexual contacts with the child'. In more than half the cases the 'contact' consisted of the girl seeing male genitals (though Kinsey noted that some exposure may have been accidental). In 9 percent of cases the contact was entirely verbal. The remainder involved fondling with no genital contact (31 percent), genital fondling (27 percent), oral-genital contact (2 percent) and coitus (3 percent).[15]

Saphira took Kinsey's one-in-four figure for 'sexual contacts' and redefined it as 'sexual abuse'. But there was no way she could use his findings regarding the males involved to support her claim that 'one in 16 girls will be molested by her father or stepfather before her sixteenth birthday'.[16] Kinsey found that 52 percent of the males were strangers, 32 percent were friends or acquaintances, 9 percent were uncles, 4 percent were fathers and 3 percent were brothers.[17]

When Kinsey's figure for the number of women who experienced some form of pre-adolescent sexual contact with their own fathers is presented as a proportion of all the women in his sample, his results show that fewer than one girl in 100 had any sort of sexual contact with her own father. Also, since over half the pre-adolescent sexual experiences in Kinsey's sample were visual or verbal, and 31 percent fell into the ambiguous category of 'non-genital fondling', Kinsey's findings indicate that fewer than one girl in 300 experienced any sort of genital contact with her own father.

Kinsey's findings also failed to support Saphira's claims that most sexual abuse victims suffered long-term damage. Kinsey found that little physical harm was reported, but 80 percent of respondents said they had been upset or frightened at the time. He noted: 'A small portion had been seriously disturbed; but in most instances the reported fright was nearer the level that children will show when they see insects, spiders or objects against which they have been adversely conditioned.'[18]

At the time of the publication of Saphira's *The Sexual Abuse of Children* in 1981, Kinsey's 30-year-old American study was the only major source of statistical information on human sexual behaviour available. But, with the escalation of interest in child sexual abuse, new surveys – concerned with sexual abuse rather than sexual behaviour – soon proliferated.

None of the recent surveys is comparable with the Kinsey report, or with each other. They vary in their definitions of 'child' and 'sexual abuse', in the populations studied, in the research methods used and in the analysis of the data. One of the most frequently cited recent American surveys was conducted by Dr Diana Russell in 1978. Like Saphira, Russell was a radical feminist. Prior to her survey, she authored *The Politics of Rape* (1975) and edited the *Proceedings of the International Tribunal on Crimes Against Women* (1976). In *Mental Health News*, Hilary Haines hailed Russell's study as the first major random-sample survey since Kinsey.[19] However, on closer examination, Russell's face-to-face questionnaire seems designed to uphold, rather than test, her radical feminist view of male sexuality. Of the 50 percent of Russell's sample who agreed to be interviewed, 38 percent (1 in 2.6) reported sexual abuse before the age of 18. As Haines pointed out, Russell achieved this startling result despite her definition of abuse being limited to direct physical contact. But (as Haines failed to point out) Russell's definition included everyday aspects of family life like unwanted hugs and kisses. Also, in contrast to Kinsey's age-based definition of adult–child sexual contacts, Russell's definition included 'sexual abuse by peers and other children'. In one instance Russell classified 'unwanted but non-forceful kissing by a cousin' as sexual abuse.

Though she found that child sexual abuse was alarmingly common, Russell suspected the true figure was higher still. 'There may be a significant number of women who have repressed such experiences from their conscious memories,' she wrote in 1983.[20] Russell provided no scientific support for that claim, but, thanks to the early-'80s proliferation of recovered memory stories, none was needed. *Michelle Remembers* (1980), and the books and articles that followed in its wake, persuaded feminist therapists and their clients that if they kept up the therapy for long enough, memories of sexual abuse were bound to surface. *Michelle Remembers* – which was later shown to be a hoax – also revived a belief that had fallen into disrepute in the wake of the great witch-hunts: that children could be brutally molested as part of satanic rituals.[21]

Gender politics and feminist anger were powerful influences on the early '80s expansion of the repressed memory movement. In a 1983 anthology of writings about incest edited by counsellor Ellen Bass, a contributor who had recovered incest memories during therapy wrote, 'My healing began with my simultaneous decision to accept myself as a lesbian and enter therapy.' Another counsellor wrote of her recovered memory experience, 'I have met and loved my rage.'[22]

In New Zealand, the repressed memory beliefs popularised by *Michelle Remembers* found a ready audience among followers of a mysterious home-grown form of analysis known as Primary Activation Therapy. This therapy is based on the belief that virtually everyone has been sexually abused in childhood, and everything from stammering to short-sightedness can be blamed on repressed memories of child sexual abuse. Primary Activation therapists extract lurid accounts of these supposed memories from clients using the paint-by-numbers instructions in the Primary Activation manual. To speed the extraction, the manual provides graphic descriptions of the basic 'P' (paedophile) scenes that therapists are expected to uncover.[23]

Around the world, radical feminist theorists and anti-pornography activists hailed the rising tide of repressed memories as proof that child sexual abuse was rampant. But it wasn't proof at all; it was an unfounded theory based on the belief that human memory is essentially accurate, and that traumatic memories can be repressed and recovered years later. To say that this belief is debatable would be an understatement. Battles over the nature of memory have raged in homes and courtrooms, in scholarly journals and at learned conferences around the world. In the arenas of politics and the law, the rage and righteousness of the recovered memory movement often prevails, but when the debate focuses on matters of science, memory researchers like Elizabeth Loftus usually win hands down. In studies on more than 20,000 subjects, Loftus has demonstrated that human memory is remarkably fragile and inventive, that eye-witness testimony is often unreliable, that false memories can be triggered in up to 25 percent of individuals merely by suggestion, and that memory can be altered simply by giving incorrect post-event information.[24]

In the early '80s, while Primary Activation Therapy was being practised in secret in New Zealand, the public learnt about the sensational side of the repressed memory debate, and about local initiatives in the field of child sexual abuse, through the popular media. Driving the initiatives was a loose coalition of feminists (led by Saphira and Haines), child protectionists (led by Zelas and Geddis) and anti-pornography activists of religious-conservative and feminist persuasions. In theory, the Society for the Promotion of Community Standards was concerned with depictions of nudity and sexual acts, while Women Against Pornography was concerned with the exploitation of women, but in practice both groups campaigned against the same sexually explicit magazines and videos, and both groups were subjected to the same hostility and derision from the same disrespectful sections of the community.

When the anti-pornography groups turned their attention to child pornography, the hostility and derision evaporated. Not only was child pornography totally unacceptable to the general public, it offered sexual abuse campaigners a welcome answer to some troubling questions like: why were so many men with no histories of mental illness or crime apparently molesting their own and other people's children? How were they getting away with it? Why was there so little physical evidence when (if the flood of recovered memories was to be believed) child sexual abuse was widespread and had been going on for years? To these questions the anti-pornographer's ultimate fantasy (an ultra-secret international multimillion-dollar kid-porn conspiracy orchestrated by Satan-worshippers) provided the answer. To everyone who believed that men were black-hearted predators, and that child sexual abuse was rampant, it made perfect sense.

• • •

During the first half of the '80s the primary focus of the child abuse awareness campaign was on legislative change and professional education. High-level committees were formed (the National Advisory Committee on the Prevention of Child Abuse in 1981; the Advisory Committee on the Investigation, Detection and Prosecution of Offences Against Children in 1985). The Department of Justice and the Institute of Criminology undertook a victim-oriented study of rape in 1982. National conferences were held (the Justice Department conference on rape, and the Mental Health Foundation conference on child abuse in 1982; the YWCA Rape and Sexual Violence to Women and Children Conference in 1983; the Child Abuse Prevention Society seminar in 1984; the Family Violence Conference in

1985). Organisations were established (the Incest Survivors Group in 1981; the Child Abuse Prevention Society, and the Help Foundation in 1982; Women Against Pornography in 1983). Overseas experts toured New Zealand and New Zealand experts toured overseas. High-profile books appeared (Rush's *The Best Kept Secret* and Smith and Pazders' *Michelle Remembers* in 1980, Saphira's *The Sexual Abuse of Children*, Sgroi's *Handbook of Clinical Intervention in Child Sexual Abuse* and Dworkin's *Pornography* in 1981, Russell's *Rape in Marriage* in 1982, Kempe and Kempe's *The Common Secret*, Russell's *Sexual Exploitation* and Masson's *The Assault on the Truth* in 1984). Multidisciplinary child abuse teams were established in 1982. Saphira's 'knicker sticker' campaign was launched (6000 stickers reading 'Children, don't let an adult put a hand down your pants – tell someone about it' appeared in 1983). Old laws were changed. New laws were introduced. And throughout the early '80s seminars were held for the frontline troops in the battle against child sexual abuse. The key messages were: 'one out of four girls will be molested before she turns eighteen', 'the man will usually know the child', 'one in five child molesters will be the father, stepfather or foster father', 'only a third of sexually abused children tell anyone', 'most women who were molested as children experience some difficulties in their adult life', 'the victim must be believed', 'the victim must be protected' and 'wherever possible a female counsellor should assist the sexually abused girl'.[25]

These messages were rarely questioned by the mainly female seminar participants, not only because they were based on Miriam Saphira's work (which had been endorsed by the Police, Social Welfare and Justice departments), but also because they were seen as part of the ongoing war against male oppression (a war that had gained new urgency in 1981 when popular Wellington feminist Leigh Minnitt was murdered by her husband). Besides, anyone who challenged the radical feminist analysis of child sexual abuse laid themselves open to accusations of being 'sexist' and 'in denial', and of wanting to put the clock back to the bad old days when victims were disbelieved.[26]

The first two accusations were unfair to those expressing honest concern. The latter was a self-serving myth – while we can never know what proportion of children were disbelieved, a search through back issues of *New Zealand Truth* reveals that, throughout its 65-year history prior to the rise of feminism, it was commonplace for children's complaints of sexual molestation to be taken seriously, for child suspects to be prosecuted, and for child witnesses to be believed by juries. But – and this is another reason why few women questioned Saphira's claims – respectable women did not read *Truth*.

In response to Saphira's campaign, existing organisations concerned with the welfare of women and children turned their attention to child sexual abuse. At a YWCA conference on 'Rape and Sexual Violence to Women and Children' in 1983, the keynote speaker quoted a US claim that 66 percent of men had a 'conquest mentality' towards women (and could therefore be justifiably called 'rapists'), observing: 'Well, we can be pleased that not all men rape, but surely that 34 percent who don't must understand that as long as we have to fear the 66 percent (and we can't tell who is who) then we have to treat all men with fear and suspicion.'[27]

During the early '80s many new radical feminist organisations were formed. One of the first, Christchurch-based Incest Survivors' Group, was headed by Lynda Morgan, who, in 1992, became one of three Department of Social Welfare staff responsible for interviewing children in the Christchurch Civic Crèche case. Between 1982 and 1987 Morgan and her group distributed information kits nationwide, participated in television and radio programmes, addressed public meetings and provided counselling to sexual abuse victims.[28] In 1984 the Christchurch *Press* reported:

> Linda [sic] Morgan regards the high incidence of child sexual abuse in New Zealand as a 'statement' about our society. 'It says what our society is – bloody sick,' she says. 'For any woman it's a normal childhood thing to be molested in some way' … There is so much of it that Linda Morgan calls it an epidemic.[29]

Initially, the invisibility of the epidemic was a problem. How can you prove there's an epidemic when few children complain? Clearly, the challenge facing abuse campaigners was to identify the non-disclosers and get them to disclose.

In 1982 Miriam Saphira admitted that victims of unreported abuse were difficult to identify. However, once Suzanne Sgroi's *Handbook of Clinical Intervention in Child Sexual Abuse* (1981) became available, investigators were able to use her list of behavioural indicators to identify alleged victims. In 1984 Eileen Swan, coordinator of Auckland's Help Foundation, discussed indicators of child sexual abuse at a national seminar attended by 300 child protection workers. Swan's list (which was actually a list of behaviours that most young children display at some time) included: eating, sleeping and elimination disturbances; regressive behaviour; excessive masturbation; irritability; sophisticated knowledge of sexual acts; excessive attempts to manipulate the genitals of others; psychosomatic complaints; school problems; phobias, fears; secretiveness; lack of friends; stealing, lying; manipulative, seductive and compulsive behaviours; truancy.[30]

Like Patricia Bartlett of the Society for the Protection of Community Standards, Swan seemed unable to accept that the natural curiosity of young children about sex could be healthy and harmless. 'Any signal or statement from a child about sexual activity should be noted as a cry for assistance,' she said. She also warned colleagues not to be misled by what could seem, to the uninitiated, a normal, healthy relationship between the child and the man she dubbed 'the offender'. 'While the interactions between child and offender may appear to be positive and affectionate, this in itself is not an indication that sexual contact did not occur or that there has not been any psychological damage to the child,' she said.

Having identified the victim, the next step, obtaining a disclosure, presented further challenges. Despite being assured that it was safe to disclose, and despite being assured that they would be believed, many children stubbornly insisted that they had not been abused. This all-too-common outcome could have caused a crisis of confidence in the child protection movement. But, thanks to American psychiatrist Roland Summit's 'Child Sexual Abuse Accommodation Syndrome', the crisis was averted.

Summit's syndrome was not research-based and its construction lacked intellectual rigour (by his own admission it was 'entirely impressionistic'). Nonetheless, it has been invoked in hundreds of child sexual abuse cases worldwide (including the Christchurch Civic Crèche case) to 'prove' that children who show behavioural signs of abuse but insist they have not been abused really have been abused, that children who have made vague allegations and have later retracted those allegations really have been abused, and that children who *don't* show behavioural signs and who consistently deny being abused really have been abused.[31]

The counter-argument to Child Sexual Abuse Accommodation Syndrome goes like this: even if we accept the child protection movement's exaggerated statistics about the prevalence of child sexual abuse (that one in four children has been abused), this still means that three out of every four children (75 percent) have not been abused.

Therefore, in the absence of any conclusive evidence, when a child denies being abused, there is a 75 percent chance that the child is telling the truth.

In Britain, child protection entrepreneur Arnon Bentovim (a child psychiatrist at London's Great Ormond Street Hospital for Sick Children) developed an interviewing technique based on Summit's theory. Bentovim used 'anatomically correct' dolls (with penises, vaginas, pubic hair and breasts) and questions designed to elicit disclosures from children 'who could not, or would not, talk about possible abusive experiences spontaneously'.[32] According to Bentovim's colleague Dr Eileen Vizard, the technique involved:

(1) *Free play period.*
(2) *Undressing the dolls and naming body parts.*
(3) *Types of touching* – Nice/appropriate. Not nice – bad/inappropriate. Icky – funny/confusing. The therapist asks child to say or to show with dolls what sort of touching is nice, not nice, i.e.:
  (a) Child says or shows own example of nice touching.
  (b) Child blocks; therapist demonstrates examples of stroking or smacking using dolls.

(4) *Naming of dolls* – Child may spontaneously name the perpetrator and identify a doll with that name early on/at any stage in the interview. Therapist now uses this named doll in further re-enactment. If child blocks, therapist asks child to pick a doll which has done a rude thing to a child, and to name the doll. If child blocks again, for fear of consequence of disclosure, therapist should firmly nominate a doll as the alleged perpetrator, based on referral information.

(5) *Re-enactment of the abuse* – Scene set by asking child for details of room, furniture, clothes, time of day etc when the abuse happened. Child asked directly to show possible abuse with dolls, i.e. 'Has anything rude/sexual happened to you? Show me with the dolls.' If child does this, therapist to ask child to show if any other types of abuse happened, e.g. buggery, oral and genital contact etc. If child blocks here, therapist to ask directly if these abuses occurred or not. If child cannot show any abuse spontaneously, therapist to ask child direct (non-leading) questions about types of abuse, i.e. 'Did he touch you?' (pointing to dolls); 'Where?'; 'What with?'; 'Can you show me on the dolls?' The therapist continues with direct questions, to clarify if other forms of abuse occurred: 'Did he touch you on the fanny?' If child unable to do any of this spontaneously, therapist may wish to help child by offering:
(a) Multi-choice questions – 'Did he touch you there or there?'
(b) Hypothetical questions– 'Supposing Uncle Jack had touched you there (like you told the social worker) would it have been with a private bit of his body, or not with a private bit?'
– These questions are very helpful for blocked/frightened or denying children.
– Therapist should also ask if other people were involved; if so, what were their names etc.

(6) *Recapping, reassurance and* relief.[33]

That the mutually reinforcing combination of Summit's baseless syndrome and Bentovim's coercive interviewing technique was accepted without question by radical feminist investigators intent on proving that child sexual abuse was rampant should come as no surprise. What seems more surprising is that it was also accepted, and therefore validated, by many professionals in medicine and the law. This may have been because the success of the feminist-led child sexual abuse awareness campaign had sent a clear message to the child psychiatrists, paediatricians and family lawyers who had hitherto considered themselves leaders and innovators in the child protection field. That message was: If you don't accept the radical feminist analysis of child sexual abuse you will not be allowed on the bandwagon, and if you don't get on the bandwagon you will be left behind.

By invoking Summit's syndrome, and by basing their interviews on Bentovim's technique, New Zealand child sexual abuse investigators were able to greatly improve their detection rates. In the second edition of her book (in 1985) Miriam Saphira noted:

> The number of [child sex abuse] cases reported to the Police has doubled since the first edition was published. These cases came to notice because the children told someone who responded or someone noticed changes in the children and asked the right questions.

• • •

In 1985 a group from the Department of Psychological Medicine at the University of Otago tapped into the *zeitgeist* with the first of two women's mental health surveys. Questionnaires were sent to 2000 women. In follow-up interviews, 314 women were asked, among other things, whether they had ever been sexually abused during childhood. Almost 10 percent said they had.[34]

A decade earlier, the majority of respondents would have regarded child sexual abuse as a serious but uncommon phenomenon. But by 1985 most would have learnt that the number of women claiming to have been sexually abused in childhood was increasing dramatically. Studies of the spread of alarming ideas indicate that, having learnt of this trend, many women in search of explanations for their own troubles would have found it easy to believe that they too had been victims of childhood abuse. They would also have found it easy to believe that what they had previously regarded as inconsequential sexual experiences were actually deeply traumatising episodes of sexual abuse.

Outbreaks of this sort of behavioural contagion – in which the distress of sufferers may be severe, but for which no objective evidence of any ailment can be found – have occurred throughout recorded history. Between 1872 and 1990, more than 100 outbreaks have been reported in the scientific literature. The forms the outbreaks take reflect the anxieties prevalent in the cultures in which they occur. In all cultures, outbreaks tend to be preceded by periods of heightened anxiety and are commonly triggered by emotionally disturbed women.

At the start of an outbreak the contagion usually spreads along pre-existing social networks. Later, when the media becomes involved, prior social relationships become irrelevant. Though the complaint may be distressing, it confers on participants secondary benefits like attention, status, sympathy, leisure, camaraderie, relief of tedium and financial compensation.[35]

The phenomenon has been described as 'mass hysteria'. Whether the Christchurch Civic Crèche case was an example of mass hysteria has been widely debated. But before we can address the debate, we need to address the question What is 'mass hysteria'? In fact the term is misleading. 'Mass' implies close physical contact between the afflicted – as at the Nuremberg Rally or during the group suicide of a religious cult – but that is not necessarily the case. The 'Invasion from Mars' panic that took place in the United States on 30 October 1938 following a radio broadcast, is an example of the way media-spread anxiety can break out among geographically isolated individuals and small groups.

'Hysteria' is another confusing term. It has its roots in the belief that certain illnesses in women could be attributed to the capricious wanderings of the womb around the body. By the 16th century, scholars had recognised that the notion was anatomically groundless, and that men too could exhibit the symptoms of hysteria, but the term persists because the condition it describes – the expression of psychological distress in the form of physical 'illness' – is unquestionably real. Hysteria is also unquestionably contagious, but these days the term 'mass hysteria' is regarded with suspicion because it suggests that the afflicted are mentally disturbed. In fact, while this may be true of the leaders of an outbreak, it is generally untrue of the followers. Indeed, the willingness of followers to share the beliefs current in their community indicates that they are in sound mental health. For most people caught up in a communal panic it is the *ideas*, rather than the *individuals*, that are the problem.

Many contemporary epidemiologists believe that outbreaks of mass hysteria are infrequent and short-lived in Western society. In a 1973 article in *Psychological Medicine*, Benaim and his colleagues noted, with the complacency of Victorian missionaries: 'The fact that they do not spread so widely [in Western society] may be due to the fact that people are less credulous, more sophisticated, and less bound to unquestioning faith.'[36] Two other explanations should be considered: the first is that hysteria as a concept has become so unfashionable that many researchers wouldn't recognise the condition if they fell over it; the second is that – judging by the outrage provoked by McEverdy and Beard's 1970 paper on Royal Free Disease (a mysterious ailment that struck down more than 300 people, mainly nurses, and led to the temporary closure of London's Royal Free Hospital in 1955) – any researchers who recognise the condition in a Western society would be well advised to keep quiet about it.

Hysteria as a diagnosis has fallen into disrepute. In the '60s anti-psychiatrists like Thomas Szasz argued that hysteria was a label used by the powerful to control the powerless who behaved disruptively (and who therefore did not know their place). In the '70s feminists seized on this socio-political analysis and made it their own. Hysteria, they declared, was a label invented by misogynists for the purpose of belittling women and reinforcing patriarchal oppression. In 1980 hysteria was dropped from the *American Psychiatric Associations Diagnostic and Statistical Manual.*

Nowadays mainstream psychiatrists use the term 'somatoform disorder' to describe representations of personal distress in the language of physical complaint. However, because the 'somatoform disorder' label suggests that sufferers may have overreacted to, or even imagined, the trauma to which they attribute their problems, the diagnosis is not looked upon kindly by sexual abuse therapists. They prefer the label Post Traumatic Stress Disorder (PTSD).

PTSD is a controversial diagnosis developed in the guilty aftermath of the Vietnam War. Its symptoms include all the normal emotional responses to severe trauma, and the rare, but well-known, lingering disturbances that may occur in trauma sufferers with a predisposition to neurotic disorder. Because this grab-bag of symptoms is as unoriginal as it is all-encompassing, many mainstream psychiatrists regard PTSD as a fashionable collage rather than a genuine disorder.

In personal and public disasters, counsellors often use PTSD as a Trojan horse with which to invade the privacy of shocked survivors, even though everyday experience suggests that such people would be better off with a kind word and a nice cup of tea. Furthermore, studies of survivors of the Mount St Helens eruption show that psychiatric symptoms are not – as therapists would have us believe – common responses to trauma, but rare responses, usually confined to those with some pre-existing vulnerability. (Only 3.6 percent of the Mount St Helens eruption survivors developed psychiatric symptoms – most commonly clinical depression or morbid anxiety. Within two years most symptoms had resolved. After two years, the only people still afflicted were those with the sort of life-long vulnerabilities that would have put them at risk of developing neurotic disorders in even the most tranquil of circumstances.)[37]

Unfortunately the mischief done by PTSD does not end with its propensity to turn mentally healthy survivors into victims in need of treatment. Therapists with an interest in child sexual abuse also use the label to medicalise the commonplace emotional vicissitudes, personal disappointments and career shortcomings complained of by their adult clients. This 'post-traumatic' explanation encourages disaffected individuals to blame their troubles on some past trauma, even if no objective evidence of any such trauma can be found.

With the emergence of Somatoform Disorder and PTSD as psychiatric diagnoses, the term 'hysteria' has been largely abandoned by the mental health professions. Nonetheless, the term persists in the vernacular heartland where it has come to mean somatisation plus drama – the sort of high-pitched representations of personal distress in the language of physical complaint that have become the staple of talk-shows.

Thus 'hysteria' and 'histrionics' have become confused. This is unfortunate, because in reality most people with hysterical illnesses/somatoform disorders (such as, say, blindness with no organic cause), and most people caught up in outbreaks of mass hysteria/epidemic anxiety (such as, say, those that occur in response to imaginary gas leaks), seem calm and sensible, and show no signs of histrionic behaviour.

• • •

Between the first Otago women's mental health survey in 1985 and the second in 1989-90, the child sexual abuse awareness campaign gathered supporters and speed, and mainstream professions in medicine and the law struggled to get a grip on the steering wheel.

Prominent child protection workers made overseas study trips. Top-level conferences were held. Influential organisations were formed (the Family Violence Prevention Coordinating Committee in 1986, Christchurch's Sexual Abuse Therapy and Rehabilitation Team in 1987, Doctors for Sexual Abuse Care in 1988). Reports on the problem were published by the Accident Compensation Commission and the National Advisory Committee on the Prevention of Child Abuse in 1986, by the Commission of Inquiry into Violence in 1987, by the Advisory Committee on the Investigation, Detection and Prosecution of Offences Against Children, the first Otago sexual abuse survey, the Mental Health Foundation and the Royal Commission on Social Policy in 1988 and by the Committee of Inquiry into Pornography in 1989.

Among the influential visitors who toured New Zealand during the late '80s were: child witness expert Dr Gail Goodman in 1987; radical feminist anti-pornography campaigner Catharine MacKinnon in 1988; Astrid Heger, the paediatrician who misdiagnosed mass child sexual abuse in the McMartin preschool case in California, in 1989; satanic ritual abuse expert Pamela Klein in 1990.

Influential books appeared: Diana Russell's *The Secret Trauma* in 1986; Saphira's *For Your Child's Sake* in 1987; Bass and Davis's *The Courage to Heal* in 1988; the Family Violence Prevention Coordinating Committee booklet *Reach Out* in 1990. There were also children's books: *Katie's Yukky Problem*, *Daniel and His Therapist* and *Megan's Secret* by Lynda Morgan in 1985; Jenny Hessell's *What's Wrong with Bottoms?*, and Hayward and Carlyle's *Too Close for Comfort*, in 1988; Saphira and McIntyre's *Look Back, Stride Forward* in 1989. And there were sexual abuse prevention programmes for children: *Keeping Ourselves Safe* in 1988; *Feeling Safe* in 1990.

Old laws were changed, new laws were introduced and high-level initiatives were taken. In 1987 multidisciplinary sexual abuse teams were established in South Auckland, Lower Hutt and Christchurch. In 1988 the Minister of Social Welfare increased funding for child abuse services by $20 million per year.

Feature articles in the *Woman's Weekly* in October 1986 ('RAPE: What victims should know about compensation') and in *Broadsheet* in November 1987 ('Accident compensation for sexual assault'), and a 1987 Accident Compensation Commission leaflet advised women that counselling and up to $10,000 in lump-sum compensation was available to anyone who had been sexually assaulted after 1 April 1974, even if no one has been charged and no complaint had been laid.

• • •

While most developments in child sexual abuse detection and treatment impacted on women and children, the highly influential 1988 Telethon impacted on the whole community. The televised charity event followed the tradition established by New Zealand's first 24-hour Telethon in 1975, which captured the hearts, minds and wallets of the nation. Further Telethons were held annually, and later biennially. Each was a countrywide festival of giving and togetherness. Each raised funds for a designated cause.

Not that the cause really mattered. To the organisers, Telethon was a hugely successful publicity stunt. Don Hutchings, organiser of the first eight Telethons, told *Metro*, 'We quite honestly got to the point where we sublimated the cause and promoted the festival ... we could do Telethon for a three-legged dog.'[38]

The cause for Telethon '88 was not a three-legged dog, but it did turn into something of a Cerberus. The aim was 'to reduce the level of violence in our communities'. The Telethon public relations officer turned to Mental Health Foundation publications for inspiration, and the 'one in four' sexual abuse claim leapt off the page and grabbed him by the lapels. As a result, in the month leading up to the festival, the nation was saturated with the 'one in four' claim in radio, television and print advertisements.

Two advertisements stood out. One featured a photograph of four babies. The headline read: 'ONE OF THESE CHILDREN WILL BE SCARRED FOR LIFE'. The text began, 'One in four girls will be sexually abused before they turn 18. Half of them by their own father.' The other advertisement featured a photograph of a frightened little girl in bed. Behind her, in the darkened doorway, was the ominous silhouette of a man. The headline read: 'IT'S NOT THE DARK SHE'S AFRAID OF'. The text began: 'Some children treasure Dad's goodnight kiss while others live to dread it. Because some fathers don't stop there.'

Interested parties in the fields of politics, justice, welfare and health hailed the Telethon campaign as a long-overdue attempt to make the wider community 'face cruel facts'. Many in the wider community did not take kindly to the attempt (and given that incest convictions nationwide for the previous year totalled 19, one can hardly blame them).[39]

A bewildered letter to the *New Zealand Listener* echoed the questions that ricocheted around the nation:

> This is a terrible accusation against fathers. Would such an accusation result in mothers seeing their husbands as potential molesters of their own daughters and what would such suspicion do to their marriage? And how reliable is the evidence for fathers molesting their own daughters? What assumptions have been made to support this contention? The statistics are necessarily based on some sort of sampling technique. How big and how representative are the samples? Have reputable mathematical significance tests been applied to the results?[40]

Several prominent individuals sprang to the defence of the 'one in four' figure. Member of Parliament Marilyn Waring said: 'There is evidence to support the claims, including the leading world study on sexual abuse from the Kinsey Institute, which says that almost all men behave in a sexually offensive manner and those that don't are nonconformists'. Despite the controversy, on Telethon Day the hype and hoopla prevailed: $5.5 million was raised.[41]

When the party was over, the 'one in four' claim was subject to further analysis. Articles in the *Listener* and *Metro* criticised the Mental Health Foundation for supplying exaggerated figures, the Telethon organisers for exaggerating them further, and the advertising agency for compounding the problem. Those who previewed the advertisements were criticised for allowing the hyperbole to pass unchecked.[42] In response, the accused parties defended the 'one in four' claim, defended themselves, denied they were anti-family or anti-men and invoked the concepts of 'denial' and 'backlash' to explain the fuss.

• • •

The second Otago women's mental health survey took place in 1989–90. A questionnaire was sent to 3000 women, and follow-up interviews were conducted with 497.[43] Throughout the survey period it was almost impossible to watch television, listen to the radio, attend a film, open a newspaper or magazine or glance at a display of newly published books without being reminded of the sexual abuse issue. One of the most influential books of the period was *The Courage to Heal* by Ellen Bass and Laura Davis. The book was aimed at women who had no memories of being abused, but who thought they might have been. Just about anything – feelings of inadequacy, fear of success, lack of motivation – was presented as possible evidence of sexual abuse. Bass and Davis told readers, 'If you don't remember your abuse, you are not alone. Many women don't have memories, and some never get memories. This doesn't mean they weren't abused.' To help readers recover their memories, many suggestive, self-hypnotic techniques and 'survivor' stories of child sex abuse (including ritual abuse) were included in the book.

Under the circumstances, it is perhaps not surprising that the level of retrospectively reported child sexual abuse rose from almost ten percent in the 1985 Otago survey to 32 percent in the 1989–90 survey.[44] Some of the increase may have been due to the broader definition of sexual abuse and the later cut-off age for childhood used in the second survey. Also, the *zeitgeist* may have encouraged some genuinely abused women to disclose their abuse for the first time, but the finding of 'a stable amount of sexual abuse in this community during the last 50 years' is not so easily explained. Why didn't the abuse rate fall during World War II, when a substantial proportion of the adult male population was away overseas? When challenged on this point, a member of the Otago research team suggested that the men who had remained at home had taken up the slack. All things considered, the possibility that the survey may have been contaminated by over-reporting seems a more likely explanation.

The second Otago survey also studied the long-term effects of retrospectively reported child sexual abuse. The researchers distinguished between non-contact abuse (exposure, spying, indecent suggestions, pornography and so on), non-genital contact (touching of breasts or buttocks, inappropriate kissing and so on), genital contact, attempted intercourse, and intercourse. They found no relationship between non-contact and non-genital sexual abuse in childhood and poor mental health in adulthood. However, they did find a relationship between serious child sexual abuse (repeated genital contact or intercourse prior to the age of 12) and poor adult mental health (primarily anxiety and depression). But, even among women seriously abused in childhood, poor mental health was the exception rather than the rule; 75 percent of the victims of serious child sexual abuse were found to be mentally healthy adults.

The Otago researchers found poor mental health to be more common in women from dysfunctional families who had experienced some combination of serious physical, emotional and sexual abuse. No clear relationship was found between the type of abuse suffered and the symptoms displayed. Mentally disordered women who had been abused as children – physically, emotionally or sexually – suffered from the same sort of psychological disturbances as mentally disordered women who had not. No cases of PTSD or Multiple Personality Disorder (the ailments claimed by sexual abuse campaigners to be common and lasting after-effects of child abuse) were found. The researchers concluded:

> The message for therapists is that when evaluating the relevance of childhood abuse to beware an exclusive and potentially exaggerated focus on the traumas of sexual abuse which may obscure both the relevance of other forms of abuse and the unfolding of other damaging developmental influences.[45]

Other retrospective community studies from around the world have reported prevalence rates of child sexual abuse ranging from 3 percent to 62 percent. Some variations may be accounted for by differences in the definitions used and the survey methods employed, but, even if all the known variables are standardised, the results of such studies will still be tainted by those great unknown and unknowable variables: the levels of over-reporting and underreporting.

Scholars in search of child sexual abuse prevalence rates that do not depend on the inherent unreliability of retrospective self-reporting have turned to contemporary reports and conviction rates for their statistics. One of the most carefully planned and randomised American surveys using this approach, the 1981 *National Study of Incidence and Severity of Child Abuse and Neglect*, found the prevalence of sexual abuse among American children to be 0.2 percent.[46] In pursuit of a comparable figure for New Zealand, I asked Dr Phil Silva, director of the Dunedin Multidisciplinary Health and Development Research Unit, about his ongoing study of the physical, intellectual, emotional and social development of a cohort of 1000 Dunedin children born between 31 March 1972 and 1 April 1973.

'Phil,' I said, 'how many cases of child sexual abuse did you pick up?'

'None,' he replied.

So what is the answer? Is the true prevalence of child sexual abuse higher than one in four, lower than one in 1000 or somewhere between? Do 'most women who were molested as children experience some difficulties in their adult life', or is sexual abuse just one of many adverse childhood experiences that may or may not cause lasting harm? Clearly, the only answer is: *we don't know*.

• • •

In the absence of any definitive knowledge about the prevalence and consequences of child sexual abuse, those involved in the investigation and prosecution of the Christchurch Civic Crèche case had to base their handling of the case on the beliefs, assumptions, educated guesses and tentative conclusions recorded in the official publications of the time.[47] These can be summarised as follows:

- Child sexual abuse is a widespread problem with serious long-term consequences.
- All males are potential child molesters.
- High priority must be given to discovering and treating victims of child sexual abuse, and to convicting and punishing offenders.
- The incidence is so high that any given accusation of molestation cannot be dismissed as improbable; rather, it is highly probable.

In the absence of any definitive knowledge (but with the findings of this chapter to rely on), I too must approach the Christchurch Civic Crèche case with a collection of beliefs, assumptions, educated guesses and tentative conclusions. These are:

- Child sexual abuse happens. It may or may not cause lasting harm. The long-term effects are difficult to determine because traumatic sexual abuse usually occurs in association with other detrimental childhood factors.
- Late-'70s estimates of the extent and severity of child sexual abuse were inflated by the sexual–political agendas of the researchers.
- False estimates from the late '70s fuelled a child sexual abuse panic.
- During the '80s, the panic gained official credibility. Resources were poured into publicising, detecting and treating the perceived problem. Estimates of the extent and severity of child sexual abuse were further inflated as a result.
- All estimates of the prevalence of child sexual abuse are contaminated by unknown and unknowable levels of under-reporting and over-reporting.
- There is probably no way of ever knowing the truth.

CHAPTER 3

Crimen Exceptum

TO THE AUTHORITIES of the 16th and 17th centuries, witchcraft was *crimen exceptum*, a crime distinct from all others. In 1580 the great French legal scholar Jean Bodin wrote: 'Proof of such evil is so obscure and difficult that not one out of a million witches would be accused or punished if regular legal procedures were followed.'[1]

Exceptional crimes require exceptional counter-measures. With witchcraft, as with child sexual abuse, the perpetrators and victims were rarely obvious. To identify them, special investigative techniques had to be devised and special investigators had to be trained in their use. To secure convictions, special laws had to be passed.

With regard to physical signs, witch-finders were accused of interpreting haemorrhoids and the scars of childbirth as 'witches' marks'. In much the same way, present-day medical investigators have been accused of interpreting normal variations in the appearance of the hymen and the dilatation of the anus as signs of sexual abuse.

When it came to behavioural signs, the afflicted could be particularly helpful. During the great witch-hunts, William Somers, 'the Boy of Nottingham', exhibited all the signs of demonic possession after studying a pamphlet on the *Witches of Warboys* and receiving coaching from an exorcist.[2] In much the same way, a key child witness in the Christchurch Civic Crèche case exhibited all the signs of satanic abuse after his mother had studied *Ritual Child Abuse: Discovery, diagnosis and treatment*.

But because most physical and behavioural signs of witchcraft were inconclusive, and because even the clearest signs could be caused by something else, the confessions of alleged perpetrators, and the spectral evidence of alleged victims (the dreams, visions and hallucinations of those said to be 'bewitched'), were the most important evidence of all. In Scotland and continental Europe, witch-hunters extracted confessions by torture and the threat of torture. In England, where torture was banned and witch-suspects were consequently less willing to confess, witch-hunters had to rely on the spectral evidence of alleged victims. Nowadays sexual abuse counsellors use 'dream work', 'guided imagery', 'visualisation' and 'psychodrama' to elicit the modern-day equivalent of spectral evidence from their clients, and, as was the case during the great witch-hunts, children, adolescent girls and mentally unstable adults have been fruitful sources of such evidence.[3]

Once the evidence against a witch-suspect had been collected, the case had to be proved in court. This was no mere formality. The crime of witchcraft went onto the statute books of Europe at a time when suspects were entitled to know the charges against them and the identity of their accusers. The evidence of children, interested parties and convicted felons was normally inadmissible. It was generally accepted that juries should have no interest in the conviction of the accused, that confessions should not be extorted by threat or force, and that witnesses should not be intimidated or bribed and should give evidence only on matters of which they have first-hand knowledge. But witchcraft was *crimen exceptum*. It was not amenable to the normal principles of proof. So the laws had to be changed to make witch-convictions possible. In the final analysis, it was the law changes that swept away the rights of suspects to a fair trial, and the near universal acceptance by a normally sceptical judiciary that the coerced evidence of witchcraft was reliable, that made the great witch-hunts possible.[4]

In New Zealand over recent years the rights of suspects in sexual abuse cases have been similarly eroded.

3.i: The Rise of the Sexual Abuse Specialist

Before we consider the late '80s law changes that facilitated the conviction of sexual abusers, we need to consider the early '80s law changes that facilitated the emergence of sexual abuse specialists. The foundations for those changes were laid during the previous decade when a series of statutory provisions giving greater financial independence to women created a secure platform on which the big guns of family law reform could be assembled, and from which a fresh salvo of ground-breaking legislation could be launched.[5]

Prior to 1980, divorce was not to be undertaken lightly. You needed a two-year separation, four years living apart, or grounds like desertion or adultery. In a contested case you had to hire a private detective and present your evidence at a public hearing in the High Court (and, more often than not, suffer the indignity of having the whole tacky saga reported in *Truth*). Less titillating but equally stressful issues of custody, access and property were commonly dealt with in the District Court.

Behind the legislative reforms of the early '80s, with their provisions for counselling and mediation, no-fault divorce, closed-court hearings and restrictions on the publication of proceedings, was the well-intentioned belief that family breakdowns were a private matter. But privacy gained meant accountability lost. As Justice Felix Frankfurter of the United States Supreme Court observed:

> One of the demands of a democratic society is that the public should know what goes on in courts by being told by the Press what happens there, to the end that the public may judge whether our system of criminal justice is fair and right.[6]

As well as being private rather than public, New Zealand family courts applied a blend of established and new provisions to make the proceedings informal rather than formal, inquisitorial rather than adversarial (i.e. in the nature of an inquiry conducted by a judge, rather than in the nature of a contest between two sides with the judge acting as referee). As in all civil courts, proof to a criminal standard ('beyond reasonable doubt') was not required – proof 'on the balance of probabilities' was sufficient. Another existing provision, that allowed a court dealing with family issues to 'receive any evidence that it thinks fit, whether it is otherwise admissible in a Court of law or not', came into its own with three new provisions. The first allowed Family Court judges to call their own witnesses. The second allowed them to appoint a lawyer to represent the child. The third required judges to determine custody, access and protection issues according to 'the best interests of the child'.

Judges used to applying the relatively straightforward rules of the past – the 'mother principle' (that young children should be with their mothers), the 'father principle' (that older boys should be with their fathers) and the principle that siblings should be kept together – found that determining the best interests of the child was no easy matter. When there was no tangible evidence and when, as normally occurred in Family Court cases, the children did not give evidence, judges came to rely on the opinions of expert witnesses (primarily psychiatrists, psychologists, counsellors and social workers) and counsel for the child when making custody and access decisions.

Another feature of the Family Court legislation was its provision for counselling. The idea behind counselling is that, when your life is in a tangle, talking things through with a sensible, sympathetic and discreet outsider can help clarify the problems and find a workable solution. Before there were counsellors, people took their troubles to clergymen and doctors, to teacup readers and astrologers, and to trusted friends.

Counselling as a modern specialty began in New Zealand in the wake of World War II. Most of the first wave of counsellors were trained by psychiatrists. In the postwar years, medically trained psychiatrists were drawn into the public debate over war neuroses, marriage breakdown, and delinquency, but they did not normally treat emotionally distressed members of the community. This was partly because psychiatrists were expensive and there weren't many to go around, and partly because most people in crisis did not want to be labelled as mentally ill. Fortunately (and psychiatrists were as aware of this as anyone else), you didn't need years of specialist medical training to help someone suffering from ordinary emotional distress – an empathetic layperson with minimal training and good communication skills could do the job just as well. So the stage was set for the training of counsellors.

As it turned out, psychiatrists weren't even needed to train counsellors, but before anyone realised that, psychiatrists had established a beachhead for themselves among socially concerned middle-class folk with an interest in worthy causes. From their place in the community, they trained counsellors, commented on social issues and fought a series of losing battles on two social fronts.

On one front were the anti-psychiatry forces of the '60s and '70s, spearheaded from within by psychiatrists Thomas Szasz and R.D. Laing, and from beyond by a range of social and political groups that regarded psychiatry – with its drugs, shock treatments and surgical intrusions into the brain – as a tool of the Establishment. Anti-psychiatrists sought social change by forming communes, collectives and all manner of self-help groups; and personal change by studying meditation, self-actualisation and personal growth.

On the other front were the swelling hordes of psychologists with arts and science degrees. Many psychologists believed that their new specialty held the keys to curing everything from asthma to xenophobia, and their utopian claims were just what the nation's decision-makers wanted to hear. From the '70s on, employment opportunities for psychologists proliferated. To keep pace with the demand, psychology departments expanded, postgraduate courses were established, and increasing numbers of people studied the subject because it was fashionable and the job prospects were good.[7]

During the 1970s, psychiatrists and psychologists clashed over the nature of mental ill-health and who was best qualified to treat it. Psychiatrists argued that mental disorders – and especially major illnesses like schizophrenia – were best treated with judicious drug use (which could be prescribed only by the medically trained) and psychoanalysis. They also sought to extend their territory by labelling alcoholism and drug abuse (the latter formerly regarded as a crime) as mental disorders, and by calling for an increase in the number of psychiatrists. For their part, psychologists made a virtue of their drugfree approach and advocated treatments based on behaviour-modification techniques.

If the disputes between psychiatrists and psychologists were really about the merits of different therapeutic approaches, they would have been resolved by a 1977 article in *American Psychologist*. The report summarised the results of 375 studies of therapeutic outcomes and concluded that, while therapies for the mind were statistically effective in reducing psychologically painful symptoms, no approach could be said to be best. Also, while it was helpful for those providing verbal therapies to be 'empathetic', and for those providing behaviour-modification therapies to have some knowledge of behavioural principles, in general the credentials and experience of the therapist were unrelated to the client outcome. This may have been because, at that time, people sought help for their personal difficulties only when two essential preconditions were met: they were at a very low ebb, and they wanted to make improvements to their lives. These factors probably ensured that, unless the therapist was grossly incompetent or unethical, the client could only improve.[8]

During the counselling-infatuated '80s, as more and more people sought counselling, and more and more people who didn't want it had it thrust upon them, and more and more untrained and unsupervised counsellors went into business, the essential preconditions for therapeutic effectiveness applied less often and therapeutic outcomes were consequently far less certain. A survey in 1997 reported that counselling for women who had miscarried produced no sustained benefits, that bereavement counselling had no effect on the quality of life of people close to deceased cancer patients, and that depression among spouses of suicide victims was unaffected by counselling.[9] But back in the '70s, there was little doubt – on the whole, counselling worked.

In any event, the clashes between psychiatrists and psychologists were more about resources and power than about therapeutic effectiveness. The psychologists, seizing the drugfree moral high ground, went on, through sheer weight of burgeoning numbers, to colonise the new territory opened up by the psychiatrists' expanding definitions of mental disorder. By 1980, though psychiatrists were moving from mental hospitals and into community clinics, most were still doing the same unglamorous work they had always done – treating people with severe and disabling mental illnesses.

During the '70s, most psychologists and psychiatrists occupied paid positions in educational, penal and health institutions, and most lay counsellors worked for church-run organisations or groups like Marriage Guidance and Youthline. Throughout the decade, counselling was never more than a middle-class cottage industry. Even when publicity surrounding the 1977 Telethon (of which the Mental Health Foundation was the beneficiary) encouraged New Zealanders to seek counselling as a first rather than a last resort, the idea didn't catch on. But, with the establishment of the Family Courts in 1980, large numbers of people who may not otherwise have felt the need or want of counselling accepted it for two compelling reasons: it was compulsory and it was free. And large numbers of people took up a career in counselling for another compelling reason: Family Court counsellors were paid. Initially, most Family Court counsellors were trained by Marriage Guidance, but Family Court coordinators were free to appoint anyone they thought fit.

The early '80s were opportune times for the cottage industry of counselling to expand into a major occupational sector. In the wake of the controversial 1981 Springbok rugby tour, scores of disillusioned social activists gave up trying to change the world and set about trying to change themselves. Also, between 1981 and 1985 the New Zealand unemployment rate escalated and the real disposable incomes of full-time salary and wage earners plummeted. These pressures, along with an increase in single-parent families and a growing trend for women to combine motherhood with a career, increased the demand for flexible, part-time work for women.

Becoming a counsellor was an attractive option: no prior qualifications were needed; there was a wide range of optional training courses and no generally agreed training standards; the hours were flexible; the job market was expanding. Young women took up counselling in droves, and brought with them a medley of young women's motives: to help the needy; to overthrow oppression and injustice; to empower the powerless; to do the right thing; to be part of the action.

The growth of the counselling industry – at first within the Family Court system and later throughout the wider community – coincided with Miriam Saphira's child sexual abuse awareness campaign. But to deal with an epidemic on the scale envisaged by Saphira there could never be enough formally trained counsellors. To meet the demand, a profusion of enthusiastic, self-appointed feminist counsellors with an interest in alternative therapies and a disdain of recognised qualifications entered the field. According to a 1989 survey, most sexual abuse counsellors had acquired their specialist knowledge from seminars and books, rather than from recognised courses of study.[10]

To unearth child sexual abuse on the expected scale, the counsellor first had to accept that sexual abuse was everywhere. After that, finding signs of it was easy. When she had found the signs, the counsellor had to establish an empathetic relationship with the alleged victim. A sense of victimhood helped. Being a sexual abuse survivor was a good starting point. Failing that, any grievance, when analysed in terms of radical feminist theory, could bring a counsellor to the realisation that she too had been screwed, if not by the patriarch, then certainly by the patriarchy. (The constitution of the National Collective of Rape Crisis and Related Groups of Aotearoa states: 'Bodily rape cannot be isolated from the rape many women feel of their land and their culture', and 'Rape is … upheld by the patriarchal and colonial society'.)[11]

Once an empathetic relationship had been established, the counselling could start in earnest. *The Courage to Heal* urged alleged victims to remember and talk about every repugnant detail of the alleged abuse, whether they wanted to or not, to 'allow yourself to obsess', to visualise revenge, to fantasise about murder and castration, and to seek retribution through the courts.[12]

To provide therapy on the *Courage to Heal* model, counsellors needed the prurience to delve, on a daily basis, into the lewd and tacky details of other people's real and imagined sex lives, and the moral certainty to respond decisively to the intimacies uncovered. Traditional counsellors – those non-judgemental folk who helped people identify their own problems and find their own solutions – were generally unsuited to the task. Scientifically oriented psychologists were usually too cautious to be suitable. Metaphorically speaking, sex abuse counsellors needed balls. After all, they had already identified the problem (sexual abuse), and the solution (punish the offender). All they needed was the power and authority to convince even their most recalcitrant clients to see things their way.

Counsellors with authoritarian impulses were best suited to the task. As Theodor W. Adorno et al. observed in *The Authoritarian Personality*, authoritarian people crave power, favour severe punishments and think in rigid, oversimplified categories. They believe that wild and dangerous things go on in the world. They have an exaggerated concern with sexual goings-on and a punitive attitude towards violators of sexual mores.[13]

For all these reasons, work in the sexual abuse field was highly attractive to authoritarian feminists, and especially attractive to authoritarian lesbian feminists who, unlike their heterosexual sisters, were free to apply radical feminist theories to real-life situations, unrestrained by conflicting loyalties to the traditional family and the opposite sex.

In a 1997 article in *American Psychologist*, therapist Laura Brown described her philosophy this way:

> ... the job of the feminist therapist is the subversion of patriarchy in the client, the therapist, and the therapy process ... the initial and ultimate 'client' of feminist therapy is the culture, with the first responsibility always to the project of ending oppression that is at the core of feminism.[14]

This is not to suggest that all New Zealand sexual abuse workers were authoritarian lesbian feminists, or even authoritarian feminists, but the literature of the period indicates that authoritarian feminists set the style and pace of the child sexual abuse prevention movement in the '80s. As sexual abuse workers, they may not have been consciously sadistic in their dealings with men, or unaware of the distress their analyses and actions caused, but, convinced that male sexual violence was an insidious and overwhelming evil, they were prepared to do whatever had to be done to combat it. It was probably primarily from a sense of grim necessity that they adopted slogans like 'Believe the child' to justify interpreting whatever children said (or didn't say) as evidence of sexual abuse; slogans like 'Act immediately' to justify disbelieving and punishing the alleged offender; and slogans like 'Protect the child' to justify breaking up families.

Initially, most paid sexual abuse specialists worked for the Department of Social Welfare (DSW) or the Family Court, and unpaid sexual abuse specialists worked for Women's Refuges and Rape Crisis Centres. In theory, they worked alongside their clients, but in practice the moral weight of their unshakable convictions and – in the case of DSW social workers – their statutory right to seize children they considered 'at risk' meant that sexual abuse specialists wielded enormous power over their emotionally and economically vulnerable clients.

To maintain the illusion that using child protection means to achieve radical feminist ends was justified, child sexual abuse experts unleashed regular displays of outrage and urgency throughout the '80s. In her address to a 1984 child abuse prevention seminar, Julie Sutherland, from DSW in Hamilton, effectively urged the 300 sexual abuse workers in her audience to tear apart families by driving out the men, or removing the children, even when there was little or no evidence of abuse:

> ... the child's protection is the first consideration, and that will mean their removal from home or the offender's removal ... In situations where there is not enough evidence for prosecution, or where the family denies it, or where the child does not feel ready to discuss it – there again, the child still needs protection.[15]

Sutherland supported her call for immediate intervention with extravagant claims about the magnitude of the problem: 'Whether sexual assaults have been occurring once or a thousand times the later long-term effects are the same. There are of course no levels or degrees of sexual abuse.'[16]

• • •

Throughout the '80s, as sexual abuse specialists pursued their mission with unchecked zeal, the level of reported child sexual abuse escalated. When DSW, the police and counselling agencies began setting up child protection teams and specialist sexual abuse teams, the reporting rates received an extra boost. The teams were based on procedures advocated in the 1986 report of the National Advisory Committee on the Prevention of Child Abuse, headed by Dr David Geddis.

David Geddis had been promoting Henry Kempe's concept of multidisciplinary child protection teams since the early '70s, but it was not until the National Advisory Committee on the Prevention of Child Abuse was established that his campaign took off. From the outset, the committee scorned parent-focused methods of helping needy families, and advocated early, vigorous professional intervention. In 1983 Geddis and his colleagues drafted new child protection laws. In 1984 their Child

Protection Bill was about to be introduced into parliament when Prime Minister Robert Muldoon called a snap election. After the election, the Bill was referred to a working party. Then in 1986 a new Children and Young Persons Bill was introduced into parliament.[17]

As well as working for legislative change, the National Advisory Committee on the Prevention of Child Abuse published *Guidelines for the Investigation and Management of Child Sexual Abuse*.[18] The report comprised five papers: 'Police and Department of Social Welfare Investigative Procedures and Liaison', 'Child Protection Team and Specialist Child Sexual Abuse Team Procedures', 'Interviewing and Therapy', 'Medical Diagnosis and Examination' and 'Legal Intervention'. Among the 'assumptions and principles' on which the papers were based were the claims that 'Children often fail to report or recant their reports of child sexual abuse' and 'Children reporting sexual abuse should be presumed to be telling the truth'. Since children rarely make unprompted reports of sexual abuse to police or DSW staff, the latter statement really meant 'Adults reporting sexual abuse on behalf of children should be presumed to be telling the truth'.

The report advised police and DSW staff to select personnel for sexual abuse work on the basis of their 'sensitivity, interest, aptitude and skill', and to provide them with 'specialist training prior to undertaking sexual abuse enquiries and investigations'. Starting from the premise that all sexual abuse allegations should be believed, the report called for the removal of the perpetrator from the home, counselling for the victim and the non-offending parent, and changes to the criminal justice system to overcome 'the potential psychological hazards and social and legal barriers to effective prosecution and Court Room performance by the child'.[19]

In 1986 it would have been unthinkable to question those apparently worthy recommendations. So it was only when sexual abuse workers began putting the report into action that its recommendations were revealed to be explosives buried in a minefield of ideology.

Much of the damage was perpetrated by over-enthusiastic social workers who transformed two-parent, heterosexual families into one-parent, woman-led families at the first suggestion of abuse. These interventions could occur even if there was no physical evidence and both parents and the child insisted that no abuse had taken place. Furthermore, any woman who insisted that she would have known if abuse had occurred and was certain it had not, was likely to labelled as incapable of 'keeping the child safe'. The National Advisory Committee report stated:

> If the non-offending spouse, parent or caretaker is unable or unwilling to take protective action ... then the following option can be considered: a request to the Department of Social Welfare to take complaint action to have the child placed under the supervision of the Department of Social Welfare.[20]

By 1987 increasing numbers of people were complaining to government departments about the devastation caused to their families by false accusations of child sexual abuse. By 1988 they were complaining to members of parliament. By 1989 they were complaining to the media.

One much-publicised case began in the North Island two months after the controversial 1988 Telethon. In response to the media outcry, Minister of Social Welfare Michael Cullen asked retired judge Ken Mason to review the case. After a one-month investigation, Mason provided a 40-page report.

As an example of the process by which sex abuse specialists inflated unsubstantiated concerns into devastating (but still unsubstantiated) accusations, this case is not unusual. Its significance lies in the fact that, to the best of my knowledge, it is the only case of this sort that has been fully and independently documented.

• • •

In 1988, four-year-old Mary was living with her mother, Ms A, and her mother's partner, Mr A. There was stress between Ms A and her ex-husband over Mary's weekend visits and Mary was unsettled as a result. A counsellor suggested that Mary might have been sexually abused. Then Ms A noticed a rash near Mary's genital area.

Dr E, a general practitioner, found no genital trauma or evidence of penetration. She said the rash might have resulted from sexual abuse but was not in itself evidence of assault; it might also have occurred innocently. She stated, 'While these findings were inconclusive I felt that, in conjunction with Ms A's expressed concerns, it was important that the situation be assessed more fully.'

Mary was referred to her local Child and Family Clinic and from there to the Help Foundation. These developments strained Ms A's relationship with Mr A. On the way home from a Help interview, Mr A put Ms A and Mary out of the car and made them walk. Mary alluded to this incident at her next Help interview.

A Child Protection Team meeting was called to discuss the case. The Help therapist said that Mr A was potentially violent (a belief based on Mary's comment about the car incident) and that there were strong (but unspecified) indications that Mary had been sexually abused (even though the child had made no disclosure). The meeting was told that Dr E had confirmed the abuse (even though she clearly had not). The police agreed to interview Mr A. Ms A agreed to send Mary to stay with relatives until the matter was resolved.

When Mr A was told of the accusation he took a drug overdose and spent two days in hospital. After his discharge he went away for a few days. 'I thought it was probably better if we split up for a while till this was resolved so there could be no question that I could be abusing her,' he told the *Dominion Sunday Times*.

He returned to find his home deserted. Ms A told Judge Mason that she had separated from Mr A at that time because she needed breathing space, not because she believed that Mr A had molested her child. Her father had died the same week. Mr A created an altercation at the funeral because he could not find out where Ms A was living. A few days later he created an altercation at the home of one of her relatives. As a result he was charged with two offences and remanded in prison for five weeks.

The day after the funeral Ms A was called to a Child Protection Team meeting where it was agreed that 'Mary had been abused and most likely by Mr A. Then, as a DSW social worker explained to Judge Mason, 'Ms A was told that if she and Mr A got back together again complaint action would be taken and her child would be removed from her.' The social worker justified the move by citing departmental policy ('If a child is being abused in the household we either have to remove the child or the abuser'). She also attacked the Mason inquiry: 'I am concerned that we are not having an enquiry about protecting that child because the child has gone back into that household ... Somewhere we have to start believing the child and stop denying this happens because it does.'[21]

This outburst seems particularly irrational for two reasons. First, because 'believing the child' should have meant believing that abuse had not occurred, since Mary consistently denied that she had been abused. Second, because no one involved in the case had suggested that sexual abuse does not happen.

Over the weeks following her father's funeral, Ms A expressed doubts about the sexual abuse claim to another DSW social worker, who urged Ms A to accept counselling. The social worker indicated to Judge Mason that the purpose of the proposed counselling was to persuade Ms A that Mary really had been abused.

For Ms A, the issue was resolved when she was advised that the police had interviewed Mr A and had found no evidence of any offence. 'That was the reason I thought it would be okay if I went back to Mr A,' Ms A told Judge Mason.

Mr A, Ms A and Mary then moved to another town. Four days later a social worker faxed their nearest DSW office:

> L [DSW social worker] thinks there may be a psychiatric history with this woman. Mary on Child Protection Register because of belief that she has been sexually abused by Ms A's ex-defacto, Mr A. I am concerned that we be certain he is not back with her as it was indicated that complaint action be taken if they reconciled ...[22]

On the basis of that fax, a DSW social worker and a police officer removed Mary from the family home and placed her in foster care. A general practitioner examined her next day. He found no signs of sexual abuse, and diagnosed her rash as 'thrush, possibly as a reaction to antibiotics used to clear up an ear infection'. Mr A complained to the Minister of Social Welfare but received no response. Over the next 10 days Ms A, Mr A and Mary were interviewed, individually and together, by Dr F, a DSW-appointed psychiatrist. She reported:

> I found no evidence of sexual abuse either in what Mary told me or in her behaviour. She was extremely upset that she cannot stay with her mother and Mr A at home. She cried and pleaded with me to send her home straight away. Ms A has a very good relationship with Mary ... I saw Mary in the presence of Mr A and her mother and again I found no evidence of anything worrying in their relationship.

Of Mr A's alleged violence, she wrote: 'Mary told me that she likes Mr A ... she told me that he does smack her on the leg sometimes ... She does not mind and says that her mum smacks her sometimes too.'[23]

A DSW social worker responded with a file note: 'Dr F's report is extremely biased and will probably be challenged on these grounds.' She told Judge Mason that she did not regard her response as heavy handed.

In December, after a three-week separation, Ms A was given interim custody of Mary. In February, DSW withdrew the complaint action. In March, Mr and Ms A took their story to the *Dominion Sunday Times*.

In an internal report to the Minister of Social Welfare a DSW officer wrote: 'I do not consider that there is any case established that requires an apology. Nor do I consider there is any case for costs or compensation from the department for its actions to date.'[24]

Despite these assurances, the Minister asked Judge Mason to review the Mary A case and several other cases, and to report on whether any DSW staff actions, or any laws, regulations, bylaws or practices under which the staff operated were unreasonable, unjust, oppressive, unlawful, improperly discriminatory or wrong, and to recommend appropriate changes.

In his report, Mason rejected any suggestion that Ms A had been blackmailed into separating from Mr A, but acknowledged that 'Ms A's perception that she was being blackmailed may be a valid one'. He expressed sympathy for the 'necessary, unenviable and emotionally distressing role' performed by social workers, but he also addressed their conduct:

> In my view the complaint action of 15 December 1988 was inexcusable. It was unreasonable and unjust. It compounded the hasty and precipitate action taken on 30 November 1988. It proceeded in the absence of comprehensive enquiry and discussion with DSW staff in other districts and the Help therapist. It flew in the face of two medical reports by Dr F which DSW had initiated. In summary, it proceeded in the absence of accepted, professional social work practice.

Despite these strong words, Mason concluded:

> I see no need for disciplinary action against any social worker referred to in this report. I believe that the process of this enquiry in itself has been a learning experience for all concerned. I anticipate that the errors and omissions so apparent in this case will not be repeated by the workers concerned.[25]

This conclusion is difficult to understand. There is nothing in Mason's report to indicate that the social workers had learnt anything whatever from the experience. Indeed, their responses suggest that they remained defiantly unrepentant.

Mason's terms of reference did not address the question of bad faith, but the issue may have been raised during the inquiry. He wrote:

> I reject the notion that one or more of the social workers in this case have acted in bad faith. I believe that those workers whom I interviewed were very conscious of the statutory requirement 'to keep the child safe' and I am satisfied that at all stages that was the priority which motivated their decisions and actions.[26]

There is no precise legal definition of 'bad faith' but it carries an odour of dishonesty, fraud and malice. Since the social workers acted with the best of intentions and from a sincere conviction in their own rightness, the concept of bad faith does not seem applicable here. But since they arrived at their convictions through the suppression of doubt and with reckless disregard for dissenting opinion, rather than through honest investigation, the concept of good faith does not seem applicable either. More importantly, the question of whether the social workers acted in bad faith is a red herring. DSW procedure manuals make it clear that social workers who act honestly ('in good faith') may face disciplinary action if they perform their duties in an incompetent or negligent manner.

A more significant point – raised by Mason's finding that the social workers were following statutory requirements – is the question of whether the departmental emphasis on keeping the child safe, to the exclusion of all other considerations, contributed to the problem. On this matter, child protection workers are adamant: when it comes to weighing children's rights against parents' rights, the rights of the child are paramount. This claim – built on a world view in which social workers are selfless carers who rescue vulnerable children from the predations of selfish parents – is an example of the way in which child protection rhetoric is used to achieve authoritarian ends. In reality, the issue is not children's rights versus parents' rights; the issue is the rights of statutory authorities versus the rights of parents. If the question is rephrased: 'Who knows what is best for a child – the parents who have cared for her unconditionally from birth, or the social worker to whom she is just another case?' the answer is, almost invariably, the parents. But, even in terms of children's rights, Mason could have recommended that social workers consider the right of a child *not* to be removed from her home and placed among strangers against her will without proper evidence and due process.

Though Mason seemed baffled by the inability of DSW staff to accept that there was no evidence of sexual abuse, he did not address the possibility that they were in the grip of a collective delusion about the prevalence of sexual abuse and the dangers it posed – a delusion that meant any suggestion of abuse would almost inevitably be confirmed. Instead, despite his own evidence that the social workers had consulted widely before taking action, Mason attributed most of the problems in the case to poor communication and a lack of clear protocols.

For Mr and Ms A, he recommended payments of $3000 and $8000 for the disruption and distress they had experienced, plus an apology from a senior DSW official and reimbursement of their out-of-pocket expenses. Mr and Ms A regarded the compensation as inadequate and threatened legal action. Before responding, the minister consulted the Acting Director-General of Social Welfare. He replied:

> While Mr Mason did not believe the Department's officers acted in bad faith, it is conceivable that a Court and specifically a Jury might do so. It is impossible to determine with any accuracy what damages might be awarded but they would almost certainly be in excess of what we have offered for an out-of-Court settlement. My advice would be that it would be better to increase our offer a little in the hope of getting a settlement.[27]

DSW's next offer, of $15,000 to Ms A and $10,000 to Mr A, was accepted.

The Acting Minister of Social Welfare welcomed the Mason report and said that proposed legislative changes would prevent further false accusations of sexual abuse. The Opposition social welfare spokesman said they would do nothing of the sort.

• • •

As casualties of the upsurge in child sexual abuse allegations began looking for help, sexual abuse counselling, a major segment of the burgeoning counselling industry, began to grow unchecked. Some troubled women referred themselves or their children for counselling. Some unruly children were referred by health professionals who thought the counsellor would determine whether or not they had been abused. But, as the case of Mr and Ms A demonstrates, it is often impossible to determine with any certainty whether or not a child has been sexually abused. Additionally, rather than determining whether or not any abuse has occurred, sexual abuse specialists just tend to assume that it has. This is because sexual abuse counsellors are philosophically and financially committed to diagnosing and treating sexual abuse. Indeed, even if a counsellor finds that a child's misbehaviour is caused by jealousy of a new baby, and even if she knows how to help the family deal with it, there is next to nothing in the public purse to provide counselling for that. So if a counsellor wants to be paid, she has little choice but to diagnose sexual abuse.

This funding distortion arose as more and more money was demanded (and provided) for sexual abuse services. Some funding came from fee-paying clients and private charities. Some came from government agencies.[28] But the single most important source of funding was the Accident Compensation Commission (ACC).

By the time the Christchurch Civic Crèche case arose in 1991, ACC had enabled scores of under-trained and poorly supervised sexual abuse counsellors to acquire official recognition. To understand how this situation arose, we need to understand how ACC works.

• • •

The aim of the 1974 ACC Act was to provide prompt and effective treatment for all accident victims. But, during the passage of the Bill through parliament, two provisions for lump-sum compensation were added (one for physical disability, the other for 'pain and mental suffering' and 'the loss of ... capacity for enjoying life') as trade-offs for the abolition of the right to sue.

As with all accident-compensation schemes, ACC carried the risk of inadvertently encouraging its beneficiaries to maximise their agony in order to maximise their gain. Opportunists (such as the man who sought compensation for having a cottonbud lodged in his ear, even though the bud was quickly removed and no injury was suffered) could be relatively easily identified. Claimants suffering from compensation neurosis posed a greater problem. After relatively trivial accidents, such claimants developed disabling symptoms that were unresponsive to medical treatment but improved dramatically once money changed hands. In his book on the ACC Act, Judge Blair observed:

> It must be expected that the introduction of the Accident Compensation Act will increase the incidence of compensation neurosis. The Act gives the right of compensation for accidents to persons who previously had no such rights, e.g. housewives and sportspersons ... It accordingly must be accepted that accident or litigation neurosis will become more common.[29]

The original Act provided cover for 'the physical and mental consequences' of 'personal injury by accident'. Sexual assaults were covered, subject to ACC being satisfied that an assault had taken place and an injury had been suffered. However, in response to concerns that rape victims could be denied ACC-funded treatment if they showed little or no evidence of 'actual bodily harm', the definition of 'actual bodily harm' was extended to include 'pregnancy and mental or nervous shock' where these occurred as a result of 'rape' (or, after 1985, 'sexual violation'), 'sexual intercourse with a girl under twelve' or 'infection with a disease'. Other sex crimes, like attempted sexual violation and indecent assault were not itemised in the ACC legislation until 1992. Nonetheless, as a result of precedents established when rejected ACC claims were appealed, the range of sexual abuse claims accepted by ACC at the time of the Civic Crèche case in 1991 far exceeded those itemised in the legislation.

Claimants had to satisfy ACC that they were genuinely injured (and not malingering), and that the injury was caused by an accident (and not by disease, infection or ageing). In rape claims the 'actual bodily harm' was usually in the form of 'mental or nervous shock'. So the ACC assessor had to determine whether the claimant really did suffer from 'mental or nervous shock', and whether the shock really was the result of rape.

A further complication was that ACC was, in theory, a no-fault scheme, so the rights and wrongs of claims were not usually investigated. However, with claims involving sex crimes or medical error, even if ACC was satisfied that the event had occurred (sexual intercourse in the case of a rape claim, medical intervention in the case of a medical error claim), the claimant was not eligible for compensation if the intercourse was consensual or if the medical intervention was appropriate but had failed to achieve the desired result. In both cases, ACC had to be satisfied that the perpetrator was at fault before compensation would be paid.

Interestingly, ACC has always handled medical error claims and sexual assault claims very differently. This difference reflects the influence of two very different groups of treatment providers. In terms of feminist stereotypes, the medical treatment providers could be characterised as powerful, wealthy, white, middle-class and male, while sexual abuse treatment providers could be characterised as powerless, poor, oppressed and female. If this is indeed the case (and the stereotypes undoubtedly have some validity) then a comparison of the outcomes of medical error and sexual abuse claims suggests that the allegedly powerful providers have had less influence on the policies and practices of ACC than the allegedly powerless ones.

To understand the relative influence of these two groups we need to first understand what is meant by 'natural justice'. Legal textbooks describe the principles of natural justice as minimum standards of fair decision-making imposed by common law. Over centuries of legal precedents these principles have been refined into two cardinal rules: that *no person shall be condemned unless he/she has been given notice of the allegations against him/her and a fair opportunity to respond*, and that *the decision-maker shall have no material interest (by way of gain or detriment) in the outcome*. Centuries of legal precedents have also established that the principles apply to any administrative decision (and not just to court proceedings) in which a person may be adversely affected.[30]

From the inception of ACC, whenever a medical error claim was received, the alleged perpetrator was notified and invited to comment, all relevant evidence was considered and independent advice on the claim's validity was sought. According to Lynda Angus, head of ACC's Medical Misadventure Unit (MMU), the unit receives around 2500 claims per year. When the claim involves no more than one person's word against another, it is normally rejected. This approach embodies two elemental concepts of justice: the first is that anyone accused of an offence should be presumed innocent until proven guilty; the second is that, in the absence of corroborating evidence, it is often impossible to determine whether or not an offence has occurred. In all, about 40 percent of claims are accepted, but most of these are for medical mishap (i.e. for a serious, rare and unforeseen complication of a medical procedure for which the health professional is not to blame, but which is deemed to be an 'accident' and therefore eligible for ACC assistance). Only 15 percent of claims accepted by the MMU are for medical error.[31]

Accurate statistics for sexual abuse claims are not available because the Sensitive Claims Unit (SCU) does not have an effective recording system, but, according to Lynda Angus (who heads both the SCU and the MMU), the SCU receives around 12,000 claims per year. 'Working on feel and anecdotal evidence we think we accept around 85 percent. The only claims we decline are those that clearly don't fit the Schedule [the list of sexual offences covered by the 1992 ACC Act] or those for which we never get enough information,' she told me.[32]

The believe-the-victim philosophy that underpins this high acceptance rate means that, in relation to sexual offences, ACC has effectively replaced the presumption of innocence with the presumption of guilt. This approach makes sexual assault claims easy to administer. When you believe the victim, you don't need any input from the alleged perpetrator (in fact he is never invited to comment, or even advised that a claim has been lodged). You don't need to investigate the claim. You don't need independent advice on its validity. You just need an ACC assessor to accept it. Lynda Angus explained:

> We don't go around questioning whether people have been sexually abused or not ...
> We occasionally get people who have been named – or think they've been named – as perpetrators who ring up and say, 'I believe so and so has lodged a claim and it's all false.' We don't actively pursue that because we feel that a person who has gone to the lengths of going to a doctor and saying, 'I want to lodge a claim,' and going to a counsellor and going through the whole story, must have some psychological need, and that we should help them deal with it.[33]

It was not always so. Throughout the '70s decisions on ACC cover for rape were largely left to the courts. If the alleged offender was found not guilty, it was ACC policy to reject the claim. Then, in 1980, a landmark ACC Appeal Authority decision changed everything.

It seemed like a clear-cut case of rape. The man admitted that the woman had struggled during the assault. But the woman was a teenager who had spent the day in the pub before going off with a gang member, and the unsympathetic Christchurch jury probably felt that it served her right. As a result of the not-guilty verdict, ACC rejected her claim, but the decision was overturned on appeal. Judge Blair ruled:

> The phrase 'within the description of' [in the ACC Act], where it applies to rape, means that a complainant ... does not have the onus on her ... to prove beyond reasonable doubt that rape had been committed. She need go no further than to satisfy the Commission that what happened has the ingredients of rape. These ingredients are penetration of the female by the male without her consent.[34]

Over the following decade Judge Blair's phrase 'the ingredients of rape' was used to argue that non-penetrative indecencies should be covered by ACC, even though his decision shows that he had in mind a much narrower definition of 'the ingredients of rape'.

Following that landmark judgment, ACC disregarded verdicts in criminal cases, and the burden of proof required for the acceptance of sexual assault claims went from 'beyond reasonable doubt' to the Commission 'must feel an actual persuasion that entitlement exists'.[35]

By 1987 the range of sexual assault claims acceptable to ACC included: 'any sexual or intended sexual act, or experience, which is forced onto an adult or child without their consent ... providing the assault happened after 1 April 1974.'[36]

Sexual assault victims could claim counselling costs, compensation for loss of earnings, medical and dental fees, transport costs, payment for damaged clothing and lump-sum awards of up to $17,000 for 'permanent damage to bodily functions' and up to $10,000 for 'loss of enjoyment of life'. In practice, most sexual abuse claims were for counselling costs and 'loss of enjoyment of life'.

As a matter of policy, ACC required treatment providers to be professionally qualified. Among those providing counselling, general practitioners, psychiatrists and psychologists had statutory registration, and members of the New Zealand Association of Psychotherapists, and the New Zealand Association of Child Psychotherapists, were bound by the standards, ethics and disciplinary procedures of their professional bodies. These practitioners were paid a fee for service by ACC.

By contrast, most sexual abuse counsellors had had no formal training and were not registered practitioners nor members of a recognised professional body. Most worked for sexual abuse treatment centres like Help (in Auckland and Wellington) or START (in Christchurch), and each centre had at least one qualified professional on its management team. On that basis the treatment centres, rather than their individual counsellors, were accepted as ACC treatment providers and reimbursed for fees claimed on behalf of their counsellors. Between the 1986–87 financial year and the 1988–89 financial year, total ACC payments to counsellors escalated from $147,308 to $1,205,677. Seventy percent of those payments went to counsellors working for sexual assault treatment centres.[37]

Lump-sum payments for 'loss of enjoyment of life' showed a similar increase. In the 1987–88 financial year 700 lump-sum payments were made to sexual assault victims. By the following year the number had risen to over 1500, and most recipients were paid the full $10,000. At the same time, more than $1 million of ACC funding was poured into sexual abuse education, research and prevention programmes. In summary, by 1989, sexual abuse services were costing ACC over $17 million a year.[38]

In December 1988, with a budget blowout looming, the ACC board decided to stop payments for all paramedical treatments from the end of the month. Word of the change leaked out on 19 December and it was confirmed on 20 December. That day, for osteopaths, chiropractors, podiatrists, occupational therapists, acupuncturists and counsellors, the ACC gravy train jolted to a sudden stop. Then, in a dramatic illustration of the power of 'the sex abuse industry' to bend the government to its will, on 23 December the ministers of ACC, Women's Affairs and Social Welfare announced that, as an interim measure, ACC would 'continue to pay for counselling services under an administrative delegation from the director-general of social welfare'.[39]

Funding for the interim measure was appropriated under the Disabled Persons Community Welfare Act. As ACC managing director Jeff Chapman observed, using the Act to fund sexual abuse counselling required a liberal interpretation of the statute, 'but it has been in no-one's interest to question the legal basis'.[40]

At the same time, all sexual abuse counsellors were given provisional ACC registration on an individual basis. This arrangement was supposed to last six months, but it kept being rolled over while debate raged over who should pay for, and who should provide, sexual abuse counselling.[41] Jeff Chapman noted:

> Many persons offering sexual abuse counselling services are largely untrained. Ultimately it has to be accepted that untrained persons should not be paid by the Government or the Corporation to counsel people in psychological and emotional distress … The reaction of some groups which employ unqualified counsellors is likely to be vocal and negative with widespread media coverage. These groups are unlikely to be appeased by a grandparenting clause which enables time to obtain basic qualifications and training.[42]

In 1989 and 1990 regulations were passed to allow the resumption of ACC-funded treatments by psychiatrists, psychologists, psychotherapists, general practitioners, chiropractors, acupuncturists, occupational therapists, osteopaths, physiotherapists, and podiatrists. Lay sexual abuse counsellors were, strictly speaking, not included, but their funding continued under the Disabled Persons Community Welfare Act. Then in 1992 responsibility for sexual abuse counselling funding returned to ACC because, at that point, everyone providing sexual abuse counselling was given extended interim registration.

In summary, the procedural changes to sexual abuse counselling funding between 1988 and 1992 ensured that, by the time the Christchurch Civic Crèche case erupted in 1991, the majority of sexual abuse counsellors were as poorly trained and poorly supervised as they had always been. This is not to suggest that more training and supervision per se would have produced better counsellors. As the research into therapeutic effectiveness cited earlier in this chapter shows, empathetic individuals with good communication skills can become effective counsellors with a minimum of training and supervision. The problem was that sexual abuse counselling tended to attract women with authoritarian feminist impulses who were trained by authoritarian feminists in authoritarian feminist methods. So instead of swelling the ranks of compassionate and effective counsellors, training and supervision on this model just produced better-trained authoritarian feminists.

3.ii: *Crimen Exceptum*

During the first half of 1989 public outrage over false allegations of child sexual abuse, sparked by *Dominion Sunday Times* publicity of the 'Mary A' case, rose to a nationwide crescendo when TVNZ and *North & South* featured investigations into the controversial 'Ward 24 case' in Christchurch. The message to child protection workers was clear: if you want to convince the doubting public that child sexual abuse really is an overwhelming and insidious evil, indiscriminately accusing men of sexual molestation isn't enough – you have to make the accusations stick.

Making the accusations stick meant increasing the number of convictions in the criminal courts. Child sexual abuse allegations had been dealt with in the Family Court for almost a decade, but in the eyes of the public the outcomes were suspect. After all, the proceedings took place in secret, the children involved did not normally give evidence and could not therefore be cross-examined, opinion and hearsay evidence were admissible and a lower standard of proof was required. Furthermore, Family Court judges did not have to identify the perpetrator, even when the abuse was ruled to have been proven. All they had to do was determine future custody, access and protection issues on the basis of 'the best interests of the child'. This situation was unsatisfactory to prosecutors who wanted perpetrators convicted, and to suspects who risked losing their marriages, families, homes, savings, jobs and reputations if a Family Court judge ruled against them, but who were denied the right to be tried by a jury of their peers and to be presumed innocent until proven guilty.

Before the child protection movement could increase the number of convictions in the criminal courts, it had to meet three challenges. First, it had to close ranks (as the 'Mary A' case showed, investigations by dedicated sexual abuse workers could be derailed by independent-minded police officers and doctors). Second, it had to change the law to ensure that the sort of evidence used to convince Family Court judges that sexual abuse had occurred 'on the balance of probabilities' could be used to convince criminal juries 'beyond reasonable doubt' that sexual abuse had occurred. Third, it had to persuade influential decision-makers to join the crusade. The man who worked tirelessly throughout the 1980s to achieve those ends was Dr David Geddis.

To encourage the child protection movement to close ranks, the Advisory Committee on the Prevention of Child Abuse recommended that all abuse allegations be investigated by 'specialised personnel, trained and working together'. As a result, child protection teams sprang up in towns and cities nationwide. The existence of these teams ensured that input from independent-minded professionals into the evaluation of child abuse allegations was effectively excluded.[1]

It was only when David Geddis sought statutory authority for child protection teams that his plans began to founder. The first sign of trouble came when the select committee considering the 1986 Children and Young Persons Bill was inundated with complaints about the Bill's complexity, and about the National Advisory Committee's professional, monocultural bias, its inadequate consultation, its lack of concern for family support and the sweeping powers it sought for child protection teams.

After the 1987 election, a working party appointed by Minister of Social Welfare Michael Cullen recommended that the Bill be rewritten, and that Maori and Pacific Island groups be consulted. Geddis and his supporters reacted by attacking the minister, by making emotional claims about the prevalence of child abuse and by falling back on the slogan most favoured by child protection workers when their power and resources are threatened: children will die!

The battle between Geddis and Cullen came to a head early in 1989 when the Minister returned the Bill to parliament not only stripped of its Geddis-promoted provisions (no mandatory reporting, no child protection teams, no National Register of Children at Risk, no National Committee for Child Protection), but also stripped of the 'paramountcy principle' contained in the previous Children and Young Persons Act 1974 ('the interests of the child or young person as the first and paramount consideration'). After lengthy and heated debate the Children, Young Persons, **and**

Their Families (CYPF) Bill was passed. The resulting Act nailed its colours to the mast in a bold opening statement:

> An Act to reform the law relating to children and young persons who are in need of care or protection or who offend against the law and, in particular – (a) To advance the wellbeing of families and the wellbeing of children and young persons as members of families, whanau, hapu, iwi, and family groups.

As it turned out, the change in legislative direction was not as dramatic in practice as it was in theory. This was partly because the paramountcy principle that had vanished from the CYPF Act (which addressed abuse and neglect issues), persisted unchanged in the Guardianship Act (which addressed custody and access issues). Also, the pressure on social workers to transform themselves from child savers to family support workers (as required by the CYPF Act) was outweighed by the pressure on them to be financially accountable (as required by the 1988 State Sector Act and the 1989 Public Finance Act). Being financially accountable meant doing work that could be measured, and it was easier to measure the number of children being sent for counselling and the number of parents being subject to complaint action than to measure the benefits of setting up things like afterschool programmes. Consequently, despite the changes heralded by the 1989 CYPF Act, most DSW social workers went right on doing individual casework (instead of family-support work).

Though the National Advisory Committee's 1986 report, *Guidelines for the Investigation and Management of Child Sexual Abuse*, failed to gain legislative support, for nearly three years it provided unofficial practice guidelines for sexual abuse workers nationwide. The official guidelines issued in 1989 (the police *Policy and Guidelines for the Investigation of Child Sexual Abuse and Serious Child Physical Abuse*, and the DSW *Draft Guidelines for the Investigation of Sexual Abuse*) were based on the National Advisory Committee report. Like the parent document, both sets of guidelines advised that child sexual abuse allegations should be believed. Both advocated the use of specialist police-DSW sexual abuse teams. Both recommended that medical examinations be carried out by 'doctors endorsed by the Sexual Abuse Team'. In a telling slip, both often referred to the alleged offender as 'the offender', and both advocated his removal from the family home. Both were, in effect, blueprints for the continuation of a heavily interventionist child-saver approach to child protection.

While Geddis fought, and ultimately lost, his public battle with the Minister of Social Welfare, behind the scenes key members of his National Advisory Committee for the Prevention of Child Abuse (including Christchurch child psychiatrist Karen Zelas) regrouped on another committee established by the previous Minister of Social Welfare. This was the Advisory Committee on the Investigation, Detection and Prosecution of Offences Against Children. Here they turned their attention from legislation to protect alleged victims of child sexual abuse, to legislation to prosecute alleged offenders.

Most people heard about Geddis's second wave of legislative proposals when the report of the Advisory Committee on the Investigation, Detection and Prosecution of Offences Against Children (*A Private or Public Nightmare?*) was released on 7 November 1988. At the time it seemed like just another discussion document. Nobody guessed, and hardly anybody knew, that its proposals were already being turned into law. Even the Minister of Social Welfare was unaware of the legislative activity until the day of the report's release, when Minister of Justice Geoffrey Palmer advised him that:

> it is proposed to include a number of provisions relating to children's evidence in sexual abuse cases in this year's Law Reform (Miscellaneous Provisions) Bill ... In drawing up the present proposals my department had the benefit of an advance draft of the National Advisory Committee's report provided on a confidential basis.[2]

Palmer also advised Cullen that a soon-to-be published paper from his department would reach similar conclusions to the report of the Advisory Committee. The research for that paper (*Child Sexual Abuse Study: Role of expert witnesses in criminal trials*) comprised a review of the literature covering 'a relatively small proportion of the information available' and interviews with 32 'persons experienced in the field of child abuse' (10 child psychologists, one child psychiatrist, two paediatricians, nine specialist social workers, six police officers and four counsellors). The researchers did not consult any judges or lawyers, which, in view of the expertise they could have brought to the topic, raises questions about the comprehensiveness and impartiality of the report.

That this Geddis-inspired legislation was prepared without benefit of open scrutiny or debate under a Minister of Justice with a professed concern for government accountability is further cause for concern. Prior to entering parliament in 1979, Geoffrey Palmer, law professor and constitutional law expert, complained that too much power resided in executive government, and that there were insufficient safeguards against its abuse. After 10 years' first-hand experience of the legislative process (including five years as Attorney-General and Minister of Justice) he revisited the problem in 1992: 'Real power is with the executive ... cabinet ministers can and do dominate caucus which meets in secret and does not function as an instrument of accountability ... it is possible to change too much too quickly and with too little public input.'[3]

Nothing illustrates these points better than Palmer's own handling of the preparation and introduction of the Geddis-promoted changes to the laws of evidence. The vehicle for these changes, the Law Reform (Miscellaneous Provisions) Bill, has been used annually since 1981 to introduce amendments that are considered too important to be included in the routine Statutes Amendment Bill, but not important enough to require their own legislation. The 1988 Law Reform (Miscellaneous Provisions) Bill contained 202 clauses affecting more than 50 different Acts (covering everything from race relations to wandering stock). It was introduced by Palmer late at night, under urgency, on what was expected to be the last sitting day before parliament broke for Christmas.[4]

At the time of the Bill's introduction, most members of the Press Gallery were staking out the offices of Prime Minister David Lange and Minister of Finance Roger Douglas as their feud over the speed and stealth of the government's legislative reforms approached flashpoint. But, even if they had been in the House that night, and even if the resignation of Roger Douglas from his Ministerial portfolio had not preoccupied the Press Gallery next day, a piece of legislation described by Geoffrey Palmer as a 'washing up Bill' would probably not have attracted much attention.

Three days before Christmas, newspaper readers were advised that persons wishing to comment on the Law Reform (Miscellaneous Provisions) Bill should send 20 copies of their submissions to the Justice and Law Reform Select Committee by 3 February 1989. Though the Acts to be amended were listed, no information was provided on the nature of the amendments, or where such information could be obtained.

Under the circumstances, it is hardly surprising that eight of the 11 submissions to the select committee on the Geddis-promoted amendments to the Crimes Act, the Evidence Act and the Summary Proceedings Act came from David Geddis and his supporters. Three further submissions arrived too late to be considered.

In July 1989 the Geddis-promoted amendments were reported back to the House essentially unchanged. Two weeks later, still embedded within the Law Reform (Miscellaneous Provisions) Bill, they sped discreetly through their second reading with the enthusiastic endorsement of the Opposition. In November 1989 the now-separated Crimes Amendment Bill (No. 3), Evidence Amendment Bill (No. 3) and Summary Proceedings Amendment Bill (No. 2) sped through their third readings, again with the enthusiastic endorsement of the Opposition.[5]

While their legislative initiatives were moving through parliament unnoticed by the wider community, David Geddis and his supporters held workshops and seminars nationwide to promote their report, *A Private or Public Nightmare?* However, articles in the *New Zealand Law Journal* (in May and August '89), and in the *Family Law Bulletin* (February '90), made it clear that had news of the changes been promulgated earlier, there would have been many more unfavourable submissions to the select committee.[6]

Of particular concern to critics was Geddis's claim that child sexual abuse was, in effect, *crimen exceptum* – a crime distinct from all others. In 1986 the same concern was raised by evidence expert R.A. McGeehan (later Justice McGeehan). In a paper for the Advisory Committee on the Investigation, Detection and Prosecution of Offences Against Children, McGeehan argued that there were no special aspects of child abuse prosecutions that would warrant any departure from normal courtroom rules and procedures. Shortly after preparing that paper, McGeehan was appointed to the High Court bench, whereupon his involvement with the Advisory Committee ceased. However, in *A Private or Public Nightmare?* he is listed as a committee member and the title of his paper ('Prosecutions – Offences against Children – Standard Rules of Evidence – Applicability') appears on the list of 'Background Papers Prepared by Committee Members'. This gives the misleading impression that a jurist of McGeehan's stature supported the report's conclusions, when the opposite was the case.

Unlike McGeehan, Geddis argued that child sexual abuse should be treated as a special case in the criminal courts:

> Throughout this Report the Committee has detailed those areas where child victims of sexual abuse, and the nature of the crime itself, differ from most other cases dealt with by the criminal justice system. However at present the same rules of evidence apply. In the view of this Committee this ought not to be so. As they apply to cases of child sexual abuse some of the rules of evidence are over-restrictive and irrational in a number of matters of detail. They are also open to the more fundamental objection that as a rigid set of rules they are too inflexible to enable justice to be done.[7]

Complaints that the rules governing courtroom procedures are 'too inflexible to enable justice to be done' are nothing new. So, before we take a closer look at the changes sought by the National Advisory Committee (the changes that made the conviction of Peter Ellis possible), the question must be asked: what are the traditional rules governing courtroom procedures, and why do lawyers and judges think they matter?

• • •

Broadly speaking, all human communities have generally accepted rules governing the rights, duties, freedoms and obligations of their citizens, and generally accepted procedures for dealing peacefully with breaches of, and disputes about, those rules. In our society, when a serious breach of the rules (a crime) is suspected, a court of law is required to determine whether the crime really was committed, whether the suspect really was responsible and, if so, what punishment he or she should suffer as a result. The courts fulfil this role by providing the suspect with a fair trial. Nowadays, most of our ideas on what is meant by a fair trial stem from our collective beliefs about human rights. The essence of these beliefs can be found in key legal documents from the Magna Carta to the present day, but their international codification is relatively recent.

The Universal Declaration of Human Rights was adopted by the United Nations in 1948, in the wake of the Holocaust. At the time, people were painfully aware of the boundless capacity of ordinary human beings to demonise and persecute other ordinary, law-abiding human beings who had done them no harm. In Nazi Germany even the law courts, whose role in more sober times was to stand as a bastion of rationality between the suspect and the lynch mob, had failed to protect the innocent when prejudice and delusion ruled. The preamble to the Universal Declaration of Human Rights reflected the shared horror from which it was born, and the shared vision for a better world to which it aspired:

> Whereas recognition of the inherent dignity and of the equal and inalienable rights of all members of the human family is the foundation of freedom, justice and peace in the world,
>
> Whereas disregard and contempt for human rights have resulted in barbarous acts which have outraged the conscience of mankind, and the advent of a world in which human beings shall enjoy freedom of speech and belief and freedom from fear and want has been proclaimed as the highest aspiration of the common people ...[8]

These ideals formed the basis for the International Covenant on Civil and Political Rights. New Zealand ratified the Covenant in 1978, and in doing so agreed to observe certain fundamental rights in its domestic law. These rights included the right to life and liberty; the right to freedom of movement, freedom of expression and freedom of association; the right to equality before the law; and the right to be secure against unreasonable search and seizure. The Covenant also covered the rights of persons detained, arrested and charged. These included the right to be informed in detail of the nature and cause of the charge; the right to a fair and public hearing by an independent and impartial court (though the press and public may be excluded in some circumstances); the right to be presumed innocent until proven guilty according to law; the right to be present at the trial and to present a defence; the right to free legal aid if the accused person cannot afford to pay for it; the right to examine witnesses for the prosecution; the right to obtain the attendance of, and to examine, witnesses for the defence under the same conditions as the prosecution; and the right not to be compelled to testify or to confess guilt.[9]

• • •

The traditional rules and procedures in our criminal courts serve to uphold the rights itemised in the Covenant. For example, the provision in the Crimes Act that 'Except as otherwise provided in this Act, there shall be one uniform procedure in respect of all offences' acknowledges the principle of equality before the law. The requirement that each charge shall 'apply only to a single transaction', and shall 'contain so much detail of the circumstances of the alleged crime as is sufficient to give the accused reasonable information concerning the act or omission to be proved against him' enables the suspect to provide an alibi if he or she was somewhere else at the time. In a further acknowledgement of the accused's right to be informed, the Summary Proceedings Act requires that the police provide the defence with copies of all relevant information when a person is charged with an offence.[10]

Once a trial begins, anyone (apart from the accused) who knows something about the case and is considered legally competent (i.e. anyone who is capable of giving a rational account of what he or she has seen and heard) may be called to give evidence and be cross-examined. The right of accused persons *not* to give evidence flows from the presumption of innocence: accused people do not have to prove their innocence, in the eyes of the law they are already innocent; if their accusers think otherwise the onus is on them to prove it.

The accused and the witnesses are normally required to appear in court in person. This serves to deter dishonest witnesses (in that it is harder to tell a lie about a person 'to his face' than 'behind his back'). It also allows the jury to observe the demeanour of the accused and the witnesses in each other's presence, and to see and hear the witnesses give evidence and be cross-examined. By means of these observations juries evaluate the credibility of each witness, and the credibility of each witness's evidence, and thereby determine whether or not the accused is guilty beyond reasonable doubt.

The established laws of evidence and courtroom procedures help to ensure, but do not guarantee, the reliability of the evidence. For example, the requirement that, prior to giving evidence, witnesses swear an oath (or make a solemn affirmation) to tell the truth reminds them that they have a duty of truthfulness greater than that required in the ordinary course of social conduct. Another requirement, that ordinary witnesses testify only on relevant matters of which they have direct personal knowledge, ensures that juries will not be misled by irrelevancies, or by hearsay and opinion evidence of unknown and untestable reliability. To further protect the reliability of the evidence (by ensuring that witnesses are not manipulated into saying whatever their counsel want them to say), lawyers are not allowed to ask leading questions during their witnesses' evidence-in-chief.

Ensuring that the opinion evidence of expert witnesses is reliable and fair poses special problems. Because claims made by articulate and skilled experts may have more impact on lay juries than the same claims made by anyone else, criminal courts have traditionally accepted only well-qualified people with reputations for independence and objectivity as expert witnesses. Also, expert witnesses are normally allowed to give evidence only on matters beyond the knowledge and experience of common jurors, but about which there is a sound body of reliable research data (e.g. the chemical analysis of stains). These restrictions recognise that, while experts may be authoritative in their specialist fields, their opinions on other matters are worth no more than anyone else's. The same distinction – between the use of specialist expertise for advice, and lay common sense for decision making – is reflected in the practice of leaving the ultimate decisions/opinions – about who and what to believe, and whether or not the suspect is guilty beyond reasonable doubt – to the collective wisdom of 12 lay people with no personal or professional interest in the case.

Despite all the safeguards, some untruthful evidence, whether from determined liars or genuinely mistaken witnesses, will inevitably come before the court. In the final analysis, the only way that evidence can be properly tested is by careful, thorough and vigorous cross-examination. For this reason all questions, leading or otherwise, are normally allowed during cross-examination (provided the questions are relevant and are not used simply to oppress).

Finally, to discourage juries from reaching verdicts based on prejudice, judges routinely instruct them to ignore all gossip, innuendo and media reports, and to reach their verdicts solely on the basis of the evidence presented in court.

• • •

When Geoffrey Palmer became Minister of Justice in 1984, he began a campaign to enshrine the principles of the International Covenant of Civil and Political Rights into New Zealand law. In the debate leading up to the passage of the Bill of Rights Act (1990), Palmer argued that without restraints on the powers of government, and guarantees of fundamental freedoms for the people, it would be too easy for enthusiastic but misguided politicians to pass laws that eroded the rights of New Zealand citizens. As if to prove the point, he used his executive power in 1988 and 1989 to push the Geddis-promoted amendments to the Crimes Act, the Evidence Act and the Summary Proceedings Act through parliament.

The Geddis amendments were introduced at a time when measures to protect sexual offence complainants in general (rather than child sexual abuse complainants in particular) were already in force. When the earlier measures were introduced, judges already had general discretionary powers to modify existing procedures for any sort of trial. They could disallow questions they considered irrelevant or oppressive. They could clear the court, allow a traumatised witness to give evidence from behind a screen, prohibit the identification of witnesses and the publication of evidence, and allow the introduction of written evidence if 'the Court is of the opinion that the interests of justice so require'. But those powers were exercised sparingly, even in sexual offence cases. According to feminists, this was because judges (who were almost exclusively male) were insensitive to women's concerns. According to traditionalists, it was because judges believed that justice should be seen to be done and evidence should be tested by vigorous cross-examination. In any event, the effect of the law changes of the '70s and '80s was to transform provisions that had been exceptional and discretionary for all cases into provisions that were routine and sometimes mandatory for cases involving sexual offences. As a result, by the time the Geddis-promoted amendments were introduced in 1989, sexual offences had already acquired special status within the justice system. This special status, and the public anxiety surrounding the issue, meant that the deleterious effects of the amendments on the suspect's right to a fair trial were either overlooked, or applauded.

Among other things, the amendments extended the 1985 restrictions on public access and media scrutiny from the narrowly defined 'cases involving sexual violation' to the broadly defined 'cases of a sexual nature'. They also replaced the requirement that child witnesses appear in person in court with a provision allowing complainants under the age of 17 in cases 'of a sexual nature' to give their deposition at the preliminary hearing, and their evidence at trial in the form of a pre-recorded, videotaped interview with a DSW interviewer (or via closed-circuit television, or from behind a screen). Another amendment restricted the defendant's access to the evidence against him. While defendants are normally entitled to copies of documents, the amendment stated that: 'the defendant shall not be entitled to a copy of the videotape, but shall be entitled to view the videotape within the Court precincts in the presence of an officer of the court.' A further amendment gave judges the power to disallow 'intimidating' or 'overbearing' cross-examination (in addition to their existing power to disallow 'irrelevant' or 'oppressive' cross-examination).

Prior to these amendments becoming law, they were tested at a trial in Timaru. As it happened, the judge discharged the defendant on the grounds that there were 'substantial and material' contradictions in the children's evidence, so the experiment was not a triumph for the prosecution. Nonetheless, defence lawyer Douglas Taffs was troubled by the evidentiary changes. He told the *Christchurch Star*:

> this new legislation is intrinsically designed to operate on the basis that the child is telling the truth which is splendid if the child is telling the truth; that it should be protected from the trauma of a criminal trial and relieved of the burden of telling the story at depositions. But it seems to me that no one is prepared to face up to this enormous problem that arises when the child is either lying, or possibly blaming someone to protect someone else or, indeed, in some way fantasising. In that case all these safeguards

become devices to further the child's lies or fantasies or transference of blame and I don't see how that squares with the principle that a man is innocent until proven guilty.[11]

Among the most far-reaching of the Geddis amendments were the provisions allowing child psychiatrists or child psychologists to testify on matters of opinion that were within the everyday experience of ordinary people, and about which there was no reliable, research-based body of knowledge. These matters were:

(a) The intellectual attainment, mental capacity and emotional maturity of the complainant ...

(b) The general development level of children of the same age group as the complainant ...

(c) Whether any evidence given during the proceedings by any person ... relating to the complainant's behaviour is, from the expert witness's professional experience or from his or her knowledge of the professional literature, consistent or inconsistent with the behaviour of sexually abused children of the same age group as the complainant.[12]

The latter provisions allowed expert witnesses to confound juries with unscientific material like R.C. Summit's 'Child Sexual Abuse Accommodation Syndrome', or a list of everyday child behaviours said to be consistent with sexual abuse.

The Geddis amendments also addressed the judge's directions to the jury:

(a) ... the Judge shall advise the jury not to draw any adverse inference against the accused from the mode in which the complainant's evidence is given.

(b) The Judge shall not give any warning to the jury relating to the absence of corroboration of the evidence of the complainant if the Judge would not have given such a warning had the complainant been of full age.

(c) The Judge shall not instruct the jury on the need to scrutinise the evidence of young children generally with special care nor suggest to the jury that young children generally have tendencies to invention or distortion.[13]

In contrast to the provisions for expert witnesses (which were based on the premise that child witnesses are different from adult witnesses and juries need expert help to understand them), items (b) and (c) were based on the premise that child and adult witnesses are essentially the same. The latter provisions were based on the work of American sexual abuse specialist Dr Gail Goodman.

In the early 1980s Goodman established that if neither the interviewer nor the child had any motive to make a false report, and if the child was interviewed in a neutral style with minimal use of leading questions, reliable evidence could be obtained. More recently, Ceci and Bruck found that, by repeating questions, by asking leading questions, and by characterising the person being discussed as bad or dangerous, interviewers can easily lead small children to fabricate stories. They also found that children will readily change their stories to agree with a friend's experience or to conform with what they think an adult wants to hear. However, when the New Zealand law changes relating to children's evidence were drafted, Goodman's findings were the last word on the subject. *A Private or Public Nightmare?* concluded:

> we found no evidence to suggest a child victim is a less reliable witness than any other ... Our review of the literature and our experiences do not support a blanket statement that children are highly suggestible about events of personal significance such as sexual abuse.[14]

• • •

The law changes relating to children's evidence were introduced at a time when suspects in child sexual abuse cases were already having a hard time defending themselves. A general loosening of restrictions on the admissibility of hearsay and similar fact evidence meant that suspects faced a greater risk of being found guilty by innuendo. Furthermore, the law restricting cross-examination of rape complainants about their previous sexual histories with anyone other than the accused was also being applied to child sexual abuse cases. This meant that evidence of a child's previous sexual abuse, or previous false allegations, or previous sexual activity with peers, could be ruled inadmissible. These restrictions hampered the ability of defence lawyers to provide alternative explanations for the sexual allegations, precocious knowledge, or sexualised behaviour of underage complainants.[15]

A further problem for defendants was created by the increasing numbers of women counselled on the *Courage to Heal* model who were laying complaints of long-term sexual offending that had occurred many years earlier. In a 1992 judgment, President of the Court of Appeal Sir Robin Cooke observed:

> Mr De Cleene contended that the balance has swung too far against the defence in sexual abuse trials. He mentioned the difficulty of defending charges based, as here, on events many years past ... He dwelt on the difficulty, if the range of dates is wide, of raising alibi defences or of cross-examining on details with a view to shaking the complainant's story ... Mr De Cleene pointed also to the changes introduced by Parliament to reduce the ordeal of complainants and to remove what have been perceived as outdated obstacles to successful prosecutions of guilty persons ... Beyond question it is true that all this legislative activity, combined with the approach of the Courts ... has significantly shifted the balance in sexual trials, especially perhaps those relating to child abuse ... other developments ... have also moved the balance towards the prosecution. These include ... DNA testing ...[16]

Cooke's comment on DNA testing is revealing. As an investigative tool, DNA testing helps protect the innocent as well as convict the guilty. By suggesting that DNA testing favours the prosecution, Cooke demonstrated that even the president of the Court of Appeal could have difficulty invoking the presumption of innocence when dealing with people accused of sexual offences. This may have been because he regarded such offences as exceptional crimes for which established judicial procedures were ill-equipped to cope. 'The evil of this kind of offending appears to be virtually worldwide,' he said. 'While the Courts cannot solve the social problem, a response to it in the Courts invoking a technical legal doctrine of some obscurity seems unsatisfying.'[17]

The same impatience with legal procedures that were acceptable as long as they protected innocent people accused of ordinary crimes, but were unacceptable when they hindered the conviction of witch suspects, pervades the writings of judges during the great witch-hunts. Their solution was to insist that, because witchcraft was *crimen exceptum*, the rules of evidence had to be changed to allow the admission of spectral evidence (the dreams, visions and hallucinations of people considered to be bewitched). Spectral evidence had a powerful impact because it was disgusting, titillating and grotesquely obscene. It was also vivid, emotive and convincingly articulated. But it could never be proved or disproved, and there was never any conclusive corroboration, so accepting or rejecting it was entirely a matter of belief. The Salem witch trials, which resulted in the execution of 19 people in 1692, came to an end when the Governor declared spectral evidence inadmissible. In *Historical Essays Concerning Witchcraft* (1718) Bishop Francis Hutchinson, a critic of the witch trials, wrote of the impossibility of mounting a defence against spectral evidence:

> in other cases, when wicked or mistaken people charge us with crimes of which we are not guilty, we clear ourselves by showing that at that time we were at home, or in some other place, about our honest business. But in prosecutions for witchcraft, the most natural and just defence is mere jest. For if any wicked person affirms, or any crack-brained girl imagines, or any lying spirit makes her believe, that she sees an old woman, or other person, pursuing her in her vision … such fantastic notions … leave the lives of innocent men naked without defence against them.[18]

• • •

David Geddis persuaded New Zealand's key politicians, judges, lawyers and bureaucrats to make child sexual abuse a special case within the justice system by stressing the vulnerability and innocence of young children. In sexual abuse prosecutions, he argued, the trauma of a courtroom appearance could damage both the quality of the child's evidence and the quality of the child's life. Therefore, in the interests of justice and in the interests of children, the rules and procedures had to change.

This was not the first time these arguments had been put before government. In 1975 the Minister of Justice asked the Criminal Law Reform Committee to consider 'The Position of Young Witnesses in Cases Involving a Sexual Offence'. In particular, the committee was asked to consider an Israeli scheme that allowed a Youth Examiner to interview the child in private, and to give evidence in court on the child's behalf.[19]

At that time child witnesses in New Zealand sexual abuse cases were treated no differently from other witnesses. If they were considered legally competent, they had to give evidence in court and answer questions put to them in cross-examination. However, their vulnerability was not entirely disregarded. Judges had the discretion to suppress the names of child witnesses and exclude the public from the court. They could also allow parents to remain in an otherwise cleared court (and there are cases on record of children as young as three giving evidence from their mothers' laps). Furthermore, as in all court cases, judges could disallow cross-examination they considered irrelevant or oppressive.

It was the Criminal Law Reform Committee's view that the existing procedures and rules of evidence had, over centuries of fine tuning, brought the scales of justice to a delicate balance, and they did not want that balance altered without good cause.

To test the claim that children were unable to testify freely in the existing system, the committee studied a random selection of police files. They found that one in 10 child molestation prosecutions was not proceeded with because of the child's unsuitability as a witness. No comparable estimate was made of the proportion of adult molestation cases not proceeded with because of the adult complainant's unsuitability as a witness. Nor is it clear what proportion of unsuitable child witnesses were considered incompetent, what proportion were considered unreliable (that is, their evidence was not considered honest and truthful), and what proportion were considered competent and reliable but were too distressed to testify. In any event, 90 percent of the reviewed cases did proceed and the children involved, whose ages ranged from three to 16 years, gave evidence and were cross-examined.

On the question of whether appearing in court and being cross-examined caused long-term harm to a child, the committee reported:

> We are not aware of any reliable scientific research done on that issue. Most of the published material appears to present the views of what adults thought children ought to feel. None of the professional persons who discussed the issue with us was able to provide evidence that harm commonly resulted from the court experience as opposed to the sexual experience.[20]

Having found no reason to support the call for greater protection for child witnesses, the committee found even less reason to support the Israeli Youth Examiner scheme. They concluded that courtroom use of the Youth Examiner's hearsay and opinion evidence, in place of the child's first-hand evidence and cross-examination, would reduce the reliability of the evidence but increase the likelihood of that evidence being believed (because of the 'expert witness' status of the Youth Examiner). They further noted that, since there was no reliable, research-based body of knowledge on the interpretation of children's comments and behaviour, opinions on that subject were matters of common sense that should be left to the collective wisdom of the jury.

By the time the same calls for reform arose again in the late '80s there was still no reliable, research-based body of knowledge about the interpretation of children's comments and behaviour, or about whether the quality of the child's evidence or the quality of the child's life would be adversely affected by his or her participation in court proceedings. Nonetheless, the proposed changes were instituted virtually unopposed. This was partly because the law changes were passed in relative secrecy, and partly because the bureaucrats, politicians, lawyers and judges responsible for implementing the changes were, by the late '80s, on the defensive.

So much had happened in the intervening decade. Pressure groups of every sort had learnt to couch their grievances in the rhetoric of human rights. Miriam Saphira's message that child sexual abuse was an insidious and overwhelming evil had become child protection orthodoxy. Playwright Mervyn Thompson had been tied to a tree and had 'rapist' spray-painted on his car. Laws giving special status to sexual violation cases had been passed. The Cartwright Inquiry into cervical cancer treatment at National Women's Hospital had put the knife into the male-dominated medical establishment. The 1988 Telethon had spread sexual abuse anxiety throughout the community. The 'believe the victim' message had permeated the child protection, police and justice systems. Fathers had become afraid to bathe and toilet their own children. Child sexual abuse prosecutions had escalated. Sexual abuse counselling had become a growth industry. ACC payments to sexual abuse victims had skyrocketed.

As a result, by the late '80s, white middle-class men were suffering from white middle-class male guilt and were anxious to atone. In the public arena, political correctness ruled. Few men were prepared to openly question the notion that all women were oppressed (even when the claim was made by tenured female academics on high salaries), or that all men were dangerous sexual predators, or that society was being torn apart by rampant child sex abuse. Political opportunists, and men with wives and daughters active in the feminist and child protection movements, were particularly vulnerable to the tyranny of good intentions, as were liberal men in positions of power. As liberals they were anxious to show that, despite their complicity in the recent free-market reforms, they were committed to protecting the weak and oppressed. As males they were anxious to show that they really were sensitive and caring. As leaders they were anxious to show that they could act decisively in a crisis. So when the National Advisory Committee on the Prevention of Child Abuse urged government and the courts to make some inexpensive procedural changes that would protect innocent children from the predations of evil men, the government quickly obliged.

The 1989 amendments to the Evidence, Crimes and Summary Proceedings Acts came into force on 1 January 1990. The associated Evidence (Videotaping of Child Complainants) Regulations came into force just over six months later. Over the more than two years between the introduction of the regulations, and the start of depositions in the Christchurch Civic Crèche case, judges weighed the requirement to 'minimise stress on the complainant' against the requirement to 'ensure a fair trial for the accused'. More often than not, they ruled in favour of the complainant.

One of the most influential judgments was made in a 1990 appeal against a ruling by Justice Roper that the videotaped interviews in a case were inadmissible. Roper rejected the videotapes for three reasons: it was sometimes difficult to determine whether a complainant was talking about his or her own experience or about something heard from another child; the interviewer engaged in prolonged probing and sought confirmation of accounts given her by the children's mothers; and it would be virtually impossible to cross-examine the complainants on statements made in a 'play' atmosphere eight months earlier by showing them the videotapes prior to cross-examination.

In his Court of Appeal judgment, Sir Robin Cooke said that the purpose of the 1989 Evidence Amendment Act was 'to ensure that the old technicalities of evidence and traditional approaches to the giving of evidence, even the contents of evidence in matters such as hearsay, shall not necessarily prevail'. He acknowledged that many of the interviewer's questions were of a 'somewhat leading or coaxing character', but ruled that 'in the spirit of the new legislation' the videotapes were admissible.[21]

Other appeal judgments 'in the spirit of the new legislation' were made on the competence of child witnesses. In the past, judges required child witnesses to promise to tell the truth (after first satisfying themselves that the child knew the difference between truth and lies, and understood the implication of making a promise). Under the new legislation, that role passed to the DSW interviewer, and the manner in which the interviewer tested the child's competence was the subject of several appeals. In 1991 the Court of Appeal ruled that the interviewer's approach should not be 'over-refined or pedantic'. In 1992, it ruled that the competence test was met by the following exchange:

> 'We need to make an agreement that we only talk about real stuff, the truth, can we do that?' Child nods. 'Is it OK that we only talk about the truth?' Child nods.[22]

With regard to expert witnesses, in 1987 Justice McMullin ruled in a Court of Appeal judgment that a psychologist's evidence in a sexual abuse case was inadmissible because:

> The psychologist's belief that the complainant was telling the truth was also a belief that the events she described did in fact occur. The admission of the psychologist's evidence would inevitably lead the jury to learn of her opinion ... If the complainant was a competent witness ... it was for the jury to make their own assessment of credibility.[23]

McMullin also stated that expert opinion should be admissible only in recognised branches of science, a point he reiterated in a 1988 judgment.

> Before a psychologist or other similarly qualified person can be allowed to give evidence that a particular child has exhibited traits displayed by sexually abused children generally, it must be demonstrated in an unmistakable and compelling way, and by reference to scientific material, that the relevant characteristics are signs of child abuse.[24]

But once the Geddis amendments came into effect, everything changed. Thereafter, expert witnesses could base their testimony on their professional experience, so scientific evidence was no longer required. Also, they were allowed to comment more freely on matters that were for the jury to decide. As the Court of Appeal observed in a 1992 judgment, expert evidence 'will usually be especially important in assisting the jury to evaluate the truth of the complainant's evidence'.[25]

All this legislative and judicial activity meant that, by the time the Christchurch Civic Crèche case erupted in 1991, many of the traditional safeguards that protected the reliability of evidence in criminal cases no longer applied in child sexual abuse cases. Because corroboration was no longer necessary, sexual abuse complaints were not always thoroughly investigated. Also, child complainants no longer had to appear in court in person. They were no longer required to deliver their evidence-in-chief without leading or coaxing. Their evidence was no longer tested by unhampered cross-examination. Instead, juries viewed prerecorded interviews with child complainants conducted by interviewers trained in the beliefs and methods of the child protection movement, and observed cross-examinations conducted via videolink. Also – regardless of their personal evaluations of the credibility of the children, and the credibility of the children's evidence – jurors were encouraged, by the hearsay and opinion evidence of experts, to believe whatever the child witnesses said.

By the time the late '80s and early '90s evidentiary and procedural changes for child sexual abuse cases had been implemented, the power structure had changed. At the investigative stage, control of the collection of evidence had moved from the relatively objective police to the clearly partisan sexual abuse specialists. At the prosecution stage, control of the presentation of the child's evidence-in-chief had moved from judges and lawyers in a courtroom to sexual abuse specialists in video recording studios.

As a result, by 1991 effective control of the investigation and prosecution of child sexual abuse had shifted from the justice system to the child protection movement. At that point the elevation of sexual offences against children to the status of *crimen exceptum* was complete. After that – in New Zealand in general and in Christchurch in particular – suspected child molesters were prosecuted more vigorously, and convicted more often.

Chapter 4

Christchurch Possessed

4.i: The Place

When the Christchurch Civic Crèche case seized headlines in 1992 the allegations shocked the nation, but the fact that the bizarre claims arose in that southern city came as no surprise.

Christchurch, a city flat as conformity, was founded in 1850 by wealthy and pious Church of England settlers. Driven by visions of an orderly and hierarchical slice of England in this far-flung colony, they created an elegant provincial capital on the swamps and sand dunes of the Canterbury Plains. At the city's heart they built a cathedral surrounded by noble public buildings. Along the peaceable river Avon they created genteel suburbs and verdant parks and gardens. The ruling elite believed that their power and wealth were the deserved consequence of their own innate superiority, and they encouraged the less privileged to embrace those beliefs with humility, deference and gratitude. More than 140 years later Christchurch remains a class-conscious city.

This snobbery, imposed from above, seems to have provoked in those below a defiant eccentricity. Throughout its history Christchurch has been as famous for its cranks and zealots as it has been for its Englishness and its class distinctions. This is not to suggest that other cities are devoid of eccentrics and fanatics, it's just that in most places, if they are not insulted, assaulted or ignored, they are, more often than not, patted on the head and told to keep taking the pills. But Christchurch is a place where messianic zealots gather a following, attract influential patrons and go on to change the world.

Some people blame the hot nor'wester. Some blame the smog, or the lead content in the air. Some blame the topography. 'Strange things happen in Christchurch because it's so flat,' people say. For entirely prosaic reasons, there may be an element of truth to this observation. The flatness of the city makes it easy for anyone with a bright idea to gather together enough like-minded people to turn any theory – be it dazzlingly enlightened or downright flakey – into action. And for more than 100 years that is exactly what Christchurch people have been doing.

In the late 19th century Christchurch was the epicentre of the prohibitionist movement and the campaign for women's suffrage. In the early years of this century a prison reform movement flourished in the city. During World War I, while jingoistic patriotism prevailed elsewhere in the Dominion, Christchurch was a hotbed of pacifism. After the war, a campaign for the purification of the white race through the elimination of mental defectives, homosexuals and other 'weak and impure elements' seized the public imagination. Around the same time visiting faith healers and religious revivalists drew thousands to their rallies. In 1935 Viennese philosopher Karl Popper arrived in the city. During an unhappy eight-year stay he wrote *The Open Society and Its Enemies*.[1]

In 1940 Christchurch-born Maurice Bevan Brown returned from 17 years' experience of outpatient psychiatry in Britain. Until his death in 1967 he worked tirelessly to convince Christchurch people that there was more to psychiatry than the institutional care of the mentally ill. He practised office psychotherapy, trained lay analysts and gave public lectures on everything from natural childbirth to war neuroses. His book *The Sources of Love and Fear* (1950) challenged the rigid child-rearing methods promoted by the Plunket Society at that time.[2]

In the wake of World War II the ripples generated by Bevan Brown and others led to the establishment of several national mental health bodies in the city. These included the Marriage Guidance Council, the Association of Psychotherapists, the Manic-Depressive Society, the Schizophrenia Fellowship and the Association of Clinical Psychologists.

Nowadays New Zealand's only sex-change surgeon works out of one of the city's more conservative suburbs, and the public face of Christchurch's eccentricity is displayed each lunchtime by a scattering of entertainers and evangelists in Cathedral Square. From 1974, the most spellbinding of these has been the Wizard, a self-styled 'living work of art' whose enchantments, controversies, and drought-breaking rain-dances spread his fame far beyond his adopted city.

Politically speaking, Christchurch is a hotbed of fundamentalist extremes. The city has spawned fundamentalist Christians (armed and unarmed), fundamentalist Marxists, fundamentalist Trotskyites, fundamentalist Greenies, fundamentalist Maoists, fundamentalist New-Agers, fundamentalist white supremacists, fundamentalist sceptics, fundamentalist gays and a group of fundamentalist anti-communists infamous for their sledgehammer attacks on Lada cars.

Christchurch has been the setting for some of the most bizarre crimes in recent New Zealand history. In 1954 two adolescent girls murdered the mother of one of them by hitting her over the head repeatedly with a brick. In 1964 six adolescent boys were charged with beating a homosexual draper to death with their fists and boots in the Hagley Park toilets. The not guilty verdicts sent shockwaves around the nation. In 1984 a disturbed woman with a morbid preoccupation with the occult was convicted of the murder of three infants and the attempted murder of three more. She was probably the nearest thing to a satanic baby killer the city has ever known. In the early 1990s Christchurch's reputation as a setting for bizarre crimes reached its apogee. First came the Civic Crèche case, then the 'body in the garden' case, then the 'poisoned professor' case.[3]

• • •

There were also imaginary crimes. In recent years, one of the strangest and most persistent has been the Great Christchurch Child Pornography Ring. Though no tangible evidence of its existence has ever been found, the belief that a paedophile ring was abducting local children and filming their forced participation in obscene rituals enjoyed widespread popular currency in the late '80s and early '90s.

Conspiracy theories of this sort are the product of an elemental human need for explanations. When people feel threatened by a widespread invisible evil, a conspiracy theory is bound to follow. How else can you explain the lack of evidence?

The appeal of conspiracy theories spans the social spectrum. For the oppressed they provide an explanation for their powerlessness; for the powerful they provide a focus for their fears. Human history is replete with conspiracy theories. The major ones are about groups of malefactors seeking world domination for their own evil ends. This century Zionists, Germans, Japanese and communists have been the subject of major Western conspiracy theories.

Some conspiracy theories have a real-life basis, but the two phenomena – conspiracy theories and real-life conspiracies – should not be confused. In the fantasy world of conspiracy theories hundreds of people may be involved, often over decades. The conspirators inevitably include people in high places. Everyone is sworn to secrecy. The whole operation is extremely efficient. No one leaves tell-tale evidence. No one blabs. No outsider notices anything suspicious.

In real life, even small-scale conspiracies – like the burial of Doug Gardner in Gay Oakes' Christchurch garden – rarely go undetected. There is usually at least one insider who can't keep the secret, and at least one outsider who notices something amiss. There is nearly always evidence to be found. In the unusual event of a conspiracy going undetected for years – like Kim Philby's infiltration of British Intelligence with Soviet agents – the temptation for the conspirators to boast about their exploits later often proves irresistible.

In Western societies, conspiracy theorists often invoke Christianity's arch-enemy Satan to describe the unseen evil they fear. Sometimes they accuse members of the feared group of belonging to a cult of Satan-worshippers who practise infanticide, cannibalism and degenerate sexual orgies. At different times over the past 1800 years lepers, Jews, heretics, Cathars, Knights Templar, witches, Freemasons, gypsies and numerous religious minorities have been accused of membership of satanic cults.

In 1980 the publication of *Michelle Remembers* revived the satanic cult conspiracy theory and applied it to child molesters. The book described horrendous sexual and physical abuse allegedly suffered in the 1960s by co-author Michelle Smith during her childhood in a satanic cult. The cult's activities were apparently so well hidden that none of Michelle's school friends or teachers, and none of the workmates or acquaintances of Michelle's parents ever noticed anything suspicious.[4]

Michelle Remembers was later shown to be a hoax, but the cult it described was an idea whose time had come.[5] By 1980 the twin beliefs that men were dangerous sexual predators and child sexual abuse was rampant were spreading rapidly throughout the Western world. As a result, increasing numbers of child sexual abuse cases were being reported. The upsurge was most marked in centres where sexual abuse specialists were active. 'How come nobody noticed all this abuse until you came along?' people wanted to know. *Michelle Remembers* provided the answer.

Following the publication of *Michelle Remembers*, hundreds of troubled women began 'recovering' memories of satanic abuse, usually during therapy. Throughout the '80s these self-proclaimed survivors spread the satanism scare in books and magazines, in seminar rooms and conference halls, in television and radio programmes.

Most mainstream child protection workers were prepared to believe that large-scale child sexual abuse was occurring in their midst, but many found the term 'satanic' a bit over the top. So to make the belief more credible, they coined alternative names: ritual abuse, ritualistic abuse, cult abuse, multi-victim multi-perpetrator abuse, sadistic ritual abuse, multidimensional sex rings, sadistic abuse.

The definition of ritual abuse used in Pamela Hudson's 1991 book *Ritual Child Abuse: Discovery, diagnosis and treatment*, and adopted by the former Civic Crèche parents who formed the organisation End Ritual Abuse, stated:

> Ritual abuse … is a brutal form of abuse to children, adolescents and adults, consisting of physical, sexual and psychological abuse, and involving the use of rituals. It usually involves repeated abuse over an extended period of time. Physical abuse is severe, sometimes including torture and killing. Sexual abuse is usually painful, sadistic and humiliating, intended as a means of gaining dominance over the victim. Psychological abuse is devastating and involves the use of ritual indoctrination which includes mind control techniques.[6]

Other characteristics of ritual abuse allegations are: disclosures are usually made long after the alleged events and are usually preceded by intensive interviewing and therapy; searches by doctors for signs of bodily harm, and by police for bones, bodies, burial sites, pornography and ritual garments are fruitless; when ritual abuse cases are brought to court the primary issue before the jury is whether or not to believe the victim; defendants usually maintain their innocence, even following conviction.

4.ii: The Fever

Once the seeds of the ritual abuse scare had dispersed into the ether, it was probably inevitable that they would reach New Zealand. Once they reached these shores, it was probably inevitable that they would find some fertile imaginations in which to take root and grow. It was probably inevitable that the pornographic elements of the scare would raise more anxiety than the satanic ones in this secular nation, and it was probably inevitable that the scare would escalate into a full-blown, cult-abuse panic in Christchurch because, by the mid-'80s, Christchurch was the epicentre of a nationwide web of child protection workers dedicated to the investigation, detection and prosecution of sexual abuse. When we follow the threads of the web most of them lead back to child psychiatrist Dr Karen Zelas.

Karen Zelas graduated in medicine from Otago University in 1964. From 1966 to 1971 she was a psychiatric registrar at Christchurch's Sunnyside (Psychiatric) Hospital. Her duties included part-time work at the local Child Health Clinic.

Child Health Clinics were established in the 1950s to assist school children with emotional, social, intellectual and behavioural problems. Initially, each clinic was headed by a paediatrician who received part-time assistance from a psychiatrist, a psychologist and a social worker. By the 1970s some clinics also employed child therapists. At that time the only employment available to New Zealand psychiatrists who wanted to work with children was at Child Health Clinics.[7]

Zelas's work as a psychiatric registrar was her first step towards specialist qualification. In 1971 she sat the British examination that entitled her to work as a consultant psychiatrist in New Zealand. Then, like most New Zealanders who qualified around that time, she stayed in Britain to obtain further experience, and to sit the slightly more demanding Royal College of Psychiatrists membership examination.

When Zelas returned to New Zealand in 1973 she took up the position of full-time child psychiatrist at the Christchurch Child Health Clinic. By then, management of the clinics had passed from the Department of Health to hospital boards. This change, along with the growth of educational psychology, meant that the clinics were moving away from being support units for schools, and towards becoming child psychiatry outpatient clinics. The Christchurch clinic staff worked as a team, with the psychiatrist as team leader. They provided medical, psychological and social assessments and treatment plans for referred children.[8]

In March 1974, in an interview with the Christchurch *Press*, Zelas took on the additional role of spokesperson on child mental health issues. Of the few child psychiatrists in New Zealand at that time, she was the most articulate, assertive and photogenic, and she soon acquired a high media profile. In addition to her clinical work, she attended overseas conferences, advised decision-makers, and addressed allied professionals and community workers. By the late '70s it was these extracurricular activities, rather than her clinical expertise, that gained her the reputation of being a committed professional, working at the cutting edge of her field.[9]

Throughout the '80s and '90s Zelas's reputation for excellence continued to grow. In a 1994 Court of Appeal test case on sentencing for incest, the court commissioned its own report from Karen Zelas ('a leading consultant psychiatrist in this field in New Zealand') and received oral evidence from her. In his 24-page judgment, Sir Robin Cooke mentioned Zelas approvingly 20 times, and quoted extensively from her submission.[10]

In 1996 a judge told me: 'She's extremely able ... Her qualifications run to about three pages ... She is regarded as one of the authorities in the field of sexual abuse and child abuse in New Zealand ... She's published a lot of research ...'[11]

At the second Ellis appeal in 1999, when presented with research demonstrating that experts could not distinguish between true and false allegations of child sexual abuse, Justice Thomas expressed confidence that Dr Zelas could in fact do so.

Such comments illustrate the high regard in which Karen Zelas was held by the New Zealand judiciary at the time, but tell us little about the realities of her career. Though she does indeed have an impressively long string of letters after her name, within her profession her qualifications carry less weight than one, hard-earned fellowship of the Royal Australian and New Zealand College of Psychiatrists (FRANZCI).

The first set of letters (MB ChB 1964 Otago), is Zelas's graduating degree in medicine. The second and third sets are her primary specialist qualifications – her English Diploma of Psychological Medicine and her Membership of the Royal College of Psychiatrists (DPM 1971 RCP Lond. and RCS Eng., MRC Psych 1973) – both of which were acquired from relatively undemanding courses of study and examination. The fourth set, her membership of the Royal Australian and New Zealand College of Psychiatrists (M. 1975 RANZCP), was acquired without examination under a 'grandparenting clause' when the college was established. The fifth set, her fellowship of the same College (R 1979 RANZCP), was acquired by election at a time when such elections were commonplace. The sixth set, her membership of the New Zealand Association of Psychotherapists (MNZAP 1981), was acquired by presenting a paper to an NZAP conference.

Also, contrary to the judge's claims, Karen Zelas has conducted no research and has only a few lightweight articles to her name.[12]

Her reputation for excellence is a product of her knowledge of other people's work, her media and networking skills and the sheer force of her personality. From the late '70s on, these qualities ensured that, whenever a child psychiatrist was needed for a media comment or a government working party, Karen Zelas was nearly always it.

In the early '70s, when Zelas was pursuing her specialist training in London, most British child psychiatrists were aware of Henry Kempe's claim that baby battering was epidemic in America. However, they were confident that, thanks to the welfare state, cruelty to children was largely a thing of the past in their country – the emotional problems of young children were a much greater concern.[13]

When she returned to Christchurch in 1973, Zelas brought with her the family-centred approach to child psychiatry pioneered by D.W. Winnicott. Winnicott believed that children should be cared for by adults with emotional ties to them because such adults were most likely to place the child's needs first. According to Winnicott, impersonal child-rearing systems could meet the child's physical and intellectual needs, but could not replicate the intimacies of family life that were the primary source of a person's value and self-realisation. To maximise the benefits of family life, he encouraged parents to give their children security and unconditional love in their early years. He believed that most childhood emotional problems could be prevented by parental education and support or, failing that, ameliorated by family therapy. As Zelas explained to the Christchurch *Press* in March 1974, rather than separating problem children from their parents, the latest trend in Britain was to treat whole families together.[14]

Three months later she restated her family-centred philosophy in a vigorous attack on childcare centres. As in the previous interview, she drew her authority from 'studies overseas' (in this geographically isolated country, basing one's claims on 'studies overseas' is a time-honoured method of winning respect for any cause). Zelas told the *Press*:

> Day-care centres and crèches, while being beneficial to working mothers, could have detrimental effects on children. Studies overseas ... show that this is the case, but the seriousness of the problem may not be apparent here until these children become adult citizens.[15]

She also criticised feminists for their denigration of the mothering role, and argued that children need a constant mothering person during their first three years of life. 'If a mother becomes frustrated or dissatisfied … she needs help to provide what the child requires, not to go out and leave the child to someone else,' she said. She added that the help could come from 'good husbands as well as from professional bodies'.

Though professional opinion was divided over the significance of the mother's role, in the early '70s most New Zealand child health workers shared Karen Zelas's view that families with problem children should be supported. However, following Henry Kempe's 1973 visit to this country, Dunedin Hospital paediatrician Dr David Geddis took up his call that families with problem children should be policed.[16]

In 1977 Geddis's sphere of authority expanded dramatically when he was appointed medical director of the Plunket Society and – along with Dr Karen Zelas – a member of the newly established Child Health Committee of the Board of Health.[17] By then the first International Congress on Child Abuse and Neglect had been held in Geneva, and the journal *Child Abuse and Neglect* had been established. News of these developments sent a clear message to child health workers: child abuse is the new frontier, and David Geddis is leading the charge.

Geddis and Zelas attended the second International Congress on Child Abuse and Neglect in London in September 1978. In an interview with the Christchurch *Press* following the Congress, Zelas indicated that her interest was moving from emotional trauma unintentionally inflicted by inept parents, to physical trauma deliberately inflicted by abusive parents. 'We have no reason to be complacent about the incidence of child abuse in New Zealand,' she said. She also referred to Kempe's notion of a basic conflict between parents' rights and children's rights, and suggested that while most physical and emotional abuse was perpetrated by mothers, 'Sexual abuse, which we now know is more common than most people had realised, is most often carried out by the father'.[18]

Zelas's change of allegiance from the teachings of Winnicott to the teachings of Kempe brought with it a change in therapeutic approach. She told the *Press* that her clinic's shift from working with parents to focusing on the child's development in a safe environment was 'abreast of forward thinking overseas'.

As Zelas's fame spread, the Christchurch Child Health Clinic grew in size and importance. In 1979 it became the Child and Family Guidance Centre and Zelas became its director (but her role of chief clinician remained unchanged). By then the clinic had nine full-time and several part-time staff. One part-timer was child psychiatrist Dr Bill Watkins, who also worked half time as a lecturer in Psychological Medicine at the Christchurch School of Medicine. The other new staff were mainly social workers and child therapists. As a result of the staffing increase, more multidisciplinary teams were formed. But, because Zelas was away a lot and Watkins was only there half time, medical supervision of the teams was less than optimal.

The growing demand for the clinic's services and the shortage of medical staff meant that, by the early '80s, the Child and Family Guidance Centre could no longer provide comprehensive medical evaluations for all referred children. Instead, more or less by default, psychologists, social workers and therapists began taking increasing responsibility for conducting assessments and drawing up treatment plans.

In 1980 Zelas's outside responsibilities increased when she was appointed to the National Advisory Committee on the Prevention of Child Abuse. At first the committee focused on the physical maltreatment of children by distraught mothers. When radical feminists protested that sexual abuse by fathers was a more pressing problem, committee members responded with caution. In June 1982, when the Christchurch *Press* devoted a full page to Miriam Saphira's work, Zelas warned that investigations of child sexual abuse allegations 'should not become a witch-hunt to find out if it happened'. 'One of the potential problems of vigorous investigation might be the impact of it on the child, and that impact should never be lost sight of,' she said.[19]

Such caution was not well received by the leaders of the sexual abuse awareness campaign. At the 1982 Mental Health Foundation Conference on child abuse they launched a counter-attack.

The paper presented by Lynda Morgan of the Christchurch Incest Survivors Group created a sensation. Unlike the other speakers, who based their claims of expertise on their academic qualifications and clinical and research experience, Morgan based hers on her experience as an incest survivor. Also, while other speakers gave unemotional, scientific papers on aspects of physical abuse, Lynda Morgan and Miriam Saphira gave emotional papers on sexual abuse.[20]

The Incest Survivors Group had begun meeting in October 1981. Its five members were united by their memories of incest (which covered 'the whole range of sexual abuse, from touching to all kinds of sexual activity'), by their anger that 'none of the molesters was apprehended at the time and none has ever been charged or brought to court', by their hostility to conventionally trained mental health experts, and by their conviction that women who had experienced incest were best qualified to help others in the same situation.[21]

After a year of gruelling self-help therapy, the group members still felt far from healed. But they did feel angry and strong. So, taking their unresolved problems with them, they set out to change the world. Morgan's presentation to the Mental Health Foundation Conference was their first public statement.[22]

In her paper, Morgan attributed the problem of sexual abuse to the patriarchy, and to its primary prop, the heterosexual family. Until these institutions are dismantled, she warned, 'we will suspect all men – including you men here.'

Ironically, in view of her later role in the Civic Crèche case, one of Morgan's demands was for increased childcare subsidies. 'If this or any government really cared about children, they would be setting up childcare centres,' she said.

For women already damaged by sexual abuse, Morgan advocated the Incest Survivors Group's approach to therapy. 'Talking about the assaults with as much physical and psychological detail as possible is the best way of releasing emotions of fear, grief, anger, guilt and self-negation,' she said. According to Morgan, the anger generated by this therapy often spilled over into members' daily lives ('in the form of vulnerability towards or sexual rejection of partners and hostility towards males, male relatives and male children'), and into their perceptions of the wider world:

> ... we are all extremely sensitive towards and feel much distress and anger in reading reports of sexual assaults and rape of women and children ... We consistently felt that molesters and rapists are protected by the courts and some of us felt we would like to harass and humiliate the offender ...[23]

In May 1983 many New Zealanders with a professional interest in child abuse raised their expertise by attending the lectures of Dr Donald Bross, lawyer and medical sociologist from the Henry Kempe Centre, who visited New Zealand as a guest of the Family Courts Association.

During his visit, Bross spoke to several Christchurch groups about the ferment of prosecutions and law changes that had accompanied the upsurge in child abuse and neglect reports in the United States. In retrospect, his comments to the Christchurch *Press* seem prophetic:

> Cases of sexual molestation, child abuse and neglect were occurring with alarming frequency at child care centres in the United States, Dr Bross said. 'In Colorado last year, 17 separate pieces of legislation were introduced dealing with sexual molestation of children ... Each one was in response to a case of molestation of a child by a teacher or child care worker, and there was a general outrage in the community about it.'[24]

Though Bross's message resonated with their concerns, to the radical feminist lobby, any presentation by a white middle-class professional could not go unchallenged. When Eileen Swan of the Auckland Help Foundation addressed a child abuse seminar in 1984 she warned against 'having too many white middle-class professionals moving in' because 'there is an element of middle-class cover-up that goes on'.[25]

When Swan issued her warning, Dr Karen Zelas was on a 10-week study tour of trends in the diagnosis and treatment of child sexual abuse overseas. On her return she and Christchurch lawyer Laurie O'Reilly took seminars for health and legal professionals nationwide. A family lawyer recalled:

> Laurie and Karen were pioneers. It's exciting to be a pioneer in any field. Their message was that vulnerable people were being abused by powerful people in a very intimate way. For family lawyers it was a hard message to resist. People work in family law because they care about the weak and the needy. It was hard to stand back and look at that message in a detached way. You got drawn in. Before you knew it you were wanting to get in and do something about it.[26]

Zelas's status and personality made a major impact:

> She was accepted as some sort of guru. People thought whatever Karen said must be right. She could walk into a room and make a few remarks and people would say: 'Gosh she's wonderful, she's such a good person, such a good presenter.' That was the level of the debate. It was like you were letting the side down if you questioned anything she said.[27]

By the end of 1984 Zelas was a child sexual abuse expert to child protection workers and lawyers nationwide. Then at a family violence conference in September 1985 radical feminists attacked her 'white middle-class professional arrogance'.

'They were incredibly cruel,' recalled a shocked delegate. 'They reduced her to tears.' Zelas responded with a poem, 'Pain', which was published in the conference report.[28]

Throughout the three years prior to Karen Zelas's emergence as a sexual abuse expert, Christchurch feminists and child protection workers trained by Miriam Saphira and Lynda Morgan had been uncovering child sexual abuse on a grand scale. However, because few cases were professionally validated, they had little impact on the official statistics. The change came when Zelas began applying her newfound expertise. Between 31 March 1984 and 31 March 1985, sexual abuse referrals to the Child and Family Guidance Centre increased by over 360 percent. The following year the increase spread to Ward 24 and Glenelg Children's Health Camp.[29] From then on, any troubled family that stumbled into the currents that swirled between those three Christchurch institutions risked being torn apart by accusations of child sexual abuse.

• • •

Ward 24, Christchurch Hospital's 10-bed child psychiatry inpatient unit, opened in 1982 with child psychiatrist Philip Ney as its half-time director. From the outset, the unit was controversial. The controversy was theoretical (Are child psychiatry inpatient units a good idea?) and practical (What on earth does Ney think he's doing?).

Regardless of the presenting problem, children were admitted to Ward 24 for five weeks. On admission, each child was allocated a primary therapist who was responsible for his or her day-to-day care and therapy. Primary therapists were nurses or 'child and family workers'. The latter were chosen for their 'personal qualities indicative of a genuine interest in working with children'. They were the only clinical staff employed by the hospital board who did not have traditional health care qualifications. This would have been of little consequence had they been adequately trained and supervised. But Professor Ney believed that obligatory supervision would create an unnecessarily hierarchical staff structure which would not be conducive to the development of a therapeutic environment. So he allowed unqualified and untrained staff to treat troubled children as they saw fit, and to consult specialists only when they considered it necessary to do so.[30]

From the outset, Ward 24 staff made the diagnosis and treatment of child sexual abuse a priority. When Lynda Morgan addressed the November 1982 Mental Health Foundation Conference, she said: 'We want to congratulate Ward 24, Christchurch Hospital, on the work they are doing with abused, specifically sexually abused children, and with their mothers.'[31]

• • •

At the Child and Family Guidance Centre and Ward 24 the move towards large-scale diagnosis of child sexual abuse was led by poorly supervised junior staff. At the other key Christchurch institution, Glenelg Children's Health Camp, the initiative was taken by senior staff.

Like the other five permanent children's health camps spread throughout New Zealand, Glenelg was established in the 1940s for the purpose of improving the health of needy children. Over the years, problems like tuberculosis and malnutrition declined, problems like poor bladder and bowel control stayed more or less constant, and problems like anti-social behaviour and low self-esteem increased. Despite the changes, health camps continued to provide the same regime of sunshine, fresh air, exercise, good food, rest and routines. Generally speaking, it seemed to help.[32]

After six years in general practice Dr Dianne Espie was appointed medical officer of health responsible for Glenelg Children's Health Camp in 1981. She had no postgraduate qualifications in paediatrics, psychiatry or gynaecology, but during the 1980s she attended many seminars on child abuse and counselling, and thereby became a child sexual abuse expert. By 1985 she was diagnosing increasing numbers of sexual abuse cases in the course of her work.[33]

• • •

As the number of sexual abuse cases identified at the Child and Family Guidance Centre, Ward 24 and Glenelg began to escalate, the number of Family Court custody, access and guardianship cases involving sexual abuse allegations also began to climb. For Family Court judges, determining whether or not a child had been sexually abused seemed a near-impossible task. Like water divining, it appeared to require a special skill. They usually relied on the advice of experts in reaching their conclusions. And whenever an expert was needed, Karen Zelas was the obvious choice.

As a witness, Zelas excelled. 'She's calm and measured. She comes across as sincere and reassuring. Unflappability is her greatest strength,' said one lawyer.[34]

'She's an articulate and polished performer. She handles cross-examination very, very well,' said another.[35]

'Judges relied heavily on Karen Zelas,' explained a legal academic.

'It was such a new field, and Karen came across as scientific and professional. They found that tremendously reassuring.'[36]

As the Christchurch child sexual abuse statistics continued to climb through 1985 and 1986, so did the time Zelas devoted to, and the income she derived from, her work as an expert witness. Her absences from the Child and Family Guidance Centre had brought her into conflict with the Canterbury Hospital Board earlier in the decade, and her February 1986 appointment to the Advisory Committee on the Investigation, Detection and Prosecution of Offences Against Children would have given the board further cause for concern. With the Sixth International Congress on Child Abuse and Neglect scheduled for Sydney in August 1986, and the National Advisory Committee's report, *Guidelines for the Investigation and Management of Child Sexual Abuse*, scheduled for release soon after, a further upsurge in the child sexual abuse allegations, and in Zelas's court work, could be anticipated. Against this background, in August 1986 Zelas caught the wave and took what was, for a New Zealand child psychiatrist, an unprecedented move: she left the public health system and went into full-time private practice.

The Sixth International Congress on Child Abuse and Neglect was the first that the influential International Society for the Prevention of Child Abuse and Neglect had held in the Southern Hemisphere. With 1600 delegates it was the largest child abuse conference in Australian history. The 70-strong New Zealand delegation included David Geddis, Laurie O'Reilly, Karen Zelas and the new director of Ward 24, Bill Watkins.[37] (Six months earlier, following the departure of Professor Ney, Watkins had exchanged his half-time job at the Child and Family Guidance Centre for a half-time job as director of Ward 24, while continuing his other half-time job as lecturer in Psychological Medicine at the Christchurch School of Medicine.)

Among the luminaries who addressed the Sydney Congress were Arnon Bentovim, inventor of the Great Ormond Street technique for interrogating unwilling children; Roland Summit, who originated Child Sexual Abuse Accommodation Syndrome; paediatrician Astrid Heger and social worker Kee MacFarlane from Children's Institute International (an abuse investigation unit in Los Angeles); and David Finkelhor, a New Hampshire sociologist and researcher of sexual abuse issues.[38]

The work of Summit, MacFarlane and Heger was of special interest because in 1983 they had uncovered evidence of a cult of sexually perverted Satan-worshippers, not behind the barricades of an armed encampment in wildest Wyoming, but behind the ordinary fence of the apparently ordinary McMartin preschool at Manhattan Beach, California. For astonishment value, this was the equivalent of a Norwegian folklorist uncovering a tribe of trolls under a rock in his front yard. But Summit, MacFarlane and Heger were authoritative, articulate and convincing, and Finkelhor supported their findings with research showing that, following the McMartin discovery, other investigators had uncovered similar cases all over North America.[39]

Getting the kids to talk in such cases was apparently not easy. At a court hearing prior to the Sydney congress, Summit explained:

> the investigator must wait to build a trusting relationship and hope to find some
> way to pry open the window of disclosure. That usually requires multiple interviews,
> ingratiation, and separation from the alleged perpetrators. Direct questioning may be
> unproductive unless coupled with confrontation, presenting the child with a reassurance
> that the examiner already knows what happened. The investigator either provides a
> hypothetical [scenario] based on experience with other cases, or assures the child that
> another victim has already broken the secret.[40]

In the McMartin case, MacFarlane (as principle interviewer) and Heger (as medical examiner) used anatomically correct dolls and hand puppets to encourage, cajole, threaten and bribe children into disclosing abuse. In a videotaped interview recorded during the investigation, Heger told a girl who repeatedly denied being abused, 'I don't want to hear any more "no"s. No, no! Detective Dog and we are going to figure this out. Every little boy and girl in the whole school got touched like that ...'

Heger also examined children's genitals and diagnosed redness, lax anal tone, vaginal and urinary infections, hymenal openings of more than four millimetres and irregularities in the smoothness and symmetry of the hymen as signs of sexual abuse. If none of these signs were present, she reported that her findings were 'consistent with a history of sexual abuse'. After interviewing and examining around 200 children, MacFarlane and Heger concluded that four-fifths had been sexually abused.[41]

In the United States during 1987–90, flaws in the work of Summit, Heger, MacFarlane and Finkelhor would be scrutinised in the course of legal proceedings surrounding the McMartin case. No convictions were obtained, but the case lasted seven years and cost $13 million, making it the longest and costliest criminal prosecution in American history.[42] In Britain during 1987–88, flaws in Arnon Bentovim's work would be scrutinised in the course of Lord Justice Elizabeth Butler-Sloss's inquiry into the Cleveland case – a scandal that erupted when it was revealed that 121 children, controversially diagnosed by two doctors at Middlesbrough General Hospital in the County of Cleveland as sexually abused had been removed from their homes in the space of a few weeks.[43] But in 1986 the McMartin and Cleveland scandals were yet to break. At the Sydney congress, the contributions of Summit, MacFarlane, Finkelhor, Heger and Bentovim were received with enthusiasm and respect.

After hearing from the experts, delegates to the Sydney congress returned to their own countries to search out sexual abuse victims and perpetrators with renewed vigour.

4.iii: The Epidemic

The National Advisory Committee's 1986 report *Guidelines for the Investigation and Management of Child Sexual Abuse* was released in New Zealand immediately after the Sydney congress. Its primary effect was to transform the slogans of New Zealanders like Miriam Saphira and Lynda Morgan, and of overseas experts like Gail Goodman, Arnon Bentovim, Roland Summit, Astrid Heger, Kee MacFarlane and David Finkelhor, into mainstream child protection orthodoxy.

In Christchurch the report's release coincided with the abduction and drowning of six-year-old Louisa Damodran.[1] Though there was no evidence that the little girl had been sexually assaulted, this horrifying crime made the National Advisory Committee's report seem particularly timely. Local child protection agencies adopted it as a practice manual, and a child protection team (CPT) was established in accordance with its recommendations. The CPT was based on the principle that 'A coordinated approach to the reporting, investigation and management of child abuse cases will enhance protection of the child, accountability of the offender and, if desirable, partial or full reintegration of the family'. The CPT chair was Dr Karen Zelas. Her deputy was Dr Dianne Espie. Team members included family lawyer Laurie O'Reilly and Crown prosecutor David Saunders, together with representatives of the police, Barnardo's, the Plunket Society, Maori and Pacific Island groups, the departments of Health and Social Welfare and members of the legal, psychological and psychiatric professions.[2]

Whenever the CPT considered a case, it weighed the risks of removing the child from the family against the risks of leaving the family intact, and reached a decision based on 'the best interests of the child'. In cases of severe physical abuse the balance of risks was tipped in favour of intervention (because, without intervention, the child could die). But in cases of sexual abuse the balance was less clear. According to the National Advisory Committee's report, victims of child sexual abuse may suffer headaches, abdominal pains, obesity, anxiety, depression and low self-esteem. As it happens, victims of broken homes may suffer the same symptoms. This means that, even in clearly proven cases of child sexual abuse, any intervention is likely to cause the very problems it is intended to prevent.

The CPT had no statutory authority. Consequently, its practice of sharing confidential information about individuals without their knowledge or consent raised serious privacy issues, and its directions to DSW social workers and police officers to remove children from their families raised serious questions of accountability.

For most occupational groups, the duty of confidentiality is an ethical and common law matter, but for hospital board employees it is a matter of law. For this reason the Canterbury Hospital Board declined to join the CPT. However, in defiance of the board, and in defiance of the law, staff of the Child and Family Guidance Centre and Ward 24 joined the CPT and were actively involved in its work.[3]

In addition to the inter-agency CPT, in 1986 Christchurch DSW formed its own Child Abuse Team, and in 1987 Christchurch police formed their own Child Abuse Unit.[4] After that, child sexual abuse reports in the city escalated as never before.

In the Christchurch *Press* of 17 July 1987, under the headline 'Dramatic increase in child abuse', Dianne Espie reported that she had examined 40 sexually abused children already that year; most had shown signs of previous penetration. Next day, Detective Sergeant John Ell reported that 60 child sexual abuse cases, some involving children as young as 18 months, had been reported to police since 21 April. Two weeks later Bill Watkins, director of Ward 24, said he would not be surprised if there were 200 child sexual abuse cases in Christchurch each year. Around the same time he advised government that the majority of children in his ward 'have been or currently are being abused'. By the end of the year 110 cases had been referred to the CPT. On 30 December a social worker told the *Press* that reports of child abuse of all kinds received by Christchurch DSW had exceeded 700 for the year – a fivefold increase over the previous year.[5]

As the *Press* report of 17 July indicates, the 1987 avalanche of sexual abuse reports began with Dianne Espie's medical examinations of children. Most of the examinations took place at Glenelg Health Camp where manager Madeleine Harrison used a list of alleged indicators to identify suspected victims. Harrison was a nurse who became manager of Glenelg in October 1986. She 'attended all training seminars possible and kept up to date with the literature' on the diagnosis of sexual abuse. Her list of indicators included attention seeking, wetting and soiling, immature and regressive behaviour, masturbation, sleeplessness, nightmares, sexualised behaviour and complaints of stomach pains. She found the indicators to be common among children admitted to Glenelg. This is hardly surprising – children removed from home and placed among strangers often display such behaviours – but to Harrison they were deeply sinister. In 1988 she reported that, of the more than 250 children who passed through the camp the previous year, 117 had probably been sexually abused, one had probably not been, and the rest were in doubt.[6]

Madeleine Harrison referred suspected sexual abuse victims to Dianne Espie, who conducted medical examinations and diagnostic interviews. Their unrelenting search inevitably brought male staff at Glenelg under suspicion. Staff member Alan Fort's problems began in June 1987 when he was 'approached by a senior staff member who was very concerned at the number of girls being sexually examined by Dr Dianne Espie without any consent by parents'. Shortly afterwards another male staff member, Anthony B, was dismissed for 'inappropriate kissing and cuddling' of a 10-year-old boy at bedtime. 'I have not been informed of the date of alleged incident, nor who reported it,' Mr B protested. '… the reason given seems also to imply that some sort of sexual activity went on … The very idea that I could even be suspected of this makes me sick to the stomach.'[7]

The following month Fort, too, was dismissed. 'Glenelg still have not told me to this day why I was dismissed and what the allegations were,' he complained two years later.[8]

Questions of parental consent of the sort that concerned Alan Fort always loom large when there is a risk that a medical intervention will cause long-term harm, and this was certainly the case with Espie's examinations of children. Using controversial methods, she diagnosed sexual abuse on an unprecedented scale and, as a consequence of her work, fathers were accused of molesting their children, families were broken up and children suffered.

In response to a complaint to the Medical Council, Espie claimed that, as medical officer of health, she had legal authority to examine the genitals of children without parental consent. She further claimed that, since parents had signed a general consent form when their children were admitted to Glenelg, consent had already been given.[9]

Espie conceded that obtaining parental consent for any medical procedure was 'ideal', but argued that 'consent from a parent was not appropriate or may not have been appropriate … when the allegation was of intrafamilial sexual abuse'. This view echoes the National Advisory Committee's report: '… incest will likely entail a lack of awareness or a desire for concealment on the part of the presenting parent or parents.

Consent ... may be best obtained on general grounds in these circumstances.'[10]

According to Grant Gillett, Professor of Medical Ethics at the Otago Medical School, this approach is ethically unacceptable:

> The requirement for parental consent protects vulnerable children in an adult-dominated world. With medical interventions, parents have a responsibility to weigh the benefits to the child against the risks. One of the risks of a sexual abuse investigation is that the family will be broken up, which is a momentous disruption to a child's life. In my view, even with interventions where the risks to the child are negligible, suspending parental consent on the basis of an 'allegation' isn't good enough. Parental consent should be suspended only when there is strong evidence that the parents do not have the best interests of the child at heart. Any surgeon who wants to do an appendectomy on a child against the parents' wishes has to present enough evidence to convince a court that parental consent must be suspended to safeguard the child's welfare. And that's just for a four-centimetre cut in the abdomen and two days in hospital, which is piffling compared to the harm done to a child by breaking up its family, so why should the standards differ?[11]

Having embarked on her investigation without parental consent, Espie followed the National Advisory Committee report's recommendation that doctors include in their medical examinations a diagnostic interview/medical history using anatomically correct dolls ('to aid precision in eliciting the history'), and a physical examination. 'In most cases the history is more likely than the physical examination to yield important information,' the report noted, but that was not Espie's experience. Although she conducted some searching interviews, she found that many suspected abuse victims would not, or could not, speak of the problem. But, when she examined the genitals of the girls according to the report's instructions, she was usually able to conclude that sexual abuse had occurred. The National Advisory Committee's report stated:

> Measure the transverse diameter of the vaginal opening, using a paper tape cut to 1 cm lengths. If it is greater than 4 mm in the prepubertal child it is probably abnormal. The vaginal opening varies but studies by Cantwell indicate that an opening of greater than 4 mm is suggestive of previous penetration.[12]

When H.B. Cantwell published her findings in 1983, her four-millimetre rule was hailed as a definitive indicator of child molestation. But by 1987, when Espie began using it to 'prove' that sexual abuse had taken place, it was being seriously challenged. By the end of the decade it had been totally discredited.[13]

The damage done to families by Espie's misplaced reliance on the four-millimetre rule was compounded by her gynaecological ineptitude. In May 1987 eight-year-old Anna C was admitted to Glenelg suffering from toileting problems. After examining Anna on 22 June 1987, Espie reported: 'No hymen. Transverse diameter of vaginal opening = 6 mm.' This report does not make sense. Promoters of the four-millimetre rule taught doctors to measure the transverse diameter of the hymenal opening because the hymen has a distinct margin, i.e. though the hymen is not particularly easy to measure, it is easier to measure than the tissues surrounding it. Furthermore, congenital absence of the hymen has never been reported and could not occur without associated major genito-urinary abnormalities. The hymen may become stretched and torn, but it never completely disappears. Remnants of hymen can be seen in girls and women who have experienced repeated penetration or who have given birth vaginally. Espie's failure to find the hymen, and her measurement of something other than the hymen, suggests that she did not know what she was doing.[14]

Espie's gynaecological ineptitude was matched by her ineptitude as an interviewer. After reviewing transcripts of her audiotaped interviews with Anna, Dr Herbert Kean, a senior British police surgeon with postgraduate qualifications in obstetrics, child health and medical jurisprudence, reported:

> ... interview with A on 22.6.87 ... most of this haphazard and unconstructed interview is a fishing expedition. D makes such statements as 'So you think the yukky touching might have started when you were four. Is that right? It looks a wee bit stretched down there.' A answers most of the questions with either 'Mmm' or 'No' or 'I don't know'... D is obviously getting a bit desperate by p. 12 ... She asks 'What sort of rude things have people done to you?' A replies, 'Only the doctors have done rude things – no one else has.' When asked 'O.K. so who are the people who have touched your vagina?' A replies, 'No one'. D then says 'O.K. how come it has got so big then?' ... [3.7.87 interview] D tells A that she really knows who the adult is and spends the interview time to get confirmation of her belief from A. There is some suggestion ... that if A tells Trish, Trish will tell the judge and A will be allowed home. In spite of this coercion the interview was completely inconclusive. Another report dated 3.7.87 tells of the interviewer writing all the family names on a piece of paper and asking A to cross them all off except those who yukky touched her. This ploy was obviously unsuccessful as A crossed all the names off except her own ...[15]

Espie's approach to interviewing was in breach of the National Advisory Committee report guidelines, which stated: 'Leading questions (e.g. those which imply the nature of the act or the identity of the perpetrator) must not be used'. However, though Espie used the report to justify her use of the four-millimetre rule, she ignored it when justifying her use of leading questions. 'I found that use of leading questions was of therapeutic value where a child was having great difficulty talking about possible abuse,' she told the Medical Council.[16]

At the 3 July interview, Espie introduced Anna to anatomically correct dolls. Eight years later Anna recalled:

> I remember when Dr Espie showed me what to do with the dolls it was like a follow-the-leader thing. I thought, okay that's what I'm supposed to do and played with the dolls too. However, no matter what I did, she just kept on going on about how someone had touched me and kept asking me questions about Dad. I think that at some point, either after I had left Glenelg or just before then, I actually did say that Dad had touched me – there just seemed no other way out of it.[17]

On the day of that interview, the police visited Mr C at work, and Dr Espie called Mrs C to Glenelg. Mr C was told that Anna had been sexually abused (but not by whom), and Mrs C was told that her husband had molested Anna. Two days later Anna was taken from Glenelg to a foster home.

On 8 July, Mr and Mrs C's application to regain custody of Anna was rejected by a Family Court judge. Social worker Trish Ross passed on the news to Anna:

> I … took her to the park to explain that she would not be going home. Anna was very upset and cried openly … I talked with Anna about how when the judge and other people knew who it was who had done the bad touching, then we could work out what needed to change … Anna cried a little more and stated that she would tell Dr Espie who it was. I cuddled Anna for some time telling her she was very brave …[18]

After eight weeks in foster care Anna revisited Dr Espie. She recalled:

> I have seen the notes recording a time on 28 August 1987 when I apparently wanted dolls to 'show you what Dad did'. The notes say that I put the male doll's finger inside the vagina of the girl doll, and then said 'Will I be able to go home now I've told?' That's very much what I remember of the whole time – that no one would believe that Dad hadn't touched me, and that the only way I could get out of it and be allowed to go home was if I said he did.[19]

Trish Ross advised Mr and Mrs C that 'it would be most unlikely Anna could come home … if Mr C was also in the home', so on 8 September he moved out. But it took until 27 October for the department to be satisfied that Mrs C 'understood and supported Anna and would protect her from her father'. At that point Anna was allowed home, but she remained in formal DSW custody until the charges against her parents – that Anna was 'in need of care, protection or control' – were resolved in the Family Court.[20]

The complaint action against Mr and Mrs C was originally set down for 5 November. That day Jill Pengelly, counsel for the child, sought an adjournment until 14 December in order to obtain a report from Karen Zelas. Around the same time Mr and Mrs C were sent for counselling on separation issues with Trish Allen, a counsellor who worked in the same suite of offices as Karen Zelas.

All the while, Anna's DSW file continued to grow. Curiously, inserted between two administrative notes, both dated 3 December 1987, is an undated and unsourced newspaper article from Britain commenting on news that two Cleveland paediatricians had discovered, in under six months, more than 200 children 'at risk' of sexual abuse. The article stated:

> Some [paediatricians] believe that vaginal size of more the five millimetres is 'associated with sexual abuse in a high proportion of cases,' and so can be used as evidence. Certain police surgeons disagree. Dr Raine Roberts from Manchester, writing in the *British Medical Journal* last year, said: 'Not only is the measurement impossible to do with any degree of accuracy, but the hymen dilates and contracts, and can vary, in the same child, from a pinhole to a centimetre, depending on whether she is relaxed or apprehensive, warm or cold … and because of this, some examiners may well be finding evidence where there is no abnormality.'[21]

The presence of this article indicates that, when DSW was preparing its case against Mr and Mrs C, the department was aware of the controversy surrounding hymen measurements. But DSW carried on regardless.

Dr Zelas's report wasn't ready by 14 December, so the case was adjourned until 3 February the following year. When it was finally heard, Zelas told the court, '…in my opinion Anna has been sexually abused and her father is the perpetrator.'[22]

Judge McAloon said he was 'particularly impressed with the evidence of Dr Zelas and Dr Espie … I must accept in this particular case that sexual abuse has taken place and that the defendant is responsible for it,' he concluded. Initially, Mr C was allowed limited access to his daughter. But when Anna began receiving counselling from Heather Broadhurst at the Sexual Abuse Therapy and Rehabilitation Team (START), access was terminated.[23]

Her counselling notwithstanding, Anna was unhappy. In 1991 she began running away from home. In 1992 she began running away from foster homes and living on the street. Eventually she made her way to her father and in 1993 Mr C applied for custody of Anna. In 1994 Judge Kean placed her in her father's care and instructed DSW to leave Mr C and Anna alone unless they approached the department for help. 'I am living with Dad now and we get on well,' Anna reported in 1995.[24]

START, the organisation to which Anna was sent for counselling, was founded in 1987. Its purpose was, and still is, to provide therapy and support for sexually abused women and children. Signatories to its application for incorporation included Dianne Espie, three former Ward 24 staff (child and family workers Heather Broadhurst and Judy Collins, and social worker Fran Erikson), a psychotherapist from the Child and Family Guidance Centre (Sue Dick), and the paediatrician husband of a Christchurch Family Court counselling coordinator (Terry Caseley). The woman who would lay the first complaint against Peter Ellis in the Civic Crèche case (Ms Magnolia) and her mother (Grandma Magnolia) were also active in the organisation. START's solicitor was Jill Pengelly, who served as counsel for the child in many sexual abuse cases.[25]

START's philosophy included the belief that 'children do not lie about sexual abuse'. START counsellors based their understanding of sexual abuse on 'An analysis of sexual abuse which incorporates the socio-political context in which abuse occurs, i.e. the patriarchal structure of society.'

In the real world, people send their children for therapy because they want them to get better, but when children went to START, they sometimes got worse. The START information leaflet warned:

> Children in therapy can become upset and difficult ... Feelings come out [that can] cause your child to play up, act grumpy, have bad dreams and generally be difficult. Seeing your child like this after a session can cause you to feel really angry at them, at us, at yourself and ... might make you feel like giving up ... It's really important at this time to seek the support of the mothers' group ... Ending therapy can make you feel better but it cannot help your child.[26]

According to START, if the child didn't get better, the mother was to blame. Under the heading: WILL MY CHILD GET OVER THIS? the leaflet stated:

> The most important factor in your child's recovery from sexual abuse is you, their mother. By believing what your child has said, by not blaming them and by working hard to be close and loving with them and protecting them from further abuse, you give them a very good chance of recovery ...

To further tighten START's grip on the mother's fragile self-confidence, the leaflet suggested that she too may recover memories of sexual abuse. The section headed WHEN YOU HAVE MEMORIES OF YOUR OWN stated: 'Knowing that your child has been sexually abused may remind you of similar experiences you had in childhood or adolescence ... SEEK HELP FOR THIS NOW.'[27]

• • •

In mid-1987 Sue Dick, the Child and Family Guidance Centre (CFGC) therapist who helped establish START, obtained what was probably Christchurch's first ritual abuse allegation.

The D children, whose parents were embroiled in an acrimonious marriage breakup, were referred to CFGC by Women's Refuge. Sue Dick suspected sexual abuse and, after a two-hour videotaped interview with the girl and a three-hour videotaped interview with the boy, she confirmed it. The plot thickened when the girl's comment that she did not like 'the story with the witch in it' prompted another round of interviews. The children told Dick that their father, his fiancée and her 12-year-old daughter dressed up as witches and subjected the children to indecencies. They talked about a black hat with a purple pompom, green and pink hair and a blue costume with a red spider on the front. They said the woman chased them, screaming and yelling, with long false fingernails outstretched.[28]

These allegations became the police Child Abuse Unit's first multi-offender case. There was no supporting evidence (no wigs, no costumes, no false fingernails, no medical evidence), but the investigators hoped that when Mr D saw the videotapes he would break down and confess. He didn't. So they decided to prosecute.

When the prosecutor showed the children around the courtroom they ran amok. When he asked them what Daddy had done they said nothing had happened. So the charges were withdrawn, but the aborted prosecution did not go to waste. A few weeks later, in an article in the *Christchurch Star*, the case was used to illustrate the need for law changes to spare children the stress of appearing in court in person.[29]

Following the article, leaflets were distributed around Mr D's neighbourhood, identifying him and his fiancée as the deviants in the *Star* article. After that, the couple received threatening phone calls and slogans were painted on their shop.[30]

• • •

From 1987 the dramatic rise in sexual abuse allegations in Christchurch was matched by an equally dramatic rise in ACC payments for sexual abuse counselling. For the year ended 31 March 1987, ACC paid for 184 sessions at two counselling centres in the city (which works out at a modest 0.6 counselling sessions per 1000 people, while the comparable rates for Auckland and Wellington were 5.5 and 4.0 per 1000 respectively). After that, the Christchurch rate began to climb. In the 1987–88 year ACC paid for 1.5 sessions per 1000 Christchurch people. The year after that – the year that START opened for full-time business – the city's rate hit a national high of 16.6 ACC-paid sessions per 1000 people. That year ACC was paying six sexual abuse counselling centres and 21 individual counsellors in Christchurch at $50 per session, but most of the counselling payments were going to two centres: START (for 1177 sessions in the 1988–89 financial year) and the St Albans Medical Centre (for 1595 sessions over the same period).[31]

The START total is no surprise. Just about everyone in Christchurch knows someone who received sexual abuse counselling from START in the late '80s, but the St Albans Medical Centre total is a mystery. At $50 per session, ACC would have paid the centre $79,750 for sexual abuse counselling in the 1988–89 financial year. Yet, despite extensive enquires, I have been unable to find anyone who has had – or knows of anyone who has had – sexual abuse counselling from the St Albans Medical Centre (and the privacy laws prevent me from finding such people by any other means).

• • •

By early 1988 sexual abuse allegations were coming thick and fast in Christchurch and inevitably a conspiracy theory arose to explain them. The stories told by the D children had already convinced investigators that ritual abuse was happening in the city, but that involved only one family, and the number of cases being diagnosed suggested something bigger. By then most Christchurch abuse investigators had read *Michelle Remembers*. So they knew what to look for, and before long they tended to find it.

The Great Christchurch Child Pornography Ring scare has all the hallmarks of an urban myth. There is no hard evidence of its existence but many people believe in it. The story of its discovery comes in many versions. Each is a bewildering mix of supposition, imagination and verifiable fact. The version given here is drawn from media reports, interviews, a feverish potted history compiled by some of the parents involved and a paper on 'Ritual Abuse and the Law' presented at a 1993 women's law conference.

The investigation began in March 1988 when a doctor from Ward 24 advised police that children in the ward were telling horrific stories of multi-victim, multi-perpetrator sexual abuse. Investigators began interviewing child complainants, children named by child complainants, and children who went to the same schools or lived near child complainants. But, as the potted history records: 'disclosures taking a long time and children so scared hard to get them to talk'.

By May the children had begun to talk. They talked of being taken to private homes and a gay bar. They talked of 'video cameras, bright lights, knives, guns, a rich man in a suit, lots of adults and other kids, photographs of naked children, black clothing, drugs and needles, a rich man with a scar on his hand, an old rusty white car and a flash red car with leopard-skin seats', and about abuse that was 'child to child, adult to child and lots of horrendous extras'. As the stories grew, the police alerted the principals of five Christchurch schools believed to be in the ring's recruitment area.[32]

When two children identified a neighbouring teenager as their abuser, Detective Brent Hyde arrested him. When the children said the lad had taken them to the pornography ring, Hyde let him go in the hope that the teenager would lead him to the conspirators. But he didn't.

This did not impress Hyde's superiors. They told him to come up with hard evidence or close the inquiry. So, in August 1988, around 30 police officers executed simultaneous search warrants on half a dozen Christchurch properties. As a result, an elderly man was arrested for possessing photographs of naked schoolgirls, but nothing else was found. At that point the investigation was closed and Hyde was sent on leave. He resigned later in protest at what he claimed was a coverup.

Periodically thereafter, Hyde's supporters took their concerns to MPs and the media. At such times the file on the alleged paedophile ring was dusted off, and rumours of ritual abuse and child pornography again filled the Christchurch air.

As recently as September 1991 – 11 weeks before the first complaint in the Civic Crèche case – Detective Inspector Roger Carson attempted to lay the rumours to rest. He told the *Christchurch Star* that the alleged ring had been intensively investigated since March 1988 and, though the names of several prominent businessmen had been given to the police, a lack of hard evidence had resulted in the file being closed. He added that the case had got so 'out of control' towards the end that 'everyone but the Queen' was being implicated.[33]

In a telling aside, Carson said the operation had 'built up a profile of young homosexual men working as a group'. Since virtually all the alleged perpetrators of sexual abuse at that time were husbands and fathers, and virtually all the alleged victims were girls, this police interest in the activities of homosexual men is surprising. However, in the light of Adorno's work on the authoritarian personality, it is understandable.[34]

By its very nature, the police force attracts people with authoritarian impulses and trains them in authoritarian methods. Adorno found that authoritarian people have an exaggerated concern with sexual goings-on and a punitive attitude towards violators of sexual mores. It was probably impulses of this sort that drove some Christchurch police officers of the late '80s to collect information on the activities of law-abiding young men who happened to be homosexual.

For homophobic police officers, the late '80s must have been a frustrating time. Prior to the passage of the Homosexual Law Reform Act in 1986, male homosexuality was a crime. Officers with a prurient interest in the private lives of gay men could pursue their quarry confident in the knowledge that the law was on their side. However, once homosexuality was legalised, the police could investigate gay men only when they suspected them of committing other crimes. In the late '80s, the idea of suspecting gay men of that most perverted crime, child sexual abuse, was probably highly attractive to homophobic police officers.

But during most of the Great Christchurch Paedophile Ring scare the primary focus of the child protection movement was on heterosexual men. It wasn't until November 1991, when Ms Magnolia accused Peter Ellis of molesting her son, that some of the more homophobic members of the Christchurch police again had the opportunity to investigate the private lives of homosexual men.

• • •

Despite the police's failure to find evidence of organised abuse, the numbers of heterosexual men accused of child sexual abuse kept climbing. In the 20 months prior to October 1988, 58 Christchurch men were convicted of child abuse, rape, incest, sexual violation and indecent assault. But, according to START therapist Heather Broadhurst, that was the tip of the iceberg. She told the *Star* that, over a six-month period, START had identified 61 men responsible for abusing 105 children. She said 67 of the children had been abused by more than one adult, and added that when a single disclosure was pursued by START therapists, it could lead to a cluster of victims among playmates and siblings of the disclosing child. Because of the apparent scale of the problem, Broadhurst was angry that only four alleged perpetrators had been sent to prison (but she added that another two had committed suicide and one was given probation).[35]

In September 1988, after reading about the support group formed for parents accused in Britain's Cleveland scandal, former Glenelg staff member Alan Fort established PAIN (Parents Against Injustice) 'to help a growing number of parents falsely accused of sexually abusing their children'. Within weeks he was contacted by more than 150 families nationwide. The majority of those families came from Christchurch.[36]

In 1987 and 1988, 270 cases of child abuse were referred to the Christchurch Child Protection Team.[37] The numbers indicated a problem of Cleveland proportions, but while the British scandal resulted in a judicial inquiry, in New Zealand the authorities didn't want to know. In November 1988, when PAIN wrote to MPs calling for 'a ministerial inquiry into New Zealand's handling of child sexual abuse', only Rangiora MP Jim Gerard showed concern. He passed PAIN's letter to Social Welfare minister Michael Cullen with a worried note: 'The group raises two very important points – if they are correct. 1. Parents, innocent of child abuse, are having their children removed from their homes. 2. Parents are being accused of sexual misconduct without sufficient reason, with evidence obtained by questionable methods.'[38]

PAIN's letter was distributed around the time that the report of the National Advisory Committee on the Prevention of Child Abuse, *A Private or Public Nightmare?*, was published. When MPs weighed the professional support for this report against the lack of professional support for PAIN, they concluded that PAIN had no credibility. Some child abuse workers even claimed that PAIN was a front for organised paedophilia.[39] Government advisors assured their ministers that the real problem lay with the under-diagnosis, rather than the over-diagnosis, of child sexual abuse, and that PAIN's complaints were part of the 'backlash'. Their ministers saw no reason to disagree.

On 28 March 1989 Michael Cullen rejected PAIN's call for a full-scale inquiry, but ordered an independent review of 'four recent child abuse cases which ended with charges being dismissed because of lack of evidence'. But, before the review could take place, nationwide outrage erupted over a *Frontline* television documentary about sexual abuse allegations in Ward 24.

• • •

The *Frontline* programme focused on the story of Cleo F, who suffered from tubrous sclerosis. At four and a half she was mentally and physically retarded. Her inoperable brain tumours were causing headaches, tantrums, epileptic fits and bursts of repetitive behaviour. They were likely to limit her lifespan. Her parents had twice visited Australia for expert advice. They were actively involved with IHC, the Epilepsy Society and the Child and Family Guidance Centre. Cleo would soon be starting school and her parents were keen to make it a positive experience. So in March 1988 they sought help from Ward 24 in managing her behaviour.[40]

On her first day in the ward Cleo made round objects from playdough which she called 'diddles'. By her therapist's own admission, they did not resemble penises. But when Cleo cut them up, and sucked and licked them, the therapist suspected sexual abuse.[41]

Over the next six weeks Cleo was subject to 18 therapy sessions, some lasting more than two and a half hours. Fifteen of the sessions were disclosure interviews. Their purpose was to obtain information about the perceived abuse, and to identify the perpetrator.[42]

The number of disclosure interviews was a spectacular breach of the guidelines in *Guidelines for the Investigation and Management of Child Sexual Abuse*, which stated: 'The number of interviews with the child victim [note: not the *alleged* victim] should be kept to an absolute minimum ... in most instances only one detailed interview with the child will be necessary'. However, there was an escape clause: 'In some instances ... it may be necessary to establish a trusting relationship with the child over several interviews before the child feels free to divulge detailed information.' Even in terms of the need to establish a trusting relationship, it is difficult to regard 15 interviews as anything other than excessive.[43]

Cleo's primary therapist, Karen Dennison, was a nurse with no experience in disclosure work, so the interviews were conducted by occupational therapist Colleen Shaw while Dennison took notes. As it happened, Shaw had worked with only three alleged victims of child sexual abuse, so her experience was also limited.[44]

Cleo made no explicit disclosure. No medical evidence of abuse was found. But some of her comments, and the way she played with anatomically correct dolls, convinced Shaw and Dennison that she had been sexually abused by her father.

A week before Cleo was due to leave Ward 24, her therapists broke the news to Mrs F, and asked her not to mention their suspicions to anyone. They also invited Mrs F to observe Cleo's final disclosure session at which, they said, she was ready to tell her mother about the abuse. As Mrs F watched, Cleo picked up the daddy doll, said it was 'the diddle man' and threw it out the door. Then she climbed onto the therapist's knee and asked for a jellybean.[45]

Because Dennison's notes were the only evidence in the case, the *Frontline* team was keen to get them independently evaluated. No one in New Zealand would look at them, but *Frontline* eventually found two British experts – child psychotherapist Dr David Pithers and family psychiatrist Dr Elizabeth Tylden – who were prepared to comment. Pithers reported:

> These sessions are gratuitously painful for the child … The way Cleo was treated cannot be justified whatever the outcome … The interviewer's ineptitude is startling … The transcripts are very unsafe from an evidential point of view … The impression is of adults using a child for their own purposes.[46]

Tylden was equally unimpressed. 'I cannot understand how any suspicion fell on the father in this case,' she said. 'I believe these interviews pervert the course of justice, corrupt the innocent and destroy not only the self-confidence of the child but the stability of the whole family.'[47]

But suspicion had fallen on the father, and as far as the Ward 24 staff were concerned, it was justified. Before Cleo was discharged, Mr F was called to the hospital and confronted by Shaw, Dennison and Ward 24 director Dr Bill Watkins. They told him that his daughter had been sexually abused, but refused to name the suspected abuser. Instead, they called in Mrs F. 'They think it's you,' she said. Mr F was then warned that if he went home, even for one night, Cleo would be put into DSW custody.[48]

At CPT meetings on 9 and 30 May 1988 the DSW representatives opposed complaint action being taken against such apparently cooperative parents, particularly when the identity of the abuser was unclear. They were also troubled by the number of interviews, the inexperience of the interviewer, the style of interviewing, the presentation of dolls in an undressed state, and the use of jellybeans. But the police proceeded with the complaint action. Both parents were accused of 'avoidably delaying the development of Cleo and neglecting and ill-treating her'. Mr F was also accused of sexually abusing her. At that point Mr and Mrs F hired a lawyer and contacted *Frontline*. 'To me, there's no way they should get away with what they've done to this child. And they shouldn't be able to do it to other children,' Mrs F said.[49]

By the time the case came to court, Bill Watkins was much less confident. He expressed reservations about the evidence and conceded that the interviewing and recording techniques were unsatisfactory. Patricia Champion, a psychologist who had known Cleo since she was 22 months old, questioned the therapist's competence. But the doubts counted for nothing when counsel for the child Isabel Mitchell called Karen Zelas as her expert witness.[50]

In a judgment delivered almost a year after Cleo had been admitted to Ward 24, Judge Mahon demonstrated the ease with which Family Court judges, free from the constraints of traditional courtroom rules and procedures, may destroy a man's reputation without first finding him guilty. Mahon declared himself satisfied that Cleo had been sexually abused, even though the standard of proof fell short of that required for a criminal charge. He said there was insufficient evidence to identify the perpetrator, but he believed it to be a close family member, most probably the father. Having satisfied himself on these points, he then drove an intractable wedge between Cleo's parents:

> While I have reservations about some of the evidence given by the mother, I am satisfied she is fiercely protective of her daughter Cleo, and that now being aware that Cleo has in the past been sexually abused, she has taken and will continue to take every possible precaution to ensure that there is absolutely no possibility of that occurring again. The complaint is dismissed.[51]

• • •

The experience of Ben G and his family at the hands of Ward 24 staff was also mentioned in the *Frontline* programme. The case had featured in the *Christchurch Star* two weeks earlier, and was among those that the Minister of Social Welfare wanted reviewed.

Ben was the second of four children. His older brother Ashley and younger brother Chris were normal kids. His baby sister Holly had an artery defect and was on the waiting list for surgery. This caused no particular problems to her parents, except that they had to protect her from chest infections. But Ben was different. Mr and Mrs G were concerned about his misshapen head, his poor coordination, his constipation and his withdrawn behaviour. But it wasn't until he started school that the quest to find out what was wrong with him began in earnest.[52]

Ashley was a good kid at school, but Ben was alternately aggressive and withdrawn. As a witness in a later complaint action brought against Mr and Mrs G, Ben's headmaster testified that the couple were helpful and cooperative, and willing to take up the school's suggestions for managing their son's behaviour. The public health nurse who visited the G home testified that, apart from Ben's disruptive behaviour and poor coordination, she had no concerns about the family.[53]

In 1987 and 1988 Ben was referred to two consultant physicians who were eminently qualified to diagnose his underlying biological condition. One was paediatrician and START founder Terry Caseley, who had a long-term interest in mental handicap. The other was child psychiatrist Bill Watkins, director of Ward 24.

If Caseley or Watkins had correctly diagnosed Ben's condition when he was first first referred to them, his family may have been spared the nightmare that was to follow. But it wasn't until 1992 that Caseley identified Ben's problem as Williams Syndrome. Children with Williams Syndrome have a characteristic 'elfin' appearance, with a wide mouth and upturned nose. They are verbally fluent, poorly coordinated, hypersensitive to noise and prone to constipation. When correctly diagnosed and treated with understanding, they are friendly, sociable and anxious to please in their relationships with adults. When incorrectly diagnosed and treated inappropriately, their anxiety, distractibility, obsessiveness, irritability and difficulty relating to peers, along with their general retardation, often cause problems.[54]

In 1987 Ben was labelled a disturbed child, and that label unleashed a witch-hunt. Mr and Mrs G allowed him to go first to Glenelg, then to the Child and Family Guidance Centre and finally to Ward 24. They were concerned about the unsettling effect of these moves on their son, but they wanted to know what was wrong, and they wanted guidance on managing his behaviour. They thought the professionals would help.

Ben was admitted to Glenelg on 15 September 1987. While he was there, manager Madeleine Harrison wrote two reports on him. The report for his parents was 'neutral to encouraging'. The report for Harrison's colleagues suggested that gross parental emotional, physical and sexual abuse were the most likely causes of Ben's problems.[55]

Ben was admitted to Ward 24 on 26 January 1988. Despite having his stay extended far beyond the normal five weeks, and despite being under the constant scrutiny of sexual abuse diagnosticians, for a very long time he showed no signs of having been molested. Finally, on 18 April, he said something that therapist Moira Eason interpreted as evidence of sexual abuse. After that, Jill Donnelly, a therapist with no previous experience of disclosure work, interviewed him relentlessly.

Between April 18 and 22 June 1988, Ben was subject to 32 disclosure interviews. Sometimes he had two interviews a day. Some interviews lasted almost three hours. Some took place long after his normal bedtime. Only one interview was videotaped. Records of the other 31 sessions were reconstructed from notes taken by another staff member, or written up from memory by the interviewer.[56]

Donnelly introduced Ben to anatomically correct dolls at the first interview, and at every session she steered the conversation towards sexual matters. Eventually Ben grasped what she wanted, and as session built on session, he drew on the Williams Syndrome behaviours that seemed most appropriate to the occasion (anxiety to please, verbal fluency, obsession with violent themes and a tendency to exaggerate). He told her about a neighbouring farmer being gored by a bull, about seeing a pig's head split open with an axe, and about an episode of *All Creatures Great and Small* in which a veterinarian put cream on his arm and inserted it into a cow to untangle the legs of twin calves. Then, with encouragement from Donnelly, Ben wove these yarns into tales of strange costumes, bloody deeds and obscene rituals involving his family, their neighbours and various farm animals, including a donkey.[57]

On 11 May 1988, when Ben had been in Ward 24 for 15 weeks, the Child Protection Team met to consider his case. There was no medical evidence of abuse. But, on the basis of Bill Watkins' assertion that 'Ben's disclosures indicate that sexual abuse occurs within the home, within the entire family and on a regular basis', a decision was made to take complaint action against both parents in relation to all four children. It was further agreed that Mr and Mrs G would have no access to the children until the court hearing.[58]

Until 12 May 1988, Mr and Mrs G were unaware that any accusations had been made against them. That day, Mrs G was home with 16-month-old Holly and three-year-old Chris when five carloads of police and social workers rolled up the drive. They brought warrants to uplift the children, a search warrant and summons to appear in court the following week.[59]

While social workers carried off the screaming children, the police searched the house for evidence of cult abuse. They removed a hearth broom (found by the hearth); a plastic shape (found under the cot); two magazines and a page of advertisements (found under the mattress in the main bedroom); a black nightie (found in the duchesse); a donkey whip (found on the living-room wall); a candle (found on a shelf by the hot-water cylinder); a yard broom (found outside the back door); a jar of vaseline (found in the bathroom cabinet); and two chair spacers, three lengths of dowel and a piece of grey pipe (found at various locations around the house).[60]

While the search was in progress, Mrs G was taken to the police station and grilled for seven hours. At the same time Mr G was picked up at work. Unbeknown to his wife, he was grilled at the same police station. The Gs found out later that all their children had been taken into state custody. For five days no one would tell them where they were. On the fifth day Mrs G was contacted by DSW because Holly, who had been breastfed until the day they were separated, was ill. After that, Mrs G was allowed an hour a day of supervised access with her baby at the DSW office.[61]

On 17 June 1988, after having no contact with her other children for more than a month, Mrs G was called to DSW. She was expecting to be reunited with her offspring, but she saw only counsel for the children Keith Hales and a DSW officer. They told her that if she did not leave her husband and start divorce proceedings she would never see her other children again. When this issue was raised in court, Hales described it as a 'misunderstanding'. However, two letters – one from Hales to the court registrar, the other from DSW to the Housing Corporation – support Mrs G's version of events.[62]

By late July, divorce proceedings had been instituted and Mrs G was allowed to see all her children for an hour a day. By then they had been medically examined. No signs of abuse had been found. Also, Ben's older brother had been subject to disclosure interviews conducted by incest survivor Lynda Morgan (who had joined the Christchurch DSW Child Abuse Team in October 1987), and his younger brother had been subject to disclosure interviews conducted by a Ward 24 therapist. Neither child disclosed abuse.[63]

Around the same time Karen Zelas was asked to report on 'the current effects on the children of separation from their mother ... and whether ... the children should be returned to her care'. In her report, Zelas said she had read the Ward 24 notes on Ben, and observed the children interacting with their mother on two occasions. Her conclusions would have set D.W. Winnicott spinning in his grave. She said that nine-year-old Ashley and six-year-old Ben were coping adequately and should remain in foster care. Three-year-old Chris presented more of a problem. 'I have some concerns about Chris's emotional development,' she wrote, 'but I do not think this is attributable to the separation. I am therefore of the opinion that it is not warranted to place Chris in a situation of undetermined risk by replacing him in his mother's care.' However, she recommended that baby Holly be returned to her mother, provided that Mrs G continued to live with her parents.[64]

Mr G was not allowed near his children for four months. Then, when he saw them for an hour of supervised access, Ben was so upset that all further contact with his father was denied. However, Mr G continued to see Ashley, Chris and Holly for one closely supervised hour a week.[65]

The 17 days of court hearings began on 29 August 1988 and were not completed until 20 January 1989. After weighing the evidence and the arguments, Judge Kean delivered his 92-page judgment on 2 March 1989.

He expressed grave reservations about the inexperience of the interviewer, the use of leading questions, the number and timing of the disclosure sessions, the inadequacies of the transcripts and the suggestive use of anatomically correct dolls. He said he was not sure where fact ended and fantasy began. He dismissed the complaints and suggested, prophetically, that there could be an alternative explanation for Ben's behaviour which 'the professionals have simply not been able to determine'.[66]

In all, from the day their four children were removed from their care, it took Mr and Mrs G 10 months to get them back. By then, their marriage was over.

Four weeks after the judgment the *Christchurch Star* published a feature on the Ben G case. 'Literally hundreds of therapists, psychiatrists, police officers and social workers in this country are devoting every waking hour to dealing with this flood of misery and horror,' wrote journalist Cate Brett. 'The work is new, urgent and under-resourced; not surprisingly mistakes are being made.' Lest anyone think that innocent men were being swept away in the flood, Brett included the baseless claims (which she described as 'fairly compelling facts') that 'more than 90 percent of sexual abuse disclosures are valid', and that 'men who sexually abuse children commonly deny the abuse ... Some are pathological liars ...' To drive home the point, she noted that a PAIN affiliate had recently been convicted of sexual abuse and sent to prison for seven years, still protesting his innocence. 'Such outcomes do little for PAIN's credibility', she wrote.[67]

That was the case of Mr H. The charges of rape, indecent assault and inducing an indecent act arose when the children of his first marriage and the children of his ex-wife's best friend were counselled by START and the Child and Family Guidance Centre. Subsequently, Dr Margaret Metherall of Doctors for Sexual Abuse Care examined the children. She found that the hymens of the three younger girls were irregular in appearance, with aperture diameters of six, five and two millimetres respectively. She reported that it was 'highly likely that some form of vaginal penetration' had taken place with the first girl, and that 'an attempt at vaginal penetration' may have been made with the second. Further tests on the third girl revealed that she had lax anal tone, and that her hymen could not be fully penetrated with an adult finger. Metherall therefore reported that anal penetration and attempted vaginal penetration may have occurred with that child. The fourth girl had already reached puberty. Metherall found that her vaginal entrance admitted two fingers without difficulty. She reported that while this finding was consistent with the use of tampons it also raised the possibility of 'vaginal penetration of some other sort'.[68]

At his sentencing, Mr H told Justice Holland: 'I want you to know I am innocent of these allegations and I wish an inquiry to go into the children's counselling.' Justice Holland told the man he was sick.[69]

For her *Star* feature on the Ben G case, Cate Brett interviewed DSW psychologist Dr John Watson (who had nothing to do with the case) and reported that 'as an expert on forensic interviewing ... he concludes that Ben has been sexually abused'.[70]

Along with this presumption of parental guilt came the presumption that, when cases were dismissed by the courts, abused children were being returned to their abusive parents. Over the weeks following the dismissal of the Ben G case, Watson used the presumption to press for more resources for child protection.[71]

• • •

The *Frontline* programme featuring the cases of Cleo F and Ben G rushed to air on 13 April 1989 in the face of a threat of suppression by the Crown Law Office. It was rescreened several days later. Television and radio stations nationwide were inundated with calls, and the programme provoked a flood of letters overwhelmingly supportive of the families involved. A petition calling for a public inquiry into Ward 24 collected 800 signatures in two weeks.[72]

Nine months earlier, the report of Judge Silvia Cartwright's inquiry into cervical cancer treatment at Auckland's National Women's Hospital was presented to government. As a result of the *Frontline* programme, and Rosemary McLeod's follow-up article in *North & South*, thousands of hitherto uninterested New Zealanders called for a Cartwright-style inquiry into the diagnosis and treatment of child sexual abuse nationwide. The clamour, which continued all year, finally began to fade when Leader of the Opposition Jim Bolger assured radio host George Balani that a judicial inquiry, covering past and present procedures for the handling of child sexual abuse allegations and reviewing cases in which families may have been damaged by misdiagnosis, was urgently needed.[73]

But the government that saw fit to order a judicial inquiry into cervical cancer treatment at National Women's Hospital did not see fit to order a judicial inquiry into child sexual abuse treatment at Christchurch Public Hospital. Instead, Minister of Health Helen Clark left it to the Canterbury Hospital Board to organise an internal inquiry, and Minister of Social Welfare Michael Cullen asked retired Judge Ken Mason to review a clutch of complaints from Christchurch people. And when Jim Bolger became prime minister in 1990, he didn't order a judicial inquiry either.

4.iv: The Ongoing Malaise

For child protection workers, the *Frontline* programme was devastating. Overnight, in the eyes of the public, they were transformed from demon hunters into demons. But they were not demons. They were not driven by sadism or insanity or malice. At heart, the overwhelming majority of Christchurch child protection workers were ordinary, decent people who wanted only to do good.

We work long hours for little pay under stressful conditions, they told me. We perform deeds of kindness and caring far beyond the call of duty. We act with the best of intentions. We are well regarded by friends and colleagues. We are dedicated to making the world a better place. Those who accuse us of wrongdoing are malicious ingrates.

That people accused of being monsters would want to prove they are not is understandable. However, this emphasis on their own goodness also served to convince Christchurch child protection workers that at best they were incapable of doing harm (and therefore no harm was done), or at worst that if any harm was done it was minor (and therefore more than compensated for by their goodness). Consequently, though the evidence that they had harmed innocent people was overwhelming, their confidence in their own virtue enabled healthcare workers involved in the Ward 24 controversy to convince themselves that they had done nothing wrong.

The position taken by defenders of Ward 24 highlights one of the great paradoxes of life. There are few monsters in the world. In the grand sweep of human existence, the harm inflicted on innocent people by criminals and psychopaths is minuscule compared to the harm inflicted by ordinary, well-intentioned citizens going about their daily work in a spirit of duty, loyalty and service.

According to Hannah Arendt, even Adolf Eichmann – who masterminded the mass transportation of Jews to the death camps – was no monster. 'The trouble with Eichmann was precisely that so many were like him, and that the many were neither perverted nor sadistic, that they were, and still are, terribly and terrifyingly normal'. To call this evil 'banal', as Arendt did, is not to trivialise it. What made this evil so dangerous was that it was so easy. No exceptional human qualities were required to bring it into existence. The wind had only to blow in the right direction, and the evil spread like wildfire.[1]

In *On the Objective Study of Crowd Behaviour*, L.S. Penrose analysed the spread of ideas through human societies. He found that, like the spread of infectious diseases, the process requires an infective agent (an idea), a means of transmission, and a susceptible population. The upside of a toxic idea is that it offers hope to those who feel oppressed, and gives meaning and purpose to those whose lives seem empty. The downside is that it creates stereotypes – in-group good, out-group bad – and thereby paves the way for the demonisation and persecution that follow.

Penrose found that a group may have a different standard of collective morality from the individuals within it, and that a change of opinion among a few members may easily alter the attitude of the whole group if the other members are divided or indifferent.[2]

History suggests that once a pathogenic belief has infected the wider population, all that is required for it to reach its full destructive potential is for everyone to behave normally. Like working people everywhere, Christchurch child protection workers carried out their assigned tasks because they had been told it was their duty to do so, and that their efforts would contribute to the common good. Even if they did not entirely believe these claims, and even if the work was unpleasant, it was generally easier to comply than not.

The human propensity for obedience to authority was studied by Stanley Milgram in a famous 1963 experiment. Milgram recruited citizens of New Haven to serve as 'teachers' in a 'learning experiment'. Each 'teacher' was required to administer what he believed were electric shocks of increasing magnitude to a 'learner' every time a mistake was made in a 'test'. The 'learners' were really actors, who screamed, begged for mercy and lapsed into silence as the pretend shocks became more severe. Whenever the 'teacher' hesitated, a man in a white coat instructed him to continue. Milgram found that 65 percent of people were prepared to torture a man to within an inch of his life when instructed to do so by someone in authority. Like working people everywhere, Milgram's experimental subjects were more concerned with following orders than with the wider implications of their work.[3]

In his study of collective persecution, Tzvetan Todorov found that once people have consented to perform tasks in their working lives that they would find morally repugnant in their private lives, they adopt various habits of mind to make the job easier. They compartmentalise their lives, they separate their immediate responsibilities from the wider picture, and they fall back on clichés ('it doesn't matter what job you do, as long as you do it well', 'somebody has to do it').

According to Todorov, when confronted with the effects of their conduct, people whose moral compasses had become so disoriented that they have ended up doing harm when they thought they were doing good rarely admit to any wrongdoing. Instead, they resort to excuses. When the first excuse ('It never happened') collapses under the weight of evidence, the second excuse ('I had no idea it was happening') is embraced with enthusiasm. Todorov found that, when real, such ignorance is more or less a matter of conscious and deliberate effort. He also argued that the third excuse ('I was just obeying orders') is the excuse of subhumans with no conscience or free will, that the fourth and fifth excuses ('It was someone else's fault' and 'the system is to blame') are the excuses of bureaucrats, and that the final excuse ('everyone was doing it') is the excuse of children.[4]

• • •

In response to the *Frontline* programme, the Canterbury Hospital Board and the Christchurch child protection services began to fight back. Their responses indicate that the only question most of them asked themselves was, 'How can we justify what we've done?' Apart from Social Welfare Minister Michael Cullen's proposal that DSW compensate Mr G (which was overruled by his departmental legal advisor), and Hospital Board member David Close's proposal that the board apologise to and compensate the F and G families (which was overruled by his fellow board members), I have found no indication that anyone connected with the investigation or prosecution of the controversial cases ever asked him or herself, 'Could we have made a terrible mistake, and, if so, what can we do to put it right?'[5]

Nobody admitted that the interviewing techniques were grossly unreliable. Nobody admitted to having done anything wrong. Nobody apologised to the families involved. Above all, nobody admitted that the allegations of sexual abuse against the parents of Cleo F and Ben G were without foundation.

Instead, child protection workers dismissed the *Frontline* programme as a biased and sensationalist outrage. Newspaper headlines proclaimed: 'TV item on child abuse raises ire', 'Hospital scapegoat, says child specialist', 'Mistakes small price to pay to protect children', 'Child abuse expert slams *Frontline*', '*Frontline* impact worries prosecutor'.[6]

Child psychiatrist Karen Zelas told *Star* journalist Cate Brett that the programme was 'misleading and inaccurate and may well be defamatory'. Later, an article in *New Zealand Doctor* reported that Zelas was 'adamant the child [Cleo F] was a sexual abuse victim'.[7]

The aggrieved parents wanted a commission of inquiry into the handling of sexual abuse allegations nationwide. But in a front-page story in the *Christchurch Star* on 24 April, Cate Brett argued that an inquiry could become 'a vehicle for undermining a decade of progress'. In this regard, the criticism proffered by the British experts on the *Frontline* programme was particularly worrying. Brett wrote:

> Dr Tylden … said the consistency in all the transcripts she read [of evidential interviews conducted elsewhere in New Zealand] led her to assume the problems extended beyond Ward 24. Such a conclusion from a British expert closely associated with the Cleveland inquiry has provided powerful ammunition for groups like Christchurch's Parents Against Injustice. For more than a year PAIN has been mouthing 'Cleveland' to a largely sceptical and indifferent media. At this moment *Holmes* show host Paul Holmes and Television New Zealand are debating the wisdom of taking a second bite of the cherry, as PAIN seeks to implicate other agencies such as Child and Family Guidance, the Sexual Abuse Treatment and Rehabilitation Team and Glenelg Health Camp in the Ward 24 debacle. Wittingly or not, *Frontline* has tapped into a deep well of ignorance, fear and mistrust which is now threatening to overwhelm every therapist, social worker, police officer and psychiatrist working in the field. The ultimate victims, of course, are the children.[8]

The Canterbury Hospital Board did not want an independent inquiry either. But the public demand for accountability could not be ignored. So on 22 April 1989 psychiatrist Les Ding, medical superintendent of Sunnyside Hospital, was directed to undertake an internal inquiry. The Christchurch Patients' Rights Group was unimpressed. 'To ask a doctor to investigate his or her colleagues is like asking the police to investigate themselves,' complained spokesperson Helen Chambers.[9] According to Grant Gillett, Professor of Medical Ethics at the Otago Medical School, Chambers' suspicions were well founded:

> In a professional healthcare setting, even if the person conducting the inquiry is from a different institution, there's a presupposition about treating one's colleagues as brothers. One doesn't like to find fault with colleagues who are doing their best in a fairly well-intentioned way. There are elements of 'there but for the grace of God go I' and 'this person could be sitting in judgement on me in the future' and 'we all have to do a difficult job in difficult circumstances'. Also, the medical gaze tends to focus on the narrowly defined medical problem, so wider social issues are marginalised. For all these reasons,

medical investigators are predisposed to be sympathetic towards colleagues who may have not acted well ... The predisposition is magnified if the investigator is employed by the organisation being investigated. In such situations there is greater collegial closeness, and all sorts of informal considerations concerning the investigator's good regard and future career come into play ... It's not a matter of conspiracy, or any intention to distort the facts, it's just that people from within a profession don't have the impartiality and detachment to make findings on the basis of evidence that can stand up under severe cross-examination, regardless of the professional courtesies involved.[10]

The 1975 report of the internal inquiry into cervical cancer treatment at National Women's Hospital illustrates this point. In 1973 three senior hospital clinicians were asked to review the case notes of 29 patients treated at the hospital for cervical cancer. Bur they considered only 13 cases, and concluded that 'the agreed policy was followed' in all of them. The report stated that 'all staff members involved ... acted with personal and professional integrity'.

In her independent inquiry into the same issue 12 years later, Judge Cartwright noted: 'It is astounding and of grave concern that the Committee ... chose to avoid the central issue: were patients at risk of developing invasive cancer, or of having the diagnosis of invasive cancer delayed as a result of [the treatment programme at National Women's Hospital]?' Another concern was that the review committee, having found that invasive cancer was subsequently diagnosed in all 13 reviewed cases, expressed no sense of alarm.[11]

In the Canterbury Hospital Board internal inquiry, Dr Ding was required to investigate the complaints and allegations about Ward 24 raised in the *Frontline* programme. His terms of reference covered staff training, staff supervision, interviewing techniques and the role of Ward 24 in sexual abuse prosecutions. He was also asked to determine whether any matters arising from his investigation warranted further inquiry or action.

In the course of his six-week investigation, Ding interviewed 13 present and former Ward 24 staff, four Child and Family Guidance Centre staff and 16 other people, including child psychiatrist Karen Zelas, DSW psychologist John Watson, Senior Sergeant John Ell, paediatrician Terry Caseley, START therapist Heather Broadhurst, Crown Prosecutor David Saunders and counsel for the child in the Cleo F case, Isabel Mitchell. He did not interview Mr and Mrs F, Mr and Mrs G, their lawyers, Patricia Champion (the expert who criticised the interviewers in the Cleo F case) or the British experts who contributed to the *Frontline* programme. Ward 24 director Bill Watkins was on study leave at the time. He proved difficult to contact, and his contribution was limited.[12]

Like the internal inquiry into cancer treatment at National Women's Hospital, the Ding inquiry avoided the central issue: were families being destroyed by accusations of sexual abuse on the basis of evidence obtained by questionable methods? Also, like the report of the National Women's internal inquiry, the Ding report showed that, no matter how honourable and well intentioned the investigators, internal inquiries are often little more than damage-control exercises. The opening summary of the Ding report stated:

1. The power of the media once again demonstrated its effectiveness in initiating self-examination by a health service. However, the ethics and even the legality of its tactics are questionable.
2. Unlike the Cleveland situation, there was no evidence of overenthusiastic diagnosis, excessive reliance on single medical findings or breakdown of inter-agency and inter-professional working relations. What was in question was the style and standard of the evidential interviews involved in the two cases … If anything, the Ward approach erred on the side of over-caution manifesting in excessive persistence in the pursuit for evidence.
3. The Canterbury Hospital Board was mindful of the demand from some quarters for a public inquiry. At this point the nature of the allegations would not justify that …
4. Court judgments on the two cases were released to me on the condition that [their] contents would not be disclosed. I did not, for ethical reasons, seek permission for such disclosure, although such disclosure may assist the Canterbury Hospital Board's effort to refute the allegations made against Ward 24.

Ding could not ignore the evidence of unprofessional interviewing and inadequate supervision in Ward 24, but he minimised the problem by arguing that the criticised procedures were not confined to Ward 24, and he excused those responsible by suggesting that the problems were a legacy of the previous director (who had left more than three years earlier). Ding suggested that, had the present director been aware of the problems, he would have corrected them.[13]

There can be no doubt that keeping tabs on his staff was difficult for Bill Watkins. Some feminist therapists refused to discuss their work with men, and male staff were barred from working with sexually abused children. Also, the demands of Watkins' two half-time jobs – one as an academic, the other as director of Ward 24 – limited his contact with patients. But most children spent at least five weeks in the ward, and, at weekly ward rounds each child's primary therapist reported to senior staff on 'what had been happening day to day with the child'. A team decision was then made about 'how to carry on'.[14] Furthermore, no matter how inadequate his knowledge of ward procedures, Watkins presented his therapists' findings to the Child Protection Team and defended their work in the courts. This suggests that, if he was genuinely unaware that untrained and unsupervised therapists were subjecting children in his ward to excessive numbers of coercive, lengthy and badly recorded interviews at odd hours of the day and night, then his unawareness could only have been achieved by means of what Todorov called 'conscious and deliberate effort'.

Another explanation offered by Ding for the ongoing deficiencies in Ward 24 procedures was that 'the Director ... has never received any negative feedback from the [Child Protection] Team, Crown Prosecutor's Office or the Court on its past work with sexual abuse'. Not only does this claim discount the negative feedback from Judge Kean in the G case, it suggests that the Child Protection Team (CPT) was as blind to the deficiencies in the interviewing techniques as were the staff of Ward 24 themselves. Yet most, if not all, CPT members must have been aware of the recommendation of the National Advisory Committee on the Prevention of Child Abuse that only one evidential interview be conducted. After all, the CPT was based on a recommendation of that committee. CPT chair Karen Zelas and CPT member Laurie O'Reilly were members of the committee, and CPT deputy chair Dianne Espie relied on the committee's report for her determinations of hymen measurements. All this suggests that, if CPT members were genuinely unaware of the deficiencies in the interviews conducted at Ward 24 (and the same deficiencies in the interviews conducted at Glenelg Children's Health Camp, START and the Child and Family Guidance Centre) then, like Bill Watkins, they could have achieved their unawareness only by means of 'conscious and deliberate effort'.

As well as minimising and excusing the problems in Ward 24, and failing to address the possible harm inflicted on children and their families by these problems, Ding also failed to consider whether the expenditure of large amounts of healthcare time, energy and resources on dobbing in suspected criminals, and collecting evidence against them, could be ethically justified.

The ethical principles underpinning the provision of healthcare focus on the provider's responsibility to his or her patient, and the provider's duty of confidentiality.[15] So the primary ethical question raised by the *Frontline* programme, and left unaddressed by the Ding report, was this: how do the principles of healthcare ethics apply to cases of suspected child abuse, where the healthcare provider's responsibilities are complicated by the status of the patient and the intrusion of law enforcement considerations into the therapeutic relationship?

With children too young to make rational decisions about their own wellbeing, the therapeutic relationship has to be extended to include the child's parents. However, because the welfare of the child is paramount, in situations where parents are blatantly violating their child's best interests, society may intervene to protect the child. According to Alan Goldman, author of *The Moral Foundations of Professional Ethics*, the rights of healthcare professionals to intervene on behalf of children have two major limitations:

The first is that the damage must be potentially drastic, if we are to respect the family as the social unit for raising children. The second is that doctors themselves are not to be granted authority to override parents generally. The courts are the proper source of overriding decisions. Doctors are responsible for petitioning their rulings, and in emergencies medical personnel may have to act on their own out of necessity. The latter responsibilities do not represent special authority for doctors, but simply the duty shared by all to report and prevent even well-meaning parental abuse ...[16]

With regard to the intrusion of law enforcement considerations into the therapeutic relationship, most healthcare codes of ethics stress the provider's duty not to disclose confidential information without permission, unless required by law to do so. However, the provider does have the discretion to disclose without permission if the patient or the community is in imminent danger.[17]

In situations where the danger is not imminent, the need to preserve the therapeutic relationship usually takes priority. For this reason, most healthcare providers resist police pressure to report or disclose confidences about crimes, and resist vigorously pressure to covertly collect information for law enforcement purposes. The Royal Australian and New Zealand College of Psychiatrists Code of Ethics states:

- If required to divulge information, psychiatrists shall as far as possible divulge only that information relevant to the case at hand, avoid highly sensitive and personal speculation, and take care to separate factual information from opinion.
- Where the purpose of the psychiatrist's intervention is not inherently therapeutic (for example forensic psychiatric assessment), its nature shall be made absolutely clear to the person involved.[18]

These ethical considerations have two important implications. The first is that interventions in cases of suspected child abuse cannot be justified unless there are strong indications that the child is in imminent danger. The second is that it is unethical for healthcare workers to let parents believe they are pursuing a therapeutic relationship with a child when they are in fact pursuing a forensic one. These considerations invite the conclusion that, in the late '80s, there were ethical problems in Ward 24 as well as procedural ones.

According to the Ding report, the procedural problems were caused by deficiencies in staff training and supervision, but the ethical problems cannot be so easily explained. While it is true that there were untrained and unsupervised staff on the ward, there were also a properly trained psychiatrist, a properly trained clinical psychologist and several properly trained nurses. These people not only allowed the questionable practices to continue; in many instances they actively supported them.

This suggests that the problems of poor practice in Ward 24 were secondary to a more serious problem: the political misuse of psychiatric theory and treatment.

Les Ding wrote: 'I am satisfied that Ward 24 has taken adequate steps to rectify their methods of evidential interview.' His satisfaction was based on the 'Sexual Abuse Diagnostic Guidelines' drawn up by Bill Watkins in December 1988. These distinguished between therapeutic and diagnostic interviews, and recommended that someone other than the child's primary worker conduct the diagnostic interviews. They also made tentative suggestions about the number and duration of interviews, and the use of leading questions and anatomically correct dolls. But the ethical issues were not addressed. The Ding report indicated that evidential interviews would be conducted less often in Ward 24, but it was Social Welfare Minister Michael Cullen who pointed out that they should not be conducted there at all.

By the time the Ding report was released in June 1989, the Specialist Services Unit (SSU) of DSW had set up its own evidential interviewing facility in Christchurch. Psychologist Dr John Watson was the unit's director. Child psychiatrist Dr Karen Zelas trained and supervised the interviewers. One of the unit's first interviewers was Sue Sidey (who would become one of the three interviewers in the Civic Crèche case). Thereafter, virtually all formal evidential interviews for Christchurch court cases involving allegations of child sexual abuse were recorded on videotape at the SSU.

• • •

Despite the findings of two internal inquiries (that there was no reason for DSW to apologise to or compensate the parents of Mary A or Ben G), the question of whether families were being destroyed by false allegations of child sexual abuse continued to concern Michael Cullen, so he asked retired Judge Ken Mason to review some recent cases dismissed by the courts. This was not the commission of inquiry that the parents of PAIN wanted, but it gave them cause for hope.[19]

The ambit of the Mason review was never clear. Newspaper reports described it as covering 'a cluster', 'a smattering', 'a number', and 'several' recent cases. In an interview with Cate Brett on 29 March 1989, Cullen said that four cases would be reviewed initially, and that 'the person heading the review will be given an open brief, with the freedom to examine other cases if necessary'.[20]

When Mason took up the review, the terms of reference he negotiated with DSW required him to 'inquire into and review' only one case (that of Mary A), and to 'report on whether any further inquiry or review ought to be undertaken' into another case (that of Ben G).[21]

During his one-month investigation, Mason thoroughly researched the Mary A case. His 40-page report was highly critical of the social workers' actions. He recommended that DSW apologise to the couple, reimburse their out-of-pocket expenses and make ex-gratia payments for their disruption and distress.[22]

Over the same period Mason read the DSW file and judgment on the Ben G case. He also received written submissions from the lawyers for Mr and Mrs G, and was briefed by the regional solicitor for DSW Christchurch. The G children were held in state custody for 10 months, which must have caused their parents considerably more disruption and distress than that caused to Mr and Ms A by having Mary taken from them for three weeks. Nonetheless, in a two-page report, Mason advised that 'no further inquiry or review ought to be undertaken'. But he did recommend that DSW give consideration to the rights of defendants in future complaint proceedings.[23]

That issue was addressed in the Children, Young Persons, and Their Families Bill, which Cullen introduced into parliament under urgency two weeks after the *Frontline* programme. The child protection movement was infuriated to discover that, though the Bill came in the guise of the second reading of the David Geddis-inspired 1986 Children and Young Persons Bill, it was a totally rewritten package. The new legislation restricted the rights of statutory officials to arrange and conduct medical examinations on children without parental consent, and gave children the right to have a support person of their choice present during the examination. Most importantly, instead of giving child protection teams statutory authority, the new legislation created family group conferences. These helped ensure that decisions about the welfare of children could not be made without the involvement of the child's parents.[24]

But the new legislation also increased the power of statutory officials to intervene in cases of suspected child abuse. In particular, it overrode existing legislative restrictions on the disclosure of private information when reporting suspected child abuse. The Bill was passed in May 1989 and became law seven months later.

Towards the end of 1989 Michael Cullen asked Judge Mason to comment on another 10 complaints of false allegations of child sexual abuse from Christchurch. In his 19-page report Mason itemised and commented on each family's complaint. Their concerns were essentially the same. They began with a child admitted to Ward 24 or Glenelg, or treated by the Child and Family Guidance Centre, or counselled by START, and ended with accusations, forced separations, broken marriages, lost jobs, lost homes and lost families. Mason's comments were also essentially the same: 'No information has been provided as to the extent of that organisation's [START] involvement ... I see no grounds for Ministerial intervention ... It would be necessary to know more about the circumstances of this alleged incident [removal of a child by DSW] ... I see no grounds for Ministerial intervention ... In the absence of more explicit information [about coercive counselling at the Child and Family Guidance Centre] I see no ground for intervention by the Minister'. And so on.

Mason noted that his recommendations were likely to compound the complainants' 'sense of deep grievance', particularly in view of the fact that they were 'based solely on a perusal of the papers supplied'. He asked the minister to forward his report to Rangiora MP Jim Gerard, and he offered to meet with the complainants.[25]

When they met with Mason and Gerard on 15 December 1989, the complainants were unaware of the contents of Mason's report. 'That was unfortunate as a prior knowledge of my views may well have resulted in some of the problems being ironed out at our meeting,' Mason wrote to Gerard in February 1990.[26]

Mason was expecting to console people who knew they had lost, but instead he was faced with people who still had hope, and who would not take no for an answer. His letter to Gerard continued:

> I explained to the meeting that more detail and fact, as distinct from emotion, would be required before I could recommend ministerial intervention. I suggested that each complainant spell out in simple direct terms the nature of the complaint, that each complaint be supported by facts, names, dates etc. and that, wherever possible, each complainant should confine himself/herself to not more than three pages.

He advised Gerard that he would be overseas for five weeks, and asked him to have the information ready on his return. However, as the judge explained nine months later, there were problems:

> I left New Zealand on 17 February and returned on 28 March ...[and] My wife and I were overseas from 3 June to 12 July ... I received information from most of the complainants on 26 February, 5 April, 9 May and finally on 26 May. Contrary to my expectations and my specific request the volume of material ... runs to some hundreds of pages! I felt bound to read the material but ... was unable to start until late July/early August.[27]

Following an inquiry from PAIN in early August, Mason assured Cullen's secretary that a report would be forthcoming in about three weeks. When the report had not appeared by October, Mr H, by then an inmate of Paparua Prison, became suicidal. So, in response to another call from Cullen's secretary, Mason provided an urgent report on the complaints of Mr and Mrs H. 'I recommend that you take no further action in this case and that you decline the invitation to institute a formal Inquiry,' he wrote. He added that, with respect to the other complainants, 'My enquiries ... have almost been completed and my tentative view is that in these cases also there is no cogent evidence to justify ministerial intervention.' He advised that his final report would be delayed. 'I am leaving for the United States later today,' he explained.

• • •

Judge Mason's response meant that, by the end of 1990, PAIN had been effectively discredited and the Christchurch child protection movement had been effectively vindicated. Also, recent law changes made it easier for child witnesses to give evidence in court. Christchurch agencies involved in the investigation, treatment and prosecution of child sexual abuse were busier than ever.

CHAPTER 5

And a Little Child Shall Mislead Them

5.i: Enter the Devil

The most extensive and expensive child abuse investigation in New Zealand history began with the enigmatic comment of a four-year-old boy, Geoffrey Magnolia. Exactly what Geoffrey said, and what he meant, have never been clearly established and the questions are now probably irrelevant. This is because, like the chain of events that led to the child pornography ring scare in Christchurch, the chain of events that led to the Christchurch Civic Crèche case had a certain inevitability.

In the early 1980s, the McMartin case in California triggered an epidemic of ritual abuse allegations in day-care centres that spread across the United States and around the world, so it was probably inevitable that allegations of that sort would arise in New Zealand sooner or later. Christchurch was the epicentre for the investigation, detection and prosecution of child sexual abuse in New Zealand, so it was likely that the first New Zealand allegations would arise in that city. Many Christchurch child protection workers sent their preschoolers to the Civic Crèche, so it was likely that the first allegation would be made there. Ms Magnolia was a sexual abuse worker with a history of mental instability, so it was likely that she would make the first allegation. Peter Ellis was the only male childcare worker at the centre, so it was likely that he would be her target. Some Christchurch police already regarded homosexual young men with suspicion, so it was likely that they would pursue the allegations against Peter Ellis with enthusiasm.

As a man, Ellis risked being accused of child sexual abuse from the day he began working at the Civic Crèche in 1986. In 1989 the risk increased. This was because, in response to the *Frontline* programme, support for fathers accused of molesting their own children increased. In an interview in *New Zealand Doctor* in September 1989 Karen Zelas observed: 'Fewer cases of child sexual or physical abuse are being reported in New Zealand because of the negative backlash against those who in good faith are trying to protect children.' Between 1986 and 1989 there were 33 to

36 criminal prosecutions for incest each year, but in 1990 the total fell to 12.[1] For sexual abuse investigators, any drop in the statistics was cause for concern. At a theoretical level it undermined their alarmist claims about the prevalence of sexual abuse and the damage it caused. At a practical level it threatened the continued funding of programmes dedicated to the detection and treatment of the problem. This encouraged them to look for abuse beyond the family, and in the 1990s the spotlight fell on male teachers.

Mr N, a Christchurch teacher's aide convicted in April 1991 of sexual offences against six girls, and the physical assault of a boy, had little family or community support, so he was a vulnerable target. Also, as it turned out, he was genuinely guilty of at least one offence.

At the sentencing of Mr N, Justice Holland said, 'I am not aware in New Zealand of a Court having to deal with a school teacher on charges of indecent assaults of this kind with young girls.'[2] Though I have not checked the records, I find it hard to believe that Mr N's was the first case of this sort in our nation's history. Anecdotal accounts of sexual impropriety by teachers are certainly not unknown. In *I Passed this Way* Sylvia Ashton-Warner wrote of her teacher at the age of 10: 'I did learn the strange excitement of being pressed close to a man's body ... he was picked up years later for this very sort of thing.' But the allegations against Mr N may have been the first in the 1990s upsurge of such cases.[3]

Whatever its national significance, the case was important locally because many former Civic Crèche children attended that school and because, when the crèche case erupted six months later, the Mr N case was used by sexual abuse workers to 'prove' two key arguments. The first was that it was possible for a teacher to molest children in the presence of other children and staff without any adult noticing anything amiss, and without any child saying a word to anyone about it. The second was that, were it not for the skills of the police Child Abuse Unit and the DSW interviewers, crimes of this sort may never be revealed. The only difference between Mr N and Peter Ellis, sexual abuse workers told me, was that Mr N had the decency to plead guilty. My research has revealed that the Mr N case was not quite as it seemed.

The story began on 26 January 1990, when, after a lifetime of manual labour, Mr N began work as a teacher's aide at a city primary school. He was a stranger to Christchurch. His marriage had broken up. He was an isolated and lonely man. He had no training or experience of teaching. His appointment was based on his fluency in the Maori language.[4]

On 3 October 1990, when Mr N was away at a funeral, a girl described by fellow pupils as 'the school gossip' sparked a rumour that he had been dismissed for putting his hands down girls' panties. On learning the reason for the buzz in the classroom, the teacher upbraided the children for gossiping, and urged them to tell an adult if any such thing happened to them. Afterwards, seven-year-old Zena approached the teacher, burst into tears, and said that Mr N had done it to her. Zena was the troubled child of a dysfunctional family. She openly masturbated herself and attempted to masturbate other children. At the time of her disclosure she was in therapy at the Child and Family Guidance Centre. The principal and Zena's mother were immediately notified of the disclosure. The chair of the school's board of trustees was notified that evening.[5]

That day and the next, the story spread like wildfire. Children talked to one another and to their parents. The 'school gossip' named girls she believed were involved and a concerned parent notified their parents. These parents, in turn, questioned their children and worried about their behaviour.

On the morning of 4 October, when the principal asked Mr N about the allegations, he said they were not true. The following afternoon – after discussions involving parents, staff, the chair of the board, the Ministry of Education, the School Trustees Association and the police – Mr N was advised that the matter was being investigated by the police and he would be suspended in the meantime. The board chair recalled:

> ... he was visibly upset and weeping. He began by apologising and said he was sorry it had happened ... he did not want to bring shame on the school or have the child suffer ... He made some reference to the fact that he knew it was wrong but didn't know how to deal with the temptation ... I drew his attention to the fact that others may have been involved. He replied, 'I don't think so'... The principal read out a number of names from the class list ... he said, 'No, no, no', but when the name 'Jenny O' was read, he said, 'Perhaps, maybe it was an accident'.[6]

On 9 October Constable Donna Scott of the Child Abuse Unit conducted a videotaped interview with Zena. On 10 October a meeting for parents of children in Mr N's class was addressed by the police. On 11 October Detective Ken Legat interviewed Mr N. There was no lawyer present. The interview transcript conveys the impression of a guilty, ashamed and remorseful man who was anxious to confess all:

> Q: As you are aware there has been a serious allegation made, what can you tell me about that?
>
> A: I am going to admit the allegation.

Mr N explained that sometime in June he had become disturbed by Zena's masturbation. He added that on some occasions when he was sitting on the floor reading to children she had put her hand on his trousers over his penis, and on one occasion she had pulled down his fly. He said that he had touched her 'private parts' three times.

A: The first time it ever happened I was reading a story, all the children were around. There were three sitting on my lap and Zena happened to be one of them. That's when I put my hand between her legs.

Q: What was she wearing?

A: Slacks.

Q: Did you touch inside or outside her clothes?

A: Outside.

---------------- [line]

Q: You are saying that you have only touched Zena's vagina three times on top of her clothes?

A: No, the third time I went into her panties.

He said he put his hand into her panties when Zena was sitting on his lap during a bus trip.

Q: Did you rub her vagina?

A: Just felt it, yes.

Q: Why did you do it?

A: I don't know, I honestly don't know.

Mr N then viewed Zena's videotaped interview, and responded with frank disbelief. 'A lot of that is fabricated,' he said. 'For a start there is no way I have that much time to do what I am supposed to do with her.' When Legat asked if he had touched Jenny O and another girl, he said that he had cuddled them, but nothing more[7]

During the three weeks between Mr N's first and second police interviews, five more girls were interviewed by Constable Scott and DSW interviewer Sue Sidey. The girls said that Mr N had put his hands down their panties in front of other children and staff in the morning before school, in the playground during morning break, at their desks when he was checking their work and in the class library.

'The lawyer told me not to come,' Mr N told Detective Legat at the start of his second interview, but he agreed that he had come voluntarily. When Mr N denied the new allegations, Legat tried a new tack. 'Have you taken any drugs that would distant [sic] your memory?' he asked. 'I don't think so,' said Mr N, but the suggestion that he may have forgotten committing the offences took root. Legat insisted that the children were telling the truth, and persisted with his questioning. Eventually Mr N gave up.

Q: You are not too busy to touch the children?

A: I don't remember.

Q: You are saying that it might have happened but you don't remember?
A: I don't remember.

Then came the bombshell. Mr N admitted that he had a sexual problem, and gave a muddled account of an occasion 27 years earlier when, at the age of 19, he had spent a month in jail for what he called 'perving' at a woman.

A psychiatric evaluation followed. Mr N confessed that he had been troubled all his life by fantasies of women's underwear, voyeurism and indecent exposure. He said on one occasion in the '70s he had exposed himself, but this had not resulted in any criminal charges. He assured the psychiatrist that, until he had become disturbed by Zena's masturbation, his sexual interests had focused on adolescent and adult women.[8]

While the criminal aspects of Mr N's sexual behaviour were unacceptable, his life-long fantasies cannot be so readily categorised. They were, and are, such staples of the advertising industry and men's magazines that they are probably considered seriously abnormal by only two categories of people: the old puritans, who regard them as sinful; and the new puritans, who regard them as politically incorrect. As the son of a clergyman, Mr N's past self-image was shaped by the old puritans; as a confessed sex offender, his present self-image was shaped by the new puritans. The psychiatric report noted that he felt guilty, ashamed and remorseful, and had made several suicide attempts, but was willing to receive treatment.

When the members of the school appointments committee found out about Mr N's conviction they were devastated. If they had thought to ask, or to check his criminal history, this blot on his record would have stopped him getting the job.[9]

His second police interview ended in confusion, but Mr N returned two days later to finish the job. As on the previous occasions, no lawyer was present. The transcript of his third interview indicates that Mr N's confidence in his own memory had by then collapsed.

'Even when I am talking to the doctor, I want to try and remember,' he told Detective Legat. 'I want to find out what's wrong ... I want to find why my mind is blocked ...'

'Is there anything else you want to say?' asked Legat, at the end of the unproductive interview.

'How sorry I am whatever happened,' said Mr N.

Two months later, on 10 January 1991, Mr N was interviewed by the police about two new allegations. This time his lawyer was present. The first allegation, of physical assault, brought to a head issues that had dogged Mr N's police interviews, and, indeed, his whole short-lived teacher's aide career.[10]

According to preschool teachers who have worked in both Maori-language and English-speaking preschools, the different ways that New Zealand's two main cultures relate to children often cause confusion. One problem area is the robust physicality that most Maori regard as normal. In the course of daily life, Maori kids tend to be pushed around, shouted at and hit when they are naughty; and hugged, stroked and kissed when they are unhappy. By contrast, politically correct Pakeha believe that the child's permission should be obtained before any touching can take place. Also, Maori adults do not as a rule modify their behaviour in the presence of children. Indeed, many Maori regard the Pakeha view that swearing and arguments are unsuitable for children's ears as ineffably precious.

Mr N was unaware of these things when he took up his teacher's aide appointment. He was the only Maori on the teaching staff of a liberal, middle-class school.[11] There were bound to be misunderstandings. In the course of Mr N's eight months at the school, the classroom teacher complained to the principal on at least three occasions about his swearing, his 'over-familiarity' and his striking of children. During his second police interview, misunderstandings of this sort caused confusion in relation to Jenny O.

> Q: Did you ever touch her in an inappropriate manner?
> A: How do you mean?
> Q: ... Did you ever touch Jenny O?
> A: I suppose I might have.
> Q: In what way?
> A: I just put my arm round her shoulder.
> Q: Did you ever put your hand on her bottom?
> A: I used to pat all of them on the bottoms.
> Q: Was that under or over the clothes?
> A: Just outside.
> Q: Did you ever touch Jenny O round the vagina area?
> A: Not that I know of.

In Mr N's January 1991 interview the same sort of mixed signals were exchanged over an allegation of physical abuse. The complaint related to an occasion when Steven had created a disturbance while Mr N had the class seated on the floor in front of him. The classroom teacher recalled:

He shouted at Steven, 'Don't talk when I'm talking. Pay attention.' Steven smirked ... [Mr N] shouted 'Don't you laugh at me' and within a split second, he had grabbed Steven by ... the ear and pulled him off the floor ... He then pushed him to the very front of the room and pushed him to the floor. He then smacked him across the side of the head ... Steven bit his lip and started to sob and the defendant just continued his teaching.[12]

Steven gave a less sinister account of the incident to the police and added, for good measure, that he had seen Mr N put his hands down a girl's panties.[13] For his part, Mr N recalled pulling Steven's ear, but he was not sure whether he had hit him.

At his January 1991 interview Mr N was also confronted with a new allegation from Zena. She said he had taken her to the corridor by the girls' toilet, pulled down her panties, taken out his penis and rubbed it on her vagina. This claim fell so far outside the possibilities of misinterpreted cuddles that Mr N was in no doubt. 'And that's most definitely lying,' he said.

'Why didn't she say that in the first place?' he added, as if to underline the ridiculousness of the allegation. Legat said that, after seeing him hit Steven and yell at other kids, the children were too scared to say anything.

'When I am on duty they all come around me,' Mr N protested. 'If they were that scared they wouldn't come near me ... I loved those kids and was proud of them. They are a great bunch of children.'

At the end of the interview Mr N was charged with assaulting Steven and sexually violating Zena. 'The one about Zena is definitely wrong,' he said. 'I don't know why she is saying that.'

The depositions were heard on 16 March 1991. Mr N was committed for trial on five charges of sexual violation, 10 charges of indecent assault and one of physical assault. The offences were said to have taken place in various public places around the school, often in the presence of other adults and children. Curiously, none of the charges related to the incident in the relative privacy of the bus, to which he had confessed.[14]

On 16 April 1991 Mr N pleaded guilty to all charges and was jailed for two weeks while pre-sentence and victim-impact reports were prepared. During that period he was also assessed by the Kia Marama sex offenders' unit. On 30 April 1991 he was sentenced to eight years in prison.

According to his lawyer, at the time of his guilty plea Mr N was adamant that the more serious charges were untrue. However, because he accepted that there was some truth in the minor charges, he did not want to put the children through the ordeal of a court hearing. Also, he was consumed with guilt, shame and remorse. He knew he had a problem and was anxious for treatment.

The Kia Marama report made the same point. It stated that Mr N acknowledged offences against two girls but did not remember offending against any others. He denied rubbing his penis on Zena's vagina. On the basis of these findings, the report concluded that he was minimising the extent and degree of his offending. However, it also noted that he was eager for treatment.[15]

In any event, regardless of how Mr N had pleaded, according to a member of the prosecution team, it was a case that Mr N's lawyer could never have won. First, there was Mr N's partial confession. Second, there was the credibility that any Christchurch jury would have afforded to the professional parents the Crown intended to call as witnesses. Third, there was Dr Margaret Metherall's report that two of the girls' hymens showed irregularities. By 1991 such irregularities had been known to be meaningless, but Metherall told the depositions hearing that they indicated, in Zena's case, 'recent trauma by attempted penetration', and in another case, 'suspicion of trauma due to penetration'.

At the time the Mr N case was little more than a five-day wonder. There were two items in the Christchurch *Press* about the court proceedings, and an article about the need for safeguards when hiring school staff. It wasn't until the Civic Crèche case erupted six months later that the Mr N case made national headlines.

On 15 December 1991, three weeks after Peter Ellis's suspension, an article about the Mr N case by Christchurch journalist Amanda Cropp appeared in the *Dominion Sunday Times*. If the headline – 'When the enemy emerges from within' – did not frighten the wits out of anxious crèche parents, the rest of the article would have done the job. 'Police say [Mr N] was gradually working his way through the whole class and describe him as one of the most audacious offenders they've ever dealt with,' reported Cropp. She also claimed:

> He abused children in the playground in front of other pupils. He sexually violated a child in the girls' toilets and his use of condoms suggested that the offences were carefully planned *[note: there is no mention of condoms in the court record]* ... [Mr N] thought nothing of molesting children while [the teacher] was busy in another area of the open plan classroom. The offending occurred almost daily for ten months. Even when the first allegations came to light, [Mr N] was able to molest another girl before being formally suspended.[16]

In the article Constable Scott explained that the signs of abuse were subtle and could easily be attributed to other things. Detective Legat urged teachers to contact the police at the first suspicion of abuse. The chair of the school board of trustees agreed. 'You can bring in the police at the rumour stage, and they are not going to react in a cackhanded way which is going to destroy someone's reputation,' she said. Anyway, if they did needlessly destroy a reputation, she considered that a small price to pay. 'If you make a mistake it's really sad,' she said. 'But adults can stand on their own two feet, children can't.'

On 16 December 1991 Mr Larch, spokesperson for the Civic Crèche management committee, faxed the article to Alistair Graham, manager of the city council department responsible for the crèche. In his covering note, Mr Larch said the article was 'of interest and comfort'.[17] The 'comfort' was presumably drawn from the article's implicit assurance that the police could be relied upon to investigate the Civic Crèche case in a careful and responsible manner.

As previously discussed, at the time of the Mr N case a ritual abuse scare was ripening in Christchurch. The seeds of the scare were carried to New Zealand in books, magazines and the electronic media, and by two influential people: American therapist Pamela Klein, and Upper Hutt police officer Laurie Gabites. In May 1990 Klein described the diagnosis and treatment of ritual abuse to a child sexual abuse conference in Wellington. The same year, Gabites collected information on the issue in the United States. Following his return, he helped found the Ritual Action Group (also known as the Ritual Action Network) early in 1991.[18]

Klein, an expert witness in many American ritual abuse trials, was also the Typhoid Mary of the ritual abuse scare in Britain. Nine months after her New Zealand visit, affidavits presented to a Chicago court showed that she had exaggerated and falsified her qualifications. The judge ruled that Klein was 'not a legitimate therapist as the term is defined by Illinois law'. But by then in the US, Britain and New Zealand the seeds of her noxious message had been sown, and satanic panic was spreading unchecked.[19]

Klein's message found a receptive audience because it came at an opportune time. Over the previous 40 years, heavily jowled Russians and narrow-eyed Asians had provided the templates onto which Western conspiracy theorists could project what Jung called 'the archetype of the enemy'. Over the same period, hating people of other races, religions and sexual orientations within one's own society had become increasingly unacceptable. So when the communist states of Eastern Europe collapsed, and the West made peace with its old enemies in Asia, Westerners were left with only one category of people whom it was socially acceptable to hate: paedophiles. Compared to the enemy without, this enemy within was dangerously close, and fiendishly difficult to identify. To people who felt threatened by such an invisible and elemental fear, Klein's message made sense.

In her address to the Wellington conference, Klein described her method of extracting from children as young as five what she believed were repressed memories of ritual abuse. These 'memories' – revealed in drawings, play activities and conversations – included ceremonies involving anal and vaginal rape, spiders, ghosts, skeletons, knives, crucifixes, tombstones, fires, high priestesses, infanticide, cannibalism, being buried alive with 'creepy crawly things', and death threats.[20]

Prior to Klein's visit, claims of occult practices were not unknown in New Zealand. At least once a year for as long as most people could remember *Truth* had run a sensational story, illustrated with photographs of candles and tombstones, about a cult of satanists celebrating Black Mass in some godforsaken part of the country. But, apart from a few Christian fundamentalists, hardly anybody took those stories seriously. However, following Klein's visit, notions of this sort enjoyed a wider currency.

In 1991 the influential Ritual Action Group (RAG), whose members came from 'government departments, community organisations, the clergy, the law, the media, the police, counsellors and survivors of ritual abuse', carried Klein's teachings throughout New Zealand.[21]

The year began with an eight-part National Radio series (*Free to Fly*) aimed at adults who were sexually abused as children. Listeners who thought the series was not for them were advised by producer and RAG member Dianne Stogre Power that 'many survivors have no idea they've been sexually abused'. Her list of adult manifestations of child sexual abuse included 'low self-esteem; an inability to trust; alcohol, drug and sex addictions; eating disorders; a need to be totally in control, to be a super-achiever; a pervasive sense of guilt; self-harm including attempted suicide; and the ability to absent oneself mentally'. Having invited listeners to attribute every emotional vicissitude, personal disappointment, career shortcoming and 'nameless dread' to child sexual abuse, Stogre Power guided her newly diagnosed victims along *The Courage to Heal*'s path to recovery. The first step was to name the problem: child sexual abuse. The next was to find a counsellor who could help the alleged victim remember and talk about the alleged abuse and confront the alleged abuser. Anyone who questioned the delayed recollections was said to be 'in denial'.[22]

From 7 January 1991, heavily promoted, half-hour episodes of *Free to Fly* played three evenings a week. Each Thursday episode was followed by a nationwide toll-free talkback session with radio diva Sharon Crosbie. In May 1991 the series was replayed on Tuesday and Thursday mornings. In June, July and August 1992 it was replayed again on Friday evenings. Listeners were invited to send in for the *Free to Fly* booklet and cassette copies of the series.

During the first repeat broadcast in May 1991, police officer and RAG member Laurie Gabites claimed that pornographic photos of New Zealand children had surfaced in California, and former detective Brent Hyde complained that the Christchurch child pornography ring investigation two years earlier should never have been shelved.[23]

During 1990 and 1991, as child sexual abuse concerns escalated, ACC counselling and compensation payouts spiralled. In his 1991 annual report, ACC chair Colin Beyer noted that the commission's expenditure was increasing ahead of inflation, and he singled out sexual abuse compensation as 'the only area where we pay out considerably more than we could ever have foreseen'.

'We pay out in the range of $30 to $50 million a year on sexual abuse claims,' he said. 'I feel uneasy about this because of the ease of misrepresenting a situation. It is also almost impossible for us to check the veracity of claims, particularly when they relate to events that took place 10 or 15 years ago.'[24]

Beyer's concerns were well founded. The sexual abuse awareness campaign attracted many well-meaning people in its early years, but in the late '80s, as sexual abuse became *crimen exceptum*, the campaign became an arena where money, power, trendiness, moral righteousness and an absence of accountability could be found in abundance. These qualities made it an attractive haven for the deluded, the incompetent, the corrupt and the criminal, and, as John Ralston Saul observed in *The Doubter's Companion*, 'In public life, bad people, like bad money, drive out good.'[25]

In the early '90s dishonesty within the sexual abuse awareness campaign was facilitated by dishonesty within ACC and DSW. At a grassroots level there were the people who made a false ACC claim and received a $10,000 windfall in return, and the therapists who counselled them at ACC's expense. At the heart of the bureaucracy there were the RAG members who promoted ritual abuse beliefs under the aegis of the DSW-sponsored Family Violence Prevention Coordinating Committee. At the top there was Jeff Chapman, managing director of ACC from 1985 to 1992, whose extravagance and deceit at the taxpayer's expense led to his imprisonment for fraud in 1997.[26]

Because there is rarely any corroborating evidence, statistics for false ACC sexual abuse claims are as unattainable as statistics for true ones. However, COSA (Casualties of Sexual Allegations) has collected scores of examples of successful claims where the complainant has subsequently retracted the allegation, or where the alleged perpetrator has proved on the basis of time, place and circumstance that the alleged abuse could not have occurred.[27]

A highly publicised case of ACC fraud involved troubled Christchurch psychology student Simone Doublett, who came to believe during counselling that she was a victim of ritual abuse. In an interview with the Christchurch *Press* following her retraction, she traced her problems to the death of her brother some years earlier. She said she wanted sympathy and attention, and she wanted to hurt and punish her family. Telling lies about sexual abuse served both goals. 'Everyone was talking sexual abuse,' she said. 'It was like everybody was very sorry for somebody who had been abused ... From the fifth form I started building myself up to believe that I had been abused.'[28]

Doublett began receiving counselling from Christchurch psychologist Dr Lynne Haye in February 1991. At Haye's suggestion she applied for ACC compensation and received a $10,000 payout. Haye encouraged her to write and talk about her dreams and fantasies. Before long, Doublett was recounting lurid tales of infant sacrifices and sexual assaults. Haye, having studied ritual abuse, believed the lot.[29]

A simple medical examination would have revealed that Doublett could not have experienced the abuse she reported, but to Haye that was out of the question. 'How would you feel if I asked for that? I've never heard of anybody doing it. This was not a criminal case,' she told journalist Martin van Beynen.

Nonetheless, Haye admitted that she had consulted a 'senior Christchurch policeman' who was apparently equally gullible. He considered tailing Doublett's alleged abusers, and warned Haye that his colleagues could not be trusted; there were suspected satanists in the ranks.

After two and a half years of counselling Doublett had had enough. In August 1993 she advised Haye, ACC and her university lecturers that the abuse had never happened, and she began repaying ACC. Whereupon ACC charged her with fraud, and the Psychologists Board advised her that she would be denied registration on graduation. Haye's registration was unaffected, and she was not required to repay the $4000 she had received from ACC for counselling Doublett.[30]

Doublett's retraction did not make headlines until 1995, when the ACC case against her came to court. However, in 1991 her allegations helped convince Christchurch therapists and police officers that ritual abuse was a reality in their city.

• • •

Between the grassroots misuse of ACC payments by people like Haye and Doublett, and the executive criminality of ACC managing director Jeff Chapman, the bureaucratic transgressions of RAG member Raewyn Good flourished.

Good was executive officer of the DSW-sponsored Family Violence Prevention Coordinating Committee (FVPCC) from 1986 until October 1992. During her term of office she promoted FVPCC's work to politicians, bureaucrats and the public in relentlessly 'holistic' and 'bicultural' terms. Between 1988 and 1992 her efforts drew more than $1.3 million in ACC grants. Also, the halo effect of her politically correct rhetoric, together with her forceful management style, ensured that, between 1986 and 1991, nobody involved with FVPCC made an issue of the fact that the unit's accounts were never audited. So it wasn't until 1992, when someone realised that the Ritual Action Group was operating out of the FVPCC office, that questions concerning the unit's financial accountability were seriously addressed.[31]

A DSW audit uncovered evidence of extravagant spending and misleading record-keeping in FVPCC, but the department dealt with the problems internally. A police investigation established that, during 1991 and 1992 (when ritual abuse allegations were being levelled against staff of the Christchurch Civic Crèche), Raewyn Good, together with RAG colleagues Jocelyn Frances and Ann-Marie Stapp, used DSW and ACC funding and facilities, and a $5000 grant from the Roy McKenzie Foundation, to organise unauthorised $80-a-head ritual abuse workshops around New Zealand. Workshop attendees were told that babies were being killed and eaten nationwide in satanic rituals led by evil and powerful men. Judges, policemen and church leaders were said to be involved.[32]

The first major RAG workshop took place at a high-profile Family Violence Prevention Conference in Christchurch in September 1991 – 11 weeks before the first complaint was laid in the Civic Crèche case. Initially it seemed like a mainstream conference: Christchurch mayor Vicki Buck welcomed everyone; Principal Family Court Judge Patrick Mahony made some opening remarks. After that, the 270 delegates attended a week of sexual abuse workshops and seminars. Christchurch High Court Registrar Peter Fantham demonstrated the use of closed-circuit television for child witnesses; Miriam Saphira took a session on 'Stopping Child Abuse'; RAG member Raewyn Good chaired sessions on 'Recent Research' and 'Cultural Facilitators of Violence'; RAG member Laurie Gabites took a session on 'The Adolescent Sexual Offender'; RAG member Chris Ravenswood took a 'Regression (Trance) Workshop' and RAG members Ann-Marie Stapp and Jocelyn Frances took a 'Ritual Abuse Workshop'.[33]

During the conference, reputable newspapers presented the claims of Stapp, Frances and Gabites as reliable news. The *Sunday Star* reported:

> Systematic ritual sexual, physical and psychological abuse of children is being practised by devil worshippers and other closed New Zealand cults, according to research to be presented at a family conference this week ... Frances says there is clear evidence of satanic ritual abuse in New Zealand and more, it appears to be prevalent ... there is also a sex ring in Christchurch associated with the manufacture of pornography ... 'An example is a child may be bonded – emotionally – to a dog. The cult orders the child to kill the dog... The child is then made to drink the blood and parts of the dog's body will be used on the child – particularly the dead animal's sexual organs. Photographs are taken ... and then distributed to hard core pornography links around the world.' Frances' claims are backed by Gabites ... He says pornographic photographs of New Zealand children are being sent to the United States as part of a paedophile network.[34]

The *Sunday Times* reported that American counsellor Mitchell Whitman had been contacted by several ritual abuse victims during a recent New Zealand tour, and senior DSW advisory officer Anne Caton was taking the claims seriously. The Christchurch *Press* reported that in the US ritual abuse 'occurred at preschools and summer camps without parents knowing'. Most newspapers quoted Frances and Stapp's definition of ritual abuse ('physical, sexual and psychological abuse that is systematic, ceremonial and public'). Most noted that their claims were based on memories recovered by a handful of women during therapy, but that detail failed to provoke journalistic scepticism.[35]

No one asked: if ritual abuse was, and is, widespread and public, why has no outsider ever stumbled across a ceremony in progress, or evidence that a ceremony has taken place? And if all that child pornography was, and is, being produced, why has no locally made hard-core 'kiddie porn' ever been found?

At that time the only explicit child pornography found by New Zealand police and customs officers had been imported from overseas, and nearly all of it was more than 20 years old. According to a 1996 *Guardian* investigation, this is because child pornography was commercially produced in Europe for a short period in the '70s, and in relatively small quantities. Since then, these '70s images have been reproduced and transferred whenever and wherever new technology has become available. The investigators concluded that the much-hyped child porn sweeping the internet consists of images from the '70s, topped up with pictures from clothing catalogues and the sort of photographs of naked children that can be found in any family album.[36]

The unquestioning media coverage of the Ritual Action Group's claims demonstrates the ease with which normally responsible journalists can succumb to sensationalism. Cynics may say they were more interested in breaking a big story than in finding the truth, but Penrose's work on crowd behaviour suggests that their failure to question may be a normal human reaction to an unreasonable and ill-defined threat.[37]

According to Penrose, if a communal threat is clearly defined, those affected will generally react calmly and rationally. By contrast, an improbable and poorly defined threat can cause mass panic. During the terrible days of the Blitz, Londoners coped with remarkable equanimity; but during the 1938 'Invasion from Mars' radio broadcast, panic swept America. Studies of this panic have found a close relationship between the condition of being frightened and an inability to question the authenticity of the information received. The improbable nature of the events narrated, and the impossibility of the rapid time sequences described, should have aroused scepticism. Instead, they enhanced the frightening effects of the programme by making the events seem supernatural. In the psychopathology of panic, the doctrine of Tertullian, '*credo quia impossibile*' (the more impossible, the more terrifying if true), attains a new significance. In some situations the intellect may become so swamped with fear that it effectively ceases to function.

Of course not all journalists lose their nerve when faced with seemingly impossible claims, but even the most level-headed journalists may fail to uncover the truth when their primary sources are carriers of a highly contagious delusion. TV3's *60 Minutes* investigation of the phantom Christchurch child pornography ring, broadcast on the opening night of the Family Violence Prevention Conference, was a case in point.[38]

The programme was television journalist Melanie Reid's first major investigation. 'I was hell-bent on going after the big story,' she recalled six years later. 'There was only one big story in Christchurch at that time and that was the paedophile ring. And I was going to get to the bottom of it.'[39]

She interviewed all the obvious people: the newspaper journalist who covered the story (Cate Brett); the detective who led the investigation and resigned in protest when it was closed (Brent Hyde); the therapist who treated the children involved (Heather Chambers, formerly Heather Broadhurst of START); the former matron of a Christchurch children's home (Rose Robinson); the police officer who closed the investigation (Detective Inspector Roger Carson); and the mother of two of the children involved. She flew to Melbourne and interviewed two Australian 'child pornbuster' detectives, and made an unsuccessful attempt to interview a man believed to be involved in the ring. With the exception of Inspector Carson, everyone Reid interviewed portrayed the porn ring as a terrible reality. Hyde said: 'The children spoke of adults having sexual connections with them, making them do indecencies on adults. And all this was on film ... There seemed to be no doubt that there was an organisation videoing children for a pornographic maker ... It looks like a mafia setup ...'

Chambers was equally emphatic: 'I know it happened. I'm absolutely convinced, not only that it was operating but that it probably still does ... We're talking about photographic evidence of children being sexually abused.'[40]

'So where's the hard evidence?' asked Reid. In a 1997 interview she recalled the response:

> There was this theory that 95 percent of paedophiles don't get caught. They're highly organised. They're very clever. They have friends in high places ... These experts explained it all to me. If I raised an eyebrow it quickly went down because there was always an answer – with literature and more literature to back it up. It all fitted together. It all made sense.[41]

In the absence of any locally made child pornography, Reid had to make do with a scratchy old foreign clip. 'This material was made overseas,' she explained in a voice-over, 'but it's typical of the sort of kid porn that would be produced in New Zealand.'

After effectively transforming Christchurch's phantom child pornography ring from an unsubstantiated rumour to a well-hidden reality, Reid concluded with a call for evidence: 'People know it exists but they can't prove it ... unless someone comes forward with photographs or videos no one will be prosecuted.'[42]

Six years later, Reid looked back on the episode with discomfort. At the time, though, she found the specialists she interviewed to be authoritative, plausible and persuasive, and the programme she made faithfully reflected their views:

> The media and public were being fed some disturbing messages and I reported them. Child pornography. It's happening. Here is a policeman. Here is a child welfare person. Here is a sex abuse expert. Here is a family. Here is some child pornography. Here is an Australian cop. Here it is. It's all here. But there wasn't anything tangible. I know because I did the story. It was really all hearsay.[43]

Compared to some newspaper coverage of the Ritual Action Group's bizarre claims, the *60 Minutes* story on the Christchurch child pornography ring was relatively restrained, but the nature of the medium, and the nature of the message, encouraged viewers to believe the worst. By the time the Family Violence Prevention Conference was over, a ritual abuse/child pornography ring scare had been unleashed in Christchurch. From then on, it was just a matter of time.

5.ii: A Model for Early Childhood Education

In the 1980s, once a ritual abuse panic had been unleashed in an American community, it tended to drift awhile in the murky waters of rumour before attaching itself, leech-like, to some unfortunate childcare centre. But not to any childcare centre; many such panics attached themselves to the most highly regarded preschools in their districts.

Virginia McMartin opened her day-care centre at Manhattan Beach in California in the mid-'60s. By the early '80s her work with young children had won her the town's most prestigious service award. Over the same period Violet Amirault, proprietor of the Fells Acres Day Care Centre in Malden, Massachusetts, developed her facility into the most respected early childhood unit in the area. Yet in 1984 the lives of both these middle-aged women were shattered by accusations of sexual depravity and sadistic molestation involving children in their care.[1]

Despite the previously unblemished records of childcare workers like McMartin and Amirault, and the lack of tangible evidence of child porn rings or ritual abuse cults at any preschool anywhere in the United States, throughout the '80s most American child protection workers treated ritual abuse claims as unquestionably true. Between 1986 and 1988 an influential survey of the alleged problem was conducted by a team led by New Hampshire sociologist David Finkelhor. This government-funded study considered 270 'substantiated' cases of child abuse, involving 1639 children, that were said to have occurred in American day-care centres between January 1983 and December 1985. Because not all alleged cases were reported, the researchers estimated that the 'real' figure for the period was around 550 cases involving 2500 children.

Finkelhor's team regarded a case as 'substantiated' if one child protection agency believed it to be true. Consequently, many 'ordinary' cases that had been rejected by police, prosecutors and the courts were included in the survey, as were more than three dozen cases involving patently absurd and impossible acts of ritual abuse.

On the basis of this manifestly unsound research, Finkelhor and his colleagues drew some startling conclusions. Their report, *Nursery Crimes: Sexual Abuse in Day Care* (1988), became the Bible for ritual abuse believers worldwide.[2]

The similarities in the abuse stories collected by Finkelhor's team from different day-care centres could be explained by the networking of therapists, and by their reliance on the same books and training manuals, but Finkelhor favoured a more sinister explanation. 'The occurrence of very similar ritualistic allegations in cases that clustered in certain regions, such as Southern California or the Pacific Northwest, have suggested to some investigators the possibility that large-scale organisations or cults may lie behind some of the ritualistic abuse', he wrote. To Finkelhor, the lack of tangible evidence proved how clever the cults were. 'Those perpetrators who were using day-care abuse for the production of pornography were apparently effective in disposing of it before it could be discovered.'

One of Finkelhor's most influential findings was that, while solitary acts of abuse were normally perpetrated by men, 40 percent of the perpetrators of group abuse were women. He also found that, compared to abuse committed by solitary men, multi-perpetrator, female or mixed-gender abuse was more likely to involve force or threats and include penetration, child-to-child sex acts, pornography and ritualism, and was more likely to cause serious and lasting harm.

When it came to characterising these sadistic female child molesters, Finkelhor was stumped. The accused women ranged in age from 16 to 77. Most were wives and mothers. Most had recognised childcare qualifications. They had no criminal records, or histories of drug or alcohol abuse. Indeed, 'Many had been highly regarded in their communities as church and civic leaders, intelligent businesswomen and generally law-abiding citizens'.

As one would expect, these highly regarded women ran highly regarded childcare centres. Many centres were so highly regarded that welfare agencies used them to give children from problem families a haven of stability in their otherwise chaotic lives. Most preschools in the Finkelhor survey were licensed; 82 percent had been inspected by the licensing authority in the year of the alleged abuse. Many centres had open-plan layouts; parents were free to come and go at any time. One of Finkelhor's 'substantiated' cases of ritual abuse took place in a centre with large windows and a playground facing a busy street corner. He concluded that 'traditional indicators of quality in day-care such as experience, education and reputation are not guarantees against the possibility of sexual abuse'.

Many of the children in the cases investigated by Finkelhor came from dysfunctional families. Reports of previous sexual victimisation were common. Many of the mothers were said to be emotionally unstable and marginally employed, and to suffer from drug and alcohol addictions and mental illness. Finkelhor concluded that backgrounds of this sort increased the vulnerability of children to sexual abuse in day-care.

Another significant finding was that day-care staff rarely detected or reported abuse. Instead, most complaints were initiated by dysfunctional mothers. At a 1989 ritual abuse conference, Roland Summit explained:

> Eccentric, alienated, unsocialised and paranoid personality types are needed to ferret out allegations of child sex abuse in the face of lack of evidence and conventional, well-socialised parents and professionals (who reinforce denial for their own mutual belief) ... It takes somebody paranoid to continue to express suspicion and to take the child from doctor to doctor until someone confirms that maybe there is abuse.[3]

As well as needing paranoid mothers, preschool ritual abuse cases needed disclosing children. According to Finkelhor, most children initially disclosed to parents 'spontaneously' or in discussions prompted by parental concerns – though deciding whether a disclosure was 'spontaneous' or 'prompted' often posed problems. Should a child singing a dirty song be classified as a 'spontaneous' disclosure, wondered Finkelhor, or as behaviour warranting further enquiry? The possibility that the child may have been simply having fun – and that, as Freud might have said, a dirty song is sometimes just a dirty song – does not seem to have occurred to Finkelhor. To further complicate the picture, some 'spontaneous' disclosures were triggered by sexual abuse prevention courses or television programmes. Others occurred 'after the child had been home for a period of time because of vacation, sickness or simply refusing to go to school'.[4]

Most prompted disclosures arose when parents questioned or examined their children. In some cases, concerned parents rook their children to therapists or doctors who diagnosed abuse. Parental suspicions were most commonly aroused by children's fears and nightmares. However, as Finkelhor noted, these were difficult to differentiate from normal developmental problems.

Finkelhor found that initial disclosures were at the mild end of the spectrum. It could take weeks, months or years of therapy before a child was able to talk about the horrors of multi-victim, multi-perpetrator abuse. Furthermore, ritual abuse disclosures were not always well received by parents. 'The cases of parental denial even in the face of investigators' convictions tended to be multiple-victim cases ... Such intractable denial can be explained, if not condoned,' he noted disapprovingly.

In *Nursery Crimes*, Finkelhor's message to an anxious world was that even the most prestigious day-care centres could harbour depraved, Devil-worshipping pornographers, and that seemingly kind and capable childcare workers could be perverted child abusers in secret.

The third issue of *Child Abuse and Neglect* for 1991 featured articles on the ritual abuse controversy. Most authors treated *Nursery Crimes* as an authoritative source of information on the subject.[5] In 1992 *Nursery Crimes* would have a profound effect on the development of the Christchurch Civic Crèche case.

• • •

The central-city Christchurch Civic Child Care Centre (popularly known as the Civic Crèche) opened in November 1976 in a building on the corner of Montreal and Hereford streets that became part of the Arts Centre complex. Initially, the crèche was a joint venture between the city council and the Christchurch Technical Institute.

Crèche ownership was not a new thing for the Christchurch City Council. In the depths of the Great Depression it had established the Cathedral Square Community Crèche.[6] From its inception, the Cathedral Square facility was ostensibly for the convenience of shoppers. To the conservative element in Christchurch society, shopping was an appropriate activity for wives and mothers. Consequently, until '70s feminism revolutionised attitudes towards the role of women, this 'shoppers' designation, together with its council ownership, conferred on the Cathedral Square crèche a measure of respectability that the backyard nurseries and philanthropic charities – the sort of facilities that had provided childcare for the children of widows, deserted wives and solo mothers since the days of Minnie Dean – could never hope to enjoy.

In the late '50s political activist Sonja Davies publicised the squalor of backyard nurseries and persuaded the government to set health and safety standards. Once the 1960 Child Care Centre Regulations were in place, Davies went on to unite childcare workers from facilities as diverse as shoppers' crèches and industrial nurseries into one organisation, and to develop a training programme for them.[7] But it wasn't until '70s feminists set out to persuade the nation that childminding services were not dumping grounds for the neglected offspring of unnatural, dysfunctional and irresponsible women that childcare centres emerged from their shadowy past and into the heart of a raging debate.

Most people agreed that mothers needed time to themselves, and that small children did not need their mothers every hour of the day. But everyone had their own ideas about how much of what sort of care, at what age, was best for small children. Broadly speaking, the concerns of feminists for women's rights, and the concerns of alternative lifestylers for children's liberation, were pitted against the concerns of child health professionals for the attachment needs of small children, and the concerns of religious conservatives for traditional family values. While argument raged, women with young children entered the workforce in droves.

When an early-'70s survey of Cathedral Square crèche users revealed a demand for half- and full-day childcare for mothers engaged in work and study, the Civic Child Care Centre was established. At its opening in November 1976, the chair of the Technical Institute Council described the facility as 'a model for early childhood education'. The following year a member of the institute's council stated that 'no other childcare centre in the country was the equal to the Christchurch centre'. At that time mainstream New Zealand recognised two sorts of early childhood services: one offering a few hours' education per week to the three- and four-year-old children of full-time mothers; the other offering full-time childcare to the infants, toddlers and preschoolers of working mothers. Facilities like the Christchurch Civic Crèche helped break down these stereotypes.[8]

In 1978 the Technical Institute withdrew its involvement, leaving the city council fully responsible for the Civic Crèche. In 1981 the council established a committee of council and parent representatives to handle the crèche's day-to-day management. The management committee's responsibilities included budgeting, staff appointments and policy matters. Overall financial responsibility was retained by the council.[9]

At regular intervals over the following decade moral conservatives and fiscal purists argued that, because childcare was not a core council activity, the council should sell the crèche to private enterprise. But there was always enough support, inside and outside the council, to keep the crèche in council ownership until its closure in 1992.

In January 1989 the crèche moved from the Arts Centre site to the Cranmer Centre, a two-storey building three blocks north along Montreal Street that housed a range of voluntary service organisations. At the time of the crèche closure these included: Marriage Guidance Council, THAW (The Health Alternatives for Women), Schizophrenia Fellowship, New Zealand Childcare Association, International Master Practitioners Guild (meditation and yoga), Eating Disorders Resource Centre, Home Birth Society, Epilepsy Association, ADARDS (Alzheimers and Related Disorders), SPELD (learning disabilities) and GROW (mental health). Several employees of these organisations used the Civic Crèche for their preschoolers. A 1989 crèche brochure offered:

> quality childcare for children aged 18 months to 5 years from many different racial, cultural, social and economic backgrounds. The Centre is open between 7.30 am and 5.00 pm, Monday to Friday, and takes children on either a full day or part day basis. The minimum number of hours per week is 8. The Centre has 12 children in the nursery area (18 months to 3 years) and 24 children in the preschool area (3 years to 5 years). The Centre is also licensed to take two school-age children as part of a holiday and after-school programme. A full range of stimulating and creative activities are offered, with a special extension programme for the 4 year olds. Included in the children's learning

experiences are Taha Maori, non-violent play and non-stereotyping. The balanced programme gives ample opportunity for both structured and free play activities. The convenient, central city location means the children have access to a wide range of extra-curriculum activities. Visits to the Botanical Gardens, Hagley Park, the Avon River, the Public Library and the Town Hall are a regular feature ... The Centre employs 11 permanent staff and is an equal opportunity employer, with male and female staff and a mixture of races and cultures.[10]

At the Arts Centre the nursery was upstairs. The preschool was downstairs. Children in the nursery were known as 'Wombles'. Children in the preschool were known as 'Big Kids'. In the Womble End the focus was on cuddling and nurturing. With the Big Kids, self-esteem, independence, cooperation and education were fostered. In both sections most activities took place in a large playroom with a kitchen and toilets attached. There were also two sleep rooms and a supervisor's office in the nursery section, and a second playroom in the preschool section.

At the Cranmer Centre, the Womble End and the Big End were side by side in a suite of rooms on the ground floor. The main playroom of each section opened through French doors to a picket-fence-enclosed outdoor play area. Indoors, a kitchen and staffroom opened into a short corridor between the sections. The corridor also contained the Big Kids' lockers.

In addition to the playroom, at the Womble End there was a sleep room, a room with laundry and toileting facilities and a 'quiet room' (which contained the Wombles' lockers and, paradoxically, a piano). At the Big End the toilet area (comprising a lobby with handbasins, plus two children's toilets and an adult's toilet) opened off the playroom. The toilet lobby could also be entered from the staffroom. The supervisor's office was on the far side of the playroom. At any time the supervisor could look directly from her office across the playroom and into the Big End toilet area.

On the crèche enrolment form, parents recorded their children's attendance times, provided basic personal and health information and signed an agreement that included the statement: 'I agree to my child being taken on outings from the Centre on foot or by pushchair or car in accordance with the Centre guidelines for such outings.'

The 'guidelines for such outings' were requirements relating to staff/child ratios, staff rosters and child attendance times. The staff/child ratios (1:4 for Wombles, 1:8 for Big Kids) meant that, by the time the crèche filled for the day, there were always at least three staff on duty in each section. During the busiest hours two extra staff were employed to maintain staff/child ratios during lunch and tea breaks. Throughout the day children were never left unattended, inside or outside, even when they were asleep.

The supervisor worked a 37-hour, five-day week (7.30am to 4pm or 9am to 5.30pm with an hour for lunch). She contributed to staff/child ratios between 10am and 1pm and spent the rest of the day on administrative tasks. The other permanent staff worked nine-day fortnights (i.e. they had one working day off every two weeks).

The staff shifts changed daily. The two staff who worked the 7.30am–3.30pm shift on Monday worked the 8.30am–4.30pm shift on Tuesday and the 9.30am –5.30pm shift on Wednesday. On Thursday they went back to the 7.30am shift. During the first and last hour of the day, when only two staff were on duty, they jointly supervised the children who arrived early or left late at the Womble End. This arrangement ensured that no staff member was ever in sole charge of a whole section of the crèche.

Weather permitting, the Womble staff took all their charges for a half-hour walk each morning in big prams and three-seater pushchairs. Big Kids walks (involving one or two staff with up to five children each) normally took place in the afternoon. The children and adults who went on Big Kids walks varied, depending on who was present that day, who wanted to go and who had time before the scheduled end of their crèche day. If a student teacher went along, two extra children were allowed to go. In addition to the organised walks, whenever a crèche worker went to the dairy or post office, he or she usually took a couple of Big Kids along. Once or twice a year the whole crèche (with additional parent helpers) took a day trip by bus or car to somewhere like the local wildlife park.

To give focus and variety to the crèche programme, the centre had a different theme each week. At monthly staff meetings, the previous month's themes were evaluated and the coming month's themes were brainstormed. The themes for February 1991 included 'Yellow' ('fruits, vegs, flowers, sunflowers; wear yellow; tints & shades; sun; collage; songs; different languages') and 'Boats and Floating Things' (walnut boats, corks, floating/sinking). The evaluations read: 'Yellow – colours always useful. Floating – wet clothes a nuisance; Kite flying great!'[11]

In 1991 the 11 permanent staff ranged in age from 20 to 53. They all had at least one appropriate qualification; some had several. There was a Karitane nurse, a kindergarten teacher, three Playcentre supervisors and three primary school teachers. Six staff had one or more qualifications in early childhood education from the Christchurch College of Education, the Christchurch Polytechnic, the New Zealand Childcare Association or the British Royal Society of Health. Eight had children of their own; one was a grandmother. The longest-serving staff were two women who had worked in the nursery since 1980. The five staff arrested in 1992 had worked at the centre for between five and nine years. Three had children of their own. The four arrested women had come to the crèche with prior experience and qualifications in working with young children. Peter Ellis had completed the field-based training for the New Zealand Childcare Association's Certificate in Childcare during his five and a quarter years at the centre.[12]

The Department of Social Welfare regarded the Civic Crèche as a 'superior childcare facility' and 'an excellent community resource'. In June 1991, the Christchurch DSW childcare liaison officer wrote: 'My dealings with the centre have been numerous, with many of the Department's clients subsidized to use this service. It is reassuring to know that these children are receiving such caring and consistent attention.'[13]

Over the years, scores of high school pupils, trainees from the New Zealand Nanny School, people on employment schemes and students from the Christchurch College of Education studied and worked at the Civic Crèche. These extra adults were not included in the staff/child ratios. During five-week blocks, college students participated in the crèche programme, observed interactions between children, parents and staff, and completed assignments of the centre's activities. While they were there, college lecturers visited and checked on their work. These students and lecturers were knowledgable, detached and impartial observers. They had ample opportunity to identify problems at the crèche, and every reason to report them. Over the years their reports were entirely positive.

In 1986 a college lecturer stated, 'It's a privilege for my students to work at the Civic.' In 1988–89 the same enthusiasm was conveyed to a student who later joined the crèche staff: 'The Civic was held up to us as *The Best. The Model Centre*. It had innovative programmes. It had a wonderful atmosphere. It had children from both sides of the tracks and they all got along beautifully. It was multiracial and it was marvellous. Everyone wanted to go there on section.' Even in 1991, the year of Peter Ellis's suspension, the college's Director of Early Childhood Programmes heaped praise on the centre's 'high quality programme', its 'respect for the needs of each child and his/her family' and its commitment to the 'fostering of gender equity, bicultural and multicultural awareness and the encouragement of creativity and independence in children'.[14]

I have found no evidence that the police interviewed any College of Education students or lecturers in their search for independent observers of the crèche, though they did interview the administrator, a cleaner and the staff of some of the organisations based in the Cranmer Centre. They did not interview Schizophrenia Fellowship employee David Close, even though, as a city councillor and justice of the peace with no personal connections with the crèche, he would have been a reliable and independent witness. Between January 1989 and June 1991, Close spent 20 to 30 hours a week in rooms directly above the Civic Child Care Centre. He was usually there in the morning, and often in the afternoon as well. He recalled:

> Every time I got up from my desk I could look through the window at the children. At morning tea time I would often stand at the window and look down. It was a very happy scene of children playing and learning. From time to time there would be a little outbreak of crying as a child got sand in his eyes, or somebody grabbed a toy off somebody else, but there were always appropriate interventions from the staff. On wet days I would hear them singing 'Puff the Magic Dragon'. Day after day, week after week, I heard the happy sounds of children's play coming up from that area below.[15]

• • •

There is no written history of the Civic Crèche, but the available documentation – a reasonably comprehensive collection of correspondence, photographs, attendance records, notices to parents and minutes of staff and management committee meetings – goes back to the early '80s. Those who knew the crèche, as parents, staff, council officers or education specialists, divide its history into three colourful chapters, each named after a crèche supervisor: the Liz Little chapter; the Dora Reinfeld chapter; the Gaye Davidson chapter. In memory, the hues of each chapter flow through to enliven the next, while, at the end, New Zealand's biggest child sexual abuse case stains the story like a great toxic chemical spill, pouring back through time, poisoning everything in its path. Whatever their views on the guilt or innocence of the Civic childcare workers, those who talk of crèche history cannot do so without reference to its unhappy demise.

Though Liz Little left the crèche in May 1983, and Peter Ellis had no contact with the place until August 1986, in 1992 the ghost of the Liz Little chapter came to haunt his life. This was partly because, at a time when the student radicals of the '70s were becoming the parents of the '80s, the crèche was a place where traditional ideas on acceptable childcare practice were questioned. The Civic's non-sexist, non-racist, non-violence policies were put in place in those early days. Toys, stories and nursery rhymes became gender neutral. War toys were banned. Freedom of expression became a cardinal value. Junk piled higher and higher and mobiles hung lower and lower. The line between creativity and chaos became increasingly blurred.[16]

Though it became modified over time, the political correctness instituted in the Liz Little era was a continuing feature of the Civic. Most people applauded it, or took it for granted, but for Susannah, who joined the Civic staff in 1989 from a background in Kohanga Reo, it was sometimes hard to take:

> You weren't allowed to identify a child's gender. I got into trouble for saying things like 'You're a lovely little girl' or 'Come on, son'. Gaye said to me, 'Su, I don't personally give a damn, but the parents are really into this.' … I was responsible for the Taha Maori, so I suggested we say a karakia before lunch. It was a management strategy more than anything – a way of getting the kids to sit quietly for a moment, instead of diving for the

food. There were all these discussions about what was appropriate. I spent ages writing a 'prayer' that didn't refer to God. I managed to make it sound like an ode to conservation, which went down really well with parents ... Christmas was another problem. We'd put heaps of energy into celebrating Chinese New Year and all sorts of things that had no particular relevance to our culture. I said, 'Accept who you are. What's wrong with children knowing the Christmas story?' But it was Civic philosophy because 10 years ago people had decided – no Christmas story.[17]

Another legacy of the Liz Little era was the interpersonal tension sown in the political ferment of the early '80s. 'Why has this man got it in for you?' I asked former supervisor Gaye Davidson's ex-husband, after reading Mr Ash's statement to the police at the time of the crèche case. 'He's never forgiven me for leaving the Trotskyites after the Springbok Tour,' he replied.[18]

Much of the political ferment took place at a large gothic-looking house in Avonside Drive. In a *New Zealand Listener* article on the crèche case Bruce Ansley described it as 'one of those inexplicable nerve junctions of the city ... a magical place whose currency was ideas, where radicalism was the norm, where people of the Left gathered, talked, acted'. It was, in effect, an urban commune, and over the years at least seven Civic Crèche workers lived at, or visited, the place. One of the Civic's first male childcare workers lived – and in 1984 killed himself – in the house. One of the house's residents was so committed to non-sexist childrearing that she refused to tell anyone the gender of her baby.[19]

None of this had anything to do with Peter Ellis. 'I'm probably the only person involved in the crèche case who's never been near the place,' he told me gloomily. Indeed, the only relevance of the house in Avonside Drive to the case lies in the fact that Ms Magnolia, the woman who triggered the investigation, made a statement to the police about her time as an occupant of the house, and about the sex life she shared with some of its inhabitants. As a result, the police tried to link the house to Peter Ellis, to child pornography and to some of the city's best-known homosexuals, massage-parlour proprietors, video-store owners and habitual criminals, but to no avail.[20]

The Civic Crèche entered a new era when Playcentre-trained Dora Reinfeld became supervisor in 1983. In articles in *North & South* and the *Listener*, Reinfeld was credited with pulling the crèche back from the brink of anarchy, though staff and parents who were there at the time regard this as an overstatement. 'Dora is very good at blowing her own trumpet,' observed Mr Sycamore, whose three children attended the crèche between 1982 and 1992. But he conceded that the place 'could have done with a bit of tightening up'.[21]

Under Reinfeld's supervision, children were taught to wash their hands after painting and before eating, to stop standing on the piano, to stop climbing in and out the windows and to stop saying 'fuck' all the time. Reinfeld also put a stop to the children's masturbation and sex play, and changed the centre's non-sex-role-stereotyping policy from gender neutrality to gender balance – which meant that boys were allowed to play with trucks, but not too much. Nudity continued to be a feature of outside play ('take your clothes off before you run under the hose'), but Reinfeld insisted that children wear knickers inside. And she introduced staff to the latest ideas on the detection and prevention of sexual abuse.[22]

With a change of supervisor, and a move away from revolutionary theories, the radical ideologues on the staff moved on, leaving behind a group of sensible, caring and professional childcare workers. To the staff who remained, Reinfeld's management style was a mixed blessing. They approved of her ideas, but found her dictatorial manner difficult to accept. 'We feel we're always being observed ... everyone feeling angry', someone wrote in the minutes of a staff crisis meeting in 1986.[23]

In 1987 Reinfeld was appointed lecturer in early childhood education at the Christchurch College of Education, and Gaye Davidson was appointed supervisor of the Civic Crèche. Davidson held a British Royal Society of Health Certificate in Child Care. After owning and operating her own crèche for three years, and working for Barnados for 18 months, she had begun working at the Civic Crèche in 1984.

In the wake of the crèche case, one of the explanations given for the downfall of the centre was that 'standards slipped' following Reinfeld's departure. A vigorous proponent of this view was Reinfeld herself. 'She says that if the guidelines, policies and administrative systems that were put in place during her time at the Civic survived under Davidson, the abuse would not have happened,' Cate Brett wrote in *North & South*.[24]

But crèche staff who experienced the transition are adamant that standards did not slip. Jan Buckingham, who had worked at the crèche since 1985, recalled: 'For me the crèche improved once Gaye became supervisor because she was strictly fair and very approachable and very caring. But she had expectations and we delivered them. We certainly didn't slack.' Sandi, who joined the staff in 1987, agreed: 'As a boss Gaye was fantastic. She was very professional. She never let matters ride. She was very direct in her dealings with staff.'[25]

Of the parents I spoke to who worried in advance about Reinfeld's departure, only one couple, Mr and Ms Aspen, felt that crèche management standards did slip. They said that one day their daughter came home with sweets. They had wanted to shield their child from lollies, softdrinks and potato chips until the age of eight, so this was a problem. They complained to Davidson. Then, concerned that the complaint may not be taken seriously, they asked the now-departed Reinfeld to intervene, which she agreed to do. To add to their concern, on a couple of occasions their daughter was out walking when they came to collect her. They also worried about the amount of dressing up and face painting at the crèche ('I have no problem with fantasy and having fun, but it seemed like they were doing it all the time'); about the posters on the noticeboard ('There was a flyer for "Lesbians for a Nuclear Free Aotearoa"... it is absolutely of no consequence to me whether someone is gay ... but the crèche seemed to have become a lesbian collective'); and about some of the other parents ('one had mixed feelings about children from such allegedly deprived backgrounds in the same crèche as their child'). So when their daughter was four and a half they sent her to a church school.[26]

Other crèche parents shifted their four-year-olds to more traditional preschools, but most couples who did so were not unhappy with the crèche, they just thought a structured environment would better prepare their child for primary school.

A counterweight to the Aspens' criticism exists in the form of a character reference written for Davidson in 1990. It states:

> I have known Gaye Davidson since 1986, when my daughter first started attending the Civic Child Care Centre. Since then, Gaye was appointed Supervisor, and I served two terms of office as Chairperson of the Management Committee. As Chairperson I worked closely with Gaye, covering a wide range of responsibilities, from staff to parents, and from budgets to a full relocation of the centre to its present site. During all this time, I found Gaye to be thoroughly professional in all her dealings with the children, parents and staff, with a high degree of expertise in performing her duties as working Supervisor, handling the day to day running of the centre as well as being a child-care worker. Gaye was also responsible, in conjunction with myself and the other members of the Management Committee, for developing, refining, and continuing the many policies and philosophies which have worked towards establishing and maintaining the Civic Child Care Centre's valuable reputation. I also came to know Gaye in a private capacity, and her family, meeting together on many social occasions, maintaining this contact still, and I found that in both her professional and private lives, she has always demonstrated the same open, warm, friendly, honest, reliable and caring nature. Gaye is a strong and vibrant person, and I can only strongly attest to her good character and believe she is a valuable asset to the Christchurch Civic Child Care Centre.[27]

The greatest outpouring of parental support for the Civic came in April 1991, when the city council voted to divest itself of crèche ownership. Among the 90 signatures on a petition opposing divestment were Mr and Ms Magnolia (who would lay the first complaint against Peter Ellis), Mr and Ms Arbutus (whose child's allegation would lead to Ellis's arrest), six parents whose children would become complainants in the court proceedings and nine of their supporters. The petition praised the staff for their 'strong commitment to their vocation and to the centre's philosophies of fostering the physical, emotional, social, cultural, creative and cognitive development of the children in their care'.[28]

In addition to the petition, 53 individuals and groups wrote to newspapers and the council, and made oral submissions to a special council meeting. Among their number were two MPs, three educational bodies, 12 future complainant parents and six of their supporters.[29]

At that time, 32 of the 78 families using the crèche were on low incomes,[30] but when it came to writing letters and making submissions, professional parents led the charge. Ms Rimu, who was new to Christchurch, was mystified by their passion:

> I remember coming home from a meeting and saying to my partner, 'These are middle-class parents with well-paid jobs! They shouldn't be relying on the council to provide them with childcare.' I thought if the Council relinquished the crèche we were perfectly capable of running it as a parent cooperative. But these very committed people were determined to 'Save the Civic'.[31]

The parental passion also astonished Susannah, who had never met anyone who worried about the gender of nursery rhyme characters before she joined the Civic staff:

> They had good educations and good jobs. They were financially secure. But when it came to parenting they were as insecure as any parents I've met. They over-analysed everything. They needed to get everything right – to be the perfect parent, to provide the perfect experience, to produce the perfect child – because they had no excuse not to.[32]

Ms Rimu made the same point:

> These parents were very, very intense. I'm much more laid back. I don't expect the structures my children are in to be perfect. No system is going to suit every individual child. You take the best and provide what you can from home. But that wasn't how these parents felt. They were very articulate, very well-connected, very credible, very well educated. They wanted everything to be perfect. They wanted someone to make it perfect. And they wanted someone to blame if it wasn't.[33]

Some professional parents told me that they agonised at length over placing their preschoolers in childcare. They wanted the best for their offspring, yet they were abandoning them to strangers for their own selfish and mercenary reasons. Year round, the volatile odour of parental guilt hung over the crèche like petrol fumes.

Bur among crèche families, the intense, professional parents were just one part of a diverse group. Ms Sycamore recalled:

> One of the attractions to us was that the crèche catered for a wide variety of people. There were people on social welfare subsidies who were stretched with their parenting skills. There were young people with strong views on how to parent, who were lost in the forest of this new game of raising children. There were relaxed, everyday, two-parent families where both parents worked. There were some very academic people. The staff coped with this amazing range extraordinarily well.[34]

Most parents on social welfare subsidies were solo mothers, or women in the throes of relationship breakups. Some had histories of drug or alcohol abuse. At the time of the crèche case, backgrounds of this sort were more common among the dozen or so families who were the source of ritual abuse allegations, and the more than 40 families who sought lump-sum compensation for the alleged abuse of their children (but uncommon among the 17 families whose children became involved in the court proceedings). A solo mother – whose child never disclosed any sexual abuse by any crèche worker – recalled her response to a compensation offer:

> This counsellor said, 'You know you can claim $10,000 from ACC.' She didn't even say 'up to', she just said '$10,000'. I was on the benefit and that was a lot of money. Everyone was doing it. I didn't have a problem. Where do I sign? No problem. None whatsoever. The counsellor put in a report saying that my daughter was completely screwed up. I wondered if she'd got the kids muddled up, or maybe she wrote the same report for everyone. Anyway, the money came through really quickly.[35]

When scandal engulfed the crèche in November 1991, the parent group split. Some stood firmly behind the staff, some became complainants. Others supported one group or the other. Most walked away. To the bewilderment of the staff, the groups they considered most likely to support them – the parents who had enthused over the crèche's politically correct policies, and the parents they had supported through their personal crises – were the ones who turned on them when the chips were down.

By the time the case reached the courts, the parents who did not walk away had formed two distinct groups. The flag bearers for one group were the parents of complainant children, and, for the other group, the parents who appeared as witnesses for the defence. In addition to their views on the crèche case, the members of these groups differed in their occupations, in the duration and stability of their relationships and in the number of children for whom they were joint biological parents.

Among the seven parents who became defence witnesses and their partners there were four teachers, two restaurateurs, a nurse, an accountant, a dentist and a financial director. None were unemployed, and none were social workers, counsellors or therapists. All were in stable long-term relationships. They had, between them, an average of three children per family. There were no twins.

Five of the 21 complainant parents in the trial of Peter Ellis worked in the sexual abuse field. The rest came from a range of occupations. One couple had four children, the rest had one or two. One parent was not in a relationship at the time of the trial. Some parents had children by other relationships. There were three sets of twins. (For those who wonder about the relevance of twins, it could be argued that, because of the closeness of twins, an alarming idea, once sown in the imagination of one twin, may be quickly transmitted to the other.) Three complainant children had close relatives who were members of parliament. Several had influential grandparents. When the trial was over, guilty verdicts were returned on charges involving seven children. Five of their parents worked in the sexual abuse field.

The sorts of people these complainant parents were, and the lives they led, would become major elements in the development of the crèche case. But the central element was Peter Ellis himself.

5.iii: Peter Ellis

'I always knew Peter was a little bit different,' Lesley Ellis said of the eldest of her four children. 'I think I always knew Peter was homosexual.' Despite being primarily homosexual, Ellis also had sexual relationships with women. Over the 11 years prior to his imprisonment, he had, in order, a five-year relationship with a man, a two-year relationship with a woman and a four-year relationship with a man.[1] I therefore thought it prudent to ask him how he defined himself. He wrote:

> Gloria Gaynor says it best (in song): 'I am what I am.' I say, 'I am Peter therefore.' My family says, 'You are Peter and we love you.' My friends say, 'You are Peter, please don't change.' ... In a relationship with a woman I was, for want of a better word, bisexual, and with a man I was monogamous – point is, I actually never stopped to observe the boundaries as each of these people were, first and foremost, my partner and friend. Their actual sex was a minor detail that wasn't my problem and seldom appeared to be a problem for anyone I knew. A case of 'He is Peter therefore.' ... I am happy being me.[2]

At the time of his arrest on 30 March 1992, 34-year-old Peter Ellis was a qualified and experienced preschool teacher. Both his parents were teachers, but the path that brought him to his chosen career – like everything else about him – was unconventional.

On leaving school at the end of 1975, Peter Ellis picked tobacco, travelled overseas and worked in restaurants. In the early '80s, after a period on the dole, he found part-time work in a bakery, which gradually built up to full-time work. A couple of years later, when he left the bakery and went back on the dole, the authorities found he had received more than his entitlement in dole payments during his earlier transition to full-time work. As a result, in 1986 Ellis was convicted of 'misleading a social welfare officer'. For this, his first offence, he was sentenced to 80 hours' community work.

Faced with a choice of serving his sentence at an animal shelter or the Civic Child Care Centre, Ellis chose the crèche. It was a choice that Detective Colin Eade would later regard as deeply suspicious. After all, Ellis kept dogs, cats, rabbits, ferrets, budgies, fantail pigeons and fowls. He was fond of animals. Why didn't he go to the animal shelter? According to Ellis, the decision was a practical one. He could ill-afford the return bus fare to the shelter each day. He had enough animals already and did not want to be tempted to take more. The big house in Hereford Street where he boarded was an easy 20-minute walk from the Civic. He got on well with kids. So he chose the crèche.

Allowing people convicted of minor offences to serve their community sentences at the Civic Crèche, provided they were suited to childcare work, was in keeping with the centre's non-stereotyping, give-everybody-a-fair-go philosophy. For the placement of Peter Ellis, the issue of his suitability was inextricably linked to his sexuality. It wasn't just that he was a man – having male staff had always been part of the Civic ethos. It wasn't just that he was homosexual – gay men had worked at the Civic before him. With Ellis, the issue was that he was (if not to himself, then certainly to the world at large) blatantly homosexual. He wore bright clothes and makeup. He had long hair, long fingernails and rings on almost every finger. He walked with a mincing gait. He had a sharp tongue and an outrageous sense of humour. Working with Peter Ellis would be like working with Julian Clary or Quentin Crisp. An item on the agenda of the crèche staff meeting of 18 August 1986 read: 'Probation people want to know how we feel about a homosexual working in the Centre.'[3]

In the months preceding that meeting, homosexual rights had been vigorously debated. Some folk argued that homosexuality was a normal variant in the human condition; others claimed it was a gross perversion. In July 1986 the Homosexual Law Reform Bill was passed by five votes after a clause banning discrimination on the grounds of sexual orientation had been dropped. Among those opposing the Bill was New Zealand's top-ranking police officer, John Jamieson. 'I can't divorce my private life and belief from my professional life,' he told the *New Zealand Herald* in 1993. 'My general response to my job is permeated by my Christian beliefs and ethics.' Among his beliefs was a conviction that homosexuals should not be allowed to work with children.[4] But, unlike Jamieson, the Civic Crèche staff were progressive liberals. In August 1986 they made Peter Ellis welcome.

More often than not, people sentenced to community work at the Civic came in for a few hours and then wandered off, never to be seen again, but Peter Ellis worked two energetic 40-hour weeks. In her August 1986 report, supervisor Dora Reinfeld wrote: 'Peter ... provided some hilarious puppetry shows – one of which we had to abandon as staff and children "got out of hand".' By the time Reinfeld made her next monthly report, Ellis was a relieving childcare worker.

'Peter Ellis has fitted in extremely well and puts lots of energy into programme planning. Fantastic team spirit,' she wrote.[5]

Peter Ellis also impressed the crèche parents. When the centre closed for a three-week summer break on Friday 19 December 1986, Ms Cypress asked him to babysit her three-and-a-half-year-old-daughter Zelda for the two-and-a-half working days left before Christmas.

Ms Cypress was a stressed and busy woman. She worked by day, and pursued university studies at night. Zelda had been in full-time childcare since she was a year old. Ms Cypress later admitted that she and her husband spent little time with Zelda during her preschool years, and the child was often 'the meat in the sandwich' of their domestic problems.

On the days Ellis babysat Zelda in December 1986, Ms Cypress dropped her at 404 Hereford Street on the way to work and picked her up on the way home. According to Ellis, he took Zelda into the kitchen for food and drinks, and into the living room to watch *Playschool*, but he never took her to his bedroom or any other upstairs part of the house. Most of the time he and Zelda wandered the town – Christmas shopping, looking at decorations, visiting pet shops and admiring the festive grotto in a big department store. In a statement to the police five-and-a-half years later, Bruce, the owner of 404 Hereford Street, said:

> I have no recollection whatever of seeing the child or her mother. I had told Peter that under no circumstances was he allowed to keep a child at the house. At all. My house has tempting things for little fingers to break and I am adamant about that. So he apparently took her out for walks or whatever. On one of those days I was putting up Christmas decorations, and that's something I can't do when anyone's in the house. She may have come in for a drink of water, but I can't remember seeing her.

On at least one occasion during the nine months between Peter Ellis's arrival at the crèche in August 1986 and his departure from 404 Hereford Street in May 1987 a group of crèche children and staff went to see his animals at the house. Five and a half years later, the stories told by former crèche children to anxious parents and sexual abuse investigators led police to regard the house in Hereford Street as a hotbed of ritual abuse and child pornography. It would therefore be useful to know when and how often crèche children visited 404 Hereford Street, which staff accompanied them, and what happened while they were there.

The crèche attendance registers of the period – in which walks were normally recorded – have not survived. Some staff recall visiting the place, but their vague and disparate recollections tell us more about the fallibility of memory than about the events in question. However, there is general agreement on four points: that children were taken to see Ellis's animals on one occasion during Dora Reinfeld's time at the centre (that is, between Ellis's arrival in late August 1986 and Reinfeld's departure in late January 1987); that three or four staff, and eight to 10 children, went along; that they saw lots of baby animals (kittens, puppies, baby ferrets, day-old chickens and newborn angora rabbits); and that Ellis provided juice and biscuits for the visitors. Ellis recalled telling the children that, if they wanted to stay with him, he would put them in cages with the other baby animals. 'They thought it was a great joke,' he said. Bruce recalled that Ellis had sought his permission for the visit. 'It seemed a nice thing to do. But when a procession of women and children came through the gate I retreated upstairs until they had gone,' he said.

No one could remember exactly when the visit occurred or who went on it, but my best guess is that it took place soon after the crèche reopened on 12 January 1987 following the Christmas/New Year break, because Reinfeld's school-age son went along, and that was the only time the crèche was open and schools were closed when Reinfeld and Ellis worked at the Civic. Also, crèche attendance figures were at their lowest in early January (because most crèche families were away on holiday). Indeed, early January was probably the only time all year when staff/child ratio allowed three or four childcare workers to leave the centre with eight to 10 children for an outing lasting more than an hour.

In January 1987 only two of the 21 children who were the subject of charges against Ellis attended the crèche (Zelda Cypress and Molly Sumach). They would have been three-and-a-half, and two-and-a-half years old respectively. Because of the difficulty people have in remembering anything before the age of four, if Zelda or Molly went on the trip to 404 Hereford Street, it is unlikely that either of them would have remembered it.

Some crèche staff also visited 404 Hereford Street outside working hours, usually to collect Ellis for a meeting or social function. On at least one of those occasions crèche parent Ms Kowhai and her children were also visiting Ellis. These other visits have made it difficult for the adults involved to remember who was present on which occasion.

In February 1987 Gaye Davidson replaced Dora Reinfeld as crèche supervisor. In May 1987 Ellis and his menagerie left Hereford Street and moved in with Ms Kowhai. From there, at the end of 1988, he divested himself of most of his animals and moved into an upstairs flat on the corner of Colombo and Armagh streets. A year later he moved to a flat in Tancred Street with room for animals in the back yard. He lived there until his imprisonment in 1993.

As far as any adults can remember, and as far as the crèche records show, there were no crèche visits to 404 Hereford Street after Reinfeld left, either during the three months that Ellis still lived there or after he had moved away. There are no adult memories or written records of any crèche visits to Ellis's other homes.

During Reinfeld's time, apart from her praise for Ellis's work, the only other surviving comment about him appears in the minutes of the September 1986 staff meeting: 'Support Peter in toileting girls'.[6]

In retrospect, that comment seems as harmless as a patch of disturbed soil above a double-chambered landmine. One chamber was primed by Ellis's reluctance to toilet children, especially when they had soiled themselves. 'It's an aspect of childcare I don't find particularly attractive,' he told me. 'Peter would make any excuse to get out of it,' confirmed Sandi. 'He hated poos or wees or sick or snot or anything like that.'[7] Ellis's unwillingness to pull his weight in cleaning up children was an ongoing source of irritation to his female colleagues.

The other chamber was primed by the conflicting messages with which male childcare workers were bombarded. One was that young children benefited from contact with men in nurturing roles. The other was that men could not be trusted around small children.

By the mid-'80s child molestation allegations in Christchurch were escalating at an alarming rate. As a leading-edge supervisor, Reinfeld responded by introducing 'one of the very first child sex abuse prevention programmes in day-care'.

For adults, Reinfeld's programme included a rule that male staff were to be chaperoned during nappy changing.[8] For children, her programme was based on audiotapes of two episodes of *Grandpa's Place* (a children's radio programme), and on two children's books: Jan Hindman's *A Very Touching Book* (1983) and Lynda Morgan's *Katie's Yukky Problem* (1986).

The books distinguished between 'good' and 'bad' (or 'yukky' or 'secret') touching, and told children which people were allowed to touch which parts of their bodies for what reason. They also told children to say 'no', and tell a responsible adult, if the wrong person touched them in the wrong place, in the wrong way, for the wrong reason.

Programmes of this sort are used widely throughout the Western world. Supporters claim that children who have been taught the rules of touching are less likely to be sexually abused than those who have not.[9] Critics claim that the rules are impossibly complex and confusing for small children. Lucy Sullivan, of the Department of Psychology at the University of Sydney, wrote:

> Imagine explaining to a two- or three-year-old, as parents have seriously been instructed to do, that mummy can touch you here, here, here and here, and daddy can touch you here, here, here but not here; brother and aunty can touch here and here, but not here and here; uncle can only touch here, but you must let the doctor (even more remote) touch here, here, here and here.[10]

Guidelines issued to teachers in recent years, and anecdotes from the community, suggest that sexual abuse prevention programmes of this sort cause diffuse anxiety and undue sexual self-consciousness in both children and adults. As a result, the risks of children misinterpreting casual affection or routine toileting assistance as abuse have increased, and healthy, unselfconscious, physical contact between children and adults has become largely a thing of the past.

Complainant parents whose children attended the Civic Crèche between 1986 and 1991 used *A Very Touching Book* and *Katie's Yukky Problem* to impress the rules of touching on their children from an early age. Yet these children did not complain of being sexually abused by crèche staff until 1992 (by which time they had left the crèche). There are two possible explanations for this: either no abuse took place; or 'good and bad touching' programmes don't work.

In February 1987 Gaye Davidson became crèche supervisor and Peter Ellis was accepted for the field-based New Zealand Childcare Association training course. In March, Davidson and the crèche management committee recommended Ellis for a permanent appointment to the preschool section of the centre. Dora Reinfeld was one of his referees, but Alistair Graham, head of the city council unit responsible for the crèche, was not enthusiastic. At that time – as the probation officer's query shows – people could question the suitability of gay men for childcare work without fear of being labelled homophobic. By 1997, when I interviewed Graham, they could not. This constraint made for a very circumspect conversation.

> AG: The only time I've actually challenged an employment recommendation was when Peter was appointed. Now that's not just because he was a male – and that was something different too in childcare, it really was: was Peter the most appropriate person to appoint to a childcare centre?
>
> LH: Why did you question it?
>
> AG: I'd seen Peter. He'd been discussed often at parents' meetings. I just wasn't sure he was the most appropriate person to have in a highly rated childcare centre.
>
> LH: Why?
>
> AG: The council was questioning whether they should be involved in childcare. Anything that was seen as different or controversial we had to manage very carefully. I had real reservations about Peter.
>
> LH: What would you say those reservations were?
>
> AG: About his ... his ... style ... his ... character ... his ... manner ... um ...
>
> LH: What was it about them?
>
> AG: Well, just ... I didn't ... just little glimpses I had on the occasional interaction – I don't recall absolutely those reservations now. But they [Davidson and the crèche management committee] persuaded me – don't be such a conservative old so and so.

An issue that Alistair Graham would have raised, had he been aware of it in 1987, was Ellis's fondness for alcohol. This was not an issue at his trial, but because he was widely condemned in the forum of public opinion as an alcoholic who should never have been allowed near children, the matter needs to be addressed here.

Alcohol, mainly in the form of sweet sherry, was a regular feature of Ellis's life for some years prior to his placement at the Civic Crèche. During a stressful period in 1984 he began drinking heavily. His employer suggested he take time off to get treatment. After an assessment, treatment was not recommended, but Ellis reduced his alcohol consumption.

The crèche placement was Ellis's first day job in years. While most tipplers work during the day and drink in the evening, Ellis's usual pattern had been to drink during the day and work at night. During periods of unemployment, the daytime drinking continued. Consequently, when he began working at the crèche, he thought it reasonable to call into a nearby bar at lunchtime.

I found no mention of Ellis's drinking in the crèche records of Reinfeld's time, and she did not mention it in an interview with city council officer Sally Latham at the time of Ellis's arrest.[11] According to Latham, Reinfeld thought that Ellis's childcare work was 'brilliant', and that he had a good relationship with children and parents. Latham also reported that, shortly after he began work at the crèche, Reinfeld gave Ellis two warnings: one for being too familiar with a female staff member; the other for dealing too harshly with a situation involving a child. (Ellis recalled only the first occasion. He said that Reinfeld took exception to him bumping Solvig's breast when they were horsing around. However, he felt that, considering the size of Solvig's breasts, Reinfeld was making a mountain out of a molehill.) Later, in an interview following Ellis's conviction – a time when Reinfeld would have been under pressure to defend her decision to employ him – she mentioned his alcohol consumption. She said she had warned him about his drinking. The differences between Reinfeld's two interviews illustrate an important point: the stories people tell about the past vary with the circumstances of the telling.

Reinfeld's reported later comments also raise the issue of what exactly constitutes a 'warning'. According to the Christchurch City Council's procedures for dealing with employees whose work is not up to standard, the supervisor initially 'speaks to' or 'counsels' the employee. If that doesn't work, the supervisor issues a formal oral warning. This advises the employee that if he or she doesn't shape up a written warning is likely to follow. Written warnings are serious. They detail the complaint and advise the employee that any further transgression of the same sort may result in dismissal. Such warnings normally stay on the employee's file for 12 months. Then, if there are no further problems, the warning is removed. However, if the employee is persistently troublesome, a final warning may be issued. If this goes unheeded, he or she may be dismissed.

Latham reported that Reinfeld's warnings were withdrawn from Ellis's file after 12 months. This implies that the warnings were in writing, but the records of the period show that Reinfeld held Ellis in high regard. She wrote and spoke of his work with enthusiasm. She encouraged him to train as a childcare worker. She took him onto the crèche payroll. She acted as his referee. These are not the actions of a dissatisfied supervisor. The time factor also needs to be considered. Given the steps that must be undertaken before a written warning is issued, there would hardly be time to issue one, let alone two or three, warnings between Ellis's first day on the council payroll (10 September 1986) and Reinfeld's last day at the crèche (late January 1987). Then there is the matter of Ellis's employment status. After completing his community service Ellis worked for Reinfeld as a relieving childcare worker. His official status was 'casual'. This meant that, if his performance was unsatisfactory, she could have sent him on his way. There was no need for a formal warning. These points suggest that if Reinfeld 'warned' Ellis back in 1986, for whatever reason, she did not – as was later assumed – put him on written notice.

However, there is evidence that when Gaye Davidson became supervisor she did warn Ellis about his lunchtime drinking. In her first report to the management committee she stated that 'Peter has been a great success with children and parents alike'. But she also registered concern about his drinking, even though 'in no way has it interfered with his work'. Davidson told me that those comments referred to Ellis's lunchtime drinking. She said that when she made it clear to him that going to the pub at lunchtime was no way for a childcare worker to behave, he stopped the practice.

Four years later, when Ellis became offensively drunk at a crèche parents' party, Davidson reprimanded him, and discussed the problem with a council personnel officer. Again the point was made that he was a good childcare worker. Notes of the discussion were placed on Ellis's file but no further action was taken.

Two references to Ellis's drinking over a five-and-a-quarter-year period, neither of which indicated it affected his work, is hardly cause for serious concern. However, by his own admission Ellis was 'an enthusiastic drinker', and during the 19 months between losing his job and the end of his trial there were times when he drank heavily.

On 22 June 1993, Ellis was sentenced to 10 years in prison. That evening a group of his supporters gathered to discuss the implications of Crown Solicitor Brent Stanaway's successful prosecution. They wondered how Ellis would cope without his alcohol, and without his pets – especially the puppies named after police officers, and the hens named after his female colleagues (the big placid one was Jan, the fussy little one was Marie, the bossy one was Gaye). 'Maybe he'll get a spider called Stanaway,' someone suggested. In the event, Ellis acquired no creepy crawlies, real or hallucinatory, and experienced no alcohol withdrawal symptoms in prison.[12] This suggests that his alcohol consumption was not as great as his critics claimed.

While no one ever saw Peter Ellis behave in a sexually inappropriate way with any child, there were a couple of aspects of his behaviour which, along with his drinking, came under scrutiny at the time of the crèche case. One area of concern was the risque comments that sometimes peppered his conversations with adults. 'Stupid gay-boy talk', as one acquaintance put it.

Ellis's sexual conversations were kept out of the earshot of children, and related to the activities of consenting adults in private. Often they involved no more than a passing innuendo. ('Peter,' I said, 'I'll need some biographical background on you.' 'How graphic do you want it?' he replied, arching an eyebrow.) Sometimes he discussed unconventional adult sexual practices with people he regarded as friends. On other occasions he sought to shock the shockable. During the police inquiry a couple of crèche workers recalled that during 'Black Week' (the week in August 1991 when the theme at the centre was Black), Ellis told them he used felt pens to paint his partner's penis black.

When he was drunk, Ellis's risque comments could cross the border from funny to boorish. But on such occasions it was his drinking, rather than his conversations, that concerned his colleagues.[13] It wasn't until the crèche inquiry of 1991–92, when the activities of consenting adults in private became the subject of intense police interest, that Ellis's conversations became an issue.

The other aspect of his behaviour that came under scrutiny during the crèche inquiry – his boisterous and teasing interactions with children – was often cause for comment, and sometimes cause for concern, throughout his childcare career.

In a 1996 survey of men in childcare, Dr S.E. Farquhar of Massey University found that the interactions of male preschool teachers with children differed from those of their female colleagues in four main ways: men were better at controlling unruly children; they were more physically interactive; they were more involved in children's play; and they had more fun. These same qualities, together with his creativity, featured in descriptions of Peter Ellis's work given to me by parents and staff of the Civic Child Care Centre.[14]

Ellis's ability to control unruly children was recognised and used by staff, parents and children alike. Susannah used it for her Taha Maori programme: 'Peter could keep a group focused for longer than any of us. When I wanted to take children for singing, I'd get Peter to bring them together and keep them quiet while I did the nice stuff in front. He was great. He'd try really hard to do whatever I wanted them to do and the kids would follow him.'[15]

Several staff recalled parents using the threat 'I'll tell Peter!' when their children were misbehaving. Some staff admitted to using the threat themselves. As for the kids, Ellis said they often ignored the childcare worker nearest them and sought him out when they wanted to 'tell on' someone: 'They'd take great delight in dobbing someone in, knowing full well that they'd get a better reaction from me. I'd say, "I told you not to pick flowers. The flowers are for everyone. You picked them. Go inside."'[16]

Ellis's physical interactions with children were more vigorous than those of his colleagues. When they played 'What's the Time Mr Wolf?' he'd chase the children, snapping and snarling, threatening to eat them up. He'd even chase them through the tunnel (the concrete tunnel in the outside play area at the Arts Centre site; a folding canvas tunnel at the Cranmer Centre site). He told television journalist Melanie Reid:

> I got down to the children's level. I was prepared to do wheelbarrow races. I wasn't just prepared to sit in the corner and read stories. We were out there to have fun. We were in the sandpit digging great big holes, not just making sandcastles. I'd have a slide down the slide. I'd get on the swings and have a swing. When we went for a walk in the gardens we'd run under the sprinklers and hide in the piles of leaves.[17]

His boisterous games were a constant source of astonishment to Sandi:

> He'd do things that really shocked me, but the kids loved them. Like he'd line them up with a mattress on the floor behind them. Then he'd hurl another mattress at them. This line of kids would fall back, sandwiched between the two mattresses. It was the funniest most bizarre thing. They'd beg him: 'Can we play the mattress game?!'[18]

Ellis's teasing was another aspect of his work that his colleagues had mixed feelings about. 'He'd play silly games,' Susannah recalled. 'Like an annoying brother, or a silly uncle, or the family tease. The kids seemed to like it. In fact they'd often initiate it. But it wasn't my style.'

The problem was that sometimes Ellis didn't know when to stop, and on those occasions excited kids suddenly became crying kids. Like the time he pretended to take the noses off children, and pretended to put them back on other children. It was all good fun until he pretended to throw a child's nose over the fence. It landed on a car. The car drove off …

For Gaye Davidson, supervising Ellis could be hard work. In her September 1988 report she wrote: 'As Peter sometimes tends to overdo activities and can also step over the boundaries of centre policies, Marie's [Big End head teacher] influence works well here. Fortunately he responds well to having limits put on his activities, but it can be tiring keeping an eye on him …'[19]

When a couple of little heads got banged together, Davidson put a stop to the mattress game. When she saw that Ellis had hung a child on the picket fence by his overalls, and that other kids were begging to be hung up too, she put a stop to that game. And so on.

The centre policy that Peter Ellis transgressed most often was the non-smoking one. Taking a group of children for a walk in the Botanic Gardens provided an ideal opportunity for a cigarette or two (when the children were running about freely, or when they were sitting quietly finishing the iceblocks he bought them as a treat). When he couldn't get away from the crèche during the afternoon, Ellis sometimes had a clandestine cigarette in the toilet.

One of the most admired aspects of Ellis's work was his creativity. Ms Maple recalled one of his midwinter creations:

> He'd arrived early and turned some climbing equipment into a mountain in the middle of the playroom with lots of white newsprint on top for snow and lots more scrumpled up into snowballs. The children came in and climbed the mountain and had a snowball fight. There was mess everywhere, but the kids had a wonderful time.[20]

Keeping an eye on Ellis's creativity was, for his supervisor, more hard work. One day he filled the wooden fort with paper snowballs, but when a child hiding under the 'snow' got jumped on, Davidson stopped the game. Another day, when Ellis took the children outside to paint in the rain, they clashed again: 'Gaye said, "It's raining. You can't." I said, "But it's warm rain. It's dry rain. It's not drenching rain." We sprinkled Lux flakes around and painted on the wet concrete. The rain made the paint spread out. The kids had a great time.'[21]

Most parents were initially cautious of Ellis. When the time came for her daughter to join the Big Kids, Ms Mahogany decided to check him out:

> I went and observed Peter because I wasn't sure about him. I thought he was queer. I decided he was actually very good with children. I watched him making pancakes. He had children in a group around the electric frypan. I liked the way he chattered about the pancakes, and let the children flip them over, but at the same time he knew where everyone's hands were – they weren't touching the cord and they weren't going to get burnt – and they were all getting their share of pancakes.[22]

Mr Mahogany was also hesitant at first:

> My first impression was that he was an exhibitionist homosexual. I thought, crumbs, I don't want my kids involved with him. But when I got to know him I kept scolding myself for that impression, because I felt very much at ease with him. I found he had the same sort of feelings about life as I had.[23]

Ellis's boisterous games attracted Ms Beech's attention: 'He'd have the kids sitting on the floor in a pretend boat singing, "Row, row, row your boat, gently down the stream. Throw the children overboard and listen to them scream." Then they'd all tip over and scream. They absolutely loved it.'

Several parents commented to me on Ellis's teasing. Most concluded that, because the children he teased were the ones who enjoyed it and sought it out, it wasn't a problem. Mr Sycamore recalled:

> We'd go through this performance every morning. 'Oh dear, look who's here,' from Ellis. 'Oh fancy you being on today,' from Keziah. Peter would tease and she would give it back. The sparring would go on. They were obviously glad to see each other. We knew she was going to have a good day.[24]

As his colleagues perceived it, Peter Ellis enjoyed 'having a good gossip' with parents. The fact that parents often turned to him for child-rearing advice never ceased to amaze them. He spent more time talking to parents than tidying up, they complained. For their part, parents valued the interest Ellis took in them and their families. Ms Rimu recalled: 'I had a miscarriage and Peter was lovely then. He was also very tuned into my daughter. Working at the crèche wasn't just a job to him. He was clearly interested in the children as individuals. He remembered things they'd told him that made them special.'[25]

Supervisor Gaye Davidson told me that most of the time Ellis was not 'over the top'. Complaints about him were more likely to come from his colleagues than from parents, and those complaints were infrequent. However, his work went through a rough patch in late 1988/early 1989. 'He was having domestic problems and he wasn't able to come to work and leave them behind,' recalled Davidson. 'He was starting to be a little bit aggressive in his handling of the children.' On 15 December 1988 Davidson issued him with a verbal warning about his 'performance and conduct'. On 7 February 1989 Alistair Graham issued him with a written warning, in which he advised Ellis that he had:

> 1. demonstrated a lack of support and seeming indifference to children's emotions (e.g. leaving children for whom you were responsible to cry unconsoled);
>
> 2. been frightening children with either threatening physical posture, excessive physical force or blatant verbal threats, (e.g. standing over children using your height as a means of power, throwing items to or at children using your strength in an excessive manner, and generally verbally threatening children in your care);
>
> 3. consistently being sarcastic in a manner which knowingly causes unnecessary concern and bewilderment to the young children in your care. The effects of this sarcasm is disturbing to the children … This written warning will remain in force for one year.[26]

According to Ellis, the letter referred to incidents in which:

> I threw a pillow at a child during a pillow fight. He fell over and thought he was hurt. I saw he wasn't, but Debbie made a soothing noise and he burst into tears. She accused me of being insensitive and complained to Gaye. I think [Molly Sumach's] parents complained around that time too. [Molly] asked me what I thought of her pink dress. I said I liked her blue overalls.[27]

As Ellis saw it, his comment to Molly was a fun way of starting a conversation:

> If a child asked me what I was doing, I might say, 'I'm standing on my head juggling six elephants.' Back would come the reply, 'No you are not!' My rejoinder, 'Then what am I doing?' Nine times out of ten the child would know what I was doing, and I'd have started a conversation with a child that was thinking for itself. Obviously the child that didn't know what I was doing would be informed, though it is possible that a child went home and told its parents that I was standing on my head juggling six elephants.[28]

Alistair Graham's warning had the desired effect, but it was not removed from Ellis's file after a year. When the police seized his file in April 1992 it was still there.

• • •

Ultimately, the person on whom greatest responsibility fell for deciding whether Ellis was an appropriate person for childcare work was Ms Rata, Ellis's tutor in the New Zealand Childcare Association (NZCA) training programme. The NZCA's field-based programme was designed for people already working in childcare, and especially for people who lacked the confidence, the secondary qualifications and the financial resources to pursue early childhood education courses in tertiary institutions. Ms Rata was a Kohanga Reo mother when she undertook her NZCA training. After completing the course in 1987 she provided Maori input for the NZCA programme. In June 1988 she joined the NZCA permanent staff. As one of three Christchurch-based tutors she was responsible for a group of 10 students who were, at that stage, halfway through their training. Peter Ellis and Susannah (who began the course as a Kohanga Reo mother and went on to join the Civic staff in 1988) were members of that group.

In 1995, when I recorded separate interviews with Ms Rata and fellow tutor Alison Mary, the wounds created by the crèche case were still raw. It was impossible to discuss Ellis's training without first addressing the impact of the allegations against him on their lives. For her part, Ms Rata had been in and out of the Civic a lot, as a crèche parent and as Ellis's tutor, but when the allegations arose she was thrown into confusion:

> The Civic was a high-quality centre, but the whole childcare community turned incredibly nasty when this thing blew up. The initial reaction from most people was – no, no, it couldn't have been – followed by doubts. Even I doubted, because I didn't know what the accusations were. It was all so hush-hush and confidential. You can't fight shadows if you don't know what shape they're taking. You can't say – this didn't happen – if no one will tell you what they're talking about. The backlash against people who said 'No! I didn't see anything. I didn't! I didn't!' was really, really ghastly. I began to think: what's wrong with me? I didn't see anything. This whole thing has been a major trauma in my life. The consequences are so ongoing. I've leaked more tears into my pillow about this furore than anything else.[29]

NZCA tutors were required to keep in touch with the realities of childcare work by spending a week each year at an early childhood centre. Early in 1991 Alison Mary spent a happy week at the Civic. But, when the allegations arose in November of that year, that experience, along with the rest of her 30 years in preschool education, suddenly seemed to count for nothing:

> I was in a bad way as far as my professional judgement went – thinking, what am I doing in childcare if I can't pick up something like that going on? Our friends – who knew less about it than we did – were so convinced it had happened. Yet I never sensed anything amiss during my week at the Civic, and I have great confidence in my ability to sense a centre. It's not intuition. It's the experience and knowledge you gain from working with preschool children for so long. The Civic children were free to express themselves. If they didn't want to do something, they didn't. I can't understand how anything bad could have happened without those kids just walking away. And there were so many people around. A constant procession of adults coming and going. Finally I got to thinking it can't have been going on. I would've picked something up. Suddenly I found myself, a lesbian feminist, on the side of this guy who was accused of sexual abuse. I used to be quite friendly with some of the counsellors, and some of the complainant grandmothers. They don't speak to me any more.[30]

During the three-year NZCA course students spend four days a week at their own centres and one day a week at the NZCA tutorial room. In addition to instructing students, and setting and marking their assignments, tutors visit students at their centres three times a term and make formal observations of their work.

In the course of her observations, Ms Rata would spend up to an hour watching and making notes, and a further half hour discussing her observations with the student:

> We'd go over everything that had happened. 'What did you do? Why did you do that? Could you have done it some other way?' When something crops up – when children are fighting or whatever – there are so many possible ways of dealing with it. I'd say, 'You dealt with it this way, which is fine. What other ways could you have used?' It was the really effective, one-to-one, teaching aspect of my work.[31]

As Ellis's tutor, Ms Rata had to cope with the same sort of exuberance that Gaye Davidson had to cope with as his supervisor: 'Peter both delighted and infuriated me. He mostly delighted me before he was mine to take responsibility for. I became infuriated occasionally thereafter. He was so bouncy. He loved to challenge anything and everything.'

'He thoroughly enjoyed his training,' she continued. 'He was continually surprised at how much he'd learnt, and delighted by it. He was very pleased and proud when he had finished. I don't think he was particularly career oriented. He was just happy to be where he was.'

Her observations of Ellis covered all the issues that featured in the crèche investigation. On the question of his relationships with children, her recollections were strongly positive:

> It's hard to make generalisations, but the Civic children were fairly sophisticated, well-behaved, sure of themselves, open and heading towards cocky. They got on really well with Peter. They used to mob him in a friendly sort of way. They challenged him. He challenged them. But I always felt that Peter knew what he was doing. I know there've been heaps of people second-guessing how he might have been too rough or too loud. I know there've been people who've felt, after the event, that children were scared of him, that he ruled with a rod of iron. I didn't see any of that.[32]

A recurring topic in Ms Rata's discussions with Ellis was his sophisticated use of language:

> Peter loved word play, and so do I. I'm not talking about sexual innuendos, just sophisticated use of language. Once when we were talking with children, I made some comment about calling a spade a spade, and not the interface between man and nature. Peter questioned the appropriateness of my language, and so he should have. But he went on to talk about window cleaners being transparent wall maintenance engineers. This sort of chit chat went on. A lot of it went past the children. It may have sounded sarcastic, but it wasn't supposed to be. I discussed it with him later and gave it a lot of thought. In the end I decided that I was happy to have a wide range of language available to children in childcare. I told him there were one-to-one situations where sophisticated language wasn't appropriate, but if the other staff were talking to children in a maternal sort of way, it was fine by me if he used sophisticated language. I've been censured for that since, but it seemed to make sense at the time.

In considering whether Ellis was ever 'too rough' with children, Ms Rata took her Kohanga Reo background into account:

> When I was doing my training I made a dreadful faux pas in a mainstream childcare centre. A child was going to thump another child with a block. I was right there so I grabbed the hand and said, 'Hey careful, don't do that!' I didn't hurt him. I just grabbed

the hand. The poor child dissolved into tears. He wasn't used to being grabbed like that. In Pakeha centres, staff are supposed to deal with situations like that using words.

But Ms Rata insisted that, by any reasonable standard, Ellis's boisterousness was not a problem:

> I saw him involved in rough-and-tumble games several times. Jumping off things onto mattresses, doing somersaults, that sort of thing. It seemed to me that he always came off worst, with kids piling up on top of him. I was unaware of any injuries or accidents, and the activities were always completely up to the kids. They didn't have to take part if they didn't want to. It was the children who wanted rough and tumble who were there. He'd pick them up and throw them in the air and twirl them around. The more sedentary staff were disinclined to do that, so I thought Peter's interactions were a positive thing.[33]

Peter Ellis graduated with a Certificate in Childcare from the New Zealand Childcare Association on 31 January 1990. From a professional point of view, the rest of that year and most of the next went well. When Ms Rata took six weeks' maternity leave in October 1991, Ellis and Susannah job-shared as relieving tutors in her absence. On 10 November 1991 Alison Mary sent them letters of thanks, and references 'for who knows what purpose'. In Ellis's reference she wrote that he had:

> … shown initiative and reliability in this task. He has related well with trainees, introduced them to new learnings, organised his tutorials and workshops efficiently, involving children from the Civic Centre on a number of occasions. He is committed to the Treaty and shared many practical ideas on carrying out this commitment in childcare centres.[34]

But before the month was out, Peter Ellis's career as a childcare worker had come to an abrupt end.

5.iv: The First Allegation

'There were earlier disclosures of sexual abuse at the Civic Crèche that were not acted upon,' Wendy Ball told me. 'There were two written disclosures that came out at the depositions hearing, but not at the trial.'

'Let's make sure we're talking about the same things,' I said. 'One incident concerned [Kane Juniper]. The other related to an episode in the Childcare Association rooms. Right?'

'Yep. But they're historic to me. I came in after the initial disclosure by [Geoffrey Magnolia].'[1]

Wendy Ball came to Christchurch from Sydney in 1989. When the crèche case arose in 1991 she was lecturing at the Christchurch College of Education and studying for a Master of Law degree at the University of Canterbury. During the case she liaised with Detective Eade and some of the complainant families. After the trial she acted as spokesperson for the complainant parents. Since then, as senior lecturer in law at the University of Waikato, she has written and lectured on children's evidence in sexual abuse cases. In a paper presented to the 1995 conference of the Australian Association of Trauma and Dissociation (an organisation formed in 1992 to alert Australians to the dangers of ritual abuse), she compared the Civic Crèche case to the Mr Bubbles case, a preschool ritual abuse case in Sydney that collapsed in 1989 when the judge ruled that the children's evidence had been contaminated by excessive and leading questioning.[2]

Wendy Ball and Ms Magnolia were friends. When Geoffrey Magnolia made the comment that sparked the crèche case in November 1991, Ball heard about it soon afterwards. Her knowledge of the 'earlier disclosures' came later.

The 'earlier disclosure' involving Kane Juniper was a nebulous parental worry, never put in writing, which in 1992 mushroomed into a terrible certainty. In 1994 the Junipers joined End Ritual Abuse, an organisation formed 'to educate the public on ritual abuse, and … act as a support group for those survivors and families who have been involved in ritual abuse'.

In 1989 Kane's parents enrolled their son at the Civic Crèche on the recommendation of friends, and because their friend Suki worked in the Womble End. In May 1990, when he was two-and-a-half years old, Kane was moved to the Big End. In retrospect, Gaye Davidson was adamant that she would not have moved him if she did not think he was ready, but his mother was anxious and Kane was unsettled.[3]

Ms Juniper's anxieties revolved around three questions. Was Kane ready for the Big End? Was he being looked after properly without Suki (and, in particular, were the Big End staff protecting him from the aggressive Mikey Ash)? Could the flamboyant Peter Ellis be trusted near her child?

In December 1990 Mr and Ms Juniper shifted Kane to a Montessori preschool. They took a cake for him to share with the other children on his last day at the Civic, and told the staff they thought the Montessori programme would better suit their son.[4]

Ms Juniper later claimed that she began suspecting Ellis of sexually abusing her son around Kane's third birthday. If that claim were true, her failure to withdraw her son, or to take any other action at the time is difficult to understand. The crèche attendance register shows that Kane spent more than 70 hours at the Civic between his birthday in early November and his departure in December. During his last week he spent two full days and two half days at the centre. Also, by her own admission,

Ms Juniper did not discuss her concerns with her partner or her mother until the following year, and she never approached the crèche supervisor about them. Nor did she lay a complaint with the council or the police. Nonetheless, she did not keep her fears entirely to herself.

Mr and Ms Juniper belonged to a community action group. Several members, including Mr Dogwood, Mr and Ms Juniper and Mr and Ms Ash, sent their children to the Civic. One member, Suki, was on the crèche staff. It was in separate conversations with Suki, and with Mr and Ms Ash, that Ms Juniper shared her fears.

At a party soon after Kane left the Civic, Ms Juniper told Suki that Kane had come home from crèche one day with a thread hanging down his trouser leg. When she pulled the thread, Kane said 'ouch'. On investigation, she found the thread caught around his penis. 'That's a silly thing to do,' she said. 'Peter did it,' Kane replied. In recalling the conversation more than five years later, Suki could not remember whether Ms Juniper described the thread as string or wool, or cotton from an unravelling seam, and she could not remember whether it was said to be wrapped, or tied, around the boy's penis.

In response to Ms Juniper's worries, Suki said, 'Look, I don't think Peter would have done that. He's a bit different. He's flamboyant. But I think he's safe.' However, she offered to pass on Ms Juniper's concern to Gaye Davidson. 'Ms Juniper said, "No, no. I'm quite happy now that I've talked to you. And please don't tell [Mr Juniper] about it,"' Suki recalled.[5]

Soon afterwards Suki went overseas, and though Ms Juniper forgot about the 'thread around the penis' incident, she continued to worry about Peter Ellis. In December 1990 she shared her worries with Mr and Ms Ash.

In describing Mr and Ms Ash, it is difficult to know where to start. Their commitment to non-sexist child rearing was such that they taught Mikey to call them 'Mummy Jean' and 'Mummy Trev'. Mr Ash was the man who never forgave Gaye Davidson's ex-husband for leaving the Trotskyites after the Springbok Tour in 1981. Also, Mr and Ms Ash were serial accusers. In the years leading up to the crèche case, they accused Mikey's natural father of sexually molesting his son, and Mr Ash accused two university lecturers of sexually harassing female students. During the crèche case they accused Peter Ellis, Gaye Davidson's ex-husband and the entire crèche staff of sexually abusing children.[6]

Despite hearing about Ms Juniper's concerns in December 1990, and despite Ellis becoming offensively drunk at a party at their home in February 1991, Mr and Ms Ash continued to send Mikey to the Civic for eight hours a day, two or three days a week, until he turned five in April that year.[7] This suggests that they did not regard any crèche staff as a danger to children at that time. But when Mr Juniper finally heard about his partner's fears early in 1991, he reacted more strongly.

Around April 1991, when he was researching an article on the case of the school Maori language assistant convicted of child sexual abuse, Mr Juniper told friends he and his partner had withdrawn their son from the Civic because the child had been sexually abused by Peter Ellis. He said they didn't tell the crèche supervisor because they didn't think she would care. When this story reached Gaye Davidson she phoned Ms Juniper immediately. 'I was concerned for two reasons,' Davidson recalled. 'If it hadn't happened, they were spreading malicious rumours. If it had happened, and they hadn't reported it, children were at risk.' But Ms Juniper assured Davidson that there was no cause for concern:

> She apologised for what Mr Juniper had said. She said it wasn't true. She said if they had any concerns they would've felt comfortable talking to me about them. She said if she thought her child had been abused there was no way she would have left other children in danger.[8]

At the crèche case depositions hearing, Ms Juniper accepted Davidson's account of the conversation.

About three weeks after being reassured by Ms Juniper, Gaye Davidson received an anonymous phone call from a woman who accused the crèche of harbouring a child molester. Davidson invited the caller to come in and talk to her. She said she would need more details before she could act. The caller declined to do so. Davidson did not connect this complaint with the Kane Juniper episode, which, as far as she knew, had been resolved.[9]

At the crèche case depositions hearing, Kane's grandmother – an influential force in some of Christchurch's worthy causes – said she had made the anonymous phone call. 'I rang … because I felt Ellis was an unsuitable, an unsafe, person to be working with children and I realised that people do not stop abuse without an interception,' she said.

So that was Wendy Ball's first 'earlier disclosure', and the facts show that she was wrong on three counts: it did not involve a disclosure of abuse; it was never put in writing; and, far from being ignored, it was taken seriously and responded to promptly by the crèche supervisor.

The second 'earlier disclosure' was made in October 1991. It took the form of a child's comment, noted by a student working with a group of Civic children in the Childcare Association rooms. A four-year-old girl playing with a naked, anatomically correct doll was heard to say, 'This is his penis. You can suck on this. It has blood on it when it comes out of the girl.' The student made a written report to Gaye Davidson, who immediately arranged for the child to be interviewed by DSW. The issue was resolved when the child disclosed that she had seen her parents engaged in sexual activity.[10]

So that was Wendy Ball's second 'earlier disclosure'. This time there was a statement by a child and a written report. However, Ball was wrong on two counts. First, far from ignoring the issue, Gaye Davidson responded promptly and appropriately. Second, the disclosure had nothing to do with Peter Ellis or anyone else on the crèche staff.

By the time Ms Juniper had shared her worries about Peter Ellis with Suki, Mr and Ms Ash, Mr Juniper and Grandma Juniper, the genie was out of the bottle. For most of 1991 the overwhelming parental support for the Civic Crèche prevented the genie from insinuating itself into the imaginations of other crèche parents, despite the troubling stories with which they were bombarded (newspaper stories of a paedophile being employed as a school Maori language assistant, *Free to Fly* radio stories of repressed memories of horrendous abuse, grapevine stories of therapists treating adult victims of ritual abuse and Ritual Action Group stories of satanic cults in preschools). But it was too good to last. On 20 November 1991 Ms Magnolia laid her complaint.

• • •

As noted earlier, in *Nursery Crimes*, Finkelhor reported that parents of children allegedly molested in day-care centres were often described in negative terms (such as 'emotionally unstable' or 'marginally employed'). Roland Summit claimed: 'Eccentric, alienated, unsocialised and paranoid personality types are needed to ferret out allegations of child sex abuse in the face of lack of evidence.'

But to spark a mass panic, the complainant not only needs the ability to discover an unseen threat, he or she also needs the ability to convince others to believe in it. This takes a special sort of person. Ms Magnolia was one such person. Dr Iben Browning was another. Browning was a self-taught climatologist who predicted that a catastrophic earthquake would strike the Mississippi Valley on 3 December 1990. Though scientifically groundless, the prediction triggered a mass panic. Schools and factories closed on the day, and groups such as Red Cross wasted precious funds in their efforts to calm the public. A review of the panic found that the media was duped by Browning because he appeared to be well qualified and to have a sound track record, and his predictions appeared to be scientifically plausible.[11]

Another perspective on the sort of people who initiate mass panics emerged from an investigation into an outbreak of hysterical fainting in a classroom of adolescent girls. The researchers found that when the young woman who triggered the outbreak was admitted to hospital, she triggered an outbreak of hysterical pregnancies on the ward. They concluded that she had an 'epidemiological personality'.[12]

Adults with epidemiological personalities may also trigger a variant of the condition known as mass psychogenic illness by proxy. In this disorder, one group (usually parents) attributes an imaginary illness to another group (usually children). One such epidemic occurred in an elementary school in Georgia in 1988. It began with a discussion among mothers of the symptoms exhibited by their children in the two weeks since school had begun for the year. The symptoms – which included pallor, dark circles under the eyes, headaches, fatigue and nausea – were attributed to a gas leak at the school. Over the next two months the school's gas fittings were checked. Parents picketed the school and contacted the news media and a lawyer. Public health officials were called in. The officials found that the school's air and water were clean, that the school's teachers had noticed none of the claimed symptoms and that no child had been seen by a doctor in relation to the parental concerns.[13]

Another such outbreak, described as 'a phantom epidemic of gonorrhea', occurred at a Pennsylvania elementary school in the 1960s. Public health officials conducted clinical and laboratory investigations and studied the spread of the outbreak. They concluded:

> Even though the existence of multiple cases of gonorrhea could not be confirmed, there was strong evidence of an epidemic of quite a different kind, an epidemic of panic based on the spread of rumours ... a striking feature of the episode was the fact that a small group of parents, supported by very little scientific evidence, created sufficient unrest to force the closing of a school.[14]

In the control of a mass panic, the role of the authorities – be they seismologists, public health officials or experts in some other field – is pivotal. If the authorities move quickly to investigate the complaint and reassure the afflicted, the panic is likely to subside. If the authorities validate the panic it is likely to grow and spread. The epidemic of 'mysterious gas poisoning' on Jordan's West Bank in March and April of 1983 is a case in point. It started among schoolgirls. Official tests for toxic gases were negative, but the PLO rejected the test results, and in doing so validated and inflamed a pre-existing communal fear of Israeli toxic gas attacks. After that, the epidemic spread to other girls' schools (but not to boys' schools) and to the general public. By the time the panic was over, more than 900 people had been afflicted.[15]

As with epidemic diseases spread by bacteria or viruses, treating the afflicted is rarely enough. Carriers must be identified and quarantined if the epidemic is to be brought under control. According to German philosopher and psychiatrist Karl Jaspers, the importance of quarantining epidemiological personalities during episodes of hysterical contagion was recognised as far back as the 16th century. He noted that during outbreaks of demonic possession in convents: 'When the Bishop ordered house-arrest and isolation of the nuns the epidemic immediately died down, while it tended to grow rapidly when it was fought by priestly exorcism of the devil in public.'[16]

These days, when an outbreak of mass hysteria occurs among schoolgirls, isolating the instigator is relatively easy. But when an outbreak is instigated by someone perceived to be an 'expert' (as in the case of Dr Browning and his earthquake prediction), isolating the carrier is rarely possible.

• • •

Ms Magnolia, instigator of the Civic Crèche case, was the child of a well-known Christchurch family. Her mother was involved in women's issues. Her late father often stood for public office.

Ms Magnolia's first contact with the Civic Crèche was in the early '80s, when she was a solo mother with one child living in the urban commune in Avonside Drive. It was a period of great upheaval in her life. She recovered memories of child sexual abuse, abandoned her patriarchal surname and made a suicide attempt. She kept scrapbooks of newspaper items on court prosecutions for sexual offences. 'Collecting these clippings was a politically motivated and laborious obsession,' she told a women's conference at the time.[17]

After leaving Avonside Drive, Ms Magnolia boarded with a man who later owned a shop dealing in adult videos. The man had nothing to do with the Civic Crèche but Ms Magnolia named him, and everyone she could think of who had passed through the Avonside Drive house, in statements to the police during the crèche inquiry.

After extensive therapy, Ms Magnolia returned to university to study 'violence against wimmin and wimmin's health' in the 'capitalist, racist patriarchy'. She became a counsellor and tutor in drug abuse, eating disorders, group skills and child sexual abuse. She joined START. She wrote a handbook on sexual abuse. On the subject of sexual abuse, she was an expert.

Ms Magnolia's tutoring sometimes went off the rails. During one course she had a sexual relationship with a student. In another she did Tarot card readings. 'A couple of women objected,' recalled a course participant. 'But the younger women were clearly in her power.'[18]

Students also went to her for counselling. A former student recalled:

> X: I went to her to sort out some sexuality issues, and to sort out my appalling relationship with my parents. I was also claiming $10,000 from ACC for loss of enjoyment of life. I could have done with $10,000 at that time. I really did believe that I'd had a loss of enjoyment of life, so I was entitled to that money. She wrote a report and I got the $10,000 alright.
>
> LH: Ummm. My understanding is that you're supposed to have been sexually abused to qualify for ACC money.
>
> X: Oh, we threw in a couple of later sexual episodes to cover that.[19]

In August 1989, when Ms Magnolia's son Geoffrey was 18 months old, he began attending the Civic Crèche. In January 1991, when he was almost three, he became a Big Kid. He normally spent eight hours a day, four days a week at the crèche.

Geoffrey was a lovely baby, but Ms Magnolia worried about him a lot. He threw tantrums. He woke at night with pains in his legs. Sometimes she noticed redness around his anus. Sometimes he didn't want to go to crèche. Sometimes he was fussy about his clothes. He used words like penis, vagina and breast in an insulting way.[20]

Because of her background and interests, the chances of Ms Magnolia coming to suspect that her son had been sexually abused were probably greater than most. Of all the men in her son's life, Peter Ellis was the one with whom he spent the most time. So it was probably inevitable that Ellis would be the target of her accusation.

When Ms Magnolia laid her complaint on 20 November 1991, no one thought to question her timing. Everyone assumed that she complained that day because Geoffrey had 'disclosed' two days earlier. On closer inspection, this assumption seems flawed.

First, there is the 'disclosure' itself. The comment that triggered the crèche case – 'I don't like Peter's black penis' – was not a clear disclosure of abuse. 'What am I supposed to have done?' Ellis wanted to know. In relation to Geoffrey Magnolia, that question has never been answered. Ms Magnolia claimed that Geoffrey made the comment on three occasions – to his father, to his mother and to his grandmother. There were no other witnesses to these conversations, and Geoffrey never repeated the comment or made any allegation of abuse in his three DSW interviews.

Geoffrey's language and behaviour, and Peter Ellis's role as his caregiver, were the raw materials for Ms Magnolia's complaint, and those raw materials were available to her throughout his year in the Big End. In theory, Ms Magnolia could have turned them into a complaint at any time.

Indeed, had she wanted to, Ms Magnolia could have laid a complaint without waiting for Geoffrey to do or say anything worthy of concern. In the section of her handbook entitled 'Children who do not tell' she wrote: 'A child who has been abused or is currently being abused may or may not show any signs of the trauma they experience … Some children experiencing emotional, sexual and physical abuse continue to play, smile, laugh, attend school and do well …'[21]

Throughout 1991 the likelihood of Ms Magnolia making a complaint was poised, like the hands on the Doomsday Clock, at a few minutes before midnight. From time to time the risk increased or decreased according to the stresses in Ms Magnolia's life, her day-to-day impressions of Ellis and the level of sexual abuse anxiety in the Christchurch air. More often than not, the risk increased.

Early in 1991 Ms Magnolia's father died suddenly. The family was devastated. Three-year-old Geoffrey, who had been close to his grandfather, was taken to farewell the corpse before the coffin lid was closed. His mother told him the coffin was going to be burnt. Ms Magnolia later recalled that the family's energy was focused on supporting Grandma Magnolia, and Geoffrey received little attention at that time.[22]

In August 1991 the weekly themes at the crèche were: Birds; Smell and Taste; Bodies; Black; and Insects. During Body Week they bathed dolls, did foot and hand painting, made cut-out body and face shapes and compared navels (I've got an in-y, you've got an out-y').[23] Had Ms Magnolia asked, she would have learnt that they didn't discuss genitals that week. She didn't ask; she just worried, and drew her own conclusions.

In early September Christchurch was buzzing with stories of ritual abuse and child pornography prompted by media coverage of the Ritual Action Group's message and the child pornography ring scare. That buzz wasn't enough to trigger a sexual abuse complaint at the Civic Crèche, but the anxiety and suspicion it sowed among Christchurch sexual abuse workers drove the hands on the Doomsday Clock a little closer to midnight.

In late September Ms Magnolia visited Ellis on his day off to buy a puppy. Geoffrey said he wanted to call it Blossom. Ellis didn't care what he called the little black dog, but he thought the lad should be clear about its gender. 'Look,' he said, turning the puppy over. 'It's a boy.' During that visit Ms Magnolia noted that Ellis's flat was untidy, that Ellis had been drinking and that his partner was drunk. After that, she worried about Ellis a lot.[24]

Despite her worries, Ms Magnolia and her partner handed Geoffrey over to Peter Ellis whenever his shift and their arrival at the crèche coincided. Ellis recalled:

[Mr and Ms Magnolia] actually had a harder time of handing [Geoff] over than [Geoff] had of letting them go. They gave him the message – Mummy and Daddy are going, darling, give us a kiss and burst into tears to prove that you love us and don't want us to go and that we really aren't bad parents. I wasn't amused and my face probably showed it.[25]

Ms Magnolia later claimed that her son developed a growing reluctance to attend the crèche and a growing dislike of Ellis throughout October and November 1991.

At the end of October, the alarm bells sounded by the Ritual Action Group were amplified by terrifying stories from across the Tasman. On 29 October, listeners to Radio New Zealand were advised that the entire Australian police force was on the alert for covens of baby-eating satanists. On 30 October a New Zealand priest announced that he had been contacted by victims of a local satanic cult. He was sure that such cults had operated here in the past. He thought the *60 Minutes* programme on the Christchurch child pornography ring showed that they still did.[26]

Less than three weeks later, two events occurred that together jerked the hands on the Doomsday Clock to midnight. One was the visit of Dr Astrid Heger to

Christchurch. Heger was the paediatrician who, in 1983, had misdiagnosed child sexual abuse on a grand scale in the McMartin case in California. In 1989 she came to New Zealand to help set up Doctors for Sexual Abuse Care (DSAC). In 1991 she returned on a DSAC-sponsored lecture tour. On 19 and 20 November 1991 she was in Christchurch, leading a training session for physicians and sexual abuse specialists.[27]

The other defining event of 19 November 1991 was the introduction of the Accident Rehabilitation and Compensation Insurance Bill into Parliament. The purpose of the Bill was to replace the 1982 ACC Act in general, and to abolish the provision for lump-sum compensation for 'loss of enjoyment of life' in particular.[28] For those who still hoped to benefit from the lump-sum scheme, there was no time to lose.

On 20 November Ms Magnolia advised Gaye Davidson of her belief that Peter Ellis had abused her son. She said she would keep the boy home until Ellis was removed from the crèche. Davidson immediately sought advice from the city council administration. Later that morning she and council personnel officer Barbara Newman visited Mr and Ms Magnolia at home.

When the Magnolias learnt that Ellis had the day off, they sent three-year-old Geoffrey back to the crèche that afternoon. Then, when they heard that Ellis would be suspended next morning, Geoffrey's crèche attendance continued, uninterrupted, until the end of the year. But on the morning of their complaint, Geoffrey was at home. While his parents were talking to Gaye Davidson and Barbara Newman, he hung around, eavesdropping on the conversation.

'I said, "Do you want me to take [Geoff] out and play?"' Davidson recalled. 'We went to his bedroom and I read him a couple of books. Then we walked around outside until they had finished talking. I was later accused of coercing him at that time.'[29]

Barbara Newman asked the Magnolias to put their complaint in writing. She explained that copies of the complaint would be supplied to Ellis and his union, and a hearing would be held within four days. At 5pm that day a four-page letter, handwritten by Ms Magnolia and signed by both parents was delivered to the council.[30]

'To whom it may concern,' the letter began. 'We would like to voice our serious concerns about Peter Ellis … we have cause to suspect that Peter may have been involved in inappropriate sexual behaviour with or around our son …'

According to the letter, Geoffrey first made the comment 'I don't like Peter's black penis' to his father around the middle of October 1991. Mr Magnolia had asked the boy whether he had seen Peter's penis or whether it was just a story. Geoffrey said it was just a story, so Mr Magnolia took no further action.

Geoffrey allegedly made the comment again when he was in the bath with his mother on the evening of Sunday 17 November. 'I asked him whether he had seen it and had he touched it and he said no, then clammed up,' Ms Magnolia reported. 'I resolved to ring Gaye then had two very busy days.' Curiously, despite her concerns, Ms Magnolia sent Geoffrey to the crèche from nine to five on both those days.[31]

At this point Ms Magnolia's credibility must be seriously questioned. She had spent the best part of the previous decade proclaiming that, at the first suspicion of sexual abuse, the child must be protected and the abuser must be confronted. Yet, when her own son allegedly disclosed, not only did she fail to complain, she sent her child back to the scene of the alleged abuse, and into the care of the alleged abuser.

Events came to a head in the evening of Tuesday 19 November (the day of Astrid Heger's seminar and the introduction of the new ACC legislation to parliament). Geoffrey allegedly said to his grandmother that he had not wanted his father to leave him at the crèche that morning because he didn't like Peter's black penis. 'At this stage we began to get considerably more concerned that there had been something going on and began to see meaning in [Geoff's] previously odd behaviour,' Ms Magnolia wrote. Her concerns revolved around Geoffrey's famous comment, his interest in genitals, his tantrums and his clinginess, and around her misgivings about Peter Ellis. She indicated that she had been worrying about these things since Body Week at the crèche, and had discussed them with 'Maree [sic] (another crèche worker)', 'Ali Locke (a counsellor)', and with 'our family therapist Ann Casely [sic]'. That evening, she questioned Geoffrey closely, and with a cavalier disregard for the contaminating effects of leading questions:

'Will you tell me what happened with Peter and his penis?'
'No, I won't.'
'Did Peter hurt you?'
'No.'
'Did Peter scare you?'
'Yes.'
Then Geoffrey said, 'I don't want to go to crèche any more.'
'Do you want to go if Peter isn't there?'
'Yes.'
'Was Peter's penis scary?'
'It was dark-y. Scary.'
'Is Daddy's penis scary?'
'No you silly mummy.'
'Is yours?'
'Noo-o.'

Geoffrey then told his mother a story: 'If Peter came to this house he would be a monster. If he was a monster and he was here you'd be asleep Mum in your bed and you'd wake up and see the monster and you'd be surprised.'

In closing, Ms Magnolia signalled her intention to spread her anxiety throughout the crèche community: 'We are concerned for other children at the crèche as well.'

• • •

On the day Ms Magnolia laid her complaint, Peter Ellis's mother and grandmother returned from a trip abroad. His mother arrived exhausted; his grandmother arrived with galloping Alzheimer's. 'You rest,' Ellis told his mother. 'I'll take tomorrow off and look after Grandma.' But when he phoned Davidson, she declined his request.

'This is a family crisis,' he protested.

'Well, just come in for an hour then,' Davidson said. She had been instructed to bring him to the council at 9.30am, and was not allowed to tell him why.

Ellis immediately phoned his colleague Jan Buckingham.

Playcentre-trained Buckingham had been on the crèche staff since 1985. She was a busy mother of four, with foster children as well. Ellis was a single man. Their paths had rarely crossed prior to April 1987 when they spent three days together at an in-service training course on a marae. Then, in May 1987, Ellis moved in with Ms Kowhai, two blocks from Buckingham's home. Jan Buckingham recalled:

> Neither of us had transport, so when our shifts coincided he'd walk to my place and we'd bus into town together. He'd often call in on his way home for a cup of coffee. We got to know each other really well. He has an amazing sense of humour. He made me laugh. He really did. He got to know my family. He used to tell me his troubles and woes. I'd pat him on the head and dish out what was probably unnecessary and unwanted advice and he'd go his own sweet way.[32]

In mid-1989, when Buckingham's marriage collapsed, she asked Ellis to take her husband as a boarder for a few weeks while she sorted out her life. When Ellis's own crisis struck on 20 November 1991, he asked Buckingham whether anything untoward had happened at work that day. As far as she knew, nothing had.

At the city council next morning Peter Ellis and Gaye Davidson met with Barbara Newman and Alistair Graham from the council administration and Angela Counihan from the Southern Local Government Officers Union. Peter Ellis was informed of the complaint, given a copy of the Magnolias' letter and advised that he had been placed on paid leave. Ellis, who had assumed the complaint was about his boisterousness with children, was devastated. A formal hearing was arranged for the following Monday. Ellis was told not to contact Mr and Ms Magnolia, or any crèche parents or staff. Davidson was instructed to keep the matter to herself.

While council officials kept an open mind and proceeded with caution, Ms Magnolia showed no such restraint. She was convinced that the abuse had occurred, she was convinced it was widespread and she was determined to let everyone know. She later conceded that she had been advised to keep the matter to herself, but had no intention of doing so:

> I intentionally didn't listen to that because I have a strong belief that secrecy in sexual abuse cases keeps it happening and I felt it needed to be talked about ... I rang the parents of friends that [Geoff] played with because I was concerned for those kids. I didn't initiate contact with others. Several people rang me and if I heard things about them then I would tell them and recommend they talk to the parents concerned.[33]

The first complaint had only just been laid, but, like a careless match tossed into the tinder-dry landscape of a Canterbury summer, it set off an inferno.

CHAPTER 6

A Complaint Has Been Made

6.i: The Scapegoat

When Ms Magnolia laid her complaint it sparked an inferno because the climate was right and the wind was blowing in the right direction. Anxiety over the dangers that men posed to young children had been smouldering nationwide for more than a decade. In Christchurch, rumours of clandestine pornography rings and satanic cults had driven the anxiety of sexual abuse workers to fever pitch. By the early '90s, evil seemed to be everywhere.

The practice of symbolically expelling evil from a community by means of a scapegoat can be found in all societies throughout human history. The process involves a complex of mental, emotional and social mechanisms that enable people to claim righteousness and purity for themselves, while attributing hostility and evil to the despised scapegoat.

In some societies the process is controlled by ritual. Indeed, the term 'scapegoat' comes from an ancient Judaic ritual in which, each year on the Day of Atonement, the sins of the people were symbolically transferred to a goat, which was then released into the wilderness. This ritual left the people feeling purged, and for the time being guiltless. In *The Golden Bough*, J.G. Frazer described purification rituals involving rocks, plants, animals and humans as scapegoats. Of human scapegoats, he wrote:

> Whenever Marseilles ... was ravaged by a plague, a man of the poorer classes used to offer himself as a scapegoat – prayers were uttered that all the evils of the people might fall on his head. He was then cast out of the city or stoned to death by the people outside the walls ... such sacrifices were not confined to extraordinary occasions of public calamity ... Abdera in Thrace was publicly purified once a year, and one of the burghers, set apart for the purpose, was stoned to death as a scapegoat or vicarious sacrifice for the life of all the others ...[1]

Frazer also noted that in societies where the sacrifice of innocent victims was no longer tolerated, condemned criminals were sometimes used 'for the sake of preserving the old ritual in a form which will not offend the new morality'.

In Frazer's Victorian world view, societies with scapegoating rituals were superstitious and unenlightened. However, everyday experience suggests that the scapegoating impulse remains universal, and the only difference between 'primitive' societies and our own is that our society has no formal scapegoating rituals.

In *The Nature of Prejudice*, Gordon Allport noted that scapegoats are generally selected on the basis of pre-existing prejudices. In this regard, authoritarian Christchurch feminists had a pre-existing prejudice towards men, and authoritarian Christchurch police had a pre-existing prejudice towards homosexuals. Allport also found that visibility and marginality were important factors. People who looked and behaved differently, and who lacked strong support networks, were easy targets.[2]

If a scapegoat is to fulfil his purpose, the community must be persuaded to unload all the evil in its midst onto him. In *Faces of the Enemy*, Sam Keen noted that when the mass hatred required for this process is generated by people unconscious of their own paranoia, projection and propaganda, a notional enemy with near-omnipotent powers and a degraded moral character is created that may seem as real and objective as a rock or a mad dog.[3]

• • •

From the day the first complaint in the crèche case was laid, the certainty of Ms Magnolia and her supporters that they were good and right, and that anyone who questioned them was bad and wrong, was unassailable. Thereafter, from a bunker at the centre of the firestorm, they defined the issues and set the agenda for the investigation. Their stance was governed by two imperatives: the need to believe the growing wave of allegations; and the need to act decisively. Through their passion and certainty they ensured that anyone who wanted to wield power in the crisis had to do so on their terms.

Beyond the centre of the firestorm was the confused majority. To their disparate responses they brought their various personalities, personal circumstances and life experiences. Some people walked away. Some were swept along in the excitement. Some tried to douse the flames. Many doubted the validity of the allegations, but few raised their voices in protest.

• • •

When Suki went overseas in March 1991, Debbie Gillespie, a trained primary school teacher who had been on the crèche staff since 1988, was appointed head of the Womble End. Sharleen, a 20-year-old kindergarten teacher, was appointed to the position vacated by Gillespie at the Big End.

For Sharleen, joining the Civic Crèche staff was the biggest thrill of her life.[4] Her colleagues were less enthused. Sandi recalled:

People said the network of staff was so tight that we didn't let her in, but that's not true. A lot of staff came and went. They always fitted in beautifully. The woman who replaced Peter was a lovely person. But Sharleen just didn't fit in. She was a clock watcher. In her first week she drove me mad going 'One more hour and 15 minutes to go-oh,' as she walked around. 'One more hour and ten minutes to go-oh.'[5]

Significantly, the faults that Ellis and his colleagues found with Sharleen were virtually identical to the faults that Sharleen and her colleagues found with Ellis. She loved to be centre stage, they told me. She didn't pull her weight. She gossiped with parents. She dressed inappropriately (Ellis suffered from psoriasis and sometimes wore trackpants with no underpants. Sharleen sometimes wore a white miniskirt for no reason that her co-workers could fathom). Her conversations with parents and staff sometimes went beyond the bounds of sexual propriety (she once asked a crèche father to photograph her in her underwear as a treat for her boyfriend).

Human nature being what it is, there was no love lost between Sharleen and Ellis, and Ellis teased her mercilessly. In response to her clockwatching, he turned back the clocks. When Sharleen pinned a photo on the staff noticeboard of her rather large self on a rather small donkey, Ellis provided a word-bubble for the person in the photo holding a second donkey: 'Here, Miss, I think you're going to need two!' In my interview with her, Sharleen remembered Ellis as a man who could be both kind and cruel, and she never knew what to expect.[6]

When Gaye Davidson returned from the city council on 21 November 1991 she told the crèche staff that Peter Ellis was on indefinite leave. She was not allowed to tell them why. There was to be no discussion or speculation. They were not to contact him. For an upfront supervisor this was totally out of character. 'Gaye was strung out,' recalled Sandi. 'She didn't say anything, but you could see she was under major stress.'[7] Sharleen seized the opportunity to acquaint Davidson with her latest complaints about Ellis. The rest of the staff just worried. As soon as Jan Buckingham got home she phoned him:

> I thought it was ridiculous. I'd been stewing over it all day. He's a colleague. He's been put in limbo-land. I said, 'What's going on?' He said, 'I'm not allowed to tell you.' I kept putting questions to him. He kept answering 'Yes' or 'No'. By the time I'd finished I'd figured out what the complaint was, and who had made it. So Peter thought that he may as well read me the letter.[8]

Figuring out what Geoffrey had said and why was another matter. That evening, and over the coming months, Ellis and his colleagues considered the possibilities. Ellis thought Geoffrey's comment must have something to do with the puppy Ms Magnolia had bought from him the previous month. Was the boy upset because his mother had bought a honey-coloured female puppy for his sister? Had he said,

'I don't like Peter's black puppy?' or 'I don't like Peter's puppy's black penis?' Or was Geoffrey talking about his recently cremated, swarthy-complexioned grandfather, also named Peter? Did his comment have something to do with 'Black Week' at the crèche? Had a child rolled black playdough into a 'penis'? Had he overheard someone saying that Ellis had painted his partner's penis black? Did the stuffed paper rocket made by crèche worker Marie Keys have anything to do with it? A year or two earlier the rocket had provoked an outbreak of hilarity of the sort that can erupt in any workplace at any time. 'Someone attached it to the ceiling at an unfortunate angle,' Debbie Gillespie recalled. 'Everyone who saw it burst out laughing and suggested a name – but it had to be Peter who painted "Genitalia Too" on the side.' The deed was done while Davidson was at lunch. As soon as she returned she made him take it down. But by November 1991 that episode seemed too old to be relevant.

Ultimately, the question of what Geoffrey said and what Geoffrey meant, and to what extent his reported comments may have been contaminated by his mother's questions and suspicions of Ellis, remains a mystery.

'You've got to get a lawyer,' Buckingham told him on the evening of his suspension. 'What for?' said Ellis.

At Jan Buckingham's insistence, Peter Ellis contacted Chris Knight, her family solicitor. English-born Knight ran a solo practice specialising in civil and family law. On Friday 22 November Peter Ellis entered his life. Over the coming months, Knight observed him closely:

> I don't profess to be an expert in picking a child abuser. However, I have met a number of them. There were a couple of things about Peter that contrasted with my experiences, and which led me to believe him. The first was that, even though he always denied any wrongdoing, he was never dismissive of the allegations. He always exercised himself acutely as to whether there could be any truth in them. The other thing was, he always had an anxious concern for the children. He was never angry with them. He never called them liars. What distressed him was that the children he had loved and worked with were being made to go through these hoops because of him. There were times when he was depressed. There were times when he had drunk a bit. He was very, very scared. He felt very vulnerable. You could have excused him if he started blaming the children. But he never did. The love and a closeness which Peter continued to feel for the children contrasts with the abuser who at some level will regard children as objects. That was never there with Peter. It was totally absent.[9]

The day after his suspension, Ellis met Peter Lawson, secretary of the Southern Local Government Officers Union. Unlike the lawyers in the case, whose ethics required them to put their clients' interests first, everyone else who dealt with Ellis in an official capacity had to weigh their commitment to justice for Ellis alongside other, often competing, interests. In Lawson's case, these interests included his commitment to his employer, to his union members and to the public good. At times of social unrest, the weight of community feeling can unbalance the judgement of officials. During the crèche case, Lawson stood out as one who kept his head while all about were losing theirs. Yet it cannot be said that he was a remarkable man. His most distinguishing quality, along with his common sense and steady nerve, was his ordinariness.

Lawson and Knight met with Ellis on Friday 22 November to prepare a response for the council hearing the following Monday. Both men were concerned about the damage that could be done to Ellis's reputation and livelihood if the complaint was mishandled. They knew the council had no experience in child sexual abuse investigations. They feared the issue would not be treated with the confidentiality it deserved. Furthermore, there was no 'specific allegation of misconduct' to answer.[10] They therefore advised Ellis not to attend the complaint hearing. Lawson recalled:

> Angela Counihan and I went along and said that as far as we were concerned the allegation was unclear and without foundation, and that it was quite improper for the council or the union to start interviewing children or investigating the issue in any way. We said it was a matter for the police. We rather naively believed that the police would handle it properly. I guess that was our first mistake. We told the council that if a complaint wasn't laid with the police by midday on Friday [29 November], then Peter should be reinstated.[11]

Next day, Ellis endorsed his union's position in a letter to the council, and added: 'I am completely unaware of any actions of mine that could have led to the letter from Mr and Ms Magnolia dated 20-11-91. I can also advise you that should a complaint be laid with the police I intend to defend the charges made.'[12]

While all this was happening, Gaye Davidson maintained her silence and Jan Buckingham kept her knowledge to herself, and the imaginations of the other crèche staff ran riot. They figured that Ellis was in serious trouble. Most assumed the problem related to his boisterousness with children. But Sandi had another theory: 'My first thought was: he's been to the pub at lunchtime. A parent has noticed but we haven't. I thought: that's it – he's down the road.' It was almost a relief for Sandi when Susannah visited Ellis and reported back to her colleagues. 'I thought – oh phew, he hasn't been drinking. The parents are worried over something or other, but it's all going to be sorted out.'[13] A couple of days later Debbie Gillespie approached her supervisor. 'I said, "Gaye, it's okay, we all know." It was just awful her carrying that burden on her own.'[14] From Davidson's point of view, it was a harrowing time:

> I was really, really confused. I kept thinking: it can't have happened. But did it happen? Has something happened? What could have happened? Where did it happen? I couldn't believe that something could have happened. But I couldn't dismiss it either, because he

was being accused. I often wonder about the outcome if we'd all stood behind Peter at that stage and said: This is crap. But none of us knew whether it was or it wasn't. I didn't know what to do. I was consumed with guilt at not being able to support him. Once I found out what the charges were I knew I'd made a huge mistake in not supporting him right from the start.[15]

To add to the pressure, during the week following Ellis's suspension, a two-person team from the Education Review Office (ERO) was in the crèche every day, making an inspection. As well as meeting the management committee and staff, and spending a week observing the crèche, the ERO team talked to 20 or 30 parents and city council officials. Gaye Davidson told the team that a staff member was on leave while a complaint against him was being investigated. They were untroubled by the news, and gave the centre a glowing report.[16]

Though the crèche staff knew about the allegations within days of Ellis's suspension, Davidson confided in only one parent: management committee member Ms Arbutus.[17] But the mystery proved too much for another parent, Ellis's former tutor Ms Rata:

> The atmosphere was brittle. The smiles were too bright. The staff were a little bit too happy. 'Hey, what's going on?' 'Can't talk about it.' 'Where's Peter?' Evasion. Looking back, that experience gave me confidence in my own senses. I realised that if there was ever any problem at the Civic, I would have picked it up. I found out where Peter lived and went to see him. I burst out laughing when he told me what had happened. I said, 'And have you got a black penis?' He assured me that he hadn't.[18]

On Monday 25 November Geoffrey Magnolia made no disclosure in his DSW interview, but this did not divert his parents from their mission. Between 20 and 25 November they spoke to many present and former crèche parents. They also heard about the alleged 'earlier complaints', and about Ellis hanging a child on the picket fence by his overalls. A social worker friend of Ms Magnolia arranged a DSW interview for her own former-crèche child. In response to some 'non-leading questions', another crèche child told his father that a boy had to 'fight Peter off in the bedroom'. But a staff report on crèche sleep routines effectively ruled out that room as a venue for indecencies:

> Children from both the nursery and preschool area are sent for a sleep around 12–12.15pm. Children from the preschool are toileted and prepared for bed by the person on the 8.30 shift. This person then takes them through, sets up their bedding and places them to bed. At this stage there is normally always a nursery worker in the room and if that is not the case, more than one nursery worker is moving in and out of the sleep room as they put the children to bed. Once the children are settled in bed, the preschool caregiver leaves the sleep room and two nursery workers stay in the room. The majority

of these preschool children are sent from the nursery, upon waking, to any available caregiver in preschool for dressing/toileting. Any afternoon sleepers are prepared and taken to bed by the 8.30 caregiver and usually awoken and dressed by the 9.30 shift caregiver, occasionally by a nursery worker or supervisor. At this stage there can be up to four children in the room. At any time the inside of the sleep room can be viewed by people passing by through the windows in the two entry doors.[19]

Mr and Ms Magnolia also discussed their concerns with council officials. In his notes for the planned complaint hearing on Monday 25 November, personnel manager Marshall Wright wrote:

We are under pressure from parents of the boy that we should tell all other parents and staff ... We know from the grapevine [that] a lot know ... We understand that other children may be going for 'disclosure' interviews (nothing official to us) – Whole matter has the potential for getting out of hand and damaging the crèche.[20]

At a meeting with council officials the following day (Tuesday 26 November), Mr and Ms Magnolia kept the pressure on. Marshall Wright told them that spreading word of the allegation would be inflammatory and defamatory, but they were free to lay a complaint with the police if they wished. The Magnolias said they had already done so. When the possibility of Ellis returning to the crèche under close supervision was raised, Ms Magnolia said she would help other parents go to the police. She felt that further witnesses to Ellis's misconduct could be found among children who had since left the crèche.[21]

Following that meeting, union secretary Peter Lawson faxed Ellis's lawyer, Chris Knight: 'I have just received advice from Marshall Wright ... that the complainants have been advised that due to lack of evidence the Council will reinstate Peter Ellis unless a formal complaint has been laid with the police by 3.00 pm on Friday 29 November.'[22]

Despite the council's efforts to contain the situation, by Wednesday 27 November Chris Knight sensed it was getting out of control. That day he advised Mr and Ms Magnolia that where sensitive allegations were involved, 'the only body or organisation to whom information should be communicated is the police'. His letter continued:

I have received information from several independent sources which seem to indicate:
a) That you have communicated directly with Peter's employers.
b) That you have circulated your above letter and that it has got into the hands of several persons.
c) That you have discussed the situation with a number of people including Civic Child Care Centre personnel and other parents whose children attend the Centre.

d) That there is doubt that you have filed a complaint with the police. (Certainly Peter has received no approach from the police.)

As you are also aware, Peter is absolutely shattered by the suggestions that you have made, and totally denies any inappropriate conduct. He has been further distressed by the feedback he has been getting ... He feels that his reputation has suffered irrevocable damage and that he may lose his job. Fears have also been expressed to me ... that the reputation of the Centre has also been damaged by your actions.

You will be aware that damages for defamation in circumstances such as this could be extremely heavy.

My purpose in writing is to advise you immediately to stop all discussion of this matter with anyone but the police or persons authorised by the police. If you have not yet filed a complaint ... then you must either do so immediately or withdraw your suggestion that Peter has been involved in anything improper. You must also ... show your solicitor this letter, as I shall need to discuss with your solicitor the implications of your actions to date.[23]

As it happened, the police officer Ms Magnolia spoke to when she phoned the Child Abuse Unit on Monday 25 November was Detective Colin Eade. He jotted down her complaint, and noted that, though her son had disclosed no abuse at his DSW interview, a second interview had been scheduled. Of Peter Ellis he wrote: 'He is apparently homosexual.'[24]

For the first three months of the investigation Detective Eade was in sole charge. Thereafter he was almost single-handedly responsible for dealing with the parents, children, doctors, interviewers and psychologists involved.[25] From the outset, one of Eade's most enthusiastic supporters was Ms Arbutus, the crèche management committee member to whom Gaye Davidson had confided. On Tuesday 26 November Ms Arbutus took her four-year-old son to play with Geoffrey Magnolia.[26] Following that apparently innocuous event, Ms Arbutus and Colin Eade joined forces.

At the time Gaye Davidson held Ms Arbutus in high regard: 'I thought she was a really lovely, supportive woman. She believed in the crèche. She worked really hard for the crèche.' So when Ms Arbutus suggested that she and Davidson discuss the Ellis situation with council management, Davidson arranged a meeting. 'She was really strong and really upfront,' recalled Davidson. 'She said she thought it was disgusting that it had been kept a secret. She thought that everyone should know.'[27]

Gaye Davidson and Ms Arbutus met with personnel officer Barbara Newman on Wednesday 27 November. Newman recalled:

[Ms Arbutus] wanted to know what the council's position was. I don't know whether she wanted more – whether she wanted me to say how terrible, how shocking it was, how wrong Peter was and how right everyone else was, and how we had to get rid of him. I just explained our position and where we were in the process. In retrospect, I think she saw that as supporting or covering up or protecting Peter.[28]

At that meeting Newman discovered that, contrary to the council's wishes and without the council's knowledge, plans for a meeting to inform crèche parents of the allegation were proceeding apace. Newman's notes read:

> Discussion with [Ms Arbutus] to inform me on what action the management committee is intending to take with regards Peter Ellis incident. Specialist Services Unit Welfare Dept – Social Welfare Worker Welfare Dept – Child Abuse Team personnel Police Dept. [Ms Arbutus] suggested someone from city council management should be there ... Nature of meeting to inform/educate parents on process for complaints they may have regarding their children ...[29]

Later that day Colin Eade phoned Barbara Newman. Her memo of the conversation made three points. The first was that, though he had been contacted by only two parents and had no evidence of abuse, Eade believed he was onto something big:

> Colin Eade has taken on the responsibility on behalf of a number of parents. Two have already been in touch with him to lay complaints about Peter Ellis ... He believes more parents will be getting in touch ... no definite allegations but what was coming through [was that] children were afraid of Ellis.[30]

The second was that, though Eade had never visited the crèche or met Peter Ellis, he believed that Ellis was a feared and dangerous person: 'If Peter should return to the crèche at the moment, Colin believed there would be a mass exit of children. [Also] Peter could tamper with the evidence and this would be in itself a criminal offence.'

The third was that Eade had seized control of the decision-making (even with respect to Ellis's employment), and was calling the shots:

> [I said I] would get back to Colin on the question of his [Ellis's] future/return to the crèche ... Subsequently spoke to Colin Eade again to arrange a meeting time with him for Alistair [Graham] and myself. Not possible at the moment ... 1.30 pm today had been our suggestion – more likely now to be late next week.[31]

Notes made by Barbara Newman two days later indicate that Colin Eade also told her that he was organising the parents' meeting. Her 29 November notes read: 'Spoke with Colin Eade regarding his Monday [2 December] meeting of parents ... He said that it was not his meeting, he was just attending it. I queried this as I had taken it from his Wednesday conversation that he was organising it and running it ...'[32]

On 26 November, Gaye Davidson had assured Barbara Newman that 'the majority of parents think Peter is okay', and Alistair Graham (manager of the council unit responsible for the crèche) has raised the possibility of his reinstatement. However, after hearing about Eade's 27 November phone call to Barbara Newman, Graham considered moving Ellis to some other area of council work. The final note on Newman's memo of 27 November read: 'Redeployment for Peter? Library Unit (Alistair).'

Alistair Graham was greatly concerned by news of a meeting to inform crèche parents of the allegations. Now that the police and the semi-autonomous crèche management committee were involved, the matter seemed out of the council's hands. However, in a last-ditch attempt to control the situation, he sent a memo to Gaye Davidson:

> I ask that you do not involve yourselves with the initiation of, the planning of, or attendance at, any meetings proposed by parents relating to matters currently under police investigation at the Centre. I ask that this also be conveyed to staff. Further, you should refrain from comment or dialogue with parents on this matter.[33]

• • •

There were two council representatives and seven parent representatives on the crèche management committee. The supervisor and another staff member also attended the monthly meetings. Topping up the parent representation was a casual and continuous process. As children turned five and went to school, parents moved on and new ones were found to take their place. Ms Jacaranda's experience was typical: 'I suppose I looked like the sort of person who wouldn't mind giving a bit of time. Gaye approached me. Would I be interested? I said, "What does it involve, Gaye?" She said, "Oh, it's nothing, just a short meeting once a month. It's pretty social really."'[34]

At each management committee meeting Davidson reported on budget and occupancy rates, and raised routine matters like fee structures, maintenance requirements and the purchase of new equipment.

After receiving the Magnolias' complaint on 20 November, Davidson did not attend the management committee meeting that evening, but she put in her usual report and the usual discussions followed. Committee members also discussed crèche management procedures with an ERO inspector, and planned their Christmas function.[35] Everything seemed to be ticking over smoothly. Then the following week Ms Arbutus called her fellow parent representatives to an urgent meeting.

Ms Gingko arrived for the Thursday 28 November meeting to find another parent waiting outside: 'She said, "There's been an accusation. It involves Peter." I felt the blood drain out of my face. My heart stopped. In seconds life went from being a breeze to absolute turmoil.' To add to the confusion, Gaye Davidson and the council representatives did not appear. Instead Ms Arbutus arrived with Detective Colin Eade.[36]

Ms Arbutus presented herself as the mother of an abused child. She even claimed that *her* son had come home from crèche and said, 'I don't like Peter's black penis'. She said she had arranged a DSW interview for him, and added that her daughter, who was almost seven and had never been a crèche child, was scared of the place.[37]

'[Ms Arbutus] was the emotional driver of that whole episode,' recalled a committee member. 'She knew there were things wrong, that we had to act and this is what we had to do. She said, "We've got this anger, we've got to use this anger as positive energy to do something and not just sit around."'[38]

Colin Eade presented himself as a concerned and authoritative police officer with very grave news. The impact of his contribution suggests that, no matter how ill-founded a person's response to a crisis, if they have status, and appear calm and confident, their views are likely to prevail. Eade said that four crèche parents (two current, two past) had contacted him with concerns that Ellis may have sexually abused their sons. He was satisfied that the children needed formal interviews. The investigation could take months. Whatever the outcome it was unlikely that Ellis would ever work in childcare again. Yet the council was talking of reinstating him, and personnel officer Barbara Newman was being 'difficult'. He was 'talking about an offence'. It was all a great worry.[39]

'You are not stupid people,' he said, and he was right. There was a social worker, two lawyers and three teachers present at that meeting. 'This is serious,' they said. 'What do we do now? We can't just do nothing. We must let everyone know. We need to hold a meeting. And we need to talk to the council.'[40]

By the end of the evening Detective Eade and Ms Arbutus had done such a good job of persuading the management committee to adopt the 2 December meeting as their own that when I interviewed them five years later, they all assured me the meeting was their idea in the first place.

At the close of the 28 November meeting each parent had taken away a list of names from crèche attendance registers. Over the next couple of days they phoned the people on their lists with an alarming and mysterious message: 'There is going to be an urgent meeting at the Civic at 7.30pm on Monday to discuss concerns that have come from the children. Childcare will be available. There will be outside agencies involved. In fairness to those involved I cannot discuss this further.'[41]

At that stage in the inquiry, no child had disclosed any abuse. The concerns that prompted the 2 December meeting had come not from children but from anxious parents. However, the phrase 'concerns that have come from children' enabled Colin Eade and Ms Arbutus to trigger, first in the management committee and then in the wider crèche community, the unquestioning 'believe the children' response that had been implanted in the nation's psyche over the previous decade. In fact, what crèche parents were being asked to do was 'believe on behalf of children', and that is precisely what many of them did. For Ms Gingko, informing the 20 parents on her list was a nightmare:

> It was just horrific. Ringing them. Saying who I was. Saying there was going to be a meeting. Would they please come. No, I couldn't tell them what it was about. Rumours were flying. Some said, 'Is it about Peter?' I said, 'Yes, it is.' Someone rang and said, 'You phoned my sister-in-law and she's in a total panic because kids have been molested.' I said, 'No, that's not what I said.' It was awful. Absolutely awful.[42]

Ms Rowan declined to discuss the reasons for the meeting with the people on her list (though many already knew). However, she did confide in a couple of friends: 'One said, "How bloody ridiculous." The other flew into a panic. I should have known then what was going to happen.'

Over the same period, other parents received more sinister messages. Ms Hawthorn recalled:

> I was put in touch with a parent who had a counselling background. She told me that she had it on good authority that Peter Ellis had abused a child. He had chosen this child because the parent was a sexual abuse counsellor and he wanted to be caught. She was busy networking to make sure all parents would know what Peter had done.[43]

Ms Linden was phoned by Ms Hickory, who said that a meeting was being held because Ellis had been abusing four little boys. Mr Mahogany received a call from a woman who identified herself as a crèche parent: 'She said that other parents had come to her with evidence of misbehaviour by a member of the crèche staff. She said I should check out my children for sexual abuse.'[44] Ms Cork received a call from a parent who had already arranged a DSW interview for his child. He said there was a distressing problem at the crèche – a suspicion of sexual abuse. Ms Cork recalled:

> It suddenly explained the incredible trauma we'd had with our child for the last three years. He had a very good school, but in his first year he did things like break rulers over his knee. He ripped up a book. He didn't have the social skills you would expect of a child who had been to a good preschool. In his second year he would do things like hide in the wardrobe at the back of the classroom and shut the door. He would stuff food in his mouth. These were bizarre behaviours which I believe have links with what happened at the crèche ... The biggest thing is – he was totally off-task. I know a lot about sexual abuse ... there's an inability to make eye-contact with an adult. There's extreme fidgetiness ... He didn't want to read ... The reading recovery teacher thought he was psychologically disturbed. When he was put in a room with her, he behaved like a sexual abuse victim – he tried to stuff the arm of his t-shirt in his mouth. He thought – Here we go again, I'm going to be mistreated. That's what I think. But it's supposition because he hasn't really disclosed very much at all ...[45]

• • •

Management committee members left their 28 November meeting wound up and ready for action. Next day, Mr Larch, Ms Arbutus and Mr Beech marched off to confront the council administration. Mr Larch – a lawyer with leadership aspirations – was their spokesperson. They wanted to see city manager John Gray, but they had to settle for Alistair Graham, Barbara Newman and second-tier manager Rob Dally. There were still no disclosures of abuse, and Ellis had still not been interviewed by the police, but by then the panic had developed its own momentum. Notes of the meeting refer to the 'gravity' of the situation and the 'problem in establishing how widespread'. They also indicate that Ms Arbutus was in fighting mode: she 'wanted to know what counselling there would be for parents'; she didn't want union secretary Peter Lawson to attend the 2 December meeting; she didn't want Ellis reinstated; and she wanted Barbara Newman out of her life.[46]

By the end of that meeting it was clear that the council's efforts to prevent a brushfire had failed. However, for Alistair Graham, there was consolation in the fact that Mr Larch was spokesperson for the crèche management committee. '[Mr Larch]'s reaction was a very responsible one,' Alistair Graham recalled. 'We were dealing with some very strong-willed parents, and he was trying to remain rational and sane and calm throughout the whole thing. I was thrilled that we had someone of his calibre to deal with.'[47]

Most of the crèche staff heard about the parents' meeting after work on Thursday (28 November), when Barbara Newman came to remind them not to discuss the Ellis situation with parents, and to instruct them *not* to attend the Monday meeting. They respected the first message, but rejected the second. When Monday night came, they went along.

Peter Lawson heard about the parents' meeting when someone from the council phoned him on Friday afternoon (29 November) to advise that the Magnolias had laid a complaint with the police, and that Ellis would not be reinstated in the meantime. Lawson immediately made plans to attend the Monday meeting on Ellis's behalf. 'I was concerned that it was going to turn into a witch-hunt. That they were going to solicit more complaints,' he recalled. A phone call from Mr Larch, advising him that he would not be welcome, and a phone call from Colin Eade assuring him that there was to be no soliciting of further complaints, failed to reassure him. However, when he learnt that city manager John Gray and council officer Rob Dally were going, Lawson agreed not to attend. 'At that stage I had faith in them to try and keep a lid on things,' he told me.[48]

When Chris Knight left work on Friday 29 November for a weekend out of town, he knew nothing of the parents' meeting scheduled for the following Monday. Nonetheless, he was deeply anxious about the Ellis situation. So he asked a young criminal barrister, Rob Harrison, to keep a watching brief on it in his absence. As a result, when the Ellis case finally went to court, Harrison was counsel for the defence.

Harrison was well regarded in Dunedin, where he had worked for 10 months before establishing his own practice in Christchurch. However, almost without exception, members of the Christchurch legal fraternity portrayed him to me as an inexperienced upstart, and an outsider.

While his legal colleagues were free with their opinions, Harrison was more reticent. At first he declined to talk to me. Then he agreed to talk about the facts of the case. Finally, after I had goaded him at length about the sorts of things his learned friends were saying, he agreed, reluctantly, to tell me a little about himself.

He grew up on the West Coast. After what he called 'varied and optional lifestyles' (working as a bushman, a short stint in the army, beginning an arts degree at the University of Canterbury), he became an unenthusiastic law student. During his final two years he gave up attending lectures:

> I got someone else to take lecture notes and I sat the exams. The rest of the time I worked as a devilling clerk in a criminal barrister's chambers, and at the Community Law Centre. I was paid something like $1.35 an hour, but it was the experience that mattered. I researched the law for certain cases, interviewed witnesses, interviewed the punter in the slammer, went to the crime scene, wrote it up, prepared the case from start to finish to go to court. It's valuable experience. You learn how to do it. Sometimes my senior would say – I haven't got much work for you, but there's a trial on, tell me what's happening, sit there all day and watch it. I thought he was wanting to get rid of me, but he wasn't. He was providing me with invaluable experience. Watching the major players of the day conduct jury trials gives you a good understanding of how the law works. When I left university I was streets ahead of my peers in terms of knowing what happens in a criminal court.[49]

His degree was structured towards corporate law, but his experiences in criminal law changed that: 'I saw the relevance of the law. I saw people who genuinely needed help. The richness of life experience, the people you meet – the flotsam and jetsam and the real gems – it's almost addictive.'

After graduating in 1987 Harrison worked in a law firm in Timaru, where he practised all aspects of the law and began working his way up the grading scale for lawyers receiving state-funded legal aid. Within the Christchurch legal establishment, the speed of Harrison's ascent was regarded as unseemly, even though the gradings were assigned by their own District Law Society. Harrison attributed his rapid ascent to the formative years he spent in the criminal barrister's chambers, and to the work he packed into his two years in Timaru.

In 1990 Rob Harrison moved first to Dunedin, and then to Christchurch, lured by the prospect of more interesting work and a growing personal relationship with TV3 journalist Rose Daly. In December 1990 he opened his own practice.

'Rob Harrison's a humble barrister operating from very cheap premises who does nothing but criminal work – work that no one else would do,' a Christchurch corporate lawyer told me.[50]

'That's true,' admitted Harrison, when I put the comment to him. 'I once defended a man on a charge of threatening to kill his lawyer. The registrar was desperate, "Will you take the case, Mr Harrison? I can't get anyone else to do it."' He made no apology for his 'very cheap premises' and 'criminal work':

> When I hung up my shingle in Christchurch I had to do legal aid work because I'm a barrister. I'm not allowed to advertise. The local solicitors weren't going to refer clients to someone they didn't know. I could have gone into a law firm that did criminal work, but I'd done that and I wanted more autonomy. I had to start somewhere. So, yes, I did work that corporate lawyers wouldn't deign to let near their designer decor. By 1991 I was doing very, very well financially. I worked from 'very cheap premises' to keep my overheads down. The law has to be accessible. Defending an action shouldn't cost people their houses and the clothes they stand up in. Big law firms have high overheads because they're chasing the corporate client. Of course they don't do the sort of work I do. They'd have nightmares if my sort of tattoo-festooned skinhead came strolling through the door. They'd call the police. They'd count the artworks on the walls when they left.[51]

On 29 November 1991 Rob Harrison told Peter Ellis that he was available any time, should he need a criminal lawyer. But it wasn't until Ellis was arrested four months later that Harrison again entered the picture.

• • •

On the day of the parents' meeting, the crèche inquiry moved from the private to the public arena. Under the headline 'Allegations of abuse', the Christchurch *Press* of 2 December 1991 reported: 'A Christchurch Civic Crèche worker has been suspended after allegations a child was sexually abused.' In what may or may not have been a coincidence, that same day a community newspaper reported that a local DSW coordinator of volunteers was forming a support group for families of sexual abuse victims.[52]

Christchurch city manager John Gray responded to the *Press* item with an urgent memo to the mayor and councillors confirming that a complaint had been made. He did not mention that a meeting was being held for crèche parents that evening, and, given the closing comment in his memo ('It is not a matter suitable for public debate'), he probably wished that it wasn't.

6.ii: The Meeting Was Somewhat Volatile

The item in the Christchurch *Press* on 2 December 1991 alerted the hundred or so crèche parents who crowded the Big End playroom that evening to the reason for the meeting: a Civic childcare worker had been suspended following an allegation of sexual abuse. Apart from that worrying snippet, most parents had no idea what was going on. Mr and Ms Sycamore tried to find out:

> We asked other parents. No one seemed to know anything. The staff were tight lipped. Then [Ms Magnolia] arrived. There was this dramatic scene where she stopped in the doorway and burst into tears. A couple of parents rushed over and supported her to a seat. Then this group sat in a huddle, crying and hugging each other for the rest of the evening.[1]

At least three of the four parents who had laid complaints with the police and arranged DSW interviews for their sons were among the group of distressed parents: Ms Magnolia (who triggered the investigation), Ms Arbutus (who sounded the alarm in the management committee) and Ms Ngaio (who would be chief spokesperson for the group at this meeting).

• • •

Whatever their later feelings about the crèche, the Ngaios were happy with the centre when their son Derek left for school the previous January because they gave the staff a $75 donation. They were still happy when the 'Save the Civic' campaign was mounted because they sent letters of support to the mayor, two MPs and four city councillors. '... the Civic attracts a high calibre of trained childcare workers. This is reflected in the broad range of families who are attracted to this Centre and in the exceptional quality of the social, cultural and educational policies and practices which the Civic maintains,' they wrote. When the 1991 May school holidays came along, they must have still been happy because they sent Derek back to the crèche for the holidays. Nonetheless, when the rumours about Peter Ellis arose, the allegations provided the Ngaios with an explanation for their son's developmental problems.[2]

The crèche workers also worried about Derek. 'There was something not quite right about him,' Susannah recalled. 'He was poorly coordinated. He couldn't relate to other children. He had toileting problems. But at the same time he was verbally very fluent.' Derek had a wide mouth and a turned-up nose. His physical problems included a hernia and constipation. His behavioural problems included extravagant fears and obsession.[3]

'Has [Derek Ngaio] ever been checked out for Williams Syndrome?' I asked a health professional who knew the family. (My question was prompted by memories of the damage caused to the G family when their son's comparable symptoms were misdiagnosed as the effects of sexual abuse. 'No one would dare suggest it,' she replied.

When Ms Ngaio heard about the original allegation in the week leading up to the 2 December meeting, she contacted Ms Magnolia 'to offer her support … recognising that she must be feeling quite shattered, shocked …' Then the Ngaios questioned their son. 'I can remember my partner and I … saying something along the lines we had heard some children were beginning to talk about some things they found scary at crèche,' Ms Ngaio told the court at Ellis's trial. At that time the scariest things Derek could think of were that Peter had tickled him, and had stolen a gherkin from his friend's lunch. The lad also told his mother that 'Gaye did wicked things', but he couldn't remember what they were. At that point Ms Ngaio consulted Child and Family Guidance therapist Sue Dick (who had uncovered Christchurch's first ritual abuse case) and laid a complaint with the police. Then, after a visit from Detective Eade, she arranged a DSW interview for her son.[4]

• • •

The parents who witnessed Ms Magnolia's dramatic entry into the 2 December meeting concluded that something dreadful must have happened to her child. The presence of city manager John Gray and another council official down the front, and the ashen-faced crèche staff huddled in a corner, seemed to confirm their fears, as did management committee spokesperson Mr Larch's announcement that representatives of the Police Child Abuse Unit and the DSW Specialist Services Unit would address the meeting. Everyone waited anxiously for more information. To their mounting frustration, none was forthcoming.

Detective Eade acknowledged that a member of the crèche staff has been suspended. He said there were 'concerns' rather than allegations. He said there was no cause for alarm. He invited parents to phone him if they were worried. 'Which staff member?' someone asked. He could not say. 'Is the staff member present?' No. (At that point everyone scrutinised the beleaguered staff.) 'What has he done?' He could not comment.

DSW interviewer Sue Sidey spoke next. Sidey had joined the Christchurch DSW Specialist Services Unit in 1989. Prior to that she had worked as a counsellor for the Auckland Help Foundation. It was the first time she had addressed a public meeting, but she was not ill-prepared. She had discussed her presentation with her supervisor, Dr Karen Zelas. Also, on the previous Friday (29 November) she had attended a meeting to review DSW sexual abuse investigation policy. The review meeting was one of four held around the country. Under the heading 'Truth', the report on the review meetings stated: 'It was generally agreed that the guidelines need to continue to stress that all complaints must be presumed to be true.' Under the heading 'Ritual Abuse', it stated: 'Some felt guidelines should acknowledge its existence and provide some guidance.'[5]

At the 2 December parents' meeting Sue Sidey declined to discuss the allegations alluded to in the morning paper. Instead, she advised parents to watch their children for rashes, abrasions, nightmares, dinginess, bed-wetting, tantrums, general behaviour changes and oral sex with other children or toys. She also encouraged them to read their children books like Jan Hindman's *A Very Touching Book* and Lynda Morgan's *Katie's Yukky Problem* and to contact her if they had any concerns, but she cautioned them against questioning their children too closely. She explained that interviewing was a skilled task best left to specialists, and that disclosures could be difficult to obtain from children who had been bribed with gifts or sweets.[6]

'Can't we at least talk to our kids about it?' someone asked. Sidey said that would be all right, and suggested asking 'Is there anyone at kindy you don't like?' as a suitable question. 'Crèche,' muttered the restless crowd. 'Not kindy. Crèche.' Someone asked Sidey about her training. The reply was not reassuring. She said there was no special training course for interviewers; they learnt on the job.

'The most awful thing was they wouldn't tell us anything about the allegations,' Ms Cedar recalled. 'There was lots of innuendo and no specifics. It made you want to rush home and grab your kid and say, "What's been going on at crèche? Have you got a sore bottom? Tell me what happened?"'[7]

Neither speaker mentioned sexual abuse, and this increased the confusion. Had anything happened? If it hadn't, why call a meeting? If it had, what was it? While most parents were puzzling over these questions, Ms Magnolia's supporters made their move. Ms Sycamore recalled:

> Suddenly this enormous leap took place. One minute Sue Sidey was saying, 'Go home and look at your children. Ring us if you've got any worries.' Next minute [Ms Ngaio] was laying into John Gray: The children can get counselling through ACC, but what about the parents? These parents need counselling! This is a council-run crèche. The council must pay for it. Are you going to give us an undertaking now that counselling will be available?' John Gray was going, 'Yes! Yes! Yes!'[8]

Ms Ngaio's outburst sent the embattled staff further into their corner. What have you done to our kids? the aggrieved parents seemed to be saying. Why did you allow this to happen? Then an Australian father began asking some pertinent questions.

'What are you talking about?' he said. 'Is the allegation of a sexual nature?'

'Yes, it is of a sexual nature,' conceded Eade.

'Well, what are you talking about? Are you talking about groping, or are you talking about penetration?'

'I can't comment. We're still investigating.'

'This is just like the Mr Bubbles case,' the father complained. (The Mr Bubbles case? What's he talking about? wondered his listeners.) 'There's an assumption of guilt here I find very disturbing,' he continued. 'I employ staff. I can't treat them this way. I can't have allegations running around without putting them to them.'

At that point some people started to shout and scream. A few more burst into tears. Others walked out. 'We want nothing to do with your witch-hunt,' they said.

When it was over, a social worker parent approached the two older women who had worked in the Womble End for more than a decade and gave them a big hug. 'We know you're not involved,' she said.

'This is frightening,' Ms Sycamore said to her husband on the way home. 'Why are they setting this man up?'

Mr Sycamore tried to sound reassuring. 'That policeman seemed a sensible, non-excitable fellow,' he said. 'I'm sure he can handle it.'[9]

• • •

For every parent at the 2 December meeting there was one overriding question: has anything happened to my child? In the fear-filled wake of the meeting they reviewed every aspect of their child's behaviour in minute detail, and drew their own conclusions.

Ms Elm remembered the rare occasions when her daughter didn't want to go to crèche, and the odd time when she didn't want her father to put her to bed: 'I thought – Oh dear, that's peculiar, perhaps … Then I thought – No, that's not peculiar. It's absolutely normal. It's got bugger all to do with sexual abuse.'[10]

Ms Maple was more pragmatic. 'J and I decided that the nature of the child we have – the way he talks to us and we talk to him – meant we would have known if he felt anything wrong – anything violating – any sort of mistreatment at all,' she told me. 'He would have chatted to us about it in the same way that he chatted about everything else in his life.'[11]

Mr Beech based his conclusions on his daughter's behaviour in Ellis's presence. 'Two or three times each term I'd drop Tania off when Peter was on the early shift. I'd have a cup of coffee with the staff at the Womble End. Then Peter would say, "Well, we'd better get down to our end." My daughter would trot off with him quite happily. She was never clingy. There was never a problem in any shape or form. I decided the accusations just didn't ring true.'[12]

Ms Willow recalled a day when her daughter didn't want to be left at crèche. 'She was standing there crying. Peter was holding her by the shoulders and saying, "Just go, Mum, she'll be fine." I'm sure she was. At the time it seemed perfectly normal.

But when I started worrying about leaving my daughter with somebody who wasn't safe, I looked back on that incident as a terrible, horrible thing.'[13]

In the course of her agonising, Ms Mahogany remembered the worst story her son had ever told about Peter Ellis:

> Leo said they'd gone for a walk in the Botanic Gardens. When it was time to go back this boy sat down and said he wouldn't go. Peter said, 'The rest of us'll go and leave you here' and they began walking off. The boy started screaming and crying, then he raced up to join them. I thought: there's plenty of us have done that![14]

But since virtually every young child displays some of the signs mentioned by Sue Sidey in the course of an average year, most parents felt that the only way to find out if anything untoward had happened was to ask.

'Did Peter ever do anything horrid to the kids?' Ms Willow asked her daughter.

'He tripped up Michael,' she said. 'And one time he pulled a kid out of the tree.'[15]

Having considered her parents' concerns, Nina Elm raised the subject with her mother when they were out in the car.

> She said, 'Peter did do something awful to me once.' I thought: here we go. Disclosure. Just drive slowly. She said, 'He dyed my hair pink.' Which he did. When she was four she went through this obsessive pink phase – pink knickers, pink socks, pink everything. On the way to crèche one day I said, 'There's Undine's mother. She's got red hair.' Nina said, 'I'd like to have pink hair.' We talked about it when we got to crèche. Peter said, 'I can make your hair go pink. You just wrap it in wet crepe paper. It washes out.' I said, 'That would be fun – go for it!' When I got back Nina's hair was bright pink. The trouble was it didn't wash out. So that's what Nina remembered about Peter – six weeks of fading pink hair. But she still wanted to go back to see him after she'd left. Foolishly or not, I believe that if he'd done anything dreadful to her she wouldn't want to go back to see him.[16]

Despite the parental questioning, there were no disclosures of abuse from any children in the wake of the December 1991 meeting. Furthermore, though both Colin Eade and Sue Sidey gave out their phone numbers, they received only one expression of parental concern during the remainder of 1991.[17]

At that stage in the inquiry, the lack of disclosures made believing whether or not one's child had been (or may have been) molested by Peter Ellis a matter of parental choice. After reviewing their experiences of the crèche, and after receiving reassuring responses from their children, most parents chose not to believe. However, a few chose to believe.

The believers included the four parents who had already laid complaints with Colin Eade (Ms Magnolia, Ms Arbutus, Ms Ngaio and Ms Laburnum); Ms Cork (who diagnosed abuse on the basis of her son's poor reading skills and his inclination to stuff food and clothing into his mouth); Mr and Ms Mulberry (parents of the child whom Ellis had hung on the picket fence by his overalls); Mr and Ms Lime (parents of the child who claimed that another lad had to fight off Ellis in the bedroom); Mr and Ms Palm (colleagues of the Ngaios); other present and former crèche parents who worked in the sexual abuse field; close friends and relatives of the Magnolias and the Ngaios. Because of Ellis's homosexuality, most believers assumed the problem was confined to boys.

Immediately after the 2 December meeting, 13 core believers formed a mutual support group. Seven of the 13 worked in the sexual abuse field. Another held an influential position on the staff of the Christchurch City Council. Over the coming weeks they met regularly to ensure that their concerns were 'handled properly by the crèche hierarchy', and to discuss what they believed were behavioural indicators of sexual abuse. They also tried to figure out where the supposed abuse could have happened, and why it had gone undetected for so long. Over the same period, sceptical parents – having satisfied themselves that their kids were okay – got on with their lives.

At that stage, in the absence of any disclosures from children, all the investigators had to go on were the innuendos of a few agitated parents. As counterweights to those innuendos, there was the open-plan centre with adults coming and going all day, and the positive experiences of the scores of sexual abuse workers who had used the Civic over the years. Those people were trained to spot sexual abuse where others may overlook it. Their children were trained to speak out if anyone touched them inappropriately. Their failure to notice anything amiss during Ellis's time at the centre provided strong support for the sceptics' argument that no sexual abuse had taken place.

Further support for the sceptical view can be found in the speed with which the rumours spread in the wake of Ms Magnolia's allegation. If unsubstantiated rumours of child molestation at a Christchurch childcare centre could permeate the crèche community and the child protection services within days, was it really possible for real, large-scale abuse at the same preschool to stay hidden for almost six years?

Nonetheless, the investigators pushed on with their inquiry. The Christchurch *Press* of 3 December reported that specialist interviewers would be attempting to ascertain whether any children who attended the Civic Child Care Centre had been sexually abused. A police spokesman said the investigation would be 'reasonably long'. Next morning a Christchurch radio station carried the union response: 'Peter Lawson says despite police investigations there's been no proof of the allegations, and he believes the employee should be reinstated until it's proven otherwise. He says the union will consider taking legal action if need be.'[18]

Everyone agreed that the police investigation had to run its course, but in the meantime the council, the union and the management committee had important decisions to make. A summit meeting was held on Wednesday 4 December.

Angela Counihan, who represented the union at that meeting, wanted Peter Ellis's employment contract honoured. Everyone else had other concerns. None of them had much to do with justice for Ellis. City manager John Gray and second-tier manager Rob Dally wanted to protect the council from scandal. Alistair Graham and senior community adviser Martin Maguire (who liaised between the council and the crèche on a day-to-day basis) wanted to save the Civic's reputation as a high-quality centre. Management committee spokesperson Mr Larch wanted to return the Civic to the happy place it used to be. To all these people the answer was simple: Peter Ellis had to go. To personnel manager Marshall Wright, personnel officer Barbara Newman and the in-house solicitor Peter Mitchell, the answer wasn't so simple. If Ellis were to be removed, he had to be removed in a lawful manner.

In the morning of 4 December Mr Larch faxed a bold three-page letter to meeting chairman Rob Dally. This move reinforced the impression that Mr Larch was calm, organised and in control, and that his views should be taken seriously. Mr Larch's letter detailed what he claimed, and believed, were the concerns of parents. But it made no mention of the concerns of sceptical parents about the nebulous nature of the allegations and the prejudicial manner in which they were being handled. Instead, Mr Larch focused on the demands of the believers.

In his letter Mr Larch chided John Gray for failing to assure parents that Ellis would not be reinstated without prior consultation with the management committee. Since Mr Larch had already stated that he did not want Ellis reinstated while doubts existed, this was an implicit demand that Ellis not be reinstated at all.

Mr Larch also reminded the council that the management committee did not want to deal with Barbara Newman, and offered a suggestion that shoved the agenda of the vociferous believers right up the noses of the council administration. His letter stated:

> In order that the matter may be handled in the best possible manner it may be appropriate for the Council to engage some professional help in dealing with the situation. To this end it may be appropriate if the personnel department and perhaps those immediately involved in the ongoing investigation spoke with the child abuse educator at the Department of Social Welfare. We understand that this person provides education in child abuse matters ... her input at this stage could be invaluable.[19]

Council officers were generally sympathetic to Mr Larch's proposals but they were a little concerned that he did not appear to know his place, and they opened the 4 December meeting by addressing this issue.

'The council gave me a very clear message,' Mr Larch recalled in a 1996 interview. 'If you rock the boat, if you're aggressive and outspoken and go to the media, we will simply close the Civic. We're in control here. We are consulting with you. We want to work with you. But if you upset us we've got this big stick we can hit you with.'[20]

Rob Dally advised the meeting that interviewer Sue Sidey was still dealing with concerns – rather than complaints or allegations – from four families. She expected the interviews to be finished in the coming week. She said that children had made further negative statements about Peter Ellis.

In his notes Rob Dally also recorded Sue Sidey's comment that 'Peter Ellis is not a suitable person for a childcare centre'. As it happened, Sidey had no expertise in preschool education, and had never met Ellis or seen him at work. But in the heightened anxiety of the time Sidey was prepared to offer such advice, and Dally was prepared to note it.[21]

After receiving Dally's report, the 4 December meeting discussed Mr Larch's letter item by item, and generally accepted his proposals. Then Martin Maguire tabled a list of DSW-approved sexual abuse counsellors. The meeting agreed that counselling should be available to parents whose children had gone through the interview process, and to Peter Ellis and the other crèche staff.[22]

I asked Maguire why the city manager had agreed to provide sexual abuse counselling for parents, when there was no evidence that any sexual abuse had taken place.

'To be honest, I'm not sure that John Gray actually understood what counselling was about,' he replied. 'I think he just wanted to fix the problem. He wanted to be seen as a good corporate citizen. He probably thought that providing counselling would set everyone's minds at rest.'[23]

Some of the counsellors on Maguire's list had been involved in the Ward 24 and Glenelg controversies, and in the case involving the school Maori language assistant. In his memo Maguire stated that former START therapist Sara Crane was 'recognised among other counsellors as perhaps the leader in her field'.[24]

In any event, the only parents who sought counselling in 1991 were the two complainants whose children had long since left the crèche (the Ngaios and the Laburnums).[25] But, as the case mushroomed in 1992, the counselling process brought scores of vulnerable and uncertain parents under the influence of sexual abuse workers who were convinced that the alleged abuse had occurred.

• • •

In the weeks leading up to Christmas 1991, child abuse anxiety was transmitted to the city council administration by three separate, but interconnected, carriers: crèche management committee spokesperson Mr Larch, the police/DSW investigation team of Colin Eade and Sue Sidey, and the parent support group that had formed around Ms Magnolia.

None of the carriers had any evidence of abuse. But what Mr Larch lacked in evidence he made up for in energy and organisation, what Eade and Sidey lacked in evidence they made up for in authority and innuendo, and what the support group lacked in evidence they made up for in passion.

In the wake of the initial allegation, the support group members were like the survivors of a house fire, picking over their charred memories of the crèche. In the process they found many familiar keepsakes, transformed, almost beyond recognition, into ugly and deformed fragments which they flung at the council and the crèche management committee in a frenzy of rage and revulsion.

When their daughter was at the Civic, the Palms were typical crèche parents. They supported the centre's non-violent, non-stereotyping policies. They discouraged Lara from playing with dolls, and taught her the correct names for genitalia. When she was four, Ms Palm told a crèche worker: '[Lara] said, "I've got a clitoris." I'm proud of her for owning her clitoris.' But when the accusations against Peter Ellis arose, the Palms looked back on their daughter's preschool years with alarm rather than pride.

Ms Palm recalled an occasion the previous summer when children were playing naked outside and Ellis painted leaves and flowers down their backs and legs. At the time most parents thought it charming. One even took photos. But supervisor Gaye Davidson felt that Ellis had taken face painting too far, and told him not to do it again. In December 1991 Ms Palm redefined the episode as 'buttock painting' and 'unacceptable behaviour'.[26] To sceptical parents, the complaint was ridiculous:

> The 'buttock painting' incident is now legendary. Most people had no problems with it whatsoever. I can just see those complainant parents going on about how nudity in children is the most beautiful thing in the world and isn't it great that no one has any hangups. Then, when the spectre of sexual abuse was raised, they launched themselves from one end of the spectrum to the other without stopping for breath in the middle.[27]

Another legendary incident – the occasion when Ellis hung Derwent Mulberry on the fence – occurred about three weeks before Ms Magnolia's initial complaint. At the time Ellis was lining up a group of children for a game and Derwent kept pushing to the front, so Ellis picked him up by the shoulder straps of his stout overalls and hung him on the picket fence. The other kids thought it was a huge joke, and begged to be hung up too. The children were happy, but Davidson felt that Ellis had overstepped the boundary of acceptable childcare practice. So she put a stop to the game and phoned Ms Mulberry.

In bursts of activity on 5 and 12 December, members of Ms Magnolia's support group bombarded council officials and the crèche management committee with complaints about Ellis. These involved one-off incidents (buttock painting, fence hanging and gherkin stealing), and ongoing concerns (tickling and intimidating children, gossiping with parents and drinking heavily outside working hours).

Ms Magnolia's supporters also concluded that Ellis's activities could not have gone unnoticed by his colleagues. At first they attributed the problem to staff negligence and institutional mismanagement. Later, they concluded that the other childcare workers were sexual offenders too.

• • •

On Friday 6 December the council made its first attempt to remove Peter Ellis from the crèche payroll. At a meeting with personnel manager Marshall Wright, union secretary Peter Lawson and community adviser Martin Maguire (who had been delegated by the council to act as Ellis's 'support person'), Ellis was told that reinstatement was not an option. Wright expressed some sympathy for Ellis, and invited him to consider redeployment. 'No,' said Ellis. 'I want my job back.'[28]

Shortly afterwards, in a letter to the council, Mr Larch put his opposition to Ellis's reinstatement in writing:

> ... having considered the situation from all positions and weighed up the conflicting factors the Management Committee are firmly of the view that it would simply not be possible for the staff member to return to childcare duties at the Civic Child Care Centre ... the Management Committee ... do not see reinstatement as an option in this situation.[29]

Before posting the letter Mr Larch circulated it to the management committee. 'I am under some pressure to forward a letter capable of being shown to the Union,' he explained.[30] The other lawyer on the management committee was not happy: '... as you know, my concern is whether we should be writing such a letter at this stage, and I don't want the letter to be used to absolve the council from any responsibility on this issue.' However, she acknowledged that Mr Larch's letter 'reflects how we, as a committee, feel, and how the issue of possible abuse in the context of childcare creates almost a "special case", i.e. guilty or innocent, right or wrong, once trust in a person is questioned, it never fully returns, and as you so rightly say, childcare survives on trust.'

The other committee members were just grateful that Mr Larch was handling the problem, and were happy to let him get on with it. Most of them had trouble believing that Peter Ellis was guilty of anything, but they wanted to keep the Civic afloat, and they were prepared to toss Ellis overboard to achieve that end. Besides, there seemed no alternative. In fact there was an alternative, but no one realised that until much later.

In 1992 Ms Magnolia enrolled Geoffrey in another childcare centre. Later that year, when the crèche case was reaching a crescendo, she accused a gay male childcare worker at the second centre of sexually abusing her son. That complaint was handled very differently. The details will be discussed later, but at this stage it is worth noting that, when both cases had run their course, Peter Ellis was in jail and the other gay male childcare worker accused by the same woman of abusing the same child was still working in early childhood education.

• • •

During Geoffrey Magnolia's second interview, on 4 December 1991, he informed interviewer Sue Sidey that 'Peter scares some of the kids'. He said his mother had told him. But he denied that Peter scared him. When Sidey asked, 'What about the black penis?', Geoffrey said, 'I'm not going to tell you today.'[31]

The following year, when Sidey asked Nadia Rimu about the crèche she too refused to discuss it. That worried her parents, but by 1997 they were far less concerned. 'We've got another four-year-old now,' Ms Rimu explained. 'When she doesn't know something she'll say, "I'm not telling you." Four-year-olds do that. If they don't know, they've got too much pride to say, "I don't know."'[32]

Ms Magnolia was devastated by Geoffrey's failure to disclose. 'She was angry, crying with rage,' crèche worker Susannah recalled. 'I couldn't understand it. She thought her child had been abused. He'd gone for an interview and revealed nothing. Why wasn't she relieved?' Around that time, Childcare Association tutor Alison Mary was confronted by Ms Magnolia in the foyer of the Cranmer Centre.

'I am not a mad woman, Alison!' she said.[33]

In his 9 December interview Derek Ngaio told Sue Sidey that Peter had tickled him, and had stolen his friend's gherkin. He said the tickling was on the outside of his clothes. He identified his chest, waist and legs as the tickled areas. He added that his Mum tickled him too, which he thought was a bit mean. In her report, Sidey stated that the boy's memories of the crèche had faded, and he showed no anxiety that would be consistent with sexual abuse.

Sidey completed her interviews on 20 December 1991, and Colin Eade reported to the council the same day: '... enquiries into the Child Care Centre are complete ... To date there have been no disclosures of any sort of indecent touching by any person employed at the Child Care Centre.'[34]

However, in Eade's view, the inquiry had not been in vain. Though he had no expertise in preschool education, and had never met Peter Ellis, he expressed firm opinions on both issues:

What has come out of these interviews very clearly is that the children had a general fear of Peter Ellis. It is possible that this fear may affect their behaviour for some time to come. It also appears that he has handled some of these children roughly.

It is clear to me that Peter Ellis should not be involved in any way in the supervision or care of children. I believe that we were very lucky to have this brought to our attention at this stage. If he had continued on at the Centre, things could have got worse.[35]

Eade did not expect the case to be reopened, but he did not rule out the possibility. 'It is possible that Sue Sidey will be contacted by other parents in the future but it is unlikely that these children will disclose sexual abuse,' he wrote. 'The investigation is complete as far as the Police are concerned. If anything further develops in 1992 I will advise you.'

6.iii: Reinstatement Is Not an Option

On Monday 23 December 1991 union secretary Peter Lawson was called to a meeting at the city council. He was hoping to have good news for Peter Ellis in time for Christmas, but the council had a different agenda. 'I was confronted [by] about four senior managers who advised me that Peter Ellis was being dismissed,' Lawson recalled. 'I had a bitter argument with management over that, but they decided to go ahead anyway.'[1]

Personnel manager Marshall Wright knew that employers were not supposed to rely on police findings when dealing with complaints against employees. But city manager John Gray had no qualms about doing so. 'The council had a letter from the police saying that Ellis was not an appropriate person to be employed in childcare. That was the trigger that changed suspension to dismissal – just a simple statement like that,' Gray told me.[2]

When Lawson was shown notes of the 2 December parents' meeting, his indignation increased:

I had been given an assurance that there would be no soliciting of further complaints, but that was really one of the main themes – telling people what to look for and how to lay a complaint. They might not have said 'We want you to lay complaints' but that was the whole thrust of the meeting.[3]

From the union point of view, the only good thing to come out of the 23 December meeting was that Ellis's suspension was extended while redeployment options were considered. Next morning, Peter Lawson and council administrator Alistair Graham broke the news to Peter Ellis. Graham recalled:

> I told him, 'Look Peter, we know you love the Civic, but you've got to understand that you can't go back. It won't survive if you go back.' By then parents were leaving – not a lot, but some. Rumours were everywhere. So, regardless of his guilt or innocence, it was inappropriate for Peter to return.[4]

While it was true that rumours were rife, and that crèche numbers had fallen slightly, a fall in numbers was normal at that time of year. In December 1991 there were only three unexpected withdrawals from the crèche roll: Geoffrey Magnolia, and the children of management committee activist Ms Arbutus. At that stage the remaining crèche families – even Ms Magnolia's supporters who still had children at the Civic – were apparently prepared to wait and see which way the authorities jumped before reviewing their children's childcare arrangements.

After Alistair Graham's approach had failed, the task of persuading Ellis to go quietly fell to his council-appointed support person, Martin Maguire. 'I went to him with instructions from Marshall [Wright] to offer him up to ten grand to get out. Whether that had any official sanction from John Gray I don't know, but I was obviously there to see if he would take the bait. He wasn't interested.'[5]

'What did he say?' I asked. The offer seemed like a good test of Ellis's guilt. If he really was a paedophile who had almost been caught, wouldn't he just take the money and run?

'He wanted his job back,' said Maguire. 'He wasn't dismissive. He just said, "No." He had a point to prove; he was innocent and he wanted his job back.'

'What was his attitude towards his job?'

'He loved it. Loved it. And he wanted it back.'

In late 1991 and early 1992 Maguire visited or telephoned Ellis most days. His impressions were, to say the least, mixed:

> From the beginning he was adamant that he was innocent. He was stunned that all this was happening to him. I think that increased his drinking. His partner obviously had an alcohol problem. I'd say Peter was borderline. Around the back of the house there was a wall of flagons – I'm not joking – a complete wall of empty flagons. He was always pleased to see me. He was quite flamboyant. At times he was very funny. He made two passes at me of a sexual nature. I never knew whether to believe the stuff he told me about his sexual experiences. He claimed that he had been sexually abused as a child. He was quite graphic about all sorts of stuff that I didn't think was quite normal.[6]

When I asked Ellis about these conversations he insisted there was no truth in his wild talk. He said he was never sexually abused as a child, and that he made the comment to 'wind up' Maguire. This is entirely possible. Caution was not one of Ellis's strengths. Many people familiar with his risqué conversations – his teasing and his desire to shock – insisted that it was his tongue, rather than his actions, that got him into trouble. When his former colleague Suki heard he had been suspended following an allegation of child sexual abuse, her first thought was: Bloody Peter, what's he said? 'He has such a bizarre sense of humour,' she told me. 'I often used to think – You gotta watch it, boy – not everyone'll think that's funny.'

In any event, throughout his many conversations about sex, whether drunk or sober, with Martin Maguire or anyone else, Ellis never showed any interest in, or approval of, sex with children.

• • •

Most New Zealanders take a break over the Christmas–New Year period, but in 1991–92 sexual abuse workers nationwide abandoned their holiday plans in favour of working on submissions to the select committee considering the new ACC legislation. The closing date for submissions was 15 January. However, after a storm of protest from women's groups, it was extended until the end of the month. Despite the rush, 367 written submissions and 194 oral submissions were received.

Among the organisations with strong Christchurch links that presented submissions were the New Zealand College of Clinical Psychologists; the Joint Methodist–Presbyterian Public Questions Committee; the Royal Australian and New Zealand College of Psychiatrists; the National Collective of Rape Crisis and Related Groups of Aotearoa; the New Zealand Association of Psychotherapists; the New Zealand Association of Counsellors; Doctors for Sexual Abuse Care; and The Health Alternatives for Women (THAW). THAW was housed in the same building as the Civic Child Care Centre. Some THAW workers sent their children to the crèche. When women phoned THAW for legal advice, they were often referred to Ms Magnolia's friend Wendy Ball.

The discussions required for the preparation of submissions on the ACC Bill would have made child molestation a hot topic among social activists nationwide. The process would also have helped spread news of the allegations at the Christchurch Civic Child Care Centre around the country.

• • •

On 10 January 1992 council personnel manager Marshall Wright visited Peter Ellis with union secretary Peter Lawson. Wright reiterated that reinstatement was not an option and offered Ellis redeployment or $10,000 in voluntary severance. Ellis said he wanted his job back.

On 20 January, after a meeting with Peter Ellis and his lawyer Chris Knight, Peter Lawson advised Marshall Wright that Ellis was seeking reinstatement. At that point, Wright drafted a letter terminating Ellis's employment.

Peter Ellis's dismissal letter outlined the events of the previous two months: the initial unspecified 'allegations which had been made concerning your behaviour'; the meetings, the provision of a support person and the offer of counselling; the letter of 18 December advising that the management committee was opposed to his reinstatement; and the letter of 20 December advising that, in the opinion of Detective Eade, 'Peter Ellis should not be involved in any way in the supervision and care of children'. The dismissal letter also pointed out that redeployment and voluntary severance had been offered and rejected. It concluded: 'The City Manager, having carefully considered all options available, has now come to the conclusion since you can no longer be employed for the purpose for which you were originally engaged that your employment should be terminated. Please take this letter as notice of same. You will be paid through to 14 February 1992.'[7]

Peter Lawson and Chris Knight responded by bringing Employment Court barrister Tony Couch on to Peter Ellis's defence team. Couch's first impressions of Ellis were vivid:

> Peter was quietly spoken, but he very clearly denied any impropriety. He was pretty detailed in his denial. What came across very strongly was that he loved his job. He loved working with kids. He cared about those kids. He was fairly dishevelled and he had very long fingernails, but the important thing was that he was very aggrieved at losing his job – not so much because he felt he'd been treated unfairly, although he did feel that – he was very genuinely aggrieved because it was a job he loved.[8]

At a meeting with Ellis, Lawson and Knight, Couch addressed the central questions surrounding Ellis's dismissal, and concluded that Ellis had good reason to feel aggrieved:

> I formed the view that his dismissal was wide open to challenge because the council had either omitted, or I think refused, to tell Peter what the allegations were. He'd been dismissed on the basis of allegations that he didn't know the substance of, so obviously he didn't have the opportunity to respond to them. It was a grossly unjustified dismissal in employment law terms. It was also wide open for challenge by judicial review. At the time, I regarded it as an open and shut case.[9]

The crèche reopened after Christmas on 13 January 1992 with a steady daily attendance level and a shorter-than-usual waiting list. Apart from Ellis's absence, the centre carried on more or less as usual. In the lives of some crèche children, Ellis was of minor significance and they were unconcerned by his absence. But to others he was a favourite and they missed him a lot. Ms Rata recalled:

> When he didn't come back after the holidays some of the kids who really loved him became quite angry to hear his name. It reminded me of a little girl whose parents had

split up – the grief-fury of being let down by a loved figure. The significance of Peter to those children needs to be acknowledged. When the bond was cut so suddenly their distress turned to anger and a feeling of being let down. Later, when people asked their kids about Peter doing mean things, they had an opportunity to get even. In all the psychobabble that's been thrown around about the innermost souls of these children, I'm surprised this fairly obvious point hasn't been raised.[10]

The crèche staff had no idea whether Ellis would return, but when they learnt in early January that the investigation was over and no abuse had been found, they were reasonably optimistic. That news, together with a glowing report from the Education Review Office, was a huge relief. Ellis was not a child abuser. The Civic was a good and safe place. They figured that once the council had sorted out Ellis's employment, and issued a statement clearing the reputations of Ellis and the crèche, all would be well. Most staff assumed that Ellis would return to childcare work, if not at the Civic then at some other centre; it was just a matter of time.

• • •

After the Christmas break, Ms Magnolia's support group resumed their meetings. By mid-January their discussions would have included two worrying items of new information: the first was that Ellis was seeking reinstatement; the second was that he was bisexual. To anxious parents, the latter meant that girls were also at risk. At that point they began worrying about their daughters as well as their sons.

In particular, they worried about the dozen or so children that Ellis had babysat over the years, and the handful of children that were his favourites. Most of the babysat children were cared for by Ellis for short periods on one or two occasions (usually to give their mothers a break during a domestic crisis). However, there were four children with whom he had had extended contact outside the crèche: Zelda Cypress, Gary and Ethan Kowhai and Yelena Holly.

Ellis's babysitting of Zelda Cypress during the two-and-a-half working days left after the crèche closed for Christmas 1986 has already been discussed. His babysitting of Gary and Ethan Kowhai took place while he was living with their mother in 1987–89. His babysitting of Yelena Holly took place while her mother worked nights in late 1991 and early 1992. Like his other babysitting arrangements, Ellis's babysitting of the Kowhai and Holly children grew out of his interest in, and his concern for, the lives of crèche families.

In late 1986 Ms Kowhai's life was a mess. Early in 1987 her estranged husband gained custody of Gary and took him to live in another town. Ms Kowhai recalled:

> The Civic to me was like a haven. When Peter was there he focused on me as someone to help. I was a needy person because [Gary] had been taken away from me. Peter tended

to fill that gap. Around Christmas 1986 we met up at a party. After that we spent a lot of time together. He started coming to my place with alcohol. I wasn't much of a drinker but I realised once I'd had a few drinks that I didn't worry about [Gary] anymore. Peter moved in around May 1987.[11]

During the two years that Ellis lived with Ms Kowhai, she regained custody of Gary and formed a relationship with another man. Over the same period Ellis babysat her children on many occasions. After Ellis moved out, Ms Kowhai continued to visit him with her children. She first heard about Ms Magnolia's allegations from Ellis himself. For a few weeks she supported him.

Ms Holly was another stressed and busy woman whom Ellis had befriended. After separating from her drug-addict husband, she was desperate for babysitters. Her daughter Yelena spent eight hours a day, four days a week at the Civic. Ms Holly asked crèche staff to help out in the evenings as well. Peter Ellis, and Debbie Gillespie's partner Belinda (a relieving crèche worker), offered their services. From around May 1991 Ellis babysat Yelena Holly about once a week at her home.

In the wake of Ms Magnolia's allegation, Ms Holly's sympathies were initially with Ellis. 'Are you coming to the meeting tonight?' someone asked, as she was leaving the crèche on 2 December. 'I'm not having any part of your witch-hunt,' she replied.[12] After that Ms Holly increased Ellis's babysitting to about three nights a week until mid-February 1992, when she told him not to come that evening. Following that phone call, Ellis never heard from Ms Holly again.

Throughout January, Ms Magnolia's supporters continued to question their children about Ellis and the crèche. They also contacted other crèche parents and advised them to do the same. By late January, alarming stories about Ellis were circulating among crèche children. Sandi recalled:

> [Yelena Holly] used to sit on my knee and have long chats. She'd say things like, 'Peter's been naughty. Peter's been really naughty. He's going to go to jail. My mum says Peter's going to go to jail cos he touches children's bottoms and you're not supposed to do that.' I never knew what to say. I couldn't say 'No, he hasn't' because I didn't know. It was a horrible turmoil of a time.[13]

Interestingly, the comments that Yelena made to Sandi were almost identical to the comments that Detective Eade made to Yelena's mother. Ms Holly recalled:

> Detective Eade came around to see me and spoke to me and told me what to say ... I needed a step by step guide ... I told her that Peter had been very naughty ... Then I talked to her about the policeman coming round, that [Peter] was probably going to be in a jail ... I talked to her about jail ... and tried to ram home to her that there was no way that she could be hurt by him any more ... Colin Eade ... told me to explain to her that she was safe ...[14]

Regardless of whether they had been abused or not, Eade's instructions conveyed a powerful message to crèche children: Peter Ellis is evil and must go to jail, and you must help us put him there.

As well as questioning their children, concerned parents read them the books recommended by Sue Sidey (*Katie's Yukky Problem* and *A Very Touching Book*). The potential for these books to make children anxious about physical interactions with adults has already been noted. The use of these books in conjunction with questions about Ellis would have effectively redirected the children's anxieties from physical interactions with adults in general, to physical interactions with Ellis in particular. Also, for children who couldn't see the point of their parents' questions, these books provided the answer: Mum and Dad wanted to know if Peter had done any yukky (or bad, or secret) touching. In *Katie's Yukky Problem*, Lynda Morgan wrote:

> A bad touch was when someone who was bigger and older, usually someone you knew, touched your body in a way that made you feel yukky and uncomfortable ... the touch might be on your breasts, bottom or vagina, or it may be a hug or a kiss that you don't like. Sometimes the person says it's a game or a secret and asks you not to tell anyone.[15]

In *A Very Touching Book*, Jan Hindman wrote:

> Secret touching may happen with someone you love a lot! Someone whom you would feel bad about getting into trouble if you told the touching secret. Secret touching may happen with a trick – or a promise not to tell ... You may be promised treats or fun or extra love.[16]

In so far as Ellis was a man, and a favourite with most crèche kids, he fitted the scenario. They loved his tricks and treats, and if you counted the iceblocks he bought them on walks to the gardens (and insisted they finish before they returned to the crèche), he had secrets with them too. All the children had to do was figure out whether he had ever touched them in a yukky or bad or secret way, and tell a grownup. According to the books, kids who told about yukky touching were rewarded with lots of cuddles and praise.

Figuring out whether Ellis had touched them in the wrong places wasn't too difficult. According to Morgan, even a hug could qualify as bad touching. In any event, in the course of rough-and-tumble play with Ellis, a great deal of random bodily contact took place.

Figuring out how the touching felt was more difficult. Hindman named four feelings: happy, sad, scared, angry. Morgan described bad touches as feeling yukky or uncomfortable. So how was a child supposed to describe the gleeful anticipation of hiding from Peter during a game of 'What's the Time, Mr Wolf?', or the sensation of wet clothes after running through a sprinkler with him in the gardens? The best that most kids could come up with was 'scared' or 'yukky'.

By late January, despite more than eight weeks of parental questioning and readings of the recommended books, no present or former crèche children· had made any disclosures of sexual abuse. However, the possibility that there was no abuse, and that Ellis should be allowed to get on with his life, was not something that Ms Magnolia's support group was prepared to accept.

At the 2 December meeting Mr Larch had invited parents with concerns about the management of the crèche to put their complaints in writing. This should not have been difficult for angry, articulate people with serious concerns. But by January 1992 Mr Larch had received only one written complaint. It was from the Palms, whose daughter had left for school almost a year earlier and who, prior to Ms Magnolia's initial allegation, had been fully supportive of the crèche.

The Palms complained that, during their daughter's three-and-a-half years at the Civic, Peter Ellis tickled her, took food from her lunch and painted her buttocks. Because 'these behaviours did not go unnoticed by other staff', they felt there were important questions to be answered. These were:

1. …what specific responsibilities are given to staff to ensure that only appropriate interactions with children are maintained?
2. What happens when complaints are reported to staff members and what procedures exist for addressing and investigating complaints?
3. What employment policies exist for responding to a series of complaints made about the behaviour of one staff member?[17]

At the end of December a second member of Ms Magnolia's support group wrote a letter of complaint. Unlike the Palms, who sent their letter to the council and the management committee, Ms Lime just sent hers to the council.

The Limes' six-year-old daughter had attended the Civic from 18 months to five years of age. Their three-and-a-half-year-old son Clayton was still enrolled there. Ms Lime's letter addressed three concerns:

1. The possible harmful effects on my children as a consequence of having attended the Civic.
2. My own personal concerns about the behaviour and professionalism of a particular staff member, and
3. The practices and procedures at the Centre that allowed this situation to develop.

Of the first concern, she wrote:

> I have talked at length with Clayton. What has emerged is that he has been asked to keep 'secrets' by ... Peter Ellis. I have not been able to elicit what these secrets might have been. Clayton has also said that during a 'fighting game' with the same staff member Clayton 'got hurt'. This 'hurt' seems to have been associated with his knee. No further information has been forthcoming ... at various times Clayton has been frightened by the over vigorous games ...and also by his teasing and 'bullying behaviour'. The above information leaves me with grave fears about the situation in which I placed my child ... I would like therefore to make a formal complaint ...

Of the second concern she wrote:

> I have long been personally concerned about the relationship that Peter had with the children at the Civic ... On a number of occasions I witnessed Peter teasing children, indulging in name calling and overly physical games. While at no time did I see children distressed by these interactions ... in fact some were positively 'excited' by it ... I did not think it was either appropriate behaviour for a childcare worker or that it behoved an environment in which I wanted my children to spend a significant portion of their formative years ... I now regret that I didn't act at the time and also that I cannot remember enough of the details surrounding these instances to make a formal complaint ...

Of the third concern she wrote:

> Why were the boundaries between worker and child, not only in the wider professional arena but also within the more defined scope of the Civic's charter, not clearly delimited and, if and when these boundaries were crossed, was not appropriate action taken? I surmise ... the behaviours ... have continued over a period of years ... I recommend that a complete and thorough enquiry, financed by the Council, be undertaken into the above-named practices and procedures.[18]

Over the month in which those two complaints were sent to the council, Peter Ellis received five supportive letters from crèche families, and a 'thinking of you' card signed by three crèche staff. Union secretary Peter Lawson advised the council and management committee of this support. But when the decision was made to terminate Ellis's employment, it counted for nothing.

Whether the complaints counted for anything is a matter of debate. 'We make our decisions based on the facts,' council personnel manager Marshall Wright assured me. He acknowledged that there were 'all sorts of worries going one way and another', but insisted that, 'At the end of the day it has to be a management decision – weighing up all the factors and deciding what to do.'

According to Employment Court barrister Tony Couch, in late January 1992 the council administration was not as calm and rational as Wright made it sound: 'I seem to remember the council was really scared. They were really frightened of this whole child abuse thing. I think they knew they hadn't treated Peter fairly, but they were in a bit of a funk. I know John Gray took it over personally, and he was having real difficulty coping with it.'[19]

For his part, city manager John Gray told me he could not remember much about the period. 'My memory's not selective, I assure you,' he added. I had never suggested that it was.[20]

• • •

Having spent two months harnessing their anger and directing it towards ensuring that Ellis never worked in childcare again, Ms Magnolia's supporters must have been upset by the news that he was seeking reinstatement.

'It was like I'd pushed the start button for this whole case to start rolling again,' Ellis recalled. 'It was like I'd turned round and said – Right, I haven't done it, I want my job back. The answer was – Ohooh, let's go and round up a few more [allegations], we don't want him back.'[21]

By the end of January the children of Ms Magnolia's supporters had been subjected to two months of parental interrogation. They had been read books about sexual molestation. They had been told that Ellis was a bad man, and were asked leading questions about him. Research into the suggestibility of children has shown that influences of this sort can prompt children to make false allegations.[22]

Ms Arbutus (the driving force behind the 2 December meeting) obtained the first disclosure. Astonishingly, it did not come from either of her crèche children, but from seven-year-old Mandy, whose contact with the Civic was limited to 10-minute visits when she called in with her mother to collect her younger siblings.

The nature of Mandy's disclosure, and the circumstances under which it was obtained, is a mystery. Ms Arbutus gave her notes of the event to Detective Eade. But around the time that Ms Arbutus complained to the police that Eade had propositioned her, the notes disappeared.

The DSW guidelines in use at the time of Sue Sidey's evidential interview with Mandy on 30 January 1992 advised: 'do not use leading questions'; 'if possible get the child to recall a specific incident'; 'encourage the child to relate incidents from the beginning'; and 'do not interrupt, correct or challenge the child'.[23]

Once Sue Sidey had satisfied herself that Mandy knew the difference between truth and lies, and had obtained a promise from the child that she would tell the truth, the interview proper began. Mandy said she had come to talk about 'yukky touching' on 'private parts', but the interview transcript shows it was Sidey who introduced the idea that Mandy had been touched in that way.

Sidey's report stated that Mandy gave details 'to indicate attempted digital penetration over her clothing, and touching under her clothing, in a way consistent with a child who has experienced sexual abuse'. But Mandy's claim that the touching happened at the Big End in the presence of other children and adults, including her own mother, did not appear in the report. Nor did Sidey admit that her attempt to obtain a detailed description of a specific incident was a dismal failure.

Mandy said she was playing the xylophone 'and he was on stilts when he came along and –'

'Now hang on,' said Sidey. 'Was he on stilts or not?'

'No.'

Sidey reminded Mandy to tell the truth. Then Mandy continued: 'He came along and he touched, touched, touched, touched me, touched, touched, then I said no and then I ran away and so did him because he didn't want to be caught because I always knew it was him.'

After the interview, Sue Sidey told Mr and Ms Arbutus that Mandy had made a disclosure consistent with sexual abuse by Peter Ellis. Within hours the news had surged through the sexual abuse awareness networks of Christchurch like a high-voltage electric shock. That day, another phase of the Civic Crèche case began.

6.iv: The Police Investigation Has Been Reactivated

DSW interviewer Sue Sidey advised Detective Eade of Mandy Arbutus's disclosure shortly before he returned from his summer vacation on Monday 3 February 1992. At the time he was the only police officer involved in the case. To city council officials and crèche parents he seemed calm, authoritative and trustworthy, and they looked to him for guidance.

Up to that point Eade's career had been unremarkable. In the 16 years since he and his senior colleague Brian Pearce had joined the police, Pearce had risen to the rank of detective inspector, but Eade was still an ordinary detective. To his fellow officers, Eade was a bit of a loner.

Within Christchurch child protection circles, the failure of the Police Child Abuse Unit to crack the Great Christchurch Child Pornography Ring, despite years of trying, still rankled. Sexual abuse workers who could not accept the obvious – that no evidence of a porn ring meant that none existed – had another explanation. They believed that people who abused children on a large scale were extremely clever and had influential friends. They also believed that the police investigation of the alleged ring was inadequate, and they suspected a high-level coverup.

As a rising tide of ritual abuse beliefs swept over Christchurch in 1991, many sexual abuse workers began to wonder whether the alleged child pornography ring was really a cult of perverted Satan-worshippers. These considerations meant that, by the time Detective Eade reactivated the crèche inquiry at the end of January 1992, some parents and sexual abuse workers had come to regard ritual abuse at the Civic Crèche as a possibility, and secrecy as a top priority. Consequently, though news of Mandy Arbutus's disclosure triggered a fresh wave of worrying, networking and child-interrogation among Ms Magnolia's supporters, at the margins of the network a curtain of obfuscation fell. Council administration, crèche management committee members and Civic staff knew that some parents were still highly critical of the crèche, but, apart from that, they were (in the words of childcare worker Jan Buckingham) 'blissfully, naively, stupidly unaware' of what was going on.

Ms Mulberry responded to news of Mandy's disclosure by announcing the removal of her children from the crèche in two angry letters, one to her neighbour and former friend Peter Ellis, the other to supervisor Gaye Davidson. To Ellis, she wrote:

> We trust children when they say things because children do not know how to lie ... we trust all the accusations toward you are real ... the Civic ... is not a caring place and never was; as more of your activities with children come to light. M and I hope to never see you on the street, but if we do ... I will not acknowledge you ...[1]

In her letter to Davidson, Ms Mulberry blamed all the recently alleged but supposedly longstanding problems at the crèche on inadequacies in Davidson's supervision. This claim does not stand up to scrutiny. In the course of examining every episode used by Davidson's critics to support their complaints about her, and every other episode I could find in which her supervisory abilities were tested, I found abundant evidence, even in the words of the complainants themselves, that Davidson acted promptly and appropriately on every occasion. Ms Mulberry's account of the time Ellis hung her son on the fence is a case in point. Ms Mulberry said that Davidson phoned her immediately after the incident and invited her to lay a complaint. According to Ms Mulberry, Davidson did this because she knew her son would go home and tell his mother, and Davidson wanted to 'get in first'. Ms Mulberry's account illustrates two important points: the first is that she was well aware that Davidson had responded quickly and firmly to the incident; the second is that both Ms Mulberry and Davidson knew that if anything untoward happened at the crèche, there was every likelihood that the kids would go straight home and tell their parents.

Despite all the evidence to the contrary, Ms Magnolia's supporters believed their revised view of Gaye Davidson with a passion. In her letter to Davidson, Ms Mulberry wrote:

Since the allegations of abuse were first raised, more and more incidences [sic] and information from other parents has surfaced, some dating back years. The anger and concern we felt at the beginning has been fuelled by the knowledge that this was not an isolated incident ... It concerns and upsets us greatly that you never acted on these appropriately, thus placing children (ours included) in a situation of danger ... It brings into question your own abilities as a supervisor.[2]

• • •

The next of Ms Magnolia's supporters to spring into action was Ms Lacebark. During Kari Lacebark's three years at the Civic Child Care Centre, Ms Lacebark served on the management committee. During the Save the Civic campaign the Lacebarks signed the petition and wrote a letter of support to the Christchurch *Press*. When Kari turned five and left for school, her parents gave the staff a $50 donation.[3]

Ms Magnolia and Ms Lacebark were friends. Grandma Magnolia and Grandma Lacebark were influential figures in Christchurch feminist circles. So, when Ms Magnolia began spreading word of her allegations, Ms Lacebark was among the first to know. Initially, she thought the problem just concerned boys, so she didn't join Ms Magnolia's support group, but she did attend the 2 December meeting. 'I took from that meeting that there were concerns and these could involve girls as well. Nobody said it was girls. It was just that we should consider all our children,' she told Detective Eade later.

Ms Hawthorn, who sat next to Ms Lacebark at the 2 December meeting, recalled: 'She was really emotional – shaking and freaked out.' Crèche worker Jan Buckingham also noted Ms Lacebark's reaction: 'For me, alarm bells began ringing about her that night. I thought – Oh Lord, she's drinking all of this in. You could see the cogs going.'[4]

Next day, Ms Lacebark began questioning her daughter:

I just said to her, 'Do you remember much about the crèche?' She said, 'Yes.' I said, 'Who did you used to like at the crèche?' She listed two friends. I said, 'Who did you used to like who used to look after you?' She listed basically everybody. She listed Marie, Debbie, Gaye and Peter. Then I asked her if there was anyone she didn't like who looked after her. She said, 'No one.' Then I asked her if she liked Peter. She said, 'No, not really.' Then I left it. At that stage I remember thinking it wouldn't have happened to [Kari] because she was so up front and she would have told me ... Sue had talked at the meeting about indicators ... [Kari] showed none of those. It just nagged me, it just stayed in my mind ... I wondered if anything had happened ...[5]

As well as worrying about her daughter, Ms Lacebark worried about Yelena Holly. Of the dozen or so children babysat by Ellis, only two – Yelena Holly and Zelda Cypress – became complainants in the court proceedings. The path by which

Yelena Holly became a complainant began when she went to play with Kari Lacebark on 6 February 1992.

That day Ms Lacebark put her seven-month-old son on the floor with his nappy off and Yelena rook a great interest in his genitals. 'She started touching his penis. I told her not to and she carried on,' Ms Lacebark recalled. 'She was certainly inquisitive. She was having a good look.' When Yelena began running a little car over the baby's genitals, Ms Lacebark became angry. When Yelena threw a tantrum, Ms Lacebark sent her and Kari outside.

Afterwards, Ms Lacebark discussed Yelena's behaviour with Ms Magnolia and Ms Arbutus, and with Detective Eade and DSW interviewer Sue Sidey. Following those discussions, Ms Lacebark again invited Yelena to visit. 'I wanted to see if she would do it again,' she told Colin Eade later. So Ms Lacebark again put her baby on the floor with his nappy off and, sure enough, Yelena again made a beeline for his penis.

• • •

To those outside the curtain of secrecy surrounding the revived investigation, the hostility emanating from Ms Magnolia's supporters was like the distant rumble of thunder – vaguely ominous, but probably nothing to worry about. To those who knew no better, the worst was over. They were confident that, once some outstanding concerns had been dealt with, all would be well.

To crèche staff and Childcare Association tutors the outstanding concern was Ellis's dismissal. 'They [the council administration] thought Peter was unsuitable for childcare work,' recalled Jan Buckingham. 'That really got up our noses because we didn't think they had any qualifications to make that judgement.' The nebulous grounds for his dismissal compounded their concern. 'We felt really insecure as childcare workers. They seemed to be saying that if a child said something negative about you – which could happen anytime if you're doing your job properly – you could be down the road with a tainted reputation,' Susannah explained.[6]

On 3 February the Childcare Association tutors wrote to the council administration, questioning the grounds and manner of Ellis's dismissal, expressing confidence in his ability as a childcare worker and stressing the importance of men in childcare. 'We ask for immediate reinstatement and a public apology,' they wrote.[7]

The city council administration's outstanding concern was the challenge to Ellis's dismissal. '[Employment Court lawyer] Tony Couch was firm that we were procedurally wrong and that he had a strong case for personal grievance/ reinstatement,' council administrator Rob Dally noted after a discussion between himself, Couch and personnel manager Marshall Wright on 10 February.[8]

The crèche management committee's outstanding concern was the letter of complaint Mr Larch had received from Mr and Ms Palm before Christmas (about food stealing, buttock painting and general mismanagement at the Civic). Mr Larch's draft reply of 23 January took a conciliatory stance, but when the management committee considered the complaint at their 5 February meeting they were less sympathetic. The minutes of that meeting read: 'Letter from [Palms] to [Mr Larch] – very upset about whole business; attacking Gaye. Much discussion.' A couple of months later, when news of this brief, unflattering comment reached the Palms, they instructed lawyer Gerald Nation to write to the management committee on their behalf, demanding an apology. Mr Larch's apology was prompt and unreserved. But, in retrospect, management committee member Ms Rowan was unrepentant:

> Our view was – if they were that concerned, why did they leave their child at the creche for the best part of four years? These were intelligent, capable, well-connected parents who weren't taking responsibility for their own child. If I had a child in a situation where I felt something was wrong, I'd do something about it. If I still wasn't satisfied, I'd do something else. These people just left it. And here they were, years down the track, blaming someone else for whatever problems they had with their kid.[9]

• • •

At the time of their first allegation against Peter Ellis, the Magnolias announced that they would be removing their son from the Civic. But they did not do so immediately. Instead, they sent Geoffrey back to the scene of his alleged molestation for five to eight hours a day, four days a week, until the end of the year.[10]

The five weeks during which Geoffrey continued to attend the Civic gave his parents time to arrange another crèche for the new year. It also gave them an opportunity to examine the Civic through the darkened lens of their beliefs, and to find sinister justification for doing what they planned to do anyway.

The Magnolia's letter of 10 February was addressed to 'Gaye and the staff of the Civic'. Copies were sent to the management committee, the city manager and the mayor of Christchurch.

'... we removed [Geoffrey] from the crèche at the end of last year because of our concerns for his safety and welfare while in your care,' they wrote. They said they were 'mostly satisfied with his care on a daily basis and personally liked, admired and appreciated staff members', and 'appreciated the prompt action taken to suspend Peter following our complaint'. But they had three major concerns.

The first was that 'the ongoing inappropriate behaviour ... could not have occurred without at least tacit support (or ignoring) from other staff'. The second was their 'shock and considerable further stress and distress to have staff "go cold" on us ... and appear angry with us for taking action to protect our child, and other children'. The third was that they continued 'to be disturbed by comments on the grapevine that it's all blowing over and not as bad as first thought. We want to let you know that neither of these statements are at all accurate and that the distress and disclosures are continuing.'[11]

• • •

By mid-February the rumours in circulation were having an adverse effect on the crèche. While daily attendance numbers were holding steady, the waiting list had plummeted. On 17 February, management committee spokesperson Mr Larch decided to act. In a draft newsletter to crèche parents he announced the good news:

> Specialist Services of the Department of Social Welfare completed their evidential interviews immediately prior to Christmas and the Police Child Abuse Unit have indicated that on the basis of that report no Police prosecution will proceed as there was no disclosure of abuse.

He mentioned that 'the Council and the staff member concerned are having continuing discussions in relation to future employment options' and he promised to report again when he had more information. On a more upbeat note, he invited parents to peruse the excellent Education Review Office report, and closed with new year greetings to all.[12]

Next day (18 February), after obtaining council administrator Alistair Graham's approval of the newsletter, Mr Larch faxed it to other management committee members for comment. The following day, as he was preparing to send out the newsletter, Detective Eade phoned him with shattering news: the investigation had been reopened.

Eade's timing deserves close examination. Despite ongoing parental questioning, Sue Sidey had recorded no further disclosures from present or former crèche children since Mandy Arbutus's evidential interview on 30 January. Indeed, the only vaguely relevant events between 30 January and 19 February were the two occasions (on 6 and 13 February) when Yelena Holly had taken an interest in the Baby Lacebark's penis. So why did Eade choose Wednesday 19 February to advise Mr Larch of the revived investigation? I can think of three possible reasons.

The first is that Eade had heard about the forthcoming parents' newsletter, and was alarmed by the possibility that Mr Larch's reassuring news would turn the rumour that 'it was all blowing over and not as bad as first thought' into a self-fulfilling prophecy. The second is that on Wednesday 19 February the hottest, driest, fiercest nor'wester of the year (the wind that is said to drive people mad) was howling through Christchurch.[13] The third (which may be related to the other two), is that Detective Eade may have been galvanised into action by the statement he took from Ms Lacebark immediately prior to phoning Mr Larch.

When Ms Lacebark had questioned her daughter after the 2 December meeting, Kari's responses had been reassuring, but Ms Lacebark had continued to worry, to network and to question her daughter. When she heard that Ellis had taken children on walks, she asked Kari about that. When she heard that a child had complained of Ellis wiping his bottom too hard, she asked Kari about that too. Kari's replies were non-committal, but Ms Lacebark drew her own conclusions. These were that Ellis had taken Kari to the gardens by herself, where he had bought her an iceblock and threatened her with dire consequences if she told; and that Ellis had taken Kari into the toilets and shut the door.

On 19 February, immediately after taking Ms Lacebark's statement, Eade phoned Mr Larch. 'Possible charge of indecent assault!!' Mr Larch noted. 'Investigation still very much on … may take a considerable time to bring to a conclusion.' Following that conversation, Mr Larch redrafted the reassuring paragraph of his newsletter to read:

> While it had been hoped that Specialist Services would have completed their evidential interviews immediately prior to Christmas unfortunately this has not turned out to be the situation as new concerns have arisen. The Police investigation is continuing in close liaison with the Department of Social Welfare and it is not clear when these enquiries will be completed.[14]

Mr Larch also added a sentence about Peter Ellis's employment prospects: 'At this stage we are able to say with some certainty that the staff member concerned will not under any circumstances be returning to the Centre.' Then he faxed his revised newsletter to Alistair Graham, who phoned him back immediately demanding to know what was going on. 'I think you'd better ring the police,' said Mr Larch.[15]

After speaking to Colin Eade, Alistair Graham phoned Mr Larch with an even more alarming message. In the course of that conversation, Mr Larch crossed out the revised portions of his newsletter, and made additional notes:

> Police (!) & Council unhappy with para 2. Please delete. As yet Police do not wish Peter/legal reps, or staff to know case has been reopened. (Includes Gaye!). Council unaware of situation prior to my speaking to them today after discussion with Colin Eade. Concerns relate to children who knew Peter inside and outside Centre. Both male/female. Not now pupils, i.e. gone for some time. THIS INFORMATION IS HIGHLY CONFIDENTIAL DO NOT DISCLOSE 'TO ANYONE'.[16]

Mr Larch then produced a bland final draft of his newsletter. It had been a bad day. But it still wasn't over. There was a management committee meeting that evening. Mr Larch recalled:

> The committee was saying – Why can't we send out a notice saying the investigation's finished? In the end I said, 'I'm going to make a cup of tea and walk around the garden.

You might like to look at my file while I'm gone.' A nod was as good as a wink. That's how I got around the problem of not telling anyone. I didn't tell anyone. I assume they read my file – but I don't know that.[17]

Thus, through the chain of events recounted above, Detective Eade formally reopened the Civic Crèche investigation on Wednesday 19 February 1992 on the basis of one equivocal evidential interview and the vague worries of a few anxious parents.

• • •

Inspired by Eade's interest in their activities, Ms Magnolia and her supporters stepped up their worrying, their networking and their interrogations. Finally, in late February 1992, after three months of parental questioning about Peter Ellis, nudity, sex, breasts, vaginas, penises, ejaculation, bottoms, scariness, naughtiness, soreness, secrets, yukky touching, toileting, poos, wees and the crèche, the kids started talking dirty.

From late February on, whenever an indecency was mentioned by a child, that child was asked to name the other children who were present. Then the parents of the named children were informed, and they, in turn, interrogated their own children. By this means, waves of fresh allegations multiplied and spread among Ms Magnolia's supporters with the speed and virulence of a sociogenic Ebola virus.

On the evening of Thursday 20 February 1992 Ms Magnolia told Ms Lacebark of Audrey Walnut's revelation. According to Ms Magnolia, Audrey (a child with close family connections to the Magnolias) said that Ellis took herself, Kari Lacebark and Ali Tamarack into the crèche toilets and showed them his penis. Ms Lacebark responded to this news by interrogating Kari. 'I ... told her word for word what Audrey had said,' she informed Colin Eade later. Kari said she remembered the episode, and added – in response to further maternal questioning – that Derek Ngaio and Lara Palm had sucked Ellis's penis. Then she said something about a cup.

Ms Lacebark admitted to asking her daughter leading questions before and during that conversation. Furthermore, the notes she made were not recorded during the discussion, but jotted down afterwards, so they were probably both inaccurate and incomplete. Her notes about the cup aspect of the conversation read:

K: He said it was a cup.

M: A cup? What did you have to do with the cup?

K: We had to drink from it.

M: Did you drink from it?

K: Yes, yucky stuff came out of it. He used to put water from a hose into a cup and then stuff from his penis and make us drink it. I didn't like it.

As it happened, engaging the children in culinary activities was one of Peter Ellis's specialties. Pancake making was popular, though some children found the accompanying lemon sauce too sour for their liking. In winter, children often helped Ellis make pumpkin or mixed-vegetable soup which they drank from cups. On one occasion, as part of a biology/cooking lesson, Ellis sliced up kidneys and discussed their biology with the children. During 1992, as anxious parents interrogated their offspring about Ellis and the crèche, elements of these culinary activities found their way into the conversations.

Immediately after her discussion with Kari on 20 February Ms Lacebark reported back to Ms Magnolia, who advised Ms Ngaio and Ms Palm of the revelations the same evening. First thing next morning (Friday 21 February), Ms Lacebark informed Colin Eade of Kari's comments about Ellis. 'It relates, at the very least, to her engaging in oral sex with him,' Eade wrote. This was, at the very least, an overstatement. According to Ms Lacebark's notes, Kari said that Derek Ngaio and Lara Palm had sucked Ellis's penis, but she did not include herself in that activity, and since neither Derek nor Lara had mentioned oral sex or any other obscenity, Kari's comment was no more than an unsubstantiated rumour.

Nonetheless, the Ngaios and Palms were understandably alarmed.

On Saturday 22 February both couples checked out the rumour with their children. The Ngaios told Derek that some children had been talking about Peter. However, apart from recalling Ellis's tickling and gherkin stealing, the boy had nothing to say. But when the Palms took a similar approach, Lara figured that her parents wanted more, and she did her best to oblige:

> She said that it was hard to remember ... We gave her lots of reassurance. We said she was okay to talk and she was safe. We said it was okay and we knew that it was hard to talk. We said that it was okay and would help to take the scary feelings away. I then said to her that some of the children had talked about scary things happening to them and they said that it had happened to her ... We both asked questions about whether there was anything that Peter did that was scary or that she didn't like ... she wouldn't elaborate ... I then asked [sic] her that other children had said that Peter had put his penis in their mouths and that they had said that it happened to [Lara] too. [Lara] nodded and said, 'I thought that would be it.'[18]

Three days later (25 February), Ms Palm told Colin Eade about the conversation. '[Lara] has disclosed to her mother after some leading ... that Peter had put his penis in [Lara's] mouth and had touched her vagina,' he noted.

After Ms Lacebark had reported to him on Friday 21 February, Eade contacted Ms Holly and told her of his suspicion that Yelena had been abused. Ms Holly did not move in the same circles as Ms Magnolia, so Eade's news came as a shock. Ms Holly phoned Ms Lacebark the same day. Then, on Saturday 22 February, she broached the subject with her daughter:

> I told her that Peter had been very naughty … she said, 'How?' I said, '… he's got children to suck his penis.' She went, 'Oh, yuk.' I said, 'Has he ever done that to you?' She said, 'No.' Then I talked about the policeman coming around, that [Peter] was probably going to be in a jail … She said that he put things up her bottom, he put cakes and biscuits, and that it hurt.[19]

According to Ms Holly, Yelena also said that Ellis made her 'drink yukky drinks and he puts piddle in them' – a claim made by Kari Lacebark two days earlier that would, in the days ahead, also be made by Lara Palm and Derek Ngaio.

The claim that Ellis gave the children drinks containing urine indicates that, at this early stage in the investigation, Ms Magnolia's supporters were finding evidence of ritual abuse that fitted the checklists of allegations in *Ritual Child Abuse: Discovery, diagnosis and treatment* by Californian therapist Pamela Hudson.

Until now, the role of Hudson's checklist in the initiation and development of the crèche case has gone unrecognised. Indeed, spokespeople for the investigation have insisted that, until August 1992, the case was a large-scale but otherwise conventional child sexual abuse investigation. They say that it wasn't until Bart Dogwood made his August disclosures indicating that Peter Ellis, his friends, his mother and several members of the crèche staff were depraved devil-worshippers that the possibility of ritual abuse was ever considered. But the 'drinking urine from a cup' allegation gives the game away.

There are two fatal flaws to the allegation. The first is that making children drink urine is not something that real-life paedophiles ever do. The second is that 'urophiles' (people aroused by sexual activities involving urine) do not use cups. Dr John Money of Johns Hopkins University, an international authority on paraphilias (sexual perversions), explained:

> The urophile is, by definition, the one who gets turned on by drinking urine or by being urinated upon. Typically he gets his partner to urinate directly in his mouth, with no cups or other utensils. I have never read or encountered a case of urophilia in which the urophile was turned on by getting children (or anyone older) to drink urine either out of a container or out of his penis. Pedophilia and urophilia are two different, non-overlapping, paraphilias.[20]

Money's comments – based on more than 50 years' experience of studying and treating paraphilias – are supported by a survey of pornography on the internet conducted by researchers from Carnegie Mellon University ('Marketing pornography on the information superhighway: a survey of 917,410 images, descriptions, short stories and animations downloaded 8.5 million times by consumers in over 2,000 cities in forty countries, provinces and territories'). The survey revealed that purveyors of cyberporn are highly sophisticated niche marketers who cater to every taste, no matter how disgusting or bizarre. The author noted that pornographers avoided using paedophilic terms (like 'young' or 'teen') when describing images related to urophilia (or any other adult paraphilia) because they were keenly aware that customers who sought paedophilic images were not interested in other paraphilias, and vice versa.[21]

My own survey of the child sexual abuse literature suggests that a belief that paedophiles are interested in perversions involving urine and faeces exists only in the fevered imaginations of ritual abuse investigators. There is no mention of such perversions in Miriam Saphira's books on child sexual abuse, or in any other basic texts on the subject. Even adult 'ritual abuse survivors' rarely include these perversions in their accounts.

However, in his book on sexual abuse allegations in American day-care centres (*Nursery Crimes*) David Finkelhor stated: 'In the McMartin case ... the ritualistic elements that children have come to talk about include, among other things ... the drinking of blood and urine.' The same allegations were made at Ritual Action Group seminars throughout New Zealand in 1991 and 1992. But, for Ms Magnolia and her supporters, the primary source of the allegation was probably Pamela Hudson's *Ritual Child Abuse* – first, because the book provided a convenient checklist of allegations, and, second, because the book went on sale in Christchurch in January 1992, immediately prior to the reopening of the crèche case.[22] Hudson claimed that children ritually abused in childcare centres commonly display these symptoms:

1. Acting out of sexual acts.
2. Sudden extreme fear of the rain, the bathroom, bathing or washing hair.
3. Nightmares, night terrors.
4. High anxiety, separation anxiety.
5. Temper tantrums, disruptive behaviour.
6. Eating problems, refusal to eat meat, catsup, spaghetti or tomatoes.
7. Fear at bedtime, refusal to sleep alone, fear of the dark, refusal to go to bed.
8. Vomiting for no apparent reason. Frequent complaints of abdominal pain.
9. Medical findings commensurate with sexual assault.
10. Toileting problems.
11. Dazed, drugged or groggy appearance when returned from care provider.

Hudson also claimed that ritually abused children commonly make allegations about:

1. Group sex, and molestation by other children.
2. Molestation by adult strangers, day-care workers or babysitters.
3. Being locked inside a cage or 'jail'.
4. Being threatened that the abusers would kill their parents, siblings or pets if they told anyone about the abuse.
5. Being buried in a casket, coffin or box.
6. Being held under water.
7. Being threatened with guns or knives.
8. Being bled, being drugged orally or injected with needles.
9. Being photographed or filmed during the abuse.
10. Being tied by ropes, wires or cables, hung from hooks, placed in closets, spread over an inverted pentagram or placed on an inverted cross.
11. Being abused by people wearing robes and masks, and carrying candles.
12. Participating in mock marriage.
13. Being defecated and urinated upon, and having to ingest urine or faeces.
14. Seeing and having to participate in the torture and killing of animals. Having to drink animal blood and having blood poured over their heads.
15. Being operated upon.
16. Being tortured and sexually assaulted.
17. Seeing small children and babies killed, carved up and eaten, and sometimes participating in these activities.
18. Being taken away from the care provider, and travelling by car, airplane, helicopter or unusual conveyance.
19. Being taken to churches, other day-care centres, people's homes and graveyards for more terrorising, torture and sexual assault.
20. Being taken to underground places like caves, crypts, 'the hole', or tunnels for more terrorising, torture and sexual assault.[23]

Hudson based her checklists on telephone interviews with the parents of 12 children involved in 11 cases of alleged ritual abuse in childcare centres across the United States. Of the 'urine drinking' allegation, she wrote:

> Gallup child reported having to drink a 'pee' punch. The McMartin child consumed the 'devil's round'. The Washington children said feces were smeared on them, they were urinated upon, had to drink/eat urine and feces, and had both injected into them. The Campbell child said she had to drink her 'pee' and eat her 'poo'.

Toileting accidents are a major concern for small children. It is hardly surprising that the four-to-six-year-olds in Hudson's survey, when questioned about naughtiness and bottoms, came up with stories about urine and faeces. It is also hardly surprising that, when the names of childcare workers were included in the adults' questions, the same names appeared in the children's answers. The surprising part – given the leading nature of the questions and the improbable nature of the answers – is that sexual abuse investigators accepted the children's responses as concrete descriptions of real-life events.

• • •

In February 1992, while the members of Ms Magnolia's support group were observing symptoms in their children and extracting allegations from them that fitted the items on Hudson's checklists, the crèche staff were respecting the council's instructions not to discuss the Ellis issue with parents or children, and the council administration and the management committee were respecting Detective Eade's instructions not to tell the staff that the investigation had been reopened. Consequently, among Civic childcare workers, ignorance prevailed. 'The whole situation got away on us,' recalled Sandi. 'It was well and truly out of control before we twigged to what was happening.'[24]

The staff had waited weeks for the council or the management committee to issue a statement clearing the Civic Child Care Centre's good name. By late February their patience had run out. After documenting their concerns, they presented them to Mr Larch: 'Why did the Management Committee indicate that reinstatement of Peter was not an option?' they wanted to know. 'Who did they consult before taking this action? Why were the staff deliberately excluded from this process?' They also questioned the expertise of police officers in childcare matters, and closed with two requests: 'We would like it publicly stated through the media that there was no evidence of sexual impropriety or abuse at the Civic … We ask that the Management Committee take our concerns seriously and communicate our feelings to the City Council.'[25]

'[Mr Larch] wasn't interested in discussing our concerns,' recalled Susannah. 'We found out later that he already knew the investigation had been reopened. He was having big boys' meetings at the council about it.'[26]

• • •

On 27 and 28 February five-year-old Kari Lacebark recorded two interviews with Sue Sidey. On each occasion Detective Eade monitored the interview from an adjacent room.

'Evidential interviewing is simply a process that allows the child to tell their story, and for that story to be recorded in a way that can be repeated,' DSW chief social worker Mike Doolan explained to me in a 1997 interview. 'It's like taking a statement from a competent adult, only using a methodology that recognises childhood and the way that children tell their stories. There ought to be no influence from the interviewer in the process – other than to provide the environment and the facility for the kid to be able to express themselves.'[27]

In the Civic Crèche case, the charges laid were based solely on videotaped interviews with former crèche children. Hundreds of hours of interviews were eventually recorded with more than 100 children. But only 53 hours and 25 minutes of interviews with 19 children were introduced as evidence in court.

At the depositions hearing, around 35 hours of interviews involving 14 children were played. At the conclusion of that hearing, Judge Anderson committed the five defendants for trial, but made no comment on the quality of the interviewing.[28]

Pre-trial, Justice Williamson spent around 39 hours watching most of the 44 videotaped interviews with the 14 children who were involved in the case at that stage. Then he rejected the defence's pre-trial submission that 'the procedures followed in this case by the Police, the parents and the interviewers were so wrong and oppressive that the resulting videotaped interviews and the children's oral evidence should be excluded on the grounds of unfairness.'[29]

When the case went to the Court of Appeal, Ellis's counsel, Graham Panckhurst QC (later Justice Panckhurst), argued that the interview process was seriously flawed, and the limited selection of interviews played at the trial effectively concealed those flaws from the jury. He urged the court to view the videotapes and consider the disclosure process as a whole. But, after viewing no videotapes, and after considering only selected excerpts from the interview transcripts, the Court of Appeal concluded:

> The professionalism of the three women who conducted the interviews is obvious from the transcripts ... There was criticism about some of their questions and of the way some evidence was elicited, but we are satisfied that this is of no real moment ... From the extracts of the transcripts to which we have been referred, the interviewer can be seen in some cases to be following up information received from a parent, but without inappropriate persistence or leading, and we do not accept the submission that they were working under an agenda with the object of obtaining disclosures of abuse in the belief that it had occurred.[30]

In the wake of the court proceedings, the standard of interviewing became a public issue. Senior DSW social worker Mike Doolan recalled:

I did much of the work involved in convincing government that this criticism was unfair, that there was an attempt at disinformation, a defence-led contention that the evidential interviewing process was biased, that the children were asked leading questions, that they were set up – I'm not saying it can't happen, but our staff of specialist interviewers are highly-trained, professional people. I know they would not buy into a witchhunt of that sort. All our interviewers felt under a cloud. It was important that somebody was seen to be defending them and that's what I did.[31]

His apparent unfamiliarity with the contents of the interviews raised a worrying question. 'In response to the criticisms, did anyone go back and look at the interviews?' I asked.

'Not to my knowledge,' he said defensively. 'But all interviews are reviewed. There's a peer review process, and there's a supervisory process as well. But if you're saying – No – There was nothing put forward that convinced me of the need to do that. The criticism was coming from defence-based groups and they had reasons for making those claims other than them being true. I certainly wasn't prepared to put the staff through any inquiry on that basis. It would have dealt a death-blow to morale.'

The endorsement of the highest court in the land was, to Doolan, his trump card: 'When the Court of Appeal actually praised the professionalism of the evidential interviewers and the processes they used, that to me was an affirmation of them. I used that on many occasions, writing to editors and so on, nationwide.'[32]

• • •

Kari Lacebark had her first interview with Sue Sidey on 27 February 1992. It lasted 44 minutes. The transcript is 33 pages long. On page eight, Kari repeated some of the comments she had made a week earlier in response to maternal questioning (that Ellis had shown her his penis in the crèche toilets, and had put it in Lara Palm's and Derek Ngaio's mouths). Then, having said her piece, Kari tried to bring the interview to an end: 'Can we have a wee break now?' (p. 8); 'I want to have a break of talking' (p. 9); 'Getting tired' (p. 13); 'When will we be finished?' (p. 16); 'I feel sick' (p. 21); 'Can I go back now?' (p. 22); 'Can I go?' (p. 29); 'I want to go' (p. 30).

Throughout the interview, Sidey invited Kari to elaborate on her story. On page 11 she obtained another disclosure:

S: Hey you know what you saw happen to [Lara] and [Derek]?
K: Yeah.
S: Um, Peter's penis go in anybody else's mouth?
K: In my mouth.
S: What did it feel like when it was in your mouth?

K: Feeled rough.
S: Mm.
K: Baby stuff came out of it.

(Regardless of what did or didn't happen at the crèche, and regardless of what the Lacebarks may have said to her about Ellis, Kari had probably heard about 'baby stuff' from her parents prior to the arrival of her baby brother seven months earlier.)

When Sidey sought details of the 'penis in the mouth' incident, Kari said it happened 'lots of times', 'once a day' and 'only on Mondays and Fridays'. She said Peter's hands were near her knees at the time. Her attempt to demonstrate the offence with dolls added to the confusion:

K: Ah, he was I were on the toilet – I sit on the toilet and do wees then he – sat on me.
S: He sat on you? Walked up and sat on you?
K: I don't know.
S: Did he sit on you?
L: Yes.

When the videotape was shown at his trial, Ellis scribbled a note to his lawyer about a game he played in the crèche armchair. It involved pretending to sit on a child and asking, 'Where she's gone?'

'She's behind you!' the other kids would shout. 'No, that's just cushions,' Ellis would reply.[33]

On the subject of walks, Kari said the only thing she didn't like about them was that they made her tired. After that, Sidey addressed the issue of secrets. From the prosecution point of view, this issue was critical. If Sidey could establish that Kari had been threatened or bribed into silence, the credibility of her delayed disclosures would be greatly enhanced. The relevant section of Kari's transcript (pp. 29–30) reads:

S: Hey, [Kari], you know when you had to suck Peter's penis, what did he say? Did he say anything or not?
K: No. Can I go?
S: Soon. Did he say anything or not?
K: No.
S: So I was wondering if anyone told you not to tell or not?

At that point, Kari recalled her walks with Peter.

K: He said that if, if I give you ice, I give you a iceblock promise not to tell anybody and I did I wanted to.

Towards the end of the interview, Sidey returned to one of Kari's earlier comments – that Yelena Holly had touched her vagina:

S: Mm. And [Yelena], [Yelena] touched your fanny once?
K: Yeah. Can you – now can I go?
S: Yeah, nearly. Nearly finished. And, have any big people ever done that to your fanny before or not?
K: No, only Peter's only.
S: Pardon?
K: Peter's only …
S: When? When did Peter touch your fanny?
K: Don't know. No, he didn't. Only touched me.
S: He only touched you what?

After reading a note that Colin Eade had pushed under the door, Sidey continued:

S: You said Peter touched your fanny and I said – where – and you said – no, he didn't, he only touched you – what?
K: He only touched me here [indicates groin area].
S: What did he touch you with?
K: I don't know.
S: What? What?
K: His penis. I want to go.
S: Yeah. I know, yeah.
K: Can I please go?
S: Pretty soon. We just talk about that one. What did that make you feel like there on your body? When his penis …?
K: It feeled the same.

Sidey invited Kari to demonstrate the touching with dolls, but Kari had had enough.

S: Come and sit down here.
K: I don't want to.
S: Okay.
K: I want to go home.
S: All right. If … Would you … Urm, when his penis touched you there, were your clothes on or off?
K: On.
S: They were on. What about his clothes?
K: They were on.

S: They were on too?
K: Yeah. But not his trousers.
S: How did his –
K: I want to go.

Finally, Sidey struck a deal: 'Could you come back another day and tell me the other things if we have a break now?' When Kari agreed, she was allowed to go.

At the trial of Peter Ellis, Count 20 of the 28-count indictment was based on this interview. It read: 'that Peter Hugh McGregor Ellis did sexually violate Kari Lacebark by having unlawful sexual connection with her occasioned by the connection of her mouth with his penis.' Ellis was found guilty on that count.

• • •

On learning that Kari had disclosed abuse in her evidential interview on 27 February, Mr and Ms Lacebark joined Ms Magnolia's support group. That evening they met with Ms Magnolia, Mr and Ms Ngaio, Mr and Ms Mulberry, Mr and Ms Palm and Detective Colin Eade. The reason for Eade's presence, and the nature of the discussion, has never been revealed.

Next morning (Friday 28 February), Sue Sidey re-interviewed Kari. The interview lasted 40 minutes. The transcript is 28 pages long.

'I just don't want to come back here tomorrow,' Kari announced. 'Last time I didn't really like it here … it was a bit too long.' At first she just played with dolls. It wasn't until page 17 of the transcript, when Sidey encouraged her to undress an 'anatomically correct' doll, that the opportunity to talk about genitals arose:

S: What's this called?
K: Vagina.
S: Who's seen your gina?
K: Peter. You can stick your finger in.

That exchange was followed by three more pages of questioning ('Where were you when Peter saw your vagina?', 'What did he see it for?', 'Did anyone else at crèche see your vagina in the toilets?', 'Was that cos he was helping you with the toilet or something else?' 'Did he see your vagina cos he was helping you or doing something else?', 'What was he doing when he saw your vagina?', 'When he was going to the toilet?', 'What did you see?', 'What did his penis see, ah do?', 'And whereabouts were his trousers?', 'Did anything else happen to your vagina or not?'). But apart from saying that Peter had seen her vagina and she had seen his penis in the toilets, Kari had nothing to add.

Then, when Sidey asked Kari to show her 'what Peter's penis did' on a female 'anatomically correct' doll, she rubbed its genital area. More questions followed:

S: Yeah what did that feel like on your vagina?
K: It felt not very nice.
S: And whereabouts were his trousers when that happened?
K: I don't know. You can fit your finger up here because it's a doll.

------------ [line]

S: ... whereabouts were his trousers when he did that?
K: On him.
S: Yeah, whereabouts on him?
K: Here.
S: Were they up here or down there or down there or–?
K: Up here.
S: So how did, were his clothes on or off when his penis–?
K: On on on on on on ...

------------ [line]

S: Was it hard or soft or hanging down or standing up or what was it doing?
K: Hard, bit hard.

------------ [line]

S: How many times had Peter's penis been there?
K: One time.
S: And whereabouts did that happen?
K: Can you hold the dolls?
S: Whereabouts did that happen?
K: I don't know.
S: When his penis went there, whereabouts were you when that happened?
K: In the toilets.
S: And were your pants on or off?
K: On.

------------ [line]

S: Did his penis touch you on top of your clothes or underneath?
K: Underneath.

    ------------ [line]

S: Were you standing up or sitting down?
K: Standing up.
S: And what was he doing, was he standing up or sitting down or kneeling?
K: Kneeling.
S: And so his pants were up, so what about his fly, was that open or shut?
K: Pardon?
S: You know his fly, the zip on his pants.
K: Oh, shut.

Then Sidey produced an anatomically correct male doll ('Oh look out,' she said. 'We took the trousers off, silly us') and she asked Kari to demonstrate the incident using same-sized male and female dolls. Heedless of the implications of her demonstration, Kari continued to insist that both she and Ellis had their clothes on during the touching.

'How did the penis touch you if it was in there?' Sidey asked. Finally, when Kari was asked to demonstrate the incident again, she pulled the doll's pants down. However, she was adamant that it happened only once, and that she was standing up at the time.

Having dealt with that point, Sidey broadened the scope of her questioning: 'Did any other parts of his body touch your vagina or not?', 'Did he touch your vagina anywhere else?', 'Did it happen anywhere else or not?', Anything else touch you?' Kari answered 'No' to all those questions, and made a final plea. 'I don't want to end up coming here tomorrow or the next day.'

At the trial of Peter Ellis, Count 21 of the 28-count indictment was based on this interview. It read: 'that Peter Hugh McGregor Ellis between 1 May 1989 and 30 July 1991 at Christchurch indecently assaulted [Kari Lacebark] a girl under the age of 12 years in that he touched the complainant's vagina area with his penis at the crèche.' Ellis was found guilty on that count.

• • •

By 4 March, apart from the disclosures recorded from Mandy Arbutus and Kari Lacebark, the crèche case was running entirely on rumours, and no one was promoting those rumours more energetically than Colin Eade. Mr Larch's report of the meeting that day between himself, Colin Eade and council officers Rob Dally, Alistair Graham, Marshall Wright and Martin Maguire reads:

At this stage the Police consider that they are looking at more than ten victims of sexual abuse but that may increase to between 20 and 30 given the scale of the offending. Some offending took place at the Centre but it is likely that in all situations where the staff member was in contact with children those children were at risk. For the long term benefit of any children affected it is necessary to make contact with them and offer the children the opportunity of discussing the matter should they wish ... Also agreed that a further [parents'] meeting would be held incorporating Colin Eade (who would be able to be more explicit in regards to the offences that have now arisen as opposed to the concerns previously) ... Disclosure from Colin Eade that we are probably talking about indecent acts and maybe attempted sexual intercourse (please note this information is highly confidential and do not disclose) ... Colin Eade also expressed some concern in regards to the staff member attempting to end his life ... which he indicated would have a bad effect on both the parents and the children involved.[34]

Colin Eade had never met Peter Ellis. Furthermore, Ellis was never suicidal at any stage of the crèche investigation. However, Eade was plagued by thoughts of taking his own life. This suggests that Eade's concerns had more to do with himself than with Ellis.[35]

On 5 March Yelena Holly told Sue Sidey that Peter had put raisins and sandwiches in her bottom. However, despite considerable prompting, she made no other disclosures. According to sexologist Dr John Money, there are around 40 different sexual perversions. Some of them are very weird and some of them are very disgusting, but none involve the use of raisins or sandwiches (or, for that matter, cakes or biscuits – the foods cited by Ms Holly in her statement to the police a week earlier). Nonetheless, Sidey regarded Yelena's story as a serious disclosure, and Eade regarded it as a serious offence. Count 24 of the 28-count indictment that Ellis faced at his trial charged that: 'Peter Hugh McGregor Ellis between 1 May 1991 and 1 February1992 at Christchurch did indecently assault [Yelena Holly] a girl then under the age of 12 years in that he placed food against her anus with his finger at her home'. Ellis was found not guilty on that count.

• • •

Throughout February and March 1992, in the imaginations of Ms Magnolia and her supporters, the case continued to grow. When Detective Eade and Constable Diane Smith met with the crèche staff after work on the day of Yelena's DSW interview, Eade painted an alarming picture. Jan Buckingham recalled:

> He said Peter was guilty. He'd been offending under our noses. The abuse had been going on for years. It was one of the biggest child sex abuse cases in the Southern Hemisphere. It was going to make headlines around the world. Peter had involved other people. Children had been taken away in cars. They'd been taken to QE II [swimming pool].

Our jaws were on the floor. Our eyes were out on stalks. We'd never seen anything, never heard anything, never suspected anything. Gullible fools – we dropped into his lap like ripe plums. We thought – Well, you're a policeman. You're a professional. You must know what you're talking about. It must be true.[36]

At that meeting the behaviour of Sharleen, the youngest and most insecure of the Civic staff, would have signalled to Eade her vulnerability to police pressure. 'Sharleen was sitting on the floor wearing this little white mini-skirt with her legs apart, and Colin Eade was sitting opposite her,' recalled a staff member. 'We were cringing with embarrassment, thinking – Sharleen, do something.' However, at that stage, Sharleen was not alone in her vulnerability.

Eade told the crèche staff that it would be easier for all concerned if Ellis confessed. 'Is there anyone here who feels they could go and talk to him?' he asked. Jan Buckingham and Susannah volunteered for the job. When they visited Ellis the following Sunday they had two messages: the first was that the investigation was continuing; the second was that his colleagues thought he was guilty. For Ellis, the first message was a shock but not a surprise – a phone call from Ms Kowhai a few days earlier had warned him that something was up.

Ms Kowhai had heard about Ms Magnolia's allegation in November 1991 from Ellis, and for a while she was supportive. However, by March 1992 her sister had joined the rumour network: 'She told me that Peter had put sandwiches up little girls' vaginas and stuff. The whole thing sounded absolutely horrible. She told me to ring Colin Eade and Sue Sidey.'[37]

To Eade, Ms Kowhai was a key witness. With her neediness, and her history of dysfunctional relationships, she was also a vulnerable one. She told Eade that Ellis had lived with her for two years and had babysat her children. Eade asked her to maintain contact with Ellis.

'In the beginning I wasn't going to go against Peter,' Ms Kowhai told me. 'I did in the end. Because …' She paused before continuing. 'The more I sort of began to realise what had happened, the more I realised that my loyalties lay with my children and not with him. Also because of the way I was talking to Colin Eade about Peter, and talking to Peter about what Colin Eade and the police were doing, I was right in the middle. I was getting really screwed up in the head basically.'[38]

Shortly before Jan Buckingham and Susannah visited Ellis, Ms Kowhai phoned him. 'I abused him. I yelled at him. I said, "How dare you! How could you do such horrible things?" I said, "You're gonna go to jail!"' On Sunday 8 March, when his colleagues came to deliver the same message, they got as far as telling Ellis that the investigation was continuing before losing their nerve. So they went back a few days later to finish the job. Susannah recalled:

It was a very cruel thing that we did. We told Peter the staff were abandoning him. We talked for a while about the allegations, and speculated about who was making them. When we came away I said to Jan: 'His conscience is clear.' Then we had this conversation where we tried to figure out how he could have done all those things and not have known. There was no way I could pick up anything that made me feel –Yep, we've got him. I just felt a heel. We were supposed to shock him into a confession. All we did was shatter him. It was all a bit yukky and scary – Peter can be the baddie over there, and we'll be the goodies over here. I still feel terrible. I feel as if we're as responsible for Peter going to jail as any counsellor or family, in terms of the way we cooperated with the police.[39]

CHAPTER 7

Parents in Terror of Abuse Discovery

7.i: There Seemed to be No Logic to It

Ellis's colleagues advised him of the reactivated investigation on Sunday 8 March 1992, and he notified his defence team the next day. Employment Court lawyer Tony Couch phoned Detective Eade for more information, and was shocked by his attitude: 'He used some very coarse language to describe Peter Ellis. He basically said, "This bloke is a child molester and we're going to get him."'[1] The following day (10 March) Ellis's solicitor, Chris Knight, faxed a complaint to the district superintendent of the Christchurch Police. After outlining the history of the investigation, Knight wrote:

> Mr Ellis has now been advised, informally and through friends, that a continuing and widespread inquiry is being undertaken ... Mr Ellis has been told that a number of obscene and graphic activities are alleged to have been carried out by him on various children and that details of these alleged activities are well known amongst parents and workers involved with the Civic Child Care Centre. He has also been advised that members of the child abuse unit are actively soliciting children and parents ... I have had discussions with Detective Eade today who advises me that he is not prepared to provide me with any information concerning the above nor is he prepared to contact Mr Ellis concerning the matters ... I am of the view that the handling of this matter by the child abuse unit has been inappropriate ... it is well past the time when full disclosure should have been made to Mr Ellis as to the nature and extent of the allegations ...

Knight also made an urgent Official Information Act request for 'the full file relating to Mr Ellis'; 'full disclosure of all statements made by any witnesses'; 'full disclosure of any videotaped interviews in respect of any children concerned with the investigation'; 'full and explicit details of the basis of the current investigation, the parameters of the inquiries, and the reasons why Mr Ellis has not been provided with any information regarding these matters'; and 'such further or other information as is necessary properly to inform Mr Ellis as to the matters covered in this letter'.[2]

Detective Inspector Roger Carson advised Knight by mail that his application would be dealt with 'in due course', and passed the letter to Eade without comment. On 16 March Eade replied: 'I intend to report on this to the Detective Superintendent when time permits. I will not be commenting on the reasons I do not believe the information should be released and I will not be commenting on the obvious criticisms you have voiced about the way I am conducting this investigation.'[3]

• • •

Following the first formal disclosure in the crèche case (by Mandy Arbutus on 30 January 1992) there was a sharp increase in the number of children referred to Christchurch DSW for interviews. In February 1992 there were 81 referrals (compared to 60 the previous February). In March 1992 there were 103 referrals (compared to 60 the previous March).[4] Four of the Civic Crèche children interviewed during that period became complainants in the court proceedings. They were Kari Lacebark, Yelena Holly, Lara Palm and Derek Ngaio. Their mothers were among the most energetic parental networkers and child interrogators of all the crèche parents.

Sue Sidey's interviews with Derek Ngaio (on 9 December 1991), Kari Lacebark (on 27 and 28 February 1992) and Yelena Holly (on 5 March 1992) have already been discussed. These were followed by Lara Palm's first interview (on 9 March), and Derek Ngaio's second interview (on 10 March).

Apart from Lara Palm's knowledge of, and interest in, her clitoris, there was nothing unusual about her behaviour during her three-and-a-half years at the Civic Crèche. However, as was the case with many formerly happy crèche children, Lara's behaviour deteriorated after she began disclosing abuse. According to Ms Palm, between 22 February '92 (when she first suggested to Lara that Ellis had put his penis in her mouth) and 9 March '92 (when Lara was interviewed by Sue Sidey), her daughter's bad dreams worsened markedly.

Like most anxious crèche parents, the Palms continued to worry, to network, to question their daughter and to send her to therapy throughout 1992. During that period Lara was able to capture her mother's undivided attention by saying, 'Mummy, I have been doing some more remembering about the crèche.'

Under cross-examination at the trial of Peter Ellis, Ms Palm said that she and her partner asked their daughter 'direct questions' about Ellis and the crèche. She agreed that 'Did Peter make the children look at each other's penises?' was one such question. Along with most of Ms Magnolia's personal and professional supporters, Ms Palm believed that because (in theory at least) her daughter was free to answer 'yes' or 'no', this was not a 'leading question'.[5]

Garrow and Casey's Principles of the Law of Evidence defines 'leading questions' as: questions that suggest the desired answer (for example, 'Then he hit you, didn't he?'); questions that put words into a witness's mouth; and questions posed on the basis of an unproven fact (for example, 'What did X do after he hit you?', when it has not been established that X did hit the witness). The author, Sir Maurice Casey, claimed that not all questions that require 'yes' or 'no' answers are leading. 'The test is whether the question is put in such a way as to indicate to the witness the required answer,' he wrote. According to Casey 'Was it raining?' passed the test, while 'It was raining, wasn't it?' did not.[6]

Questions that require 'yes' or 'no' answers may not always be 'leading' in a strictly legal sense. However, as anyone with experience of young children would know, questions that invite a child to imagine a scenario that may not have occurred ('Did Peter make the children look at each other's penises?') can be highly suggestive.

The manner in which an adult's questions are framed is just one factor that may affect the reliability of children's reports of past events. Ceci and Bruck (*Jeopardy in the Courtroom: A Scientific analysis of children's testimony*) found that children tend to provide the answers they believe adults want to hear, regardless of their own knowledge of a topic. Also, children do their best to answer adults' questions, even when the questions are bizarre. (When asked nonsensical questions like 'Is milk bigger than water?' or 'Is red heavier than yellow?', most five-to-seven-year-olds will reply 'Yes' or 'No', rather than 'I don't know'.) Furthermore, when asked the same question more than once, children often change their answers. (They appear to interpret the repeated question as 'I must have given the wrong answer the first time.')[7]

Ceci and Bruck discovered that the problems of everyday adult–child conversations were magnified when topics with legal implications were discussed, and that the magnification was compounded whenever a child was re-interviewed on the same topic, and whenever anatomically correct dolls were introduced into the conversation. Interviewers (be they parents, police officers or specialist interviewers) with *a priori* beliefs about what had happened were found to use repeated, suggestive and leading questions to encourage children to provide the answers they expected. They also presented negative stereotypes of alleged offenders to children, and failed to explore other possible explanations for the children's comments or behaviour. Ceci and Bruck concluded that evidence obtained from children using interviewing techniques of this sort could be unreliable.

In the crèche case, most complainant parents admitted to asking their children leading or direct questions before their children made any disclosures. Many also admitted to continuing to ask such questions for months afterwards. Some parents made notes of their children's more significant comments at the time, or recounted them soon afterwards to Ms Magnolia, Detective Eade or Sue Sidey, who in turn made their own notes. On one occasion, after Lara Palm had 'done some more remembering about the crèche', Ms Palm tape-recorded her disclosure. But none of these notes or tape-recordings provided complete verbatim accounts of the parents' questions or the child's answers. Furthermore, for the great bulk of the uncontrolled and extended parental interrogation of crèche children that began in 1991, continued throughout 1992, and was still going in 1993, no notes or records of any sort were made. The DSW evidential interviews were the tip of a great child-interrogation iceberg. But because they were recorded on videotape and used in evidence, they were the only part of the iceberg that was available for detailed scrutiny during the court proceedings.

• • •

At Lara Palm's DSW interview on 9 March, when Sue Sidey asked her who Peter was, she replied with a negative stereotype ('he's a very mean man and he wants children to feel all scared'). Then she made one of the clearest, most spontaneous and most detailed disclosures of the entire crèche investigation: '… it was lunchtime there and we are eating at the table and I had a gherkin in my lunchbox and he just came along and nicked it out and ate it.' But Sidey wanted more.

'What else do you remember?' she asked.

Lara said that Peter played 'drinking games', and she repeated the allegations that her parents had coaxed from her two weeks earlier: that he had put his penis in her own and other children's mouths, and had touched her own and other children's 'private parts'. In contrast to the fluency and detail of her account of the gherkin incident, she was unable to provide coherent descriptions of any of the other alleged transgressions. However, she was able to give a reason for her delayed disclosure: 'He just said don't tell your parents or else you'll um turn into a gherkin and get eaten up.'

At the trial of Peter Ellis, Counts 27 and 28 were based on this interview. Count 27 read: 'that Peter Hugh McGregor Ellis between 1 January 1989 and 31 January 1991 being a male sexually violated [Lara Palm] by having unlawful sexual connection with her occasioned by the connection between his penis and her mouth at the crèche'. Count 28 read: 'that Peter Hugh McGregor Ellis between 1 January 1989 and 31 January 1991 at Christchurch indecently assaulted [Lara Palm] a girl under 12 years of age in that he touched her vaginal and anal area with his hand at the crèche'. Ellis was found guilty on both counts.

• • •

Next day, the eccentric Derek Ngaio had his second DSW interview. Derek's return should have alerted Sue Sidey to the possibility that the crèche investigation was being driven by something other than child sexual abuse. In his first interview in December 1991 Derek said that Ellis tickled him, and stole Lara Palm's gherkin.

In her report Sidey said that Derek 'did not appear to show anxiety that may have suggested he had experienced sexual abuse'. She also noted that his memory of the crèche had faded. So why did she agree to interview him again? He'd had no contact with Ellis or the crèche in the intervening three months. However, he had played with Lara Palm, and his parents had worried and networked and interrogated him intensively. Under the circumstances, Sidey should have realised that whatever Derek had to say about Ellis and the crèche was more likely to reflect the anxieties of Ms Magnolia's support group than his own experience.

The DSW 'Evidential Video Interview Guidelines' for non-disclosing children in use at that time state that 'a further interview or two may be warranted in particular cases', and that 'this should be a joint team decision supported by supervisors'.[8]

According to DSW chief social worker Mike Doolan, the professional supervision system ensures that no DSW staff member works alone, and no staff member's work goes unscrutinised. 'It would take collusion for something to go wrong,' he told me. 'I'm not saying that doesn't occur – we've dealt with it when it does happen – but we've got some pretty good protective mechanisms in place.'[9]

Sue Sidey's professional supervisor was Dr Karen Zelas. Like most sexual abuse workers, Sidey held Zelas in high regard. 'The quality of her supervision was extremely good; really objective and very professional,' Sidey told me. 'She was a safety valve for me all the way through. She was also extremely knowledgable. She knew child development. She knew memory. She knew the interview process because she had helped to set up the unit.'[10]

In an affidavit presented during pre-trial arguments in the crèche case, Zelas stated: 'I have provided supervision to the evidential interviewers on a weekly basis, during which we have discussed matters of interviewing technique as well as broader aspects of evaluation. Review of their videotaped interviews has been an integral part of this supervision.' At the trial of Peter Ellis, Zelas testified that the supervision included 'an element of consultation about individual children'. The supervision took place at group meetings, in one-to-one sessions and during telephone consultations. 'At times I was ringing up Karen for supervision at breakfast,' Sidey recalled.

In her role as an expert witness in child sexual abuse cases nationwide, Dr Zelas routinely advised courts that:

> The number of interviews required by a child is variable, most commonly one to three. One of the most common factors influencing the number of interviews is the child's level of anxiety. Other factors include: clinical evidence that the child is blocking or avoiding significant topics; gradual or incomplete disclosure of abuse; confused or inconsistent information.

None of these factors applied to Derek Ngaio's first interview. As Sidey's supervisor, Zelas would have – or should have – known that. Also, since Sidey knew about the parental networking and questioning of children that had taken place in the intervening three months, Zelas would have – or should have – known about that too. But, despite all the contra-indications for doing so, Derek's second interview was allowed to proceed.

On 10 March Derek Ngaio told Sue Sidey that his friend Lara could remember 'drinking games'. Derek's own knowledge of the games appeared to be entirely hearsay, but Sidey interrogated him at length on the subject. 'He was making these yukky drinks with wees and making children drink it because the trick he played on them to make them do it is if you don't drink it you'll turn into a pumpkin and turn into pumpkin soup,' Derek told her.

Sidey did not explore the possibility that Derek might have combined Lara's comments about 'drinking games' with his own memories of eating pumpkin soup from a cup at the crèche, and added a touch of the Cinderella story for good measure. Instead, she seized on the notion that Ellis had made Derek drink his urine from a cup, and questioned him closely on that theme. The boy did his best to be helpful, but, unlike most of the children interviewed during the crèche investigation, he was stumped for answers:

> S: And how did the wees get into the cup?
> D: I think he might put the cup underneath his penis and done wees in it.
> S: Okay did you see that happen or not?
> D: I can't remember.
> S: Okay right, so which children did the games happen with?
> D: I can't really remember it very well.
> S: Oh we know [Lara], don't we.
> D: Yep.
> S: Yeah and who did you see drinking?
> D: I can't remember.
> S: Okay and how many times did you see it happen?
> D: Don't know.

To the question 'So it [Peter's penis] went in [Derek's] mouth is that right?', the lad replied, 'I think so.' Undeterred by his uncertainty, Sidey asked Derek how it felt and how it tasted, to which he replied 'yukky' and 'horrible'. However, apart from saying that the activity took place 'in the toilet rooms' he was unable to provide further details.

The vagueness Derek displayed in his second interview was similar to the vagueness he displayed in his first. But by March '92 Sidey was no longer prepared to attribute his uncertainty to the fading of memory with time. 'I feel that [Derek's] responses of "I think so" are related to his anxiety surrounding his experience and his fear of disclosing', she wrote in her report.

When the Ellis case went to trial in April 1993, Count 26 of the 28-count indictment stated: 'that Peter Hugh McGregor Ellis being a male did an indecent act with [Derek Ngaio] a boy aged under 12 years in that he urinated into a cup from which the said boy drank at the Crèche.' Ellis was found not guilty on that count.

• • •

The transformation of Derek's videotaped comments into a count at the trial of Peter Ellis took place in five stages. In theory, the process could have been aborted at any stage.

In the first stage Sue Sidey, in consultation with her supervisor Karen Zelas, reviewed Derek's videotape and concluded that a disclosure of sexual abuse had been made. In the second stage, Detective Eade concluded that Derek's disclosure was evidence of a criminal offence and grounds for a charge against Peter Ellis. In the third stage the charge was placed before District Court Judge Anderson at the depositions hearing. In the fourth stage Crown solicitor Brent Stanaway placed Derek's charge on the draft indictment for the Ellis trial. In the fifth stage Justice Williamson rejected defence counsel Rob Harrison's pre-trial submission that Derek's charge was too unreliable to put before the jury.

The 'drinking urine from a cup' story was a fantasy that existed only in the overheated imaginations of ritual abuse believers. Yet (with the exception of Judge Anderson, who was not required to evaluate the credibility of the evidence) every professional who passed that fantasy along its five-stage journey to the Ellis trial took it seriously. Through their actions, they lent authority to the ritual abuse beliefs on which the crèche case was based.

This is not to suggest that Brent Stanaway and Justice Williamson believed in ritual abuse. But they accepted the urine-drinking allegation (and other equally unlikely allegations) for two compelling reasons. First, they had confidence in the reliability of disclosures obtained by interviewers under the supervision of Karen Zelas. Second, they had no reason to suspect that ritual abuse beliefs played any part in the early stages of the case. This was because, at Ritual Action Group (RAG) workshops throughout New Zealand in 1991–92, and in RAG literature distributed over the same period, ritual abuse believers were warned that anyone who spoke out on the subject would likely have their comments dismissed as 'a fantasy in the minds of people who have been working with sexual abuse for too long' or as 'something that has been invented by people who are paranoid and see conspiracies everywhere'. In a similar vein, Pamela Hudson warned readers of *Ritual Child Abuse* that parents, child protection workers and journalists who were open about their ritual abuse beliefs risked being ostracised by their peers.[11]

Child health clinicians whose interest in ritual abuse was more scholarly than populist also avoided the term. In the third issue of *Child Abuse and Neglect* for 1991 (which was largely devoted to 'the ritual abuse controversy'), readers were advised to use terms like 'multidimensional sex rings' when dealing with alleged outbreaks of large-scale and perverted child sexual abuse.

Fear of losing their credibility was just one reason for the ritual abuse investigators' secretiveness. My interview with Sue Sidey suggested that another reason was fear itself:

> LH: Okay. You've got your nose to the grindstone interviewing kids. The ripples seem to be spreading. The concern seems to be building. Did you get a feeling of the mood in Christchurch as the year progressed?
>
> SS: Well, I was in the thick of it … My main impression was that there were a lot of very anxious and frightened people. People were beginning to fear for their safety, you know.
>
> LH: What were they fearful of?
>
> SS: Well, they were worried about – you know – people were beginning to worry, from all quarters, about retributions – about their ongoing safety because of their involvement. Are their children safe? You know.
>
> LH: Yeah, but what did they feel was the nature of the threat?
>
> SS: Well, they felt like people were going to get them!
>
> LH: Who? Ohhhh! You mean the extended web of –
>
> SS: Mmm. Mmmmm.
>
> LH: … abusers and umn …
>
> SS: Oh – um, yeah. [When a look of astonished disbelief crossed my face, Sidey drew back from specifics.] Or maybe. You know. Sort of. Worried, I think, that there may be … People were scared because they thought they would be – their children or themselves might be silenced in some way. You know. [Her 'you knows' were becoming imploring. As if, to Sidey, the problem was self-evident – it could not be, and did not need to be, articulated.
>
> LH: But how? By whom?
>
> SS: Well, by attack or whatever.
>
> LH: From?
>
> SS: Well, from people who were trying to silence them. You know. The fears went to that extent.
>
> LH: Yeah. Yeah. I accept the fears. But I can't focus on where they felt the threat was coming from.

SS: Well, they would. Here were, say, people who might know, because they had been abused in some way, or knew people who were being abused, or they were, um, they were scared that they would be the object of other people trying to shut them up and threaten them, so that they wouldn't tell any more what had happened to them.

LH: [puzzled silence]

SS: I mean, it may or may not have been a rational fear, but I think people do get fearful like that sometimes. They were just scared. You know.

LH: Yeah. I accept they're scared. I just can't, um. I mean, who did they think was going to shut them up? And how? Or hadn't it focused as specifically as that?

SS: I think they were scared that people were going to come and get them and their children. You know. People who were supporters of the alleged offenders. Or even the alleged offenders themselves. Sort of thing.

LH: Oh.[12]

• • •

Throughout the crèche investigation Detective Eade advised concerned parents to have their children examined by a member of Doctors for Sexual Abuse Care (DSAC), even if the child had made no disclosure of abuse. During these examinations the child's ano-genital region was inspected, and swabs and blood samples were taken. The swabs – from the anus, throat and vagina (in girls) or urethra (in boys) – were tested for sexually transmitted diseases like gonorrhea, chlamydia, trichomonas and herpes. The blood samples were tested for syphilis and Aids.

Immediately after Ellis's arrest, Rob Harrison arranged for his client to be tested for sexually transmitted diseases, including Aids. When Harrison advised Eade of the results on 4 May, he hoped the negative findings would quell the panic and spare children the ordeal of a medical examination.[13] But in the months ahead Eade continued to recommend that former crèche children have full medical examinations and STD tests.

These examinations caused the anxiety levels of already anxious parents to escalate. First, because the mere mention of the examination was an invitation to imagine the worst. Second, because the examination was embarrassing, uncomfortable, even painful, for the child. Third, because DSAC doctors always reported their findings in the most alarming manner imaginable.

The DSAC *Manual for the Medical Management of Child Sexual Abuse* was based on the work of Dr Astrid Heger, the paediatrician who misdiagnosed child sexual abuse on a massive scale in the McMartin preschool case in California. Doctors were told to avoid statements like 'the examination was normal' or 'no evidence of sexual abuse exists'. Instead, the phrase 'this examination is consistent with the allegation of sexual abuse' was recommended. Consequently, every medical examination of a crèche child, no matter what the outcome, allowed ritual abuse believers to put another tick against the item in Pamela Hudson's checklist that read 'Medical finding commensurate with sexual abuse'.[14]

In mid-March 1992 Dr Margaret Metherall examined Kari Lacebark and found that the child had asymmetrical puckering of the anus. Kari had made no allegation of anal assault, and Ms Lacebark knew of no trauma that could account for the 'suspicion of scarring' (though she did recall that her daughter had been constipated). Nonetheless, Metherall reported: 'The significance of this lateral verge defect is uncertain, but must raise a suspicion of scarring due to trauma in this area. In my view the findings of this examination are supportive of the allegation of sexual abuse.'

At the trial of Peter Ellis, Metherall presented a more realistic assessment of her findings. '[I]t is possible that those folds resulted from healing of a tear to the anus but it could also be a normal variant, a congenital variant in the shape of the anus,' she said. But by then the damage was done. In the 14 months between Kari's medical examination and Ellis's trial, rumours that there was medical evidence of anal penetration in the crèche case fed the flames of panic. 'Oh well,' people said, 'if there's medical evidence, it must be true.'

• • •

By mid-March, despite the mounting anxiety among crèche parents, and the growing numbers of children being interviewed and medically examined, only five children (Mandy Arbutus, Kari Lacebark, Yelena Holly, Lara Palm and Derek Ngaio) had said anything in their DSW interviews that could be interpreted as disclosures of sexual abuse. For Colin Eade, the reality of having five alleged victims and one alleged perpetrator must have been a concern. If his expectation of large-scale offending was to be realised, he needed more formal disclosures involving more victims, more perpetrators and (because no parent had ever seen any evidence of sexual abuse at the crèche) more venues.

With her apparent evidence of anal penetration, Kari Lacebark was potentially a key witness. But Kari had made it clear that she wanted no more interviews. However, once when an important visitor had come to call, and Ms Lacebark had promised to take her and Yelena to McDonald's afterwards, Kari agreed to one more interview.

'Colin came to our house,' Kari told Sue Sidey on 18 March '92.

'And what did he say?' asked Sidey.

'I was scared of going to jail,' replied Kari.

Sidey did not pursue the topic. Eade produced no job sheets of his visits to complainant parents. Consequently, to this day, little is known about the nature and extent of his home visiting. However, we do know that, at this stage in the inquiry, Eade wanted more disclosures.

Timothy Cork (whose mother had concluded, on the basis of his poor reading skills and his habit of stuffing food and clothing into his mouth, that he was a victim of ritual abuse), was also visited by Eade prior to his DSW interview. Mrs Cork recalled:

> Colin Eade came round because he wanted to talk to Timothy before he had his disclosure interview [on 20 March]. He said there'd been an enormous web of intimidation and fear, and he wanted to tell Timothy that he didn't have anything to lose by telling the truth. He said children were told that their houses would burn down, that their parents would disappear and be killed. He said he'd never encountered anything like it in the police force. So he did have a talk to Timothy. I remember him saying to me, 'He's gotta go, Peter Ellis has got to go down.'[15]

Despite Eade's best efforts, Timothy Cork made no disclosure. But Kari Lacebark was more forthcoming. According to Ms Lacebark, after playing with Yelena Holly, Kari reported that Ellis had put food into her bottom, and had made some additional allegations. The new allegations would have electrified anyone with an interest in ritual abuse. They included: that stuff came out of Ellis's penis and into her vagina; that Ellis made her eat poos and rubbed it around her nose; and that she was one of a group of children who were taken by car to Ellis's house where men had stood in a circle around them with their pants down.

The new allegations appeared in notes made by Ms Lacebark in the days following Kari's second DSW interview (28 February). But when Kari went for her third interview (18 March) she had another story to tell.

'I know lots of things to do with Peter,' she said at the start of the interview (which would last 38 minutes, and produce a 26-page transcript). 'Peter used to took take me for a swim … And it wasn't fun because he came in with us and he kept putting our head under the pool … I nearly drowned in there because I was only little.' In response to further questioning, Kari said that Ellis had taken her and Yelena to the QE II pool by bus, and that no other children or teachers had gone on the trip.

Crèche records show that no staff ever took any children to the QE II pool, or to any other Christchurch swimming pool, and that Kari and Yelena never went on an outing from the crèche alone with Ellis. However, Ellis recalled lining up chairs to make a pretend bus and 'driving' a group of children to the crèche paddling pool (which, for the purposes of the game, had been renamed 'the QE II pool'):

Kari's 'near drowning' story was probably shaped by her mother's questions, by her memories of 'driving' to the crèche paddling pool and by her recent experiences of learning to swim. As it happened, it was a story that anyone searching for indicators of ritual abuse would regard as highly significant. According to Pamela Hudson, children ritually abused in day-care centres were often subjected to 'water torture' by being held underwater in bathtubs, in backyard swimming pools and in boating ponds, and by 'being placed in cages and lowered into the Pacific Ocean'.[16]

After obtaining details of the 'near drowning' allegation, Sidey went in search of other venues for the alleged abuse. 'Where else has Peter taken you?' she asked.

'He took nowhere else. He took us to his house,' she said, at which point Sidey suggested that they make Peter's house with toy furniture.

'He'll probably be inside … not on the streets because he knows that he'll probably be in trouble for doing all those nasty things.' Kari said.

'What's the worst thing?' asked Sidey.

'Putting my head under,' said Kari.

'Yeah, what's the worst thing he did to your body?'

'Touching it.'

'Whereabouts?'

'With his penis, about here, my leg.'

'Leg' was not the answer Sidey was looking for. 'What's it called, what parts that he touched round there?' she asked.

'My bottom,' said Kari.

Kari then wanted to make her own house and put Peter in jail.

'This is Gregory in his cot there and now he's got twins,' she said. 'We haven't got twins but I just want to make twin babies for us.' In theory, the DSW dolls and toy furniture were concrete representations of reality, but, like many children interviewed in the course of the crèche inquiry, Kari regarded them as play materials that could be used in any number of creative and changeable ways.

While Kari played, Sidey pursued the allegation that Ellis's penis had touched Kari's bottom. As in her previous interviews, Kari gave contradictory answers to questions about how often it happened ('every day I went to the crèche', 'about seven times'), how it felt ('not very nice', 'don't know', 'it felt sore'), where their clothes were, and whether either of them was standing, sitting or kneeling at the time. Kari remained adamant that the alleged offence had happened in the crèche toilets.

When Sidey presented Kari with male and female anatomically correct dolls and invited her to 'show me what happened', Kari placed the penis of the male doll first against the vagina, and then against the anus, of the female doll – and thus, to Colin Eade who was monitoring the interview from an adjacent room, not only had Kari confirmed Dr Metherall's suspicion of anal penetration, she had demonstrated vaginal rape as well. After that, Kari had had enough. 'Can we have a little break of talking?', 'I said I want to have a break of talking' (p. 17). 'I really want to go' (p. 18).

'Oh I want to go home.' Then, apparently recalling the promise that had helped her to escape from previous interviews, 'We'll come tomorrow' (p. 20). 'I want to come back tomorrow' (p. 21). 'I want to come tomorrow because I want to have my lunch' (p. 23). 'I could come another day' (p. 24). 'Oh let me go home. I want to go', I'll come back', 'I want to go okay I do', 'Come on I'm going to take my stuff (p. 25). Finally at page 26 of the transcript, five-year-old Kari was allowed to leave.

At the trial of Peter Ellis, Count 21 of the 28-count indictment was based on this interview. It charged that 'Peter Hugh McGregor Ellis between 1 May 1989 and 30 July 1991 at Christchurch indecently assaulted [Kari Lacebark] a girl under the age of 12 years in that he touched the complainant's vaginal area with his penis at the crèche'.

Ellis was found guilty on that count.

Next day, Yelena Holly had her second interview. She repeated her story about Peter putting his penis into children's mouths at the crèche, and added that he put yukky stuff into her mouth when he was babysitting at her home. But then she ruined the impact of her disclosures by saying she knew these things because her mother had told her.

• • •

After breaking the news to the crèche staff that the case had been reopened, and telling them that Peter Ellis had been offending for years under their noses, Detective Eade sought their cooperation. He said anything they could remember about the paedophile in their midst would be helpful. They all tried desperately to remember something. No one could recall seeing or hearing anything indicative of sexual abuse, but most of them could think of something negative to say about Ellis. Between 11 and 19 March, Constable Diane Smith took their statements.

The police inquiry was uppermost in the minds of the Civic staff when they met with Rosemary Smart after work on 18 March to discuss her council-funded review of management practices at the crèche. Smart was the director of the Campbell Centre (the counselling and psychotherapy wing of Presbyterian Support Services). Her academic training was primarily in education and social work. She was a registered psychologist and a member of the New Zealand Association of Psychotherapists. More than 20 years earlier she had worked as a Playcentre supervisor. Over the previous decade she had been, successively, an assistant psychologist in the Justice Department, a social worker with the Canterbury Hospital Board and a lecturer in social work at the University of Canterbury.[17]

The only publication by Smart listed in any major database is her address to the 1994 Australian Family Therapy Conference, entitled 'Expertosis: Is it Catching?' In the address Smart linked her disillusionment with rational thought and the scientific method (which she equated with money, power and the patriarchy) to her long and bitter struggle with the health authorities over the mental illness and suicide of a family member.[18]

'I was reviewing the management and policy of the crèche,' Rosemary Smart told me. 'I was not looking for: did this happen, didn't this happen? I was very, very clear all the way through that wasn't my brief.'[19]

City council administrator Alistair Graham agreed: 'The review was our attempt to restore the credibility of the crèche,' he said. 'We thought the only way to do that was to have an independent, professional person look at how it operated, to see if there were some ways that we could improve its operation, and to make some recommendations.'[20]

'It was a management review,' his colleague Martin Maguire confirmed. 'It had nothing to do with Peter Ellis.'[21]

The review's terms of reference covered management practices, staff supervision, codes of ethics and complaints procedures. 'Did it have anything to do with sexual abuse?' I asked. Maguire conceded that it did: 'You couldn't go into that childcare centre and disregard the trauma that had just happened there and not reflect on how that possibly may have happened and make some recommendations. We were quite clear that it wasn't to be a witch-hunt, but we wanted some guidelines.'

In my interview with her, Smart defended the professionalism of her review, and refuted journalist David McLoughlin's suggestion that she had been influenced by one of the more vociferous complainant parents. 'I followed an academic approach,' she said. 'I didn't have time to do an exhaustive review of the literature, but I reviewed the latest stuff at the time. It had nothing to do with anybody else's influence … I kept myself very detached.'[22]

In retrospect, Martin Maguire was less confident. 'The whole thing took off like a brushfire,' he recalled. 'For somebody like Rosemary to write a report when Christchurch was a seething cauldron of rumour and counter-rumour and suspicion and satanic ritual abuse and satanic worship and all that sort of stuff. It would have been bloody difficult to go into that situation and write something that was totally dispassionate.'

When Rosemary Smart met with the crèche staff for the first time on 18 March 1992 she made a positive impression. 'She came across as someone who was here to support us, here to help us,' recalled Sandi. 'We could air all our problems and all our worries. We could let the whole lot out and she'd be there.'[23]

In the course of the meeting some staff voiced concerns about the statements they had made to the police. There were things they may have overstated or understated. There were things they could have said differently. 'I thought maybe there was more stuff there that might be pertinent, that they hadn't talked about,' Smart recalled. So she sought the staff's permission to read their police statements, and they gave it willingly.

Smart returned to observe the crèche for a couple of hours the following Tuesday morning (24 March), and for a similar period next afternoon. At the time she was favourably impressed. 'I actually felt it was running very well,' she told me. 'I walked in and felt quite good about the crèche.'

• • •

By the time Rosemary Smart made her observations of the crèche, a letter had been dispatched to present and former Civic parents, and a scandal had exploded into the media.

The letter, signed by city manager John Gray and crèche management committee spokesperson Mr Larch, began: 'The Christchurch Police are currently investigating allegations of sexual abuse against a long term former staff member of the Civic Child Care Centre. While we do not wish to cause undue alarm, this matter is being taken seriously.' The letter advised that a 31 March meeting at Knox Hall would be addressed by Detective Eade, Sue Sidey and child counsellor Sara Crane (a former START therapist with an interest in ritual abuse). 'For additional information there will be a social worker, a psychologist dealing with persons who offend against children and information from the Accident Compensation Corporation.'[24]

On Friday 20 March 1992 TVNZ viewers learnt that police were investigating allegations of sexual abuse involving up to 50 children at the Christchurch Civic Child Care Centre. By Saturday the rest of the media had picked up the story. On Monday a front-page headline in the Christchurch *Press* proclaimed: 'Parents in terror of abuse discovery'. Readers were informed that the investigation was believed to involve about 200 children of both sexes. It would probably take months. 'It is a horrifying situation that is getting worse and worse,' a parent told the paper.

In response to the publicity, Peter Lawson, secretary of the Southern Local Government Officers Union, issued a press release expressing 'grave concern at the highly emotive and misleading media handling of the allegations'. He pointed out that a police investigation the previous November had found no case to answer, and that the worker's dismissal was not because of any evidence of sexual abuse. 'The worker concerned has still not been interviewed by the police,' he said. '[I]n the hysteria of the moment … the rights of the worker are being completely ignored.'[25]

Grandma Magnolia responded with an angry letter to Peter Lawson: 'It is unfortunate that you have chosen to expose your ignorance to the media and, by so doing, compounded the pain that dozens of Christchurch parents, and more particularly those small children affected by their attendance at the Civic Crèche, are currently suffering. It is deep water you have, apparently innocently, waded into.' She urged Lawson to talk to experts in the sexual abuse field to 'really hear what happens when a child is brave enough to finally tell, what happens when an alleged abuser is required to front up to his actions (usually TOTAL denial) ... I think eventually you may have reason to feel truly appalled at what you have chosen to support through the media,' she said.[26]

The same day (23 March) Ellis's solicitor, Chris Knight, faxed Detective Inspector Carson. After pointing out that he had received no response to his fax of 10 March, other than a formal acknowledgement, Knight wrote:

> Commencing on Friday afternoon (20th of March) the matter has received major publicity in all media ... This publicity now appears to have reached hysterical proportions ... Media coverage and advice being given to parents appears to be inflammatory, suggestive, misleading and contradictory. The matter appears to have got well out of control. In the context of the above your continuing refusal to provide my client with any information whatever is a scandal ... In addition to the information that was previously sought you are now asked to disclose:
>
> a) Reasons why no police statement issued to the media has pointed out that the childcare worker concerned was pronounced innocent by the police of any molestation as recently as December last.
>
> b) What steps are being taken to ensure that any evidence now received will be fair, impartial, objective and free from any influence whatever from the inaccurate, incomplete and distorted media coverage.[27]

That evening TVNZ quoted a police spokesman (presumably Colin Eade) as saying that it was too early to interview the man at the centre of the investigation. 'There are still children we want to speak with,' he said. Eade's aim was to get all the 400 or so children who had attended the crèche since 1986 formally interviewed at least once. Only when that goal was accomplished did he intend to interview Peter Ellis.[28]

Next morning (24 March), Chris Knight received a letter from Detective Inspector Howard Broad, ostensibly in reply to his fax of 10 March. 'Given the difficult and sensitive nature of these investigations, and in this case the scale of the inquiry, the time delay is neither unusual nor unacceptable,' Broad wrote, before declining Knight's request for information.[29]

'It was like a police state investigation going on,' recalled Knight. 'Something was driving it, but there seemed to be no logic to it. There seemed to be no control. There seemed to be no direction. Common sense had flown out the window.'[30]

7.ii: Peter Was as Good as Hung

Five nights a week, for most of every year since April 1989, Paul Holmes has interviewed the movers and shakers of the day. TVNZ publicity describes *Holmes* as 'a challenging and provocative perspective on news and events'. Critics describe it as infotainment. It is the most-watched current affairs programme on New Zealand television. On 23 March 1992 New Zealand's leading child sexual abuse expert, Dr Karen Zelas, was interviewed by Paul Holmes about the Christchurch Civic Child Care Centre inquiry. Regardless of the content of the item, the interview signalled that the case was An Issue of Great National Importance.

Zelas urged crèche parents not to conduct their own interrogations.

> There is a real risk if they start to try to speak with their own children about it that unintentionally in their effort to get to the truth they might introduce ideas to the child by the way in which they ask questions of the child. Then they may finish up in a position that it'll become impossible to know whether or not their child actually has been abused.

The formal disclosures obtained in the investigation to that point had come from children who had been questioned vigorously by their parents (Mandy Arbutus, Kari Lacebark, Yelena Holly, Lara Palm and Derek Ngaio). Therefore – according to Zelas's own criteria – their disclosures were unreliable.

In the *Holmes* interview, Karen Zelas advised parents to 'note any changes in their children's behaviour or any particular anxieties they may have developed'. She listed fears about going to the crèche, sexualised behaviour, nightmares and sleep disturbances as possible indicators of sexual abuse. She said that parents whose children had long since left the crèche would have to cast their minds back 'to try to identify whether there were changes in the child's behaviour'. She said the long-term effects of sexual abuse could include anxiety, sleep disturbances, relationship problems, sexualised behaviours and problems at school. In adolescence these could evolve into 'antisocial behaviours, sometimes promiscuous behaviour, depression, anxiety, alcohol and drug abuse'.

Among young children, behavioural upsets of the sort mentioned by Zelas are common. Prior to the *Holmes* interview, most present and former crèche parents would have attributed such upsets to everyday stresses (like moving house or starting school), or to family crises (like the birth of a new baby or the breakup of a marriage). But Zelas's message – that their children could have been sexually abused without them noticing, and that if the problem wasn't diagnosed and treated their children's lives could be ruined – prompted many parents to re-examine their offspring's behaviour in a new and sinister light.

Having sown alarm among many previously unconcerned crèche parents, Zelas invited them to contact the investigating agencies. 'The actual interview process itself is a very gentle one, particularly with young children,' she said, before closing with a mention of the meeting for parents scheduled for the following week.

Zelas's *Holmes* interview effectively validated the sexual abuse panic that was engulfing the crèche. For a professional who regarded herself as a rational and dispassionate expert, it was a deeply compromising performance. Fourteen months later, when Zelas appeared as expert witness for the prosecutions in the trial of Peter Ellis, she minimised the significance of her supervision of Sue Sidey, and gave the impression that the *Holmes* interview never happened. During her cross-examination by Ellis's barrister Rob Harrison, this exchange took place:

> H: Between the meeting at the crèche [2 December 1991] and the meeting at Knox Hall [31 March 1992] what involvement did you have in the inquiry?
>
> Z: ... I had no official involvement. The only involvement I had in that period was as supervisor to Sue Sidey, and that was an intermittent contact. We had no contact from shortly before Christmas until late January, and we met I think two or three times over the next few weeks.
>
> H: Didn't you also appear on the *Holmes* show on 23 March 1992?
>
> Z: No. Not that I'm aware of. What was the topic of that? If I did it was about a different topic.
>
> H: There was a programme viewed on 23 March 1992 – *Holmes* programme about the Civic Crèche inquiry.
>
> Z: No. I haven't been on TV about the Civic Crèche inquiry. I certainly don't remember it.

Finally, after Harrison had read an extract from the Holmes interview aloud to the court, Zelas conceded, 'If you say so then I must have. I actually don't recall doing that interview.'

In the context of a criminal prosecution in which the reliability of memory, and the credibility of Dr Zelas, were important factors, it was an extraordinary admission.

• • •

As the panic escalated, concerned parents continued to question their children, and to send them for medical examinations, therapy and DSW interviews.

At Kari Lacebark's fourth interview on 27 March (which would last 38 minutes and produce a 26-page transcript), Sue Sidey opened with: 'I know that you've been to some places with Peter. Where are all the places that you've been with him?'

For Kari, Sumner Beach came to mind. 'He showed us a big fish and it had a little thing on its back,' she said.

Crèche records show that no staff took any children to any beach during Kari's time at the centre. However, on cold winter days crèche workers sometimes put sand, shells and driftwood in the emptied water trough and made a pretend beach indoors. There were fish at the crèche, too: pretend fish in games, songs and artwork; real goldfish in a fish tank. There were also trout in the river where they went to feed the ducks; golden carp and perch in ponds at the Botanic Gardens where they went for walks; fish in tanks and streams at Willowbank Wildlife Park where the whole crèche went for day trips. The most recent trip to Willowbank was in September 1991.

'Well, where else has he taken you to before?' Sidey asked again (p. 4).

'Taken us – I think he took us to this place where a big fish. Willowbank,' said Kari.

'Where else have you been with Peter?' Sidey persisted (p. 5).

'Nowhere else, just ever go to Willowbank,' Kari replied.

A 1989 briefing paper to the Minister of Social Welfare on evidential interviews stated:

> The interview has to follow the rules of evidence. The interviewer cannot suggest that any particular thing happened or ask if any particular person was involved. The interviewer can only encourage the child or young person to tell everything s/he knows about it and try to get as much detail as possible.[1]

If Sue Sidey had conducted her interview according to these guidelines, she would have stopped asking Kari where she had been with Peter at this point, but she did not. Her persistence would have conveyed to Kari that she was supposed to come up with another venue. She was probably relieved when Sidey told her what that venue was.

'I think you've told that you have been to his house before,' Sidey said.

'Yeah,' Kari conceded.

After that, Sidey focused on the alleged visit to Peter's house (pp. 5–24).

S: So um who lives with Peter?

K: Oh he lives by himself.

S: Right, and does he have some friends?

K: Um of course he does, yes, lots of friends, bad friends. His family don't like him though.

S: How do you know that?

K: Because Mummy told me.

S: Okay so [Kari], what about his bad friends, what sort of people are they? Are they men or women?

K: Men and women.

S: And how do you know he's got bad friends? Have you met his friends before or not?

K: Yes I have.

S: Where did you meet his friends?

K: Um at his house.

S: Yeah and what was his friends' names?

K: Can't remember.

S: Oh and what were they doing when you went there, his friends?

K: They were showing the penis and the gina.

Kari's answers showed that she was misinformed (e.g. Ellis did not live by himself, and his family loved him very much). They also showed that her misinformation had come from her mother. But when the opportunity to explore the issue of maternal contamination arose ('And how do you know he's got bad friends?'), Sidey appeared to head off another 'Because Mummy told me' response by suggesting alternative answers ('Have you met his friends before or not?').

In response to further questioning, Kari said that a man named Joseph 'teased' her with his penis. But when Sidey invited her to demonstrate the 'teasing' using naked anatomically correct dolls, the pubic hair on the male doll threw Kari into confusion.

K: What is it?

S: Have you never seen that before on a–

K: No.

S: ... near a penis.

K: No. What is it?

S: What do you think it is?

K: I don't know.

Clearly, Kari did not know what pubic hair was. This revelation, when combined with the anatomical confusion that Kari displayed in her first interview ('it [Ellis's penis] sticked out from the side of his body'), should have cast doubt not only on the 'organised abuse at Peter's house' disclosure, but on all Kari's earlier disclosures about indecent exposure, and oral and genital contact with Ellis's penis. But Sidey was undeterred.

'Show me with this doll how the man teased you with his penis,' she said.

In her report, Sidey stated that Kari 'demonstrated genital contact between two dolls' but she made no mention of Kari's failure to recognise pubic hair.

'Kari's anxiety, the way in which she has disclosed (at times through demonstrations) and the detail she has given which includes feeling states, is consistent with a child who has experienced sexual abuse over a period of time on several occasions,' Sidey reported. 'Kari's disclosure included detail consistent with there being at least one other perpetrator.'[2]

The police were unable to identify the location of the alleged 'teasing'. Nor could they establish the identity of the mysterious Joseph. But they laid a charge anyway. At the trial of Peter Ellis, Count 23 of the 28-count indictment read: 'that Peter Hugh McGregor Ellis between May 1989 and 30 July 1991 at Christchurch did indecently assault [Kari Lacebark] a girl under the age of 12 years in that he took the child to an unknown address where an unknown man put his penis on her vagina'. Ellis was found guilty on this charge.

• • •

Whenever an indecency by Ellis was alleged in a DSW interview, Sidey asked the child if he or she had told anyone at the crèche about it. In her first interview (27 February), Kari Lacebark said she told Marie and Debbie about Peter being naughty, but they did nothing about it. In her first interview (9 March), Lara Palm said she told Debbie, Jan, Marie and Gaye about Peter putting his penis in kids' mouths. She said they tried to make him stop but he didn't listen. In Kari's fourth interview (27 March), when Sidey pressed her for the names of Peter's bad friends, she came up with: Julie, Arnie, Joseph, James, Jemma, Harry, Gina and Melissa. There were no childcare workers' names on that list.

'Where were the other teachers?' asked Sidey. 'Where was Gaye and Marie and them ones?'

'I don't know where,' said Kari. But later in the interview she said, 'Marie came and got us.'

Interestingly, when Kari and her mother first discussed the allegation of organised abuse at Peter's house, Kari said that someone else had driven the children, but her mother had not believed her. Ms Lacebark's notes read:

How did you get back to the crèche?

Daddy picked us up and took us back.

I don't think Daddy remembers this.

No, it was Marie. She picked us up and took us back to the crèche.

Since Marie Keys could not drive, this version of Kari's story was even more unlikely than her previous one. Nonetheless, claims of this sort – that Ellis's colleagues were aware of his offending and (at best) did nothing to stop it, or (at worst) actively supported it – fuelled, and were fuelled by, the anger that complainant parents and their supporters were directing towards the crèche staff. On 20 March, concerns about the Civic childcare workers reached the highest levels of government. That day, in response to a request from the Prime Minister's Office, the Christchurch City Council administration provided the Ministry of Education with the names and qualifications of the current crèche staff.[3] Around the same time three of Ms Magnolia's supporters vented their rage on the staff in writing.

Despite her concerns about the crèche, Ms Birch (a member of Ms Magnolia's support group) continued to send her child to the Civic until 5 March. Then on 16 March she attacked the staff for their 'wall of silence'. 'I expected to hear of great concern for the young children who were brave enough to speak up to their parents. I also expected the children to be believed, and the staff to encourage and support these young children and their parents,' she wrote.

For their part, the staff were constrained by council instructions not to talk to parents or children about Ellis, and by their mixed feelings about the case. 'Parents were looking at us with new eyes,' crèche worker Susannah recalled. 'They were expecting warm fuzzies and group hugs every five minutes. We just didn't know how to respond.' In her 23 March letter Ms Magnolia's sister accused the crèche management and staff of 'subtly freezing out the very people who have finally put a stop to the ghastly alleged offending of your staff member ... What did you think prompted the [Magnolias] and other parents to make the complaints?' she asked. 'Malice? A sense of mischief? Voyeuristic pleasure? What? ... I think you should resign.'

The third angry letter came from Grandma Walnut, a woman with close family ties to the Magnolias. Audrey Walnut did not become a complainant in the court proceedings but her grandmother was in no doubt that she had been abused. 'I feel I must express my deep concern over the sexual abuse against my granddaughter while she attended the Civic Crèche. We were all shattered to discover the depths to which the "childcare" worker sank and also the cover-ups that followed,' she wrote. 'I would like the crèche closed.'

In the midst of these outpourings, several crèche parents phoned the council to say they had no concerns and would not be attending the 31 March meeting. Management committee spokesperson Mr Larch also received a poignantly supportive letter from a former crèche parent. It read:

> When this problem arose late last year it caused immediate panic and stress for me. However, after thoughtful consideration and discussion with my family doctor, and observance of Justin's behaviour past and present, I came to the conclusion that the likelihood of abuse to Justin was nil. Justin's dad Stuart died of cancer last year. One of the reasons for the mental well health and stability of Justin and me throughout Stuart's entire illness was the knowledge and belief that the Civic Crèche was giving Justin the

stable loving environment needed at a time of family stress. I therefore do not think it is necessary nor do I wish Justin to be involved with any interviews ... Justin has now settled into school extremely well. He is a normal, healthy, intelligent child, which I feel in a large part is due to his attending the Civic Crèche ...

• • •

On Thursday 19 March 1992 Detective Eade reported to Detective Inspector Howard Broad on the crèche inquiry. On Monday 23 March Broad briefed Detective Superintendent Stokes and Detective Inspector Carson on Eade's report. In August 1988 Carson had closed the Great Christchurch Child Pornography Ring investigation. In September 1991 he told the *Christchurch Star* that the porn ring inquiry had got so 'out of control' that 'everybody but the Queen' was being implicated. In view of that experience, the prospect of another large-scale child sexual abuse investigation in the city must have concerned him.[4]

During the meeting between Broad, Stokes and Carson, the merits of the case against Ellis, Eade's handling of the inquiry and the manner in which the investigation should proceed were discussed. The first issue – the merits of the case – was relatively straightforward. Eade had assured Broad that 'five clear disclosures have been made by individual children of abuse ranging from indecent assault to anal intercourse', and Broad had no reason to question his claim. Responsibility for interpreting the children's disclosures rested not with Eade, but with interviewer Sue Sidey and her supervisor Dr Karen Zelas, and they were acknowledged experts in the field.

Stokes and Carson accepted Broad's assurance that Eade had solid evidence of child sexual abuse. Most importantly, that evidence comprised five videotaped interviews. This meant that, unlike the porn ring investigation – which had taken place before the law changes allowing the use of such videotapes as evidence in court – in the crèche investigation the police had 'something to put in front of a jury'.[5]

Stokes, Carson and Broad also considered Eade's handling of the case. At that stage they had before them two letters of complaint from Ellis's solicitor, a press release in support of Ellis from union secretary Peter Lawson, evidence of rumour and panic from the media, and Colin Eade's verbal and written reports to Howard Broad.

In his reports, Eade painted a picture of child molestation on an unprecedented scale. He said the purpose of the meeting planned for 31 March was to inform crèche parents *en masse* that their children had been sexually abused by Ellis, and to instruct them on how to talk to their offspring. Parents would also be encouraged to have their children interviewed. Eade said he did not propose to approach Ellis, or to make any decision about prosecution, until the interviewing process was completed, which he expected to take months. He noted that, among children interviewed to date, disclosures were proving difficult to obtain.[6]

In November 1997 Eade's handling of the crèche inquiry was scrutinised in a TV3 documentary.[7] This documentary affected my research in two ways: it led to an internal police report on Eades' conduct which I obtained under the Official Information Act, and it made the police extremely defensive.

In the documentary Eade stressed the centrality of his role. 'I was the person who dealt with the parents, the doctors, the interviewers, the psychologists,' he told journalist Melanie Reid. Of his own mental state, he said: 'I felt almost burnt out – pretty close to it – before the crèche case started. By the time it had finished I was beyond repair.'

Reid told viewers that senior police became so concerned about Eade's mental state during the case that they sought advice from a psychologist. 'In the past, Colin Eade had displayed signs of an obsessional personality,' she reported. 'Then, in the midst of the investigation, he was diagnosed as suffering high stress levels, insomnia and suicidal thoughts. But by that time – six months into the inquiry – the momentum against Ellis was unstoppable.'

Reid reported that Eade had propositioned a former crèche mother during the inquiry, and had sexual relationships with two others after the trial was over. A few days later TV3 reported that Eade also had an affair with a DSW employee involved in the case.

The documentary provoked demands for an independent inquiry into the case from the public, and outrage from complainant parents, child protection workers and the Police Association. Six months later the result of an internal police investigation into Eade's behaviour, conducted by Christchurch Detective Superintendent Millar, was reported in the *Sunday News* under the headline 'Crèche cop cleared by top-level inquiry'.[8]

Millar found that Detective Inspector Carson regarded Eade as 'at times depressed, under some stress and at times not totally objective', and when Ms Arbutus complained of being propositioned by Eade, Detective Inspector Broad 'elected not to confront him about the telephone call to avoid causing anxiety'. The DSW officer with whom Eade had the affair and the psychologist who treated him told Millar they thought Eade was suffering from 'stress'.[9] With regard to Eade's supervision, Millar reported:

> there was a significant and robust supervisory infrastructure in place throughout the investigation, both in the form of direct input from senior Commissioned Officers and day-to-day supervision by Non Commissioned Officers. Eade's activities, particularly in the area of specialist interviews, was only as part of a professional team including Social Welfare and health professionals ... Mr Lange from the Crown Solicitor's office

was involved from late March 1992 and monitored the investigation. He, in consultation with the Crown Solicitor in Christchurch, Mr Stanaway, provided an oversight and legal advice throughout the investigation …

Having come to the view that Eade's transgressions were of no real consequence, and that supervisory structures were in place throughout the inquiry, Millar concluded that 'Eade's psychological condition was not such that his judgment was impaired in any significant way'.[10]

At the time of the crèche case, the obvious person from the Christchurch Crown solicitor's firm of Raymond Donnelly & Co. to supervise a sexual abuse investigation was Crown prosecutor David Saunders. During the previous decade Saunders had worked closely with Karen Zelas and Detective Senior Sergeant John Ell on the development of protocols for the investigation and prosecution of sexual offences against children. But in March 1992 Brent Stanaway was appointed to the top job in Raymond Donnelly & Co., and David Saunders was smarting from the perceived snub.

'Colin, I'm not the least bit interested,' Saunders said when Eade approached him about the crèche case. 'Brent Stanaway's the Crown Solicitor now. He can worry about it. I've given my all for the Crown in the last 15 or 16 years. From now on I'm going to do the work that pleases me instead of being the Crown's loyal servant.'[11]

As it happened, responsibility for Crown input into the crèche investigation fell to Chris Lange, a junior member of the Raymond Donnelly legal team. Throughout the inquiry, Eade provided Lange with occasional verbal reports. But because Lange had little experience of child sexual abuse prosecutions and did not see Eade on a day-to-day basis, he was in no position to monitor Eade's conduct. Furthermore, since Crown solicitor Brent Stanaway had no involvement with the case until October 1992, he was in no position to monitor Eade's conduct either.

• • •

In his report, Detective Superintendent Millar indicated that Detective Eade needed to be supervised, and claimed that he had been. 'Detective Inspector Carson monitored Eade's condition and took steps to ensure that a supervisory infrastructure was in place to ensure that he had the appropriate support, guidance and oversight,' he wrote. He cited Carson's deployment of Detective Senior Sergeant Ell to the case as evidence of the 'supervisory infrastructure'. But in my interviews with them, both Carson and Ell talked of providing Eade with 'support' rather than 'supervision'.[12]

'One of my responsibilities was resourcing and workload,' Carson said. 'I wanted, among other things, to make sure Colin, as officer in charge of the case, had the appropriate infrastructure around him to support him through the whole period.'[13]

On 24 March 1992 Carson brought Detective Senior Sergeant John Ell onto the case. Ell was a leading national authority on child abuse investigations. In 1986–87 he helped to establish police Child Abuse Units and multidisciplinary child protection teams nationwide, and participated in police training and policy development. But when the Great Christchurch Child Pornography Ring investigation came to an abrupt end he moved to a less stressful area of police work.[14]

'I wanted John Ell to look at the overall workload of the Child Abuse Unit and give me a specific status report on the Civic Crèche inquiry … It was no more than that, just a business decision,' Carson told me.

'I was asked to discuss with Colin what he perceived to be the extent of the complaints at that time – to make an assessment and report back on what might need to be done,' Ell said. 'I had a discussion with Colin. To me it was just obvious that there was substance, without doubt, in what was being said by some of the children.'[15]

After that, Ell prepared information sheets for parents attending the 31 March meeting, and organised the procedures, personnel and resources he considered necessary to cope with the expected aftermath of the meeting. Then, at the end of May, he was assigned to a murder inquiry. At that point, whatever supervision he had provided for Colin Eade effectively ceased.

On 5 August, when allegations of offending by the women crèche workers arose, Ell again took up a support role in the case. For a month he worked overtime on both the murder case and the crèche case. But his involvement with both cases ceased on 4 September 1992, when he suffered a physical and emotional collapse.[16]

Back on 24 March 1992, in addition to appointing Ell to the crèche inquiry, Carson called Detective Inspector Brian Pearce and Detective Colin Eade to his office. He instructed Eade to interview and arrest Ellis no later than 26 March, and he instructed Pearce to ensure that the order was carried out. At that stage, Pearce's role in the investigation was administrative rather than operational, and it lasted only two weeks. Later in the year, when four women were named as suspects in the case, Pearce again played a short-term administrative role in the inquiry. Then, at the end of the Ellis trial, Pearce became the public face of the crèche investigation in a controversial interview on *Holmes*.[17]

In his report on television's *20/20* programme, Millar attributed Eade's 'adverse response' to Ell's appointment, and to Carson's instruction that he arrest Ellis without delay, to the effects of stress.

Roger Carson's primary reason for ordering Peter Ellis's arrest had been to bring the inquiry to a rapid conclusion, and he expected John Ell to help make that happen. But Ell had other plans.

'I was against a quick arrest and stalled it to give Colin time for more interviews,' Ell told me. 'We were able to get a little bit, a day or two. But in our system somebody has to make the final decision, and the decision was made that Ellis was to be arrested on whatever charges could be supported on *prima facie* evidence up to that time.'

However, in terms of the view of the case that Ell and Eade shared, all was not lost. 'That wasn't to say that the investigation was then ended,' Ell assured me. 'In fact it turned out to be quite the reverse.'[18]

• • •

On Thursday 26 March the city council administration hosted a meeting to review arrangements for the 31 March meeting for crèche parents. Most of the major players, and a few minor ones, were there: John Gray, Rob Dally, Martin Maguire and Barbara Newman from the council; Mr Larch from the crèche management committee; Rosemary Smart from the Campbell Centre (who was conducting a management review of the crèche); Human Rights Commissioner Carolyn Bull (who had agreed to chair the meeting); former START therapist Sara Crane (who was scheduled to speak at the meeting); interviewer Sue Sidey and supervisor Miriam Preston from DSW; two staff from the prison sex offenders' unit; and Brian Pearce, John Ell and Colin Eade from the police.

The first concern Carolyn Bull expressed – which should have been obvious to those who had attended the December 1991 meeting for crèche parents (John Gray, Rob Dally, Mr Larch, Sue Sidey and Colin Eade) was that a large meeting of anxious parents was potentially explosive. Her second concern was that the man at the centre of the investigation had still not been spoken to by the police.

Up to that point most people had regarded the 31 March meeting as inevitable, but Bull's comments allowed them to express their reservations. John Gray said the big meeting had been Colin Eade's idea. Sue Sidey suggested they arrange a series of smaller meetings instead. John Ell suggested they send out information in the mail. Brian Pearce agreed with John Ell.

But Mr Larch and Colin Eade insisted that the big meeting had to proceed. Parents were angry and they wanted answers, Mr Larch said. They would not take kindly to a change of plans. They wanted to know why the investigation was taking so long. They wanted to know when the suspect was going to be charged. There were allegations of gang rape. (This was nonsense, but Colin Eade and Sue Sidey were the only ones who knew that, and they said nothing to contradict Mr Larch's wild talk.)

By the time everyone had aired their views, the misgivings of the many had been swept away by the certainty of the few. The meeting closed with general agreement that the 31 March meeting for crèche parents would go ahead as planned.[19]

• • •

On 30 March 1992, Peter Ellis's thirty-fourth birthday began with the arrival on his doorstep of Detective Colin Eade and four other officers from the Child Abuse Unit. Their search warrant stated that the police had reasonable grounds for believing that they would find, at Ellis's home:

> Photographs showing either a child or Peter Ellis with a child, documents or writings identifying any child who has visited [the] address, a diary or diaries detailing any contact Ellis has had with children, any sound or videotapes recording children, books, magazines or periodicals relating to sexual acts, homosexuality or sexual contact with children, documents containing information on child sexual abuse or indicators of or the education on the detection of sexual abuse, clothing or personal effects of a type or size used by children.

According to the warrant, the items were sought in respect to the offences of 'indecent assault, inducing an indecent act, and sexual violation'.

Ellis began reading the warrant. Eade interrupted him to issue a formal caution, and to warn that the media could arrive at any minute. He suggested they leave for the police station immediately.

The search continued after their departure, but the police found nothing at Ellis's home, on this or any other occasion, that they could use in evidence against him. Not that they didn't try. On one visit they ripped up his floorboards. On another they carried off an item from inside a birdcage. On the inventory of seized property it was described as a 'phallic symbol/object', but it was actually an old iron shoe-last, covered in bird droppings, that had served for years as a perch.

At the Child Abuse Unit, Eade told Ellis that four children had made complaints of sexual assault against him, and the children and their parents wanted him prosecuted.

'Do you know [Mandy Arbutus], [Lara Palm], [Kari Lacebark] and [Yelena Holly]?' Eade asked. Ellis said he did.

'I believe these children. Will you tell me what you have done to them?' Eade asked.

'I'm sorry, I can't help you,' said Ellis.

When Eade described this episode to the court, Ellis scribbled a note to his lawyer: 'No mention of him saying that I was the best [paedophile] in the business, that I was in denial, that if I confessed he would get me straight onto the sex offenders' programme in prison.' Ellis also recalled that, when he failed to provide Eade with the answers he wanted, the detective said abruptly, 'Okay, we'll do it the hard way. Phone your lawyer.'

Later, in Chris Knight's presence, Eade took a statement from Ellis about his age, his places of residence, his relationships, his alcohol consumption and his work.

Then, after showing Ellis and Knight the videotape of Mandy Arbutus's evidential interview, Eade took another statement. 'I let Peter have a reasonably free rein,' Knight recalled. 'I felt it was important that his initial reactions come out. He was actually very natural and spontaneous in his various responses, and totally baffled.'

To Ellis, there were significant problems with Mandy's disclosure. The first was that she was never enrolled in the crèche. Her only visits to the centre were made at the end of the day, when she came in with her mother to collect her younger siblings. Furthermore, those visits were brief because one parent had a day job and the other had a night job, and five past five was their hectic pickup and swap-over time. Ellis said that if they were there for more than five minutes 'it was normally because I was talking to Ms Arbutus'. In any event, at that time of day there were always two staff present, and other parents coming and going. 'And I'd be tidying up to get home as soon as possible,' Ellis added.

Ellis also had a problem with Mandy's description of him. 'I was surprised that she didn't recognise my hands because children normally comment on my long fingernails and the fact that I wear a lot of rings,' he said. 'The other thing that did surprise me was the clothing she mentioned. I don't have stripy shorts, or shorts with spots on. My normal clothes are black tracksuit pants or blue tracksuit pants. I don't wear jeans as a rule. Very seldom. I'm not a jeans person.' But to Eade, these were minor points.

Q: So she hasn't got the clothes completely right, has she?
A: She hasn't mentioned my clothes correctly at all.
Q: That still takes us to the statements about the touching of her vagina. Did you ever do that?
A: No.
Q: So she is lying about that?
A: I've already answered that question. As far as I am concerned I've not touched her. She may not be lying about being sexually abused, but I've not touched her in any sexual way whatever.

Towards the end of the interview Eade's questions took an extraordinary turn:

Q: How long do you think it might take to touch a child's vaginal area?
A: I wouldn't know because I have never done anything like that.
Q: All right, you have given a lot of reasons why you couldn't have done it, but I am asking you as a man who is experienced with children if someone could touch a child's vagina out of sight of others in 10 or 20 seconds?
A: I'd be highly surprised.
Q: How about one minute?

A: This is not my field. Again, I'd be highly surprised.

Q: Two minutes?

A: I don't know how long it would take.

• • •

In November 1991 Chris Knight had put Rob Harrison on standby in case Ellis needed a barrister. Over the intervening four months Harrison had heard nothing more. Then, on 30 March 1992, he returned to his chambers at lunchtime to find a series of messages asking him to come down to the Child Abuse Unit. He arrived to relieve Knight as Ellis's interview was coming to an end. Harrison recalled:

> I sat and talked with Peter. I asked Colin Eade whether he was going to arrest him. I didn't get a straight answer. Finally, around three or four o'clock Eade announced that he was arresting Peter for the indecent assault of [Mandy Arbutus]. I subsequently learnt that he was under orders to make the arrest that day. It was staged to coincide with the meeting for crèche parents. What better way to fan the flames than to make an arrest the day before a big meeting? I said, 'Well, can we get him in front of the District Court right away?' Eade said, 'Oh, it's probably too late. I don't know how long it's going to take us to get him processed.' It was obvious they wanted to keep him in custody overnight, and that's what they did.[20]

During the day, crèche worker Jan Buckingham learnt that Ellis had been taken in for questioning. During the evening she learnt that he hadn't come home:

> I thought – Oh Peter, locked up in a cell on your birthday. So I phoned the Central Police Station and left a message – something like 'Happy birthday, hang in' – because all this time, even though I believed in my head that Colin Eade knew what he was talking about, it never got through to my heart. All the time I had this inward battle: yes he's guilty; I've been told he's guilty; these kids are making these allegations; he has to be guilty. But in my heart I knew: Hey, Peter, you wouldn't hurt a fly. It didn't fit. I used to have nightmares. My eyelashes fell out. Just stress, but not about myself at that stage. Just this inward battle.[21]

When Ellis appeared before Judge Noble next morning (31 March 1992) his trackpants were wet from sitting in a freshly hosed-out police van. (Hosing out the back of the van is an old police trick. It makes the accused look as if he's wet himself on the way to court.) Ellis was granted interim name suppression and remanded on bail for two weeks. He was required to observe a 7pm–7am residential curfew, to stay away from the Civic and to stay away from children who had attended the crèche since September 1987.

'At first I didn't realise the full weight of it,' Rob Harrison recalled. 'I was thinking, yeah, we're looking at four or five charges. It didn't look as if it was going to get any bigger.' But the media feeding frenzy concerned him deeply. 'Some things I'd seen on TV were highly emotive. Peter was as good as hung, just from the way scenes were shot – empty swings going back and forth; parents with covered faces talking about how scared they were.' Harrison resolved that he would have nothing to do with the media.[22]

With regard to television, Harrison's concerns extended from the professional to the personal. Back in November 1991, 10 days before Ms Magnolia laid her first complaint, Rob Harrison had married TV3 journalist Rose Daly. When he became Ellis's barrister, he obtained an undertaking from his wife and her boss that she would not report on the case.

'That was very hard for Rose,' he recalled. 'It automatically cut her out of the main story for the next 18 months. It also meant that I couldn't talk to her about the case because I never wanted to be in a situation where I would hear something on TV that I'd told her. I didn't want that doubt.'[23]

On the evening of 31 March 1992 radio and television audiences nationwide learnt that charges had been laid against the man at the centre of the sexual abuse controversy at the Christchurch Civic Child Care Centre, and that more charges were expected to follow. They also learnt that parents of children who had attended the centre were gathering for a meeting that evening. Crèche management committee spokesperson Mr Larch said they were relieved that firm action had been taken in the case.[24]

• • •

When present and former crèche parents began arriving at Knox Hall in the evening of 31 March, they found police ringing the building, and Detective Inspector Brian Pearce, Detective Senior Sergeant John Ell, Detective Colin Eade and the entire police Child Abuse Unit inside. For the Cedars, the defining moment came when they met a police officer of their acquaintance standing guard outside:

> We stopped to chat and she let some things slip: 'Oh this is a dreadful business. Fancy him doing those awful things to those children.' We were stunned. We had assumed that the police would look at the complaints and say, 'What a waste of time'. But she was saying, 'Oh this is terrible. It's going to be a long business. They're going to have to interview so many children.'[25]

At the door, parents had their names checked off on a roll. Then, with around 250 people packing the hall, the meeting began. Everyone I spoke to recalled the anger, fear, anxiety and distress that suffused the audience, and the long-term friendships that were severed as people took one side or the other in the heated debate. Most people also recalled at least some of the messages that were delivered.

'Parents were invited to go home and cross-examine their children, being careful not to be too specific. They were told to believe their kids, to thank them for telling, to assure them they'd done the right thing and to get straight on the phone to DSW,' Mr Sycamore recalled. 'I think parents went away with the impression that if there was a problem DSW would fix it. I don't think they grasped that the interviewers were collecting evidence for court proceedings.'[26]

'They said he'd been arrested, that counselling was available. They recommended that we get our children interviewed. It was really quite heavy,' said Ms Mahogany. 'Yet nobody told us what was supposed to have happened. When people asked, the answer was – it's *sub judice* – which I suppose was fair enough. But it just seemed to fan the anxiety.'[27]

'I remember Sue Sidey speaking,' council administrator Alistair Graham said.

> If anybody alarmed the parents it was her – talking about child abuse, what the characteristics were and what you should look out for. She seemed very consumed with the travesty of child abuse. She betrayed it in her manner and speech. She was quite emotional, I thought. After the meeting she was quite distraught. She probably had people going home and observing their kids intensely for weeks afterwards.

'They probably woke their kids up that night, looking for signs,' his colleague Martin Maguire said gloomily.[28]

Indeed, according to Mr Larch, some parents were very clear about their intentions. 'They said, "If you're telling us this has been going on and you think we're not going to question our kids, you're in Cloud Cuckoo Land,"' he told me.[29]

People also remembered Detective Senior Sergeant John Ell and child psychiatrist Karen Zelas answering questions from the floor, and city manager John Gray attempting to distance the council from responsibility for the crèche. 'I'll never, never forgive John Gray for saying that the crèche was in the hands of the management committee, and that the council just held the licence,' said an angry parent.[30]

'The council became a bit of a villain that night,' admitted Alistair Graham. 'Here we were thinking we were doing the right thing, helping the police while at the same time trying to protect the Civic and the other staff. But the whole thing developed into a bit of a slanging match.'[31]

The Civic childcare workers were the other villains that night. But, having been instructed not to attend, they weren't there. 'The air was rife with the belief that someone was going to challenge the organisers to admit that there was a lot more to come out. That people weren't being honest. That other staff were involved. Near the end somebody did stand up and ask about other staff. The answer was fudged,' Ms Rimu recalled.[32]

• • •

The Knox Hall meeting took place at a time when the Department of Social Welfare was being restructured. Three 'business units' were formed: the Children and Young Persons Service (CYPS); the Community Funding Agency; and Income Support. In mid-April, Mike Doolan arrived in Christchurch to take up the position of regional manager of CYPS. By then the Knox Hall meeting was history, and Doolan had to deal with the consequences. He recalled:

> I've always held that primary responsibility for the care and protection of children rests with parents, and the state should intervene only when they're patently unable or unwilling to carry out that responsibility. I believed, and still believe, that the meeting organised by the police and ourselves, and the offer of services by our people to over 100 crèche families was wrong. It resulted in a virtual capture of our services for more than six months. Also, even if children had been damaged at the crèche, there were no care and protection issues involved. Once we were satisfied that the police had removed the threat, or that parents had removed their children from the threat, we should have retreated. As for the criminal investigation – we have a joint protocol that governs our work with the police. When they have evidence of sexual abuse, we do the evidential interviews. Now that service was offered to every crèche family. I think that was where we went overboard. We should have offered the service – as we always do – to the police, for children who were likely to go to court. As it turned out, that would have been no more than about a dozen kids.[33]

• • •

Peter Ellis's barrister, Rob Harrison, summed up the effects of the Knox Hall meeting in a pithy analogy. 'Look at it this way,' he said. 'It's like a Ministry of Works lure. You light a stick of gelly. You toss it in the river and it explodes. Down below you've got these nets. The fish just come floating down to you.'[34]

CHAPTER 8

The Whole Crèche Thing Has Blown Up

8.i: Anyone Who Has Concerns Should Get in Touch

Ms Mahogany did not take up the invitation to have her children interviewed. 'A few years earlier I was on a social services committee,' she explained. 'The abuse team came and spoke to us. They were very strong women. I felt they would be quite intimidating for a child. So when we were urged to have our children interviewed, I thought: Oh no, not my kids.'[1]

Ms Elm, a counsellor who had seen many of her colleagues become sexual abuse specialists virtually overnight, also kept her child out of the investigators' hands:

> I said to my husband, 'I don't want any of those "experts" having anything to do with her. I'll be accused of being "in denial" for sure, but I don't have enough respect or confidence in the people who do that evidential stuff to allow Nina to be interviewed by them.' J agreed. At that stage we weren't saying she hadn't been abused. We were just saying that whatever emerged we would deal with as a family. I felt, and still feel very strongly, that if she had suffered any trauma those 'experts' would have aggravated it.[2]

But at the Knox Hall meeting there was a whole range of parents: perfectionist parents who needed someone to blame because their children were less than perfect; druggies and dropouts who needed someone to blame for their parenting difficulties; child protection workers who believed the abuse stories as if they were holy writ; parents whose children had behavioural problems for a whole variety of reasons; parents who believed in the omniscience of experts; parents desperate for reassurance that their kids were okay. For many parents, the invitation to have their children interviewed was irresistible. Ms Willow recalled: 'I don't know whether we were urged or invited to send our children to be interviewed. I think the message was: anyone who has any concerns should get in touch. Of course we had concerns! We wanted to know whether or not our children had been abused!'[3]

Detective Senior Sergeant John Ell also had concerns. One was that, in the collective anxiety of the Knox Hall meeting, parents would absorb little of what was said. So he prepared a four-page handout for parents to take home. The first page presented sexual abuse at the Civic Crèche as a serious possibility, and encouraged parents to have their children interviewed. The second page summarised the investigative process, and provided contact details for counselling, funding, medical examinations and support. The third page – a duplicate from the *Feeling Safe* sexual abuse prevention programme for preschoolers – was headed 'What to do when a child tells of his or her abuse'. The most compelling messages on the page were: 'Believe what they say'; 'Say you're glad they told'; 'Let them know they're not the only one'; 'Try not to alert the alleged abuser'; 'Seek assistance and advice'; and 'Find support for yourself'.[4]

For the crèche case information kit distributed after the Knox Hall meeting, the heading on the *Feeling Safe* page 'What to do when a child tells of his or her abuse' was changed to 'What to do *if* a child tells of his or her abuse', but two other potentially inflammatory pieces of advice ('Believe what they say', and 'Let them know too that they're not the only one') were left unchanged.

According to Ruth Corrin, writer-director of the Feeling Safe programme, the advice 'Let them know too that they're not the only one' came from her perception of child sexual abuse as an isolated, and isolating, experience. 'I wanted to say: this does happen, and it's awful, but no victim should be left feeling that he or she is the only person in history that this has happened to,' she told me. 'I never intended it to be used, as it seems to have been used in the crèche case, to imply that lots and lots of children had been molested at the centre.'

In retrospect, Corrin said she would change the other potentially inflammatory piece of advice, 'Believe what they say', to 'Take whatever the child says seriously'. But she stressed that 'Believe what they say' was included in the programme in good faith, and in accordance with the recommendations of the experts.

'But you must have known, even then, that children say all sorts of misleading and muddle-headed things that aren't necessarily believable,' I said.

'I must have known,' she agreed thoughtfully.

> But you could say that of anybody. We should have known better. We should have been able to work out what was going on in kids' heads – that they made things up, that they got ideas from all over the place. I believed – people did – that kids simply could not make up stories about sexual abuse. How could they, without any sexual experience to go on? So people were terrified for their children. It was a time of great confusion. Maybe if I'd used my head better I could have worked it out. But people weren't working it out then. It was all so new. Nobody stopped to analyse it. We thought we were doing good, and most of the time we were.[5]

The fourth page in Detective Senior Sergeant Ell's handout was devoted to information on counselling funding. The ACC section advised parents that 'victims of rape/incest' could claim counselling costs, and travelling expenses for medical treatment. It also provided information on how to lodge a claim, but it did not say that sexual abuse victims could claim up to $10,000 in lump-sum compensation. However, children were routinely referred for counselling by DSW interviewers or DSAC doctors (even if they had disclosed nothing), and counsellors routinely advised parents to apply for lump-sum compensation for their children.

The fourth page of John Ell's handout also stated that the city council would pay counselling costs for crèche parents, and any excess charged by children's counsellors over the basic ACC fee. As the investigation developed, the council also paid babysitting costs for parents attending support groups, the salary of a full-time social worker and some incidental costs incurred by crèche families.

• • •

In the days following the Knox Hall meeting about 60 parents (around a quarter of the total meeting attendance) phoned the Child Abuse Unit hotline to request interviews for their children. These requests, when added to the interviews arranged in the days leading up to the meeting, were more than enough to keep the investigators busy for months.

Apart from the handouts and the three-day police-based hotline, the net Ell put in place was woven primarily from DSW and city council resources. Its most significant features were two additional specialist interviewers (funded by DSW); a 'prosecution support social worker' (funded by DSW); and a 'counselling support coordinator' (funded by the city council).

By mid-April, when Mike Doolan took up his appointment as regional head of DSW's Children and Young Persons Service (CYPS), the DSW-resourced part of John Ell's net was largely in place.

Soon after his arrival, Doolan met Ell for the first time. By then, seven children had made disclosures of offences involving Peter Ellis, but to John Ell that was the tip of the iceberg. 'Sergeant Ell seemed to think the case was going to be huge – that there was a lot to be revealed that hadn't yet been revealed,' Doolan recalled.

> Without saying this about him personally, I thought there was a degree of heightened excitement that wasn't altogether comforting. So when he wanted resources pumped into this thing I was reluctant. I could see us getting pulled into becoming service providers to a group of competent parents when it was really an issue between them and the police.[6]

'I remember Mike Doolan phoning me,' CYPS general manager Robin Wilson confirmed. 'He said it wasn't a matter for CYPS because no children were at risk.

It was a resourcing argument as much as anything, but I was operating at a policy level and CYPS was, and still is, heavily dependent on the police. So, when the police asked for assistance, my response was to give it to them.'

When I interviewed him in 1997, Wilson had retired from CYPS. In retrospect, he had doubts, not just about the crèche case, but about the wider issues involved:

> Social Welfare was the first government agency that gave women a significant role in management. It started when I was Auckland regional manager. I opened the doors to women and got flattened against the wall as they charged through. You look back and think: was it all good? I'm sure some of it was. I helped set up the evidential interviewing units. Perhaps I was too close to see the whole scene in perspective. A lot of our interviewers were connected with the women's movement. They had reputations – Miriam Saphira at our Hamilton office, others in other places. They all seemed to run together. You'd find it difficult to question Miriam Saphira's credentials, but you'd be silly if you didn't realise that she had her own agenda. At the time I didn't see that as a problem. Now I don't know. Looking back, I'm not sure who was running the show. That's why I worry about our role in the crèche case. Were our interviewers detached and objective? I know it's been said that if they didn't create the problem they certainly gave it a good stir along.[7]

But in March and April 1992 there was no time for reflection. Robin Wilson and the senior CYPS managers, and John Gray and the senior council managers, accepted Detective Senior Sergeant Ell's expansionary plans for the crèche case, and at that point the investigation moved up another gear.

On 6 April 1992 Lynda Morgan (founder of the Incest Survivors Group) joined the interview team. Like Sue Sidey, she was based in the Christchurch DSW Specialist Services Unit. On 18 May Jan Gillanders was seconded from a Christchurch CYPS branch to become prosecution support social worker. She too was based in the Specialist Services Unit. On 25 May social worker Gen Crossen took up her appointment as counselling support coordinator. The council paid her salary and provided her with a car, but she too worked out of the DSW Specialist Services Unit. Around the same time Cathy Crawford, a specialist interviewer based in the Christchurch Specialist Services Unit, was seconded to the crèche investigation on a part-time basis.

The rationale behind the appointment of two social workers was that crèche parents who would be involved in the court proceedings, and crèche parents who would not, had to be kept separate to avoid contaminating the evidence. According to a San Diego Grand Jury report on concerns raised by ritual abuse cases in their jurisdiction, contamination is 'the act of introducing outside influences into a person's subjective experience so that either his memory of an event or his description of the event is altered'.[8] Everyone involved in the Civic Crèche investigation seemed to take the risk of contamination between the two parent groups very seriously, even though the contamination genie had long since escaped from the bottle, and there was no way that anyone could ever put it back.

In the six months between Ms Magnolia's initial complaint and the appointment of the crèche case social workers, extensive parent–child and parent–parent contamination had occurred – the former through inappropriate questioning, the latter through the sharing of information at meetings of Ms Magnolia's support group (a mix of complainant and non-complainant parents), and through the activities of other networks, both formal and informal, throughout the city.

Since some former crèche children played together and attended the same schools, the possibility of child–child contamination also needs to be considered. At the trial of Peter Ellis, some parents admitted that child–child contacts had taken place, but insisted these were of minimal significance. My interview with Ms Cedar, a non-complainant parent whose daughter was at the crèche with Yelena Holly, suggests otherwise:

> [Ms Holly] told me that [Yelena] had named our daughter as being present when some horrendous abuse had gone on. We spoke to [Opal] about it. She's very upfront. Very secure. No reason to lie. She said, 'Peter tapped me on the head with a coffee cup because I wouldn't sit down at story time.' That was the worst thing she could think of. [Ms Holly] kept phoning – trying to get us to go to parent support groups, to speak to parents whose children had named [Opal]. She told me they were having playgroups so kids could help each other remember. She asked if [Yelena] could stay at our place for the weekend. She said [Yelena] might help [Opal] remember. I agreed, but only because I thought [Yelena] could do with a break. On the way to our place, [Yelena] said, '[Opal], do you remember those dreadful things that went on at crèche?' [Opal] said, 'No.' I said, 'We're not going to talk about any of that this weekend.' [Yelena] had a lovely, pressure-free couple of days.⁹

But the risks of contamination was not confined to parent–parent, parent–child and child–child contacts. An even more significant source of contamination – which the appointments of the social workers overlooked, and indeed exacerbated – was the contamination effected by the child abuse workers themselves.

Contamination of the evidence occurred whenever a police officer suggested to a parent that Ellis had abused many children, and probably their own. For example, when Detective Eade visited Ms Willow, he encouraged her to believe the worst:

> He said that [Bo] had been named by other children. Had she talked? Can you imagine! It was like my daughter was one of a group that had been seriously abused. I said 'Is Peter guilty?' Now to be perfectly honest, I don't remember whether he said 'in my opinion' or whether he just said it. But he said 'He's guilty. Yes, he's guilty, and we're going to get him.'

By the time I interviewed her in 1998, Ms Willow had a more benign explanation for her daughter's centre-stage role: '[Bo] was, and still is, a stroppy, up-front sort of a kid. Everyone knows her name. So when kids were asked to name names, they were bound to think of her.'[10]

DSW interviewers were another source of contamination. An interviewer contaminated the evidence whenever she introduced into a formal interview an allegation she had heard from someone else. For example, when Sue Sidey said to Kari Lacebark on 27 March, 'I think you've told that you have been to his [Peter Ellis's] house before' (even though Kari had said nothing of the sort during that or any previous interview), she contaminated the evidence.

The evidence was further contaminated whenever a DSW interviewer took a comment made by a child in an earlier interview, and misreported it back to the same child in a later interview. For example, on 5 March this conversation took place between Sue Sidey and Yelena Holly:

Y: ... I didn't suck his penis I didn't, but I didn't even know ... and then little kiddies went to the toilet and then he quickly grabbed them like this and then he did poos and then he took down his trousers and just then he hold the heads like this and then they had to suck his penis about a whole minute.

S: And how did you know that they had to suck his penis?

Y: Because my mummy told, um, my friend mummy's told my mum.

S: And did, and did you know that that had happened before Mummy told you that?

Y: No.

At the end of the interview Sidey checked that point again.

S: ... you were telling me about that um Peter holding the kids' heads and them sucking his penis – was that something that you saw or something that Mummy told you?

Y: Mummy told me.

But at Yelena's second interview on 19 March, Sidey put a different spin on her earlier comments.

Y: Well he used to, he used to hold children's heads and put his penis in the mouth.

S: Yeah.

Y: And one time I saw that.

S: Yeah you did, you told me that you saw that.

Contamination also occurred whenever an interviewer invited a child to imagine how it felt to be abused. For example, when Kari Lacebark told Sue Sidey that 'he got them to touch his penis', and Sidey responded with, 'And what did they feel like when they touched it?', she encouraged Kari to make the touching experience her own.

Research by Maryanne Garry and her team ('Imagination Inflation: Imagining a childhood event inflates confidence that it occurred') has demonstrated that people may develop false memories simply by imagining fictitious past events.[11]

Therapists were another potential source of contamination. They treated crèche children and their parents in unsupervised and unrecorded therapy sessions. Many therapists treated several crèche children simultaneously. They met regularly 'to discuss therapeutic and clinical issues about the work we are doing with the children who were abused at the Civic Crèche'.[12] They encouraged parents to lodge claims for ACC lump-sum compensation (and thereby provided them with financial incentives to make abuse allegations).

'Why did you take your daughter for therapy when she'd said nothing about being abused?' I asked Ms Willow.

'I think it was just an expectation. It was something we would all do,' she mused. 'Now I think: how could I have been led? But I'm on my own. My daughter's everything to me. I wanted an expert to tell me what was going on, what I should do about it, because I couldn't figure it out for myself.'

> I'll tell you what, though. It's a bloody relief to realise that my daughter never was abused. I look at her now – she's happy, healthy, well adjusted. The only abuse was from me dragging her around those counsellors, and blaming every little thing she did on the crèche. Nothing to do with the way I was bringing her up, whether she was having a good night's sleep, whether she was eating correctly. Back then, everything was a direct result of whatever happened at the Civic. A counsellor from the Campbell Centre even gave me a children's book about ritual abuse to read to my daughter.[13]

When a therapist told Ms Willow that lump-sum compensation was available from ACC for sexual abuse victims, she lodged a claim on her daughter's behalf and received a $10,000 cheque in the mail. For each claimant, ACC required a medical certificate, a police report and a report from a counsellor, therapist, psychologist or psychiatrist on the effects of the alleged sexual abuse. In a report on Geoffrey Magnolia, Detective Eade wrote:

> He has not, in fact, fully disclosed to an evidential interviewer but was part of a group of children who were very much at risk from the suspect ... I understand that [Geoffrey] has disclosed a lot of detail to his mother. I believe that he has been physically, sexually and emotionally abused by the crèche worker.

Therapist Karen Dawson's report on Timothy Cork read:

> I have seen [Timothy] for one appointment only. He attended Christchurch Civic Crèche at the time of abuse disclosed by other children. As you know, this case has been very fully investigated by the Police and it is generally accepted that all children who attended

the crèche either experienced or witnessed very serious sexual, physical and emotional abuse. At present [Timothy] can say that Peter [Ellis] touched him on the penis; that 'Peter is scary'; and that [Timothy] gets a frightening ringing noise in his head when he is scared of the dark, and that he thinks this has something to do with what happened at crèche. On the basis of these indications and my interview with [Timothy], my assessment is that he has been completely terrified and traumatised. His present method of coping is to bury any memories of the trauma, and he is very afraid of remembering. It may not be until [Timothy] is older that therapy is useful to him.

Though charges were laid against Peter Ellis in relation to 18 families, by the time the court case was over, more than 40 families had been awarded $10,000 (or multiples of $10,000) for the alleged abuse of their children at the Civic Crèche.[14]

Contamination of the evidence by sexual abuse workers was identified as a key issue in the 1994 San Diego County Grand Jury report into concerns raised by local ritual abuse cases. The report concluded that courts should consider:

- Disallowing evaluators [specialist interviewers] who are working on the same case from conferring with each other, or with more than one alleged victim, until an independent written report has been submitted.
- Disqualifying CAPF [state-funded] therapists from taking more than one victim as a client/patient in multi-victim/multi-perpetrator cases.
- Not using therapists who are based in the same office on any one case.
- Requiring CAPF therapists to not share information with other therapists about details of sexual assault disclosed during therapy.[15]

• • •

In the wake of the Knox Hall meeting, up to five children were interviewed each day at the Specialist Services Unit. Some were interviewed several times. As a result, between 1 April and 31 May 1992 the number of complainant children rose from five to 13. The sixth complainant child to make a formal disclosure was Eli Laurel.

Ms Laurel was a friend and neighbour of the Palms and the Ngaios. In the '80s she was a colleague of Ritual Action Group founder Raewyn Good.

Eli Laurel was almost two when he began attending the Civic Crèche. One year later he moved from the Womble End to the Big End. In March 1990 his attendance increased to two days a week. In October 1991 he turned five and left for school.

Mr and Ms Laurel attended the December 1991 meeting for crèche parents. Next day, Ms Laurel asked Eli about Peter Ellis and the crèche. She later recalled that there was 'a large level of denial' at the December meeting, and that, when her son said nothing about abuse, 'I believed the biggest myth in the book – that he would tell me.'

On her return from an overseas trip in March 1992, Ms Laurel learnt that 'the whole crèche thing had blown up and children had started to disclose'. When the non-leading questions she asked Eli produced no disclosures, she took a more direct approach: 'I said to him that some children had been saying to their mummies and daddies about what Peter had done to them – like pulling down their pants and touching their bottoms ... he said Peter did wees and poos on the children's faces.'[16]

Eli's first DSW interview on 3 April lasted 56 minutes. The transcript is 44 pages long. In the course of the interview Eli passed through the three stages of disclosure described by Kee MacFarlane (the investigator who 'discovered' ritual abuse at the McMartin preschool in California) in her book *Sexual Abuse of Young Children* (which was in circulation among Christchurch sexual abuse workers from the late-'80s). MacFarlane claimed that molested children who have been silenced by threats initially deny that any abuse has taken place. Then, after careful and persistent questioning, they admit that some children were abused. Finally, after more careful and persistent questioning, they admit that they too were abused. Eli's reported claim that Peter 'did poos and wees on the children's faces' appears to have been interpreted by Ms Laurel as evidence that Eli had reached the second stage. The tenor and persistence of Sue Sidey's questioning throughout his first and second interviews suggests that she was intent on bringing him to the third stage.[17]

At the start of his first interview, Eli told Sidey his mother had promised to take him to McDonald's. This was not something that Ms Laurel, a politically correct vegetarian, would normally do. To Eli, it probably seemed like he was being rewarded for telling abuse stories.

Eli told Sidey that Peter was 'sometimes bad and sometimes good', so she asked him about the bad things. At first Eli said he didn't know or couldn't remember, but when she asked him for the tenth time (on p. 22), he said: 'He dipped people in the ponds.'

According to Peter Ellis, there was a real-life explanation for this allegation. He used to dip children's hair in the water trough and the paddling pool at the crèche, and in the drinking fountain in the park. He also let the children run under the park sprinklers and squirt the drinking fountain, but he kept them away from the river and the ponds.

Having failed to obtain a disclosure of sexual abuse, Sidey tried a different approach (p. 23). Instead of asking Eli what Peter had done, she asked Eli what he had told his parents about what Peter had done. This meant that, instead of having to remember long-ago events, Eli just had to remember recent stories.

S: ... what else did you tell Mum and Dad about the mean things?
E: Um told the good things and the bad things.

S: Yeah tell me ... what's the other mean things that you told?
E: Um, did wees in people's face.

Eli said the wees went 'in their mouths'. But, though Sidey asked him more than a dozen times, he couldn't remember which children were involved. In response to this impasse, Colin Eade pushed a note under the door and Sidey tested the 'threatened into silence' theory.

S: ... If you tell which kids it's happened to, what do you think would happen?
E: Nothing.

Then Sidey took a more direct approach. Initially, that too failed (p. 29).

S: So [Eli], um, did Peter ah, did Peter do anything to you or not?
E: No.
S: Because I heard that he did some bad things to you ...
E: Like?
S: Like um, well what were the bad things that he did to you that you don't like?
E: I don't know.

Again she asked Eli about the things he had told his mum, and again he mentioned dunking games, but Sidey persisted, and finally Eli disclosed (p. 32).

S: I heard that you told Mum that Peter had done something mean to you as well.
E: Yeah.
S: Mm, tell me what that was?
E: He done wees.
S: Wees, yeah, where did the wees go on you?
E: In my mouth.

On page 35 there was more.

S: ... where did his penis go?
E: Um there [indicates mouth].
S: Yeah, did it touch your mouth or not?
E: Um no, it went in my mouth.

But when Eli came back for his second interview three weeks later, Sidey's hard work seemed to have come to nothing.

'You said that he [Peter] was doing mean things to you,' she reminded him.

'Well no, not to me but other kids,' Eli said. As to the nature of the mean things, all the boy could remember was 'dipping people in the ponds'.

'Right, I think perhaps I could help you,' said Sidey. 'I remember some things, and we talked about mean things to do with penises.'

'Um, doing wees in people's faces,' said Eli. It was the sort of thing a five-year-old might come up with when pressed to tell stories involving himself, Peter Ellis, genitals and naughtiness.

In his first interview Eli had mentioned Mia Broadleaf, a crèche child whose parents were part of the social group to which his parents, the Palms, the Lacebarks and the Ngaios belonged. In his second interview, when Eli kept saying he couldn't remember which children Ellis had urinated upon, Sidey asked:

S: ... did it happen to [Mia] or not?

E: Um yes, yes.

'What about [Yelena]?' Sidey asked later. 'What about [Derek]? What about [Lara]?' But Eli said it just happened to Mia. Then Sidey made another attempt to persuade the boy to put himself into the 'urinated upon by Peter' scenario.

'You did tell me that Peter did some mean things to you too,' she said. 'Do you remember what you told me?'

'No,' said Eli. 'Didn't do it to me.'

'I think you told me, well you did tell me that last week, it did happen to you,' she insisted. After that, Eli conceded that 'the penis in your face' episode had happened to him.

Count Six of the 28-count indictment that Peter Ellis faced at his trial was based on Eli Laurel's first interview. It stated: 'that Peter Hugh McGregor Ellis between 1 March 1989 and 30 October 1991 at Christchurch being a male did an indecent act upon [Eli Laurel] a boy under 12 years in that he urinated on his face and placed his penis in his mouth at the crèche'. Ellis was found guilty on that count.

Later, Mia Broadleaf was also interviewed, but she disclosed nothing. Nonetheless, on the basis of Eli Laurel's allegation, Ellis was charged with indecently assaulting her. (Thus, for the purposes of this chronology, she became the seventh complainant child identified by the crèche case investigators.) The summary of the allegation relating to Mia Broadleaf in the schedule of charges presented at the deposition hearing read: 'Occasion in toilets of crèche when defendant urinated on complainant's face'. Peter Ellis was committed for trial on this charge, but Crown solicitor Brent Stanaway did not include it in the final 28-count indictment.

• • •

The eighth complainant child to make a formal disclosure was Zelda Cypress. Zelda attended the crèche full time from May 1985 to May 1988. At the trial of Peter Ellis, Ms Cypress testified that she read *A Very Touching Book*, *Katie's Yukky Problem* and

What's Wrong with Bottoms? to her daughter from the time she was about three years old.

During her two years in the preschool section of the crèche, Zelda spent more time with Peter Ellis than she did with her own parents. At the Ellis trial, Ms Cypress said: 'She was obviously very fond of him ... and would really seek him out ... Peter was very open in his admiration of [Zelda] and would often make comments about how fond of her he was.' Ms Cypress also recalled that Zelda was 'extroverted and happy' as a crèche child. But she became 'introverted and frightened' when she started school. In her role as expert witness for the prosecution, Karen Zelas said that the change in Zelda's behaviour when she started school was 'consistent with a child who has been abused' at the crèche. The expert witness for the defence, Australian child psychiatrist Dr Keith Le Page, concluded that Zelda's behavioural change was more likely due to the loss of her favourite preschool teacher.

Zelda was the oldest of the complainant children. When she gave evidence at the Ellis trial she was almost 10. Most of her evidence concerned events that allegedly occurred during the two-and-a-half days Ellis had cared for her while her mother was working prior to Christmas 1986. To recall those events, Zelda had to cast her mind back six-and-a-half years, to a time when she was three-and-a-half-years old.

When Ms Magnolia made her initial allegation in November 1991, a former crèche parent contacted Ms Cypress to express concern about Zelda's closeness to Peter Ellis. 'I said I didn't think [Zelda] had been abused, but it sowed some seeds,' Ms Cypress recalled. Then, in March 1992, a journalist from the *Holmes* programme phoned her repeatedly about Ellis's relationship with her daughter. Ms Cypress refused to speak to the journalist, but she spoke to her daughter: 'I asked [Zelda] about the crèche and who she remembered. I said, "What were they like? You tell me some stories about them." She told me she remembered Anton [a crèche child]. Then she said she remembered Peter but he wasn't that nice. I asked her why. She said, "He used to make me touch his diddle."'[18]

This disclosure came from a child who, despite being trained to speak out about sexual abuse, had made no negative comments about Peter Ellis in the four years since she had left the Civic. Her disclosure coincided with news of the crèche investigation breaking in the media, and with worrying phone calls to her mother. However, despite the surrounding circumstances, Ms Cypress was adamant that Zelda's disclosure was entirely unprompted.

The Cypresses shunned the parental networking, but Ms Cypress encountered some former crèche parents in the course of her work. At the Ellis trial, Ms Cypress said: '[Zelda's] father and myself are very clear about not allowing her to see news programmes or hear it on the radio or read it in the paper ... I myself have not initiated any discussions with her about what has been going on in the inquiry.'

Zelda's allegations were concerned solely with offences of the sort referred to in children's sexual abuse prevention books. Also, when asked to name other children, Zelda mentioned only her two closest crèche friends (unlike the other complainant children, who named each other). This suggests that the Cypresses' efforts to avoid contaminating their daughter's evidence were at least partly successful. However, short of sealing Zelda in a sensory deprivation tank for the duration of the investigation, there is no way they could have protected her from any news of the controversy.

Furthermore, though Ms Cypress was adamant that she had said nothing to put ideas into her daughter's head, recent research has shown that parents often misremember conversation with their own children. In a study reported in the *Journal of Experimental Psychology* in 1999, psychologist Dr Maggie Bruck found that while mothers could usually recall the gist of a conversation with their children, they had difficulty remembering the exact wording or the structure of the conversation. They were likely to remember incorrectly whether information was offered spontaneously by the child or elicited through questions, and to confuse specific statements they made themselves with statements made by the child.[19]

A recurring feature in Zelda Cypress's three DSW interviews (on 7 and 9 April and 28 May) was that, when making an allegation of sexual abuse against Ellis, she hid her face and tried to slide under the table. To interviewer Lynda Morgan – who knew Zelda only through her three hours and 15 minutes of videotaped interviews – she was behaving like an embarrassed and anxious abused child. To Peter Ellis – who knew Zelda from caring for her full time for two years at the crèche – she was behaving in the way she always behaved when she knew she wasn't telling the truth.

In her interviews Zelda was happy to talk on neutral subjects, but when Morgan pressed her for 'things that he [Ellis] said or did that you felt not good about' she became subdued and worried. 'Will Peter know?' she asked in her first interview. 'Will I ever see Peter again?' To Morgan, Zelda's comments indicated that she was scared of Ellis.

M: Have you always been scared of him?

Z: [Indicates no]

M: No. When did the scared start?

Z: When Mum reminded me about him.

M: Oh right. Did you used to be scared before that, before she reminded you?

Z: [Indicates no]

M: Like when you used to go to crèche, were you scared of him? No.

Morgan suggested they make a list headed 'Things that Peter said that made [Zelda] scared', which they filled in during the one-hour interview. Halfway through, Zelda told Morgan that the only place she had seen a diddle was in a book. But after more suggestive questioning she said: 'He showed me his diddle at his house ... when he was looking after me ... in his bedroom ... he said it was a secret.'

Having obtained one disclosure, Morgan concluded that Zelda had more to tell, and a second interview was arranged.

Zelda's second interview lasted just over an hour. The transcript is 24 pages long. Early in the interview Zelda said she had talked to her mother about Peter since their session two days earlier. 'Did you tell her anything that you didn't tell me?' asked Morgan (p. 3). Zelda replied with a hesitant nod. Over the next 10 pages, Morgan reminded Zelda of her previous disclosure ('He showed me his diddle'), and invited her to tell more. Finally, on page 13, Zelda drew a picture indicating that Ellis had touched her vagina with his hand. She said she told her mother about it the previous day because 'she asked me about Peter'.

In the 28-count indictment that Ellis faced at his trial, Count One was based on Zelda Cypress's second interview. It read: 'that Peter Hugh McGregor Ellis between 15 December 1986 and 25 December 1986 at Christchurch indecently assaulted [Zelda Cypress] a girl aged under 12 years at 404 Hereford Street in that he touched her vagina with his hand'. Ellis was found guilty on that count.

Over the following seven weeks Zelda had two therapy sessions with Hildegard Corbett (who was also treating Lara Palm, Derek Ngaio, Yelena Holly and Eli Laurel). She was also examined by Dr Amama Thornley (who found no abnormalities) and given a pep talk by Dr Thornley and Detective Eade (who told her that Peter Ellis was under police surveillance, so she had nothing to fear).

'After you had been to the doctor you talked about some other things that ... you didn't tell me last time,' Morgan said at the start of Zelda's third interview. But she had to repeat the question several times, and throw in lots of other suggestive questions, before Zelda disclosed that 'He made me touch his diddle', and that 'He touched me' with 'his hands and his fingers'. When Morgan asked her to indicate on a body diagram where she was touched, Zelda pointed to the vagina and anus.

In the 28-count indictment that Ellis faced at his trial, Counts Two and Three were based on Zelda's third interview. Count Two read: 'that Peter Hugh McGregor Ellis between 1 May 1986 and 1 May 1988 at Christchurch being a male induced [Zelda Cypress] a girl aged under 12 years to do an indecent act upon him namely to touch his penis at the crèche'. Count Three read: 'that Peter Hugh McGregor Ellis between 1 May 1986 and 1 May 1988 at Christchurch indecently assaulted [Zelda Cypress] a girl aged under 12 years at the crèche, in that he touched her vagina and anus with his hand'. Ellis was found guilty on both counts.

In his 6 August 1992 letter to ACC in support of Zelda's application for lump-sum compensation, Detective Eade wrote:

> ... she was involved in touching his penis a number of times, and a number of times his fingers touched her anus and vagina. On about four occasions he had contact with her vagina and anus with his penis. We are not sure whether or not there was penetration. Owing to the type of abuse involved in the offending at the Civic Child Care Centre, almost without exception, children are not disclosing the full extent of the abuse and [Zelda] may have suffered further abuse that we are unaware of.

The ninth complainant child to make a formal disclosure was Kane Juniper, who was also the subject of an alleged 'earlier disclosure' of abuse at the Civic Crèche.

When he moved to the Big End in May 1990, Kane was not fully toilet trained. In his interview with Lynda Morgan on 29 April 1992 he said that Ellis touched the cheek of his buttock apparently while checking for soiling. On the basis of that interview, Peter Ellis was charged with indecently assaulting Kane Juniper. The summary of the allegation in the schedule of charges presented at the deposition hearing read: 'While at Crèche defendant put hand under clothes and touched anal area.' Ellis was committed for trial on this charge, but Crown solicitor Brent Stanaway did not include it in the final 28-count indictment.

• • •

The tenth complainant child to make a formal disclosure was Tess Hickory. Tess entered the crèche as a Womble in April 1988. From October 1988 to November 1990 she attended the preschool section from about 9am to 2.30pm, three days a week. During that time she had two inseparable friends: Kari Lacebark and Amy Linden.

Ms Hickory knew of Ms Magnolia's initial allegation prior to the December '91 meeting. In February '92 she heard that two of Tess's friends were involved, but she did not become seriously concerned until Ms Lacebark phoned her the evening after the Knox Hall meeting. Ms Lacebark said that, according to Kari, Tess had witnessed abuse in the crèche toilets and had been to Peter's house.

When Ms Hickory was in the bath with her daughter a few days after the Knox Hall meeting she told Tess she was going to help her remember things that had happened with Peter.

Oddly enough, bathtubs were a recurring motif in the crèche investigation. Geoffrey Magnolia and Tess Hickory both made disclosures when bathing with their mothers. Kari Lacebark made disclosures when bathing dolls during a DSW interview. These activities gave parents and interviewers an opportunity to steer conversations about 'mean things that Peter did' towards genitals and nudity in a relatively unforced manner. At such times some children alleged that Ellis had molested them in the bath.

As it happened, there was no bath at the Civic Crèche, but there was a shower. Children who played naked with sand and water in hot weather were often showered afterwards. In the course of their DSW interviews some children mentioned being showered by Ellis. But – perhaps because there was no toy shower among the DSW play materials to facilitate a re-enactment – an 'abused by Ellis in the shower' scenario was not pursued.

When Ms Hickory was in the bath with Tess on 5 April she asked her daughter about Ellis's house. According to Ms Hickory, Tess said that she bathed with Ellis, and rode his horse. 'I asked her to show me and she climbed astride my stomach,' Ms Hickory reported. 'I asked her where the defendant's penis was. She laughed and said that the defendant wasn't the horse, it was a real horse, kept in the shed at the back of the house.'[20]

In the days leading up to Tess's first DSW interview, Ms Hickory suggested to her daughter that they draw a picture of Peter's house. This joint project grew into two booklets of captioned drawings about things Peter did. Ms Hickory said she drew a two-storey house because Tess told her Peter's house had stairs going up to the bedroom. As it happened, by the time Ms Hickory drew that picture, the investigation team knew that Zelda Cypress had been cared for by Ellis at a two-storey house. So Ms Hickory may have known that too. Since the only two-storey house Ellis had ever lived in was at 404 Hereford Street, Ms Hickory's drawing appeared to identify that address as the venue for Tess's 'abuse at Peter's house' allegations – even though Ellis left 404 Hereford Street in May 1987, and Tess did not start at the crèche until November 1987.

When Tess went for her first interview with Sue Sidey on 1 May 1992 she took the homemade booklets with her. The interview lasted one hour and 25 minutes. The transcript is 63 pages long.

After talking about face and body painting, Tess showed Sue Sidey one of the booklets and said Peter told her to drink his wees in the crèche toilets. According to Tess, unlike Kari and Monique (who were similarly instructed), she kept her mouth shut and the wees just went on her face. In the course of the discussion Tess often changed her story in response to Sidey's cues. A typical exchange went like this:

T: … he was sitting on the toilet … because he was doing wees.
S: Okay, does he always sit down when he does wees?
T: Yep.
S: Or does he sometimes stand up?
T: He stand he standed up I think.

At other times Tess just guessed:

S: Okay, what colour were Peter's pants that day?
T: Um they were pink, I mean black … I think they were brown.

Even after Sidey had reminded her that the penis was at the front, and the bottom was at the back, Tess insisted that Peter's wees came out of his bottom. This anatomical confusion did not deter Colin Eade from laying a charge. Charge Nine of the 28-charge indictment that Ellis faced at his trial read: 'that Peter Hugh McGregor Ellis between 3 June 1988 and 1 December 1990 at Christchurch being a male did an indecent act upon [Tess Hickory] a girl under 12 years at the Crèche in that he urinated on her face'. Ellis was found guilty on that count.

Later in the interview, Tess said she went to Peter's house with Kari Lacebark and Amy Linden. She said the only animal there was a horse, and the only other person there was Peter's mum, who was making lunch.

'What was Peter's mum's name?' asked Sidey.

'Um I think it was Sarah. No, no it wasn't – Jacinta or something like that … It was Zora,' said Tess. This was the first, albeit inaccurate, mention of Ellis's mother in a complainant child's formal interview. (In real life her name is Lesley.)

In response to further questions, Tess said that she, Kari and Amy played Snap, played with Peter's baby doll, had a pillow fight in his bedroom, rode his horse and went for a ride in his horse-drawn carriage. In an hour of questioning she had made no mention of her mother's 'bathing at Peter's house' allegation. So Sidey resorted to blatant leading ('Mum told me some stuff about a bath').

'Um I went in the bath and oh yeah and and he washed my bum,' said Tess. Once again she gave the impression that she was prepared to agree with whatever Sidey said.

S: Was that at crèche or somewhere else?
T: It was at crèche.
S: In the bath with Peter at the crèche?
T: Yes.
S: Or was it at Peter's house?
T: Um it was um Peter's house.

When Sidey said she'd heard about 'a horsey game', Tess demurred.

T: I didn't say anything about that …
S: Did Mum tell you that?
T: Yeah.

As the questioning continued, Tess said that Kari and Amy had separate baths with Peter on the same day. But Sidey wanted more.

S: Now what about something to do with the bath, is there anything that's too hard to tell me about the bath?
T: Yep. Yep, there is.

By then it must have been obvious to Tess that she was expected to come up with something really horrible.

T: Peter did wees in the bath.
S: He what?
T: He did wees in the bath.
S: He did wees in the bath?
T: Yeah – no, poos I mean.

Tess demonstrated the size of the turd with her hands, and said it floated around in the bath before going down the plughole.

The absurdity of Tess's 'bathing with Peter' allegations, the circumstances in which they had arisen, and the fact that Kari Lacebark (who was supposed to have gone on that visit to Peter's house) had not mentioned baths or horses in any of her four DSW interviews did not deter Colin Eade from laying a charge. Count Ten of the 28-count indictment that Ellis faced at his trial read: 'that Peter Hugh McGregor Ellis between 3 June 1988 and 1 December 1990 at Christchurch being a male induced [Tess Hickory] a girl under the age of 12 years to do an indecent act with him, namely a bath with him at an unknown address'. Ellis was found guilty on that count.

Four weeks later (28 May), Tess had her second interview with Sue Sidey. Again she brought the booklets of captioned drawings that she and her mother had made, and the stories continued. Tess said Peter had a tennis court at his house. She said he and his mother took her and Kari to Orana Park to see a lion. It happened once. It happened in the afternoon. It happened the same day as the bath. They went in a blue van. Tess drove. At her third interview on 3 August, Tess added that they went to a bach in the country on the day of the bath at Peter's house.

According to the crèche records, Tess, Kari and Amy attended the Big End between May 1989 and August 1990. During that time there were 40 days on which all three girls were present at the same time for three hours or more. Those hours always included the noon to 2pm period. At that time, staff who were not taking lunchbreaks had to stay at the crèche to keep the staff/child ratio at the required level. Clearly, the adventurous afternoon described by Tess could not have taken place in real life.

During Tess's second interview, Sidey questioned her at length about indecent touching. This time Tess was baffled.

> S: ... you had told Mum that someone had touched ... your vagina and your bottom.
> T: Who?
> S: With their hands.
> T: Who?
> S: And their fingers.
> T: I can't remember.

The questioning went on and on.

> S: I guess I've heard ... someone else has touched you down there with their fingers ...
> T: Who? Who? Myself? Was that a joke or something?
> S: No, no, it's not a joke ...
> T: I can't remember saying – mm – who was it?

Still the questioning continued.

> S: You told Mum that someone had touched your ... bottom and your vagina.
> T: Did I?
> S: Yeah, with their fingers.
> T: Who was it? Did I say?

At that point Sidey drew Tess's attention to another page of her homemade book. '... you also said some other things about Peter doing something with the puppy's bottom.' She asked the question four times before Tess supplied the sought-after answer: 'He put his finger in it.'

> S: Has Peter put his finger in any other bottoms before or not?
> T: ... he hasn't put it in my bottom.

Again Sidey resorted to leading.

> S: ... I guess what I've heard is that um that you said that Peter did put it in your bottom.
> T: Did he?
> S: Did you?
> T: Oh yeah.

S: Aye.
T: Did I?
S: Yeah.

After further questions of this sort Tess said that Peter also put his finger in her vagina, and that it occurred in the bath.

No charges were laid as a result of Tess Hickory's second interview, but Sidey's concluding questions ('Has Peter put anything else in your vagina or not?', 'Did any other part of him touch your vagina or your bottom?', 'Did any other part of you touch his penis?') laid the foundation for the disclosures Tess would make in her third DSW interview nine weeks later.

'For tea we're going to McDonald's,' Tess announced at the start of her 3 August interview. ('McDonald's must be making a fortune out of this case!' Peter Ellis noted when the videotape was played at his trial.) Then Tess told Sue Sidey she had come to talk about 'the bath stuff'.

T: He put his penis in my vagina.
S: What did it feel like on your vagina?
T: Feeled yucky and hairy.

She said that it went in 'just a little bit' and that her vagina felt 'normal' afterwards. With regard to the location, Tess said that it happened at Peter's one-storey house (then, with encouragement from Sue Sidey, she changed the description to two-storey). She said that Amy, Kari and 'his mum' were there, and that his mum 'kicked me and Kari'.

Count 11 of the 28-count indictment that Ellis faced at his trial was based on that disclosure. It alleged that Ellis 'did attempt to have sexual intercourse with [Tess Hickory] a girl under 12 years of age at an unknown address'. Ellis was found not guilty on that count.

Later in the interview (on page 40 of the 61-page transcript) Sue Sidey extracted another disclosure.

S: Mum said something else had touched your vagina before, is that right?
T: I can't remember, what has?
S: What else could have, what else would have touched it and make it bleed?
T: Oh, needles.

Tess said that 'Peter put some needles up our bum' in the crèche toilets. When Sidey asked '… was there blood there or not?', Tess said, 'Nope.' But after further encouragement she changed that to 'lots of blood'. Count 12 of the 28-count indictment that Ellis faced at his trial was based on that allegation. It stated that Ellis 'indecently assaulted [Tess Hickory] a girl under 12 years of age in that he touched her bottom with a needle at the crèche'. Ellis was found not guilty on that count.

• • •

The eleventh complainant child to make a formal disclosure was Julian Yew. Julian became a Civic kid at three and a half. He attended from 10.30am to 4.30pm, two days a week, until he turned five and went to school in September 1990. Over the same period he also attended another crèche and a kindergarten. According to his mother, Julian was 'a bit of a handful' during his preschool years. She said she had consulted a homeopath, a naturopath, an occupational therapist and a family doctor about his behaviour.

In November 1991 Ms Yew heard about the allegations against Peter Ellis from the supervisor of Julian's other crèche, who suggested that Julian's behavioural difficulties could have been caused by sexual abuse. When Ms Yew raised the issue with her son, he said Peter had taken him to the toilet and had said 'Ooh'.

At the end of the Knox Hall meeting, Ms Yew discussed her worries with Sue Sidey and Detective Senior Sergeant John Ell. They told her she had reason to be concerned, and advised her to have her son interviewed.

Julian's first interview on 4 May lasted an hour and six minutes. The transcript is 50 pages long. Early in the interview, Lynda Morgan told him that his mum and dad wanted him to tell her the things that he had told them. Initially, the boy talked about playing hide and seek, and about having hail put down his neck by Ellis. After that, Morgan questioned him relentlessly about secrets, penises, bottoms and 'what you told Mum and Dad'. Julian kept saying that he didn't know or couldn't remember, and that there was no more to tell. Then, on page 42, came the disclosure: 'He done wees on me.' Julian said it happened '800 times', and the wees went in his eyes, up his nose and on his teeth and hands. Later, in response to another burst of suggestive questioning, he said that Peter touched his penis.

In the 28-count indictment that Ellis faced at his trial, Count Eight was based on Julian Yew's first interview. It stated: 'that Peter Hugh McGregor Ellis between 1 February 1989 and 30 October 1990 at Christchurch being a male did an indecent act upon [Julian Yew] a boy under the age of 12 years in that he urinated on his face at the crèche'. Ellis was found not guilty on that count.

At his second interview three days later (7 May), Julian said that a boy named Andrew was run over and killed while out walking with Ellis. But, presumably because no evidence of a missing child was found, no charges were laid in relation to this allegation.

• • •

The twelfth complainant child to make a formal disclosure was Molly Sumach. Molly was the cherished only child of older parents. She began attending the nursery section of the crèche in August 1987, and moved to the preschool section in October 1988. Each morning her mother dropped her off in the morning between 9am and 11.30am. Each afternoon her father picked her up between 1.30pm and 5.20pm. Molly left the crèche in July 1989, shortly before her fifth birthday.

After the Knox Hall meeting the Sumaches discussed Ellis and the crèche with their daughter. 'We told her the police believed he had done bad touching to children,' Ms Sumach reported. 'She said, "Well if he has been doing bad touching then he should go to jail." We said, "Would you like to talk to the police about this?" And she said, "Yes."'

Molly had a lot to say in her 12 May interview with Lynda Morgan. Most of it had nothing to do with Ellis or the crèche. However, she did say that Ellis poked her crutch while the other teachers were busy with the deaf kids. Morgan did not explore the possibility that Molly had confused her school (where there were deaf kids) with the crèche (where there were not).

This allegation was the basis for Count Four of the 28-count indictment that Ellis faced at his trial. It stated: 'that Peter Hugh McGregor Ellis between 1 February 1988 and 30 July 1989 at Christchurch indecently assaulted [Molly Sumach] a girl under the age of 12 years in that he touched her vagina with his hand at the crèche'. Ellis was found guilty on that count.

• • •

The thirteenth complainant child to make a formal disclosure was Bart Dogwood. Ms Dogwood heard about the crèche investigation shortly before the Knox Hall meeting. On the basis of Ellis's arrest and the large crowd at that meeting she concluded that 'it was a serious matter and there must have been some validity to the complaints'. Next day, she asked Bart if Peter had ever touched his bottom or penis. 'Peter wouldn't do that to me,' Bart said. 'He's my friend.' This response left Ms Dogwood with 'a gut feeling that there was something more to come out', and she raised the subject with her son repeatedly over the coming weeks.[21]

On 14 April Colin Eade told Ms Dogwood that children who had disclosed to their parents were being interviewed as soon as possible, but non-disclosing children were having to wait. Curiously, that very night, Bart told his brother that Peter wobbled his dick and smacked his bum at the crèche. Next day, Bart's first interview was arranged.

At his 14 May interview with Lynda Morgan, Bart said that Peter wobbled his dick and smacked his bum when he was lying on the changing table in the toilet area of the crèche. 'I had to get changed ... because I done poos,' he explained.

On the basis of this interview, Ellis was charged with indecently assaulting Bart Dogwood. The summary of the allegation in the schedule of charges presented at the deposition hearing read: 'While in toilets at Crèche defendant touched complainant's penis when toileting him'. At the end of the depositions hearing Judge Anderson ruled that Bart had not disclosed abuse, but had talked only of being cleaned up after he had soiled himself.

• • •

However, immediately after his 14 May interview, Lynda Morgan advised Bart's mother that her son had disclosed abuse by Ellis. At that point Ms Dogwood became a complainant parent. Her entry into the activist network coincided with the appointment of the crèche case social workers. After that, what had hitherto been an informal information exchange was transformed into what amounted to a sustained campaign of state-funded contamination of the evidence.

8.ii: A Sustained Campaign of State-Funded Contamination of the Evidence

In an interview with TV3 journalist Melanie Reid in April 1993, Peter Ellis looked back over his year awaiting trial. 'This may sound potty, but my life is sort of the same,' he said. 'I get up. I have breakfast. I feed my animals. I go to my supermarket, my pet shop, they ask me how it's going. I don't have to worry about not being served. I don't have to run in and out. No one has called me names. The neighbours look out for me.'[1]

By then, Ellis had received anonymous death threats and a bullet in the mail. He had been beaten up by skinheads. In his interview with Reid he brushed aside those events as isolated incidents, but admitted to being constantly on guard, especially when he left the house.

Ellis could not drive and had never owned a car. He rarely went out during the day. His bail conditions kept him home between 7pm each evening and 7am next morning. When he reported to the police station, his mother usually drove him. When he viewed children's videotaped interviews at the Child Abuse Unit, he got a ride with his barrister Rob Harrison. When he went beyond his own neighbourhood for any other reason, he usually caught a bus. He tried to avoid public places. Walking was an ordeal.

'If I'm out walking and a toddler appears, I think: I've got to cross the road. There's a child, I don't want to be anywhere near it. I don't know who's going to suddenly point a finger and say, "He's been near my child,"' he told Reid.[2]

Between his first court appearance on 31 March 1992 and his second on 14 April, Ellis and his barrister fell into a pattern that would be repeated many times over in the coming months. Whenever Detective Eade was ready to lay more charges he would arrange for Ellis and Harrison to view the relevant videotapes. Then he would interview Ellis in Harrison's presence about the allegations they contained. After each burst of videotape viewing, Ellis would make another court appearance, and more charges would be laid against him.

On 1 and 3 April, Ellis and Harrison viewed the videotapes of interviews with Lara Palm and Kari Lacebark. On 14 April, Ellis was charged with five offences relating to the two girls. At the same time his name suppression was lifted.

From then on, the media was free to publish images of Ellis. But, lest anxious parents use newspaper photographs or television footage of Peter Ellis 'to help their children remember', Rob Harrison kept his client well away from the journalists and photographers that invariably surrounded the courthouse.

On 5, 7 and 8 June, Ellis and Harrison viewed the videotapes of Eli Laurel, Molly Sumach and Zelda Cypress. In the morning of 9 June, Ellis was charged with five offences relating to those children. In the afternoon of the same day Harrison's professionalism towards the media was put to the test when, for the first and only time, his journalist wife was assigned to the courthouse stakeout.

'It was a cold, wet, miserable winter day,' Harrison recalled. 'I hid Peter in the courthouse, and supplied him with food and coffee and reading matter. At about quarter to five I went outside. All these journalists were still standing around freezing. It was hosing down. Really, really cold. Then this wet, bedraggled figure came up to me. It was Rose.'

'Rob,' she said. 'Just tell me. Is he still in there?'

'I'm sorry, I can't tell you that,' he said.[3]

Between court appearances, Ellis's lawyers planned their approach to what was rapidly becoming the biggest child abuse case in New Zealand history. Their priorities were to obtain senior legal counsel, an expert (psychological) witness, full disclosure of information from the police and adequate legal aid to mount a vigorous defence.

For his expert witness, Ellis's solicitor approached M, a clinical psychologist in private practice whom he held in high regard. For senior legal counsel he approached Christchurch Queen's Counsel Nigel Hampton. Queen's Counsel are the most experienced and skilled of senior barristers. They represent clients in difficult cases where a specialist knowledge of the law and outstanding advocacy skills are required. By 1992 Hampton had been practising criminal law for about 27 years, and had been in solo practice as a barrister for four years. A colleague described him as 'a devastating advocate – the best criminal advocate in the South Island, if not New

Zealand'. Both M and Hampton expressed great willingness to become involved in the Ellis case.[4]

M's role was to evaluate Peter Ellis and the DSW videotapes, and, when the case came to trial, to give evidence on the appropriateness or otherwise of the children's interviews.

'I wasn't a hired gun to advocate for Peter Ellis,' M told me. 'It's unethical for forensic psychologists – or any psychologists for that matter– to act as hired guns. We can be contracted by the prosecution or the defence, bur our ethical obligation, regardless of who contracts us, is to act as impartial psychological examiners.'[5]

M met with Ellis on three occasions in April and May 1992 and made a preliminary assessment of his psychological profile. On reflection, M said it would be unethical to release the findings to me, even with Ellis's consent. On reflection, I said I didn't want them. What use would a psychological profile of the accused be if I did not have psychological profiles of his accusers?

Nigel Hampton QC's role as senior counsel was to advise Rob Harrison, and to lead the defence when the case went to court. Harrison's role as junior counsel was to attend to the day-to-day business of the investigation. Throughout the case, Knight (solicitor), Harrison and Hampton consulted regularly.

One such consultation took place in mid-May, when Detective Eade advised Ellis that he was going to arrest him for breaching his bail conditions. According to Eade, the chain-smoking, meat-eating Ellis had been seen late one evening at a non-smoking, vegetarian restaurant. When Ellis's partner, his brother and a visiting friend all confirmed that Ellis had been home on the evening in question, Eade demanded that Ellis take part in an identification parade.

'I said, "Look, Colin, I think you're being unreasonable,"' recalled Harrison. 'He just erupted. There were three or four minutes – it felt like that long – of this man screaming down the phone at me. I said, "If you've got someone who's sure it was Peter, why do you need a line-up?" But Colin was adamant. I said I didn't think Peter had to take part, but I'd check with Nigel Hampton. Nigel said, "This is madness." The line-up died a natural death.'[6]

The police's drip-feed of information was another problem for Ellis's defence team. On 5 May, Harrison wrote to Detective Eade, requesting disclosure of:

1. Copies of all interviews taken from all witnesses and potential witnesses.
2. All statements taken in relation to the investigations.
3. All notebook entries, memoranda and other data recorded by police officers.
4. All transcripts of disclosure interviews made on all children interviewed.
5. All notes of interviews relating to the initial investigation.
6. A list of all people interviewed from November 1991 to the present day.

7. Any other material that may or may not be used in any trial concerning Peter Ellis.

By the time the depositions hearing began on 2 November 1992 most, but not all, of the requested material had been supplied.[7]

• • •

In early June, Rob Harrison tackled another defence priority: legal aid. Since 1912 state-funded legal aid has been available in New Zealand for destitute persons charged with serious criminal offences.[8] Over the years the scheme has been extended to cover people charged with all but the most minor offences who are unable to pay for their own defence, and people wishing to undertake civil proceedings who cannot afford a lawyer. In theory, recipients of *civil* legal aid have always been able to choose their own lawyers, but (with the exception of people charged with treason and murder) recipients of *criminal* legal aid have not. However, in practice, the legal aid provision for people charged with serious offences has been interpreted with some flexibility by court registrars.

Harrison's legal aid application was made at a time when the scheme was grappling with a budget blowout and new legislation. In the media, the disproportionate contribution of civil legal aid to the blowout was largely overlooked. Justice Minister Doug Graham promised tighter controls on 'fees of experts engaged on behalf of the defence'. The Christchurch *Press* thundered against lawyers who were willing 'to fight a parking ticket all the way to the Privy Council if only they could, and if only the taxpayer would foot the bill', and against criminals who 'choose to plead not guilty ... not from a certainty of innocence or from a sense of injustice – or even from a belief that the prosecution will fail – but rather inspired by the attitude that it will not cost anything to have a shot.'[9]

The 1991 Legal Services Act gave court registrars the power to grant criminal legal aid to persons of insufficient means provided that they were satisfied that it was 'desirable in the interests of justice' to do so. In making their decisions, registrars were required to take into account 'the gravity of the offence', and 'any other circumstances that in the opinion of the Registrar are relevant'.

The Act also gave registrars the power to assign lawyers to criminal legal-aid cases from a list compiled by the local District Law Society. To ensure that the skills and experience of the lawyer were matched to the complexity of the case, the list was divided into categories.[10]

By its very existence, the grading system acknowledged that, in the interests of justice, complex cases required skilled and experienced lawyers. Consequently, though there was no explicit provision in the 1991 Legal Services Act or Regulations for assigning QCs to complex cases, when Harrison and Knight considered 'the interests of justice' and 'the gravity of the offence' in the Ellis case, it never occurred to them that anyone would question the need for Nigel Hampton QC to lead the defence.

In April 1992 Harrison was granted legal aid to cover the charge of indecent assault on which Ellis was arrested. By June, 10 further charges involving five more children had been laid, and Detective Eade had indicated that more were to follow. At that stage Ellis's defence team decided that Harrison should take the case through depositions, and Hampton should step in when the case came to trial. So when Harrison first applied for legal aid to cover the depositions hearing, he applied only for his own costs. These comprised an estimated 100 hours of preparation time (50 hours of viewing children's videotapes, and 50 hours of working through the statements of parents, crèche workers, doctors and DSW staff and other preparation of that sort), and three weeks of court time.[11]

At that time, in minor and routine cases the registrar fixed the amount of aid to be granted. In more significant cases the decision was made by the local District Legal Services Subcommittee (DLSS). When the Canterbury DLSS considered Harrison's application, they accepted his estimate of 50 hours' videotape viewing and three weeks' court time, but cut his other preparation time to 15 hours, and awarded him $13,950 in legal aid.[12]

By late July the anticipated number of complainant children had risen to 18. Around 8000 pages of evidence had been received and more was expected. The depositions hearing was scheduled to last five weeks. On 31 July, Knight, Harrison, Hampton and M held a case conference to plan their next move. On 11 August, Harrison advised the DLSS that Nigel Hampton QC was prepared to act as senior counsel and M was prepared to act as expert witness in the Ellis case.

'It is clear that this case is likely to be the most substantial child abuse case to be dealt with by New Zealand courts up to this time,' Harrison wrote. 'In view of the nature of the prosecution evidence disclosed to date, the [case] conference decided to present a substantial attack on the prosecution's case at the depositions hearing in the form of cross-examination of prosecution witnesses and submissions.' His legal aid request covered the estimated time required by senior counsel, junior counsel and expert witness to view videotapes, peruse other evidence, conduct research and prepare for and attend the depositions hearing. His total legal aid request, when the previous grant of $13,950 had been subtracted, came to $122,320.[13] Chris Knight recalled the response:

> It was clear that this case was far beyond the norm, and that Peter was going to need expert legal help. But we got a very, very negative response from the subcommittee. Firstly, on the grounds that the case was nothing out of the usual and therefore extra

consideration was inappropriate. Secondly, Rob's grading allowed him to represent defendants in High Court jury trials. They said he didn't need leading counsel – he could do the case himself. This completely overlooked the quite extraordinary and onerous aspects of the case. The $13,000 they gave him for deps – I think it was lifted to about $35,000 in the end (but that included psychologist's fees and disbursements) – was woefully and enormously inadequate considering the size of the case and the vast resources of the state that were being thrown into it. Also, it wasn't as if Rob was going down a well-trodden path. He had to do a huge amount of research. It was an enormous task.[14]

Having had their request for senior counsel at the preliminary hearing declined, Ellis's defence team accepted that Harrison would have to take the case through depositions, but they decided to repeat their request for senior counsel prior to trial.

Harrison expected to use M's analysis of the children's evidence in his preparation for depositions, but legal aid funding for M was a long time coming. The number of complainants continued to grow, the charges continued to mount, the crèche was closed, the four women crèche workers were arrested, the depositions hearing was rescheduled for 2 November 1992, but by mid-October M's involvement had still not been approved by the DLSS. Then, two weeks before the start of depositions, M received a chilling phone call from 'an official within the Justice Department':

> This official had heard through the grapevine that I had been approached, that I was becoming involved in the Ellis case. This person phoned to express concern – that I was getting into hot water, that I would contaminate my professional reputation if I became any more involved. This person claimed to have evidence that Peter Ellis was guilty as hell, and that if I became involved I would be seen as allying myself with Ellis. There were unspoken implications to that conversation – I wouldn't go so far as to say they were threats, because they weren't – that I would be compromising my ability to receive ongoing referrals and appointments and assignments from government departments and reputable referrers in town – that I would be committing professional suicide. I withdrew from the Ellis case as a result of that conversation. Of all the things I've done in my professional life, that's the one decision I continue to question. The frighteners were put on me. Effectively and emotionally that's what happened. I was scared shitless.

'Why are you telling me this?' I asked. The answer was twofold. First, there was a weight on M's conscience, and while authors cannot offer the traditional priestly comforts of forgiveness and absolution, they can at least provide the opportunity for confession. Second, M regarded the pressure to withdraw from the Ellis case as just one aspect of a wider problem:

> At the time of the crèche case, attempts were made and influences were exerted to suppress information that was already in the professional journals about how children can provide false information and fabricate stories. Since the Ellis trial, all discussion

on the issue has been shut down. Colleagues express disquiet in private, but within the professional groups I'm involved with – the psychologists and psychotherapists – there's total silence. I think it's partly out of shame, and partly because of the negative consequences for people who don't toe the party line. The threats and influences are still there. No one's prepared to come out and say: look, on this point, and that point, we goofed. We stuffed up. We got it wrong. We haven't learnt from the crèche case because there's been no discussion. You can produce scientific information in court about the assessment of child sexual abuse allegations, but you can't get people to hold workshops on it because it's seen as critical of the Civic Crèche process and the people who were part of it.[15]

• • •

The intensive and extensive contamination of evidence in the early months of the crèche case has already been discussed. However, compared to the contamination that followed the appointment of social workers Jan Gillanders and Gen Crossen in May 1992, the earlier contamination was modest.

Gillanders, a DSW social worker, was seconded to the crèche case on 18 May. Crossen, a nurse with social work experience, took up her council-funded appointment one week later. Gillanders' primary task was to support families involved in the court proceedings; Crossen's was to support past and present crèche families and childcare workers who were not. Both women were required to liaise with police officers, counsellors, therapists, interviewers, ACC staff, city council staff and each other.

The job descriptions provided for Gillanders and Crossen contained no explicit requirement that they 'believe the children' (or even that they believe the adults who claimed to speak on behalf of the children). But their appointments indicated that the allegations against Peter Ellis were being taken very seriously indeed.

Between 18 May 1992 and late June 1993 (for Gillanders), and between 25 May 1992 and 29 February 1993 (for Crossen), they busied themselves with a constant round of visiting families; liaising with investigators and therapists; and organising and attending support groups for mothers, fathers, couples and extended families of complainant and non-complainant children. Both social workers also attended weekly meetings with the crèche investigation team, and regular meetings with therapists. The purpose of the meetings was to 'share information (while protecting client confidentiality); offer support; identify issues, concerns, needs; plan action'.[16]

If Gillanders and Crossen had remained entirely neutral towards the accused, they would still have contributed to the contamination of the evidence through their creation and maintenance of extensive communication networks between parents, therapists, investigators and council administrators. But Gillanders and Crossen did not remain neutral, and the contribution of their open condemnation of Ellis and his colleagues to the contamination of the evidence should not be underestimated.

For Jan Gillanders, believing that the complainant children were victims of Ellis and the women who later became his co-accused was probably an expected, if unspoken, job requirement. But most people assumed that Gen Crossen, as support social worker to the rest of the deeply divided crèche community, would adopt a more neutral stance.

'We were told that Gen Crossen was there for the staff as well,' recalled crèche supervisor Gaye Davidson. 'But she made it clear on her first visit that she believed the allegations against Peter. She said, "Right, these toilets have to be painted. The colours have to be changed because this is where it all happened. We have to make it feel safe for the kids."'[17]

Crossen did not tell the staff that she believed they were guilty too, but she made no secret of that belief in her discussions with council administrators and parents. 'Gen Crossen was totally convinced that Peter and the women were guilty. Guilty as sin. Couldn't be swayed to any other point of view,' recalled council officer Martin Maguire.[18]

Initially, Jan Gillanders' caseload comprised 11 complainant children from 10 families. By the time the depositions hearing started in November 1992, her caseload had risen to 20 children from 17 families. Over the same period Crossen dealt with the 120 non-complainant families who had contacted the police, DSW or the city council for information about the investigation. In her December 1992 report she wrote:

> Clients are given general information on sexual abuse, including what sexual abuse is, an acceptance that abuse does and can occur in society, indicators of sexual abuse, ways of handling a disclosure, what can be done if a child has been sexually abused, the needs of a sexually abused child, the grief process, the healing process, appropriate therapy plus therapists in Christchurch, funding available for therapy/counselling and 'keeping children safe' information. If a diagnostic interview is requested by parents, this is arranged with Specialist Services staff, DSW ... Children are referred to therapy if necessary.[19]

To the Sycamores, Crossen was 'a pedlar of counselling industry wares'. Ms Sycamore recalled:

> She told us that Peter had molested hundreds of children. She called him a 'rampant paedophile'. I said, 'How do you know this?' She said, 'I can't tell you. It's confidential.' We weren't particularly standing up for Peter, we just wanted to know what was going on. I said, 'Our child used that crèche. She's fine.' Whenever we questioned [Crossen] this wall would go up. She would imply that the investigators had lots and lots of information. I don't believe they did. They were just trying to build up a case. When we persisted in challenging her she dropped us.[20]

Ms Rimu had a similar experience:

When the depositions hearing started, I was home with a new baby. You know what that's like? The mind works overtime. One day I got really low and rang Gen Crossen. She said, 'I'll come and talk to you. That's why we're here.' If anything convinced me the investigation was murky it was that visit. I was feeling devastated because I seemed unable to actively take sides. I would've liked to have felt strong enough to support the arrested women. I was looking for someone to talk to. I thought Gen would give me the kind of objective support I wanted, but all she did was criticise the women. She went on and on. I thought – this is not okay. This is not all right. I was very, very concerned.[21]

Mr Aspen had a negative experience at one of Crossen's support groups:

I wanted to see what support was being offered. We'd had our daughter interviewed and she'd disclosed nothing, but at the back of my mind was the thought: have we been careful enough to find out whether she'd been interfered with by Peter or anyone else at the crèche? There were six or seven people at the meeting. The facilitator asked me who I was, why I was there. I said, 'I'm just really here to learn a little more about events that might have happened at the crèche.' I got the impression that 'might have happened' was not the appropriate phrasing to use in this group. I felt like an atheist at a Christian revivalist meeting because I had not expressed my belief.[22]

Gillanders' and Crossen's networking, and their distribution of prejudicial rumours, were major sources of contamination of the evidence in the crèche case, but the problem did not end there. The day after taking up her appointment, Gillanders began assembling a library for parents and professionals involved in the case. Among the $1,093 worth of books she purchased were: *The Courage to Heal*; *When the Bough Breaks* ('a helping guide for parents of sexually abused children'); *How to Talk so Kids will Listen and Listen so Kids will Talk*; *So You're Going to Court*; *Women Changing Therapy*; and DSW interviewer Lynda Morgan's books: *Megan's Secret*, *Katie's Yukky Problem* and *Daniel and his Therapist*.[23] Under the circumstances, these titles are unsurprising. What is surprising – and indeed alarming – is that Gillanders and Crossen also distributed ritual abuse literature in the course of their work.

Spokespeople for the crèche investigation have always insisted that, until August 1992, the case was a large-scale but otherwise conventional child sexual abuse investigation. However, not only is there evidence that a checklist of ritual abuse symptoms was in circulation among Ms Magnolia's supporters from the earliest days of the investigation, but on 10 June 1992 – two months before Bart Dogwood came up with his bizarre ritual abuse allegations, Jan Gillanders bought Pamela Hudson's *Ritual Child Abuse* for the crèche case library.[24]

As it happened, Hudson's book was not the only ritual abuse publication available at that time. Crèche supervisor Gaye Davidson recalled discovering in June or July

1992 that Gen Crossen was recommending *Breaking the Circle of Satanic Ritual Abuse: Recognising and recovering from hidden trauma* to crèche parents.[25]

Gillanders also included a ritual abuse book for children (*Don't Make Me Go Back, Mommy*) in the crèche case library. In the 1993 Akiki case in California, *Don't Make Me Go Back, Mommy* was identified as a major cause of contamination of the children's testimony.[26]

The social workers' activities raise questions of accountability. Crossen was paid by the city council. But, because the council administration lacked the expertise to monitor her competence, it played no part in her supervision. Instead, according to the 'Accountability' clause in her job description, she was 'directly responsible to Manager, Specialist Services [DSW]'. This clause was presumably intended to cover Crossen's administrative supervision, because, from the time of her appointment, she received fortnightly council-funded professional supervision from Helen Campbell, a self-employed therapist. In December 1992 Campbell reported: 'I feel satisfied that she [Crossen] is working well, in a consistently supportive and ethical way with those families she is seeing.'

Jan Gillanders' job description contained no mention of administrative or professional supervision. However, the financial and employment issues traversed in her monthly reports to DSW Specialist Services Unit manager John Watson indicate that he was her administrative supervisor. Professional supervision was another matter. During the crucial first three months of Gillanders' secondment – the time when she purchased Hudson's *Ritual Child Abuse* and supported the Dogwoods prior to, and during, their son's ritual abuse allegations – she appears to have received no professional supervision whatsoever. Her DSW-funded fortnightly supervision sessions with former START therapist Sara Crane did not begin until September 1992.[27]

Whatever their formal channels of accountability, Gillanders and Crossen probably took their day-to-day guidance from the people with whom they worked. Initially, when they were based in the DSW Specialist Services Unit, their primary contacts would have been with the DSW interviewers. From 3 August 1992, when they moved to the police Child Abuse Unit in Colombo Street, their main contacts would have been with the police. From 17 August, when Gillanders and Crossen joined the expanded police investigation team at their base in Transport House, Kilmore Street, the police influence would have predominated.[28]

• • •

Gillanders' and Crossen's activities unleashed fresh waves of anxiety among crèche parents and the wider Christchurch community. As a result, many couples who had earlier decided against having their children interviewed found themselves under pressure to change their minds. The pressure on Ms Sycamore came from a relative in the sexual abuse field:

> I kept saying, 'Look, I don't think there's a problem.' Her answer was always, 'How would you know, you're not an expert. You're putting your head in the sand. You're in denial.' In the end I felt I had to go along with it – not because I had any concerns about [Glenda] – but I had to allay the fears that everyone else seemed to have about her. I had to show that I didn't support paedophilia, that I wasn't in denial, that I was a good mother.[29]

The pressure on Ms Linden came in a long, multi-pronged campaign:

> We had three or four phone calls from Donna Ellen [the DSW social worker responsible for booking in children for their videotaped interviews]. She said that [Kari Lacebark] and [Tess Hickory] had mentioned [Amy] in their disclosures. Would we like [Amy] interviewed? We said, 'No thanks. We're not worried.' Then Donna suggested she come and assess [Amy]. I said, 'Oh well, if you really think so.' She played with [Amy] for a while, and then told us that our daughter had things she needed to get out. Around the same time, Colin Eade came to visit. He said that from what other children were saying [Amy] probably had been abused, and we should prepare ourselves for the worst. Then [Ms Hickory] rang and told me some of the disgusting things that Peter was supposed to have done. She said that [Tess] had shown no signs of abuse either, but had disclosed lots, and that when [Tess] and [Kari Lacebark] played together it helped trigger memories. She offered to have [Tess] and [Amy] play together. Eventually we agreed to an interview, but we were very unhappy about it. We felt manoeuvred.

After their daughter's first, second and third interviews, Mr and Ms Linden were told that Amy had more to disclose. By her fourth interview, Amy had joined Colin Eade's list of complainant children, and Jan Gillanders had begun visiting the Linden family:

> She came round with information on support groups and counsellors. She said, 'You can claim lump-sum compensation.' I said, 'But there's no proof she's been abused.' Jan said that didn't matter. She told me to get my application in and she would fix it up. That was the final straw. I said, 'Look, I don't agree with it. I'm not taking it. It's blood money!' I was furious. I rang my husband and said, 'This is just a load of old cobblers. I don't believe Peter did anything. [Amy's] acting up, but it's just the attention she's getting. It's all just crap.' He said, 'Oh bravo! Thank God for that!'[30]

• • •

Prior to Gillanders' and Crossen's involvement in the crèche case, 13 prospective child complainants had been identified (Kari Lacebark, Lara Palm, Zelda Cypress, Molly Sumach, Eli Laurel, Tess Hickory, Bart Dogwood, Mandy Arbutus, Yelena Holly, Derek Ngaio, Julian Yew, Mia Broadleaf and Kane Juniper). In the five months between the social workers' appointments and the opening of the depositions hearing, eight more child complainants were identified (Amy Linden, Judy Balsa, Ryan Matai, Frances Pine, Jodie Alder, Fran Deodar, Ruby Hazelnut and Abigail Fir). All eight were among the 20 complainants at the depositions hearing. Three of the eight were among the 13 complainants at the Ellis trial (Judy Balsa, Frances Pine and Abigail Fir). But, at the end of the day, guilty verdicts were entered only in relation to children whose parents had delivered them to the investigation prior to the appointments of Gillanders and Crossen (Kari Lacebark, Lara Palm, Zelda Cypress, Molly Sumach, Eli Laurel, Tess Hickory and Bart Dogwood).

• • •

Grandma Magnolia is a shadowy but influential figure in this story. Crèche case records show that her grandson made his famous 'I don't like Peter's black penis' comment on 18 November 1991, but it wasn't until Grandma Magnolia heard about it two days later that her daughter laid the complaint that triggered the crèche investigation. This raises the intriguing possibility that, without Grandma Magnolia's intervention, the crèche case may never have happened. Interestingly, the records for the following year raise a further intriguing possibility: that, without Grandma Magnolia's intervention in the wake of yet another enigmatic remark by her grandson, the Civic Child Care Centre may never have been closed.

In the weeks leading up to Ellis's arrest on 30 March 1992, some of Ms Magnolia's supporters urged the council to close the crèche. But, following Ellis's arrest, crèche supporters continued to use the Civic, new families began to enrol their children and life at the centre settled back to something approaching normality. Then, in late June, a campaign to close the Civic began in earnest. Again, Geoffrey Magnolia was the catalyst. According to his mother, when four-and-a-half-year-old Geoffrey was walking past the Masonic Lodge with his parents on 23 June he pointed to the building and said that Peter had taken him there. Later, on the same walk, he pointed to a manhole cover in the road and said that Peter had pushed children down to where the caged gorillas were kept. Next day, Detective Greg Heath – who was by then assisting Colin Eade – took a statement from Ms Magnolia about these revelations. Two days later Grandma Magnolia fired off a letter to Christchurch mayor Vicki Buck:

> Rage, deep sorrow, emotional exhaustion, grief for lost childhoods – it has been more than many hundreds of us can bear. We expected appropriate action from someone like yourself, from council officers and we expected no less than the closure of the Civic Crèche ... The damage out there is on an horrendous scale ... and daily the horrors unfold ... If you wish to be fully informed you should by now be meeting with parents or better still perhaps with the two excellent social workers appointed to work with the parents.[31]

'I remember the letters,' mused administrator Rob Dally. 'There was one from [Grandpa Magnolia's] widow. I knew [Grandpa Magnolia] from way back.'[32]

Dally's colleague Alistair Graham also remembered the letters. 'The pressures were there all right, but they weren't influencing us,' he said stoutly. 'They might have influenced the police and others, but not us.'[33] Crèche supervisor Gaye Davidson's recollections, confirmed by notes she took at the time, tell a different story:

> On 3 July [council officer] Martin Maguire told me that [Grandma Magnolia] was threatening to sue the council for negligence, and that there were strong rumblings in top management about my position. Apparently some complainant families weren't satisfied with Peter's arrest – they also wanted me fired. Martin said that [city manager] John Gray wanted me 'out of the way', at least until the trial was over.[34]

At a meeting on 6 July between Alistair Graham, Martin Maguire and Gaye Davidson the issue came to a head. 'Alistair said that didn't I think it would be better for the centre if I was to leave and let someone who hadn't been through the last few months come in with fresh ideas?' Davidson noted. Next day, management committee spokesperson Mr Larch advised his fellow committee members that 'Gaye's position as supervisor, and in fact as an employee of the Council, is under serious review'.

'The political will to do away with the Centre probably now exists and may not be able to be changed,' he wrote. 'The Council have received a tremendous amount of negative feedback from parents (and more importantly their wider families) involved in the investigation and this has had a cumulative effect. I consider it appropriate now to try to redress the balance with a pre-emptive strike.'[35]

The pre-emptive strike took the form of an unctuous letter of praise and thanks to city manager John Gray. However, because Mr Larch's memo to the management committee fell into the hands of the council administration, any positive reaction Gray may have had to the letter was more than outweighed by his negative reaction to the memo.

'I wish to immediately extend my apologies,' Mr Larch wrote contritely three days later. 'The use of the words "pre-emptive strike" [was] on reflection unfortunate.'[36]

The staff of the Civic Child Care Centre were anything but contrite. 'We, the staff, fully support Gaye, and are appreciative of her skills and dedication, both as a leader and a colleague,' they wrote to John Gray. 'We are most grateful for her example and precedent.'[37]

• • •

The campaign to close the crèche began at a time when Rosemary Smart's report on the management of the Civic was approaching completion. But, in response to the support for Gaye Davidson shown by the crèche staff and management committee, the council agreed that no action would be taken on her employment until the Smart report had been released and an appropriate time had elapsed for its recommendations to be implemented.[38]

At the time of Rosemary Smart's two, two-hour visits to the Civic in March 1992 she was favourably impressed. However, by the time she interviewed the staff in mid-April her perceptions of the crèche had been coloured by her reading, by the statements that staff had made to the police and by her discussions with a handful of complainant parents.

Rosemary Smart's reading included Finkelhor's book on ritual abuse allegations in American childcare centres (*Nursery Crimes*), and Kathleen Coulborn Faller's *Understanding Child Sexual Maltreatment*. Of ritual abuse in day-care centres, Faller wrote:

> Children may report being taken to the graveyard or to a church and having sex, the sacrifice of animals and in some cases people, and the drinking of blood or other kinds of potions. Incantations and songs may be repeated. Robes may be worn. As well, emblems such as crosses, particularly upside down crosses, signs incorporating 666, pentagrams and circles, pictures of the devil, and ritual objects may be described by victims.[39]

The staff statements to the police – which were passed on to Rosemary Smart – were made in March, immediately after Detective Eade had shattered the crèche workers with his claim that Peter Ellis had been offending for years under their noses.

'That's really where things ran amok from my point of view,' crèche worker Shona recalled.

> Some of the staff tried desperately to think of something that Peter might have done. Sandi said she saw him coming out of the toilet doing up his fly. When we were overseas I saw heaps of men coming out of toilets doing up their flies when I was waiting for my husband. They get out the door before they realise they're out the door. That sort of thing was blown up out of all proportion.[40]

Smart began her interviews with the crèche staff by inviting them to read through their police statements. The staff felt the police had taken their comments out of context and were using them to discredit the crèche. But they also felt that putting the record straight in an atmosphere of rumour and innuendo would be an impossible task. 'I read through my police statement quickly and said, no, I didn't want to change it,' recalled Sigrid. 'I just thought the whole thing was crazy. I thought that everyone would wake up in a minute and realise it hadn't happened.'[41]

However, most staff seized the opportunity to tell Rosemary Smart how things really were at the crèche. 'When I interviewed them they came across as very nice people, basically. They were sort of open,' recalled Smart.

'Rosemary Smart seemed like someone who was here to support us, here to help us. So we poured our hearts out – telling her how we felt, how traumatic it was, how the centre ran.' Sandi told me.[42]

Shona was less impressed: 'Rosemary Smart sat me down and tried to put words in my mouth. She told me that Gaye never told anyone off. I said, "Gaye made it very clear when something was wrong, there's no two ways about it." She said that all the staff cared about was their social events. I said, "Once a month we had very pleasant pot-luck teas on a Sunday night in different people's homes." She reckoned they were booze-ups. I said, "They weren't booze-ups. Nobody drank much. I never saw anyone drunk at those things."'

• • •

In mid-July, Rosemary Smart delivered her draft report to the council administration. 'There were five copies,' recalled administrator Alistair Graham. 'I remember numbering them. I had one. Martin [Maguire] had one. John Gray had one. I can't remember where the other two went. This thing was to be controlled.'[43]

Alistair Graham was particularly concerned about Smart's notes on her interviews with the crèche staff. In these, Smart (who had never met Peter Ellis or seen him working with children) described what Ellis's colleagues regarded as his teasing and boisterous play as 'overt forms of maltreatment of children ranging from direct verbal attacks (insult, ridicule, humiliation) through emotional abuse (the withholding of affection or compassion) and at times physical coercion (pulling, pushing, isolation)'.

'The report was supposed to re-establish the credibility of the crèche,' Alistair Graham told me. 'I didn't want those interviews to become public. So we suggested to Rosemary that they be withdrawn.' Smart was not happy. She later recalled:

> I am really concerned about what is happening at the crèche because it's like these people cannot discriminate between what seems appropriate behaviour and what is inappropriate ... I said ... I'll take this part out, but the more I think about it, the more concerned I am, and I would really like to say to the council that I think something has to be done ... The place does not feel safe.[44]

The Smart report was completed in late August 1992. The crèche was closed in early September 1992. 'There was a very strong inference that somehow my report had caused the crèche to close. That was not the case,' Smart insisted. 'The Ministry of Education made its decision without any knowledge of this at all.' My own research suggests otherwise, but that issue will be examined later.

• • •

'Ask [Amy] if she's been to Peter's house,' Detective Eade instructed Ms Linden. He probably made the same request of other parents, because by mid-year the search was on to find a venue where children could have been abused, pornography could have been filmed and occult ceremonies could have been performed without any outsiders noticing.[45]

By then, three children had made formal disclosures involving 'Peter's house'. In March, Kari Lacebark said a man called Joseph had teased her with his penis at Peter's house. In April, Zelda Cypress disclosed genital touching by Peter when he babysat her at 404 Hereford Street. In May, Tess Hickory said Peter had a bath with her at his two-storey house. On the basis of these disclosures Detective Eade obtained a search warrant. It stated that the signatory was satisfied there were reasonable grounds for believing there were 'in any building, box, carriage, receptacle, vehicle, premises or place situated at 404 Hereford Street ... dolls, photographs or other evidence indicating the premises may have been used to commit offences of child abuse and also to allow photographs to be taken of the premises' in relation to the offences of 'indecent assault, inducing an indecent act and sexual violation'.

Bruce, the owner of 404 Hereford Street, recalled the beginning of his involvement in the crèche case:

> I'm a very private person. Retired but busy. Hobbies and things – my garden, my lovely big home with a couple of boarders. After Peter moved out I saw him perhaps once or twice a year. We just kept in touch, as you do. When he told me about the allegations I made contact more often because I thought he was being badly done by. Then in June Detectives Eade and Heath appeared on my doorstep. They said that Peter had minded this girl for three weeks at my place in December 1987. I said, 'Sorry, he wasn't here. He left in March of that year. My diaries will show that.' They said, 'This doesn't make our case any easier.' They amended the allegation to three weeks the year before. Later I found out it wasn't three weeks, it was two and a half days. I went through my diaries to show them how little I'd seen of Peter since he left. They didn't believe me. They didn't believe anything. They took away my diaries. I went down to the Child Abuse Unit voluntarily with Eade. That left the others free to poke around, but I had nothing to hide. When I got out of the car there was a well-dressed lady, probably in her forties – and her daughter, probably in her twenties – standing by the door. They were obviously there to see if they could identify me. Eade spoke to them for a few minutes. Then they went away. After that he took a laborious statement from me.[46]

Bruce's statement read:

> I can't remember Peter looking after a child at my house, even for a day ... I never gave him any authority at any time after he moved out to bring children to my house. I can recall him bringing a group of children from the crèche to my house. Another staff member was there. The children were there to see his animals and didn't go into the house.

• • •

On 31 July Ms Magnolia took her son back past the Masonic Lodge, and to the ramp beside St Elmo Courts in Hereford Street. Geoffrey said he had been to both places, and added that there were Ninja Turtles on the fire escape. Ms Magnolia included these revelations on the lists she was compiling of bizarre allegations made against Ellis and others. The lists, which went on for several pages, included a range of places Ellis was said to have taken children to, or that they 'show unnatural fear of'. These included his house and a house in Lyttelton, the Botanic Gardens and some other parks, the museum, various hotels, restaurants, carparks, hospitals, toilets and bathrooms, bridges, stairs, lifts, cellars and trapdoors. People listed as having taken part in or witnessed abuse included 'baddies', bad men (some in a circle; sometimes lots or hundreds of men), women, 'women who were really men, Maori men, a man with a ponytail, a bad man with blond sticky-up hair, rough people in ripped clothes', Ellis's mother and his (non-existent) wife and girlfriend. Twelve other people were listed but never identified. The list headed 'Other things kids have talked about or are unnaturally afraid of' included tigers, crocodiles, talking trees, skeletons, guns, explosions, black clothes, swords, cages, needles and knives.[47]

• • •

At a meeting in late July or early August Detectives Eade and Heath and a group of complainant and non-complainant parents met to plan their next move. As the police no doubt explained, more information was needed before they could identify the places and people referred to in the allegations. So the parents took copies of Ms Magnolia's lists and went home to question their children further.

8.iii: Concerns of Abuse by Other Crèche Staff (Totally Confidential)

When Bart Dogwood began attending the Civic Child Care Centre in February 1989 he was nearly three years old and his parents had been separated for almost a year. During his first six months at the crèche he lived with his mother and three older half-brothers three days a week, and spent the rest of the week with his father. After that, he lived with his father full time.

To alleviate the stress of full-time single parenting, Mr Dogwood applied for a social welfare childcare subsidy. The Dogwoods' family counsellor (who became a complainant parent in the crèche case) wrote a letter of support:

> The change from shared to single parenting was made in part because of [Bart's] perceived insecurity as a consequence of the changes in his caregivers ... [Bart] attends

8.iii: Concerns of Abuse by Other Crèche Staff (Totally Confidential)

the Civic Child Care Centre ... He is settled and happy there ... It would be of benefit for [Bart] if he was able to remain at the Civic Child Care Centre to provide continuation of care and education. It is important for [Bart's] wellbeing that he experience a secure and predictable environment ...[1]

Bart spent a year in his father's care. Then, Mr and Ms Dogwood began a trial reconciliation. After that, Bart lived with both parents, three older half-brothers and the new baby. Despite the upheavals in his home life, Bart survived his preschool years remarkably unscathed. 'While he was at the crèche and right up until before I started talking to him before his first interview [15 months after he had left the crèche], I didn't think there was any problem with him,' said his mother. 'When I had him there were no behavioural problems that I noticed,' confirmed his father.[2]

Around the time of Bart's first DSW interview on 14 May 1992 (about being cleaned up on the crèche changing table), Ms Dogwood began asking her son, at least twice a week, if Peter had hurt him in any other way. At that point Bart's behavioural deterioration began. Ms Dogwood stated: '[Bart's] toileting got progressively worse and he was pooing his pants and refusing to go to the toilet. He had severe mood swings and was often angry. There was a lot of shouting and non-compliance. This was at home but not at school ... He also went off food and got quite sick. He was very pale and wouldn't eat.'[3] By early August, Bart had reached breaking point.

By then, as a result of the confluence of two separate but related developments, the crèche case was ripe for a full-blown, ritual abuse disclosure. The first was the addition of Ms Magnolia's checklist of bizarre allegations to the ritual abuse literature in circulation. The second was Ms Arbutus's decision to withdraw her daughter Mandy from the case. In the history of the crèche investigation, Ms Arbutus and Mandy play key roles. Ms Arbutus organised the first meeting for crèche parents in December 1991. Mandy – who had never attended the crèche – made the disclosure that led to the reopening of the investigation on 31 January 1992, and to Peter Ellis's arrest on 30 March 1992.

Ms Arbutus withdrew her daughter because Detective Eade propositioned her. She had laid her complaint in early July, but it wasn't until early August, when the charge relating to Mandy Arbutus was formally withdrawn, that Eade heard about it. For Detective Eade, Mandy's departure – coupled with indications from the Lindens and the Cypresses that they also wished to withdraw their daughters from the case – may well have raised the spectre of the whole case slipping from his grasp.

• • •

On 3 August Ms Dogwood said to her son, '... at 7.30 you and Daddy and I are going to sit down and talk about the crèche. I believe you've got a lot to tell ...' Sure enough, when the Dogwoods interrogated Bart for more than two-and-a-half hours, they obtained some startling disclosures. 'It seems strange to think now that [Bart] didn't cry; in fact he seemed curiously flat and drained of feelings,' Ms Dogwood wrote.[4]

Next morning (4 August), Ms Dogwood drove Bart to 404 Hereford Street and stopped outside. Then, having satisfied herself that he recognised the building, she contacted Sue Sidey. That afternoon, Sidey conducted a formal interview with Bart that lasted over an hour.

Bart told Sidey he had had a bath with Peter at a two-storey house. He said Peter used swear words, dressed up as a witch and a judge, threatened Bart and his family, and made him do poos in the bath and eat it. He said other boys and men were present but he didn't know who they were.

'What else did he do?' asked Sidey. Bart said Peter made him touch his penis until white stuff came out of it.

'Was it [Peter's penis] hanging down or sticking out?' asked Sidey.

'Um, it was hanging down like that,' said Bart.

At the trial of Peter Ellis, defence counsel Rob Harrison asked Sue Sidey and expert witness Karen Zelas whether indecencies of that sort could be suggested to children by their parents. Sidey and Zelas replied that, when suspected victims are questioned further, only children who have actually experienced abuse can provide convincing detail of the experience. When measured against this standard, Bart's attempts to provide convincing detail of his contact with Ellis's penis were a dismal failure.

'Did any other part of you touch Peter's penis or not?' asked Sidey later in the interview.

'He put his penis up my bum,' said Bart.

'What did that make your bum feel like?' asked Sidey.

'What do you mean?'

'What did your bum feel like when you put his penis up your bum?'

'Nnnn ah what do you mean by –?'

'What did it feel like – did you know – did it feel?'

'It felt ticklish.'

'Was his body staying still or was it moving?'

'It was staying still.'

Bart said that Mikey Ash, Julian Yew and Kari Lacebark were present when Peter put his penis in his mouth and several men, including 'Robert', put their penises up his bum while Peter took photos.

At the trial of Peter Ellis, Bart Dogwood's 4 August interview was the basis for counts 16, 17 and 18 of the 28-count indictment. The offences were said to have taken place between 1 February 1989 and 1 March 1991 at 'an unknown address'.

8.iii: Concerns of Abuse by Other Crèche Staff (Totally Confidential)

Count 16 alleged that Ellis induced Bart to do an indecent act in that he 'bathed with him and touched the accused's penis'. Count 17 alleged that Ellis indecently assaulted Bart 'in that he placed his penis against the boy's anus'. Count 18 alleged that Ellis sexually violated Bart 'by the connection of his mouth with his penis'. Ellis was found guilty on all three counts.

• • •

Bart's 4 August disclosures, and the continued deterioration in his behaviour, convinced his parents that their son had more to tell. That evening his brothers quizzed him about needles, pills and trapdoors. Next morning, his parents continued the interrogation and advised Sue Sidey of the outcome. A few hours later, in an interview lasting over an hour, Sidey recorded the boy's latest disclosures on videotape. As in his previous interview, Bart was unable to identify the location of the alleged offences or the other adults present (apart from Peter Ellis and the mysterious Robert).

Later that day the Dogwoods again interrogated their son. Next afternoon (6 August), in his third DSW interview in as many days, Bart hit the jackpot. He identified the location of the alleged offences as a two-storey house in Hereford Street. He said that 20 adults were present, including Peter and his mother and crèche workers Gaye, Marie and Jan. The other adults had brown skin and slitty eyes. They wore black and white costumes and danced in a circle around a group of naked children. Marie and Gaye took off their clothes and pretended to have sex while Peter and his mother took photos. Violent and obscene adult–child and child–child acts were performed.

'So what stopped you from telling me yesterday?' asked Sidey.

'Oh I just remembered today,' said Bart.

Bart's 6 August disclosure ('the circle incident') was the basis for Count 19 of the 28-count indictment at the trial of Peter Ellis. It alleged that, between 1 February 1989 and 1 March 1991, Ellis did an indecent act upon Bart 'at an unknown address where the complainant was kicked and hit in the genital area and a needle placed on his penis by another'. Ellis was found not guilty on that count.

• • •

In August 1992 word of Bart Dogwood's sensational disclosures spread like wildfire. Children who had been named by Bart were questioned about the new allegations. Anxious mothers drove their offspring around Christchurch, inviting them to identify 'places they had been with Peter'.

On Wednesday 5 August Ms Lacebark told Kari that Bart remembered being tied up. Kari said she did too. She also remembered abuse involving Peter's mother, black and white costumes and men with slitty eyes. The same day, when Ms Magnolia took Geoffrey to 404 Hereford Street and stopped outside, he yelled, 'Take me away from here!'

On Thursday 6 August, when Ms Lacebark took her daughter to the Masonic Lodge, Kari said she had been there with Gaye and Marie. There were trapdoors and tunnels and cameras, she said. And, yes, she had been to the Parkroyal with Peter to meet men with slitty eyes. The same day Julian Yew identified 404 Hereford Street and the Masonic Lodge as places he had been with Peter. He also talked about photographs, needles and pills.

Friday 7 August was a particularly busy day. Bart identified the Masonic Lodge as a place he had been with Peter. Kari said that Gaye and Marie went to Peter's place. Geoffrey talked to his mother about trapdoors and needles at the Masonic Lodge, and about Marie and Gaye doing bad things.[5] Also on 7 August, over after-work drinks, Detectives Colin Eade and Rob Nicholl advised Detective Senior Sergeant John Ell that other childcare workers had been named as offenders in the crèche case.

• • •

During the weekend of 8 and 9 August, John Ell considered the latest disclosures. Memories of the Great Christchurch Paedophile Ring fiasco weighed heavily upon him. He recalled:

> I was very concerned about the bizarre allegations. I've seen these controversial cases before. You're damned if you do and damned if you don't. I didn't want the police saddled with sole responsibility for assessing the credibility of the children's evidence. So I got agreement from Brian [Detective Inspector Brian Pearce] and Chris [Crown Prosecutor Chris Lange] to have the children's videotapes thoroughly vetted by Karen [Zelas]. We agreed that Karen would give her comments and Chris would review the evidence, and only when he was satisfied would charges be laid.[6]

Ell spent Monday 10 August and Tuesday 11 August in meetings and planning sessions with the crèche investigation team and senior police officers. Also on the Tuesday, Ms Dogwood arrived for Bart's fifth DSW interview brandishing a copy of Pamela Hudson's *Ritual Child Abuse*. When Sue Sidey cancelled the interview, Ms Dogwood threatened to withdraw her son from the case.

On Wednesday 12 August a summit meeting was held at the Christchurch Central Police Station involving the police (Detective Chief Inspector McMeeking, Detective Inspector Pearce, Detective Senior Sergeant Ell, Detective Sergeants Hardie and Mitchell, and Detectives Eade and Hawkins), interviewer Sue Sidey, social workers Jan Gillanders and Gen Crossen and Crown Prosecutor Chris Lange. After

8.iii: Concerns of Abuse by Other Crèche Staff (Totally Confidential)

stressing the confidentiality of the meeting, Eade and Sidey outlined the history of the investigation. They said that suspicions of offending by other crèche staff had arisen early in the investigation, but when the women were interviewed – as Ellis's co-workers rather than as suspects – they gave a good impression. But now offending by some female staff had been disclosed on video. There were indications of ritual abuse. The suspected venues were 404 Hereford Street and the Masonic Lodge. Parents were becoming frantic with worry. Some were threatening to withdraw their children. Some were reading ritual abuse literature. Some were questioning their children inappropriately. As in the child pornography ring enquiry, there was talk of a police coverup.[7]

'Clearly, a compelling issue that we had to think about – and it was raised very early on – if indeed these allegations are true, or if there's any substance to them, then we have to consider the welfare of the children who were currently at the crèche,' Detective Inspector Brian Pearce told me. However, at the 12 August meeting a consensus was reached 'not to proceed with the closure of the crèche based on the information to date'.[8]

A consensus was also reached that the concerns of the most vocal parents needed to be addressed. So Chris Lange, John Ell and Jan Gillanders were dispatched to meet with them that evening. Also, to prove that the police were responding with actions as well as words, a five-officer team headed by Detective Sergeant Bob Hardie was given two weeks to investigate the multiple-offender allegations.

As a result of these developments, Colin Eade's inquiry into allegations against Peter Ellis was labelled 'Phase I', and the inquiry into other offenders, conducted by Bob Hardie and his team, was labelled 'Phase II'.

In mid-August all the police officers involved, together with social workers Jan Gillanders and Gen Crossen, moved to their own base in Transport House, Kilmore Street. From then on, the investigation proceeded under the overall supervision of John Ell.

Although on 12 August 1992 the police concluded that the crèche did not need to be closed, on 1 and 2 September they advised representatives of DSW, the Ministry of Education and the Christchurch City Council that it had to be closed immediately. During the intervening two weeks, though the parental questioning continued, no formal disclosures implicating any female crèche staff were recorded. This raises the question: what happened between 12 August and 1 September that made the police change their minds?

The closure of the crèche became the subject of extended and vigorous controversy – in the criminal court, in the Employment Court and in the forum of public opinion. However, despite all the debate, no clear reason for the closure has ever been revealed. Furthermore, by the time I came to investigate the matter, it was obvious that many of the people involved were covering their backs. In the course of my research I received so many conflicting versions of the circumstances leading to the closure of the Civic Child Care Centre that I was tempted to turn the issue into a board game. The challenge for players would be to decide who was lying, who was telling the truth, and what really happened in Christchurch between 12 August and 3 September 1992.

But to talk of truth and lies is to oversimplify the matter. Lies are never simple, and neither are the motivations that bring them into being. Even the best of people are vulnerable to tricks of memory and emotion that, like tricks of light, may conjure the past as they wanted it to be, rather than as it was.

I found police officers Brian Pearce and Bob Hardie to be sincere and honourable men. Though they abhorred homosexuality, paedophilia and pornography, they showed no vindictiveness towards the accused in the crèche case. They insisted that the decision to close the Civic Child Care Centre was made after careful consideration of the evidence. It was only when I pressed them on the nature of that evidence that their answers became evasive and contradictory. The possibility that, back in 1992, both men – along with most other right-thinking people in their city – were in the grip of a collective delusion that made rumour and innuendo seem real, was not something that Pearce and Hardie were prepared to contemplate.

'Bob Hardie and his staff were looking at the new disclosures and saying – well, can this be true? They're talking about buildings. They're talking about houses. They're talking about the crèche. Their job was to go out and try to corroborate some of the things the children were saying,' Brian Pearce told me. 'Under the Evidence Amendment Act we're not required to corroborate sex complaint evidence, but I think it's still important to endeavour to do so. So that was the thrust of Phase II.'

'Was there ever any surveillance of the crèche?' I asked. It seemed an obvious investigative step, if the centre was under suspicion.

'Surveillance of the crèche?'

'Yes.'

'No – you mean covert?'

'Yes.'

'No.'[9]

So what did Hardie and his team do? 'My brief was to establish within two weeks whether there was any reason to pursue the allegations involving multiple offenders,' Hardie told me. First he familiarised himself with the investigation and selected his team. Then he and Detective Neville Jenkins read the transcripts of Bart Dogwood's August disclosures and interviewed the core complainant parents. In the course of those interviews, the parents' subjective reality became the investigators' objective reality.

'The complaints seemed genuine,' Hardie recalled. 'The parents seemed normal, intelligent people who believed in kids. The allegations against the female staff were made under the same conditions as the allegations against Ellis. So after talking to the parents I reported back that there was no way that we couldn't pursue the allegations.'

'So how was the decision made to close the crèche?' I asked him. The realisation that the Civic Child Care Centre may have been closed on the basis of unsubstantiated allegations from disaffected parents whose children had left the centre months or even years earlier hung reproachfully in the air between us.

'It was mainly on Brian Pearce's initiative,' he said, before lapsing into a thoughtful silence.

For his part, Pearce assured me that his primary concern was for the children's safety. 'On 20 August I had a meeting with John Ell and Bob Hardie. I told them to be vigilant in terms of assessing care and protection issues with regard to the children still at the crèche,' he said, consulting his diary. By then, John Ell and Karen Zelas had met to discuss her assessment of Bart Dogwood's August interviews and Kari Lacebark's March interview. The following week Zelas put her findings in writing.

The astute combination of authority and ambiguity in Karen Zelas's report of 28 August would have done credit to the Oracle of Delphi. Zelas acknowledged that Kari and Bart had been subject to 'highly leading' parental questioning, but she also observed that 'these facts could make it easy to dismiss the children's statements as having little probative value whether or not they might be accurate'. She made no mention of the continued operation of the crèche, but she asserted that the children's disclosures concerning multiple offenders should be taken seriously. She also recommended that the police make further inquiries and look for corroboration.[10] Ell met with Zelas on Friday 28 August, and again on Monday 31 August. Those discussions left Ell in no doubt that the crèche had to be closed immediately.

'Karen Zelas said that the children were to be believed,' Bob Hardie confirmed. Then he volunteered another memory. 'We had Rosemary Smart's report about physical and mental abuse at the crèche.'

'You had Rosemary Smart's report?'

'Yeah, I'm sure we did. I'm sure it was a factor in the decision to close the crèche.'

I knew that Smart's claim of having had no contact with the police while she was conducting her review was suspect (Ell's diary recorded a meeting with her about the review on 29 June), but this was the first support I had for the staff suspicion – vigorously denied by Smart and the council administration – that her report was instrumental in bringing about the closure of the crèche.

On Monday 31 August, John Ell asked Crown Prosecutor Chris Lange for a legal opinion on the police's responsibilities in relation to the care and protection of children still attending the crèche. Lange's opinion was based on unsubstantiated allegations provided to him by the police, on Karen Zelas's assessment of the credibility of Kari and Bart, and on his own perusal of the relevant legislation. According to the DSW and Ministry of Education officers approached next day, Lange had either failed to read, or failed to understand, the relevant legislation, but the precise contents of his opinion remain a mystery.

'Following that opinion the view was formed that we'd be in some peril if we ignored the welfare of the children,' Pearce told me. So next day (Tuesday 1 September) the police embarked on a three-day round of meetings that culminated, on Thursday 3 September, in the abrupt closure of the Civic Child Care Centre.

At the time, Christchurch was in the grip of its coldest, bleakest winter in years. For day after dreary day, black skies, power cuts and crippling snowfalls blanketed the city. In every walk of life the irritability, and the sense of crisis, were palpable.

• • •

New Zealand crèches and preschools operate under the Education (Early Childhood Centres) Regulations 1990. These state that the licence of a centre may be suspended if the authority responsible for administering the Education Act 'is satisfied that it is not in the interests of children ... for the centre to continue to be open'.

In 1992 Dunedin-based Michael Deaker, South Island operations manager for the Ministry of Education, had overall responsibility for administering the Education Act in his region. Christchurch-based Bede Cooper was his deputy. Responsibility for regional early childhood centres was delegated to Christchurch-based Ministry of Education officer Grace Todd.

According to Todd, in the course of an average year three or four Canterbury childcare centres have their licences suspended for health and safety reasons (for example, as a result of concerns about lead paint or poor hygiene).

'Do you visit the centre yourself, before you suspend the licence?' I asked.

'If the Medical Officer of Health has already investigated the problem and advised the centre of what needs to be done, then we can act on his letter. When we get a notification of any other sort, the pens go down and we pay a visit. That's our absolute priority – to verify and confirm,' she said.

Todd explained that, in accordance with the regulations, when a centre's licence is suspended, the ministry provides the licensee with a suspension notice specifying the conditions that have to be met before the suspension will be lifted. If the conditions are not met within a reasonable period (normally three weeks), the licence will be cancelled.[11]

8.iii: Concerns of Abuse by Other Crèche Staff (Totally Confidential)

On 2 September 1992 police officers Brian Pearce and John Ell advised Christchurch city manager John Gray of their concerns about the Civic Crèche. On 3 September 1992 Gray advised the crèche staff that the Ministry of Education had withdrawn the centre's licence, and that he had no choice but to close the centre immediately.

In 1995 the closure of the crèche was the subject of an Employment Court case brought against the council by the 11 preschool teachers and two cleaners who lost their jobs, their careers and their previously unblemished reputations that day. In the Employment Court, only the council version of events leading up to the crèche closure was told. In this book, the DSW, police, Crown and Ministry of Education versions will also be examined. To appreciate the implications of these versions, we need to first examine the arguments traversed in the Employment Court.

Chief Employment Court Judge Tom Goddard summarised the issues this way: 'At the heart of this case is whether Mr Gray handed in the licence because of a business decision no longer to operate the crèche, or whether he did so as a means to the end of dismissing employees who were suspected of a grave dereliction of duty of which, however, he had no evidence.'[12]

In his opening submission for the staff, Graham Panckhurst QC noted that the decision to close the crèche was made following allegations of child abuse, and argued that the city council did not act as a fair and reasonable employer when confronted with wholly unsubstantiated allegations from the police and the Ministry of Education.

In reply, Tom Weston for the city council argued that, because the police had persuaded the Ministry of Education to withdraw the crèche licence prior to the 2 September meeting, John Gray was presented with a *fait accompli* – he had no choice but to close the crèche. Weston also argued that Gray was unable to advise the staff of any formal complaint because no formal complaint had been made.

After considering the arguments, Chief Judge Goddard concluded that the council had 'plainly received a very serious and very pointed complaint', and awarded the staff over $800,000 compensation for unjustified dismissal.[13]

In 1996 the Court of Appeal overturned Goddard's ruling on the ground that the council had no choice but to close the crèche, and that, therefore, the staff were not unjustifiably dismissed, but genuinely redundant.[14]

The Employment and Appeal Court cases raised two important questions that have yet to be fully answered. The first is: what information was provided by the police to the representatives of DSW and the Ministry of Education on 1, 2 and 3 September, and to representatives of the city council on 2 and 3 September? The second is: what decisions were made on the basis of that information, when were they made, and by whom?

Much rests on the answers to these questions. If the police did not tell John Gray why they wanted the crèche closed, and if the Ministry of Education did present him with a *fait accompli*, then justice was done in the crèche Employment Court case. But if the police did tell John Gray why they wanted the centre closed, and if the ministry did not present him with a *fait accompli*, then 13 unjustifiably dismissed council employees were denied their rightful compensation by the highest court in the land.

• • •

At 9am on Tuesday 1 September 1992, Brian Pearce, John Ell, Bob Hardie and Chris Lange met with DSW manager Janet Biswell. 'They wanted me to close the crèche because of the care and protection issues involved,' Biswell recalled. 'They seemed to think that childcare centres were under DSW control. I said: "No, I don't have the power to do that – you need to see the Ministry of Education."'[15]

From that point on, Janet Biswell took part in the evolving saga of the crèche closure as an observer rather than a participant. This does not mean her memories will be more accurate than anyone else's, but it does mean they are less likely to be tainted by self-interest.

At 2pm on Tuesday 1 September, Brian Pearce, John Ell and Janet Biswell met with Ministry of Education officers Bede Cooper and Grace Todd. Ell's account of the rationale behind that meeting left me unsure as to whether its purpose was to share the responsibility, or pass the buck:

> Based on my previous experience of the reluctance of some people to make hard decisions, I wanted to make sure that these other departments were involved, that it wasn't left to the police to be the bogey man. All we can do in a case like this is tell people what we know and say, 'Well, we're doing our bit, but you have some statutory obligations whether you like it or not.' I felt strongly that this was not one that the police either should be, or were required to be, the people that had to wield the big stick and do all the dirty work, all on their own.[16]

'John Ell told us the sort of new evidence that the police had found in terms of the crèche,' Janet Biswell recalled.

'What evidence was that?' I asked.

'About the female workers – activities that had been going on – drug dealing at the crèche, cannabis, that sort of thing – concerns about sexual goings-on amongst all the main parties and players and crèche parents and various other people. I think those were the two basic concerns – sexual activity and drug dealing.' These allegations were totally unsubstantiated. They had nothing to do with child abuse and everything to do with the activities of consenting adults in private. But they were all grist to the mill.

'Did he bring any documentation?' I asked. 'Did John Ell show you any evidence?'

'He didn't at that meeting – no,' she said. 'But the Ministry of Education people said we had to talk to the licensee, which was the city council. So a meeting was arranged with John Gray and some other council representatives the next day. John Ell was there, and Chris Lange. And yes, they did have evidence at the meeting with John Gray. They brought along written material and diagrammatic stuff.'

'Sorry?' I said, startled.

'They had diagrams of the various players and so on – where they all fitted.'

'Was that on sheets of paper or whiteboard?' I asked (I had heard about diagrams on whiteboard at the police headquarters – webs of lines connecting the crèche staff with each other, the Masonic Lodge and all the massage parlours, sex shops and known criminals in town).

'I think it was on sheets of paper. We didn't get to take them away.'

'But they showed them to you?' I said, checking that I had understood her correctly.

'Yes. I guess they did a really good job of convincing everyone that there were untoward activities going on.'[17]

• • •

At the 1 September meeting Ministry of Education officers Bede Cooper and Grace Todd explained that if the crèche was to be closed, there was a procedure to be followed. The first step was to advise the licensee that the licence was being suspended. At that point the centre would cease to operate. After that, it was up to the licensee to deal with whatever problems had been identified before the centre could be reopened.

'The police said the matter was urgent,' recalled Cooper. 'They said that in the interests of the children's wellbeing the crèche should be closed immediately. They also made it clear they didn't want it to reopen again in the near future. They wanted the licence terminated.'

'What information were you given about the nature of the police concerns?' I asked. After a long pause, Cooper replied:

> The police said they'd like to show us some of the evidence they had at that stage. So John Ell came to see me first thing next morning, before the meeting at the city council. He brought statements and children's interview transcripts and artwork. He said, 'Here, you pick some at random.' I remember being quite shocked at some of the things the children were saying. After working through that material for maybe half an hour, I said, 'Yes, we would have to consider suspending the licence very seriously.'[18]

• • •

According to city manager John Gray, when he arrived with staff members Rob Dally and Martin Maguire for what he believed was a meeting with Janet Biswell and John Ell at 10am on Wednesday 2 September he found waiting to meet him: Janet Biswell, Detective Inspector Pearce, Detective Senior Sergeant Ell, Bede Cooper, Grace Todd, Police legal advisor Ian McArthur and Crown Prosecutor Chris Lange. About half an hour later, the council's office solicitor, Peter Mitchell, joined the meeting.[19]

When he appeared as a witness in the Employment Court, Gray claimed that, prior to the 2 September meeting, he had no knowledge of any outside pressure to close the crèche, no knowledge of any concerns about Gaye Davidson's position as crèche supervisor, and no knowledge of Rosemary Smart's report (though the evidence in Chapter 8.2 suggests that he was aware of all those matters).

Gray said that, at the 2 September meeting, he was advised by the police that children attending the crèche were in 'serious danger', that the police wanted the crèche closed immediately, and that the Ministry of Education was prepared to suspend the crèche licence. Gray also said his repeated requests for details of the police concerns were firmly declined. When council employees Maguire and Mitchell gave evidence in the Employment Court, they supported Gray's version of events.

In an attempt to determine the truth about the 2 September meeting – and, in particular, to test Janet Biswell's recollection that the police had provided documented information on the allegations against the crèche staff – I interviewed John Gray, Peter Mitchell, Martin Maguire, Rob Dally, Brian Pearce, John Ell, Chris Lange, Bede Cooper and Grace Todd. Some of them flatly denied that the police had provided any information to the meeting. The rest became vague and forgetful when I raised the issue. In the end, I still wasn't sure about the reliability of Biswell's recollections.

Grace Todd took notes at the meeting, but they focused on licensing issues. John Gray took notes too, but under cross-examination in the Employment Court he said he had discarded them. As it happened, Rob Dally – the only council officer present at the 2 September meeting who was not called as a witness in the Employment Court – also took notes. By June 1993 the first page of his notes had disappeared, but a jotting on the surviving page is revealing. It states: 'concerns of abuse by other crèche staff (totally confidential)'. Though the information provided by that fragment is frustratingly slight, it suggests that – despite Gray's claim to the contrary – allegations of child abuse were made against other crèche staff at the 2 September meeting.

Rosemary Smart's report was also discussed. 'Mr Gray said the crèche had been subject to two separate reviews – the Education Review Office and the Rosemary Smart review. He said they'd come through with flying colours,' Brian Pearce recalled. 'I think it was John Ell who said it was his understanding that perhaps one of those reports was not all that complimentary of the management of the crèche.'

8.iii: Concerns of Abuse by Other Crèche Staff (Totally Confidential)

After the meeting Bede Cooper read the Smart report and satisfied himself that the crèche licence had to be suspended, and John Gray and his staff considered their options. Later that day someone notified the Ministry of Education that the council would not object to the crèche licence being suspended and cancelled the next day.

• • •

On Thursday 3 September, Michael Deaker, South Island operations manager for the Ministry of Education, flew to Christchurch to sign the crèche suspension and cancellation notices.

'We had the two notices prepared,' Bede Cooper told me. 'But I remember Michael being adamant that we shouldn't hand over both notices at once. He said we should hold back the cancellation letter in case the council had a change of heart overnight. There was always a chance they would decide to challenge the suspension.'[20] Even at that late stage, it seemed, John Gray was not faced with a *fait accompli*.

To everyone who had been at the long, tense meeting the day before, the meeting in Gray's office on 3 September was an anticlimax. When I asked them about it, most people could barely remember being there. But the drama was new to Michael Deaker, and his memories were vivid:

> We took the two letters with us, typed but not signed, to this briefing from Detective Inspector Pearce and his colleague, at which I was to make my own judgements in the light of what I saw and heard. They had manila folders of signed statements, and their own notes from interviews and investigations. They put those in front of me ...

'This is in the city manager's office?' I asked, astonished.
'Yes. Exactly.'
'And the city manager was there?'
'He was.'[21]

Deaker explained that his police briefing took place at a coffee table in John Gray's office. He said Gray, who was sitting at his desk throughout, appeared fully aware of what was going on.

Later, I made an independent check on the dimensions and layout of the city manager's office. Then I confirmed Deaker's recollections with Grace Todd, and discussed them with union secretary Peter Lawson.

'John Gray's office wasn't all that big as chief executive officers' offices go – about six metres long by three or four metres wide,' Lawson said. 'His desk wasn't far away from the chairs around the coffee table. I find it hard to believe he would be able to sit at his desk and ignore what was being discussed around the coffee table. There is no way he could not hear every word that was said.'[22]

John Gray had an important role to play in the 3 September exchange of letters.

His evidence in the Employment Court was that, at the 2 September meeting, his repeated request to the police for more information was denied. So why wasn't he protesting now? Why wasn't he asking to be included in Deaker's briefing? In search of a definitive answer, I tackled John Ell.

'Did you brief John Gray at all?' I asked.

'Don't have any recollection of that. Don't think so. Why?'

'It's just that other people have mentioned being briefed by you – Michael Deaker at the Thursday morning meeting; Bede Cooper said you'd run some material past him. I wondered if you'd briefed John Gray as well.'

'Oh, hang on. Yes. Well, he was the city manager. He had to be appraised. I think, from memory, before that meeting on the second at 10 o'clock Brian Pearce and I met him as a matter of courtesy because he didn't know what the hell we were doing. I think we met privately with John Gray in one of the offices there before we went into the meeting.'[23]

• • •

Michael Deaker's account of the 3 September meeting in John Gray's office continued:

> We were sitting around the coffee table and these manila folders were put in front of me: 'Read that, Mr Deaker. Read this one.' I'd skim through it. It was all stuff I'd heard about from Bede and Grace. At the end of that I was convinced that the licence had to be suspended. I went to John Gray's desk and said, 'Where's that letter, I'm going to sign it right now.'[24]

Gray responded with a prepared letter stating: 'In view of the suspension of the Civic Child Care Centre's licence, the Centre will cease to operate from today. I have no representations to make concerning the cancellation of the licence.' Whereupon Deaker signed, and handed to Gray, a notice cancelling the crèche licence.

• • •

On 4 September 1992, John Ell suffered a physical and emotional collapse that ended his involvement in the crèche investigation.[25] The same day, Michael Deaker flew to Wellington and briefed Catherine Gibson, acting chief executive of the Ministry of Education, on the events in Christchurch:

> She looked at me knowingly, and said, 'Michael, you don't think this was the police on a moral crusade, do you?' Probably a little defensively, I said, 'No, I don't.' I had no doubts at all. Then, months later, I heard Brian Pearce on the *Holmes Show*: 'I believe in a God that will not be mocked.' My mind went back to Catherine's question. I felt hollow. I thought: Bloody hell, what have I done?

CHAPTER 9

They Were All Under Suspicion

9.i: 'It was like a Police State Thing Closing in'

In 1992 John Gray was in the forty-second year as a local body administrator, and in his nineteenth year as Chief Executive Officer of the Christchurch City Council. For his decades of service to local government and the territorial army he had been awarded an O.B.E. (Military Division) in 1969, and a C.B.E. (Civil Division) in 1989. When local authority restructuring was introduced in 1989, Gray had more than 4000 employees on his payroll. By the time he retired in 1993, less than 2000 remained. Throughout the reorganisation, Gray won respect for his consultative management style and his willingness to front up when staff were made redundant.[1]

In the afternoon of 3 September, the crèche staff, their union secretary and the management committee spokesperson were called to an urgent meeting at the Civic Child Care Centre. Gray opened the 5.30 pm meeting by announcing that he was closing the crèche as of that time. There was no possibility of redeployment. His only explanation to the stunned and tearful group was that the Ministry of Education had withdrawn the crèche licence. He was not at liberty to say more. At that point, crèche supervisor Gaye Davidson phoned her lawyer Neville Taylor, and union secretary Peter Lawson turned on Gray.

'You haven't followed the employment contract,' he protested. 'You're supposed to give the union 14 days notice of a redundancy situation. I want you to withdraw this notice right now.' But, like the staff demands for answers, Lawson's demands for due process went unheeded.[2]

After Taylor's arrival and Gray's departure, Lawson and Taylor discussed the implications of the closure with crèche staff. It obviously had nothing to do with Peter Ellis; he had left the centre nine months earlier. 'We said it seemed to imply that there had been recent allegations of child abuse involving one or more of them,' Lawson recalled.

'We told them to be very careful if they were approached by the police. We said, "Don't answer any questions without having a solicitor present. These are serious times."' As if to underline the point, workmen arrived and began changing the locks.

'I lay awake that night – and every night for weeks afterwards. Thinking of the children. Picturing them. Missing them. Feeling terrible that we hadn't said goodbye,' said Sigrid. 'I didn't want to wake my husband with my crying, so I'd get up and make a cup of tea and stand at the bench and bawl my eyes out.'[3]

'I couldn't figure it out,' Susannah recalled. 'I thought – they must think we've done something wrong. I wondered if they were going to sue us for negligence. I remember thinking it was going to be awful. I didn't suspect that it was going to be as awful as it did become. But it was pretty bad that night.'[4]

• • •

During the evening of 3 September, crèche parents were advised of the centre's closure by phone, the media was advised by fax and a copy of the council's press release, together with a confidential memo from City Manager John Gray, was hand-delivered to the mayor and councillors. Later that evening, Gray advised union secretary Peter Lawson that he was withdrawing the redundancy notices and placing the crèche staff on two week's paid leave so normal redundancy negotiations could begin.

In his 3 September press release, Gray reiterated the points he had made in his earlier announcement to crèche staff, but in his confidential memo to the mayor and councillors he was more forthcoming. He said that police inquiries were ongoing, and that 'both myself and the Ministry of Education were briefed by NZ Police beforehand, and I am bound to agree with the action taken by the Ministry'.[5]

On Friday 4 September, the Southern Local Government Officers Union, and the crèche staff and parents, went in search of answers. Why had the crèche licence been withdrawn? What did they have to do to get it restored? The union tried to force the issue by announcing that it would take personal grievance claims against the council if the closure could not be reversed.

But there were no answers to be found, because Friday 4 September was the day the buck-passing started in earnest. Michael Deaker said the Ministry of Education had suspended the licence on police advice, but the centre had been closed permanently because John Gray had declined to challenge the suspension. John Gray said the decision to terminate rather than suspend the operation of the crèche was taken in consultation with the police and the ministry.[6] Then the police trumped the ministry and the council by denying all responsibility for the crèche closure. Their press release stated that the police had 'expressed some concerns' to the ministry, but the action taken was 'a matter between the Ministry of Education and the Christchurch City Council'. In a particularly bizarre touch, the police press release stated that 'parents of children currently attending the crèche should not be unduly concerned by these recent events.'[7]

Almost immediately, rumours that all the Civic staff were child abusers began to swirl. On Saturday 5 September, the Christchurch *Press* reported that 'Plans by the Methodist Central Mission to apply for a new licence for the Civic Child Care Centre may be thwarted if the centre's present staff are re-employed.' In the same item, five former crèche parents said they were 'delighted' with the decision to close the centre. One added that the police were investigating 'what could become New Zealand's biggest child abuse case'.[8]

In the evening of Sunday 6 September, Peter Lawson protested to the media that the crèche staff had not only lost their jobs, they had apparently been blacklisted from their chosen profession. He said he would be seeking an interim injunction from the Employment Court in the morning to prevent the council dismissing the workers without first confronting them with the allegations against them and giving them an opportunity to defend themselves. However, when the morning came, the council staved off the injunction by giving the crèche staff another six weeks' paid leave.[9]

From the time the police put their concerns to John Gray, he and his colleagues had been worrying about the legal repercussions of closing the crèche without prior warning.[10] In the Employment Court, when unjustified dismissal claims arise from police investigations, employers may defend themselves by claiming that the police forced their hands. But since the police were now denying they had done any such thing, that line of defence was closed to John Gray. However, the police position did offer him an alternative line of defence. If the police had indeed told him nothing, he could argue that he was unable to confront the staff with the allegations because he did not know what those allegations were.

Interestingly, on Monday 7 September, Gray stopped claiming that he had been briefed by the police, and started claiming that he had not been. In a confidential memo to city councillors and council managers, he wrote: 'I am not privy to the details about children at the Civic Child Care Centre being at risk, which the Police shared with the Ministry of Education … The real decision-making stopped short of this office.'[11] Thereafter, despite intensive cross-examination in the Employment Court, John Gray never wavered from that position.

• • •

With the crèche closure, around 50 families lost their trusted childcare facility. When the police invited concerned parents to contact them, several took up the offer.

'Why has this happened?' Mr Beech asked the officer on the end of the phone.

'Your children are safer today than they were yesterday,' was the reply. Other parents were told to 'read between the lines.'[12]

Ms Hawthorn and her friends tried to arrange a meeting. 'We wanted to give the police our impressions of the crèche. We thought there should be some balance,' she recalled. 'They said they'd only see us if we'd allow our children to have disclosure interviews. We all agreed that would be stupid because our kids were only two years old. After that, the police didn't want to know us.'[13]

In the evening of 4 September, around 50 bewildered and angry crèche supporters met to discuss their options. By then, the Methodist Mission had offered to take over the centre, but appeared reluctant to re-employ the Civic staff. Some parents wanted to support the Mission's offer. Some wanted to support the staff. All of them wanted stable childcare arrangements for their children without delay. The radical Mr Macrocarpa urged the group to sue the council. The conservative Mr Larch, who was standing for election to the city council, urged caution.

For a day or two, the Mission's plans seemed to be moving ahead. Then, on Thursday 11 September, the Mission superintendent announced that he would not be re-opening the Civic Child Care Centre, and he didn't think anyone else should re-open it either. His press release stated:

> It has been necessary for us to assume that a significant amount of child abuse occurred at the Civic. If that assumption is correct then there may be children who were victims of abuse still attending the Centre where the abuse happened. It is possible that their parents do not yet know of their abuse. Some parents may still be in denial ... The possibility that these children may be returned to the Civic would serve to compound their trauma ... it is our view that no-one should take over the running of this Child Care Centre and that it should remain closed.[14]

With no prospect of their favourite preschool reopening any time soon, most crèche families turned their backs on the controversy and got on with their lives.

'We switched right off because we had to rush around and find another childcare centre for our son,' Ms Maple explained. 'Anyway we felt totally helpless. There was a witch-hunt under way and it obviously wasn't going to stop until they had a body. We just stood back and watched it roll on with complete cynicism.'[15]

But for the crèche staff and a small group of loyal supporters, the union-assisted fight to salvage their careers and reputations continued. They made phone calls and Official Information Act requests to the council, the police and the Ministry of Education. They met with members of parliament. They complained to the Ombudsman, the Education Review Office, the Human Rights Commission and the Police Complaints Authority. They confronted Tim Langley, superintendent of the

Methodist Mission. 'He backed away down the corridor like he was terrified of us,' recalled Shona. 'It was hopeless.'[16]

By then the city was red hot with rumours, and the media was on the warpath. 'Is it true that you're getting foetuses from the abortion clinic, and eating them?' reporters asked crèche staff. 'Is it true that you're importing live snakes from Australia? Is it true that you're supplying prostitutes to judges and policemen? Is it true that you're procuring children for Asian sex rings?' One day, in a crowded supermarket, a woman told Sharleen, the youngest and most vulnerable of the childcare workers, that all the teachers from the Civic Child Care Centre should have 'child molester' tattooed on their foreheads.[17] Another day, Debbie Gillespie's former partner screamed at her, 'You're gonna get what's coming to you.' All of which raised another question for the crèche staff: What can we do to stop this defamatory talk?

On 11 September, at the invitation of the union, Gerald Nation, a partner in the old and distinguished Christchurch law firm of Wynn Williams and Co., met with the childcare workers to discuss the feasibility of suing whoever was responsible for the rumours.

'Gerald said that he thought the police had more sense than to take such preposterous stories seriously,' Susannah recalled. 'He said there really wasn't any point in suing anyone, especially when we didn't know who to sue.'

Two days before that meeting, Detective Neville Jenkins had asked Sharleen to go to the police station for an interview at 10 o'clock in the evening.

'I'll need to get hold of a lawyer first,' she said.

'Oh you don't want a lawyer, do you?' he said. 'We only want to talk to you.' Whereupon Sharleen phoned union secretary Peter Lawson. 'Help! I need a lawyer fast!' she gasped.

'The reality hit home,' Lawson recalled. 'How do you get a lawyer in the middle of the night? I said, "Stay where you are. I'll call you back in a few minutes." The first person I phoned was out. Then I realised that I only knew commercial and employment lawyers. So I got hold of Peter Ellis's solicitor, who put me in touch with a criminal lawyer. Then I got back to Sharleen. By then the police had backed off. They told her if she was going to bring a lawyer they didn't want to see her.'

Next morning, Lawson drew up a list of lawyers who were willing to be contacted by crèche staff at any time of the night or day. The following day, when the staff met Gerald Nation, the rights of citizens when approached by the police was a hot topic.[18]

'Gerald said we didn't have to answer any questions unless we wanted to, and we didn't have to go the police station unless we were under arrest,' recalled Susannah. 'This was all news to us.' Nation also reiterated Lawson's advice that they should have a lawyer present if they did decide to talk to the police.

• • •

'All through that winter, Peter was so alone, so isolated, and because he was isolated the defence was isolated too,' Ellis's barrister Rob Harrison told me. 'When the crèche closed I was sort of hopeful, really. I thought the people directly involved might start thinking about Peter again. With depositions coming up I needed people to talk to me about the crèche. I needed more contact than I was getting.'

But by then the police had convinced the crèche staff that Ellis was guilty. So when they thought about him at all, it was to blame him for their plight, and distance themselves from his tarnished reputation. Sandi was angry: 'I thought – Peter, you sod. How could you do this to us? How could you do it to the kids?' Gaye Davidson used the 'one rotten apple in the barrel' argument when people said, 'How do I know you're not all guilty?'

Behind the anger and the blame, was the fear. 'The women crèche workers were absolutely petrified,' Ellis's solicitor Chris Knight told me. 'It was like a police state thing closing in. They were all under suspicion. Enquiries were being made of friends and neighbours. It was a terrifying time for everyone on the periphery who felt they could be drawn into the vortex.'

As the waves of suspicion spread, talk of ritual abuse in preschools brought other Christchurch crèches to the edge of the vortex. Within days of the Civic closure, another one was drawn in.

• • •

Back in January 1992, Geoffrey Magnolia had begun attending Crèche X. 'He came to us because we had well articulated "keeping children safe" policies and procedures – toileting and nappy changing and so on – and also because I was there. I had cared for [Geoff] at another crèche when he was an infant. I was a friend of [Ms Magnolia],' explained Byron, one of the two male childcare workers at Crèche X.[19]

The staff and administrators of Crèche X approached sexual abuse allegations from a radical feminist perspective. In 1992, their belief in the truth of Ms Magnolia's claims about Peter Ellis and the Civic Child Care Centre was unshakable, and their commitment to supporting her and her family was absolute.

At the time, and in retrospect, the supervisor of Crèche X attributed Ms Magnolia's wilder comments to the anguish caused by her son's abuse at the Civic Crèche. However, Byron was a little more cynical:

> [Geoff] was completely terrified. His parents were completely terrified. I imagine they were terrified by their own power – they'd started something that was having a huge impact across the city and the country. Every day they had a new fear. 'Would you please keep [Geoffrey] away from the boundary fence because there's a paedophile ring and they're out to get us.' [Ms Magnolia] said the ring was planting paedophiles in every childcare centre in Christchurch. We always made time to listen to her fears. We did our

best to show that we were a safe and responsible centre. But we were raising our eyebrows to each other in private, saying, 'Which branch of the paedophile ring do you belong to?'

All year, Ms Magnolia worried about whether Byron was 'safe'. In April, Ms Lacebark told her that Kari had screamed 'It's not safe! It's not safe!', and expressed a dislike of Byron, following a visit to Crèche X. However, despite this alarming news, Ms Magnolia continued to send Geoffrey to the centre until early September.

According to Ms Magnolia, the crisis began when she collected Geoffrey from the crèche on Thursday 27 August. She found his behaviour to be 'quite weird', but he refused to tell her what, if anything, had happened. Over the coming days, she kept asking. Then, on 8 September she got her answer.

That day, Ms Lacebark told her that Kari (after apparently recalling her one visit to Crèche X the previous April) had identified Byron as 'Robert' – a man who 'hurt children'. Ms Magnolia questioned Geoffrey further, and to each of her questions – 'Did Byron touch your special parts? Have you seen his penis? Did he put his finger in your bottom?' – she received an affirmative reply.[20]

As it happened, back in 1985 Byron had worked at the Civic Child Care Centre for six months. Later, his own child had attended the Civic and Byron had served on the management committee. So it was probably inevitable that Byron would be interviewed sooner or later by the police. However, Bob Hardie assured me it was sheer coincidence that Byron was interviewed about the Civic Crèche by a member of his multiple-abuser-investigation team the day after Geoffrey Magnolia accused Byron of being a child abuser.

As the Civic workers had done earlier in the year, Byron did his best to be helpful at his 9 September police interview. He told Detective Karen McAuley that he didn't like Peter Ellis. The man drank too much, and was too fond of sleazy sexual innuendos. However, he could not recall any complaints about Ellis touching children inappropriately. After recording Byron's generally positive comments about the Civic, McAuley turned to an ongoing police preoccupation: the activities of consenting adults in private. Yes, Byron told her, the Civic staff did sometimes socialise together. Yes, a gay man called Robert once worked at the Civic. Yes, he knew about Ellis's relationship with Ms Kowhai. Yes, he thought one of the crèche workers and her husband watched porn movies. No, he didn't know of any relationships between Civic staff. Following the interview, the police praised Byron for his helpfulness. He was far more open, they said, than certain other childcare workers they could mention.

Two days later, on Friday 11 September, Detective McAuley advised the supervisor of Crèche X that a complaint may be laid against Byron the following Monday. Byron was notified immediately, and given a week's leave.

Over the weekend, the supervisor and administrator of Crèche X checked their practice manuals, consulted the police and planned their next move. Their policies and procedures, and the layout of their centre, made abuse unlikely. But they were determined to have a proper investigation. On the advice of Detective Sergeant Hardie, they agreed to say nothing about the allegation to the centre's staff until after work on Tuesday 15 September, and to say nothing at all to the centre's parents.

'Why didn't the police want you to tell anyone?' I asked.

'For the protection of the accused person,' the supervisor explained. 'It was only an allegation. The police still had to investigate it. They said that you actually aren't allowed to tell anyone when its only an unsubstantiated allegation.'[21]

On Monday 14 September, Ms Magnolia made a formal statement to Detective McAuley about Geoffrey's disclosures and the events leading up to them. 'I believe [Geoff] and [Kari] and there has not been a single thing they have said in the past which has not turned out to be true,' she concluded. Later that day, Byron was interviewed by Detective McAuley about the allegation.

'It was pretty straightforward because they'd already met me,' recalled Byron. 'I was able to say, "I am not the kind of person who would do this. I am aware of the need to protect children." Also, I could tell them where I was and what I was doing on any given day because of our record-keeping procedures.'

On Wednesday 16 September, Detective McAuley advised the crèche administrator that, as a result of Byron's interview, 'the case was as closed as it ever would be'. Next day, Geoffrey Magnolia disclosed nothing at his DSW interview. McAuley then advised the administrator that Byron could go straight back to work.[22]

Parents who heard the rumours and asked the supervisor what was happening were dealt with individually. 'I'd immediately take them into a private room and say, "What do you know? What do you need to know?" Nothing was hidden, but there was no public announcement either,' she told me.

At a professional level, the allegations against Byron were handled effectively, but at a personal level the crisis was devastating. Byron recalled:

> I was a mess. I love children. I'm good with children. Suddenly my whole life was called into question. I went back to work but I couldn't stop crying. I was dying inside. I struggled on for a while, then I dropped out. If it wasn't for the people caring for me, I'd be dead. There was a six-month period where I was relying on other people to cook for me, pay my mortgage, keep me alive. That's how basic it was.

Later in the year, when the dust was settling on the Crèche X upheaval, Ms Magnolia and her supporters kept trying to stir it up again. On each occasion, Bob Hardie dampened the crisis. In early November, when Colin Eade told Byron he was going to arrest him, Hardie told the crèche administrator there was no cause for

9.i: 'It was like a Police State Thing Closing in'

concern, and no reason why Byron could not continue in his job. Later that month, Ms Magnolia persuaded the administrator to arrange a meeting for concerned parents, but the meeting was cancelled on Hardie's advice. Then Ms Magnolia and her supporters began spreading word of the allegations by phone, and showing photos of Byron to children involved in the Civic Crèche case, at which point Hardie advised the administrator to threaten Ms Magnolia with defamation proceedings if she continued her slander.[23]

• • •

In the controversial wake of the Civic Crèche case, senior police officers have repeatedly affirmed their confidence in Detective Eade's handling of Ms Magnolia's initial complaint. When I invited Detective Sergeant Hardie to comment on the differences between Eade's response to Ms Magnolia's allegation against Peter Ellis, and his own response to her allegation against Byron, he showed no inclination to break rank.

'Different styles of policing,' he said blandly. 'Everyone to his own.'

'Two gay male childcare workers, both accused by the same woman of abusing the same child,' I persisted. 'One's in jail. The other's back working in early childhood education. The people at Crèche X reckon their man was cleared because he was innocent, and because they had good procedures. It hasn't occurred to them that your style of policing might have affected the outcome.' Hardie said nothing, but his derisive snort encouraged me to continue.

'What do you think would have happened in the Civic case, if Peter Ellis had been interviewed when the first complaint was made, instead of four months later? If the case had been shut down when Geoffrey Magnolia disclosed nothing at his formal interview? If there had been no mass meetings for parents, no support groups, no publicising of vague signs and symptoms, no urging parents to have their kids interviewed, no television and newspaper coverage?'

'I've often wondered about that,' Hardie admitted.

• • •

Throughout September 1992, the parental questioning and formal interviewing of former Civic Crèche children continued. In his fifth interview on 16 September, Julian Yew talked about tunnels, but failed to confirm Bart Dogwood's circle incident story. Kari Lacebark – the other complainant child alleged by Bart to be present at the circle incident – didn't have any interviews that month, but she did write a poem:

> Peter is bad, he puts poohs on my face, he can't stop it.
> But he might go to jail and I'll get a new dress when I go to court.

> Peter hates me. He said I'm yukky.
> Peter had a snake from Australia.
> It was dead. It didn't like the same food that the rabbits did.

Also in September, Detective Eade laid 15 more charges against Peter Ellis, and Detective Sergeant Hardie and his team stepped up their search for more offenders.

In the morning of 18 September, Bruce was walking home from the dairy with a bottle of milk and a newspaper when his property at 404 Hereford Street was 'invaded by the pagan hordes':

> It was unbelievable and horrifying. Fifteen police officers spent six hours at my place. They forked over the grounds looking for bodies. 'We know what we're looking for and we're going to find it.' They found nothing, of course. They went through the car. They went through my personal papers. They took away sackloads of my belongings. I was in shock. They said the storage cupboard under the stairs was a 'hidden cavity'. They said children were put down the laundry chute, which had been blocked off at the bottom for years. When Detective Jenkins was talking to me I started to get up off the couch. He pushed me down and called me every foul name you can imagine. He said, 'What are you going to do when you go to jail, eh?' I said, 'I'll die.'[24]

In the course of the Civic Crèche inquiry, the police seized all the videotapes they could find. Thousands of innocuous-looking tapes were viewed on fast-forward from beginning to end in case there was child pornography spliced into the middle. The cost in man-hours and wornout videotape players was huge, but no child pornography was found.

From Bruce's home, the police seized more than 80 videotapes. Some were legally classified 'adult' videotapes. None of the adult tapes were of any use to the prosecution, but one has become part of the crèche case mythology. The myth goes like this: Bart Dogwood said that Peter Ellis put a needle in his penis; Bruce had a porn video showing a needle being put in a penis. The implication of this story is that the video confirms Bart's allegation and connects Bruce to the abuse. I was told this story many times in the course of my research. Bruce was told it in the course of the crèche inquiry. His response was that he wasn't interested in such perversions and had never owned a videotape showing them. When the police returned his videos, he checked them to make sure. But for two-and-a-half years there was one tape the police refused to return.

> First, they said, 'This is an illegal tape.' But it was properly classified. Then they said, 'We have to hold it as evidence.' But it was never used as evidence. Then they said, 'We don't think it'll pass the new regulations.' So they resubmitted it. Finally it came back and I played it through. Right at the end there was a preview for a video on body piercing. It's certainly not something I'm interested in, but that's what all the fuss was about.

9.i: 'It was like a Police State Thing Closing in'

The 'hidden cavities' at Bruce's home also became part of the crèche case mythology. On 22 September, Bob Hardie phoned Bede Cooper at the Ministry of Education. '... found trapdoors and escape routes in THE HOUSE!!' Cooper noted.[25]

Bruce was a private man, a quiet old bachelor. He knew none of the women crèche workers. He knew no crèche parents or children. But in September 1992 the gossip-mongers of Christchurch transformed him into a mythological figure: the kingpin of the phantom Civic Crèche paedophile ring.

• • •

Ellis's former partner, Ms Kowhai, was another target of police attention. Detective Eade was in contact with her from the start of the investigation. Detectives Jenkins and Heath visited her on 14 September. Then, in the evening of 22 September, they asked her to come down to the police station:

> I was really scared. No one told me I could have a lawyer with me. I went down at nine o'clock and got home at midnight. I felt as if I was under suspicion from the start. They said I *must* have known what was going on. I *must* know if there's anyone else involved. They said, 'Out of the women at the Civic, who else do you think would do things like this to children? I said, 'No one.' They said, 'No, no, no. Not no one. If you had to say someone, who would it be?' Then I had to say a name. Neville Jenkins made me feel as if my kids would be taken away from me if I said nothing. I came out rethinking my whole idea of what was real. I felt as if the good feelings I used to have about the Civic were all wrong. It made me very confused.[26]

• • •

Among the extraordinary variety of Civic Child Care Centre parents, Mr and Ms Macrocarpa were in a category all their own. You could tell by their clothes, and by the dead cars on their front lawn, that they didn't give a toss about status and appearances. Terms like 'larger than life', 'anarchic' and 'feral' come to mind. Charles Dickens would have loved the Macrocarpas.

During the first meeting for crèche parents in December 1991, the Macrocarpas accused the speakers of conducting a witch-hunt, and walked out. Then, after visiting Peter Ellis and satisfying themselves of his innocence, they turned their backs on the investigation.

'Did you have your children interviewed by DSW?' I asked.

'Christ no, we're not stupid,' said Mr Macrocarpa.

Following the crèche closure, the Macrocarpas threw their formidable energy into supporting the Civic staff. They wrote letters, made phone calls and visited their Member of Parliament. When they told their MP they were supporters of Peter Ellis and the women crèche workers he said, 'If you've got any information you should go to the police.' Shortly after that, in what the Macrocarpas regard as a suspicious coincidence, the police came to them. Ms Macrocarpa recalled:

> Detective Jenkins walked in without knocking. He said, 'I want to speak to you about your association with Peter Ellis.' I told him to go away. I said, 'I know I don't have to talk to you. I'm not interested in talking to you.' He wouldn't leave. He said, 'If you won't cooperate you must be a child abuser.' I said, 'If you don't leave I'll ring someone in the police department who'll make you leave.' At which point he left.[27]

Ms Macrocarpa phoned her husband and he rushed home, convinced that the police were about to return with a search warrant. Mr Macrocarpa continued the story:

> I thought – What have we got in the house that we don't want to be hassled about? I had an AA road sign I'd been given. I wasn't sure whether it was illegal to have it, but I thought – Oh, I'll get rid of it. So I chucked it in the car along with all the videotapes – 26 of them, all three or four hours long. We knew the police were hot under the collar about videos, and we didn't want to lose ours.[28]

While the Macrocarpas packed the car, Detective Jenkins watched from across the road. When Mr Macrocarpa drove off, Jenkins followed. When Mr Macrocarpa stopped around the corner, Jenkins arrested him for receiving an AA sign. Shortly afterwards, more police arrived:

> You should have seen the looks of glee when they found the videotapes! Jenkins said, 'Okay, what's on the videotapes?' I said, 'There's music and there's children's programmes.' 'What's on the videotapes?' 'Music and children's programmes.' I don't know how many times he asked. Finally I said, 'Okay, I'll tell you: *Thomas the Tank Engine*, *Power Rangers*, *Postman Pat*, *Mickey Mouse*, *Donald Duck*, *Dire Straits*, *Queen*, *Tim Finn*, *Neil Finn*, *Crowded House*.' I went through every single one. I refused to stop until I'd come to the end. Jenkins was really pissed off. He told me I was a child abuser like my wife.

After six court appearances relating to the AA sign, Mr Macrocarpa was discharged without conviction. 'They were so vociferous,' his wife said. 'It was like we were the ideological enemy.'

• • •

Throughout September and October 1992, Ms Magnolia plied the police with the names and addresses of people from her past whom she believed were pornographers and child abusers. As a result, many of the people drawn into the vortex had only distant connections with Ms Magnolia, and no connections at all with the owner of 404 Hereford Street or the staff of the Civic Child Care Centre.

However, there was one indirect connection. Bisexual Bernard – proprietor of a second-hand book exchange and adult video store who flatted with Ms Magnolia in the early '80s – was a friend of the Macrocarpas. Bernard had never dealt in child pornography. He did not know the owner of 404 Hereford Street or any of the staff of the Civic Child Care Centre. In late September, when the police searched his home and shop they found no child pornography, and no illegal videotapes or reading matter. Bernard played no part in the crèche case court proceedings. But because he was the nearest thing to a link between the Civic Child Care Centre and pornography, stories about Bernard swirled wildly through the Christchurch rumour mill for months.[29]

• • •

On 24 September, 30 families of crèche supporters gathered at the YWCA for a fish and chip tea. Inevitably, the talk turned to the crèche closure and what might happen next. Crèche worker Marie Keys, ever the Pollyanna, said that everything would be all right, that it would all work out in the end. Jan Buckingham was more pessimistic. She could feel the storm clouds gathering.

'You don't close down a childcare centre for nothing,' Buckingham reasoned. 'When that Maori language assistant was arrested they didn't close down the school.'

'I thought that some of us were going to get arrested,' she told me. 'I thought they'd arrest Gaye because she was the supervisor, Marie because she was the deputy, Debbie because she was the senior childcare worker, me and Susannah because we knew Peter best. I almost got it right. But I thought we'd be accused of negligence, or of covering up for Peter. I never ever dreamt we'd be charged with child sexual abuse.'[30]

• • •

In the course of his enquiries into the crèche closure, union secretary Peter Lawson was told that the police had acted under Section 17 (2) of the Children, Young Persons, and Their Families (CYPF) Act. 'They said that not only did they have the right to do this, they had a responsibility to do so because the interests of the children were paramount,' Lawson recalled.

On discovering that Section 17 (2) authorised the police to do no more than 'notify the Care and Protection Coordinator', Lawson fired off a fax to Detective Inspector Pearce: 'Did you notify the Care and Protection Coordinator? If so, who was that person? Is there any other provision of that Act or any other Act … that you rely upon to take any other action … ?' Detective Inspector Broad replied laconically that Pearce was on leave, and that Lawson's fax would be treated as an Official Information Act request (which meant that the police could take up to 20 working days to reply).[31] By then Lawson had been getting the run-around for more than three weeks. Next day he issued a press release headed 'Police Accused of Acting Outside their Statutory Powers.'

After pointing out that the CYPF Act did not give the police the right to suspend the civil rights of any person, Lawson wrote: 'If they [the police] have a statutory authority upon which they acted then they should come out in the open without delay and tell the people affected what that authority is. If they do not have evidence upon which charges may be laid, then they should not cause other agencies to take action on a basis which assumes they have proof of some wrong doing.'[32]

On 30 September, a group of crèche staff appeared on the TV3 evening news, supporting Lawson's stand.

'We were really frustrated,' Susannah explained. 'We hadn't done anything wrong. The police had destroyed our reputations and they hadn't even said why. We'd written all these letters saying "What the hell are you alluding to?" but we had no answers. So we went on television and said to the police, "Put up or shut up!"'[33]

9.ii: Four Child Care Workers Arrested

In the morning of 1 October 1992, Jan Buckingham was tired from a family celebration the night before. After getting her younger children off to school she went back to bed. At 8.30am, Meg the boarder woke her from a deep sleep.

'There were three policemen standing at the end of the bed,' Buckingham recalled. 'One waved a search warrant at me. I blundered around looking for my glasses. I said, "Excuse me, I'm going to the toilet." Next thing the place was swarming with policemen. They let me phone a lawyer but I couldn't get hold of one. They wouldn't let me answer the phone or leave the property. I wish I'd known my rights.'[1]

Buckingham's teenage son was too sick to go to school that day. 'He had to sit on the bed while they searched his room,' she said. 'They turned his bed upside down. They questioned him. I said, "Surely I should be present when they're questioning him." The answer was, "No, no, no. It's just a little chat." They tapped the walls in his bedroom and said in front of him, "These sorts of wall are just right for hiding a baby's skeleton in." They took his two guitars as "evidence".'

During working hours, search warrants are normally issued by District Court Judges or Court Registrars (or their Deputies). After hours, they are normally issued by Justices of the Peace (JPs) who live in the inner-city. Curiously, the search warrants for the properties of Jan Buckingham and her colleagues were issued by an elderly suburban JP. These warrants stated that the police were looking for: photographs, documents and writings relating to children; videotapes, books and magazines 'relating to sexual acts, homosexuality or sexual contact with children'; children's clothing; photographic equipment; 'instruments or sexual aids used in sexual offending'; handwriting samples; and phone and address lists. The items were sought in relation to the offences of 'indecent assault, inducing an indecent act and sexual violation'.[2]

'They got a rake and dredged the fish pond,' Buckingham said.

'They got up on the roof and looked down the chimneys. They took away a couple of dog collars and a tinsel-and-wire Christmas decoration my daughter had made. They took a charm bracelet my mother had given me when I was a child. They took a book on beer can collecting and one on children's magic tricks. They took a fake fur coat I had made in the '60s. They found our secret stash of videos. We've got a houseful of kids and they're always taping over stuff, so when we record programmes we want to keep, we hide the tapes. My partner loves pool. The police found all his pool videos hidden in the wardrobe. They must have thought they'd struck gold.'

Around midday the police asked Jan Buckingham to go to the station for further questioning. 'I thought if I didn't go, they'd arrest me,' she explained. 'My son was home. I didn't want him to see that, so I went.'

• • •

At 8.30 that morning, Sigrid looked out the window and saw 'People jumping over the front fence. A car coming up the drive. Police cars on the road. People carrying in big bags and cameras.'[3]

While that was happening, her husband Winston arrived back from the dairy: 'They were getting out of their cars as I pulled up. Detective Nicholl wanted to know who I was. I said, "I bloody well live here. Who are you? What do you want?" He flashed a piece of paper at me. He said if I didn't cooperate I'd get arrested.'

Winston opened the front door and the police marched in. 'They handed me this piece of paper,' said Sigrid. 'They didn't say, hello, we're the police, or anything like that. Just "Read this". My mouth went dry. My whole body shook. I couldn't read it. The search warrant.'

While Sigrid sat outside, Winston checked on the police: 'I saw them looking up dolls' skirts in the bedroom. Sigrid has lots of dolls – her own, her mother's, her daughter's – there they were, looking up the skirts! We had a stack of videos. I said, "You're not taking them. You bloody well play them." So they fast forwarded a couple and said, "That'll do." But they took everything else. They took 95 condoms that I'd imported from Japan in the '70s. A couple of naughty magazines from the '70s.

'They said, "You're coming in for questioning,"' Sigrid continued. 'I knew I didn't have to go with them unless they arrested me, but I was scared they would arrest me if I didn't agree to go. So I went.'

As the police were leaving, Winston confronted Detective Nicholl. 'I hope you've got this right, because if you haven't I'm coming after you,' he said. 'There'll be a bloody inquiry after this. Just you wait and see.'

• • •

Shortly after 8.30 that morning, Susannah phoned Shona. Her voice was hushed and urgent. 'I've rung Gaye, I've rung Marie, I've rung Debbie, I've rung Jan, I've rung Sigrid,' she said. 'Everywhere I've rung a man has answered the phone and said I can't speak to them. They're all being searched.'[4]

Then Susannah phoned lawyer Gerald Nation. 'He told me to get round the staff lickety-split to make sure they knew their rights,' she recalled. 'Debbie lived closest, so I shot round there and knocked on the door. "Oh Debbie, I've just popped round for coffee." She believed me! She said, "Well, it's not really a good moment." Detective Jenkins said, "What's your name, missy?" I said, "I'm Susannah and I'm just checking that Debbie's all right – do you realise you don't have to talk to these people, Debbie?" Jenkins hated me and I hated him from that moment. Debbie said, "Oh, it's all right. I'm quite happy to answer their questions." I said, "Do you want me to stay?" She said, "No, I'm all right." I was so pissed off. I was trying to tell her by semaphore that she was allowed to have someone with her.'[5]

Debbie Gillespie was not all right, but she was determined not to show it. 'I've never been so frightened in my life,' she told me. 'I had no idea what was going to happen. After a couple of hours of police swarming all over my little house, Jenkins asked me to go down to the police station. I said, "I'll take my own car." He said, "Well, I don't know if that's possible." That was when I realised that I was going to be arrested.'[6]

Gillespie phoned her parents. 'In hindsight I wish I'd jumped in the car and gone over there,' her father said. 'But she wasn't crying or anything, and we thought the police would soon realise their mistake.'[7] Meanwhile, Susannah had arrived at Marie Keys' home:

> There were police everywhere. It was so unlike Marie. We used to call Marie and Roger 'Mr and Mrs Boring' because nothing ever happened to them. But Marie was still being Marie. She's saying, 'Oh everything's all right. Not a problem,' and I'm hissing, 'You don't have to answer any questions.' The police asked me what I was doing. I said, 'I've just come round to see what's happening. I heard it was all on. Are you coming to my place next?' I thought if they arrested me they'd really be in trouble, especially when my mother found out. They wanted me to leave. I said, 'I'd like to be here.' Marie said, 'Oh no, it's okay.' I thought: Oh Jesus! Marie has never been in so much as a protest march in her life. Anyway, we honestly didn't know – until that day none of us knew – that we lived in a police state. So off I went to Gaye's thinking – Right, I'll sort the buggers out! It seemed like a game.[8]

After nearly three hours of questioning, Marie Keys put her foot down: 'I'm not going to answer any more questions without a lawyer.' At which point Detective Marshall said, 'Arrest her', and Detective McAuley said, 'I'm arresting you on a charge of abusing Julian.' Julian? Which Julian? wondered Keys, as she too was taken off to the police station. The only time she had ever been there before was to report a stolen bicycle.[9]

By the time Susannah arrived at Gaye Davidson's home, there was a television crew outside, her property had been searched, the circular patterns on her carpet had been photographed and Davidson had been interviewed at length by Detective Legat. 'We sat and talked for about three hours,' Davidson recalled. 'At about midday he said he wanted me to go down to the station for further questioning.'[10]

Then Susannah walked in: 'Legat said he wanted to talk to me. I said, "Oh good, I'll talk to you now." Then he said something about going down to the station. I said, "I'll go now, Gaye." That was when I realised it was all for real.'[11]

After that, Susannah and some of her former colleagues gathered at Shona's home. For the previous ten years, Shona had job-shared with Sigrid in the nursery section of the crèche. Earlier that morning, when she heard that the police were at Sigrid's home, Shona assumed that she would be next.

'A friend kept ringing to check that I was all right,' Shona recalled. 'My daughter kept ringing. I told the man over the road that probably a whole fleet of police cars would be coming. Then I literally sat and waited. About 11 o'clock Winston rang. He said, "They've gone." I said, "Oh, okay, they'll be here soon." He said, "And they've taken Sigrid." I said, "Hang in there, Winston. I'll keep ringing you." So I rang him every half hour.'[12]

Around mid-afternoon, the former crèche staff at Shona's house heard that Sigrid was home. At that stage, though they feared the police would be coming for them next, they assumed that the worst was over for their colleagues.

• • •

Mr Gillespie phoned the police station in advance: 'Our daughter's been arrested, can we see her?' 'No problem,' was the reply. When he and his wife arrived at the station, he repeated his request. 'The uniformed bloke at the counter made a phone call,' Mr Gillespie recalled. 'Then he came back and said he didn't know anything about it. So we waited. And we waited. And we waited. We asked a couple of plain clothes guys who came in. We asked the bloke at the counter three or four times. No one seemed to know anything. Then we heard Gerald Nation being paged over the loudspeaker, so we knew something was happening.' After an hour and a half of fruitless waiting, Mr and Mrs Gillespie went home.[13]

The five women arrived separately at the police station. Debbie Gillespie and

Marie Keys were put in cells opposite each other. After an hour's wait, Gaye Davidson was also arrested, but she was kept apart from her colleagues. However, the police showed no interest in arresting Sigrid. 'I was asked about such things as whether I protested against the Springbok Tour or whether I was heterosexual,' she said. Then, after three hours, Sigrid was told she could go.[14] But for Jan Buckingham the isolation, and the interrogation, continued:

> The police asked question after question after question. I said I was happy to answer administrative questions. Anything else, I wanted a lawyer. When Gerald Nation came in, they started on the heavy questions. They said something about [Bart Dogwood]. I thought: [Bart Dogwood]? Who's [Bart Dogwood]? He mainly attended crèche on Mondays and Wednesdays. I rarely worked those days. He didn't know me. I lay money that kid did not come up with my name unprompted. They asked me if I'd ever seen Gaye and Marie have sex. What!!??? I was stunned at the questions. Gerald asked Detective Heath what I was meant to have done. Heath wouldn't tell him. Gerald got quite angry.[15]

That morning, Gerald Nation had contacted most of the women by phone. Then, when he heard they were being taken to the police station, he rushed down with a colleague to advise them. They found that Gaye Davidson already had a lawyer (whom she had phoned after she was arrested) and Sigrid didn't seem to need one, so they concentrated on helping Debbie Gillespie, Jan Buckingham and Marie Keys.

At that stage, Nation's only knowledge of the recent allegations against the crèche staff came from his meeting at the union a couple of weeks earlier. 'I'd picked up enough to be concerned that the women could face a raft of questions about their sexuality and their personal lives that might have nothing to do with any offending, but which could be used to create an unfair impression of them,' he told me. 'So I didn't want them to be involved in any more interviews. In the end, the three women made brief statements through us to the police in which they denied very clearly the allegations, on the basis of what little information we had about them.'

When Debbie Gillespie was arrested for 'committing an indecent act in a public place', she assumed that she had been charged with child abuse. Later, when Gerald Nation's colleague asked Detective Jenkins what the charge meant, Gillespie discovered that the police had something else in mind. Her response read:

> I have been told by the Police that the allegation is that I had intercourse with Peter Ellis in the hall outside the toilets at the Crèche. I have been told that this was allegedly witnessed by two children … I categorically deny that allegation. I have never been involved in any sexual act with him. The allegations in relation to this charge are totally untrue.

To Gillespie's parents, that charge confirmed their suspicion that the world had gone mad. 'She was supposed to have taken off her clothes,' her mother said indignantly. 'Of all people! Debbie wouldn't even run round naked at home. Not even as a joke. Let alone in front of kids at the crèche.'

Gaye Davidson, Jan Buckingham and Marie Keys were also confused by the charges they faced. These were: the sexual violation of Bart Dogwood 'occasioned by the penetration of his anus with a stick at 404 Hereford Street'; and the indecent assault of Bart Dogwood, Kari Lacebark and Julian Yew at the same address. Buckingham and Davidson said they had never been to 404 Hereford Street with children. Keys said she went there once with crèche staff and children to see Ellis's animals. All three women emphatically denied the abuse allegations.

On learning that the police intended to keep his clients in custody overnight, Gerald Nation held urgent discussions with Crown Prosecutor Chris Lange and the District Court Registrar. Then, around four o'clock, all four women were herded into the back of a police wagon and whisked off to court.

Having been advised of the arrests at a police news conference, the media was out in force at the courthouse. Inside, the police officers who came to watch were joined by a few, deeply distressed, friends of the accused. Mr and Mrs Gillespie were there because Gerald Nation had phoned them. Mr and Mrs Macrocarpa were there because they'd heard the news when they were at the police station fighting another round in their battle over the AA sign. Marie Keys' sister was there because her daughter had heard a radio announcement. Marie's husband Roger was there too, with their teenage daughter weeping on his shoulder.

'When I got home I knew things weren't right,' Roger said. 'The bed was unmade. The videotapes were gone. I made a few phone calls and found that Marie was at the police station. I rushed down. The police said they didn't know where she was. Then a member of the public told me he thought she was appearing in court.'

Initially, the women applied for name suppression. However, when they learnt it was unlikely to be granted, they advised the court through counsel that they were withdrawing the application because they did not want suspicion to fall on their colleagues. They also advised the court that they were denying all the charges because they wished to clear their names.

On behalf of the police, Crown Prosecutor Chris Lange requested that the women be denied bail.

'To my mind it was an extraordinary request, given that they were all people with no previous convictions, and three of them had families to care for,' Gerald Nation told me. 'Also, Peter Ellis was out on bail facing more than 30 charges, while Debbie Gillespie was facing one and the other women were facing four each.'

Bail was granted, but the conditions were draconian. The accused were not allowed to associate with any of their co-workers or with any crèche parents except in the presence of legal counsel. This ruling effectively isolated the women from their closest friends and supporters, and severely hampered their ability to organise their own defence. The bail conditions imposed on Christchurch's notorious Harris Gang, who were charged with shooting members of a rival gang around that time, were mild in comparison.

That evening, Susannah called at Jan Buckingham's home. 'Jan said, "Get out! Get out! You're not supposed to be here! I'll break my bail," recalled Susannah. 'I said, "I'm not talking to you I'm talking to your son." I wanted to let her know that we weren't abandoning her, because that was what the police had told the women – that the rest of the staff were ditching them.'

'I backed away down the hall,' said Buckingham. 'I was so scared, I couldn't sleep that night. I knelt on the couch looking out the front window, waiting for the police to come and take me away. Months afterwards – 8.30 in the morning – a car door slams: Oh my God, they're here, they're here. My belief in the world and the values I was brought up with was shattered.'

A week later, following an appeal to the High Court, the women's bail conditions were relaxed. By then, Gerald Nation was representing all four women.

'From October I was involved in the crèche case virtually full time for six months,' Nation recalled. 'I had support from my firm. Everyone in the office felt it was a really important case, and that we had a duty as lawyers to give it our best shot. I had staff to help with the research. The firm carried it financially without knowing when we would get paid, or if we would get paid.'

• • •

On 1 October 1992, the Christchurch *Press* carried two alarming and misleading headlines: 'Major Pedophile Network Revealed'; and 'Lawyer, Ex-priest in Pedophile Ring'. The fine print under the first headline reported that the police had found no links between child pornography and the 4000 names on an Auckland pornography dealer's distribution list, no evidence of locally produced commercial child pornography, no evidence that any paedophile investigation had been improperly halted or covered up and no evidence that 'people in high places' were involved in kid porn. However, during a nationwide investigation, the police had found some imported child pornography and 'locally produced photographs of children in various stages of undress'. The fine print under the second headline reported that imported child pornography had been found during police raids on two Wellington flats five months earlier.

Also on 1 October 1992, immediately after the women's court appearance, their identities and alleged crimes were broadcast to the nation. That evening, footage of four distressed women fleeing the camera's intrusive gaze led the television news. Next morning, front page headlines proclaimed the story. On radio, experts pontificated about child pornography and childcare centres, often in the same breath.

Radio diva Sharon Crosbie's *Nine to Noon* programme on 2 October opened with an item on the crèche case arrests. Next, day-care pioneer Sonja Davies expressed her belief in the existence of New Zealand-made child porn and her distress at the news from Christchurch. Later, Children's Commissioner Ian Hassall told Crosbie that cases of multi-victim multi-perpetrator sexual abuse had occurred in American childcare centres, so listeners should not be surprised if they occurred in New Zealand too. An extract from his interview – which effectively reasserted the great conspiracy-and-cover-up theory of child pornography – was carried on national news bulletins throughout the day. It stated:

> ... Hassall says there is a sinister element in paedophile networks around the world. Paedophiles perpetuate the common belief that sexual abuse of children is not widespread because they themselves are sexually attracted to children. He says paedophiles are quite well organised and some are fairly highly placed in positions of power. *Hassall*: 'There are quite well organised, for example, legal networks in the U.S. that are able to defend people who are charged with offences against children, and they do quite well.' Dr Hassall says that one of the reasons why the apparent rate of offences is kept down is because of successful defence lawyers.

• • •

On 1 October, Ms Willow was walking her dog when '[Ms Dogwood] drove up and wound down the car window, "The women have been arrested – blah, blah, blah – ritual abuse – blah, blah, blah – Satanic ritual abuse." Full on. The whole thing. I thought, well, if they've been arrested, it must be true.'[16]

During my research, scores of former crèche parents told me that when Peter Ellis was arrested they felt relatively detached. While they doubted his guilt, they were prepared to let the justice system take its course. But the arrests of the women were a different matter. For many parents, that event aroused such strong, in-group loyalties, detachment became impossible.

'I knew that was a fabrication of the wildest kind,' said Ms Maple. 'So far outside the bounds of reality it was laughable. They were ordinary, caring, motherly people like me and all my friends.'[17]

However, because the cost of speaking out was high, most former crèche parents kept their opinions to themselves.

'At a school function a woman said to me, "I heard you were involved in the Civic, isn't it terrible,"' recalled Ms Linden. 'I said, "But nothing happened. I know." I talked to her for over an hour about what the crèche was like, about what the complainant parents were like. At the end she said, "Do you think you might be in denial?"'[18]

'After the women were arrested I had a constant stream of people coming into my shop saying: "Isn't it dreadful, those women, what about your son, what are you going to do?"' Ms Jacaranda told me. 'I tried very hard to be staunch, but to say to some people's faces "I totally believe in their innocence" took a lot of guts. It's so hard when people are making accusations and you're trying to say: "But they're not like that, you don't know them, they're lovely women."'[19]

During October, Peter Ellis and Gaye Davidson received bullets in the mail. Davidson's ex-husband was accused of being a child molester. Debbie Gillespie's life was threatened. All the arrested staff avoided going out alone or being seen in public. All the non-arrested staff waited for the police to come.

'We couldn't sleep or eat for a whole fortnight,' said Sigrid. 'If anyone knocked at the door or the phone rang I'd jump.'

'Constantly on edge, waiting for a fight to happen,' recalled her husband. 'One night I got out of bed and went for a walk. I ended up in Tuam Street, looking at the council offices and thinking: if I can find a brick I'll whack it through the bloody window. I was that wild.'

In mid-October, Children's Commissioner Ian Hassall suggested that a blacklist of childcare workers suspected of child sexual abuse be established. Around the same time, Sharleen and Sylvia were redeployed by the city council (one as a parking warden, the other as a cashier), and Sharleen and Sandi became the focus of police attention.

Sharleen was young, attention-seeking and anxious to please. As the butt of Peter Ellis's teasing during her year on the crèche staff prior to his suspension, she was happy to complain about him when given the opportunity to do so. In Rosemary Smart's damning management review of the crèche, Sharleen's willingness to find fault with Ellis, to criticise her colleagues for their tolerance of him and to believe that he could be a child abuser were presented as virtues.

At the crèche case depositions hearing and trial, Sharleen was a witness for the Crown. It wasn't so much what she said that upset her former colleagues, as her ingratiating manner towards the police and her apparent willingness to run to them with every little tell-tale story.

'I think the other staff saw me as an ally of the police, but I wasn't volunteering. I just didn't know how to stop it,' Sharleen told me. 'I wanted to crawl into a shell and hide, but I was scared they'd arrest me if I didn't cooperate. I got lots of reinforcement from the council about how wonderful it was that I was helping the police. I was given unlimited time off to attend police interviews. Whenever the police wanted me they'd send a car to pick me up. I spent a good five to ten hours a week at the police station.

'I think I was targeted as the weak link in the chain,' she continued. 'I lived alone. I'm adopted. My mum and dad are dead. My birth mother lives in Australia. My sister was the closest person I had. Throughout this time she was in hospital.'

Sharleen's visits to the police typically began with an urgent phone call: 'You've got to come in right now – got to talk to you about this.' However, despite the apparent urgency, Sharleen was often left alone to contemplate the decor at crèche investigation headquarters:

> There were children's pictures around the walls with captions like 'thank you for saving me from the monster crèche' and 'thank you for putting bad Peter in jail'. There was a big whiteboard with 'Peter' in the middle and little offshoots to 'Gaye' and 'Debbie'. They had all these interrelationships worked out – did you know that Peter knew this person who knew this person whose uncle's friend down the road had a porn shop? I'd be left to sit and look at all this for maybe half an hour.

Then Detectives Legat and Heath would start their good cop/bad cop routine:

> One of them would keep thumping the table and saying, 'You've got to tell us everything that happened! For God's sake, children's lives are depending on this! Do you realise what he's done? How did he get away with it for six years? You know the women were involved! You must do! Surely you can come up with more than that! Why don't you go home and have a wee think about it, Sharleen? You go home and have a think.' Then the other cop would say, 'Don't give her such a hard time, mate. Don't give her such a hard time.' It was almost corny, but I didn't see it that way at the time.[20]

'What did they want from you?' I asked. The answer, it seemed, was confirmation of the unsubstantiated rumours that the police had relied upon to close the crèche and arrest the women. Sharleen explained:

> They wanted me to say I had seen things that I hadn't seen. They wanted me to say that Debbie and Peter were having an affair; that I had seen Peter taking children on the roof and dangling them from ladders; that I had seen him taking children to a house in Hereford Street. They constantly fed me bits of information. They said Peter was using children in a child pornography ring and supplying them to Asian businessmen and taking them to the Parkroyal. They told me about tunnels above the crèche and under the floor; about cages; about everyone's intimate relationships with everyone else and who was supplying drugs to parents. I totally denied all that because as far as I knew it was untrue. They gave me a book about Satanic cults. I felt obliged to read it because I'd be quizzed at the next interview. 'Did you read that? Did you read that paragraph?' I was starting to doubt what I had actually witnessed at the crèche. Things were getting twisted. So twisted.

Though she was confused at the time, in retrospect Sharleen was clear: 'I was fed a lot of bullshit by the police. I was told a lot of stuff that perhaps only existed in their minds. It was hysteria. Not just public hysteria and parent hysteria. Police hysteria.'

When Sharleen accepted the city council's offer of counselling, she was sent to Dr Karen Zelas. 'When I found out that Dr Zelas would be giving evidence against Peter

Ellis I felt so betrayed I got out,' Sharleen told me. 'I didn't feel strong enough to go to the personnel manager and say "I need counselling but I don't need this", but I went to Dr Zelas's colleague Trish Allen. I told her how disappointed and upset I felt about Dr Zelas. In the end I dropped the counselling. I felt that Trish was just pumping me for information, and I was getting enough of that from the police.'

• • •

Sandi, the other non-arrested member of the crèche staff singled out for police attention, was also the only staff member with a preschooler of her own. 'I think that gave the police power over me,' she said. She didn't recall what Detective Jenkins said, but she did recall being seized with anxiety: 'I rang him and said, "I've got to know. Are you thinking of taking my child off me?" He said, "It's a distinct possibility." I was terrified. My heart was pounding. My head felt like it was going to explode. Everything started whirling around. I sat in the corner hunched up in a ball. Yet I felt sane. It was the world that was insane.'

So Sandi took up the city council's offer of counselling: 'Just about every counsellor in Christchurch was tied up with aggrieved families. I was turned down by eight people before I found a guy who would see me. He told me I was having trouble coming to terms with the women's guilt. I said, "No, I'm not having any trouble with that! I'm having trouble with the people who say they're guilty." I never went back.'

Detectives Jenkins and McAuley visited Sandi seven or eight times, and stayed an hour or two each time. Sandi recalled:

> They asked me time and again if I was a lesbian. I kept saying, No, I'm not. 'Have you ever had a lesbian relationship with anyone?' No, I never have. Every time they went through the same rigmarole. They asked me about my ex-boyfriends, whether I'd used drugs, whether I was a heavy drinker. 'Does your husband have a drinking problem?' 'Do you enjoy pornographic movies?' 'Do you have a kinky sex life?' 'Are you into swapping partners?' 'Have you ever had sex with Peter?' 'Have any of the other staff had sex with Peter?' 'Do you know that Debbie Gillespie is a lesbian?' But whenever I said, 'Do you want to know something about the parents that are making these accusation?' Jenkins would say, 'No, I don't.' That made me really cross. They wanted every bit of dirt on us. True or untrue. But they didn't want to know the rest.[21]

Sandi's sister was a crèche parent, and she too received a visit from Detective Jenkins:

> He said the women were absolutely guilty. They must have known what Peter was doing. They were covering for him. It was like he expected me to go back to Sandi and say: 'Oh come on, you'd better spill the beans.' He said, 'Why won't the women tell us? Why won't they cooperate?' I said, 'There's nothing to tell. Has that occurred to you? The other thing is, they did cooperate with you. Fully. Right up to the time you went

in like storm troopers and ripped their houses apart.' I told him he should be looking into the backgrounds of the families making the accusations, why their children might be encouraged to say these things. He said, 'That's not the police's role. We're not doing that.' I told him our grandmother used to call at the crèche unannounced. My husband's parents used to call in unannounced at any time of the day. That was encouraged. I said, 'You're a parent. If you put a child in the bath and they'd suffered these abuses, wouldn't you notice? If your child had been defecated and urinated on and came home in different clothes, wouldn't you ask questions?' After two hours of arguing I was so upset I started to cry. I was standing there with my baby on my hip saying the police had ruined these people's lives. They would never work in childcare again and that was all my sister ever wanted to do.[22]

• • •

For Gerald Nation, the police and public attitudes to his clients were a great concern: 'People said things like, "I see you're representing that bunch of lesbians who're charged with those dreadful crimes." People seemed to have formed a strong view about the guilt of the women. It was very widespread, and the media was quite happy to promote it. The images of them at that time were very unsympathetic.'

He interviewed the four women closely about their lives and the allegations against them. 'I thought they were extremely compelling in their own defence,' he told me. 'I thought: this just doesn't seem right.' When he expressed his concerns to Detective Sergeant Bob Hardie, Hardie suggested that Nation look at the children's videotapes. When Nation looked at the videotapes he became more concerned. On 29 October he wrote to Crown Prosecutor Chris Lange, suggesting that the charges against the women were unwarranted, questioning the objectivity of the police investigation and inviting a senior detective with an open mind to re-interview the women. Around the same time, Detective Superintendent Neville Stokes, head of the Christchurch Police Criminal Investigation Branch, sought an assurance from Crown Solicitor Brent Stanaway that he was comfortable with the case going ahead.

The concerns expressed by Nation and Stokes failed to halt, or even slow, the momentum of the crèche case. When I sought comment from the Crown Solicitor's office on this outcome, I received three, mutually contradictory explanations, all from the same person. The first was that the Crown did not regard Nation's letter as a genuine attempt to halt the prosecution, but as paper-work for a future application for costs. The second was that Stanaway had taken the concerns seriously, and had reviewed the case carefully, before concluding that it should proceed. The third was that Crown Solicitors rarely, if ever, intervene to stop prosecutions. So, regardless of the concerns expressed, the case had to go ahead.

• • •

On 9 October, eight more charges were laid against Peter Ellis. Four were laid jointly with Gaye Davidson, Marie Keys and Jan Buckingham for 'circle incident' offences against Bart Dogwood, Kari Lacebark and Julian Yew. Three were for other offences against Bart Dogwood at 404 Hereford Street. One was for 'committing an indecent act in a public place' with Debbie Gillespie.

On 20 October, all five defendants made their first joint court appearance. On that occasion Debbie Gillespie was charged, jointly with Ellis, with the indecent assault and sexual violation of Fran Deodar. The interview on which Fran's charges were based was requested by Ms Deodar in the wake of the women's arrests. Fran had made no disclosure of abuse prior to the interview.

Also on 20 October, all five defendants were remanded on bail until the opening of the depositions hearing on 2 November. The November date was originally set for Ellis, but once the women were charged they too were included in the hearing. For all the accused, getting the case to court as soon as possible was a high priority. As long as the investigation continued, more charges were likely to be laid.

However, Gerald Nation did not want the advantages of a prompt hearing for his clients to be outweighed by the disadvantages of appearing in court with the notorious Peter Ellis. 'I told them they shouldn't have anything to do with him. They couldn't afford to. If they associated with him, the case against him would add to their difficulties,' he explained.

'Quite right too,' commented Rob Harrison. 'Other counsel in that position would have done the same thing.' However, because all the women's charges were laid jointly with Ellis, from the time of their arrests on 1 October 1992 until the end of the depositions hearing on 11 February 1993, the public and the media perceived Nation's and Harrison's clients as a single group. As Ellis's counsel, Harrison saw this as cause for hope.

'People are willing to believe horrible things about gay men, but when a gay male is charged jointly with four women that's bound to raise questions about the credibility of the charges,' he said.

Nowhere were these questions raised more acutely than in the minds of Ellis's former colleagues. Sandi recalled:

> It hit us: My God, Peter hasn't done anything. For a while we believed the police. But when the women were arrested we went back to our original feelings. At crèche I never felt uncomfortable about Peter caring for children. He behaved oddly, but not in the sense that you thought he was deviant. It was just Peter. He was odd. But he was a fantastic childcare worker and the kids did love him.

But by then the arrested women were fighting for their survival, and the dangers of being associated with Ellis were obvious.

'I thought Peter was innocent, but I was looking out for number one,' Gaye Davidson explained. 'I didn't want anything to do with him in case I was tarred with the same brush.'

'When I saw Peter in court I didn't know what to do,' recalled Jan Buckingham. 'I was scared. I was really scared. There were lots of aggro parents there. I avoided eye contact and came home feeling disgustingly, inhumanly low. Like Judas.'

'I suppose Peter felt abandoned,' mused Sandi. 'I think we were just so terrified for the four women, especially the ones with children. Our priority was to get them off because their families were being ripped apart.'

• • •

With the depositions hearing due to open on 2 November, the police scoured the Civic Child Care Centre, the Cranmer Centre and 404 Hereford Street for trap doors, tunnels, cages and ritual abuse paraphernalia. They checked the Masonic Lodge and other addresses suggested by complainant parents. They interviewed potential witnesses and encouraged them to believe the worst.

In particular, the police were looking for evidence to shore up weaknesses in the case against the women. Not that the case against Ellis was any stronger, but what it lacked in quality it made up for in quantity. A weakness in the 'indecent act in a public place' charge against Gillespie and Ellis was that the child witness had made no verbal disclosure. The charge was based solely on the interviewer's interpretation of the child's play with dolls. A weakness in the charges against Davidson, Keys, Buckingham and Ellis involving Julian Yew and Kari Lacebark was that they were laid solely on the basis of Bart Dogwood's circle incident disclosure. Neither Julian nor Kari had made disclosures supporting Bart's claim, and the Crown Solicitor had doubts about 404 Hereford Street as a venue for the incident. So, throughout October, the search for alternative venues, and for more disclosures implicating the women, continued.

On 28 October, Eli had his third, and Bart and Kari had their fifth, DSW interviews. Next day, Kari had her sixth interview. She said that Gaye put a sharp knife up her vagina, and Peter's mother kicked and hit her. Eli and Bart said they had sticks put up their bottoms. Bart talked about traps, tunnels and cages in the Cranmer Centre, and added Peter's mother, Sandi, Susannah and Suki to his list of offenders. Eli's list included 'Peter's mother', and men named 'Spike, Boulderhead, Yuckhead and Stupidhead'.

Over the previous couple of months, the police had interviewed Ellis's mother and Sandi at length, and made fruitless searches of their homes. Detective Nicholl had also shown Mrs Ellis an excerpt from a DSW interview in which she received 'honorable mention' from Kari Lacebark. Mrs Ellis recalled:

[Kari] had her head down. I said, 'I can't tell what she's saying.' Rob Nicholl got the transcript. He said he had to play the tape a number of times to work out what she was saying. I got the impression that what he thought she was saying was not necessarily what she was saying. There was a piece where it said in the transcript 'child indicates masturbation'. I said, 'Hang on, all she did was touch the baby's bottle!'[23]

When the police searched Mrs Ellis's home, they took an Asian mask from the wall and all the videotapes they could find. When they searched Sandi's home, they took her diaries. A typical entry read: '29 August 1991: Work was great. Outside all day, water play.'

• • •

By the end of October, the police had been investigating the Civic Crèche for almost a year, but they still weren't ready to take the case to court. With the depositions hearing due to open the following Monday, on Thursday 29 October, Chris Lange made his second application that week for an adjournment. In his ruling, District Court Judge Green stated:

> The matter of principal significance raised by the Crown is that, arising from these latest re-interviews, there is a real possibility that further people might be charged. Indeed Mr Lange put it at a high probability ... I think that the interests of justice require that this matter proceed ... It concerns me that they [the children] have been so frequently interviewed. It concerns me that there is the likelihood of further interviews. If there is any truth in the allegations ... it is very desirable ... that such recollections ... are placed well behind them rather than being revisited on such a regular basis ... The application is refused.

Weeks later, when Gerald Nation obtained a copy of Bart Dogwood's 28 October interview, he advised Sandi and Susannah that they had been named. Sandi was astounded: 'The year [Bart] was at the Civic was the year I was on maternity leave.' Susannah made ready:

> Gerald said, 'I don't want to alarm you, but if the police used [Bart's] evidence to arrest the women there's no reason why they won't arrest you, so be prepared.' I made some low-key phone calls to friends about taking the kids to school if I couldn't be there. I got the house spic and span. I chose my outfit. I ironed a skirt. The police never came. It was a real anti-climax. All I was worried about was how I presented my housewifely duties and whether I had a skirt. By then we'd realised that how people saw you was more important than what had really happened.

• • •

Rob Harrison planned his tactics for the depositions hearing in consultation with Nigel Hampton QC. Gerald Nation planned his in consultation with his colleagues at Wynn Williams and Co. Harrison's approach was based on the premise that no child sexual abuse had taken place. Nation's was based on the premise that his clients were not parties to, or were not present at, any abuse.

'At no stage did I suggest that nothing happened, because that wouldn't have helped the women,' Nation said. 'From a tactical point of view it was better for them not to be part of Ellis's fight at all.'

Support for Nation's approach can be found in the outcomes of preschool ritual abuse prosecutions in the United States. In cases in which one man and several women were accused, the man always faced the most charges and was the most likely to be convicted. But when male and female co-accused stuck together (as in the Amirault case in Massachusetts), women were likely to be convicted too.[24]

But no matter how sound their tactics, in view of the community prejudice towards their clients, both Nation and Harrison were in no doubt that if any crèche workers went on trial in Christchurch, there was a high risk they would be found guilty. So both counsel wanted to get their cases dismissed pre-trial.

In theory, a criminal case may be dismissed pre-trial either at the conclusion of the depositions hearing, or as a result of pre-trial applications. In practice, cases are rarely dismissed at the depositions stage. This is because the purpose of the initial hearing is not to consider the credibility of the evidence, but simply to determine whether there is sufficient evidence to justify putting the defendants on trial.

When Rob Harrison and Nigel Hampton considered the case against Peter Ellis, they concluded that, while there were obvious flaws in the DSW interviewing techniques and the conduct of the police investigation, those flaws were underpinned by a more fundamental problem: the contamination of the children's evidence caused by parental networking and parental questioning of the children.

'We figured that if we explored issues of contamination in depth at depositions we would have a good grounding for pre-trial arguments,' Harrison explained. 'So I went in intending to concentrate my cross-examination on those issues. After that, the plan was to put the information about contamination into a pre-trial application to have the case dismissed on the grounds of "evidence unfairly obtained". We thought we had a really strong case. We thought a High Court judge would have no hesitation in declaring the children's evidence inadmissible.'

Compared to Rob Harrison's one client, Gerald Nation's four clients faced fewer charges involving fewer children. All the charges seemed insubstantial and improbable, and the Crown Solicitor had indicated that, if they were dismissed at the depositions hearing, he would not re-lay the charges later (which, by law, he had the discretion to do). So Nation decided to mount an all-out attack on the prosecution case as it related to his clients – parental contamination, police investigation, interviewing techniques, the lot – at the depositions stage.

As lawyers, both Nation and Harrison had a primary duty to do their best for their clients, regardless of the interests of the other parties involved. So, as is usual when co-defendants in the same proceedings are represented separately, the two lawyers acted independently. In such cases, there is no requirement for defence counsel to consult each other. However, Rob Harrison thought it would be useful to do so.

'It makes good common sense to know whether the lawyer sitting next to you is going to be for you or against you,' Harrison said. 'Even if you agree to differ, it's always useful to know what angle they're planning to take, how much they're planning to ask, what witnesses they're planning to call, if any, and what those witnesses might say.'

Shortly after the women's arrests, Harrison phoned Nation and suggested they meet. He repeated the suggestion a couple of times over the coming month. But no meeting ever took place. So when the two defence counsel arrived in court on 2 November 1992 for the first day of the depositions hearing, neither had any idea how the other was planning to run his case.

CHAPTER 10

Depositions

BY THE TIME the depositions hearing began on 2 November 1992, Peter Ellis was facing 26 charges of indecent assault, 12 charges of sexual violation, six charges of inducing an indecent act and one charge of performing an indecent act in a public place. Gaye Davidson, Marie Keys and Jan Buckingham were facing three charges of indecent assault and one charge of sexual violation each. Debbie Gillespie was facing one charge of indecent assault, one charge of sexual violation and one charge of performing an indecent act in a public place. In total, the five crèche workers were facing 60 charges of sexual offending against 20 children.

In the wake of the crèche case, critics have asserted that the charges were laid in a climate of hysterical contagion, that many charges showed clear evidence of contamination, that some charges related to a child who had already been withdrawn from the case and that some charges were too absurd for any sensible prosecutor to take seriously. In a 1997 interview, a member of the investigation team rejected that criticism:

> It was a well run investigation. Colin Eade was a very thorough investigator. You never had any reason to question anything he did. Other people became involved as the case developed. We sought expert opinion where appropriate. We looked at how the allegations arose, why they arose, what they meant, whether they were reliable, how we should deal with them. The notion that we just accepted whatever the children said is simply untrue.[1]

• • •

On the first morning of the depositions hearing, an angry crowd gathered outside the court, and a belief in the defendants' guilt seemed all-pervasive. A member of the registry staff told Gerald Nation that the door he normally used to enter the courtroom was reserved for 'victims'. A veteran newspaper reporter told both defence counsel that they were wasting taxpayers' money on a hearing for scumbags.

Inside, tense clusters of spectators gathered in the public gallery. Some were there to support one side or the other. 'We felt we were doing something just by being there, and by being well dressed and looking respectable. We hoped it would help,' Debbie Gillespie's mother explained. Others were there to assess the evidence. 'We thought the only way we could ever know whether anything had happened was by sitting through the court case,' said Ms Sycamore.

Many people who wanted to be there – complainant parents, crèche critics, non-arrested crèche staff, council staff, Peter Ellis's mother – were potential witnesses, and were not allowed into court until after they had given evidence.

In the event, only 47 of the 92 potential Crown witnesses were ever called. Many potential witnesses who were not called had made statements to the police containing wild allegations about the crèche and its staff. Some allegations – especially the ones about pornography and drug dealing – carried great weight with the authorities at the time of the crèche closure and the women's arrests. Many of those allegations continued to feed the gossip mills long after the case was over. But because such allegations were unsubstantiated, and, in the context of the charges, irrelevant, they were never used in court.

In the months preceding the depositions hearing, the bald details of the charges were reported in the media. But until Chris Lange outlined the prosecution case in his opening address, hardly anybody knew what was really supposed to have happened at the Civic Crèche.

Lange said that children allegedly abused by Ellis, Davidson, Buckingham and Keys were kept in a tunnel or cavity beneath a trapdoor and made to stand naked inside a circle of adults at a Hereford Street house. When inside the circle, children were subjected to indecencies and made to kick each other's genitals. (Despite these extraordinary allegations, Lange later claimed that 'the question of ritualistic abuse did not form any part of the Crown's case against the defendants'.)[2] Lange also told the court that Ellis and Gillespie were charged with wilfully doing an indecent act in the crèche toilets, while Ellis alone was alleged to have: made children drink his urine; urinated on the faces of children; made a child eat his faeces; raped a girl; sexually violated other children using a finger or stick; and put a needle into a child's anus and made it bleed. Lange said the Crown intended to play 40 hours of videotaped evidence and present 141 exhibits to the court during the scheduled six-week hearing. At the conclusion of Lange's address, the public was excluded from court, and publication of the evidence was suppressed, while the children's videotapes were played.[3]

As it happened, only 19 of the 20 complainants had recorded formal disclosures (Mia Broadleaf, who made no disclosure, was a complainant because Eli Laurel alleged that Ellis urinated on Mia's face). The videotapes of 15 complainants were played. With the consent of the defence, the tapes of the other four complainants (who were the subject of charges against Ellis alone) were admitted without being played. This was because the procedural flaws in those interviews were less obvious, and Rob Harrison felt that screening them at the depositions stage would serve no useful purpose.

On 11 November, after six days of videotape viewing and a one-day adjournment to allow Peter Ellis to recover from being beaten up by skinheads, the adult witnesses began giving evidence. At that point, the court was re-opened and reporting by the media resumed. From time to time throughout the remainder of the proceedings, Judge Anderson issued orders suppressing the publication of certain evidence.

The first adult witnesses were the DSW interviewers. In order, they were: Sue Sidey (who conducted 28 interviews with seven complainants), Cathy Crawford (who conducted 17 interviews with five complainants), and Lynda Morgan (who conducted 13 interviews with seven complainants).

Sidey outlined her qualifications and experience, and listed the interviews she had conducted. At the completion of her evidence-in-chief, Gerald Nation began his detailed, three-day cross-examination. Rob Harrison was astounded:

> I went into depositions thinking that parental contamination was the paramount issue. The contamination came first, so whatever the interviewers did later seemed less important. But Gerald went through the theory and practice of interviewing with Sue Sidey in enormous detail. He went through the interviews involving his clients piece by piece. By the end of the first day it was pretty obvious what he was planning. I realised that I had to match him every step of the way. The media was there. The public was there. It was a battle for hearts and minds, really. I had to show that the case against my client was as comprehensively flawed as the case against Gerald's clients. The detailed cross-examination brought out a lot of information that we could use in pre-trial applications. But it also meant that I had to show my hand at that early stage. I had to ask questions that I might otherwise have kept in reserve. The upshot was that the entire defence case was revealed at depositions, and the prosecution witnesses had a good dry run before trial.

Perhaps because the tension in the public gallery was so great, the initial distance between the defence lawyers went largely unnoticed. The Crown lawyers told me that Harrison and Nation made a good team. Debbie Gillespie's parents gained a similar impression.

'Rob and Gerald worked together extremely well,' Mrs Gillespie said. 'They complemented each other: Gerald with his gentlemanly probing, Rob doing the more theatrical thing.'[4]

At the start of depositions, the distance between the accused women and Peter Ellis also went largely unnoticed. In any event, the more the women saw of the evidence against their former colleague, the more their feelings towards him thawed.

'When we saw the children's videos, we realised that the charges against Peter were a lot of nonsense,' recalled Jan Buckingham. 'I'm not proud of my doubts about him. I suppose I was just incredibly trusting and naive. I had this misplaced belief in our justice system, and in the integrity and common sense and intelligence of the people in it.'[5]

Before long, the defendants were passing notes and cracking jokes, and Ellis's talent for sketches and cartoons was being put to good effect. A surviving note reads: 'I think we should publish a Civic recipe book. Sell it for Xmas to raise funds. Noodle, tomato and poison soup, hedgehog-prickle hollandaise, kitten stew, urine sorbet. The possibilities are endless.' To which another hand had added: 'Gerald has already told us to shush!'

'We got up every morning and went to court,' Gaye Davidson explained. 'We sat there for hours listening to people saying we were child abusers. The only way we could cope with what was happening, with what might happen, was with a bit of black humour.'[6]

The outbreaks of stifled giggling from the defendants were a source of ongoing outrage to complainant parents and their supporters. In the *End Ritual Abuse Newsletter*, a grandparent with a knowledge of 'ritual abuse, child pornography rings and sex tourism' wrote: 'As I sat listening to evidence in court, and watched the behaviour of the accused staff, I began to realise that people who wield power over the weak and the vulnerable can lose all sensitivity to the enormity of what they allegedly did. These people … laughed at evidence of physical and psychological abuse, allegations of utmost depravity were greeted with smiles …'[7]

'There were grandparents in court all the time,' Debbie Gillespie recalled. 'When I saw [Grandma Lacebark] I understood the true meaning of the expression "a face like thunder".'[8]

The hearing stretched out for 11 long weeks. During that time attending court became a way of life for the participants. Each morning, Roger Keys picked up the accused women and delivered them to court. At the end of each day he took them home. Each lunchtime, the women were joined by around 30 supporters at the home of Gaye Davidson's partner.

Each morning, Peter Ellis's mother picked up her son and delivered him to court. Each evening she took him home. Each lunchtime he walked the streets of Christchurch alone. At the time of my research, those involved with the women's lunches looked back on Ellis's exclusion from their gatherings with varying degrees of self-justification, embarrassment and amnesia.

• • •

In the course of their evidence, the DSW interviewers admitted they had concerns about the reliability of some of the children's disclosures because, despite warnings to the contrary, parents had asked their children repeated, direct and leading questions, and had discussed their children's comments with other parents. The interviewers also acknowledged that their own techniques sometimes fell short of the ideal, and that some complainants had retracted their allegations.

As the defence pointed out, there were obvious problems with allegations that Ellis owned a real giraffe, that he turned a child into a frog and a cat, that he swung a child around a prickle bush by his penis, and that he put children in cages with lions and buried them in graveyards. Furthermore, since the police had ruled out the Masonic Lodge as a venue for the alleged abuse, the allegations concerning that building were clearly untrue. In response, the interviewers said that allegations of that sort were open to a variety of interpretations.

In fact, issues surrounding the interpretation of children's evidence were pivotal to the entire case. The police had found no physical evidence, no evidence of an unhealthy sexual interest in children on the part of any defendant and no adult corroboration of the children's claims. So the prosecution case depended entirely on the proposition that the children's videotaped allegations were reliable evidence of real crimes. In the aftermath of the case, critics claimed that those responsible for interpreting the children's videotapes had failed to carry out reality checks on the children's comments. As it happened, evidence to support that claim was revealed at the depositions hearing in relation to the allegations of Ryan Matai.

At the start of his first interview in June 1992, Ryan said he couldn't remember the crèche or any of its staff. But when Cathy Crawford introduced 'Peter' and 'naughty' into the conversation, he got the message. After pursuing that theme for almost an hour, Crawford summarised Ryan's litany of offences committed by Peter.

'He squeezed your arm, he smacked your bottom, he kicked your face, he choked your neck. What else happened?'

'He killed all the people with axes,' said Ryan. 'He killed all the boys not me cos I, I'm too fast for him …'

'And how did that make you feel?' Crawford asked, before seeking further examples of Peter's naughtiness.

Eventually, Crawford's apparent willingness to believe whatever he said began to worry Ryan. 'Oh he didn't really um smack me or hit me or something, I'm just joking, ha ha,' he said.

Undeterred, Crawford suggested they mark on a body-outline the places where Peter hurt him. Ryan pointed to the neck, hand and bottom.

'Now all this is true,' Crawford reminded him. Ryan told her it was not.

'I'm just really joking,' he said. 'I'm just really telling things. He pulled off my tummy button.'

'How did he do that?'

'With pliers.'

'Mmm and how did your tummy button feel?' Crawford asked. Then, when she directed his attention to the genitals on the body outline, Ryan came up with an allegation of sexual assault.

'He pulled um he put some cellotape on my penis and he took it off and blood came off with it,' said Ryan.

'Actually I'm just telling jokes,' he added. But Crawford appeared not to believe him. 'I'm just joking at the moment,' he insisted.

As long as Crawford continued her questioning, Ryan had little choice but to continue his story. He said that blood from his penis came down from the roof and went all over Peter. 'Actually there was so much blood … it was all gone and I wasn't alive,' he concluded.

At his second interview two weeks later, Ryan said he bled to death when Peter squeezed his penis with pliers and 'pulled the whole doodle right off', and recovered when Peter reattached it with cellotape. But the more Crawford pressed him for details, the more emphatic the boy's retractions became. 'I was just really tricking,' he said. 'I'm just really joking … I only joke, joking saying that, only joking, he doesn't, do you hear? … I just joking about the whole question … Do you know I'm just joking? Do you know that?'

That an imaginative five-year-old might tell stories of that sort is not in itself surprising. What is surprising, and disturbing, is the manner in which Ryan's story was handled by investigators and prosecutors in the crèche case. First, Cathy Crawford, in consultation with her supervisor Dr Karen Zelas, accepted that Ryan had made a genuine disclosure of sexual abuse. Next, Detective Colin Eade accepted that Ryan had provided evidence of an offence. Then, Crown prosecutor Chris Lange accepted that the charge of indecent assault laid by Eade was reliable enough to go to court.

Under cross-examination, Crawford's commitment to believing the child (at least when he made allegations of sexual abuse) was unshakeable. When Rob Harrison suggested that Ryan's story about Ellis being an axe murderer was a fantasy, Crawford demurred.

'If it's not fantasy, what would it be?' Harrison persisted.

'I'm not able to interpret what it could be.'

'Are you saying there's a possibility that at one stage at the crèche Peter Ellis killed all the boys with an axe?'

'No, I'm not suggesting that that be real. However, to interpret what it may mean – it's beyond my expertise.'

Crawford said that consistency in the central detail of a child's allegation was an important indicator of reliability. She explained that central detail related to what had actually happened, whereas peripheral detail related to descriptions of surroundings, and detail of time and place. With regard to Ryan's allegations, she said, 'He did give consistent central detail around being hurt.'

Harrison pointed out that Ryan also gave consistent central detail about bleeding to death after having his penis ripped off with pliers. 'You'd accept that he's making some of this up, wouldn't you?' he asked.

'It's beyond my role to assess the truth or the not-truth of a child,' she replied.

By the time she left the witness stand, Crawford had used the phrase 'it's beyond my expertise' so often that it had become a running joke. Later in the proceedings, when the court recorder's printer broke down, Judge Anderson asked the registrar to call a repairman. 'It's beyond my expertise,' he added drily.

• • •

When the interviewers had completed their evidence, a procession of 17 complainant mothers, two complainant fathers, a complainant grandmother and the occupational therapist of a complainant child passed through the witness box. In the course of their cross-examination, the defence established nine key points:

1. That the complainant parents chose the Civic Child Care Centre for their offspring because they regarded it as the best preschool in town.
2. That, during their children's years at the crèche, the complainant parents called at the centre frequently and never noticed anything amiss.
3. That the complainant children never came home from crèche smelling of urine or faeces, or with any suspicious bruises or needle marks. (But on the odd occasion some children came home wearing crèche knickers or a change of clothes.)
4. That, until the recent investigation, the complainant children never said anything about the crèche that caused their parents to make a formal complaint. (But some parents recalled comments from their children which they regarded in retrospect as evidence of abuse.)
5. That recent allegations in the media and the community prompted the complainant parents to re-examine their memories, to question their children and to discuss their concerns with other parents.
6. That, after re-examining their memories, many complainant parents came to regard their children's preschool and school-age tantrums, tiredness, headaches,

toileting problems, sleep disturbances, red bottoms, shyness, upset stomachs and clinginess as evidence of sexual abuse at the crèche.
7. That these complainant parents had formerly attributed the above problems to allergies, infections, poor hygiene, family tensions, new babies, moving house and starting school.
8. That the complainant children's behaviour since they had become involved in the crèche investigation was far worse than it had ever been when they attended the crèche.
9. That in the course of discussing the crèche with their parents, many children had made highly improbable, and often impossible, allegations.

Half the complainant parents had obtained disclosures of sexual abuse directly from their children; the other half had left that job to DSW interviewers. The parents who had obtained disclosures admitted that they had asked their children repeated, leading or direct questions, and had read them sexual abuse prevention books. However, they were adamant that their offspring's more significant disclosures were spontaneous and true.

'I sincerely believe that children do not make up things like people doing poos and wees in their mouths,' Ms Laurel said.

• • •

Next, Ms Magnolia (who was not a complainant parent because her son had made no disclosure) gave evidence and was cross-examined about her mental health problems, the stresses in her life and her interest in sexual abuse, and about her role in initiating and sustaining the crèche inquiry.

She said that, from the time of her son's 'I don't like Peter's black penis' comment, she discussed sexual abuse with other crèche parents, and made notes on their children's comments and behaviour. 'When [Geoff] first talked to me, because of my work in sexual abuse, I knew it was rare for only one child to be abused, and I knew certain profiles of abusers are attracted to work with children,' she explained.

Ms Magnolia acknowledged that crèche parents were told not to pass information among themselves. 'I intentionally didn't listen to that because I have a strong belief that secrecy in sexual abuse cases keeps it happening,' she said. She also acknowledged that she told the police of her suspicions about Asian tourists at the Parkroyal, and about ritual abuse at the Masonic Lodge, and that she collated her notes into a handout for an early-August meeting between some concerned parents and police officers.

To crèche supporters, Ms Magnolia's evidence was a revelation. 'Do you understand how it happened now?' Debbie Gillespie asked her parents. 'Do you see how it all fits together?'

• • •

The remainder of the Crown witnesses comprised five medical practitioners, nine police officers, a hotel proprietor, the administrator of Marriage Guidance, four people who had made statements critical of the crèche staff, Bruce (the owner of 404 Hereford Street) and the author of a hand-written letter on which the police placed great store. All but six police officers and one medical practitioner gave evidence before the court adjourned for a one-month Christmas break.

Four of the medical practitioners appeared in person; the evidence of the fifth was admitted by consent. Doctors Metherall and Thornley said that their inconclusive findings were 'consistent with' sexual abuse. Dr Gray said that Mia Broadleaf's hymen showed evidence of penetration. (Mia had disclosed no offence, but Ellis was charged with urinating on her face on the basis of Eli Laurel's disclosure.) However, Dr Gray acknowledged that Mia's mother hadn't been able to recall any particular time when Mia's behaviour was a concern, or any time when Mia suffered from frequent urinary infections or complained of a sore bottom. Dr Lyttle said that when she examined Judy Balsa in September, she concluded that the child's hymen showed evidence of penetration. But when she re-examined Judy in December, she concluded that the child's hymen showed no evidence of penetration.

The hotel proprietor reported that he had seen Peter Ellis taking children for a walk. The Marriage Guidance administrator (who worked upstairs from the Civic Crèche) reported that Ellis had come through her office on two occasions: once to blow bubbles from the balcony; once to retrieve a ball.

The two detectives who appeared before Christmas reported on their specialist roles. Ken Legat was responsible for the labelling and custody of exhibits. The other detective prepared a time-flow chart of child and staff attendance at the crèche. To Mr and Mrs Gillespie's horror, that detective was Michael Chappell, their nephew and godson.

'I don't care how small his role was. His cousin was one of the accused. He shouldn't have been there,' Mr Gillespie said indignantly. 'I was so wild I almost rang the vicar to ask how we could be removed from being his godparents.'

In addition to the statements of complainant parents, in the course of the investigation the police took statements from over a dozen other people criticising the centre and its staff. At the depositions hearing, four of those people gave evidence. They were: former crèche workers Sharleen and Ms Kapok (who was also a crèche parent); Debbie Gillespie's former partner Belinda (who had worked as a relieving childcare worker); and Peter Ellis's former partner Ms Kowhai.

In their evidence-in-chief Ms Kapok, Sharleen and Belinda focussed on the layout, routines, policies, procedures, staff rosters and staff/child ratios at the crèche during Peter Ellis's time there (August 1986 to November 1991). Ms Kapok worked with Ellis for four months at the end of 1986. Sharleen worked with him for nine months in 1991. As a relieving childcare worker, Belinda worked with him for two weeks in late-1990, and for less than one day a week in 1991. This meant that, in total, the three Crown witnesses who gave evidence about how the crèche functioned, worked with Ellis for only 16 months of his five-and-a-quarter years at the centre.

As it happened, the Crown had at least eight childcare workers among its potential witnesses who were well qualified to talk about Ellis's entire period of employment at the Civic. However, presumably because they were openly sceptical of the allegations, they were not called to give evidence for the prosecution.

In their evidence, Ms Kapok, Sharleen and Belinda described the Civic as a busy, well-run, open place, and Peter Ellis as a popular childcare worker who avoided toileting children. However, each woman told an additional story that lent oblique support to the prosecution case.

Ms Kapok said she went with crèche children and staff to see Ellis's animals at his Hereford Street home on two occasions in late 1986. Sharleen and Belinda said that Ellis took children on lots of walks. They also said he discussed sexual matters with them. Under cross-examination, Sharleen admitted that Ellis teased her and thought her naive. 'Anything he said I felt that it was usually embellished and exaggerated … he had a tendency to shock me,' she said.

Ms Kowhai said that Ellis drank heavily during the two years he lived with her, and that he babysat her own and other non-complainant children at her home, sometimes overnight. She also recalled an occasion when she saw him coming out of the adults' toilet at the crèche with a little girl.

By the time Bruce was called to give evidence, the earlier mood of unquestioning belief among court staff and newspaper reporters was giving way to troubled scepticism. Furthermore, with regard to the police belief that Bruce's home was the venue for organised abuse, some television reporters had been sceptical for a while. This was because, back in October when 404 Hereford Street was named on the women's arrest warrants, Bruce invited CTV and TV3 reporters on a tour of his property.

'I showed them the so-called hidden cavities: the laundry chute with a vertical 15-foot drop to the ground floor; the cupboard under the stairs; the manhole giving access to the internal plumbing; the space between two walls that was created when part of the house was turned into a flat. They fell about laughing,' he recalled.

There was also some levity during Bruce's session in the witness box. 'I had great fun,' he told me. '[Crown Solicitor] Stanaway asked me if anything strange ever happened at my place. I said, "There are ghosts of course." The conversation went on for some time. The judge was grinning. The girl transcribing the record was grinning. People were cracking up all over the place.'[9]

The last witness before Christmas was the author of a dubious hand-written letter seized by the police in the course of their investigation. This letter, together with a jointly authored piece of creative writing also seized by the police, was widely distributed at the time of the court proceedings.

'The policemen who interviewed me were like everyone else at that time – totally convinced that Peter and the women were guilty,' Childcare Association tutor Alison Mary recalled. 'When I expressed doubts they tried to sway me by showing me these pieces of writing. I said I thought they were stupid, but hardly criminal. I later found out that the bits the police were excited about weren't even written by crèche staff. It was a big fuss about nothing.'[10]

The author of the letter told the court that his links to the crèche were remote, that the letter was a work of fiction written in a moment of abject silliness and that it had nothing to do with any crèche workers. Judge Anderson placed suppression orders on both documents. (After the Ellis trial, the suppression orders were reimposed by Justice Williamson.)

• • •

During the depositions hearing, the parental networking continued and several children came up with fresh disclosures. When Mikey Ash said that crèche staff buried children alive in coffins, his mother advised Detective Eade. When Lara Palm disclosed that other adults abused her at 'Peter's house', her mother audiotaped her disclosure and booked her in for another interview. When Kane Juniper's disclosures seemed to 'support that of other children', his mother sent notes of the conversation to Colin Eade with a covering letter that graphically illustrated the paranoia of the times:

> [Mikey Ash] has told his mother that some of the children were buried over their heads in the sandpit and were given straws that had been used for bad touching to be able to breathe. [Mikey] said that [Kane] may have been one of the children. I told [Kane] this and he said he could not remember ... I feel he is repressing a memory of the sandpit ... An ongoing suspicion for me is Crèche X ... In the last few days I have learnt that a man currently working there called Byron has been identified by some of the Civic Crèche children as Robert, Peter's Friend ... I am very worried about these children and urge you to investigate the possibility of abuse occurring there now ... [Kane] has a friend who has just started attending church ... This little boy was playing churches the other week with [Kane] ... I did question him about Peter and ritual and he turns off and says he can't remember ...

Around the same time, the slogan 'The women are guilty' was painted onto the courthouse wall, former crèche worker Suki was interrogated by Interpol in London, social worker Jan Gillanders sought information on 'group/organised abuse' from 'ritual abuse workers' and the DSW-based Family Violence Prevention Coordinating Committee applauded the rise in ritual abuse awareness nationwide: 'The Ritual Action Group has provided a number of successful workshops around the country … worked alongside a number of strong and courageous survivors. Their work has enabled survivors' stories to be told and heard, despite encountering resistance from people not wishing to believe ritual abuse occurs.'[11]

Among those showing resistance to the notion that ritual abuse occurs were Christchurch City Council officers Alistair Graham and Martin Maguire.

'I must have been looking a bit sceptical, because I can remember Detective Legat saying: "You gotta decide whether you're on the side of the enemy or the side of the angels",' recalled Maguire.

'We did worry about Ken Legat, I tell you,' Graham admitted. 'He talked about Suki as if she was part of some international child abuse racket. He talked about child pornography rings, about videos being made. I'd been on the Indecent Publications Tribunal but I'd never come across the sort of things he was describing. I was investigated at one stage. My garage was bombed. I used to think: is my telephone being tapped? Am I being followed?'

'At the investigation headquarters the police had a whiteboard with a diagram connecting up all the people in the supposed paedophile ring,' added Maguire. 'They seemed to think that just about everyone was a sexual abuser. I used to walk down the street after talking to them thinking: is that person a paedophile? Is anybody on this street normal?'[12]

Over the same period, child sexual abuse was never out of the news. On 9 November, under the headline '500 Sexual Abuse Claims a Week', an ACC spokesperson reported that the rise in sexual abuse claims that had begun prior to the 1 October cut-off date for lump sum compensation claims was still continuing.[13]

• • •

In December, the veteran reporter who had earlier advised defence counsel of his conviction that their clients were guilty, advised them that he thought the case was nonsense and should be thrown out immediately. Given the number of charges against Ellis, this was not a realistic option for him. However, the nature of the evidence adduced in relation to his co-defendants gave crèche supporters hope that the women would be discharged at the end of the hearing.

'All through depositions, a lawyer friend said to us, "It's okay, the women are going to get off. Everyone knows its a load of bollocks,"' Ms Hawthorn told me.[14] But Gerald Nation's optimism was tempered with concern:

The scary thing was, the allegations against the women were incredible, the evidence against them was slight, yet the police seemed totally convinced of their guilt. They put huge amounts of time and effort and money into trying to build up a case against them. They had six or seven police officers on the job. They brought in surveyors to do sophisticated graphics of 404 Hereford Street. They took photos and a video of the house. There didn't seem to be any acknowledgement from the police that the case was weak. I found that quite frightening.

Nation's hopes for an early discharge for his clients were not shared by the Executive Judge in the Christchurch High Court. Shortly before Christmas, he indicated that he expected all the defendants to be committed for trial, and advised counsel that pre-trial applications would begin on 15 March 1993. For a case in which the 11-week depositions hearing would not end until 11 February 1993, that was an extraordinarily tight timetable.[15]

By the time the Executive Judge made his announcement, Dr Karen Zelas had been formally engaged as the Crown's expert psychological witness, Rob Harrison had been given the names of some suitably qualified Australian experts, and Gerald Nation had contacted Australian child psychiatrist Keith Le Page.

Le Page had been practising psychiatry since 1953. In the '50s and '60s he worked full time in child and family psychiatry. Since 1968 he had been in private practice, specialising in general psychiatry, with lesser amounts of child and family psychiatry. In 1985, when he found there were no guidelines for the evaluation of child sexual abuse in current psychiatric textbooks, he researched the literature and prepared his own. Le Page's guidelines were accepted by the South Australian Branch of the Australian Medical Association and presented at law conferences in Australia and New Zealand in 1990. By 1993, Le Page had been involved in about 104 child sexual abuse cases.[16]

In December 1992, Gerald Nation sought an urgent order directing that the children's videotapes be made available to Dr Le Page. In January, Harrison also engaged Le Page as his expert witness.

'I understand defence counsel approached various people in New Zealand who were simply not prepared to go head to head with Karen Zelas,' a senior Justice Department employee told me. 'They must have known she'd be too good for them, or else they agreed with everything she said.'

This view was widespread at the time of the crèche case court proceedings, but, as the experience of Rob Harrison's initial expert witness 'M' shows [see Ch.8.iii], it was self-serving, ill-informed and wrong. This is not to suggest that all the independent-minded sexual abuse experts in New Zealand were deterred from participating in the crèche case by overt intimidation. The problem is more complicated than that.

At the heart of the problem is s. 23G of the Evidence Act [see Ch.3.ii]. Section 23G allows child psychiatrists or child psychologists with 'experience in the professional treatment of sexually abused children' to give expert evidence in child sexual abuse cases. Such experts acquire their experience by working for state-funded programmes for the detection, treatment and prosecution of child sexual abuse. These state-funded programmes are controlled by DSW, ACC and Family Court administrators who believe that child sexual abuse is an extremely serious and widespread problem. Under such administrators, professionals who interpret most things children say and do (or don't say and don't do) as signs of sexual abuse are bound to receive more work than professionals who question such interpretations. Consequently, sceptical experts with the knowledge and ability to challenge Dr Zelas and her like-minded colleagues often lack the experience to qualify as expert witnesses under s. 23G. Furthermore, sceptical experts who do qualify, and who are brave enough or reckless enough to question the administrators' beliefs about child sexual abuse, are often stigmatised by professionals with opposing views, and their careers as expert witnesses tend to be short-lived as a result. For all these reasons, there is no pool of sexual abuse experts available to defence counsel in New Zealand.

• • •

Another concern for Gerald Nation was legal aid. His initial application on behalf of the women was filed in November, and declined in December. On review from a District Court Judge, the application was granted in January, subject to contributions totalling $25,250 being paid by the defendants. But it wasn't until the end of March, when the District Legal Services Subcommittee considered Nation's application for $108,000 to cover the costs of preparing and conducting the women's defence at the depositions hearing, that the legal aid contribution to his costs for the preliminary proceedings was fixed retrospectively at $43,220.[17]

• • •

The depositions hearing resumed on 19 January 1993. The Crown's remaining witnesses were Detectives Colin Eade, Rob Nicholl, Greg Heath, Neville Jenkins, Karen McAuley, Brent Marshall and Ken Legat, Constable Diane Smith and Dr Heather Lyttle. In their evidence-in-chief, the police officers described their interviews with, and their arrests of, the defendants, and their scene examinations at 404 Hereford Street, the Cranmer Centre and Civic Child Care Centre.

As they had done at 404 Hereford Street, the police prepared layout plans and took photographs of the Cranmer Centre and the Civic Child Care Centre, and scoured both venues for tunnels, trapdoors, cages, child pornography and ritual abuse paraphernalia. Their search of the Cranmer Centre was based on Ms Dogwood's

2 October visit with her son. According to Ms Dogwood, Bart said he was hung in a cage and had to kill animals and a little boy called Andrew in the hall on the second floor. Andrew was in a coffin, and Bart stabbed him with a knife in front of adults and children. Bart also said that Peter took him into the roof, and they came down a rope through a trapdoor in the ceiling.

On 19 October, in an effort to check Bart's story, Detective Jenkins accompanied by social worker Jan Gillanders and Mr and Mrs Laurel, took Eli on a tour of the Cranmer Centre. The interior of the building held no interest for Eli, but, when they reached the second floor, the boy wanted to climb onto the roof.

Following Eli's visit, Detectives Jenkins and Legat climbed onto the roof themselves. They found 'two manhole covers that are not visible from the ground' that provided access to the ceiling cavity above the Embroiderers' Guild. On entering the cavity, the intrepid detectives discovered that they could climb along the ceiling beams to the manhole above the kitchen next to the hall on the second floor.

A few days later, New Zealand Childcare Association (NZCA) tutor Ms Rata observed the follow-up of Jenkins' and Legat's discovery:

> The Civic staff told me the police were accusing them of all sorts of bizarre stuff. I didn't know whether to believe them or not until I saw police in the kitchen opposite the NZCA room. They were up a ladder taking fingerprints around the manhole. They were climbing around in the ceiling looking for coffins. They were measuring the distance to the floor, trying to figure out how Peter could have taken children through the roof and lowered them down a rope into the kitchen and put them in the oven. I had to say, "Okay, you Civic women are not crazy! You are not paranoid!"[18]

In cross-examination, defence counsel established that the police had found no improperly disturbed graves, no child pornography, no Asian connection, no cages and no material evidence of any sort to support the charges against the crèche staff.

When the Crown witnesses had completed their evidence, Gerald Nation called the accused women and their colleagues Sandi and Susannah as witnesses for the defence. Calling defence witnesses is an unusual and risky step at a depositions hearing because it gives the prosecution an early opportunity to test the strengths and weaknesses of the defence case. But Nation's clients wanted to declare their innocence at the first opportunity, and Nation wanted to adduce evidence to support his argument that the children's evidence was so unbelievable no reasonable jury could convict upon it. He also believed that, if the women were committed for trial, an application for discharge pre-trial would be considered more sympathetically if his clients had given evidence at that early stage.

• • •

In continental Europe during the 16th and 17th centuries, witch suspects were often convicted on the basis of confessions elicited by torture or the threat of torture. In England, where torture was officially banned, witch suspects were often convicted on the basis of accusations elicited from compliant and suggestible children.[19] Either way, as examples of unreliable evidence obtained by pressure or manipulation, witch confessions and witch accusations were two sides of the same coin.

From the 16th century to the present day, courts have had the power to disallow confessions elicited by threats or inducements, and complaints elicited by pressure or suggestion. Traditionally, judges have decided such matters by weighing the public interest in upholding the rights of suspects to a fair trial, against the public interest in securing the conviction of offenders.[20] Most of the time, the system works. However, injustices like the conviction of the Guildford Four during the 1980s IRA bomb scares in Britain indicate that, in times of moral panic, the pressure on judges to secure convictions can override the rights of suspects to a fair trial.

In New Zealand, the Bill of Rights Act gives judges a firm legislative basis for upholding the rights of people accused of criminal offences. Since 1990, any breach of the Act leading to a confessional statement will *prima facie* result in its exclusion from trial, regardless of the seriousness of the crime or the public outcry for a conviction.[21] Also, since 1989, the Children, Young Persons, and Their Families Act has upheld the rights of children suspected of committing offences. However, the laws that protect hardened criminals and young toughs from being pressured or manipulated into incriminating themselves, do not protect vulnerable young children from being pressured or manipulated into incriminating others; nor do they protect the people they incriminate. Consequently, when judges consider the admissibility of children's allegations that do not appear to have been provided voluntarily, they have to turn for guidance to previous court decisions on similar issues. Also, when they weigh the rights of suspects in sexual abuse cases against the public interest in securing convictions, their conclusions often reflect the messages imparted at seminars conducted by Dr Karen Zelas [see Ch.4.ii]. Those messages are: that child sexual abuse is an extremely serious and widespread problem; that children who have been intimidated into silence are unlikely to disclose voluntarily; and that, when subject to expert analysis, apparently insubstantial and unbelievable disclosures obtained through the use of persistent and leading questions can be found to be reliable. All things considered, persuading any New Zealand judge that the Civic Crèche prosecution should not proceed because the children's evidence was unreliable, was not going to be easy.

• • •

On 9 and 10 February, counsel gave their closing addresses. Gerald Nation argued that a jury trial for his clients could not be justified because of the lack of credible evidence. Rob Harrison argued that the evidence against his client should be declared inadmissible because it had been unfairly obtained. Chris Lange argued that the evidence was both believable and admissible, and that only a jury that had seen the children examined and cross-examined could determine the credibility of their allegations.

On 11 February, Judge Anderson announced his decision to a packed court. By then, Gerald Nation had prepared his clients for the worst. 'Gerald cushioned us all the way through,' Gaye Davidson recalled. 'At first he gave us the impression that our case wouldn't go past depositions. Then about halfway through he said, "I don't know whether we are going to get a discharge. I think we might have to go through with this." Even so, the judge's decision came as a terrible blow.'[22]

'It was like Judge Anderson hadn't been listening,' Ms Macrocarpa recalled. But that observation does not do justice to the attention he paid to the evidence, or to the task he faced when he came to make his decision.

If Anderson had been satisfied that a *prima facie* case had been established, he could have committed the defendants for trial without further ado (judges are not required to give reasons for their decisions to commit). Alternatively, if he had been satisfied that the evidence against the women was totally without merit, he could have discharged them forthwith (though to stand in front of the crèche case juggernaut at that stage would probably have been a foolhardy move).

Over the years, crèche critics have claimed that Judge Anderson's decision to commit the defendants indicated that he 'believed the children' and endorsed the procedures followed by the police and interviewers, but his judgment does not support that claim.

'Whatever my decision is today it does not remove the presumption of innocence in relation to the defendants,' Anderson told the court. He said his task was simply to determine whether there was sufficient evidence to justify putting the defendants on trial. 'In determining sufficiency, the judge must consider whether the evidence is capable of belief, but he is not required to believe it. If it is capable of belief, the question of whether or not it is to be believed is a question for the jury,' he explained.

Anderson then pointed out that the defence had the right to request, and the judge had the right to require, that the complainants be brought before the court and cross-examined. That option is rarely requested in child sexual abuse cases, and rarely granted. However, the Court of Appeal has ruled that if a depositions judge is satisfied that the prosecution evidence is so weak that cross-examination of the complainants, when considered together with the other evidence, may demonstrate that the complainants' evidence 'is not reasonably capable of being accepted as credible', he or she may allow the complainants to be cross-examined. Curiously, having admitted that he could have called the children had he wanted to, Anderson then argued that he had no choice but to commit the defendants to trial because he had 'not seen or heard cross-examination of the complainants.'[23]

'So why didn't you apply to have the children brought before the court and cross-examined?' I asked Gerald Nation. Anderson's ruling seemed to imply that, in his all-out effort to obtain an early discharge for his clients, Nation had left one important stone unturned. Nation replied that, in his assessment, cross-examination wasn't needed to show that the children's evidence lacked credibility. He explained:

> In my view there were so many problems apparent with the children's evidence as it was presented to the District Court that the judge could have concluded that no reasonable jury could convict the women. To have asked for permission to cross-examine the children would have undermined the whole point I was making. As it turned out, without there having been any cross-examination of the children, Justice Williamson in the High Court did eventually discharge three of the women, in part because 'the evidence against them is of insufficient weight to justify their trial' and 'a verdict of guilty would be unsafe because there is insufficient evidence upon which a jury could properly reach a verdict of guilty.'

In his decision, Judge Anderson said that defence complaints about the quality of the children's evidence were matters for the trial judge in pre-trial applications or for the jury at trial to decide. Nonetheless, his decision to dismiss three charges against Peter Ellis, and one against Debbie Gillespie, showed that he was prepared to give some consideration to the quality of the evidence. The dismissed charges related to Ryan Matai ('At unknown location defendant puts sellotape on complainant's penis and squeezed penis with pliers'); Bart Dogwood ('While in toilets at crèche defendant touched complainant's penis when toileting him'); and Jodie Alder ('When complainant in toilets defendant and Gillespie/Ellis engaged in sexual intercourse').

Judge Anderson then announced that he was committing the defendants for trial on all the other charges they faced. 'I repeat with all the force I can muster that this is not a trial,' he said. 'The defendants are presumed innocent … I would call upon the good offices of humanity, in what is a trying ordeal for a lot of people, to think and allow the process of justice to be performed calmly and reasonably in these circumstances.'

'Hang the bitches,' said a voice at the back of the court.

• • •

After the judgment, the court was cleared and the distraught defendants were led to a private room. Outside, a large crowd milled about, waiting for them to emerge.

'The women were terribly upset,' Gerald Nation recalled. 'I didn't want them being filmed leaving the court looking miserable and dejected. So I took the unusual step of making a brief statement on their behalf outside the court. It's not something that lawyers often do. It's not something I'd ever done before. At the time I just thought it had to be done because of the public prejudice they faced. When it was over I had to answer for that conduct. It wasn't the norm for defence counsel then.'

According to the Christchurch *Press* next morning, Nation told the crowd that, given the way the justice system works, his clients were disappointed but not surprised by the committal. 'They have already stated their complete innocence on oath and they will continue to do so. Every step will now be taken to ensure that ultimately justice is done,' he said.[24]

In Rob Harrison's view, with that announcement, Gerald Nation took the battle for hearts and minds too far:

> I don't think people should be defending themselves in the media prior to trial. It's paving the way for OJ Simpson-type circuses here. When defence counsel stand on the courtroom steps and proclaim their client's innocence, it encourages weeping complainants with blanked out faces to stand on the other side of the road and proclaim their guilt. Who's to be believed? There should be overwhelming silence in the media until the case is over. I accept that Gerald's motives were honorable. He wouldn't do that for personal advancement. He's not that sort of person. But it was a bad move – and it was bad for Peter Ellis. It created such a distinction between his situation and the situation of the women. Guilt by dissociation. I'd gone out of my way to avoid a feeding frenzy. Even if I'd wanted to, I couldn't have started parading my client in the media just because the women were out there. It would have made everything so much worse.[25]

CHAPTER 11

Pre-Trial Manoeuvres

AT THE TIME of the crèche case defendants' committal for trial, Peter Ellis faced 42 charges involving 19 children, Debbie Gillespie faced two charges involving one child and Gaye Davidson, Marie Keys and Jan Buckingham faced four charges each, involving the same three children. At that stage, Crown Solicitor Brent Stanaway became personally responsible for preparing the indictment (that is, the list of charges/counts the defendants would face if the case went to trial). The Crimes Act gives Crown Solicitors the power to lay new or different charges, to re-lay charges dropped at the depositions hearing, or to lay no charges at all (and to thereby abandon the prosecution), pre-trial. The Act also requires that whatever charges are laid must be based on evidence presented at the depositions hearing.

According to the Crown Law Office's Prosecution Guidelines, Crown Solicitors are required to prepare indictments 'entirely independently of the police or other investigating agencies'. They are also required to decide what charges to lay on the basis of two key questions: whether there is 'admissible and reliable evidence that an offence has been committed by an identifiable person', and whether it is 'more likely than not that it [the prosecution] will result in a conviction'. However, in practice, because prosecutors can never be sure how a trial will end, and because they are also required to consider 'the effect of a decision not to prosecute on public opinion', when they prepare indictments they often modify the charges but rarely intervene to stop a prosecution.[1]

In my conversations with him, Brent Stanaway always stoutly defended his actions in the crèche case. Nonetheless, he seemed to lack the unwavering confidence in the validity of the prosecution displayed by his junior colleague Chris Lange. This is not to suggest that Stanaway ever expressed any open disquiet, it's just an impression I got from the way that occasional zephyrs of unease escaped his lips, to be followed immediately by blustery gales of confidence. Whenever I consider the Crown Solicitor's role in the crèche case, the impression recurs.

Whatever Stanaway's views, it is difficult to avoid the conclusion that, for any experienced prosecutor well-versed in the traditional standards of criminal law, the crèche case would have seemed, in that fleeting moment between sleeping and waking, like a bad dream; a nightmare in which the prosecutor's dream-self, an honest lawman in some preacher-ridden, God-forsaken southern town, has a gun put to his head by some very powerful people. They order him to lead the lynch mob; he makes a deal. There will be no white sheets, no flaming crucifixes; one man and only one man will hang, and he must be properly convicted first.

• • •

The Crimes Act states that each charge in an indictment must 'refer to a single transaction', 'give the accused notice of the crime with which he is charged' and 'contain so much detail of the circumstances of the alleged crime as is sufficient to give the accused reasonable information concerning the act or omission to be proved against him, and to identify the transaction referred to'.[2] According to the Court of Appeal: 'If the evidence available to the Crown ... enables a charge to be made with considerable specificity as to date or place ... the prosecution should word the count accordingly ...' However, if incomplete information is provided, that doesn't matter because the Crimes Act states that 'the absence or insufficiency of such details shall not vitiate the count.'[3]

Another consideration for the Crown Solicitor was whether all the charges against all the defendants should be included in the same indictment. According to the Crimes Act 'any number of counts for any crimes whatever may be joined in the same indictment'. Nonetheless, the Court of Appeal has recognised that lengthy indictments are inherently prejudicial to the accused. This is because, even if each count considered separately is weak, a jury confronted with a lengthy indictment may find the accused guilty on the 'where there's smoke there's fire' principle. The Court therefore concluded that an indictment should contain no more than 20 charges.[4]

The Court of Appeal has also recognised that defendants facing weak charges may be prejudiced if they are tried with co-defendants facing serious charges. So for these and other reasons 'conducive to the ends of justice', two or more smaller trials are sometimes held instead of one big one. Dividing up the charges in this way is known as 'severance'.[5]

In addition to the charges already laid against the five defendants, the more than 53 hours of children's videotapes and more than 1100 pages of depositions evidence contained allegations of many other offences by many other people. The named offenders included: 'Peter's mother', 'Robert', 'Andrew', 'Joseph' and crèche workers Susannah, Sandi and Suki. Also, in addition to the sexual offences, many other offences were mentioned. These ranged from misdemeanours like driving without a licence and breaching the Zoological Gardens Regulations, to serious crimes like criminal nuisance, misconduct in respect of human remains, kidnapping, poisoning, assault, cruelty to a child, threatening to kill or do grievous bodily harm, conspiring to commit an offence, misusing fire arms, misusing drugs, manufacturing pornography, attempted murder and murder.

Decisions about whether to charge more people, and about whether to lay charges on the lesser offences, were in the hands of the police. Decisions about which indictable charges to lay against the crèche workers already committed for trial were in the hands of the Crown Solicitor. In theory, Brent Stanaway could have laid charges on all the allegations of serious non-sexual offending, even though the police had found no evidence to corroborate them. With any crime, alleged perpetrators may be charged solely on the word of alleged victims. However, when people are tried for non-sexual offences there is no ideological pressure on juries to 'believe the victim'. Consequently, without independent corroboration, juries have difficulty finding anything proved 'beyond reasonable doubt'. For this reason, laying charges on the non-sexual allegations would probably have been a pointless exercise.

In the course of preparing the indictment, Stanaway crossed six names off the list of complainant children. They were: Amy Linden (whose mother had withdrawn her from the case prior to the depositions hearing); Mia Broadleaf (who had made no disclosure); Kane Juniper (who disclosed that Ellis touched the cheek of his buttock when checking to see whether the boy had soiled himself); Ryan Matai (whose story about having his penis pulled off with pliers had been dismissed at the depositions hearing); Jodie Alder (who had two of her three charges – all based on the interviewer's interpretation of her play with dolls – dismissed at the depositions hearing); and Ruby Hazelnut (whose allegation was that 'at an unknown address defendant touched her nipples').

In addition to reducing the number of complainants, Stanaway reduced the number of charges involving the remaining children. At the depositions hearing, Fran Deodar was the subject of four charges (two each against Ellis and Gillespie). But on the first draft of the indictment, Fran's four charges were reduced to one joint charge. Also, while the other children were listed in oldest-to-youngest order on the draft indictment (as they had been at the depositions hearing), Fran was displaced to last.[6]

By then, Fran's mother had announced that she was withdrawing her daughter from the case. So the recasting of Fran's charges ensured that, when she was formally withdrawn (the day after the draft indictment was filed), her departure did not leave an embarrassing gap in the prosecution case.

When Fran Deodar was withdrawn, the remaining charge against Debbie Gillespie went with her. On 5 March 1993, Gillespie was formally discharged. Afterwards, in high-profile interviews, she talked about the effect of the prosecution on her life, and Gerald Nation outlined the circumstances of Fran's disclosure. 'I believe that if the public was able to see what was in this particular interview, how the child was questioned and what the child actually said, many people would wonder why that interview was ever used as the basis for charging Debbie Gillespie,' he said.[7]

In response to the publicity, Rob Harrison arranged for his client to meet TV3 journalist Melanie Reid. 'It was a very difficult time for Peter,' he explained. 'So much was being said about him in the media, and he was saying nothing on advice of counsel. I didn't want to fan the flames. I thought if we kept quiet we'd have an arguable case to take pre-trial about the prejudicial effect of the media. To give Peter an outlet, I said he could speak to one media person only, on condition that whatever he said wouldn't be used until after the case was over. He met Melanie and felt comfortable with her, so they went from there.' Shortly afterwards, Reid recorded her first interview with Peter Ellis.

'Debbie walked out of court the other day and said, "I'm still very conscious of what the other women have to go through", but she didn't mention you. How did you feel about that?' she asked.

'I had a bad night that night,' Ellis admitted. 'I felt hurt. I wasn't angry with her. I wasn't angry with any of the women. I felt hurt.'[8]

The complainant parents responded more strongly. Social worker Jan Gillanders reported:

> The extensive nationwide coverage was emotionally devastating to parents who felt the media had 'acquitted' her. Her various appearances on TV, in the newspaper and women's magazines was extremely upsetting in terms of her comments about her innocent colleagues and why were children believed instead of adults. Parents felt extremely powerless to respond, particularly because they had been asked by the Police and Crown Solicitor not to have contact with the media.

Gillanders also noted that the other women were hoping to be discharged. 'I remain concerned as to the effect it will have on parents if the women do not go through to trial,' she wrote. 'There are limits to people's coping mechanisms and some parents are very fragile at the moment.'[9]

On 11 March, parental concerns were aired in a widely advertised, local radio special. The programme was not explicitly about the crèche case, but it was hosted by a former crèche parent and its message was: 'mothers were also victims when a child was sexually abused'. The same day, the Christchurch *Press* featured an interview with Miriam Saphira, who was in Christchurch promoting her latest book *Stopping Child Abuse*. 'Child abuse ... applies to all kinds of abuse, from physical abuse to ritual abuse,' the article stated. 'Ritual abuse refers to the physical, emotional, and often sexual abuse that is carried out in public by members of a cult. It usually involves repeated episodes, family members and Satan worship.'[10]

• • •

Once Debbie Gillespie had been discharged, Brent Stanaway had to decide what to do with Gaye Davidson, Marie Keys and Jan Buckingham. The nature of the allegations against them, and the fact that they were wives and mothers, was likely to make convincing a jury of their guilt difficult. But the nature of the allegations against Peter Ellis was likely to make convincing a jury that he had acted alone equally difficult. Another consideration for Stanaway was that, if the manner of the women's discharge suggested that they should never have been charged in the first place, the entire investigation and prosecution would be called into question. The ultimate solution – for which Stanaway was only partly responsible – was to discharge the women while leaving the allegations of group sexual abuse against Ellis intact. The path to that solution began with Stanaway's contrived reshaping of the 'circle incident' charges.

In the draft indictment, the Crown Solicitor reduced the 16 'circle incident' charges involving three children – which had been laid equally against Ellis, Davidson, Keys and Buckingham – to two unequal charges involving the same child: one against Ellis; the other against Davidson, Keys and Buckingham. The charge against Ellis alleged that he had committed an indecent act on Bart Dogwood. The charge against the women alleged that they were parties to an indecent act committed by Ellis on Bart. At the same time, Stanaway charged Ellis as principal offender in a multi-perpetrator incident involving Kari Lacebark (the one in which 'Joseph' was said to have teased her with his penis at Peter's house), and reduced the other charges against Ellis from 34 to 28.

The gravity of the remaining charges was another consideration for the Crown Solicitor. In the draft indictment, Stanaway eliminated the three sexual violation charges against Davidson, Buckingham and Keys, and eliminated or reduced the ten sexual violation charges against Ellis in which penetration of a child's anus, vagina or penis was alleged. Thus, a charge that Ellis *sexually violated* Bart Dogwood by *inserting his penis into* the boy's anus, became a charge that Ellis *indecently assaulted* Bart by *placing his penis against* the boy's anus. Reducing the charges in that way allowed the Crown to explain away the discrepancies between the violent and bloody abuse the children said they had suffered, and the lack of physical and behavioural evidence of penetration by needles, sticks, penises and fingers, by claiming that the children were confused about what had really happened.

Having eliminated or reduced ten of the sexual violation charges against Ellis, Stanaway was left with one sexual violation charge alleging contact between Ellis's penis and a child's mouth. Unlike the other sexual violation charges, that one needed no evidence of immediate pain or lasting damage to be believed. However, instead of making do with one sexual violation charge, Stanaway upped the ante (without increasing the need for more evidence) by upgrading two other charges alleging contact between Ellis's penis and a child's mouth from *inducing an indecent act* to *sexual violation*.

With three sexual violation charges as bargaining chips, the Crown Solicitor made Ellis's barrister an offer. 'Stanaway said he'd drop all the sexual violation charges if I'd agree to a judge-alone trial [instead of a jury trial],' Harrison recalled. 'That was a major concession. It meant that if Peter was found guilty he would spend considerably less time inside. I talked it over with Nigel Hampton and some other experienced barristers. They all said: No. Don't. Not on a sexual abuse case. Don't do it.'

Around the same time, Stanaway offered to drop the sexual violation charges if Ellis pleaded guilty to one or two representative charges relating to each complainant. 'I was duty bound to put it to Peter,' Harrison said. 'The answer was obviously no.'

By then, Christchurch-born Justice Neil Williamson had been assigned to preside over the crèche case High Court trial. Williamson was admitted to the bar in 1961, and became a partner in Raymond Donnelly & Co. in 1965. He was appointed Crown Solicitor in 1968, and to the High Court bench in 1985. He was well liked and well respected in Christchurch, both as a judge and as a member of the community.

'I'd appeared before him in a couple of civil cases. I knew him to be fair,' Rob Harrison observed.

Williamson's greatest strength, and his greatest weakness, was his concern for the interests of children. In his years as Crown Solicitor, he worked closely with Dr Karen Zelas on child protection issues. In his private life, he often brought needy children into his family home. When he died suddenly in 1996, liberal theologian Father Jim Consedine told the thousand people who gathered for his requiem mass that Williamson would be remembered as a man of compassion and humility who lived by his Catholic faith.[11] In preparation for the pre-trial hearings in the crèche case, Williamson viewed most of the children's videotaped evidence, and acquainted himself with the rest of the depositions evidence.

Over the same period, Gerald Nation and Rob Harrison prepared their pre-trial applications. Nation also filed an application to have Judge Anderson's decision to commit his clients for trial reviewed in the High Court. The purpose of that application was to provide the women with another avenue of legal action, should his pre-trial applications fail. Around the same time, Harrison again approached High Court Registrar Peter Fantham for legal aid to enable Nigel Hampton QC to lead Peter Ellis's defence. Harrison recalled:

> I had more than one conversation with Fantham about it. I kept saying, 'Look, this case is huge. You've got to let Nigel take it.' He'd just say, 'You can't have Nigel Hampton. You're not entitled to counsel of choice. If you don't want the case I'll give it to the next person on the legal aid list.' By then we were getting close to trial. I talked it over with Nigel and

Peter. I knew the case really well. I felt I could do it if I had to. In the end we decided there was really no choice. So Nigel withdrew from contention, and I applied for a junior to assist me.

On 9 March 1993, Harrison was granted legal aid for Siobhan McNulty to act as second counsel. McNulty had three years' legal experience in New Zealand, and had worked in the prosecutions division of a child welfare authority in Britain. Throughout the court proceedings, Harrison also received assistance with research, typing and related matters from Bev Alexander, a recently graduated lawyer.

• • •

On 18 March 1993, Justice Williamson began hearing pre-trial applications. At the outset, he issued an order forbidding publication of the submissions and the reasons for his decisions until the trial was over.[12]

In their applications, both defence counsel sought to demonstrate that the charges of sexual perversion against their clients were unfounded, but their approaches were fundamentally different. Because his clients faced one charge involving one child, and because that charge arose late in the investigation, Gerald Nation was able to attack the investigation and prosecution of that charge without attacking the investigation and prosecution of the case as a whole. However, Rob Harrison was faced with a more daunting task. If he were to convince the judge that the charges against Peter Ellis were unfounded, he would have to demonstrate that it was not his client, but the investigation and prosecution of the entire case, that was perverted.

In Oral Judgment (No.1), Justice Williamson observed: 'In my view it is significant that the primary defence of the Accused Peter Ellis and the primary defence of the three women Accused are different in nature. With the former the defence is that the sexual acts did not take place at all; while for the latter the primary defence is that they were not present or were not parties to such acts.'[13]

This analysis meant that, if Williamson could be persuaded that Bart Dogwood's evidence identifying the women as participants in group sexual activities with children was too weak to put before a jury, he could dismiss that charge without also dismissing Bart's evidence that Ellis too was involved in such activities.

Oral Judgment (No.1) was primarily concerned with Gerald Nation's application for severance. Because the three women faced one charge involving one child, and Peter Ellis faced 28 charges involving 13 children, Nation argued that his clients would be prejudiced if they appeared in a long trial with Ellis. He therefore proposed that Ellis have two trials: one with the women, the other on his own. Also, because the charge against his clients was based on the evidence of one child, but that evidence was contradicted by the evidence of two other children, Nation suggested that the nine charges involving those three children be included in a combined trial for Ellis and the women.

The Crown and Ellis's counsel opposed severance. The Crown argued that a single trial would give the jury a better appreciation of the scale and nature of the alleged offending; Rob Harrison argued that it would give them a better appreciation of the scale and nature of the alleged contamination of evidence. Though he did not say so, Harrison also opposed severance because he felt that having his client sitting with three women for the duration of a trial would create a better impression than having him sitting alone.

Williamson accepted Nation's submission about the risk of prejudice to his clients, and the Crown's submission about the need for the jury to appreciate the scale and nature of the alleged offending. He therefore ruled that Ellis should be tried first on all 28 charges, and the women should be tried later on their one charge.[14]

As noted earlier, the Court of Appeal has ruled that an indictment of more than 20 counts is inherently prejudicial to the accused, but Justice Williamson did not address this risk in his judgment. In any event, Rob Harrison felt that two shorter trials instead of one long one was not a realistic option for Ellis:

> We were caught in a cleft stick. There was a risk that the jury would think: 28 counts, he's got to be guilty of something. But if we'd applied for severance, the Crown could have run the most believable charges at the first trial and left the rubbish to last. If Peter was found guilty at the first trial, what chance would he have of getting off on the rubbish? Anyway, we wanted the jury to see the full picture. The experience from depositions was that the more videotapes people saw, the more disbelieving they became. We wanted the jury to see how the information spread through the parents, where it started and how it snowballed. If all the complainants weren't in the same trial, establishing those links would be much more difficult.

For Gerald Nation, the judge's decision to sever the defendants (rather than to just sever the counts) came as a surprise. 'I got the feeling for the first time that Williamson was going to discharge the women,' he recalled.

• • •

Justice Williamson's Oral Judgment (No.2) concerned applications from both defence counsel to have the children's evidence declared inadmissible. 'The main thrust of [the submissions] is a contention that the procedures followed in this case by the Police, the parents and the interviewers were so wrong and oppressive that the resulting videotaped interviews and the children's oral evidence should be excluded on the grounds of unfairness,' the judge noted. The applications were made under s. 344A of the Crimes Act ('evidence unfairly obtained'), which meant that, if

Williamson ruled against them, counsel could challenge the judge's decision in the Court of Appeal prior to trial.

In his submission, Harrison argued that the December '91 meeting for crèche parents was an inappropriate response to a nebulous, innocuous and unsubstantiated remark, and that both parents' meetings (in December '91 and March '92) created a climate of fear that prompted parents to question their children directly and suggestively about Peter Ellis and sexual abuse. For his part, Nation argued that Ms Dogwood's relentless and leading questioning of her son had rendered his evidence unreliable. In response, Justice Williamson ruled that the meetings were 'entirely proper', that it was unrealistic to expect parents not to question their children and that such questioning was unlikely to lead to false testimony. With regard to Harrison's evidence of parental networking, Williamson stated, 'This exchange of information clearly occurred. The extent and significance of it, however, does not appear to me to support the sinister picture drawn by Counsel.'

In submissions concerning the conduct of the children's videotaped interviews, both defence counsel criticised the use of direct and suggestive questioning, multi-choice questioning, repeated questioning, repeated interviews and the use of anatomically correct dolls. With regard to Bart Dogwood, Gerald Nation criticised the interviewer's failure to adequately explore the context in which the child's allegations had arisen, and her decisions to interview him after his counselling had commenced, and at a time when he was obviously unwell and had been subject to intense parental pressure. To support his arguments, Nation provided an affidavit from Australian psychiatrist Dr Keith Le Page with annexures about 'the well known inquiry in Cleveland as well as American and Australian examples of such complaints by children attending preschool institutions'. To counter his arguments, the Crown provided an affidavit from Dr Karen Zelas. After considering the submissions, Justice Williamson ruled:

> The evidence of the interviews and of Dr Zelas and my own observations of the videotapes satisfies me that the interviewers who conducted these interviews were qualified, mature and trained women who were under the regular supervision of a psychiatrist with specialist qualifications in child sexual abuse cases. While there may be some legitimate criticisms about some aspects of these interviews, I am not satisfied that there has been improper conduct which should be the subject of discipline or that there are circumstances of unfairness raised by the conduct of these evidential interviews.[15]

With regard to the applications to have the children's videotapes declared inadmissible, he concluded: 'I should not exercise my discretion and make findings in relation to fairness until I have had an opportunity to hear the evidence and see the witnesses examined and cross-examined … this part of the application under s. 344A is adjourned until the trial.'

From the defence point of view, Justice Williamson had missed the point. The issue was contamination. Those responsible for the contamination had already been cross-examined at length, and their answers provided abundant support for the argument that the children's vague and contradictory allegations were the product of repeated, leading and suggestive questioning by anxious parents and determined investigators.

A further problem for the defence was that Williamson's refusal to rule on their 'evidence unfairly obtained' submissions denied them the opportunity to have that issue considered by the Court of Appeal prior to trial. However, this was less of a problem for Gerald Nation because the judge had given him hope that his clients would soon be discharged.

• • •

On Tuesday 6 April, Gerald Nation applied to have Gaye Davidson, Marie Keys and Jan Buckingham discharged under s. 347 of the Crimes Act. He argued that no jury properly directed could bring in a guilty verdict, and that, given the background to the case, it would be unfair and oppressive to put the accused on trial.

In Oral Judgment (No.3), Justice Williamson discharged the women on three grounds: first, that 'the evidence against them is of insufficient weight to justify their trial'; second, that 'the potential for prejudice against the Accused is so great that they might be convicted for the wrong reasons (such as "moral blameworthiness" or "professional incompetence")'; and third, that 'the unavoidable delay in their trial on this charge may result in hardship to the now seven-year-old child'.

In law, the first reason would have been sufficient, but Williamson claimed otherwise. 'Not one of these reasons ... would be sufficient in my view in itself,' he said. Clearly, it was a reluctant discharge.

In conclusion, Williamson issued a warning. 'Persons who are discharged under s. 347 are acquitted but they are not entitled to then conduct themselves in a manner which affects the evidence to be given in a pending trial,' he said. 'I will not hesitate to recommend prosecution for contempt if there is any comment in breach of the order [banning publication of the pre-trial submissions and the reasons for the judge's decisions on them] ... or comment which reflects generally upon the witnesses who are to give evidence for Peter Ellis or other aspects of his trial.'[16]

On Wednesday 7 April, the front page of the Christchurch *Press* featured a photo of three smiling women clutching large bunches of flowers. The headline read 'Child Care Trio Vow to Rebuild'. The *Dominion* carried the same photo and a similar item on its front page ('Women Talk of Compo – Freed Child Care Workers Vow to Clear Names'), and a full-page article inside ('Guilty Until Proven Innocent').[17]

In the Christchurch *Press* of 8 April, the women talked of compensation; a crèche parent called for an inquiry into the training of children's interviewers; DSW programme manager Anne Caton said the women's discharge had 'absolutely not' discredited the interviewing unit; and the police reminded everyone of Justice Williamson's warning. On 11 April, the lead article in the *Sunday News* was headed 'Court Gag on Crèche Four'.[18]

Though the women were gagged, comment from other quarters ran hot. Reporters estimated that the case had cost the taxpayer more than $1,000,000 and the Christchurch City Council more than $200,000; union secretary Peter Lawson said he was pressing ahead with personal grievance action against the council on behalf of the crèche staff; the *Southland Times* deplored the time taken for the system to declare the women innocent; journalist George Balani wrote: 'The Christchurch Civic Child Care Centre case continues to disintegrate ... it must be becoming clear to even the most cynical observers that all is not well in the way these cases are handled. It's time for a full and comprehensive public inquiry.' Over the same period, the graffiti slogan 'the women are guilty' appeared all over town, and a complainant grandmother appeared on the *Holmes* show.[19]

On 15 April, Williamson took the media to task over the breaches of his suppression order. After that, the only pre-trial mention of the case came in a court report about a man charged with threatening to kill Peter Ellis. The man reportedly told police he 'knew' Ellis was guilty and considered it his civic duty to 'knock him over'.[20]

• • •

With Ellis's trial scheduled to open in the Christchurch High Court on 26 April, Harrison had two pre-trial options left: he could apply for a s. 347 discharge for his client, and he could apply for a change of venue.

'I told Peter repeatedly that Christchurch was the worst place on earth to run the trial,' Harrison recalled. 'He was adamant that he didn't want to move. He'd say, "I've got my pets. I've got my support. I've got my mother. Those are more important to me." Anyway we would have still ended up with the same judge, and the adverse publicity was nationwide.'

On 15, 16 and 19 April, Rob Harrison argued two pre-trial applications under s. 347 of the Crimes Act. In the first, he submitted that the videotaped evidence of seven children (Tess Hickory, Derek Ngaio, Lara Palm, Bart Dogwood, Kari Lacebark, Judy Balsa and Yelena Holly) was so defective that no jury, properly directed, could bring in a guilty verdict. In the second, he argued that a combination of prejudicial media coverage and community anxiety would prevent Ellis from obtaining a fair trial.

Harrison supported his first application with evidence that, prior to making their disclosures, children had played together and their parents had networked, read sexual abuse prevention books to their children and put specific allegations to them. He also pointed out that many of the disclosures were contradictory and bizarre. But in Oral Judgment (No.4) the judge said that, in view of the evidence of Dr Zelas, he did not consider the children's evidence to be so unsafe or unreliable that the accused ought to be discharged on the relevant counts.

Williamson also rejected Harrison's argument that it was improper for Tess to have taken the booklets she had made with her mother ('The way to Peter's house' and 'What did Peter do') into her DSW interviews. 'In my view ... the booklets amount to no more than a note or reminder ... the witness was entitled to use such a note to refresh her memory,' he said.[21]

With regard to Judy Balsa, Harrison pointed out that in her first two interviews the child had tried to tell interviewer Cathy Crawford what her uncle had done to her brother (who had never been to the crèche), but Crawford had kept bringing the conversation back to Peter Ellis. Then, in her fourth interview, Judy made muddled disclosures of abuse by Ellis. Finally, in her fifth interview, Judy made a clear disclosure about her uncle's abuse of her brother. In response, Williamson said that Judy may have been confused, but such matters were for the jury to decide.[22]

With regard to Bart Dogwood, Harrison submitted that the judge should discharge his client for the reasons advanced by Gerald Nation on behalf of the women. To appreciate the full import of Williamson's response, we need to review the evidence placed before him. The evidence was:

- that when Ms Dogwood first asked Bart (in April '92) if Peter had ever touched his bottom or penis, Bart replied that Peter was his friend, and would not do that.
- that in his first interview (May '92), Bart disclosed that Peter had cleaned him up on the crèche changing table. Bart couldn't remember the names of the other teachers, but he told the interviewer that Peter was alright ('but he's not now'). He also assured her that no one else had done anything to his genitals that he didn't like, and that he had not seen Peter's genitals.
- that, at depositions, Judge Anderson dismissed the charge relating to Bart's first interview because there was no evidence of abuse.
- that there was nothing in Bart's demeanor in any of his interviews to suggest that he was holding back anything through anxiety, fear or insecurity.
- that at no stage did any interviewer consider it necessary to arrange another interview for Bart. All his interviews were initiated by his mother.
- that all Bart's interviews were preceded by intensive parental questioning.

- that between May and August '92, Ms Dogwood asked Bart at least twice a week what had happened at the crèche but he made no disclosure.
- that on 3 August, Ms Dogwood told Bart 'at 7.30 you and Daddy and I are going to sit down and talk about the crèche. I believe you've got a lot to tell …'
- that in his increasingly bizarre DSW interviews on 4, 5 and 6 August, and 28 October, Bart said that Peter took children to buildings with trapdoors and secret tunnels where adults threatened, molested and photographed them. The alleged crime scenes were 'Peter's house', a 'library building', a 'two-storeyed house in Hereford Street' and the Cranmer Centre. Bart said that Peter and 19 of his friends put their penises up his bum; that Peter, Peter's mother and other crèche staff shoved sticks and burning paper up his bum and made it bleed; that Peter and his mother tied up children and gave them drugs and alcohol; and that Peter's mother put them in cages and hung them from the roof. In the circle incident, which arose in his fourth interview, Bart said that Peter, Peter's mother, Marie, Jan, Gaye, 'Robert', 'Andrew' and some slitty-eyed people danced in a circle around naked children and took photos at the Hereford Street house. Then Gaye and Marie pretended to have sex, and the adults made the kids kick each other's genitals and perform other indecencies. The adults also kicked and punched the kids, stuck needles into their genitals, threatened them with knives and put them in smoking-hot ovens. At some stage, 'Andrew' put a needle up Bart's penis and made it bleed.
- that, during his interviews, Bart showed no distress consistent with the horrendous abuse he was describing. His demeanor was flat, indifferent and incongruous. On two occasions he sang.
- that, according to his parents, when he was at the crèche, Bart showed no behavioural indicators or physical injuries consistent with the horrific trauma he allegedly suffered. His toileting and other problems started after his first DSW interview. A medical examination showed no evidence of past trauma.
- that the police concluded that Bart's statements to his mother about being abused at the Masonic Lodge, being buried in a coffin, killing animals and stabbing a boy were untrue.
- that the Dogwood, Lacebark and Yew families were in close contact during the investigation. Bart alleged that Kari Lacebark and Julian Yew were involved in the circle incident. Kari and Julian failed to corroborate, and often contradicted, Bart's evidence.
- that, at depositions, adult prosecution and defence witnesses failed to corroborate, and often contradicted, Bart's evidence. Bruce said that no groups of adults and children came to his house after Ellis left in May '87 (long before

Bart, Kari and Julian started at the crèche), and that he had never owned an oven big enough to put a child in. The crèche staff said that, with or without children, it would have been impossible for Ellis and other staff to be away from crèche without anyone noticing, and that children never returned from walks looking distressed or showing signs of trauma. The police found no photos, cages or other evidence to support the allegations.

In his ruling, Justice Williamson reminded Ellis's counsel that he had discharged the women for three reasons. He said that 'the evidence of identification of the three women as being present at the time of the circle incident offence was insufficient', but insisted that 'the degree of insufficiency' did not in itself warrant their discharge. He also made it clear that his decision to discharge them did not mean that he disbelieved Bart. 'I did not reach any conclusion that the evidence of [Bart Dogwood] was generally incredible or unreliable or that the evidence was necessarily contaminated,' he said. 'I have not been persuaded that the complaints made are false or that it would be unsafe or dangerous to allow the trial to proceed in relation to them.' With regard to the circle incident, he said:

> The issue for the jury … so far as the Accused Ellis is concerned, is not only whether the events occurred but also whether he was participating in any way. The jury are entitled to have regard to [Bart Dogwood's] evidence of other sexual activities involving him and the Accused Ellis and … the evidence of other children concerning group sexual activities.[23]

By such reasoning, Williamson persuaded himself that there was no contradiction in discharging the women on the circle incident charge and sending Ellis to trial on the same charge, and on all the other charges based on Bart Dogwood's evidence. Clearly, to Justice Williamson, the claim that large numbers of depraved adults had inflicted horrendous abuse on large numbers of small children over a period of years in his city without anybody noticing had to be taken seriously.

In Oral Judgment (No.2), Justice Williamson had stated that he could not rule on the admissibility of the children's evidence (under s. 344A of the Crimes Act) until he had seen and heard the complainants examined and cross-examined. Yet here he was, in Oral Judgment (No.4) ruling the children's evidence admissible (under s. 347 of the Crimes Act) without first seeing and hearing the children give evidence. This adds weight to the suspicion that Williamson deferred the earlier ruling because he did not want his decision challenged in the Court of Appeal. (Appeals are allowed under s. 344A, but not under s. 347).

As a result of the judge's ruling, Ellis faced a full-blown ritual abuse charge at his trial. But in the draft indictment, the Crown Solicitor avoided any mention of '404 Hereford Street' (the venue identified on the relevant arrest warrants), or 'circle incident' (the activity mentioned in the relevant depositions charges) or 'sexual violation' (the circle incident depositions charge 'occasioned by the penetration of [Bart's] anus with a stick'). Instead, the draft count stated: 'that Peter Hugh McGregor Ellis between 1 February 1989 and 1 March 1991 at Christchurch being a male did an indecent act upon [Bart Dogwood] a boy under the age of 12 years'.

In his second application for a s. 347 discharge, Harrison submitted that sensational media reports and community anger would prevent his client from obtaining his minimum entitlement under s. 25(a) of the Bill of Rights Act – a fair and public hearing by an independent and impartial court – anywhere in the country. In evidence, he presented a summary of print and broadcast news, newspaper clippings, photographs of graffiti and lists of allegations collated and distributed by Ms Magnolia. He reminded the judge that images of empty swings, of angry crowds at Ellis's court appearances, of long fingernails (filmed when Ellis was slamming the door on a television crew besieging his home) and of Ellis mincing down the street with two fluffy little dogs, featured on nationwide television night after night. He said that Ellis had been portrayed as a freak and a monster, and the interviewing of over 100 children had sent ripples of horror through friends, extended family and the general public throughout New Zealand. He contrasted the women's publicity with Ellis's silence ('guilt by dissociation'), and pointed out that Ellis had been abused and assaulted, and had received threatening phone calls and a bullet in the mail.

Harrison also referred to other cases where community hostility and prejudicial media coverage had impacted on the accused's right to a fair trial. In one of the cases, Williamson himself had ruled that there was 'a real risk that a fair and impartial trial may not be possible in Christchurch' because of the effect of 'the involvement of a number of Christchurch people and events associated with this emotionally charged case; the extent of the publicity; the conduct of persons attending the District Court …'[24]

In response, Justice Williamson opined that publicity surrounding the women's discharge had assisted the accused, and that evidence of antagonism towards Ellis 'must be balanced with widespread public knowledge of unsuccessful prosecutions or public inquiries overseas which have resulted from hysteria or the actions of hypervigilant parents'. The judge therefore concluded that 'directions given at the trial and during the summing up should be sufficient to warn the jury about the very problems which this part of the application highlights.'[25]

'The trial of the Accused is to commence on Monday next, 26 April,' he said.

• • •

On 21 April, the Crown Solicitor completed the final 28-count indictment. On 21 and 23 April, counsel for Ellis and the Crown appeared before Justice Williamson to debate procedural issues for the trial.

The judge's approach to these matters was underpinned by his approach to the case as a whole. At the end of the trial he told the jury: 'the case is not a trial of the other crèche workers' conduct, nor of the conduct of the police, parents or specialist interviewers ... I emphasise that the concentration or focus must be on the charges.'[26] Since Ellis's defence was based on the proposition that the police, the parents and the specialist interviewers had acted improperly, Justice Williamson was effectively telling the jury not to concern itself unduly with the defence case. Clearly, to Williamson, the question that really mattered was whether or not the children were to be believed. In the days leading up to the trial, his Oral Judgments (No.5) and (No.6) reflected that view.

In a ruling that stands as a warning to anyone who has ever had a private conversation about sex, Justice Williamson declared that Ellis's alleged conversations about certain 'kinky' sexual practices between consenting adults in private were admissible. Statements about these conversations were obtained by the police from crèche workers Sharleen and Jan Buckingham, and Debbie Gillespie's former partner Belinda. Sharleen was the most shockable of the staff, and the person Ellis liked to tease. Jan Buckingham was his closest friend. He sometimes also confided in Debbie Gillespie, who passed things on to Belinda. (However, Belinda said that the reported conversation had taken place directly with Ellis.) In any event, the fact that only three witnesses reported such conversations indicates that Ellis did not discuss sexual matters indiscriminately. Furthermore, all three witnesses agreed that Ellis was given to flamboyant exaggeration, and they were never sure whether to believe him or not.

The conversations reported by Belinda and Jan Buckingham formed part of their depositions evidence. Belinda said that Ellis made comments about 'a Chinese man who liked wooden implements inserted in his penis'. Buckingham said that Ellis 'related various sexual exploits concerning the use of wooden spoons, straws and other implements'.

According to Williamson's Oral Judgment (No.5), an additional brief of evidence from Sharleen had been provided alleging that Ellis 'spoke to her on a number of occasions about a sexual practice known as "golden showers" and said that he enjoyed such sexual activity which involved being urinated on or urinating on other persons'.

Perhaps he did, but it is interesting to note that, despite the intense pressure she was under from the police ('Why don't you go home and have a wee think about it, Sharleen? You go home and have a think'), Sharleen did not come up with the 'golden showers' story until after the depositions hearing. She recalled:

I felt complete harassment from the police. I didn't know how to stop it. But around the time the women were discharged a friend said, 'This guy's a nice lawyer. He deals in everything.' I talked to him and he issued a statement saying I was not to be interviewed unless my lawyer was present, unless a prior time was arranged. I never heard from the police again after that, until it was time to go to court for the trial.[27]

Whether the conversations described by Sharleen, Belinda and Jan Buckingham were recalled accurately is far from clear. Whether Ellis was referring to something he had read about or something he had done, and whether he was genuinely interested in the activities or just trying to shock, is also far from clear. In any event, he was not talking about paedophilia, and no crèche child ever talked about having straws or wooden implements put up his penis. Furthermore, people who are interested in unconventional sexual practices with adults, and people who are interested in sex with children, fall into separate, non-overlapping categories [see Ch.8.i]. In other words, evidence that Ellis talked about unconventional sexual activities between consenting adults, was actually evidence that Ellis *was not* a paedophile.

Because the reported conversations proved nothing, Rob Harrison argued that putting them before a jury would be a gratuitous exercise in character assassination, but Justice Williamson disagreed. His ruling on the admissibility of evidence about Ellis's 'unusual sexual practices' was underpinned by two assumptions. The first was that innocent little children, even when questioned at length about Peter, naughtiness and private parts, were incapable of making up stories about Peter urinating on them and putting sticks up their bottoms unless they had experienced such acts. The second was that the sexual practices described by Sharleen, Belinda and Jan Buckingham were extremely rare. In fact, had he read the classified advertisements in *Truth* that week, he would have found more than a dozen advertisers offering 'golden showers' (or other euphemisms for urophilia) and several others ('all fetishes catered for') who probably offered implements as well.[28] But Justice Williamson presumably did not read *Truth*. He ruled:

> There is a special and strong relationship between this evidence and the allegations of the children as to the use of sticks and other implements in relation to their private parts and urination ... In the Accused's statements he had not denied that he did have an association with the child complainants ... A fundamental issue therefore is ... whether the association was an innocent one. On this issue the evidence contended for has strong probative force. In my view that force is sufficient to outweigh the prejudicial effect it will have.[29]

To circumvent the problem of hearsay evidence, Williamson added that 'evidence that the Accused actually carried out such activities ... is not admissible ... my ruling relates only to the statements made by the Accused to the witnesses ... as to his knowledge of these unique sexual practices and his view of them as being sexually stimulating.'[30]

On the issue of which of the children's videotaped interviews should be shown, the Crown wanted the jury to see only the interviews relevant to the charges, while the defence wanted them to see all the interviews recorded with all the complainant children. Harrison further submitted that each child should view *all* his or her own videotaped interviews or *none at all*. Otherwise, he argued, the children's minds would be refreshed only in relation to matters relied on by the Crown, and that would make it difficult for him to cross-examine them about statements made in videotapes they had not seen.

On these matters, Williamson ruled that the Crown was required to play, and the child was required to view, only the tapes on which the charges relating to that child were based ('Crown tapes'), and he placed two restrictions on the playing of other tapes ('defence-onus tapes'). First, any tapes the defence wanted played had to be relevant to the charges. Second, the child concerned did not have to view the tape.[31]

Over defence objections, Williamson also approved a Crown proposal that the jury be provided with, and be allowed to retain, transcripts of interviews on which the charges were based. In Rob Harrison's view, that decision further disadvantaged the defence:

> I wanted the jury to concentrate on the screen, not on the transcripts. I wanted them to see children that appeared to be talking about what they were doing with dolls, rather than describing what had happened to them. Also, while the jury got transcripts of Crown tapes – which they were allowed to take into the jury room – they didn't get transcripts of defence-onus tapes, or transcripts of cross-examination that might have raised doubts about the reliability of the Crown tapes.

The judge also said he would allow only limited cross-examination of children on matters unrelated to the charges (such as allegations about cages and ovens), and of parents on hearsay matters (such as discussions about ritual abuse). With regard to Harrison's plan to cross-examine the interviewers on 'interviewing techniques and the structure of interviews; background matters such as parental questioning; and the effects on the child of the interview', Williamson ruled that such questions should be directed to Dr Zelas.

When Justice Williamson had finished dictating Oral Judgment (No.6), discussion continued between judge and counsel over which of the children's videotapes could be played at the trial. Rob Harrison recalled:

> We start going through the transcripts. The Crown's relying on this tape, this tape, not relying on this tape. I said, 'I want [Judy Balsa's] fifth tape played. It explains what she was talking about in her first two interviews – when the interviewer kept asking her about

Peter hurting her, and she kept talking about her uncle hurting her brother.' Williamson said, 'No, that tape is not to be played. It's not relevant to the charges.' He'd already ruled that [Judy's] confusion between Peter and her uncle was for the jury to decide, but he wouldn't let the jury see the tape they needed to see to make that decision. The same thing happened with [Bart Dogwood's] last interview. He said [Bart's] allegation that Peter's mother hung kids in cages at the Cranmer Centre had nothing to do with [Bart's] allegations that Peter indecently assaulted him at an unknown address. Those rulings meant that the jury never got to see the developing picture, the spread of ideas, the process the kids had been through, the inconsistencies in their statements, the way they made bizarre allegations as earnestly as they made credible ones, the contamination of their evidence by parents and playmates. It made cross-examining the kids harder too. I could say, 'So [Bart], you were up in this cage?' But if he said, 'No, I never said that', I was stuck with that answer. I couldn't say, 'Look at this bit of videotape, [Bart].'

Harrison also argued that the defence-onus tapes should be played to the jury in their entirety. Stanaway expressed concern at the time that would take. After considering the issue, Williamson ruled that only the portions of the defence-onus tapes that he considered relevant could be played to the jury, the rest would have to be fast-forwarded.

On Monday 26 April 1992, the trial of Peter Ellis began.

CHAPTER 12

The Trial

12.i: The Beginning

In law, the Ellis trial was about the believability of the children's evidence. Rob Harrison therefore assumed that, as in any ordinary trial, if he could show that the children's evidence was too insubstantial, contradictory and incredible to be believed, then the prosecution case would not be proved beyond reasonable doubt and his client would go free. But the Ellis trial was no ordinary trial, and analysing the proceedings in terms of the legal issues involved can only take us so far. All things considered, it probably makes more sense to regard the Ellis trial as a dual purpose event: at one level, a formal determination of the accused's guilt; at another, a community purification ritual brought into being by years of city-wide anxiety over allegations of rampant sexual abuse, clandestine pornography rings and Satanic cults. According to this analysis, those at the centre of the proceedings – the prosecutors, the judge and the jury – served two roles: they were officers of the court, and representatives of the people in a drama as old as humanity. In the trial of Peter Ellis, the people's representatives tackled their tasks with varying degrees of doubt and certainty, reluctance and enthusiasm, compassion and indifference. But, no matter how they played their parts, the drama would end as it had to end: in the ceremonial scapegoating of Peter Ellis.

• • •

While for the court proceedings, the central legal question was whether the children could be believed, in the forum of public opinion another question was the subject of endless debate: how could so many people have got it so wrong? Most people knew that intelligent, well-educated people could make mistakes or become temporarily infatuated with unsound ideas. But on such occasions checks and balances normally kick in. Mistakes are usually corrected, irrational ideas are usually derided, and, more often than not, a fragile equilibrium is quickly restored.

Throughout the crèche investigation, the Civic staff and their supporters argued that the complainant parents, investigators and prosecutors were mistaken. But the notion that so many people could have made the same mistake about the same issue at the same time was difficult for most people to accept. When TV3 journalist Melanie Reid interviewed Peter Ellis during his trial, she returned, again and again, to the same theme: 'We're not talking about one or two children that have possibly made it up or got it wrong ... We're talking about 70 families that are convinced that you've abused their children ... It's hard to believe that so many parents, so many social workers, so many interviewers, so many police, so many professional people could have got it wrong.'[1]

In the forum of public opinion, the question demanded that Ellis prove his innocence, and found him guilty because he could not. Also, because the question went largely unaddressed at his trial, it allowed the belief – that all those innocent little children, and all those intelligent, well-educated adults, would not be making such extraordinary claims unless the claims had substance – to survive the court proceedings unchallenged.

• • •

On Monday 26 April 1993, the list of witnesses for the trial of Peter Ellis was read to the 100 or so potential jurors summoned for duty that week. Anyone with a close relationship with any witness, and anyone who could not spare six weeks of their time, was asked to advise the court. After that, the jury was selected by ballot from the assembled panel. In the process, the Crown challenged five men and one woman, and the defence challenged three men and three women. The final jury comprised nine women and three men.

Next morning, a juror advised the court that her flatmate worked with the mother of a complainant child. However, the judge did not consider the relationship close enough to cause concern. In 1997, TV3 revealed that the flatmate was actually the partner of the juror, and that the foreman of the jury was the clergyman who had officiated at the Crown Solicitor's wedding some 17 years earlier. After considering the questions raised, the Court of Appeal (in the case of the flatmate) and the Solicitor-General (in the case of the Crown Solicitor) declared the relationships to be of no great significance.

• • •

In any criminal trial, the case for the prosecution is presented first, followed by the case for the defence. In presenting their cases, counsel for both parties have a dual responsibility. English jurist Lord Reid wrote:

Every counsel has a duty to his client fearlessly to raise every issue, advance every argument, and ask every question, however distasteful, which he thinks will help his client's case. But, as an officer of the court concerned with the administration of justice, he has an overriding duty to the court, to the standards of his profession, and to the public ... Counsel must not mislead the court, he must not lend himself to casting aspersions on the other party or witnesses for which there is no sufficient basis in the information.[2]

For prosecutors, this dual role brings with it an obligation to present the Crown case fairly and completely. According to *Adams on Criminal Law*, Crown prosecutors 'must not struggle for a conviction but are fully entitled and obliged to be as firm as the circumstances warrant'. The New Zealand Law Society's *Rules of Professional Conduct for Barristers and Solicitors* states: 'A prosecutor prosecuting a criminal case must do so dispassionately and with scrupulous fairness.'[3]

Responsibility for supervising the conduct of counsel rests with the judge. He or she also controls the proceedings, sums up for the jury and determines the sentence. The judge's overriding duty is to secure a fair trial.

At the start of the Ellis trial, Justice Williamson told jurors that the ultimate decision was theirs alone. He urged them to put aside feelings of prejudice or sympathy, to disregard anything they had heard outside the courtroom and to discuss the case only with each other. He instructed them to keep an open mind until they had heard all the evidence and to make their decisions 'on a calm dispassionate consideration of the evidence' presented in court.

Williamson's instructions may have conveyed the impression that, as in any ordinary trial, the jurors were free to apply their common sense and life experiences to the evidence, and to reach their verdicts accordingly. But, in his two-hour opening address, Crown Solicitor Brent Stanaway suggested otherwise:

Some if not all of you will have come here today with preconceptions and beliefs about children, how they behave, their ability to recall events from the past and their likely reactions to traumas. They may be erroneous. The Crown will ... provide you with information which will assist you in appropriately considering the children's evidence ... You will hear evidence called by the Crown from an expert witness, Dr K. Zelas, who has been a specialist child psychiatrist for 20 years.

During pre-trial hearings, the Crown had sought permission to call its evidence in blocks. In Oral Judgment (No.5), Justice Williamson noted: 'It is proposed that the child, parent, interviewer and examining doctor give evidence, and that in respect to each child the psychologist [sic] Dr Zelas, and the police officer in charge, Detective Eade, also give evidence after each child.'[4] Since there were 13 complainant children, the Crown was proposing that Zelas and Eade give evidence 13 times. This extraordinary request suggests that the Crown was concerned that the children's evidence (the evidence on which the entire case was based) was not strong enough on its own to justify 'believing the children'.

On this issue, Justice Williamson accepted Rob Harrison's argument that allowing the jury to see and hear two important witnesses over and over again would be prejudicial to the accused, particularly in view of the fact that the defence's expert could give evidence only once. The judge therefore directed that witnesses be called 'in the normal way'. This meant that the children and their parents would give evidence first, and the other Crown witnesses (police, interviewers, expert witness and others) would follow.

The ruling also meant that the jury would not hear Dr Zelas's evidence until after the children's videotapes had been played and the children had been cross-examined via video-link. Presumably out of concern that jurors might apply their own 'preconceptions and beliefs about children' to the children's evidence and draw their own conclusions, Stanaway spent most of his opening address foreshadowing evidence the jury would hear later from Dr Zelas.

Under the guise of information on 'the general development level of children', Stanaway explained away every aspect of the children's evidence that the jury was likely to find 'bizarre or unbelievable or unconvincing'. He explained away the contrast between the school-age complainants' sensible conversations on everyday matters, and their 'vague, strange, confused or incomplete' comments about Ellis and the crèche, by claiming that they had experienced, labelled, stored and recalled the abuse with the limited understanding and language of three- and four-year-olds. He explained away their delayed disclosures by claiming that young children think literally but not logically. He said that was why, when Ellis threatened them with impossible consequences if they disclosed, they believed him and kept silent. He explained away the interviewers' relentless questioning by claiming that children say 'don't know' or 'can't remember' when they want a question repeated. He explained away the tendency for complainants to disclose more and more in each successive interview by claiming that children's memories of severe trauma may be deeply repressed. He explained away the lack of evidence of bruising or bleeding at the time, or of scars at a later date, by claiming that small children exaggerate minor injuries. He explained away the complainants' interest in playing with toys and chatting aimlessly during interviews by claiming that young children are reluctant to disclose abuse. He also claimed that the sexual knowledge displayed by some complainants 'could only come from experiencing or witnessing' the events described.

Many of Stanaway's explanations addressed contradictions in the complainants' evidence. When a child said in one interview that something happened 800 times, and in the next that it happened once, this was said to be because young children have difficulty with concepts of time and numeracy. When a complainant gave contradictory peripheral detail (e.g. about the colour of the offender's car), this was said to be because young children remember central detail better than peripheral detail. But when a complainant gave contradictory central detail (e.g. about the identity of the offender), this was said to be because the child was talking about different episodes of abuse.

The Crown Solicitor also assured the jury that, according to law, young children could be competent witnesses, and could make reliable disclosures of abuse, even when questioned in advance by parents and asked leading questions by interviewers.

• • •

Peter Ellis faced 28 charges of sexual offences against nine girls and four boys. These comprised 14 charges of indecent assault, ten charges of doing, or inducing a child to do, an indecent act, three charges of sexual violation and one charge of attempted sexual violation. At the time of the trial, the complainants were aged four-and-a-half years (one child), six years (four children), seven years (six children), eight years (one child) and nine years (one child). The offences were alleged to have taken place at unspecified times and dates between 1 May 1986 (four months before Ellis came to the crèche) and 1 October 1992 (11 months after he left the crèche, and one month after the crèche was closed). The alleged venues were: the crèche (15 offences involving ten children); an unknown address (nine offences involving four children); a child's home (two offences involving one child); the Cranmer Centre (one offence involving one child); and 404 Hereford Street (one offence involving one child).

In 26 of the charges, Ellis was alleged to be the sole offender. In two charges, other offenders were mentioned (one charge was based on Bart Dogwood's 'circle incident' allegation, the other on Kari Lacebark's allegation that 'Joseph' teased her with his penis at Peter's house). In their passage from depositions to trial, the two multi-offender charges underwent curious transformations.

At depositions, Peter Ellis, Gaye Davidson, Marie Keys and Jan Buckingham were charged as *equal co-offenders* in the circle incident. In the draft indictment, the women were charged as *parties to an offence committed by Ellis*. But, in the final indictment, Ellis was charged as *party to an offence committed by persons unknown*. Also, at depositions and in the draft indictment, Ellis was said to be the *principal offender* in the 'teasing with penis' incident, but in the final indictment he was said to be a *party to an offence committed by persons unknown*.[5] In so far as these transformations show that Brent Stanaway had trouble figuring out who to charge as principal offender in the multi-perpetrator incidents, they also show that, despite his claims to the contrary, the children did not give clear central detail on that matter.

The Crown Solicitor's decision to put Peter Ellis on trial as party to offences committed by people who were never identified or charged was unusual, but not improper. In a bank robbery, if the principal offenders escape but the driver of the getaway vehicle is apprehended, the driver may be charged as party to an offence committed by persons unknown. However, in such cases there is usually some tangible evidence of the principal offenders' existence.

In the crèche case, the child complainants alleged that groups of adults took groups of children to identified places around the city on a regular basis over a period of years. They said they were molested and tortured, and used in Satanic rituals and for the manufacture of pornography. But no tangible evidence to support those allegations was ever found. So, one has to ask, why did Brent Stanaway bother with the multiple-offender charges? Since Ellis was the only person on trial, why didn't the Crown Solicitor just charge him with the 26 offences in which he was said to be the sole perpetrator?

The answer seems to be that, given the nature of the charges, there was no way that Ellis could have acted alone and unnoticed. Because four of his colleagues had been charged and discharged, many people believed that his co-workers knew of the offending but turned a blind eye. But for Ellis to have offended on the scale alleged, negligent co-workers were not enough, he needed co-offenders as well. So when the women were discharged, Stanaway had to replace them with someone else. Also, most of the children had mentioned other people at some stage during the investigation. So even if the Crown Solicitor wanted to portray Ellis as a solitary offender, talk of other perpetrators was bound to leak into the proceedings. To cope with this problem, Brent Stanaway found a solution that was as understated as it was ingenious: he put Peter Ellis on trial with the Great Christchurch Paedophile Ring as his phantom co-defendants.

Stanaway's solution may not have worked anywhere else, but a belief in the existence of a mysterious paedophile ring that was evil, invisible and everywhere had long been abroad in Christchurch. Also, having phantom rather than real-life co-defendants made the prosecution's job very much easier. Since they had not been identified or charged, the Crown did not have to explain to the jury who Ellis's co-defendants were or what they were supposed to have done, and since they had no status in the proceedings, they could not defend themselves against the Crown Solicitor's innuendo.

• • •

Of the 57 interviews conducted with complainant children, the 21 most straightforward ones were relied on by the Crown. However, even the chosen 21 contained much that was confusing. In the course of outlining the evidence relating to each charge, Stanaway urged the jury to disregard the confusing material.

'A number of children ... talk about many things they say the accused Ellis did,' he said. 'The Crown has elected to proceed on some of those allegations but not all of them ... it is important ... that you look at what are the allegations the Crown relies on and whether or not you accept the child's evidence as regards those allegations ... if you do accept that evidence the Crown has proved its case. It need not matter at the end of the day whether you accept or reject all the other matters the children refer to.'

Distinguishing between evidence relied on by the Crown, and 'other matters', was often a delicate rhetorical operation. With regard to allegations about other people at other venues, Stanaway invited the jury to accept the generalities. 'It is the Crown's case that Ellis took children to houses where other adults were present and engaged in sexual activity with the children,' he said. However, because the adults and houses were not identified, Stanaway invited the jury to be wary of the particulars. 'You should not jump to the conclusion that simply because the children refer to a person as Peter's mother ... that the person is in fact his mother,' he said. Of Bart Dogwood's allegations, he noted: 'The Crown's case is that the complainant [Bart Dogwood] was taken to an unknown address. It could be 404 Hereford Street.'

Because the female crèche staff named in Bart's 'circle incident' videotape had been charged and discharged, Brent Stanaway's double message – accept the general but reject the particular – took on special importance. 'It was on this count only that the women were charged,' he told the jury. 'The issue of their discharge is a completely irrelevant consideration for you and I ask you to put to one side any views that you had as to the sufficiency of the case against them.' However, he also told them: 'With regard to [Bart Dogwood] and other children who talk of bizarre occurrences the Crown asks you not to dismiss what they say out of hand.'

• • •

The order in which the complainants would give evidence was an important consideration. At depositions, the police had listed the complainants in chronological order, oldest to youngest. At trial, the Crown Solicitor still put Zelda Cypress first and Molly Sumach second, but he arranged the other 11 complainants more subtly.

Putting Zelda first made sense. At almost ten years of age she was a poised and believable complainant. Ellis babysat her when he lived at 404 Hereford Street, so presenting her evidence first would alert the jury to that address early in the proceedings. Her allegations – that Ellis touched her vagina with his hand at 404 Hereford Street (Count 1), that he induced her to touch his penis at the crèche (Count 2) and that he touched her vagina and anus with his hand at the crèche (Count 3) – were at the credible end of the spectrum. Her parents had kept to themselves, and had sheltered their daughter from the growing furore, so her evidence was relatively uncontaminated. Furthermore, since Zelda's allegations went back to 1986, the Crown could reasonably hope that any juror who believed her would also believe that Ellis was a long-term child molester – a belief which could, in turn, encourage jurors to attribute the less credible allegations of younger complainants to their relative immaturity, rather than to the apparent unbelievability of their evidence.

The allegations made by the children listed second and third in the indictment, Molly Sumach and Abigail Fir, were also at the credible end of the spectrum. Molly alleged that Ellis touched her vagina with his hand (Count 4). Abigail said he poked her vagina with his finger (Count 5). Both girls said the offences took place at the crèche, and their clothes were on at the time. If jurors could be persuaded to believe those allegations, and to thereby believe that Ellis had abused many children, the chances of them believing the troubling allegations that followed would be greatly enhanced.

The four children who alleged that Ellis urinated on them at the crèche came next. The urination charges involved Eli Laurel (Count 6), Julian Yew (Count 8), Tess Hickory (Count 9) and Frances Pine (Count 13). The Crown presumably hoped the jury would find that strange allegation more believable if they heard it from four children in succession.

An additional charge laid in relation to Eli Laurel alleged that Ellis 'touched him in the anal area with a stick at the Cranmer Centre' (Count 7). Two of the additional charges laid in relation to Tess Hickory introduced 'an unknown address' into the proceedings. These alleged that Ellis bathed with her (Count 10) and attempted to have sexual intercourse with her (Count 11). A further charge involving Tess alleged that Ellis 'touched her bottom with a needle at the crèche' (Count 12).

After that, allegations involving 'an unknown address' came thick and fast. The charges relating to Judy Balsa alleged that Ellis touched her anal area with a stick (Count 14), and 'touched her vagina with his hand and penis' (Count 15), at 'an unknown address'. The charges relating to Bart Dogwood alleged that Ellis 'bathed with him and touched his penis' (Count 16), 'placed his penis against the boy's anus' (Count 17), put his penis in the boy's mouth (Count 18) and was present when 'the complainant was kicked and hit' and had 'a needle placed on his penis' (Count 19 [the circle incident]), at 'an unknown address'.

Kari Lacebark came next. Her four charges alleged that Ellis put his penis in her mouth (Count 20), touched her 'vaginal area' with his penis (Count 21) and touched her 'anal area' with his penis (Count 22) at the crèche, and that 'an unknown man put his penis on her vagina' at 'an unknown address' (Count 23).

The two children who alleged that Ellis urinated into a cup and made them drink his urine – Yelena Holly (Count 25) and Derek Ngaio (Count 26) – followed Kari.

These two similar but bizarre allegations were probably grouped together to make them seem more credible. Yelena's other allegation was that Ellis placed food against her anus (Count 24). The offences involving Yelena were said to have taken place at her home when Ellis was babysitting. The offence involving Derek was said to have taken place at the crèche.

Finally, Lara Palm's charges moved the tone of the indictment back towards the credible. Lara alleged that Ellis put his penis in her mouth (Count 27), and touched her 'vaginal and anal area' with his hand (Count 28), at the crèche.

• • •

At 2.30 pm on Monday 26 April 1992, the court was cleared of all but the people permitted by law to be present when complainants 'in cases of a sexual nature' are giving evidence. When each child witness was called, an attendant took the child and his or her support person to the video room. While the child was giving evidence, the support person was not allowed to communicate with the child, the child was not allowed to leave the witness seat and no one except the crier (who brought exhibits from the courtroom for the child to examine) was allowed to enter the room. If those requirements were not met, the attendant had to notify the judge.

The three wigged and gowned men who appeared on-screen – Justice Williamson, Brent Stanaway and Rob Harrison – did their best to set the young witnesses at ease. They asked the children about their schools, their teachers, their friends, their pets, their clothes and the toys they had brought along. Julian said that he and his dad (who was sitting behind him in the video room) were wearing identical football jerseys. Judy said she was wearing a pink t-shirt, a jumper with flowers on it, coloured jeans and white socks. Kari was wearing a new dress. Derek was wearing a pirate suit. Zelda had a new teddy. Abigail had a new Missy Bear. Eli had a new troll. Lara was dressed as a fairy.

Once Justice Williamson had satisfied himself that the child understood the meaning of 'truth', 'lies' and 'promises', he obtained a promise from the child that he or she would tell the truth. For most children, this was a straightforward process. But four-and-half-year-old Frances Pine (the seventh child on the witness list) was too overwhelmed to say anything. In response to that crisis, the Crown's expert witness, Dr Karen Zelas, slipped a note to the judge suggesting that he ask Frances to talk like a big girl, like her sister.[6]

'Perhaps if you could talk like a big girl, like your sister does,' said the judge. Whereupon Frances straightened up and looked solemn.

'Do you know what a promise is?' asked Williamson.

'No,' said Frances.

After more responses in that vein, Williamson called an adjournment and sought further advice. Dr Zelas suggested that Frances's mother sit in the video room, and though Ms Pine was yet to give evidence, Justice Williamson agreed. Then, after equipping himself with some age-appropriate questions, he made another attempt to qualify Frances as a witness.

'If I said I had a teddy bear sitting up on my head is that right?'

'Wrong,' said Frances.

'You told me before you had a doll there called Gemma wasn't it?'

'Yes.'

'If I said to you that doll's name was Margaret would that be right or wrong?'

'Wrong.'

'Today we are here to talk about real things that happened, would you agree that you will talk to me only about real things that happened?'

'Yes.'

In February 1996, Karen Zelas showed a videoclip of that session to a judges' conference. Her presentation was regarded by those present as a stunning demonstration of how to get the best out of a young and distractible child. A member of her audience recalled:

> Once the right environment was provided and the right questions were put, the judge was able to qualify the child. She did know what the truth was. She did know what it was to only tell about real things, and how important it was to do that. Once her mother was sitting in that room, the child started to talk up and started to tell things. People who were there in court would have been able to say: well, there's a child that can clearly be relied upon.[7]

Interestingly, Karen Zelas did not tell the judges' conference the outcome of Frances Pine's session.

According to the transcript of evidence, once Justice Williamson had qualified Frances, Brent Stanaway spoke to her briefly and her videotaped interview was played. Then the Crown Solicitor questioned her about the allegation on which her charge was based.

'You know it's important that we talk about real things and true things, don't you?' he said. 'We are just talking about things that really happened, do you know that?' Frances nodded.

'Do you know if I say something to you that is not right … you are allowed to tell me that, and if Mr Harrison says something wrong you can tell him too?' Stanaway continued. 'If I say your name is Bella, is that right or wrong?'

'Wrong,' said Frances.

'In the tape we have just seen … you told Sue about Peter doing wees in the crèche toilets on your tummy. Is that a real thing?'

'Wrong thing,' said Frances.
'Did that really happen?'
'No.'
'It didn't really happen?' said Stanaway. Frances shook her head.
'Did you see Peter take his pants down?' he persisted.
'No.'
'Did you take your pants down?'
'No.'
'Did you see Peter's penis?'
'No.'
'What did you see?'
'Nothing.'

At that point, Harrison applied to have his client discharged on the count relating to Frances Pine. In advising the jury of his decision, Justice Williamson outlined the child's videotaped allegations, and stated:

> Today she said to you in evidence all of those things were wrong, or perhaps more correctly, she has just not been capable of giving evidence about these matters in this Court. In a situation like this, where there is no evidence upon which a jury could properly convict ... then the Judge is empowered to deal with the matter by discharging an accused.[8]

• • •

With the other 12 child complainants, the process of qualifying them went smoothly. Once qualified, they watched the relevant Crown tapes (i.e. the videotaped interviews on which the charges relating to that child were based), and were excused while extracts from defence-onus tapes were played (i.e. extracts from that child's videotaped interviews played at the request of the defence).

When the tape-playing was completed, Brent Stanaway questioned the child briefly. By then, most complainants had had their status as victims of Peter Ellis reinforced by the adults around them for the best part of a year. Also, each child was accompanied in the video room by an adult who believed in the allegations. Under the circumstances, there weren't going to be many children like Frances Pine. Nonetheless, Stanaway was cautious. With most of the children, he simply reminded them of the importance of telling the truth, and asked them to confirm that the allegations relied on by the Crown were true.

When Brent Stanaway had finished, Rob Harrison came on-screen. In theory, the main reason for allowing children to give evidence via videolink is to protect them from intimidation by defence counsel. But, according to Harrison, no defence counsel in their right mind would bully a child. To do so would not only alienate the child, it would alienate the jury as well.

'I wanted to relax the children. I wanted them to feel comfortable enough to talk freely,' he explained. 'So I told them about my cats.' To some extent, the approach worked.

'How do you think your defence is going?' TV3 journalist Melanie Reid asked Peter Ellis during the trial.

'I think the man's been brilliant,' said Ellis. 'He's dealt with the children as children … He's read them well, and looked and listened.'[9]

DSW interviewer Sue Sidey agreed. 'I was actually very impressed with what's-his-name. I thought he'd be a real shit to those kids, but in fact he was very engaging. He was quite gentle and sensitive.'[10]

Even Bart Dogwood was impressed. At the end of his day in court, he told his mother that Peter's lawyer was kind to him: 'He really does like animals … I didn't think a lawyer would talk so much about cats in front of the judge.'[11]

In cross-examining the children, Rob Harrison sought to elicit positive memories of Ellis and the crèche, and to expose possible sources of contamination of their evidence. He asked them about the 'keeping safe' books they had read, and about the crèche kids with whom they still had contact. He asked them about the talks they had had with their parents, interviewers and therapists, and about the allegations they had made. Their replies were sometimes firm, sometimes faltering and sometimes fanciful. Most children insisted that they could remember the abuse, even if they had trouble describing it. From time to time, they contradicted themselves, their parents and each other. Sometimes they acknowledged that they may have been mistaken. To many questions, they simply replied: 'I don't remember.'

When Rob Harrison told the children that Peter denied abusing them, some were indignant: 'I just can't remember that actual picture, I just remember he did poke me in the crutch' (Molly); 'That's not true' (Tess); 'I am positive that I am telling the truth' (Julian); 'He's lying' (Bart); 'He did' (Kari); 'I'm sure I'm not mistaken' (Lara). Others were hesitant: 'He's probably lying' (Yelena); 'It's very hard to remember. I know very very well some are true, and then I think: is that one true or what?' (Eli).

In a pre-trial ruling, Justice Williamson had declared the videotapes of Derek Ngaio's and Zelda Cypress's first interviews inadmissible because they did not comply with the regulations.[12] Nonetheless, Rob Harrison could cross-examine on them. So when Zelda assured him that she could remember all her interviews, he attempted to do so.

'Do you remember what you said the first time?' he asked.

'No,' said Zelda.

'Can you remember saying … that it was only when your Mum reminded you about Peter that you became scared of him?'

'No.'

In our adversarial system, when a witness has been examined by the prosecution and cross-examined by the defence, he or she may be re-examined by the prosecution on matters raised in cross-examination. This meant that, because Rob Harrison had raised (but had failed to confirm) the possibility that Zelda's fear of Ellis had been prompted by her mother's anxiety, Brent Stanaway had the opportunity to raise (and attempt to discount) that possibility.

'Do you remember when it was you first became scared of Peter?' he asked Zelda in re-examination.

'No,' said Zelda.

'Was it when you were at the crèche or after you left the crèche?' asked Stanaway.

'I was at the crèche.'

'Why was it you were scared of him at the crèche?'

'I don't know.'

That exchange did not resolve the issue, but it was one of Brent Stanaway's more successful re-examinations. His re-examination of Eli Laurel (the fourth child witness) was one of his least successful.

In cross-examination, Rob Harrison had asked Eli: 'Isn't it true that your mum asked you if Peter had done wees in your face?'

'Yep,' agreed Eli.

'And you said yes to her?'

'Yep.'

Eli also assured Harrison that Peter, Spike, Boulderhead, Yuckhead, Stupidhead and various other adults and children had crawled, one at a time, across a ladder from a second-storey window in the Cranmer Centre to a window in an adjacent building. In re-examination, Brent Stanaway attempted to restore Eli's credibility.

'Was it [the ladder] a long way to the ground or a short way to the ground?' he asked.

'A long way,' said Eli.

'When you were going across the ladder, could people see you if they were on the ground?'

'No.'

'Why was that?'

'It just looks like a big smog or something,' said Eli.

After failing to resolve the ladder issue, Stanaway tackled the leading-question issue by asking Eli how his mother knew what Peter had done.

'One of the other parents told her and she told me to see if anything had happened,' Eli said.

'Your mum doesn't say that,' Stanaway told him. 'She says you told her that first.

Did you tell your Mum that Peter did wees on you, or did your mum tell you that was the case?'

'Some other parents rang up my Mum and told her about that, and she told me,' Eli assured him.

The next child witness was Tess Hickory. With encouragement from Rob Harrison, she spun out her story about going to Peter's bach in the country by horse and carriage. She also assured him that she was sitting in the bath with her legs straight and her feet together when Ellis touched her vagina with his penis. After his experience with Eli Laurel, Brent Stanaway did not take the risk of re-examining Tess.

Rob Harrison's biggest breakthrough came in his cross-examination of Judy Balsa (the eighth complainant child). 'Can you remember the first two tapes you made with Cathy [DSW interviewer Cathy Crawford]?' he asked.

'We first learnt about all the things Peter did and then we came on the screen and did it,' Judy replied.

'You learnt it all before you came on to the screen?'

'Yes.'

'Who taught it to you before you came on the screen and did it?' asked Harrison.

'Cathy, and she told me what Peter did,' said Judy.

Later, Justice Williamson questioned Judy himself. 'You said when you were talking to Mr Harrison that you had learnt what you were going to say ... was that before the camera was turned on?' he asked.

'Yes,' said Judy.

At that point, both counsel invited the judge to discharge Ellis on the two counts relating to Judy Balsa. Justice Williamson said he was reluctant to do so. He noted that, in her videolink evidence, Judy had distinguished between abuse by her uncle and abuse at the crèche, and had confirmed the allegations on which her charges were based. He also noted that decisions about the truthfulness and reliability of the evidence should be made by the jury. However, he concluded that a discharge was justified because there were aspects of Judy's evidence 'which appear to indicate substantial confusion on her part about times and places as well as the extent of the vital allegations'.[13] (In fact, all the complainants displayed substantial confusion on these matters, so it could be argued that, had he wanted to do so, Williamson could have discharged Ellis on all counts for this reason.) Interestingly, the judge made no mention of Judy's revelations about Cathy Crawford in his decision.

Bart Dogwood, the ritual abuse believers' key witness, was the ninth child to give evidence. In his examination of Bart, Brent Stanaway took no chances. After a preliminary chat about cricket, he said: 'I am going to ask you some questions later about what Mr Harrison asks you, but at the moment we will see what Mr

Harrison wants to ask you, right?' Under cross-examination, Bart insisted that the circle incident really happened. He said that Peter, Gaye, Jan and Marie put sharp sticks and burning paper up his bum, put children in cages at the crèche, threw them in trapdoors at the Masonic Lodge and put them in coffins and buried them in graveyards. He said that Peter put his penis up his bum, and made him do poohs in the bath and eat it, and that someone put a needle up his penis and made it bleed.

'Were there any other teachers at the crèche who did things to you?' asked Harrison.

'Yep,' said Bart, and named Sandi and Susannah.

'What about Sharleen?' asked Harrison. 'Did Sharleen do anything to you?'

'Who's Sharleen?' said Bart.

Under re-examination from Brent Stanaway, Bart insisted that there were no magic tricks, everything he described was real. After Bart, the rest of the kids seemed tame.

• • •

For the charges against Ellis, the Crown relied on: Molly's only interview; the first of two interviews with Abigail, Frances and Lara; the second of Derek's two interviews; the second and third of Zelda's three interviews; the first and third of three interviews with Eli, Tess and Yelena; the first of Julian's five interviews; the second and fourth of Bart's five interviews; the fourth of Judy's six interviews; and the first, second, third and fourth of Kari's six interviews.

With interviews played at the request of the defence, Justice Williamson allowed only the sections that he considered relevant to the charges to be played. As a result, the jury saw: excerpts from Julian's second, third and fourth interviews (all of which referred back to the allegation in his first interview that was the subject of a charge); excerpts from Judy's first and second interviews; and excerpts from Bart's first interview.

The problem the judge's ruling created for the defence is well illustrated by Bart's first interview. In the interview, Lynda Morgan took care to ensure that Bart was relaxed and comfortable. She made him promise to tell the truth. She gave him every opportunity to indicate whether he had been abused by Peter Ellis and, if so, in what way. She also gave him every opportunity to indicate whether other adults and children were involved. All Bart could come up with was a memory of Ellis cleaning him up on the crèche changing table. The contrast between that innocuous story, and the bizarre allegations in his later interviews (which were recorded after four months of parental questioning and sexual abuse therapy) was extraordinary. But because the jury had no transcript of Bart's first interview and saw only selected excerpts of the videotape, the potential impact of the contrast would have been much reduced.

Furthermore, because Bart didn't have to watch his first tape, it would have made no impact on him at all.

'I can still remember the confusion on jurors' faces when the defence tapes were played,' Rob Harrison recalled. 'They'd be flicking through the papers in front of them looking for a transcript and finding there wasn't one, wondering what the hell was going on as the video was fast-forwarded from one disjointed bit to the next. Also it was hopeless trying to cross-examine on the defence tapes. Most kids couldn't remember what they'd said in tapes they hadn't seen.'

However, Julian Yew said he could remember saying (in a tape he had not seen) that Peter had a giraffe at his house. ('Was that a real giraffe or a pretend giraffe?' Sidey had asked. 'It's real giraffe,' Julian had replied.) But when Harrison asked him the same question, Julian said, 'It was ... lying on his carpet like a dead tiger and they actually take all the bones out of it and leave all the skin.' 'He's been coached well,' Peter Ellis observed, in a note to Harrison's assistant Siobhan McNulty.

Nonetheless, Rob Harrison was heartened by Justice Williamson's insistence that the central issue was whether or not the children could be believed. By the time he had finished cross-examining them, the number of complainants had fallen from 13 to 11, and the believability of the remaining complainants had been thrown into doubt. Molly, who alleged that Ellis abused her when the other teachers were with the deaf children, admitted to confusing the crèche (where there were no deaf children) with her school (where there were deaf children); Abigail told Harrison that she hadn't seen anyone else's private parts and no one had seen hers, but Colin the policeman asked her lots of questions about Peter, and she and her mum talked about the crèche and made lots of lists before her first DSW interview; Eli, Tess, Julian and Bart put their over-active imaginations on display; Kari confirmed that her mother asked her leading questions; Yelena said that her mum and Kari told her about the naughty things Peter did; Derek couldn't remember anything; and Lara provided a graphic illustration of an implanted memory.

In response to Rob Harrison's questions, Lara said she could remember being in an incubator when she was born.

'What can you remember about that?' he asked.

'I can remember that I had wires coming off and kept kicking the tube out of my nose.'

'Has your Mum ever talked to you about when you were in the incubator?'

'Yes.'

In Rob Harrison's view, Zelda Cypress, the oldest complainant and the first to give evidence, was the only one whose credibility survived his cross-examination unscathed. 'I tried to reassure her and settle her and get her to talk,' he recalled. 'She just became more and more withdrawn. She wouldn't make eye contact. Something seemed wrong. I couldn't figure out what it was.'

• • •

While the explicit issue for the jury was whether or nor the children could be believed, the implicit issue – and, given the confusing nature of the children's evidence, the most important issue – was whether or not the adults who claimed to speak on behalf of the children could be believed.

In their evidence, the two fathers who took the witness stand immediately before their own children, and the ten mothers who did so immediately afterwards, talked about when, how often and for how long their offspring had attended the Civic Child Care Centre. They also talked about their impressions of Ellis and the crèche, their knowledge of crèche routines and their children's health and behaviour as preschoolers (memories of red bottoms, tantrums and toileting problems loomed large). With regard to the crèche investigation, they talked about how and when they heard about it, and whether they attended any meetings or joined any support groups. But the evidence of extensive parent–parent, parent–child and child–child contamination that featured in the depositions hearing received hardly a mention.

This was largely because Justice Williamson had ruled pre-trial that conversations between parents, children and other adults (and parents' notes of those conversations) were hearsay, and were therefore inadmissible in the parents' evidence-in-chief. However, that was not the end of the matter. Williamson said he would allow defence counsel 'some latitude in regard to cross-examination on hearsay matters' if he could provide the judge with legal justification for doing so. But the provision came with a warning: 'If he cross-examines concerning hearsay material then the Crown may be entitled to reexamine in relation to that material.' In other words, if the defence cross-examined a parent on an aspect of a conversation with a child, the Crown could re-examine the parent on some other aspect of the same conversation, and the defence would have no right of reply.[14]

Another factor in the sanitising of parental evidence at trial was that, after their dry run at the depositions hearing, the complainant parents had polished up their acts. At depositions, when they talked about their efforts to support each other and help their children disclose, they were accused of contaminating their children's evidence. As caring and responsible parents, they found that accusation offensive. So when they came to give evidence at trial, they were far more guarded.

In their evidence-in-chief, they recounted a version of events that they had come to believe was unquestionably true: that they had asked their children about the crèche in only the most general terms prior to their disclosures. When Rob Harrison presented them with evidence to the contrary, most parents denied or minimised the incriminating material. It was a mistake, they suggested, or a misunderstanding.

Ms Cypress said she initiated a conversation with Zelda by 'asking her what she remembered about the crèche', but had avoided further discussion. When Rob Harrison told her that, in Zelda's DSW interviews, her daughter mentioned talking about her allegations with her mother, Ms Cypress was indignant. 'I would not agree I have been having discussions about Peter and the disclosures she has made. I feel very clear about that,' she said.

In his cross-examination of Ms Hickory, Rob Harrison asked: 'Did you at some stage call Ms Linden and suggest to her that your daughter and her daughter play together?'

'I remember calling her. I don't know whether I suggested the children play together.'

'Did you not tell her that Tess had been playing with Kari and you felt it was therapeutic and that you could arrange it to try to get them to mention Peter's house?'

'I don't remember.'

'Did you also tell her of a specific allegation about Peter putting his finger into the anus of a puppy and making children suck his finger?'

'I don't remember.'

Later, Justice Williamson ruled Ms Linden's version of that conversation inadmissible on the ground that it was 'of a hearsay nature' and 'not relevant to any issue in this trial'.[15]

• • •

The Crown's procession of 13 child and 31 adult witnesses occupied 19 working days. During that time, questions concerning the playing of defence-onus tapes, the admissibility of evidence and the extent of permissible cross-examination were debated by judge and counsel in the absence of the jury on at least 25 occasions in court, and on further occasions in chambers. However, because Justice Williamson issued only nine oral judgments during that time, the arguments traversed in most of those discussions were never recorded.

In Oral Judgment (No.7), Williamson ruled that Ms Laurel's recollection of Eli coming home from crèche and saying 'Peter did wees and poohs on the children today and the children did poohs and wees on the floor' was admissible under an exception to the hearsay rule.[16]

Oral Judgment (No.8), concerned Rob Harrison's proposal to cross-examine Ms Yew about Ms Magnolia's list of bizarre allegations. Because Ms Magnolia was not a witness, demonstrating the spread of abuse beliefs among complainant parents was difficult for the defence. In cross-examination, some parents admitted contacting each other, but were adamant that little information, if any, was exchanged. So evidence about the compilation and distribution of Ms Magnolia's allegations about group abuse at 'Peter's house' was vital to the defence.

On that issue, Justice Williamson ruled that he would permit some cross-examination 'although the extent of it may have to be controlled'. He also noted that in previous (unrecorded) rulings he had 'endeavoured to set a pattern'. 'It is a trial in relation to specific charges and must remain so,' he said.[17]

In the cross-examination that followed, Ms Yew said that a meeting was held at her home in late July or early August 1992 to discuss allegations made by children about venues outside the crèche. Among those present were Ms Magnolia, Detective Eade, the Dogwoods and the Lacebarks. At that meeting, Ms Magnolia produced copies of her list.

When Rob Harrison cross-examined Ms Dogwood, she admitted to attending the meeting but insisted that she did not see Ms Magnolia's list, or consider the possibility of multi-victim, multi-perpetrator abuse at 404 Hereford Street, until after her son's bizarre disclosures of 4, 5 and 6 August.

At that point, Harrison produced Ms Dogwood's own notes. The notes headed *Monday, 3 August 1992, time 7.30pm* recorded Bart's disclosure of group abuse at a white two-storey house. The notes headed *Tuesday 8.30am* stated 'We drove passed [sic] and stopped outside 404 Hereford Street. Bart said that was the house he went to a lot.' The notes headed *Wednesday, 5 August, 4.30pm* also *Thursday 8.30am* recorded Bart's circle incident disclosure.

Of the page headed *3 August*, Harrison asked: 'Is it not correct that at depositions you said ... that those notes were written on 3 August?'

'I remember saying that and I have been extremely upset from the day that I said it because it is quite incorrect,' Ms Dogwood asserted. 'In depositions it was an extremely nerve wracking and emotional situation ... there was a tremendous amount of pressure on me and I was wrong. I did not get that information at least till mid or late August.' With regard to her note about 404 Hereford Street, Ms Dogwood said she did not take Bart to that address on Tuesday 4 August, but on another Tuesday some weeks later.

In view of the tender ages of the complainants, the horrifying nature of the allegations and the obvious distress of the parents, questioning the integrity of the parents was difficult for the defence. The atmosphere in court did not encourage it. Even when their testimony was misleading, exaggerated or over-emotional, it was not in Ellis's interest for Harrison to treat the parents with anything but sympathy and respect. However, that was not the case the following year, when Bart's mother was involved in unrelated court proceedings. On that occasion, the judge said of Ms Dogwood:

> The evidence which the applicant gave and the manner in which she gave her evidence confirmed her to be a very strong-willed person who was determined to have her own way ... a person with impassioned views who stubbornly refused to be deflected from those views ... the applicant's evidence ... was inconsistent with the evidence given by the other people

... These features together with the manner in which the applicant gave her evidence lead me to severely question the applicant's credibility and reliability as a witness.[18]

Justice Williamson's Oral Judgment (No.9) concerned Rob Harrison's wish to cross-examine Ms Dogwood about her letter protesting at the cancellation of Bart's 11 August interview. In the letter, Ms Dogwood complained that Dr Zelas had failed to take her son's disclosures about the Masonic Lodge, churches, mock marriages, graveyards, cages, dead bodies, coffins, other crèches and large amounts of money seriously because she was ignorant about ritual abuse.[19]

By cross-examining Ms Dogwood about the letter, Harrison wanted to show that her questioning of Bart was a major concern to crèche investigators, and he wanted to lay the groundwork for his later cross-examination of Dr Zelas. But Justice Williamson disallowed the proposed cross-examination on the ground that opinions about the reliability of the children's evidence were inadmissible, even when those opinions were held by people of 'different degrees of learning, viewpoint or specialist qualifications'. (The reference to 'specialist qualifications' signalled to Harrison that any application to cross-examine Dr Zelas on the same issue would likely be refused.) Furthermore, because Ms Dogwood's letter was written after the interviews on which Bart's charges were based, Williamson said he found it 'difficult ... to understand how it has real relevance to the defence in this trial.'[20]

• • •

When the children and parents had completed their evidence, Detective Legat presented the police exhibits. Then the DSW interviewers took the stand. Sue Sidey went first, followed by Lynda Morgan. By then, all the interviews conducted by Cathy Crawford had been eliminated from the case.

The restrictions placed by Justice Williamson on the interviewers' cross-examination prevented Rob Harrison from questioning them about the concerns they had expressed at depositions regarding the effects of parental anxiety, and of repeated, suggestive and leading questioning, on the reliability of the children's evidence.[21] Also, after their earlier grilling from Gerald Nation, the interviewers were far more guarded at trial. However, some discussion of interviewing techniques did take place.

Both Sue Sidey and Lynda Morgan agreed that interviewers should adopt a neutral stance and be open to the possibility that no abuse had occurred. They also agreed that open-ended questions were desirable, that pressure and coercion was undesirable and that children should be told that 'don't know' or 'can't remember' were acceptable answers. But when Harrison highlighted examples of apparent coercion or bias in their own work, they said it was nothing of the sort. All they were doing, they said, was encouraging the child to validate information already received from parents.

• • •

The next witnesses were Doctors Thornley and Metherall. In theory, because the Crown Solicitor had laid no charges of anal or vaginal penetration, the Crown needed no evidence of such penetration to prove its case. But the issue was not straightforward.

In their videolink evidence, Tess and Kari had accepted Brent Stanaway's suggestion that Ellis 'touched' their private parts, but Eli and Bart had stuck to their colourful stories of anal penetration with sharp sticks. Barr also insisted that he had penises and burning paper shoved up his bum. So with Eli and Bart, evidence of anal trauma would have been helpful to the Crown case.

Dr Thornley reported that Eli's anal area showed 'no sign of abnormality at all', and advised that 'normal findings does not mean that sexual abuse hasn't taken place'. Under cross-examination, she agreed that a child who had sticks and burning paper placed in his anus in a manner that caused bleeding would be expected to suffer acute pain and lingering discomfort.

According to Garrow and Casey's *Principles of the Law of Evidence*, a trial judge may ask clarifying questions, but a judge who descends into the arena is 'liable to have his vision clouded by the dust of conflict'.[22] Nonetheless, at the end of Dr Thornley's evidence, Justice Williamson descended into the arena. Through his questions, he established that a stick could be inserted into a child's anus without causing injury, and that, if it did, that injury could heal quickly and completely.

Throughout the trial, Williamson's interventions were an ongoing concern to Peter Ellis. 'He seems to interject at times when my lawyer is on a roll,' he told TV3's Melanie Reid.[23]

When Dr Metherall took the stand, she reported that Bart Dogwood's penis and anus were 'normal in appearance with no sign of past injury', and added that the findings 'neither confirm nor exclude a history of sexual abuse'. She also reported that she had found irregularities in the appearances of Tess Hickory's hymen and Kari Lacebark's anus. Earlier, Rob Harrison had applied to have that evidence excluded on the grounds of unfairness. He pointed out that the reported defects were not necessarily traumatic in origin, and that the relevant charges did not require proof of penetration. So, while the evidence was highly prejudicial to his client, it added nothing to the prosecution case.

But while Justice Williamson took a narrow view of relevance in relation to evidence the defence wanted admitted, he took a wider view when it came to evidence of interest to the Crown. In Oral Judgment (No.11) he took into account 'the entire evidence given in the course of the trial', 'the nature of the allegations' and 'the age and evidence of the complainants' before concluding that the medical evidence relating to Tess and Kari was admissible.[24] When little children allege horrible crimes, he seemed to suggest, admitting prejudicial evidence of doubtful relevance was entirely justified.

Under cross-examination, Dr Metherall acknowledged that little research had been done into normal variations in the genitals of non-abused children, and conceded that the irregularity in Kari's anus could be a natural defect. Also, while she considered that the notch in Tess's hymen was probably traumatic in origin, she agreed that Ellis could not have penetrated her in the way the child had described (while she was sitting in the bath with her legs out straight and her feet together).

• • •

On Friday 14 May, Detective Neville Jenkins reported on his scene examinations at the Civic Child Care Centre and the Cranmer Centre. The crèche was the venue for 15 counts. The only count located at the Cranmer Centre was the one in which Ellis was alleged to have 'touched' Eli Laurel 'in the anal area with a stick'. Earlier, the Crown Solicitor had asked jurors to concern themselves only with allegations directly related to the charges, so in theory Eli's 'stick up the bum' allegation was all that mattered. But Detective Jenkins had spent hours exploring, mapping and photographing the Cranmer Centre, and he gave the jury the benefit of his findings in his evidence-in-chief.

At the end of Jenkins's presentation, the jury (together with the judge, the accused and accompanying prison officers, counsel, court attendants and Detective Jenkins) toured the Cranmer Centre and the Civic Child Care Centre. It was Peter Ellis's first visit to the crèche since his suspension 18 months earlier.

'It was empty,' he told TV3's Melanie Reid through tears. 'It was a place that was good and fun ... a place that was full of laughter ... It made me wonder how on earth this ever happened, because the people that ran that place were all good, are good, people. The parents that went there, the parents that had children who were complainants were all good people. And something went wrong. It's nothing to do with the sexual abuse of children.'

'What was it to do with?' Reid asked.

'It was to do with people that decided that it had happened ... the police, the social welfare ...'

'Peter, there's a lot of people who'll be watching that'll be saying, "So much for the tears, so much for the sadness. You're nothing but a lowdown child abuser." They're convinced that you've abused their children,' she said.

'Probably for a long time they will,' he agreed. 'I hope one day they are actually going to be prepared to come along and say, "Hello Peter, can you tell me: did we get it wrong?" And I'll tell them. They got it wrong. Because it didn't happen. At depositions my heart went out to them … You can't help feeling sorry for these people, or feeling understanding. I still do, because I helped raise their children … I still like them. It might be stupid. But I'm cross with the people on the outside, the ones that have stirred these parents into a frenzy.'

'You say you still like them, but they're the very people that are trying to put you behind bars,' Reid pointed out.

'No, I don't think they are,' he said. 'Not really. I still think the people who are trying to put me behind bars are the five detectives, the people who have literally and utterly shaken my belief in the police.'[25]

• • •

After the official visit to the alleged crime scenes, Detective Jenkins returned to the witness stand. With regard to the Cranmer Centre, his evidence purported to show that it was possible for Peter Ellis to have taken children up to the Marriage Guidance rooms on the second floor, out the window onto the roof, up and down ladders across gables to a gully in the roof where two manhole covers were located, through the manholes into the ceiling cavity above the Embroiderers' Guild and down a rope into the kitchen opposite the Child Care Association Rooms. To ritual abuse believers, Jenkins' evidence proved that the allegations made by Eli and Bart about roofs, ladders, tunnels, trapdoors, ovens, sexual orgies, human sacrifice and devil worship in the Cranmer Centre should not be dismissed as fantasy.

In describing the Cranmer Centre roof, Detective Jenkins said that the gully in which the manhole covers were located 'showed denting in the corrugated iron consistent with a substantial amount of [foot] traffic'. However, under cross-examination, he admitted there was a benign explanation for the denting: maintenance workers went up there to clear leaves from the guttering. Doubt was also cast on the 'mysterious goings on in the ceiling cavity' scenario when Jenkins agreed that he had to be careful where he put his feet up there. 'Someone put their foot through the roof adjacent to the manhole in the kitchen,' he admitted.

With regard to the Civic Crèche, Jenkins acknowledged that, in his extensive collection of photographs, there were none of the wall between the Big End playroom and the Big End toilets. A photo of that wall would have shown three areas of constant and/or unpredictable activity throughout the crèche day: the first aid cabinet; the sink where paints and play dough were prepared; and the door into the lobby of the Big End toilets.

'You would know there were allegations of incidents in the toilet area?' Harrison pointed out.

'Certainly,' said Jenkins.

'You would know throughout most of the year the usual practice was for the door to the toilets to remain open. Do you not think it would have been important to have the door to the toilets open and photographs taken showing how much you can see of the inside of the toilets from the general play area of the crèche?' Jenkins said the omission was 'an oversight'.

• • •

The Crown's next witness was long-time Marriage Guidance (MG) administrator Toni Jones. She said that Peter Ellis had twice sought permission to come through the MG rooms and onto the roof: once to blow bubbles over the crèche play area, once to retrieve a ball. She also said that the MG staff worked long hours, and had a clear view of the roof.

All things considered, the notion that Peter Ellis could have slipped unnoticed through the MG rooms and onto the roof accompanied by a wraith-like procession of preschoolers beggars belief.

• • •

Then Peter Ellis's NZ Childcare Association (NZCA) tutor Ms Rata took the stand:

> The only reason the Crown called me was to show that Peter had access to the kitchen opposite the NZCA room. They wanted to show that he could have put kids in the oven without taking them over the roof and through the ceiling and down a rope first. I had to admit there was no reason I could think of why he wouldn't have been able to do that. We kept the kitchen key by the blackboard. Any trainee or tutor who wanted to make coffee could take it as needed. Nobody would have known or cared if Peter had taken it home and got a spare one cut.[26]

Under cross-examination, Ms Rata said that she spent hours at the Civic collecting and delivering her own children, and making formal observations of Ellis's work. She assured Rob Harrison that she was free to come and go unannounced, that children liked going on walks with Ellis and that the door to the Big End toilets was always open. In re-examination, she conceded that the door could have been closed when she wasn't there.

• • •

On Monday 17 May 1993, child psychiatrist Dr Karen Zelas took the stand. In her evidence-in-chief, she provided a list of 'behavioural characteristics of child sexual abuse'. She acknowledged that 'many of the symptoms are not solely confined to child sexual abuse', but claimed that 'clustering of a number of symptoms is more likely to indicate abuse'. Her list comprised: sleep disturbances; nightmares; mood disturbances; tearfulness; sadness; headaches; stomach aches; vomiting; separation anxiety; anxiety about school; diffuse anxiety; regressive behaviour; wetting; soiling; reluctance to go to bed; avoidance of certain activities or people; sexualised play; ritualised play; loss of concentration; over conscientiousness; striving to succeed; striving to be liked; low self-esteem; passivity; tantrums; and hostility to parents.

She said that the majority of sexually abused children either deny or fail to disclose abuse at the time it is occurring, and 'initially deny any suggestion of abuse' at a later date. She said that sexually abused children normally have 'warm feelings, loving feelings' towards the perpetrator; and often 'recant or withdraw the allegation, say they were tricking or that it wasn't true, they were telling lies ...'.

She also told the court that the complainants' headaches, sexual knowledge, unhappiness, nightmares, night terrors, toileting problems, tantrums, delayed disclosures, sleeping problems, anxiety, fear of men, aggression, hyperactivity, denial, avoidance behaviour, sexualised behaviour, nausea, red bottoms, separation anxiety, stomach aches, progressive disclosures, vomiting, gagging, fussiness and other symptoms and behaviours were consistent with sexual abuse.

• • •

Two weeks before the Ellis trial, Rob Harrison's mother was diagnosed with terminal cancer. During the trial, her condition deteriorated rapidly. On the day Dr Zelas began giving evidence, Rob Harrison discussed the situation with Peter Ellis:

> I told him we were going to have to call a break, that my mother had been given 24 hours to live. I said, 'Look Peter, if you feel this isn't going well, and I'm not able to proceed, they'll have to abort the trial. Then you could get another defence counsel and make a fresh start.' He reinforced my feeling that I was doing okay. So we marched on.

In the course of my research, several lawyers volunteered the opinion, uninvited, that Peter Ellis was convicted because his counsel wasn't good enough. A legal scholar who observed the proceedings commented:

> I get annoyed with people who say that Rob Harrison wasn't the right man for the job, that he shouldn't have done this and he should have done that. They weren't there. They didn't have to deal with issues he had to deal with. I don't think he should be criticised at all. He did a very good job. I think he generally made the right calls. Another barrister might have done some things differently, sure, but he might have got a worse result.

On Monday 17 May, Harrison advised the judge of his family crisis. Justice Williamson adjourned the court next day, and again the following day. Then, following Harrison's mother's death on the Wednesday night, Williamson adjourned the court for the rest of the week.

• • •

On Monday 24 May, Karen Zelas completed her evidence-in-chief and Rob Harrison began his cross-examination. His opening questions about the nature of memory and the suggestibility of children were predictable, and she handled them comfortably. But, without the benefit of a dry run at depositions, his less predictable questions caught her off-guard. Her biggest slip-up was to deny giving a television interview with Paul Holmes on the case, or having any involvement with the case prior to the Knox Hall meeting on 31 March 1992.

'Do you not recall being asked by Mr Holmes on 23 March 1992 … "There's a danger isn't there, parents can now start imagining change?" and your answer is "Yes, there is … There is a real risk if they start to try to speak with their own children about it that unintentionally … they might introduce ideas to the child by the way in which they ask questions … and then … it may be impossible to know whether or not their child actually has been abused"?' asked Harrison.

'If you say so then I must have. I don't actually recall doing that interview,' she said.

'Didn't you also say in that interview that there are specialist interviewers who are being set up to interview these children?'

'If you say so.'

'Would you not accept by that stage you are dealing specifically with the Civic Crèche inquiry, and you also have specific knowledge of what was happening in terms of DSW?'

'I was aware all along what was happening in general terms and procedures,' Zelas replied.

When pressed to confirm her televised warning to parents, Zelas became evasive. She said it was possible to determine the reliability of a child's interview from a careful assessment of its contents, even when prior parental questioning had taken place.

'Then why did you say on the *Holmes* programme "There is a real risk if they start to try to speak with their own children … it'll be impossible to know whether or not their child actually has been abused"?' Harrison asked.

Zelas said that she was referring to custody and access situations. Harrison pointed out that she clearly was not. Zelas said what she really meant was that prior questioning would affect the credibility of the child's evidence (i.e. it would make the evidence less likely to be believed in court). Harrison asked her why she hadn't said so, instead of warning parents that prior questioning could make it 'impossible to know whether or not their child had been abused'. Zelas replied lamely that she had not answered Mr Holmes's question as well as she might have.

'I actually thought she was going to burst into tears,' Peter Ellis wrote to Harrison's assistant Siobhan McNulty.

Harrison then moved to another topic, and tossed another unexpected question to the Crown's expert witness. 'What behaviours in young children are inconsistent with the child who has been sexually abused?' he asked.

'I haven't thought about that,' Zelas replied. But she insisted that Zelda Cypress's history of being happy at the crèche and withdrawn at school was consistent (and not, as Harrison suggested, inconsistent) with her being abused at the crèche.

Throughout her cross-examination, Zelas was adamant that when children were asked repeated, leading and suggestive questions by parents and interviewers about long-ago events, their confused and fragmentary responses could be reliable evidence of abuse.

• • •

The only evidence connecting 404 Hereford Street with organised abuse came in Bart Dogwood's circle incident disclosure. In the indictment, the Crown Solicitor located the circle incident at 'an unknown address'. This suggests that Brent Stanaway did not have much confidence in Bart's evidence. Nonetheless, when it came to presenting 404 Hereford Street to the jury as a possible location for the circle incident, and for all the other offences at 'an unknown address', what the Crown Solicitor lacked in evidence, he made up for in innuendo.

In his videolink discussions with the complainants, Stanaway not only asked children whose charges were located at 'an unknown address' (Tess, Judy, Bart and Kari) about activities involving other adults and children at 'Peter's house', he also raised the subject with three children whose charges were confined to the crèche and the Cranmer Centre (Abigail, Eli and Julian).

Adult witnesses also talked about 404 Hereford Street. Ms Cypress said that Ellis babysat Zelda there at the end of 1986. Ms Dogwood said that Bart recognised the house. Ms Kapok said that she went there on two crèche trips to see Ellis's animals at the end of 1986. Ms Kowhai said that she visited Ellis there before he left in May 1987. Detective Heath displayed his plans and photographs of 404 Hereford Street, and pointed out the 'secret cavities'. Then it was Bruce's turn to give evidence.

The police had found no evidence of child abuse, or of child pornography, or even of children at 404 Hereford Street. Bruce had always stoutly denied any wrongdoing. But when the Crown Solicitor led him through his evidence-in-chief, Stanaway gave the impression that he didn't believe a word Bruce said. In the recollections of crèche supporters, Bruce stood his ground in the face of the Crown Solicitor's onslaught. In the recollections of crèche critics, Bruce stubbornly denied everything.

At the end of Bruce's evidence – presumably with Eli's story about Spike, Boulderhead, Yuckhead and Stupidhead in mind – Justice Williamson asked him if he had a nickname. 'I hope not,' Bruce replied.

• • •

After the hotel proprietor who had seen Peter Ellis taking a group of children for a walk had testified, the witnesses to Ellis's conversations on sexual matters – Debbie Gillespie's former partner Belinda, and crèche workers Jan Buckingham and Sharleen – gave evidence. They also discussed crèche routines and staff–child ratios. Belinda recalled a game that Ellis played called 'tickle bash-ups', which involved 'tickling and possibly being hit with cushions'. She said children usually 'loved it and had a good time'. While Sharleen was on the stand, Detectives Legat and Heath sat at the back of the court. 'That was very much an ominous presence,' Sharleen recalled. 'But I said exactly what I believed to be true. Ken Legat told me afterwards that he was very disappointed in me.'

Jan Buckingham's evidence was the subject of two rulings. Oral Judgment (No.13) concerned her recollection that Ellis had talked about taking polaroid photos of adult sexual acts. The police had found no pornography of any sort at Ellis's home, and photography did not feature in any of the charges against him. Nonetheless, Justice Williamson declared Buckingham's evidence admissible because, in his view, it provided strong support for two of Bart's allegations: that Ellis took photos while a man named Robert sodomised him; and that Ellis and his mother took photos of the circle incident.

Oral Judgment (No.14) concerned Rob Harrison's wish to give Jan Buckingham the opportunity to deny the claim, made by Bart in cross-examination, that she had taken him away from the crèche on occasions other than the circle incident to places where offences occurred. Williamson ruled against Harrison's request on the ground that the matter was not relevant to the charges.[27]

• • •

Next, Detective Chappell presented his flow charts of child and staff attendance at the crèche. Then Detective Colin Eade took the stand. After he had been examined and cross-examined, he introduced, in re-examination, the 'schedule of behavioural matters'. It comprised a table with the complainants' names down one side, and 26 columns labelled A to Z across the top. Each column represented a different 'behavioural matter' mentioned in the evidence of a parent or child. In column A, every complainant who was alleged to have expressed a 'fear or dislike of Ellis' was marked with a cross. The crosses in column B represented 'reluctance/fear of attending the crèche'. Among the other 'behavioural matters' on the schedule were: fear of intruders/robbers; clothing, eating, toileting, bathing and sleeping problems; poor coordination; and fear of wolves.

Rob Harrison objected vigorously to the introduction of the schedule. He pointed out that it had no time-scale, and that many of the marked items referred to behaviours observed during the investigation, rather than while the child was at the crèche. Furthermore, the schedule was based on the unverified reports of anxious parents, and there was no evidence that any of the behaviours were caused by sexual abuse.

In Oral Judgment (No.15) Justice Williamson ruled that 'schedules and charts to assist a jury in complicated cases can be very desirable and is not improper provided that the contents are proved and that the Judge is satisfied there is no unfairness'. With regard to Harrison's objections, he said it was not 'unfair to present a summary of what has been said', and that 'the question of whether what has been said is reliable, or accurate, is a matter ultimately for the jury'.[28]

12.ii: The End

In preparing the defence case, the most important decision Rob Harrison had to make was whether to put Peter Ellis in the witness box. Outside the court, the failure of an accused person to give evidence is often regarded with suspicion. If he really is innocent, people say, why doesn't he stand up in court and say so? Inside the court, the judge may dampen that suspicion by explaining that the accused is not obliged to give evidence, and that the onus is still on the Crown to prove all the ingredients of the offence. Alternatively, the judge may excite that suspicion by observing that 'the jury might draw their own conclusions as to the accused's reasons for not giving evidence'.[1]

Some seasoned defence counsel argue that, if the accused is a presentable, articulate person with a convincing story to tell, then he should give evidence. In doing so, they say, he will satisfy the jury's desire to hear the other side of the story, and avoid any risk of provoking an adverse comment from the judge. Other seasoned defence counsel argue that the accused should rarely, if ever, give evidence. The argument goes like this: the accused does nor have to prove his innocence, in the eyes of the law he is already innocent; if the Crown thinks otherwise the onus is on the Crown to prove it. That being the case, the central question for the jury should be: has the Crown proved its case? However, human nature being what it is, if the accused gives evidence, the jury's focus may be diverted to another question: who should we believe – the accusers or the accused? When the jury has that question in mind, an innocent man who stumbles over his evidence may be disbelieved. So, the argument goes, he would be better off saying nothing.

The problem for Rob Harrison was that, in the eyes of the community, his client did need to prove his innocence. By the time all the Crown witnesses had testified, Harrison had reduced the number of complainants by two and exposed a myriad of flaws in the Crown case, but the quantity of evidence was still enough to convince most people, inside and outside the court, that Ellis must have done something. Indeed, at a social function during the adjournment for Harrison's mother's death, a woman was overheard to say that she was on the Ellis jury, and they were going to find him guilty. (An affidavit containing that information did not reach the court until after the trial. Six years later, the parties to the conversation were interviewed at the direction of the Court of Appeal. Both denied that the conversation had taken place.)

Another difficulty for Harrison was that the other witnesses he planned to call – expert witness Dr Keith Le Page, some of Ellis's former colleagues and some former crèche parents – all gave him cause for concern. The problem with Le Page was that during the bereavement adjournment (18–21 May), he had flown back to Australia to attend to other work. While he was there he had fallen ill. When Harrison opened the defence case on 27 May, Le Page had still not returned. Harrison's concern with the people who had worked alongside his client for years – and who should have been his most credible witnesses – was that their credibility had been tarnished by the closure of the crèche and the arrests of the women. The problem with the former crèche parents was that there weren't enough of them. Harrison's dream was to have a long procession of satisfied parents recounting their memories of Peter Ellis and the crèche. But most parents Harrison approached said, 'I just can't.'

Eventually a nurse, a dentist, a restaurateur and four teachers agreed to appear as defence witnesses. The most striking difference between those parents, and the parents who appeared as witnesses for the prosecution, was that none of the defence witnesses were social workers, therapists or counsellors.

After the Ellis trial, a grandparent wrote to the judge. He began by explaining that, during the three years his granddaughter attended the Civic Crèche, he would drop in for half an hour or so any time he was passing. 'I was able to have a very good idea of the atmosphere of the place, and how the staff related to the children,' he wrote. 'Peter Ellis is not a person I would like to have as a friend. He is too unlike the people I associate with. However, I cannot find any fault with him in the way he cared for my granddaughter. She liked him very much.

'I pleaded with my daughter that she appear as a defence witness,' he continued.

He said her refusal distressed him, but he came to understand it when the case came up in conversation at the hairdresser's:

> The fury and malice against Ellis and the four women was frightening. Words like 'If I could get my hands around the necks of those five mongrels, I'd soon teach them a lesson for interfering with little children' were uttered ... Normally my hairdresser is a fair minded citizen. It makes me wonder how many other parents and grandparents of crèche children were also so intimidated by public hysteria they could not bring themselves to appear as witnesses?

Four years later, a parent who took no part in the court proceedings reflected on her decision:

> When you look at a situation that doesn't involve you, you think you'll know the right thing to do, and you'll do it. But when it involves you closely a lot of other things come into play. In the end I decided to go for what was easiest for me, which wasn't necessarily what I thought was right. It was a powerful learning experience, and a great worry. What if it was me? What if I was in the hot seat and everybody deserted me for their own comfort?[3]

Another potential witness, a separated father, spoke for many in his situation: 'We couldn't support the crèche. If we did our ex-partners would never let us near our kids again.'[4]

After considering the strengths and weaknesses of the available witnesses, and the issues that had to be addressed, Rob Harrison decided that there was more to be gained than lost by putting his client in the witness box:

> Peter had been demonised, inside and outside the court, so the jury needed to see that he wasn't a monster. Strange things had been said about him, so those things needed to be put into context. His interviews with Colin Eade were before the court, but they were controlled and artificial, and no hint of Peter's personality came through in them. I knew that the more time people spent with Peter, the more they came to understand how absurd the allegations were. I felt that if the jury warmed to him there was a chance they'd look again at the children's evidence, and the only way to make that happen was to put Peter in the dock and ask him to tell his story.

• • •

On Thursday 27 May 1993, Rob Harrison opened the case for the defence. After reminding the jury of its responsibilities, he introduced his witnesses, and outlined the defence case:

> Due to the way in which most of the charges have been framed, for example that an offence occurred between 1988 and 1991, it is impossible to call evidence relating to

any specific offence. What Peter Ellis can tell you about is his recollections of his time at the crèche … what he did on walks, how he conducted himself and his recollections of the children and his relationships with the children. You will also hear evidence of how the crèche operated, the openness of the crèche … the defence will call evidence … which shows how unlikely, how impossible, it would have been for those offences to have occurred without someone seeing a traumatised child, one of the events happening, picking up on a child suffering a very serious injury to his genital area or noticing a child smelling of urine or faeces, or a child in very real fear or distress.

In court, Peter Ellis wore the suit and tie that supporters had bought him from a second-hand store. On the advice of counsel, he cut his hair and nails. In the witness box he was subdued and nervous, and his much-discussed flamboyance was nowhere to be seen. Afterwards, he wondered whether adding a headband and legwarmers to his outfit would have created a better impression.

In his evidence-in-chief, Ellis outlined his training and qualifications, described his activities as a childcare worker and firmly denied all the charges. In recalling the complainant children, he said Zelda 'thoroughly enjoyed herself at the crèche', Eli could be 'a bit grizzly', Julian was 'a full-on prospect', Tess 'had little button brown eyes and a cheeky way with her', Kari was 'a neat kid' and Lara was 'fun'.

His evidence about the functioning of the crèche was essentially the same as that given by witnesses for the Crown. Any differences that did emerge were more matters of colour, emphasis and intention, than of substance. Nonetheless, when Brent Stanaway set out to discredit Peter Ellis, he exploited those differences to the full.

A 1999 Law Commission study found that jurors generally regard aggressive cross-examination as a legitimate part of a trial, but consider 'badgering' of witnesses to be unfair and unprofessional. Presumably, in any given trial, the jurors' assessment of the fairness of the cross-examination depends on the sort of cross-examination they think the witness deserves.

In his cross-examination of Peter Ellis, the Crown Solicitor did not suggest that he was a paedophile. 'It's interesting that Stanaway never put to Peter: "You like groping little kids, don't you? You can't help yourself." There was none of that,' Rob Harrison observed. Instead, Brent Stanaway concentrated on attacking Ellis's credibility, on drawing the jury's attention to opportunities for Ellis to be alone with children and on presenting Ellis's reported conversations and behaviour in a sinister light.

About half an hour into his two-hour cross-examination, Ellis appeared to stumble. At the time, and in his closing address, Stanaway presented that apparent stumble as evidence that Ellis was an unreliable witness. Because he was an authoritative and confident prosecutor, and Ellis was a nervous defendant, the jury probably believed him. Curiously, according to the court transcript, that apparent stumble was not a stumble at all. But in view of the importance attached to the episode by the prosecution, and by people who supported the prosecution, we need to examine it more closely.

At the time, Stanaway was cross-examining Ellis on discrepancies between his evidence and the evidence of Ms Kapok. Ms Kapok recalled two visits of crèche staff and children to 404 Hereford Street in late 1986 to see Ellis's animals. She said that on both occasions they walked to the Square and caught a bus from there to Bruce's home. Ellis said there was only one visit, and everybody walked.

'How did you normally get from 404 Hereford Street – when living there – to the crèche?' Stanaway asked.

'I walked,' said Ellis. He said the walk took about 20 minutes, and that children could probably walk the distance in the same time.

'It would be possible though, wouldn't it, to walk from the crèche to the Square, catch a bus to Hereford Street, disembark and walk to Hereford Street, within 20 minutes?'

'I wouldn't know on the bus timetables because I walked.'

'Are you telling us that you never took a bus from Hereford Street to the crèche or back?'

'The buses didn't run down Hereford Street, or if they did it was very infrequent, it was far easier for me to walk. If on a rainy day I caught a bus, I would have gone and got it from the Worcester Street stand.'

'You are now saying, are you, on rainy days you did catch a bus?'

'Yes, perhaps I did. I certainly remember basically walking. Obviously if it was really pouring with rain I would catch a bus.'

'Didn't you just say to us you always walked, never took a bus?' said Stanaway. In fact, Ellis had said nothing of the sort, but the Crown Solicitor seemed to know what he was talking about, so Ellis took him at his word.

'Yes, I did say that. I'm sorry,' he said.

In retrospect, it seems hard to believe that anyone could regard that exchange as a defining moment in the trial. Nonetheless, to the prosecution, and to people who supported the prosecution, it was as if the Crown Solicitor had vanquished his foe with one blow of his broadsword, and was now displaying his head on a stake to the assembled crowd. In recalling the exchange, a member of the prosecution team told me that Stanaway caught Ellis out with a lie, and that from then on it was all over. An observer who 'believed the children', told me that Ellis was 'taken to pieces by the prosecutor' for telling 'blatant lies' about his bus journeys.

Yet that apparent stumble was so inconsequential to Rob Harrison that he couldn't recall it when I asked him about it. 'I don't think Peter did a bad job,' he said of his client's session in the witness box. Ellis supporters in the public gallery agreed. The court transcript shows that the issue was trifling, and Ellis did not lie. So how do we explain the extraordinary effect of that very ordinary exchange on the prosecution, and on people who supported the prosecution? The only explanation I have managed to come up with is that, in a perverse sort of way, the episode acknowledges what the court transcript makes clear: that, by the time the Crown witnesses had been examined, cross-examined and re-examined, the prosecution case was in trouble. By then, the fundamental flaws in the case, which had always been blindingly obvious to the defence, must also have been blindingly obvious to the prosecution (indeed, so blindingly obvious that they averted their gaze from the glare). Though they may not have admitted it to themselves, everyone in that courtroom must have realised that the evidence before the court at that stage was too vague, fragmentary and contradictory to give the jury any good reason to 'believe the children'. As a result of that knowledge, those who supported the prosecution would have been desperate for something to justify their belief in the defendant's guilt. What they needed was a reason to disbelieve Ellis. Under cross-examination from Brent Stanaway, Ellis's inconsequential stumble provided that reason.

In view of the significance attached to that episode by prosecution supporters, it may be useful to keep in mind, as we review the evidence of Peter Ellis and the other defence witnesses, that what may seem like honest and straightforward testimony at a dispassionate distance, probably seemed like lies, evasion, denials and cover-ups to many people in that emotionally charged courtroom.

In his evidence-in-chief, Peter Ellis said that he took children for walks lasting about an hour most days, weather permitting. He outlined the number of children and adults who went along, the times they went, the places they went to, the routes they took and the things they did along the way. Under cross-examination, he admitted that details of the walks were not always recorded.

'You knew you could take children for walks without noting where you were going and knowing nobody would be particularly concerned, didn't you?' asked Stanaway.

'No, that is not correct at all. I would always say where I was going, even if I had forgotten to record it,' said Ellis.

'You knew you could walk out the door with four or five children, say you were going for a walk, and no one would know where you were?' Stanaway persisted.

'No, that is not true because I wouldn't do that. It's part of the crèche policy ... We would automatically say where we were going.'

'There was no means of checking on where you had gone, was there?'

'No, there would be no means of checking.'

'So you could say you were going to the park with five children and go to Hereford Street?'

'That would apply to any person saying they were going to go somewhere and go somewhere else. There were five children and myself to say where we went and what things we did.'

Throughout his cross-examination, Ellis repeatedly denied taking Bart Dogwood to 404 Hereford Street. To those who believed in Ellis's guilt, it would have seemed like he was 'in denial'.

Ellis's games also came under the spotlight. In his evidence-in-chief, he said 'tickle bash-up' began with the announcement: 'I am going to tickle bash you!' Then he'd chased the children and tickled any that he caught. 'There was no physical hitting involved. It was just a nickname I chose,' he explained.

'Tickle bash-ups as you call them – we know about the tickling aspect of the game, what is the bash-up aspect?' asked Stanaway in cross-examination.

'That's just a bit I added at the end just for fun. It didn't have any hidden meaning. It just was tickle bash-up,' said Ellis.

'What was there different about it being simple tickling that had to have bash-up added on to it?'

'It was just a game I played with the children. They seemed to enjoy the name tickle bash-up.'

'Were there occasions you might pretend to hit children on the arm, leg or face ... the bash-up part wouldn't involve mock striking of children for instance?'

'No, it was just tickling.'

'It wouldn't involve pretending to strike a child?'

'No it would not.'

For Rob Harrison, dealing with the evidence about Ellis's conversations on sexual matters was a major challenge:

> In their evidence-in-chief, Jan Buckingham and Sharleen and Belinda talked about Peters' sexual conversations. In cross-examination, I asked them about Peter's fondness for shocking people. I didn't ask them about the sexual conversations because I didn't want to open the way for the Crown to raise them in re-examination. But the fact remained that evidence about Peter's sexual conversations was before the jury, so that evidence needed to be put into context, and the only person who could do that was Peter.

In his evidence-in-chief, Ellis said: 'I made those comments for shock tactics (in) general discussion. If I could get a bite I would aim to get a bite, which I invariably got.' In cross-examination, Stanaway covered the sexual conversations at length.

With regard to Belinda's evidence that, at a social function, Ellis had talked of a Chinaman who liked inserting wooden implements in his penis, Ellis said he'd read about the practice in a book, and had discussed it with Jan Buckingham or Debbie Gillespie. There was no Chinaman involved.

'You talked about it in a way which showed you were particularly interested in it?' Stanaway said.

'I talked about it to get bite value,' said Ellis.

'You were interested in these practices, weren't you?'

'No I wasn't.'

'You in fact were fascinated by the idea of implements being used as part of sexual practices, weren't you?'

'No I was not.'

With regard to Jan Buckingham's evidence that he had talked about photographing sexual activity with a polaroid camera, Ellis said he had taken 'photographs of my dogs and some of my chooks' but none of sexual activities.

'You were actually lying to Jan Buckingham when you said you photographed sexual activity?' asked Stanaway.

'I was having her on – lying is quite a strong word,' said Ellis. The police had found no pornography at Ellis's home. But, in his cross-examination, Stanaway implied that such evidence existed. 'Come on, you had used that camera in the way she said, hadn't you?'

'No, I had not used it in the way she said.'

'You know that [Bart Dogwood] spoke about you taking photos of him with a clicking camera. That's why you are now saying that is not true,' said Stanaway. Ellis said he may have taken photos of Bart at the crèche with the crèche camera, but he had not photographed him away from the crèche.

With regard to his alleged conversations with Sharleen about 'golden showers' (which Sharleen had remembered only after months of police pressure), Ellis said that no such conversation had taken place:

'I didn't tell that to anyone.' ... 'I certainly didn't talk to Sharleen or anyone about golden showers.' ... 'No I didn't, I'm sorry.' ... 'I didn't talk to her at all on that subject, or anyone else.'

Later, despite Ellis's repeated denials, Stanaway returned to the subject in relation to Eli Laurel's allegations.

'You urinated on him and put your penis in his mouth, didn't you?'

'No.'

'This urinating that was carried out by you was part of your fascination for that?'

'I didn't do that, no.'

'Part of your interest in this practice known as golden showers?'

'No.'

However, Ellis agreed with Stanaway that Sharleen 'was fun to bait', and that he had discussed sexual practices involving creams, sauces and raspberry jam with Susannah.

'What other foods did you refer to?' asked Stanaway.

'Only a watermelon,' said Ellis.

Finally, Stanaway put the onus of proof onto Ellis by asking him to explain why the children had made allegations against him, and why they had suffered the symptoms reported by their parents. To such questions, Ellis had no answer. All he could say was that he had not done the things he was accused of doing.

The Crown Solicitor did not suggest that Ellis was involved in a child pornography ring, but at the end of Ellis's cross-examination the judge alluded to the possibility. After questioning Ellis about the crèche visit to 404 Hereford Street, Justice Williamson asked him whether he had a friend or acquaintance called Joseph (the person named by Kari in her allegation of multi-victim multi-perpetrator abuse at 'Peter's house'). Ellis said he had not.

• • •

As the complainant parents had done before them, the parents who appeared as witnesses for the defence talked about when, how often and for how long their children had attended the crèche, and how much time they generally spent there. They also outlined their knowledge of crèche policies and routines, their impressions of Peter Ellis and their involvement in the recent investigation. They said the crèche was a busy place with people coming and going all day. Children were happy there. They never saw anything that caused them concern. Peter Ellis played rough and tumble games and took children for walks. He was artistic and flamboyant, and popular with his charges. The toilet lobby door was always open; adults and children went in and out all day to use the toilets and wash their hands (and also, Ellis recalled in a note to his lawyer, to wash play dough and glue from children's hair, sand from their eyes and mouths and paint from their clothes).

In a criminal trial, prosecution counsel cross-examine defence witnesses to undermine the defence case and enhance their own. Also, failure to cross-examine usually implies that the prosecution accepts the defence witness's evidence. In the Ellis trial, the prosecution and defence evidence about Ellis and the crèche was virtually identical. Consequently, there was nothing to be gained for the prosecution from cross-examining parents called by the defence. However, rather than giving the impression that they accepted the defence evidence, Brent Stanaway and Chris Lange gave the impression that it wasn't worth listening to.

'The prosecutors kept their heads down the whole time I was giving evidence,' Ms Mahogany recalled. 'They never looked at me. They never asked any questions. They basically ignored me.'

Ms Mahogany was also disconcerted by the limitations placed on her evidence by the judge: 'Siobhan McNulty [who took her through her evidence-in-chief] devoted quite a bit of time to asking me why I chose this crèche, and what sort of crèche I thought it was. But the judge said that I wasn't there to discuss the crèche, I was there to discuss Peter.'[5]

Because their evidence and cross-examination was limited, the parents who appeared as witnesses for the defence passed through the witness box unexpectedly quickly. When the dentist's turn came he was caught unprepared: 'I was in the dental chair when I got called. I arrived at court with a numb mouth. The judge made a joke about how I was getting a bit of my own medicine, ho ho ha ha. Everyone starts laughing. The jury's laughing at me and I'm looking at Peter and thinking: this is not fair. He's on trial. He could get a long prison term, and they're laughing at my predicament.'[6]

• • •

Dr Keith Le Page was still unwell when he arrived back in Christchurch on 30 May. That evening, he read transcripts of the evidence given in his absence. Next morning he took the stand.

Le Page outlined his qualifications and experience, discussed the nature of memory and the suggestibility of children, and stated that none of the behaviours mentioned by Dr Zelas were specific to sexual abuse. He also suggested that the complainants' reported symptoms were not caused by sexual abuse, but by other stresses in their lives.

Under cross-examination from Brent Stanaway, Le Page conceded that he usually worked for the defence in child sexual abuse cases, and that nearly all the 104 cases referred to him since 1985 involved the evaluation of information provided by the defence, rather than the assessment and treatment of allegedly abused children.

Stanaway then produced a 1988 Australian *Bulletin* article in which Le Page was described as 'a crusader for the rights of men alleged to have been abusers of children'. Le Page said he was really a crusader for a 'protocol to properly evaluate allegations of child sexual abuse'.

The previous year, Le Page had sent a copy of his protocol to the president of the Royal Australian and New Zealand College of Psychiatrists and suggested that the college develop its own guidelines. The president referred the proposal to the Faculty of Child Psychiatrists, and asked the faculty to review it in consultation with Le Page. In 1995, Le Page wrote to the NZ Attorney-General:

> During my cross-examination in the Christchurch Crèche trial in 1993 the Crown prosecutor informed me for the first time that Dr Zelas had been appointed [to review the protocol] and suggested that the implication was that the College had rejected me. The reality is that Dr Zelas refused to liaise with me for reasons unknown to me, in my opinion to the detriment of the New Zealand and Australian public.[7]

During Le Page's three-and-a-half hours in the witness box, the judge and the Crown Solicitor took him to task over his claim that the children's alleged symptoms were inconsistent with sexual abuse. In the course of a convoluted discussion, Le Page argued that none of the symptoms, singly or in clusters, were diagnostic of sexual abuse. Stanaway pointed out that Dr Zelas hadn't said they were, and suggested that Le Page had misunderstood the New Zealand legislation on the role of expert witnesses in child sexual abuse cases.

According to the defence, Le Page's cross-examination was a disaster. According to the prosecution, it was a triumph.

• • •

Susannah was the first of Ellis's former colleagues to give evidence for the defence. Her account of crèche rosters, routines and staff–child ratios was essentially the same as that given by other staff witnesses. The last three defence witnesses were Debbie Gillespie, Gaye Davidson and Marie Keys.

'You could feel the atmosphere change when the women who'd been accused gave evidence,' Rob Harrison recalled. 'You could see the jury looking at them really hard. It was like a trial within a trial.'

In Oral Judgment (No.14), Justice Williamson had ruled that Jan Buckingham could refute the allegations that Bart Dogwood had made against her only if those allegations related to charges against Ellis. As a result of that ruling, the accused women were allowed to state on oath that they had no knowledge of the circle incident or of Ellis's alleged offending at the crèche, but they were not allowed to deny that they had put sticks and burning paper up Bart's bottom. The fact that the women did not refute those allegations may have led jurors to suspect that they were true.

In her evidence-in-chief, Debbie Gillespie described the process of getting children ready for walks. Her account made the claim that Ellis could have spirited off groups of children without his colleagues noticing seem extremely far-fetched:

> To start with you get a group of children together ... sometimes that in itself was quite lengthy because it was quite a competitive thing, a lot of children wanted to go ... You would often have to toilet the children before you went, make sure they had shoes and socks on ... in winter time they would need jackets, hats and gloves – other things like making sure you had a box of tissues for runny noses. The preparation would usually take place in the main room of the Big End and in that corridor area where the children's lockers were, and the toileting in the toilet area.

Gillespie said that the toilet lobby door, and also the cubicle doors, were nearly always open. 'There would be children who liked privacy when they were using the toilets and they would close the [cubicle] door, but it was quite difficult to do because the block that they stood on was actually in the way …' She said if a cubicle door was closed she would 'check to see if someone was in the toilet and make sure the child was okay'.

Of activities involving children and staff sitting or standing in a circle, Gillespie said there were music sessions each morning, 'fruit time' each afternoon (when fruit left over from children's lunches was washed, cut up and passed around a circle of seated children) and games like 'Farmer in the Dell'.

In her evidence, Gaye Davidson confirmed from crèche records that the centre closed for Christmas on Friday 19 December 1986 (which meant that Ellis babysat Zelda Cypress for two-and-a-half days before Christmas that year, and not for 'five or nine days' as Ms Cypress had claimed).

Marie Keys, the most respected and loved of all the crèche workers, gave evidence last. When her own children were young, Keys was a caregiver for Barnardos, a Playcentre parent and president of her local Plunket sub-branch. When her children were at primary school, she served on their school committee. A few years later, she served on their high school board. 'She was the last person on earth who would ever be involved in, who would ever condone, who would ever fail to notice or keep quiet about any maltreatment of children,' Ms Rimu told me.[8]

Like everyone who gave evidence at the Ellis trial, Marie Keys could not recall children being fearful, or showing signs of pain in the ano-genital area at the crèche. However, she acknowledged that children could be upset if they fell over, or were tired or unwell.

Towards the end of Keys' evidence, Justice Williamson questioned her further: '[Lara Palm] told us that on one occasion she ran out and spoke to you about what Peter was doing and said that he was touching her. Did that happen?'

'No,' said Keys.

'Would you have remembered it?'

'If [Lara] had come out and told me Peter was touching her, or doing secret touching or whatever it was she said, I would of course have investigated, and yes, I would have remembered.'

'[Kari Lacebark] told us that she went and said to you "Peter's hurting me". Could she have said that to you?'

Keys said that children sometimes told her that Peter was being silly, in which case she would go and see what he was being silly about.

'He was usually being silly with the children playing a game, but if she had said that to me I would have investigated … I can't remember her saying that and I can't remember any incident of Peter hurting [Kari],' Keys said.

Then Stanaway asked her how she investigated children's complaints, and Harrison asked her about the demeanour of the complaining children. Keys said the children were happy when they were complaining about Ellis being silly but 'if they said he was being mean they wouldn't be happy. It would perhaps be because Peter had said: "No, you can't have your play lunch"; "No, you can't eat your food in the dress-up corner, you have to sit at the table."'

'Was there ever an occasion a child made a complaint against Peter when their demeanor was one of being scared or traumatised?' Harrison asked.

'No.'

'How many years have you worked in childcare?'

'My own children are 15 and 17. I was teaching for five years before that. I have been involved with children all those years.'

'Would you be able to read the demeanour of children quite well then?'

'I am fairly sure I can.'

• • •

At 3.45pm on Tuesday 1 June 1993, the Crown Solicitor began his four-hour closing address. His manner was measured, calm and authoritative. He attacked 'the defence contention' that 'a hysterical group of parents contaminated their children and each other with wild ideas founded on imagination and fantasy'. 'Do those parents who you have seen look the part?' he asked. 'You saw them, in the main intelligent men and women, logical and caring.' Throughout his address, Stanaway used terms like 'put up to it', 'trained', 'prompted' and 'coached' to misrepresent the defence case. (The defence contention was that lengthy and repeated questioning by parents and interviewers had led the children to genuinely believe they had been abused.) Stanaway also reminded the jury that they were entitled to convict solely on the evidence of children, and made some other general points. These were:

- that the interviewers were trained and experienced women who worked under the direction and guidance of Dr Zelas, 'an internationally recognised expert in this field'.
- that the lack of medical evidence could be explained by the tendency of small children to exaggerate minor injuries, and by 'elements of trickery, theatrics and deliberate confusing of the children by Ellis and others'.
- that Dr Zelas was better qualified and more professional than Dr Le Page.
- that the behavioural indicators reported by parents were consistent with sexual abuse.
- that the accused's sexual interests were 'similar in nature and tone to the very things that many of these children have complained about'.

- that because the accused smoked in the toilets, took children on walks, toileted them and supervised them during hand washing there were 'clearly opportunities for the accused to carry out the activities alleged'.

Then the Crown Solicitor reviewed the evidence relating to each charge, and sought to explain away the discrepancies (e.g. he suggested that the questioning conducted by parents had helped uncover deep-seated abuse, but the questioning conducted by defence counsel had simply confused the children.)

Though no giraffe skins were found during the investigation, and no adults were asked whether they had ever owned or seen one, Stanaway hailed the transformation of the real giraffe at Peter's house (in Julian's DSW interview) into a giraffe skin (in Julian's cross-examination) as evidence that the children's apparently bizarre allegations could have a real-life basis.

In fact, the most likely explanation for the giraffe story is that in 1992 many former crèche children met Harold the Giraffe, mascot of the Life Education Trust. In Tess Hickory's second DSW interview, Sue Sidey asked: 'Have you done Harold the Giraffe ... have people come to your school and talked to you about your body ... ?' But to admit that Julian's giraffe was probably inspired by the Life Education Trust mascot would be to admit that even well-meaning people could put bizarre ideas into children's heads. According to Stanaway, only child abusers using 'trickery, theatrics and deliberate confusing' could do that.

Though the Crown Solicitor avoided the term 'ritual abuse', his explanation for Bart Dogwood's bizarre evidence could have come from any ritual abuse believer's handbook. Stanaway claimed that Bart had been grossly abused by Ellis and others from an early age, and terrorised into silence. He said that's why Bart didn't disclose in his first interview, but needed 'continued questioning and support of his parents and family' before 'he felt sufficiently believed and safe' to tell. According to Stanaway, Bart's delayed disclosures of organised abuse were 'unprompted and spontaneous', and consistent with the evidence of other children. The circle incident 'was not an event which grew out of nowhere,' he said. 'Other children clearly talk of group activities where sexual acts took place involving both men and women.' His explanation for the lack of material evidence was that the offenders had destroyed it.

Of the accused, he said: 'Did you find him a convincing witness in his repeated denials that he was guilty of any of the allegations put to him?' With regard to 'the accused's own inconsistencies', he said: 'He was initially emphatic that he never took the bus and only walked. Then he backtracked considerably and acknowledged that on occasions he might take a bus when it was raining. You might think the accused was intent on distancing himself from the concept of bus trips to and from 404 Hereford Street.'

'What did you make of the accused and Bruce's repeated references to Bruce not being interested in children?' he added.

Of Ellis's sexual conversations, he said: 'How extraordinary it is that children should talk about being urinated on, how Yelena Holly should talk about food being inserted in her anus, how children should talk about sticks and needles being inserted in their sexual organs and anuses when this man has talked about those very same things.' He also suggested that, had the parents who appeared as defence witnesses known about Ellis's sexual conversations, they would not have spoken so highly of him. (Later, in his summing up, Justice Williamson claimed that the evidence about 'unusual, strange or kinky sexual practices' was not introduced to incite prejudice towards Ellis but to show a possible 'unique or unusual connection between the allegations of some of the children and the accused', but Stanaway's comments indicated that he was well aware of where the true power of that evidence lay.)

Throughout his closing address, Brent Stanaway stressed that the complainants had given *consistent central detail* of the allegations relied on by the Crown. With most of the charges, that claim was based solely on the children's affirmative responses to leading questions put to them by the Crown Solicitor in their videolink evidence-in-chief. The first question in Stanaway's 28-question series was: 'You said in the videotape yesterday that in his bedroom at his house he touched your vagina with his hands and his fingers, did that happen?' (Zelda, Count 1). He asked similar question for each charge. The last question in the series was: 'You also said to Sue in that tape, lots of times Peter did secret touching. That is, he put his hand on your bottom and clitoris. Is that things that really happened?' (Lara, Count 28). On the basis of the children's monosyllabic confirmations, Stanaway claimed that, even if their evidence was 'bizarre, unbelievable or unconvincing', the children had given *consistent central detail* of the allegations relied on by the Crown. Therefore, he argued, they were compelling and believable witnesses, and their charges had been proved beyond reasonable doubt.

• • •

At 2.15pm on Wednesday 2 June 1993, Rob Harrison began his four-hour closing address. Unlike the Crown Solicitor, Harrison worked from notes rather than a prepared script. As a result, his presentation was more spontaneous, and more frequently interrupted by paper shuffling. Observers say that he began and ended strongly, but the middle section of his address was less compelling.

Harrison pointed out that none of the children's allegations were unprompted by parental questioning. 'Not one of the children made a spontaneous disclosure of abuse, despite being read books about disclosure in situations where they were safe,' he said.

He argued that many factors in the emotional climate of the time could have led the children to make false allegations. Parents had told their children they were safe, which could have led them to believe there was reason to be scared. Because of the extensive media coverage, children could easily have known that Ellis was in trouble. Parental attitudes of support and interest in what their children had to say about Ellis and the crèche could have encouraged children to provide the answers they thought their parents wanted. Under the circumstances, the capacity for parents to put ideas into their children's minds, and for children to make things up, should not be underestimated.

With regard to the DSW interviewers, Harrison said that their job was not to seek the truth, but to encourage children to talk about abuse, and to believe everything that was said. He deplored the interviewers' failure to ask the children about their prior conversations with their parents, or about their prior knowledge of Ellis and the crèche. If such questions had been asked, possible sources of contamination of their evidence would have been revealed. Now it was too late. The complainants had been treated as victims of Peter Ellis for too long. No matter where their ideas came from, they had come to believe that the abuse really happened. Harrison also questioned Dr Zelas's multiple roles in the case, and invited the jury to consider whether she had a conflict of interest.

Harrison then reviewed the evidence relating to each child, and to each child's parents. He gave jurors three to five reasons why they should consider each child's evidence unreliable, and highlighted the evidence of parent–parent and parent–child contamination.

He also highlighted the evidence that the crèche was a busy and open place where parents could drop in unexpectedly at any time. He argued that it was beyond belief that Ellis would have used the crèche toilets to commit indecencies when he had no idea who would be coming along. How could he have avoided detection? Why would he want to commit indecencies there when he could supposedly commit them on walks? Where were the distressed children at the crèche? Where were the injuries? How could Ellis have taken children on walks, molested them, threatened them, and then returned them to the crèche looking completely normal? Harrison also protested that the Crown had twisted his client's fondness for shocking his co-workers with bizarre sexual banter into an interest in those activities.

In closing, Harrison reminded jurors that there was no other evidence to support the complainant's allegations. He suggested that they should be left with more than a reasonable doubt, and he urged them to bring back verdicts of not guilty on all charges.

• • •

At 11.25am on Thursday 3 June 1993, Justice Williamson began his one-and-a-half-hour address to the jury. The purpose of the judge's summing up is to focus the attention of jurors on matters relevant to their decisions. Judges give directions on the law, explain the roles of judge and jury, outline the issues to be decided and summarise the evidence and arguments for both sides.

In what lawyers call 'the justice game', judges are supposed to be dispassionate referees who ensure that everybody plays by the rules. Consequently, the issue of whether judges should give juries the benefit of their opinions has long been a contentious one.[9] Nowadays, in what seems like a curious compromise, judges are allowed to express their opinions, provided they tell the jury to ignore those opinions. When Justice Williamson summed up the Ellis case, he said the jury's decisions were for the jury alone to make. 'If, therefore, I appear to indicate any view on any question of fact which does not accord with your own view, then please disregard mine,' he said.

Despite his pre-trial assurance that he would take care to warn the jury against being swayed by the intense media interest in the case, the directions Williamson gave were routine. He told jurors to put aside feelings of prejudice or sympathy and to reach their verdicts on a dispassionate assessment of the evidence. He told them that the burden of proof was with the Crown, that the standard of proof was 'beyond reasonable doubt' and that each charge had to be dealt with separately ('It would be wrong ... to reason that if an accused is guilty of one charge then he must be guilty of another'). He explained the elements that had to be proved for each charge, and pointed out that the only significant issue was whether the alleged offences had occurred. In summarising the evidence, he referred to both the prosecution and defence arguments. But he devoted more attention to the prosecution case, and his comments on the defence case were often dismissive. Most of the time his personal views were implicit rather than explicit.

Justice Williamson opened his summing up with: 'The truth of the essential allegations of 11 children is at issue in this case. According to the Crown, each child has told the truth about the central matters. According to the accused, all of the children have told lies because of pressures on them from parents, other children or authorities.' In fact, neither Peter Ellis, nor his counsel, nor any defence witness had ever called the children liars. From a defence point of view, the summing up had got off to a bad start. Shortly afterwards, it got worse:

> This is not a public inquiry. It is not a trial of the crèche. Most of the parents have said they chose this crèche for their children because of its positive good qualities including the effectiveness of the crèche. Opinions about that may differ. In view of the suspicion of sexual abuse and concerns about other aspects of care the City Council may well have been justified in shutting the crèche to avoid possible risk but that topic is not the focus

of this case. Further, the case is not a trial of the other crèche workers' conduct, nor of the conduct of the police, parents or specialist interviewers …

Through those comments, Williamson gave the impression that evidence about the crèche's good qualities was of dubious value, that suspicions of wrongdoing by other crèche staff were probably justified and that defence criticisms of the investigation were irrelevant.

Throughout his summing up, the judge made several references to evidence from Ellis's co-workers that favoured the prosecution (for example, about the accused's sexual conversations), but no references to evidence from them suggesting that, because of the layout of the crèche and the way it functioned, the abuse could not have happened. Williamson also noted that, according to the Crown:

> you cannot place too much weight on the evidence of the other crèche workers because that evidence has been given with a fair amount of hindsight; that it is not impartial because they have a personal stake in the whole matter; that it was too strident. In any event, because they had never seen children or activities happening in certain ways, their evidence, even if accepted, would not have excluded sexual abuse by another carer.

The parents' evidence about their children's tantrums and toileting problems when they were three and four years old was also given with a fair amount of hindsight, and the parents and professionals involved in the prosecution also had a personal stake in the matter. But those points were never mentioned. Instead, the judge used the legislative provision for expert evidence in child sexual abuse cases to bolster the value of the parents' evidence. 'If a child says that he or she has been sexually abused then you are entitled to weigh in support of their statements the fact that they have also exhibited behaviours which have been observed by other people and which a lot of children of the same age group who have been sexually abused have also shown,' he said. He also criticised Dr Le Page for suggesting that 'a certain behaviour did not prove the child had been sexually abused'. 'Under our law he was not entitled to say that, and in any event that is not the point of the section [s. 23G of the Evidence Act],' Williamson said.

The judge suggested that contradictions in the children's evidence were of no great moment, and that jurors should concentrate their minds on the central detail. 'I suppose some people could say the four gospels Matthew, Mark, Luke and John in the Bible differ and are inconsistent in some respects, but that does not mean that the essential story they tell is untrue.' With regard to Ellis's sexual conversations, he said:

> the only significance of all the evidence about what might be termed unusual, strange or kinky sexual practices, is that it may show a unique or unusual connection between

the allegations of some of the children and the accused. This evidence is relevant if it tends to confirm the children's credibility or to refute the accused's claim that his entire association with these children was innocent.

The judge said the jury was entitled to draw inferences from the children's evidence about the accused's intentions. But he did not point out that they were also entitled to draw inferences from the adults' evidence about whether the offences could have happened. He said that when different children described similar indecencies, their evidence could indicate a pattern of offending. But he did not point out that it could also indicate a pattern of contamination of the evidence.

Finally, Justice Williamson summarised the prosecution and defence arguments in relation to each charge. At 2.00pm on Thursday 3 June 1993, the jury retired to consider its verdicts.

• • •

The jury deliberated all that day, all the next day and for most of the day after that. Each day, Ellis supporters mingled with journalists and film crews in the public area outside the court, while supporters of the complainants kept vigil in an adjacent room. Police officers patrolled the space between.[10]

On the morning of the third day, the jury returned to view two videotape extracts. At 3.30pm the same day (Saturday 5 June 1993), the foreman announced the verdicts.

The first three verdicts related to Zelda Cypress: Count 1, GUILTY; Count 2, GUILTY; Count 3, GUILTY. It was Rob Harrison's darkest moment:

> I thought: He's going to go down on them all. [Zelda] was the oldest and most credible witness. If the jury had convinced themselves that she could be believed, they had a scenario for long term offending. So all the other children could be believed. I was astounded when the not-guilty verdicts started coming in. I thought: How can they justify this? How can they believe [Eli] when he says that Peter urinated on his face, and disbelieve [Julian] when he says the same thing? How can they believe [Bart] when he talks about adults molesting children at Peter's house in one interview, and disbelieve him when he talks about the same thing in another interview? They bring in a guilty verdict on the charge that an unknown man molested [Kari] at an unknown address on an unknown date. How can they justify that?

The rest of the verdicts were: Molly Sumach, Count 4, GUILTY; Abigail Fir, Count 5, NOT GUILTY; Eli Laurel, Count 6, GUILTY; Count 7, NOT GUILTY; Julian Yew, Count 8, NOT GUILTY; Tess Hickory, Count 9, GUILTY; Count 10, GUILTY; Count 11, NOT GUILTY; Count 12, NOT GUILTY. [Ellis was discharged on charges 13, 14 and 15 during the trial.] Bart Dogwood, Count 16, GUILTY; Count 17, GUILTY; Count 18, GUILTY; Count 19 (the circle incident), NOT GUILTY; Kari

Lacebark, Count 20, GUILTY; Count 21, GUILTY; Count 22, GUILTY; Count 23, GUILTY; Yelena Holly, Count 24, NOT GUILTY; Count 25, NOT GUILTY; Derek Ngaio, Count 26, NOT GUILTY; Lara Palm, Count 27, GUILTY; Count 28, GUILTY.

Peter Ellis stood composed in the dock and complainant parents sobbed as the verdicts were read. Justice Williamson remanded Ellis in custody, and stated that in his 30 years in the courts he had never experienced such a prompt, attentive and conscientious jury.

Outside the court, in his first and only statement to the media, Rob Harrison said that the conviction would be appealed. Gaye Davidson called for a public inquiry. 'I still believe Peter is innocent,' she said. 'I have never seen any evidence of any of the things which were supposed to have occurred at the crèche and I don't see how they could have occurred. I would never tolerate or cover for anyone who abused children.' A spokeswoman for the complainant parents said: 'We are satisfied with the verdict and we applaud the courage of the children and the families involved in this legal process.'

• • •

In the two weeks between the conviction and sentencing of Peter Ellis, a pre-sentencing report and victim impact reports were prepared, and letters supportive of Ellis were submitted to the judge. The pre-sentencing report was prepared by a probation officer. 'He came into the interview convinced I was guilty, and left convinced I was innocent,' Ellis recalled. As a description of New Zealand's most notorious child molester, it was an extraordinary document:

> The overall picture gained of Peter Ellis is that of an outgoing, uninhibited, unconventional person given to putting plenty of enthusiasm and energy into his work and social activities, sometimes to the point of being risque and outrageous, thus opening himself up to being compromised or being seen to exercise poor judgement. It appears, however, that he was able to temper the more effervescent side of his nature by being caring, sensitive and understanding in such a way that both adults and children were attracted to him. Whether he used this side of his personality in a devious manner is impossible for me to ascertain. At interview I found him to be well composed and not lacking in self-esteem. He was direct and straightforward in his answers to my questions. He did not endeavour to down-play his liking for children, his tendency towards somewhat eccentric behaviour or his liking for alcohol. He was quite open about his sexual orientation but not inappropriately so ...

• • •

On Tuesday 22 June 1993, extra police with long batons were brought into the High Court for the sentencing of Peter Ellis. Justice Williamson said that the jury's verdicts were 'obviously correct' and he took Ellis to task for not facing up to the truth and seeking help at an early stage. 'Unlike almost all of those who have publicly feasted off this case by expressing their opinions, the jury actually saw and heard each of the children,' he said. 'They also heard your evidence and that of the other former Christchurch Civic Crèche workers. The jury disbelieved you. They believed the children and I agree with that assessment.'

'Every time he paused for breath I added more years to the sentence,' Ellis's lawyer recalled. Then, to Harrison's astonishment, the judge announced that he was sending Peter Ellis to prison for ten years. 'If any man had interfered with children for six years to the extent they said Peter did – traumatised them beyond belief – then even by the sentencing standards of 1993 – before the increase for sexual violation – that was light.' he said.

'I think that sentence was an acknowledgement from Williamson that he hadn't given Peter Ellis a fair trial,' a legal scholar told me. 'He failed. I think he knew he failed. The lawyer in him probably argued with the man in him over the way he handled the Ellis trial until the day he died.'

According to friends, Neil Williamson never wavered in his certainty that Ellis was guilty, but he also admitted privately that he could think of a dozen grounds for appealing the Ellis verdict. Further support for the notion that Williamson may have harboured lingering concerns about the Ellis trial – and about the psychological evidence in particular – can be found in a judgment delivered later the same year.

Justice Williamson's November 1993 judgment concerned a Crown application to introduce expert evidence to support an adult complainant's claim that she had been sexually abused as a child. If the complainant was a child, the evidence would have been admissible under s. 23G of the Evidence Act. But, because the complainant was an adult, the evidence could be admitted only with the judge's consent. In declining the application, Williamson ruled:

> A psychologist's opinion in a sexual abuse case may be a help to a jury or it may be an unjustified intrusion into their decision-making. Before a Court may allow expert evidence to be given it must be satisfied that the opinion relates to matters which are outside the ordinary experience of jurors. In addition, in sexual abuse cases, the Court must be confident that the opinion is based upon accepted facts within a sufficiently recognised branch of science ... The Court is aware from the evidence of psychiatrists, well qualified and experienced in this field, in other cases that there are sharp differences of opinion concerning the manner in which particular behavioural indicators can be classified ... The problem in allowing expert opinion testimony in situations such as this is that it may in reality be little more than a cleverly packaged endorsement of the complainant's truthfulness or that it may be perceived by the jury as an endorsement ... it is the layman who as a member of a jury decides guilt or innocence, and he should not be influenced in that onerous task by opinion that is not solidly based.[11]

CHAPTER 13

The Aftermath

13.i: The Tide Turns

On 24 May 1993, two weeks before the end of the Ellis trial, former crèche supervisor Gaye Davidson wrote to the Attorney-General and the Ministers of Justice, Police, Social Welfare and Education on behalf of the Civic Child Care Inquiry Organisation (a group that included 'the four women whose charges were dismissed, other childcare workers who lost their jobs, parents of children who were at the Centre, parents of children who were interviewed as part of the inquiry, the parents of a child who was the subject of charges brought against Peter Ellis at depositions stage but subsequently dropped ... a number of professional people ... and other people in the community').

'The purpose of this letter is to seek the establishment of an official inquiry into matters arising from the investigation of sexual abuse allegations concerning the Christchurch Civic Child Care Centre, the closure of the Centre and the prosecution of various workers associated with the Centre,' Davidson wrote. She outlined 20 concerns relating to the conduct of the investigation by police and social welfare officers, the involvement of therapists and counsellors in the process, the laws under which they operated, the damage done to innocent people and the lack of accountability of those responsible. She cited inquiries into the Cleveland and Orkney child sexual abuse scandals as appropriate models for a New Zealand inquiry, and added:

> We appreciate that the Government will not call for an inquiry when the trial of Peter Ellis is still proceeding. We are making our request for an inquiry now because:
> a. We want to make it clear that we consider an inquiry is necessary regardless of what happens at the Peter Ellis trial.
> b. We want the Government to have the opportunity to consider the request in the absence of public or political discussion of why it is necessary.
> c. We want you to be in a position to announce the inquiry as soon as the Peter Ellis trial is completed.[1]

• • •

13.i: The Tide Turns

Throughout the Ellis trial, media coverage was extensive and the nation was engrossed. By the time the jury returned its verdicts, the tide of public opinion was starting to turn. Immediately after the verdicts, concerned citizens began writing to the Minister of Justice:[2]

> 'Where was the justice done to all the people who worked at the crèche? ... Have the parents and people who brainwashed the children been given help so they don't keep offending and abusing children? ... This could happen to you or I or anyone. The laws have to be changed to give justice to all and stop initiating crime ... Every person I've spoken to says the same. Peter Ellis was set up.'

> 'I am a fairly conservative person who is obviously very pleased that the den of iniquity that apparently existed at the Christchurch Crèche has been exposed, and yet for months I have had an increasingly uneasy feeling that something is wrong with the administration of justice in this case ... I ... hope that a complete public review will be undertaken.'

> 'I have spoken to a number of people who share this disquiet and who are convinced that there may have been a miscarriage of justice in the conviction of Peter Ellis.'

On Sunday 13 June, Frank Haden's column in the *Dominion Sunday Times* was headed 'Christchurch Disgraced by Insupportable Ellis Verdict'. On Monday 14 June, Detective Inspector Brian Pearce was interviewed on *Holmes*. He defended the credibility of the children's evidence, the professionalism of the interviewers and the decision to charge the women. But it was his defence of three outspoken antipornography and anti-homosexuality activists – Members of Parliament John Banks and Graeme Lee, and Society for the Promotion of Community Standards flag-bearer Patricia Bartlett – that electrified viewers. Of pornography, Pearce said: 'It's addictive, and it's evil in every sense of the word ... for too long ... our society has mocked the Patricia Bartletts and the Graeme Lees and the John Bankses ... I actually believe in a God that will not be mocked ... I believe that this country is actually now starting to reap the harvest of liberalism and of compromise and of double standards.'[3] After that, the trickle of public scepticism became a flood:[4]

> 'What has made me write this tonight was the *Holmes* interview ... I am concerned that what would generally be considered 'justice' has not been done in this case ...'

> '[T]here was absolutely no hard evidence whatsoever to support the Police claim that there had been a whole nest of outrageous pederasts staffing the Crèche ... something must urgently be done to remedy this seemingly preposterous Ellis verdict.'

· · ·

Over the same period, in the maximum security wing of Paparua Prison, Peter Ellis was kept busy replying to supportive letters ('You don't know me but ...'). 'Even now I can keep amused,' he wrote to a well-wisher. 'I'm thinking of writing to *Dilemmas* on TV1:

> Dear Dr Phelps not wanting to be rude
> But I'd like to direct this question to Jude
> I've been convicted of horrible crimes and sent to jail
> No one listened and I didn't even get bail
> I'm not too bad and I don't even bear malice
> So please help me, kind thoughts, Peter Ellis.'

• • •

In early July, Attorney-General Paul East, Minister of Justice Doug Graham, Minister of Social Welfare Jenny Shipley and Minister of Police John Banks responded to Gaye Davidson's call for an inquiry. By then, the case that had begun with the enigmatic comment of a three-year-old boy had been passed from hand to hand through the Christchurch City Council, the Police, the Department of Social Welfare, the Crown Law Office and the Courts like a time bomb in a macabre game of pass-the-parcel. At each step along the way the parcel had grown bigger and more dangerous. All who touched it were tainted by its passing. When it reached the top levels of government and the courts the music stopped. At that point, no one needed to be told what to do. The solution was obvious: bury it.

Paul East replied that the request for an inquiry was under consideration.[5] Doug Graham wrote: 'I am not convinced that the need has been demonstrated for an inquiry...'[6] Jenny Shipley wrote: 'The matter has now traversed the court system ... I do not consider a further public enquiry into the matter to be necessary.'[7] John Banks wrote:

> I cannot for the life of me understand why you and your friends continue to support this convicted child molester ... I simply do not believe that this five year reign of terror by one of your co-workers continued by instalment almost daily without being noticed by others. I am highly critical of the decision taken to give this individual such work when he openly and often spoke of his perversions. I have no intention of seeking or supporting an inquiry.[8]

Through his response, John Banks alluded to a dilemma that obsessed the nation. If Ellis was guilty, how could the women be innocent? If the women were innocent, how could Ellis be guilty? That month, authors of articles on the crèche case in the *Listener* and *North & South* declared themselves baffled.[9]

Also in July 1993, Gerald Nation wrote to the Minister of Justice supporting his clients' call for an inquiry. 'I have always wanted to believe that there was enough protection in our legal system to ensure that an innocent person would not be convicted. Personally I am worried that in the area of child sexual abuse allegations this is no longer the case,' he wrote.[10] Doug Graham referred the letter to Paul East, who referred it to Solicitor-General John McGrath (now Justice McGrath). McGrath advised Nation that no decision would be made until the Ellis appeal was over.[11]

Nigel Hampton QC agreed to lead the Ellis appeal, with Rob Harrison as his junior. Their application for legal aid was granted, and a week in November 1993 was set aside for the hearing. When Hampton fell ill, the appeal was deferred until February 1994. However, before then, another court matter arising from the crèche case was heard.

13.ii: The Women's Costs Application

The Costs in Criminal Cases Act states that when a defendant is acquitted or discharged the court may order 'that he be paid such sum as it thinks just and reasonable towards the costs of his defence'. In determining costs, the judge normally takes all the circumstances of the case into account, but focuses primarily on two issues: whether the prosecution was reasonably and properly brought and pursued, and whether the accused brought the charges on their own heads.[12]

According to the Act, 'there shall be no presumption for or against the granting of costs'; defendants shall not be granted costs solely because they are acquitted or discharged, or refused costs solely because the proceedings against them are properly brought and continued.

The costs incurred by Gaye Davidson, Marie Keys, Jan Buckingham and Debbie Gillespie of around $114,500 were made up primarily of legal fees, calculated at cut-price hourly rates ranging from $95 to $150 plus GST. In total, the women received $55,244 in legal aid, of which they were required to pay back $32,750. The District Legal Services Committee (DLSC) also paid disbursements (for reports from psychiatrist Keith Le Page, photocopying, courier fees and so on) totalling $11,565, and authorised Gerald Nation's law firm, Wynn Williams and Co., to levy an additional charge on the women. In a letter to the DLSC, the women wrote:

> Although we do not know how we are going to pay this further liability ... we agree that Wynn Williams and Co. should be able to hold us liable for these further costs ... We are aware that the Legal Aid Fund would remunerate Wynn Williams and Co. at a

rate far less than what they would normally expect to be able to charge and we agree that we should seek to provide some top up ... We also agree that whatever sum we are personally liable for shall carry interest at the rate of 11% per annum as from 28 May 1993 if it has not been paid by that time.[13]

These arrangements meant that, as a result of being charged and discharged, Gaye Davidson, Marie Keys, Jan Buckingham and Debbie Gillespie not only lost their jobs, their careers, their reputations and their savings, they also acquired debts of $32,750 to the Legal Aid Fund, and $47,697 to Wynn Williams and Co.

The women paid their legal aid contributions relatively promptly. But, two years after their discharges, they still owed Wynn Williams and Co. $14,288 (Davidson), $2428.40 (Keys), $14,327 (Buckingham) and $13,678 (Gillespie), which they were paying off at $5 per week (Davidson and Gillespie), $10 per week (Buckingham) and $25 per fortnight (Keys).[14]

When Gerald Nation made his costs application on behalf of the women, he was optimistic that their financial burden would soon be eased. 'I thought they had a reasonable chance of being awarded costs,' he recalled. The case against them was so weak it didn't have to go to trial. They'd done nothing to bring the charges on themselves. So I prepared a detailed memorandum about the way the police had pursued the case against them, and about the sort of evidence they had relied upon. I thought it was a good opportunity for the judge to take another look at these matters.'[15]

On 29 October 1993, Justice Williamson heard Gerald Nation's application for costs on behalf of the women, and Brent Stanaway's opposing submissions on behalf of the Crown. On 15 December, he delivered his decision.[16]

With regard to the applicants' financial situations, Williamson made a series of wildly inaccurate observations. He noted the total legal aid granted, but failed to note that the women were required to pay back 60 percent of it, and that Marie Keys and Jan Buckingham had already done so. Despite evidence that the applicants were committed to paying off their debts to Wynn Williams and Co., and that Marie Keys had already paid off a substantial part of hers, Williamson suggested that they would have to pay that debt only if their costs application, or their Employment Court case against the city council, was successful. He also suggested that Gerald Nation could have applied for an increase in legal aid, even though the level of legal aid was fixed after the work was completed and all the costs were known. (The Act did not permit an increase unless there has been a change in circumstances after the level of legal aid had been fixed.) Towards the end of his judgment, Williamson noted that legal aid recipients were not usually awarded costs, and added: 'I do not consider that it is necessary for me to deal with those questions in this judgment'.

On the question of whether the prosecution was 'reasonably and properly brought and pursued', Williamson concluded that everyone involved had acted in good faith, and that there was sufficient evidence to warrant commencing proceedings. He said that he had heard Bart Dogwood give evidence about the circle incident at the Ellis trial, and had found him 'a sound and bright witness'. 'I have also heard and seen other children who made similar allegations of group abuse but who did not identify those involved,' he added.

Of Gerald Nation's concerns about the conduct of the investigation, Justice Williamson wrote: 'It is not part of the task of this Court … to conduct an enquiry into all aspects of the conduct of investigating police officers and Council officers; the competency of specialists; the tactics of the defence; or the techniques of interviewing children …'

With regard to whether the applicants were in any way blameworthy, the judge affirmed his pre-trial ruling that there was insufficient evidence to justify putting the women on trial. 'The Applicants did not bring the charges on their heads by their own conduct,' he said, and added that they were not discharged on a technicality. In making those points, Williamson acknowledged that the women were entitled to the presumption of innocence.

In his final paragraph, Justice Williamson noted that 'the Judge must ultimately exercise his or her discretion', and concluded: 'I am of the view that this is not a case for an award of costs.' Though his decision was eight weeks in the making, he gave no reasons to support his conclusion. For the women, this outcome raised a worrying question: did the judge exercise his discretion to deny them costs arbitrarily, or on the basis of fact and law?

• • •

In the Christchurch *Press* of 16 December '93, the women were reported to be 'shattered' and 'disgusted' by Justice Williamson's decision. Gaye Davidson said they weren't seeking compensation for loss of income or emotional stress, or media attention for their grievances. 'We just wanted something for our immediate legal costs,' she said.[17]

Gerald Nation's response was to consider a judicial review. 'I worked out exactly where I thought the judge went wrong and got all the papers prepared,' he recalled. 'Then I realised that there was no right of review. There was absolutely nowhere you could go with a High Court decision on costs that seemed to be based on a number of significant errors.'[18]

13.iii: The Nigel Hampton QC Appeal

Winning an appeal is never easy. Whenever a person is convicted of a criminal offence, the presumption of innocence is replaced by a presumption of guilt. So, when the case moves from the High Court to the Court of Appeal, the onus of proof shifts from the Crown to the appellant's counsel. Also, no matter how compelling the arguments, the Court of Appeal does not overturn convictions lightly.

There are many good reasons, both philosophical and practical, for the Court of Appeal's conservatism. First, there is the centrality of the jury to our criminal justice system, and the value we place on individual freedom and democratic participation in our society. The jury system gives practical expression to our communal belief that the decision to deprive a person of his or her liberty is too important to be delegated to an elite few. Second, there is the need for a justice system that seems to work most of the time because the alternative – that people will 'take the law into their own hands' – is too frightening to contemplate. A jury system that makes a lot of mistakes, or none at all, would not be credible. A fickle and time-consuming appeal system would not be credible either. So, if for no other reason than to convince the public that the justice system works, the Court of Appeal needs to run a tight ship, to issue reasoned judgments based on statute and precedent and to uphold most of the cases it considers. Even in cases where the Court finds an appellant's trial to be flawed, it may dismiss the appeal on the ground that no substantial miscarriage of justice occurred. However, as in all court cases, the ultimate question for the judges is whether the interests of justice have been served.

Most Court of Appeal hearings are presided over by a bench of three judges. However 'where the appeal raises issues of importance, including any legal, social and general economic considerations; if there are conflicting decisions of lower Courts; or if the Court is to be asked to depart from its own earlier decision', a bench of five judges may hear the case.[19] To Ellis's counsel, to the public and the media, and to former crèche workers and their supporters, the Ellis case raised issues of far-reaching importance about the investigation and prosecution of child sexual abuse allegations. But to the highest court in the land it was a standard criminal appeal. A three-judge bench, comprising President of the Court of Appeal Sir Robin Cooke, and Justices Sir Maurice Casey and Thomas Gault, was assigned to the case.

• • •

Nigel Hampton began his preparations by reading Justice Williamson's pre-trial and trial rulings:

I was struck by the restrictions placed on the way Rob Harrison could run the case, and by the effect that would have on the jury. After I'd studied the rulings, I looked at the depositions transcript and the children's evidence. I came to the view that the fundamental injustice of the case was that the jury did not see the full picture. They did not have the information they needed to appreciate the spread of allegations between families, the extraordinary breadth and depth of the interviewing, the cumulative effect of all the questioning on the children. I cannot accept that young children could be interviewed so often and for so long, over such a long period, without their memories being tainted.[20]

Nigel Hampton's appeal was based primarily on s. 385(1)(b) and s. 385(l)(c) of the Crimes Act. The former relates to points of law; the latter to issues of procedural unfairness. In his submissions, Hampton reviewed the manner in which the allegations arose and were investigated, and raised a raft of concerns about the conduct of the trial judge. He also argued that bias and publicity in the community had prevented Ellis from obtaining a fair trial, and that the jury verdicts were inconsistent.

• • •

In the weeks leading up to the appeal, Nigel Hampton worked on the case with single-minded concentration. On the morning of the appeal, he refused breakfast. 'I thought he was preoccupied,' Rob Harrison recalled. 'I thought he was keyed up and ready to go.'[21]

At 10.00am on 14 February 1994, Nigel Hampton opened the case for Peter Ellis in the Court of Appeal. He began by outlining the scale of the investigation and highlighting similarities between the Ellis case and comparable cases overseas. He described the openness of the crèche, and the history of the investigation. He talked about Ellis's highly publicised suspension, and the parents' meetings and media interest that followed. 'Parents were told to believe their children,' he said.

'Are you saying that children should not be believed?' asked Justice Gault.

'You should keep an open mind,' said Hampton.

'Isn't that for the authorities to decide?' said Gault.

'I can't see the difference between taking the child seriously and believing what the child says,' said Justice Casey.

'The child should not be discouraged by scepticism,' said Justice Cooke.

Hampton had barely resumed his account of how five crèche workers came to be charged with sexual offences involving 20 children, when Justice Cooke stopped him in his tracks.

'Would you give us an outline of the charges on which your client was convicted,' he said.

After a long pause, Hampton replied: 'We need to consider the 20 to assess the importance of contamination.'

'This is an appeal against conviction,' said Cooke. 'It is not a commission of inquiry into what happened at the crèche. Can you give us the facts on which your client was convicted?'

Again, there was a long pause. 'I kept waiting for Nigel to come back at him,' Rob Harrison recalled. 'I couldn't understand what was happening. Then Stanaway leant over and said: "Stand up and get an adjournment, he's not well." I looked at Nigel closely for the first time and realised he was really ill. But I didn't stand up. I didn't want to put down my senior, and I thought Nigel would be able to say: "I need to stop."' Then Justice Cooke called an adjournment.

'Nigel said: "I need to lie down,"' Harrison continued. 'As soon as he lay down that was it. I was saying: "Are you all right? What's the problem?" He didn't say anything. I gave him a glass of water and left [Detective Sergeant] Bob Hardie to look after him while I went to see the judges. I told them Nigel was too ill to continue and I wasn't prepared to do it on my own.'[22]

• • •

When it became clear that Nigel Hampton QC would be off work for months, Rob Harrison asked Christchurch barrister Graham Panckhurst QC to lead the Ellis appeal. Out of a sense of duty, Panckhurst agreed.

13.iv: The Graham Panckhurst QC Appeal

Graham Panckhurst was admitted to the bar in 1970. For most of his legal career he worked for the Christchurch law firm of Raymond Donnelly & Co. When his boss, mentor and friend Neil Williamson was appointed to the High Court bench in 1985, Panckhurst succeeded him as Crown Solicitor. In his years of working for the Crown, Panckhurst had prosecuted some child abuse cases, but it was his 20-year career as a fair and able prosecutor in other areas of crime that won him the respect of judges and lawyers alike. By 1992, he was ready for new challenges. In March that year, he left Raymond Donnelly to become an independent barrister. In a 1995 interview, he reflected on his chosen profession:

> If lawyers have anything to contribute to society – and I don't believe we've got a helluva lot – it's that we should be able to bring a degree of analysis and objectivity to bear when we evaluate situations. If that doesn't happen, then we're abdicating our responsibility. We're letting down our training, our experience and the contribution we have to make.[23]

• • •

The Ellis case was Graham Panckhurst's first experience of defending someone accused of child sexual abuse. He recalled:

> I came to the case reasonably fresh and with an open mind. I read the transcripts of the children's interviews, the trial evidence and the pre-trial and trial rulings. I looked at what the children had said on the one hand, and the evidence about where it was supposed to have happened and about the way the crèche operated on the other. I said: 'Right, does it marry up?' The simple answer was: 'No, it doesn't.' Everywhere I turned there was no confirmation. The evidence of opportunity wasn't there. A child said two or three other kids were present; the other kids didn't confirm it. A child said, I complained to a teacher; the teacher said, no such thing. Having made that evaluation, I came to the view that there wasn't evidence there to uphold the verdicts.[24]

To Graham Panckhurst, basing his appeal on s. 385(1)(a) of the Crimes Act ('that the verdict of the jury should be set aside on the ground that it is unreasonable or cannot be supported having regard to the evidence') was the obvious approach. But in terms of the usual run of appeals it was a bold move. Most criminal appeals are based on s. 385(1)(b) and s. 385(l)(c) ('that the judgment ... should be set aside on the ground of a wrong decision on any question of law' and 'that on any ground there was a miscarriage of justice'). In other words, most lawyers argue that their clients' convictions should be overturned because, for various procedural reasons, they did not receive a fair trial. But Panckhurst's principal argument was that Peter Ellis's conviction should be overturned because, quite simply, the jury had got it wrong.

To win an appeal on that ground, Panckhurst had to convince the Court that no reasonable jury, giving due weight to the presumption of innocence, could have convicted Peter Ellis on the evidence presented at his trial. It was a tall order, but Panckhurst was confident he had a strong case.

To support his argument, he summarised the videotaped interviews of the seven children whose allegations had resulted in guilty verdicts (Zelda, Molly, Eli, Tess, Bart, Kari and Lara), and analysed the evidence relating to the circumstances in which the offences were said to have occurred.

In his synopsis of the interviews, Panckhurst itemised the inconsistencies, contradictions and absurdities in the children's comments, the suggestive and leading questions of the interviewers and the evidence of parent–child and child–child contamination disclosed. In his analysis of the contextual evidence, he pointed out that:

- The final seven children named 21 other children as observers or participants in their abuse, but none of the named children confirmed the allegations. Some of the final seven named each other. Among other things, Tess said: that she saw Ellis defecate into Kari's mouth; that Kari went with her to Peter's house and

bach; and that Kari told her that Peter touched her bottom with a needle. But Kari said nothing to support Tess's claims. Also, Kari named five other children as parties to her abuse, but Tess was not one of them.
- No abuse was seen by any adult during Ellis's five years at the crèche.
- More than 70 families used the crèche each week. There were usually 12 children in the nursery area and 28 in the preschool section. The staff:child ratios were 1:4 (nursery) and 1:8 (preschool). Parents came and went unpredictably throughout the day.
- The preschoolers' toilets were adjacent to the main playroom. The toilet lobby door was almost always open, as were the cubicle doors (which were difficult to close). Abuse was said to have occurred in the toilet lobby and the cubicles. Some children said they saw other children being abused in the cubicles, which meant that the cubicle doors had to be open at the time.
- There was no evidence of any adult seeing anything untoward in the toilet area (but the Crown relied on Ms Kowhai's recollection that she saw Ellis coming out of a toilet cubicle with an unidentified girl, probably in 1990. She said he looked surprised and defensive).
- Four complainants said that Ellis urinated on children in the crèche toilets. Some said he defecated on them. As many as eight children were said to be involved. No children were ever observed in a soiled condition. No children complained to crèche staff about such activities.
- The maximum ratio for walks was one adult to five children. On 75 percent of walks, two adults went along. Apart from Sharleen, all the staff said that Ellis's walks were never longer than an hour and ten minutes. (But the Crown relied on Sharleen's evidence that Ellis took children on walks lasting up to two and a half hours). However, all the staff, including Sharleen, said that the walks were popular with children, and that children never returned in a distressed state.
- Zelda was the only complainant who attended the crèche when Ellis lived at 404 Hereford Street. Tess, Bart, Kari and Lara said they were abused at Peter's house (which became 'an address unknown' on the indictment). The Crown presented plans and photographs of 404 Hereford Street, and called the owner as a witness. Bruce said that at all relevant times he was retired and in residence, and that boarders were in residence when he was out of town. To his knowledge, Ellis brought children to his house only once. On that occasion another crèche worker came too. Ellis lived at three other addresses after leaving 404 Hereford Street, but the Crown did not suggest that any of them were locations for abuse. Therefore, if 'an address unknown' was not 404 Hereford Street, it was a mystery.

- Eli, Tess, Bart and Kari said that Ellis drove them by car to places where abuse occurred. But Ellis did not own a car and could not drive.
- Eli and Bart said that Ellis and his mother photographed incidents of abuse. No evidence was produced to substantiate that allegation. Ellis's mother was not called to give evidence.
- There was no medical evidence of injuries consistent with the abuse.
- Eli, Kari and Lara said that other crèche workers witnessed their abuse, or were informed about it at the time. Kari and Bart said they were abused by other crèche workers. The named workers did not confirm the allegations. To the contrary, they said they had no suspicion that abuse was occurring during Ellis's time at the crèche.

• • •

In addition to his principal argument (that the verdicts were unreasonable because the children's evidence was not credible), Panckhurst presented several secondary arguments. He contended that there was a general miscarriage of justice because the trial judge: placed unreasonable limits on the playing of children's videotapes and the extent of defence cross-examination; allowed the jury to retain transcripts of the videotaped interviews relied on by the Crown; allowed the admission of evidence about the accused's conversations on sexual matters; allowed Dr Zelas to give evidence suggesting that the complainants' allegations were credible; allowed the admission of a misleading schedule of children's behavioural symptoms; and summed up in a manner prejudicial to the defence. He also argued that the mix of guilty and not guilty verdicts for Eli, Tess and Bart was inconsistent. A further ground for appeal (for which Rob Harrison prepared the submission) was that the verdicts should be set aside as unreasonable because the children's evidence had been unfairly obtained.

• • •

At 10am on Monday 25 July 1994, Graham Panckhurst opened the case for Peter Ellis in the Court of Appeal. Rob Harrison was his junior. As before, the appeal was heard by Justices Cooke, Casey and Gault, with Brent Stanaway and Chris Lange appearing for the Crown.

Panckhurst began by outlining the chronology of the case, the grounds for appeal and the structure of the submissions. Then he moved on to his synopsis of the children's interviews. He had barely begun discussing Zelda Cypress's first interview (which Justice Williamson had declared inadmissible because it did not comply with the regulations), when Justice Gault interrupted him.

'Why are you referring to the content of an interview that was not played to the jury?' he asked.

With the air of a gentleman whose only concern was to be as helpful as possible, Panckhurst explained that, by considering all the interviews of the seven children who were the subject of convictions against Ellis, the Court could better assess the credibility of the children and the flaws in the interviewing process. He said that an examination of Zelda's first interview would show that her first disclosure arose late in a long interview, and was not spontaneous.

'But if it was not put before the jury, are we entitled to hear it now?' Gault persisted. Panckhurst explained that the trial judge's refusal to allow all the videotapes of all the children to be played to the jury was one of the grounds for appeal. He said the defence case was that, in the climate of the time, against a background of parental concern and intervention, the interviewing of the children was mishandled and had produced allegations of abuse. But the defence had been unable to properly present that case to the jury because the judge had placed unreasonable limits on the playing of videotapes, and on the examination and cross-examination of witnesses on matters of contamination.

To Graham Panckhurst, Justice Williamson's rulings and their effects on the course of the trial were secondary to the main issue: that the children's evidence was unbelievable. But what Panckhurst did not fully appreciate was that the Court of Appeal had long since abdicated its responsibility when it came to assessing the believability of children's evidence in sexual abuse cases.

Prior to 1990, the Court had considered all the cases that came before it with much the same objectivity. But when the 1989 Evidence Amendment Act eroded the traditional safeguards against miscarriages of justice in child sexual abuse cases [see Ch.3.ii], the Court of Appeal allowed its own standards for reviewing such cases to be eroded too. In the years between the introduction of the revolutionary legislation and the Ellis appeal, the fairness of the new procedures was repeatedly challenged in the courts. In a 1990 judgment on the admissibility of muddled videotaped disclosures elicited by prolonged and probing questioning, the Court of Appeal ruled that the purpose of the new legislation was 'to ensure that the old technicalities of evidence and the traditional approaches to the giving of evidence, even the contents of evidence in matters such as hearsay, shall not necessarily prevail', and that interviewers' questions of a 'somewhat leading and coaxing character' were acceptable.[25] In a 1991 judgment, the Court ruled that interviewers' efforts to ensure that child complainants told the truth should not be 'over-refined or pedantic'.[26] In a 1992 judgment on whether expert witnesses in child sexual abuse cases should be allowed to give scientifically baseless evidence, the Court ruled that evidence as to whether a child's behaviour was consistent or inconsistent with that of sexually abused children of the same age 'will usually be especially important in assisting the jury to evaluate the truth of the complainant's evidence'.[27]

By means of such rulings, the Court of Appeal effectively gave its stamp of approval to the ideological *coup d'état* that had wrenched control of the investigation and prosecution of child sexual abuse away from the relatively objective justice system, and placed it in the hands of the clearly partisan child protection movement. Consequently, when the high-profile Ellis case came along, the Court was faced with a stark choice: it could reconsider its own earlier decisions (and thereby bring the opprobrium of the child protection movement crashing about its ears); or it could ignore the controversy (and hope that it would go away).

Under the circumstances, it is perhaps not surprising that, while Graham Panckhurst focussed his attention on the unbelievability of the children's evidence, Justices Cooke, Casey and Gault focussed theirs on other matters. In particular, they focussed on the nature and effects of Justice Williamson's rulings. On the first morning of the Ellis appeal, they debated aspects of Williamson's rulings for more than two hours before deciding to allow Panckhurst to traverse both the played and unplayed tapes in his submissions.

For the next day and a half, Their Honours received Panckhurst's summaries of the children's interviews and his analysis of the contextual evidence virtually without comment. But when he moved on to his concerns about the conduct of the trial, the debate over Justice Williamson's rulings resumed.

Panckhurst pointed out that whenever defence counsel wanted to show the jury a videotape on which no charge was based, Rob Harrison was disadvantaged several times over. First, he had to persuade the judge that the requested tape contained material relevant to a charge. Second, the child did not have to watch the tape. Third, the jury did not get a copy of the transcript. Fourth, only selected portions of the tape were played. But the judges were interested only in the first point.

Throughout the hearing, Justices Cooke, Casey and Gault challenged Panckhurst repeatedly on Justice Williamson's rulings with regard to the playing of defence-onus tapes. What was Williamson's definition of 'relevant'? What did he say about the 'bizarre' tapes? Which defence-onus tapes were played? Which were not? Did the judge decline Harrison's requests or did Harrison not ask? Was the defence genuinely disadvantaged or were the judge's rulings nothing more than sensible limits to a potentially unwieldy trial?

In attempting to answer those questions, Panckhurst and Harrison were hampered by the inadequacy of the written record. The 'Crown Book' showed that, during the six-week trial, questions concerning the playing of defence-onus tapes, the admissibility of evidence and the extent of permissible cross-examination were debated by judge and counsel in the absence of the jury on at least 28 occasions.[28]

Other unrecorded discussions took place in chambers. But Justice Williamson issued only ten oral judgments during that time. So most of the arguments traversed, and the judge's views on them, went unrecorded.

Rob Harrison explained to the Court that, when Justice Williamson had finished dictating Oral Judgment (No.6) on the Friday prior to the start of the trial, discussions about the conduct of the trial continued between the judge and counsel in chambers. In the course of that discussion, arguments for and against the playing of a selection of defence-onus tapes were traversed. According to Harrison, at the end of that session, Williamson said something like, 'Well, I've set the parameters. I don't need to add to my ruling now. We understand where we are.'

Brent Stanaway confirmed that the discussion had taken place, and produced the notes he had made at the time. His notes indicated that Williamson's instructions with regard to Bart Dogwood's most bizarre tape, and Judy Balsa's tape about her uncle's abuse of her brother, were unequivocal. 'Not to be played,' Stanaway had written on the front pages of the relevant transcripts.

• • •

Shortly after lunch on Wednesday 27 July, Stanaway opened the Crown case. He argued that the defence was not hampered by the judge's rulings, and that the jury was given a full picture of the case. He noted that the jury had deliberated for a long time, and had convicted Ellis mainly, but not exclusively, on the complainants' earlier interviews. Therefore, he argued, the jury had considered the evidence carefully, and the verdicts should stand.

Stanaway's arguments about the believability of the children's evidence were based on Dr Zelas's evidence at trial. He said that children with limited understanding and immature language skills could be easily confused by fantasy games and trickery, and intimidated by threats. He said that no matter how confusing their 'peripheral details', the children had given good 'central detail' about the offences. He suggested that when Ellis took children away by car, someone else drove. That being the case, other people had to be involved.

In his submission, Graham Panckhurst had addressed only the inadequacy of the evidence of abuse by his client. When the possibility of abuse by other people was raised, Justice Cooke invited Panckhurst to comment.

'I would have rather thought it spoke for itself,' he replied.

Then, without explanation, on Thursday 28 July, the Ellis appeal was adjourned for a week.

• • •

On Friday 29 July 1994, Graham Panckhurst and Rob Harrison went to the maximum security block at Paparua Prison and handed their client a document headed: *The Queen* v *Peter Hugh McGregor Ellis*. 'Which one am I?' asked Ellis.

The document contained the sensational news that, on Monday 25 July, 11-year-old Zelda Cypress, the oldest and most credible of the complainant children, had retracted her allegations. After failing to contact Zelda's therapist, Ms Cypress had contacted the High Court registrar. On Tuesday 26 July the Court of Appeal had appointed Christchurch barrister Nicholas Till to interview Zelda and her parents. Till spoke to them that afternoon and reported to the Court next morning. On Friday 29 July, Peter Ellis held Nicholas Till's report in his hands.

Ms Cypress told Till that over the previous few months she had mentioned to Zelda that 'Peter was appealing to a higher court and saying that the children told lies.'

'I am not sure why I told [Zelda] that but on reflection think that it was to reinforce that Peter was a bad person to say that the children had told lies when they had not,' she said. 'When I said this [Zelda] was silent.'

Ms Cypress said that Zelda may have overheard her parents discussing their plans to appeal the quantum of lump-sum ACC payments made to their daughter, and to sue the City Council for negligence in their supervision of the crèche.

Zelda told Nicholas Till that she did not know that Peter Ellis's appeal was running that week until her mother told her on the evening of her retraction. She said she had been thinking about telling her mother that she had lied about Peter for a long time, and had been waiting for an opportunity to do so. The opportunity arose following a scrap with a school friend. The scrap had nothing to do with Peter Ellis, and Zelda assured Till that no one had mentioned Peter at school. The scrap escalated into a heated telephone exchange between the children's mothers. In the course of the exchange, the other mother called Zelda a liar. Afterwards, Ms Cypress spoke to Zelda about the importance of telling the truth.

'She became distressed ... said she wished she could start again ... She then said, "I want to tell you about Peter and they were lies,"' Ms Cypress reported. 'She said ... she had given the replies she thought I wanted. She said that it started with a wee story but it then got bigger.' Nicholas Till questioned Zelda closely about the crèche, her DSW interviews, the Ellis trial and her retraction. She said she thought she was telling lies in her interviews when she saw them in court, but she didn't say anything because 'she thought everyone would be mad'.

'She is plainly saying that she lied in her evidence at trial. She did not depart from that stance,' Till reported.

On receiving the news, Peter Ellis's first thought was for Zelda. 'Is she all right?' he asked. 'Are her parents supporting her?'

• • •

On 2 August, Nicholas Till re-interviewed Zelda in her mother's presence. When he asked her about the indecencies mentioned in her DSW interviews, Zelda accepted that she had made the allegations, but said they were not true. At one point she became tearful. She said she was scared her mother would be mad. She said she couldn't remember much about the crèche, or her DSW interviews, or the Ellis trial. Till reported:

> I tested her statement that she had lied from a number of different angles over a considerable span of the interview coming back to it from time to time after having pursued other points. She was adamant she had lied. She did not accept other possible explanations which I put to her, including the desire to be rid of any involvement with Peter; a perception that a clean start would solve her other unhappiness; a wish to help Peter.

Astonishingly, despite Zelda's insistence that she had lied, Nicholas Till did not 'believe the child'. Instead, he suggested that she was 'a very unhappy, confused young girl, much troubled by her part in this case'.

'I think she has chosen to withdraw her allegations as a means of removing the case and its effects from her life, coupled possibly with the wish to help Peter, who undoubtedly was a close friend,' he concluded.

• • •

On Friday 5 August 1994, the appeal resumed with submissions on Zelda's retraction. Graham Panckhurst noted that it was spontaneous and unsolicited, and had been tested rigorously. 'This is to be contrasted with the absence of any testing of the allegations against the appellant as they emerged from the complainant children,' he said. He also discounted Till's suggestion that the retraction may have been motivated by Zelda's friendship with Ellis, her contact with him having ceased when she left the crèche five years earlier.

To Panckhurst, the most important point was that, over the past two years, Zelda's allegations had been taken seriously and believed by her parents, her therapist, the police, the prosecutors and others involved in the trial process. As one of many complainants, Zelda had the support of numbers. Her allegations were believed by the jury.

'Her courage in coming forward in all the circumstances is poignant and compelling. Her action cannot be lightly discounted,' Panckhurst argued. 'Of the 118 children interviewed, six now remain in support of the convictions ... Surely the point had been reached where the fallout of complainants must be seen as alarming.'

Graham Panckhurst then highlighted Zelda's importance to the prosecution. She was the oldest child and the first witness called by the Crown. As her babysitter,

Ellis had the opportunity to offend. In his closing address to the jury, counsel for the Crown had described Zelda as a 'compelling and believable witness', and her DSW interviews as 'clear and strong'. He had described defence suggestions that Zelda was influenced by the books she had read, and by her mother's questions, as 'nonsense'. Panckhurst therefore suggested that, with such an important witness, the jury's decision to convict on her charges probably had a flow-on effect on their other decisions.

In reply, Brent Stanaway argued that Zelda's retraction lacked credibility, and that her original disclosures were indeed 'clear and strong'. He also referred to Dr Zelas's evidence that retractions were common, and did not mean that the original allegations were untrue.

• • •

In his 'evidence unfairly obtained' submissions, Rob Harrison argued that the manner in which the parents, the interviewers and the police had pursued the crèche investigation had rendered the children's evidence unreliable. In reply, Chris Lange submitted that Harrison's arguments had been considered, and dismissed, in pre-trial hearings and at the trial itself. Then Graham Panckhurst presented his closing submissions.

Panckhurst told the Court that in a trial where videotaped interviews and expert evidence assumed such importance, the grounds of appeal raised four pertinent questions: Were the children's allegations credible when measured against the contextual evidence? Did the jury have an adequate picture of the interview process and the interviews as a whole? Did the provision of transcripts, the terms and scope of Dr Zelas's evidence and the use of the behavioural schedule tip the balance too far in favour of the prosecution? Was the summing up fair and adequate in its portrayal of the defence case?

With regard to the first question, Panckhurst noted that, instead of mounting an attack on the contextual evidence, the Crown had tried to explain away inconvenient aspects of the children's evidence with terms like 'magical thinking'. Also, though the Crown claimed that the convictions were based on 'reliable central detail', his analysis of the relevant videotapes showed that they contained no 'reliable central detail' whatsoever.

With regard to the other questions, Panckhurst identified a series of points in Justice Williamson's rulings and summing up that had, he argued, individually and cumulatively contributed to a miscarriage of justice. As his presentation reached its climax, Panckhurst told the Court that, throughout the proceedings, from his earliest rulings to his summing up, the trial judge's tone had been dismissive of the defence case.

It was an extraordinary moment in the appeal. In public, in the highest court in the land, Graham Panckhurst QC was laying his commitment to the interests of justice on the line and challenging the Honourable Justices of the Court of Appeal to do the same. He was asking them to do what he had done – to put aside years of mutual respect and close friendship, and personal knowledge of Neil Williamson as a fair-minded and compassionate man – and to see what he had seen: that Justice Williamson had not given Peter Ellis a fair trial. The tension was palpable.

'What is your message, Mr Panckhurst?' said Justice Casey.

'The trial judge's rulings demonstrate that he formed a view of the case at an early stage, and that view prevailed at the trial and pervaded his summing up,' said Panckhurst.

Earlier, Panckhurst had strongly criticised Williamson's approach to Ellis's sexual conversations. In response to Panckhurst's closing criticisms, Justice Cooke challenged him to explain how the children could have come up with stories of being urinated upon by Ellis, if he had not done so.

'It is not incumbent on the defence to explain how the children came by their ideas,' said Panckhurst.

'I want an answer, Mr Panckhurst,' said Justice Cooke.

After a moment's reflection, Panckhurst said that little boys make jokes about such things. In an escalating panic, children's jokes could easily be picked up and spread. He reminded the Court that there was no physical evidence to support the allegation.

In conclusion, Panckhurst advised Their Honours that his client had instructed him not to appeal the sentence. As a crèche worker, Peter Ellis wanted no argument suggesting that offending of the type alleged did not warrant a sentence of that scale.

'The Court will take time to consider its judgment,' said Justice Cooke.

• • •

On 5 September 1994, Peter Ellis wrote:

> like the parachutist ... shoved screaming from the plane, I can only hope my chute opens, if not I plunge down to be shattered on the ground. So my time has come and like the earth rushing towards the parachutist (or should that be the other way around?) I rush headlong towards my result. 10.00 Thursday I get the thumbs – will they be up or down – I'd like to say WHO CARES – but I do. Am I a brave person, can I be strong one more time – possibly – so why do my eyes hurt and why is my mouth twitching – perhaps a sneeze ... No ... there's no spring flowers ... just walls that just maybe I will find myself on the other side of by Friday.

• • •

Shortly after 10am on 8 September 1994, Graham Panckhurst QC read the judgment of the Court of Appeal in the case of *The Queen* v *Peter Hugh McGregor Ellis* as it emerged, page by page, from his fax machine. The last page came first:

> Our overall judgement of the case is that after this long trial the jury were fully justified in their conclusion that charges against the accused had been established beyond reasonable doubt. It is significant that the trial Judge in his sentencing remarks expressed his agreement with the verdicts, describing them as 'obviously correct' ... Great risks of detection may have been run, but that is not uncommon in cases of indulgence in a perversion. The jury deliberated for more than two days and brought in carefully discriminating verdicts which can be seen as conservative. The claims that the evidence of the children was contaminated by interviewing techniques, parental hysteria or the like lack any solid basis.

In the judgment, Panckhurst's analysis of the videotapes on which the guilty verdicts were based received no mention, and the other argument in support of his claim that the children's evidence was unbelievable was dismissed in two sentences:

> The matters advanced by Mr Panckhurst about the design and operation of the crèche do not persuade us that the abuse described by the children as occurring there, particularly in the toilets, could not have happened, or that their evidence of it cannot be relied upon. Nor do his submissions about lack of opportunity for abuse away from the crèche when the children were taken on walks by the appellant.

Of allegations that Ellis took children by car to an unknown address where groups of people abused them with sticks, needles and burning paper while Ellis and his mother took photos, the Court concluded that there was nothing in Mr Panckhurst's submissions that rendered the children's stories 'inherently improbable or unworthy of belief'. With regard to Bart's stories of tunnels, trapdoors, cages and ovens, they noted that 'there were features in the house at Hereford Street which could have been in the child's mind when he was describing some of these events ...'

Though they had viewed none of the children's videotapes, Their Honours praised the professionalism of the interviewers, declared that the interviews were in accordance with 'the spirit and broad purpose of the legislation' and approved Dr Zelas's role in the case. Of Justice Williamson's rulings and summing up, the judgment stated:

> We are satisfied that the ruling about the tapes ... caused no prejudice to the defence. His ruling that the children need not be present during the playing of the defence tapes was also one given in the proper exercise of his discretion and any impact this had on the effectiveness of cross-examination seems to us more theoretical than real ... The Judge was clearly correct to allow evidence of his interest in these unusual practices to be given: the jury could see in the reference to 'golden showers' support for his conviction

on the two counts involving that unusual practice, especially as it seems unlikely that two children could have made it up or learnt of it from other sources ... We think the Judge covered the salient features of the case admirably ...

With regard to Zelda's retraction, Their Honours stated: '... we are by no means satisfied that she did lie at the interviews although she may now genuinely think she did.'

In conclusion, they quashed the three convictions relating to Zelda because of the uncertainty, but upheld all the other guilty verdicts and left Ellis's sentence unchanged.

• • •

'Graham Panckhurst had this honourable view of the justice system,' Rob Harrison recalled. 'It was obvious to him that the children's evidence was unbelievable, and he was convinced it'd be obvious to the Court of Appeal too. I kept saying: "No, no, no, the Crown'll come back at you with psychobabble and that'll be the end of it."'

'Rob warned me, but I'm afraid it didn't make any difference,' Panckhurst admitted. 'I thought the traditional safeguards against miscarriages of justice would apply. I thought the Court of Appeal would take a careful look at the evidence.'

13.v: Graham Panckhurst QC Considers his Options

On 12 September 1994, Graham Panckhurst QC wrote to Christchurch Crown Solicitor Brent Stanaway about the Ellis case. He pointed out that his first and principal appeal submission was that the verdicts were unreasonable because the children's evidence was not credible. He had supported his submission with a detailed analysis of the children's interviews, followed by a review of the contextual evidence, and had argued that the two were incompatible. In response, the Crown had argued that the children's evidence could not be taken literally, and that the jury had convicted Ellis only on allegations containing 'reliable central detail'. In his closing submission, Panckhurst had contended, on the basis of his analysis of the children's interviews, that the allegations on which Ellis's convictions were based contained no 'reliable central detail' whatsoever.

In view of the issues raised in the Court of Appeal, and the pivotal importance of 'central detail' to the Crown case, Panckhurst expressed concern at 'a major deficiency, or gap, in the Court of Appeal judgment'.

'The attack on the reliability of the central detail is not even acknowledged ... there is no examination of the interview evidence to demonstrate that reliable detail existed,' he wrote. 'My concerns at the outcome of the appeal are such that I intend to recommend that any available steps are taken on behalf of Ellis.'[1]

• • •

In theory, the British Privy Council is New Zealand's final court of appeal. In practice it intervenes in criminal cases from Commonwealth countries 'only if and when it is shown that, by a disregard of the forms of legal process or by some violation of the principles of natural justice or otherwise, substantial and grave injustice has been done'.[2]

Consequently, criminal appeals to the Privy Council are rare, and limited in nature. Between 1898 and 1994, the Privy Council agreed to hear only four New Zealand criminal cases, and overturned the conviction in only one.

While the Privy Council approach to criminal appeals is restrictive, the New Zealand approach to the provision of legal aid for such appeals is even more so. According to the Legal Services Act, legal aid for criminal appeals to the Privy Council is available only 'where the Attorney-General certifies that a question of law of exceptional public importance is involved and that the grant ... is desirable in the public interest'.[3]

In his letter to the Attorney-General of 22 February 1995, Panckhurst submitted that the Ellis case raised two questions of law of exceptional public importance: the first was whether the guilty verdicts based on the complainants' evidence could be legally justified; the second was whether allowing the jury to see only part of the complainants' videotaped evidence had denied Ellis a fair trial.[4]

In support of the first 'question of law', he enclosed his 12 September 1994 letter to Brent Stanaway, and Stanaway's reply. 'Significantly, Mr Stanaway did not endeavour to point out in the Court of Appeal judgment where the acknowledged need for good central detail has been considered, and found good,' Panckhurst wrote. 'There is no such passage in the judgment. The problem was simply not addressed by the Court.'

On the second question, Panckhurst noted that the 13 convictions left standing were based on the evidence of six children. The six had recorded 20 videotaped interviews, of which 12 were played to the jury. He noted that his concerns on that issue had been dismissed by the Court of Appeal, and quoted a passage from the appeal judgment which he described as 'the high point of the Court's thinking on the matter'. The passage stated:

He [the trial judge] was clearly right in seeking to prevent the trial becoming enmeshed in all the collateral and peripheral matters covered in the tapes not relied on by the Crown, and about exposing the jury to the playing of many hours of irrelevant material, thereby distracting them from consideration of the real issues.[5]

'Implicit in these observations is the assumption that it is acceptable for the Crown Solicitor to have the advantage of effectively pre-recorded evidence-in-chief extracted over many hours in the course of multiple interviews, and then to frame its case in such a way as to render those parts of the interviews not wanted by the Crown as "collateral", "peripheral" and "irrelevant", Panckhurst wrote. 'In this context it must be noted that the interviews not played to the jury were conducted by the same interviewers, and focussed upon the same subject matter, namely alleged abuse at the hands of people employed at the crèche.'

With regard to the public interest issues involved, Panckhurst noted that sexual abuse allegations were prevalent, and that the Court of Appeal had acknowledged that recent legislative and procedural changes had made defending such cases much more difficult. Consequently, he argued, the questions of law raised in the Ellis case were matters of fundamental and general concern that met the criteria for criminal appeals to the Privy Council.

Panckhurst also advised the Attorney-General that he had fielded 'numerous unsolicited expressions of concern' from the general public. The most troubling comments came from educationalists whose training and experience led them to question 'whether the crucial evidence was rational and safe to act upon'.

'I am available to supply any further information you may require,' Panckhurst concluded.

• • •

Graham Panckhurst's legal aid application was passed from Attorney-General Paul East to Solicitor-General John McGrath, who passed it to Deputy Solicitor-General Lowell Goddard (now Justice Goddard). Lowell Goddard passed the application to Wellington barrister and former Crown Counsel John Upton QC, and instructed him to provide an opinion. On receiving Upton's report, John McGrath advised Graham Panckhurst that 'in accordance with the practice adopted in respect of these applications' he had 'sought and considered the opinion of an independent barrister'.[6]

'I happened to be in Christchurch on business last week,' Upton reported. 'While I was there I took the opportunity of discussing this file with Mr Brent Stanaway.' With regard to the defence-onus tapes, he wrote:

Mr Stanaway told me that a number of extracts from tapes (other than those played by the Crown) were in fact played to the jury at the request of defence counsel – on a stop/start basis to show the jury precisely what defence counsel wanted them to see and no more … Mr Stanaway said that effectively defence counsel was allowed to play to the jury whatever portions of any tapes he wanted played. Mr Stanaway's recollection is that there was no occasion where there was any argument over the relevancy or otherwise of any parts of any tapes which Mr Harrison wanted to have played. On top of that, Mr Stanaway said that the defence was able to freely cross-examine witnesses as to the way in which the interviewing process was conducted … So that in other words, the jury was properly informed both through extracts from tapes played … and uninhibited cross-examination of Crown witnesses as to perceived weaknesses in the interview process.[7]

On the subject of Peter Ellis's sexual conversations (which were not part of Panckhurst's application), Upton wrote: 'Mr Stanaway said that … Ellis specifically denied ever discussing such matters in front of any of the children. Yet at least some of the children … had knowledge of adult sexual conduct of the type discussed by Mr Ellis.' Then, in a spectacular burst of illogic, Upton argued that the jury was entitled to conclude that the children's sexual knowledge 'could only have come from Mr Ellis', and that therefore, 'contrary to what Mr Ellis said, such children were involved in various types of sexual conduct with him.' The implication of this claim was that, regardless of Panckhurst's concerns, Ellis was obviously guilty, so wasting public money on an appeal to the Privy Council could not be countenanced.

'Against this background, I now come to Mr Panckhurst's request,' Upton continued. Of the two 'questions of law' raised, Upton opined that the first was a question of fact, and the second was a question of 'degree and discretion'.

'Even if I am wrong … so that one or other (or both) does involve a question of law, it is not, in my opinion, one of exceptional public importance where a grant of criminal legal aid is desirable in the public interest,' Upton wrote.

Finally – though he had not discussed the matter with Graham Panckhurst or Rob Harrison, and had apparently read only Panckhurst's application and the Court of Appeal judgment – Upton concluded:

> Contrary to what he [Panckhurst] says, there is nothing to indicate that the Court surrendered 'any proper oversight of whether the evidence was fit to be acted upon'. In addition, the Court did not countenance 'a trial process which denied effective access to part of the evidence in chief of the main witnesses'. On what I have seen, the reverse is in fact the situation. There is nothing to indicate possible injustice nor that these issues raised have any general significance outside this particular trial.

On receiving John Upton's report, the Solicitor-General advised Graham Panckhurst that his application for legal aid to take the Ellis case to the Privy Council had been declined.[8]

13.vi: *Davidson and Others* v *The Christchurch City Council*

On 3 September 1992, almost ten months after Peter Ellis had left the Civic Child Care Centre, Christchurch City Manager John Gray closed the centre without warning or explanation [see Chapters 8.iii and 9.i]. On 28 September 1992, the crèche staff instituted unjustified dismissal proceedings against the City Council, and Christchurch barrister Tom Weston was instructed to prepare the council's response.[9]

On 12 October 1992, Tom Weston wrote to union secretary Peter Lawson, urging him to consider an out-of-court settlement.[10] But the crèche staff wanted their day in court, and the compensation they sought was far more than the council was prepared to pay. Also, the council soon realised that settling that aspect of the crèche controversy behind closed doors would only further enrage their already bitterly divided ratepayers.

• • •

On 27 February 1995, the eight-day hearing of the $2.6 million unjustified dismissal claim opened before Chief Employment Court Judge Tom Goddard. The Christchurch City Council was represented by Tom Weston, with assistance from Jo Appleyard. Ten former crèche teachers (the four women who had been charged and discharged, and six others) and two former crèche cleaners were represented by Graham Panckhurst QC with assistance from Hans van Schreven. The other teacher, Sharleen, was represented by Peter Lawson.

'The rest of the staff felt very bitter towards Sharleen. They thought she let them down in the criminal court,' Lawson explained. 'It wasn't so much the evidence she gave as the way she was seen as a star prosecution witness.'[11]

In legal terms, the case was about the distinction between redundancies (where blameless employees lose their jobs through insolvency, restructuring or closure) and dismissals (where culpable employees lose their jobs through misconduct, incompetence or incapacity). In personal terms, it was about reputations and careers, and the effect of the crèche closure on both. It was about the staff of a highly regarded childcare centre having their previously unblemished reputations destroyed by allegations of child pornography and ritual abuse; and about the city manager's distinguished 46-year career in local body administration coming to a controversial end. In public terms, the case was about the questions that obsessed the nation: if Peter Ellis is guilty, how can the women be innocent? If the women are innocent, how can Peter Ellis be guilty?

Despite the narrowly defined legal issues, the wider implications of the case were not lost on the lawyers involved. Graham Panckhurst told me that he was pleased to represent the crèche staff because 'it was a further opportunity to get involved in something that might have a spillover in helping Peter'. In my interview with him, the council's lawyer Tom Weston insisted that the employment law issues were all that mattered ('I was focussing on what John Gray did over about two days ... whatever may or may not have happened in any other court, whether Peter Ellis or the women were guilty or innocent, was all completely irrelevant'). But the transcript of the Employment Court proceedings told a different story.

'Notwithstanding the fact that Mr Ellis has been through the High Court trial and an appeal, you remain firm in your own mind that he is not guilty of what he has been charged?' Weston asked Gaye Davidson in cross-examination.

'I believe in his innocence because of the operation of the crèche, the way we work together as a team,' she replied.

'When the Court of Appeal concluded that there were opportunities for these offences to occur – you differ from the Court of Appeal?'

'For the offences that are alleged to have occurred, over such an extensive period, there is no way they could have gone undetected.'

'So you would disagree with the Court of Appeal on that?'

'Yes.'

The other staff challenged by Weston on the same point were equally emphatic: the High Court and the Court of Appeal were wrong. Peter Ellis was innocent.

In terms of the employment law issues, the council's aim was to prove that the dismissals were justified because the workers were genuinely redundant (because the Ministry of Education had forced the crèche to close by withdrawing its licence). To achieve this aim, the city manager had to convince the court that he *genuinely believed* that the closure was beyond his control, even if in fact it had not been. On the other hand, if the workers believed the closure was a jack-up to enable the city manager to fire them for suspected misconduct while pretending they were redundant, that belief alone was not enough, the onus was on the workers to prove it.[12]

In addition to ensuring that both parties had a fair hearing, the judge's task was to rule on the merits of the competing claims, and determine what compensation, if any, should be paid. In such cases, the standard of proof is 'on the balance of probabilities'.

• • •

At the core of the proceedings was John Gray's response to the situation that confronted him on 2 and 3 September 1992. But, because that event did not occur in a vacuum, evidence and opinions about the causes and effects of the crèche closure featured in the proceedings. Also, because the rules of evidence in the Employment Court are relatively relaxed, information about the crèche investigation that did not appear in the criminal courts was aired for the first time in the Employment Court.[13]

All the crèche staff knew for sure was that at 5.30pm on Thursday 3 September 1992, John Gray told them that, because the Ministry of Education had withdrawn the crèche licence, he had no choice but to close the crèche and make them redundant. He said there was no possibility of redeployment, and that he did not know why the licence was withdrawn. To the staff, Gray's conduct was outrageous. He had deprived them of their jobs without warning, and would not tell them why. Next day, they discovered that Gray had met with a delegation from the police, the Ministry of Education and DSW prior to the closure. But the cloak of secrecy over that meeting prevented them from finding out why the ministry had withdrawn the licence, or what John Gray was told that prompted him to permanently close the crèche.

• • •

In his opening submission, Graham Panckhurst said:

> … the case of the applicants is that the Council did not act as a fair and reasonable employer when confronted with what were wholly unsubstantiated allegations. The applicants, as employees of the Council, were entitled to expect that matters which would inevitably affect their ongoing employment were considered reflectively and with good judgement. Also, that the process followed be one which met the requirements of natural justice. The respondent failed on both counts.[14]

In his opening submission, Peter Lawson said that the council had a contractual obligation to observe two established principles of employment law. The first was that, before dismissing employees on allegations of misconduct, the employer had to satisfy himself, on the basis of his own complete and fairly conducted inquiry, that sufficient and justifiable grounds existed for the dismissals. The second was that, for the employer's inquiry to be complete and fair, the employees had to be acquainted with the allegations against them and given an adequate opportunity to respond. 'The Respondent did not meet these obligations,' Lawson said.[15]

• • •

In their evidence-in-chief, the former childcare workers sought to show that they had done nothing to bring about the crèche closure, that the council had mishandled the situation and that they had suffered harm as a result.

All the applicants were highly critical of the city manager's handling of the crèche closure. Judge Goddard observed in his supplementary judgment:

Mr Gray's manner was variously described as unapproachable, unfriendly, not appearing to be sorry, lacking in concern for employees who were shocked and scared, very businesslike, very impersonal, very concise, insensitive, cold and clipped, cold and abrupt, treating staff with disdain and distaste as if pleased to wash his hands of the whole centre, awkward manner, lacking in clarity or honesty, making no eye contact with the staff, blunt, standing side on to the staff with his hands in his pockets, cold-bloodedly delivering his message, cold and gruff.[16]

With regard to the ongoing trauma, Gaye Davidson said that a complainant parent had taken the microphone at a recent outdoor concert and told the crowd, 'Beware, beware, there is a child molester out there.'

Jan Buckingham said she had become a virtual recluse: 'Prior to the closure ... I would assist at the school gymnastics ... take school children to sports venues and volunteer for parent help in the classroom. I used to foster children. I liked helping. Now ... I don't go to parent teacher meetings ... I don't take my children on school outings ... I have not been grocery shopping in two years.'

Debbie Gillespie recounted an occasion when Bart Dogwood's brother called her 'Kid fucker' in public, and another when Ms Dogwood followed her around a shopping mall saying loudly, 'You're a child molester. You molested my child at the Civic Child Care Centre.'

Crèche staff who had never been accused of anything said they had been denied work at other preschools. However, under cross-examination, they admitted that the council was not solely to blame for their problems, and that they had no idea what John Gray was told that prompted him to close the crèche.

'I would assume that any good employer would have a very good reason to terminate the positions of 13 people,' crèche worker Shona argued. 'He would need to have a tremendous amount of knowledge in order to do that to people's careers. I didn't know what he actually knew, but it must have been something horrendous.'

The staff also rejected Tom Weston's suggestion that, if the Ministry of Education was determined to suspend the crèche licence, and the police were determined to arrest more suspects, the crèche closure and the women's arrests would have inevitably followed. As Shona pointed out, when the management of Crèche X supported their accused childcare worker, the allegations there came to nothing.

• • •

When the staff had given evidence, Graham Panckhurst called Peter Lawson (unlike lawyers, who may not act as witnesses in their own cases, union officials may do so in employment proceedings). Lawson said that the police had no statutory authority to approach the city council – apparently with the intention of persuading the council to dismiss the crèche staff – when they had insufficient evidence to lay charges.

However, under cross-examination, Lawson denied suggesting that John Gray had details of the allegations against the staff.

'What I am saying is that unless he had something more substantial than what he has claimed to have had, he should have acted more positively in defence and in support of his employees,' Lawson said. 'He should have properly examined all the grounds upon which the police were trying to persuade him to take action, whether they were entitled to under the law.'

Lawson added that John Gray should have checked the validity of the suspension notice (which Lawson had discovered was legally invalid). After all, Gray was chief executive of a regulatory authority 'and would know very well that parking tickets or any other notice issued by any of his employees which did not comply with the regulations under which they were issued were not valid notices'.

But like the other witnesses for the staff, Peter Lawson had to admit that he had no idea what John Gray knew about the allegations against the crèche workers. However, he was sure that Gray knew more than he was telling.

'It seems obvious to me that the police would not just come along to Mr Gray and say we want you to close the Civic Child Care Centre, and that Mr Gray, without asking why, would do so,' Lawson said. 'It also seems logical to me that the police would have alleged to Mr Gray ... that some form of criminal misconduct was taking place at the centre or else he would not have acted in the way he did.'

• • •

The other witnesses for the applicants were crèche management committee spokesperson Mr Larch, and lawyer Gerald Nation. Mr Larch described his futile attempts to find out why the crèche had been closed, and his legal challenge to the closure (which he abandoned when the women were arrested). He also reported that a survey of parents at the time of the closure showed there was sufficient support to reopen the centre, provided the same staff were re-employed.

Gerald Nation gave evidence of his work on behalf of the four arrested women, and outlined the costs involved. In cross-examination, Tom Weston questioned him closely about his clients' debts to Wynn Williams and Co.

'When we came to set the fee as a firm we endeavoured to set it at a level which would provide what we thought would be adequate remuneration, but not generous remuneration, for the work that had been done,' Nation explained. 'Although we knew it would cause our clients hardship, we thought they would be able to pay if they had to.'

'The debt at the moment for three of them is growing because of the interest,' Weston pointed out. 'If the part payments being made at the moment were stopped, would you proceed to obtain judgment and bankrupt them if necessary?'

'Our firm would hesitate, and always has hesitated, before taking the step of bankrupting a client,' Nation said. 'We would make a judgment over that in all the circumstances that then applied. I would not expect it to come to that.'

• • •

In his opening address on behalf of the council, Tom Weston said:

> At best, the Police evidence can have any relevance to this case only if Mr Gray learnt of it. He did not. His evidence will be that at the meeting on 2 September ... he was told that the children were 'in serious danger' and that the crèche should be closed straight away ... Despite his repeated requests for more information he was not told why the Police and the Ministry believed the children to be in danger ... He was told that whatever was going to happen the crèche licence was going to be suspended ... From a practical point of view, they [John Gray and Martin Maguire] saw a suspension of the licence as producing the same result as a cancellation. Hence, it was agreed ... that the Council would not oppose cancellation.[17]

Tom Weston called John Gray (who had retired in June 1993), council in-house lawyer Peter Mitchell and crèche liaison officer Martin Maguire to give evidence about the events of 2 and 3 September 1992, and personnel officer Marshall Wright (who was not involved in the closure) to give evidence on staff employment issues.

In his evidence-in-chief, John Gray covered the points traversed by Tom Weston and stressed his commitment to being a good employer. Of the 3 September meeting, he said:

> I met in my office with Mr Bede Cooper who gave me a letter of suspension dated 3 September 1992. I immediately handed him my letter ... He then handed me the letter of cancellation ... The process lasted no more than five minutes ...

With regard to Michael Deaker (who signed the suspension and cancellation notices [see Ch.8.iii]), Gray said: 'I do not actually recall him being in my private office when the letters were exchanged ... although Martin Maguire now tells me he was there in the background.' Under cross-examination, Gray acknowledged that the jobs of 11 well-qualified, loyal and dedicated childcare workers were at stake. He said he did not ask how many staff were the subject of police concerns, what they were supposed to have done or when they were supposed to have done it; he did not insist on being privy to the information provided to the Ministry of Education before agreeing to fast-track the crèche closure; he did not insist on a written complaint before taking action; he did not consult the staff employment contracts before surrendering the crèche licence. All things considered, Graham Panckhurst and Peter Lawson suggested, Gray had not acted as a 'fair and reasonable employer'.

In his evidence, Peter Mitchell said that he agreed with Mr Gray's evidence. Martin Maguire said he did too.

Personnel officer Marshall Wright's evidence was not in dispute. Everyone accepted that Gray should have put the staff on two weeks' paid leave, instead of making them redundant immediately (but that error was quickly corrected). Everyone also accepted that the redundancy provisions in the staff employment contracts had been met, that the staff had been offered counselling, that two of their number had been redeployed, and that they had accepted redundancy payments on condition that their unjustified dismissal claims were not prejudiced by doing so.

• • •

In the course of my research [see Ch.8.iii], I found that the only people involved in the meetings of 2 and 3 September who supported John Gray's version of events were Gray, Mitchell and Maguire. This meant that the council's defence depended on the word of Gray and his two staff, on Tom Weston's selection of witnesses and on the ability of everyone involved to suppress, discredit, minimise, ignore or explain away the compromising documentary evidence. That documentary evidence comprised: the surviving page of council officer Rob Dally's notes of the 2 September meeting ('concerns of abuse by other crèche staff [totally confidential]'); a memo written by Michael Deaker about the 3 September meeting (which included his recollection that, in John Gray's office and in John Gray's presence, the police showed him documents alleging misconduct by the crèche staff); the letters exchanged between John Gray and Michael Deaker on 3 September (which indicated that the suspension was not a *fait accompli* until then); John Gray's 3 September memo to city councillors ('both myself and the Ministry of Education were briefed by NZ Police beforehand'); and a note handwritten by Gray on his 3 September memo to councillors ('closure necessary to create redundancy rather than dismissal situation').

In the Employment Court, Rob Dally's notes were not revealed, but John Gray was cross-examined on the other documents. He denied that Michael Deaker had met with the police in his office on 3 September. He insisted that the exchange of letters that day was a formality, and that the matter had been settled on 2 September. He was adamant that the police had told him next to nothing. Of his apparently damning 'closure necessary to create redundancy' handnote, he said: 'It may have been a note that I made to assist me in answering questions at the subsequent council meeting ... it draws a distinction in my mind between technical dismissal through redundancy as opposed to dismissal for cause – the latter in no way being relevant to this situation.'

• • •

In a 1998 interview, I asked Tom Weston how he chose his witnesses. He replied:

> The normal process is to work out what the issues are in dispute, and how you're going to structure and present your case. Then you look at who can give direct evidence of the key parts of it. Now in civil cases, if you could call someone to deal with a certain point, but don't, because you're worried about exposing them to cross-examination or whatever, adverse inferences can be drawn from their absence. Now we didn't have anyone in that category. I was determined that we would be laying our cards on the table. Plainly John Gray was going to be the main witness. Peter Mitchell and Martin Maguire were present at the meeting with the police and the ministry. I determined that they would both give evidence, even though Mitchell was a solicitor involved in giving legal advice [which meant he could have declined to give evidence on the ground of lawyer–client confidentiality]. I thought if he didn't front up there would be an inference that something was hidden.[18]

At that point, I reminded Weston that another member of the council staff was present at the 2 September meeting.

'That was one of the managers, Rob Dally,' he recalled, and went on to explain that he had interviewed Dally and the police before concluding that 'there was nothing useful that we could get from what they might say'.

'Wouldn't it have been useful to call the police as witnesses to what they did or didn't tell John Gray?' I asked.

'I can't comment on what John Gray was told, other than what's in his brief,' said Weston. Then, perhaps noting a flicker of cynicism cross my face, he added: 'As far as I know there was nothing hidden or kept back from court. My experience of John Gray is he's a man of absolute integrity. If he said something was the case, my inclination would be to trust that it was.'[19]

The main purpose of my interview with Tom Weston, and the reason the council had waived lawyer–client confidentiality for the occasion, was to find out why he did not call Bede Cooper from the Ministry of Education (who was present at both the 2 and 3 September meetings).

In his opening address in the Employment Court, Weston indicated that he planned to call Cooper. Later, when the council staff had completed their evidence, he advised the court that Cooper was not available. He was on the West Coast. He would be back in the morning. Next morning, without explanation, Weston announced that he would not be calling Cooper after all. At that point, counsel for both parties presented their closing submissions. Judge Goddard reserved his decision, and on 8 March 1995 the case came to an anticlimactic end.

• • •

The process by which I obtained the Ministry of Education file on Bede Cooper's brief of evidence, and the Crown Law Office file on the same matter, was a long and convoluted one. Phrases like 'getting the run around' spring to mind. In any event, those documents, and my interviews with some of the people involved, enabled me to piece together an interesting story.

On 6 March 1995, Tom Weston's assistant Jo Appleyard met with Bede Cooper. 'I told him that the purpose of his evidence would be to corroborate John Gray's evidence as it related to the meetings on 2 September 1992 and 3 September 1992,' she reported. Later that day, Cooper suggested some minor changes to the draft brief prepared by Appleyard, and asked her to fax him the final version before he left for the West Coast next morning.[20]

In the morning, Cooper faxed Appleyard's final version to Ministry of Education solicitor Jan Breakwell and asked her to take a critical look at it. Because she was not a court lawyer, Breakwell sought advice from Crown Counsel Neil McAteer. That afternoon, Breakwell and McAteer tracked down Cooper on the West Coast, and went through the brief of evidence with him by phone. That evening, they faxed an amended version of Coopers' brief to Tom Weston and Jo Appleyard.[21] The amendments were few, but significant.

Paragraph 10 of the 'Appleyard version' of Cooper's brief stated: 'As a result of my briefing with the Police and the Department of Social Welfare [on 1 September] I reached the view that the Christchurch Civic Crèche's licence had to be suspended immediately (at the very least) and most likely cancelled.'[22]

The same paragraph of the 'McAteer version' stated: 'As a result of my briefing with the Police and the Department of Social Welfare and after reading the affidavits and letters I reached the view that this would be an appropriate case in which to suspend the Christchurch Civic Crèche's licence immediately. However, this was not my decision to make as I did not hold the delegated authority. The delegated authority was held by Michael Deaker, National Operations, South Island.'[23]

The 'McAteer version' also noted that Mr Deaker was not prepared to suspend the crèche licence until he had sighted the police evidence, which he had done in Mr Gray's office on 3 September.

'They [the Ministry of Education] had taken out all the references to cancellation and given the impression that they went to the meeting with John Gray to consult with him and that they did not have the predetermined idea that cancellation would take place,' Jo Appleyard noted indignantly.[24]

After considering the 'McAteer version' of Bede Cooper's brief of evidence, Tom Weston decided not to call Cooper as a witness in the Employment Court. 'I formed the view that if he gave evidence he might perjure himself,' Weston told me. He assured me that the fact that Cooper's evidence had suddenly become unhelpful to the council case had nothing to do with his decision. 'That didn't really enter my mind,' he said.[25]

• • •

On 16 March 1995 (eight days after the end of the Employment Court hearing), Chief Judge Goddard announced that, to avoid further delay to the two-and-a-half-year-old case, he would declare a result immediately and give his full reasons later.

In his interim judgment, Goddard noted that the police had opened the meeting of 2 September 1992 by advising the Christchurch City manager that the investigation into the crèche was ongoing, that they considered the children to be in 'serious danger' and that they wanted the crèche closed immediately. He concluded:

> It is true that the allegation was directed at the employees of the crèche generally, and that the complaint was unspecific as to date, place and circumstances. However, the number of employees was small ... the nature of the allegations was reasonably specific, and it was plainly their commission currently that was alleged. I do not see how the respondent can say it had received no complaint within the meaning of the contract. It had plainly received a very serious and very pointed complaint ... it was for him [the city manager] to be satisfied of the facts before taking a step that could and did destroy the lives and the careers of council employees ... On these facts, I hold the dismissal on 3 September 1992 of the 13 applicants to have been unjustifiable ...[26]

In considering the level of compensation to be awarded, Judge Goddard accepted that the council could not be held responsible for the actions of the police. 'However, there is something in the applicants' complaint that the police may have been more circumspect if the council had not abandoned its employees,' he observed, before concluding that the council was answerable for 'the loss of remuneration, loss of employment and career, and for the distress occasioned by its actions ... for the branding of the applicants as child molesters'. Goddard further ruled that an indemnity clause in the staff employment contract required the council to pay the legal bills of the four women who had been charged and discharged.

On 17 March '95, a banner headline in the Christchurch *Press* read: 'Crèche Staff Win $1m Grievance Payout'.[27] While the childcare workers were delighted, their lawyers were dismayed. An award of that magnitude meant that an appeal was sure to follow, and the Court of Appeal's willingness to overturn Employment Court verdicts had not gone unnoticed in legal circles.

On 7 April 1995, Judge Goddard issued a supplementary judgment. He reviewed the evidence and arguments put before him, and noted 'some conflict in the evidence and some vagueness' among the council witnesses. He made repeated reference to the handnote on John Gray's memo of 3 September 1992 ('closure necessary to create redundancy rather than dismissal situation'), and observed:

The overall impression does not inspire full confidence in the reliability of this evidence especially as ... what happened was kept secret from the applicants until the council's witnesses gave evidence ... Some of the evidence given does not square with contemporary documents and is, in respects, unreliable for that reason as well.[28]

With regard to the claim that John Gray was faced with a *fait accompli*, the judge accepted that the Ministry of Education and the police were determined to bring about the immediate closure of the crèche, but concluded:

> I do not accept ... that the suspension of the crèche licence was inevitable; it is clear from Mr Gray's evidence that if the council had resisted, there would have been resort by the authorities to some due process ... It seems to me that the Ministry of Education could not realistically or with confidence have expected the council to acquiesce in the suspension of its licence for no reason at all that was disclosed to it, and the purpose of the deputation was to secure the council's acquiescence ...[29]

As he had done in his interim judgment, Judge Goddard rejected John Gray's claim that he had received no complaint against the crèche staff, and concluded that Gray's willingness to close the crèche so quickly and unquestioningly indicated that he believed the police allegations, and had dismissed the crèche staff for that reason.

On 3 May 1995, Judge Goddard awarded costs to the applicants. On 24 May 1995, the Christchurch City Council voted to appeal the Employment Court decision. In July 1995, apparently unimpressed by the Employment Court judgment against John Gray, Attorney-General and Minister of State Services Paul East appointed the former Christchurch City manager to his ministerial review team on whistleblowing. On 2 August, Judge Goddard issued a further judgment, clarifying a point relating to Jan Buckingham's compensation.

13.vii: More Calls for an Inquiry

In the wake of the Employment Court decision in favour of the women, and the legal aid decision against Peter Ellis, the clamour for an inquiry reached a new crescendo. A member of the public wrote to Attorney-General Paul East:

> The Christchurch *Press* recently reported that the Attorney-General turned down Mr Peter Ellis's request for legal aid to bring his appeal before the Privy Council, ostensibly because you did not view it as of significant public importance. Such an attitude shows an appalling lack of social awareness. Next to issues concerning the Treaty of Waitangi, Peter Ellis's trial and the Christchurch Civic Crèche debacle probably constitute the most significant event in recent New Zealand social history ... Most New Zealanders

are very concerned about childhood sexual abuse in our country and want to see justice done ... but how can one have any confidence that justice is being done when standards of evidence in our courtrooms seem so loose? Where in all this crazy saga ... does the truth lie? ... A thorough review of the Peter Ellis/civic care workers case will help dispel widespread public rumours and, hopefully, restore confidence in our judicial system.[1]

Spokespeople for the police, DSW and the complainant parents rejected the calls for an inquiry. Feminist activist Sandra Coney suggested that the crèche case controversy was a cynical defence-led campaign to manipulate public opinion, and that Ellis's former colleagues were not as blameless as they claimed.[2]

But by late March 1995 the government could no longer ignore the calls for an inquiry. At that point, responsibility for analysing the submissions, and for advising the Attorney-General on an appropriate response, fell to Deputy Solicitor-General Lowell Goddard.

Earlier in her career, Goddard was barrister for the Auckland Help (sexual assault) Foundation. Prior to joining the Crown Law Office, she was Senior Counsel assisting Judge Cartwright during the Inquiry into Cervical Cancer Treatment at National Women's Hospital. As the head of the Criminal Law Section of the Crown Law Office, she liaised with Brent Stanaway throughout the Ellis appeal.

Lowell Goddard considered submissions from: the Civic Child Care Inquiry Organisation (1993); Mr R. Glover, president of the Criminal Bar Association of Canterbury (1993); Mr G. Nation, barrister (1994); Mr J. Rowan, barrister (1994); Dr K. Le Page, psychiatrist (1995); and Mr G. Panckhurst QC (1995).[3]

Panckhurst's submission was prompted by his experience of representing the crèche staff in the Employment Court. 'My essential concern is that the results of the Police decision-making in this instance have been so disastrous for so many, that the internal processes behind them should be the subject of independent scrutiny,' he wrote.[4]

Le Page's submission was prompted by his experience as an expert witness in the Christchurch and Wellington crèche cases (the latter followed the Christchurch case, had a lower profile and also resulted in a conviction). 'I am writing to inform you that the legislation s. 23G of the Evidence Act under which your cases are tried is scientifically invalid and as a consequence innocent people have been imprisoned, others smeared for life and families have been destroyed,' he wrote.[5]

The other submissions suggested that the Civic Crèche case was part of a wider problem, and called for an inquiry into the investigation and prosecution of sexual abuse allegations in New Zealand comparable to the inquiries into the Cleveland and Orkney sexual abuse scandals in Britain.

'I do not believe that a Government concerned with the administration of justice can simply sit back and watch while the public debate continues,' Gerald Nation wrote. 'If the way these allegations are investigated and dealt with in New Zealand is conducive to false allegations being made then as long as these inadequacies in the system continue, children, families and those falsely accused are being hurt.'[6]

In March 1995, after consulting police, DSW and the Department of Justice, Lowell Goddard advised the Attorney-General and the Cabinet Strategy Committee that the investigation and prosecution of the crèche case, and the facts surrounding the crèche closure, had already been the subject of extensive scrutiny by the courts.[7] She added that an inquiry into 'the police decision to prosecute the women, the adequacy of the investigation and interview process and the use of expert evidence in court' could result in a renewed focus on Peter Ellis's convictions, and 'may be interpreted as a lack of confidence on the part of the Government in the adequacy of the Court process'. She further suggested that an inquiry could have a destabilising effect on the parents and children affected, and that the 'substantial costs' and 'considerable resources' required could be 'better deployed in the prevention and detection of child abuse, and the current administrative and law reform efforts in the field of sexual abuse'.[8]

• • •

By the time Lowell Goddard presented her report, the guilt or innocence of the accused childcare workers was no longer the main issue. By then feminism, religious fundamentalism, counselling services, child protection services, the Christchurch City Council, DSW, ACC, the police and the justice system were all on trial.

In any bureaucracy there are large and fragile egos. Bureaucrats generally respond to outside criticism by asking themselves: how can we justify what we've already done? It is a rare bureaucrat who ever poses the question: could we have made a terrible mistake here, and, if so, what can we do to put it right? Furthermore, when the bureaucracy under attack is the justice system, that is not the end of the matter. Beyond the egos, and the closing of ranks, there is an important constitutional issue at stake.

The separation of powers is a fundamental principle of democratic government: parliament makes the laws; the courts enforce them. In the normal course of events, each party jealously guards its patch. Judges keep the power of parliament in check by ensuring that government officials act lawfully and in accordance with the principles of natural justice, but they may not comment on government policy, or on the merits of any law. Similarly, if parliament doesn't like the way the courts are applying a particular law, it may tighten the relevant legislation, but it may not ask a judge to reconsider a decision. Also, parliament may not remove a judge from office, or reduce his or her salary. These checks and balances help ensure that neither party wields power in an oppressive or arbitrary manner. They also mean that, when there is a widespread perception that the justice system has failed, and the public is demanding that politicians do something, any response that smacks of political interference in the justice system is bound to be viewed by those affected as a major threat.

• • •

On 8 June 1995, Attorney-General Paul East announced that there would be no inquiry into the Civic Crèche case. His press release stated:

> Where the Courts have determined issues in the course of legal process, governments in the past have not considered inquiries desirable unless there is evidence of abuse of the court process or a failure of the legal system itself. In the Government's view, neither has taken place in this case.[9]

In reply, Graham Panckhurst wrote:

> I am saddened not only by the Cabinet decision but also by the decisions of each of the State agencies, particularly the Police, not to look into the concerns raised in any shape or form ... I believe a siege mentality has developed with regard to this matter. Endeavour was made to raise the concerns identified in my letter in a way which was restrained, constructive and responsible. I fear that the damage which has been done to so many innocent people will mean the Civic Crèche case will not go away. The blanket decision of the State agencies to resist any review of their actions will simply aggravate a situation which is already of widespread concern ...[10]

Among the general public, the most common response was that courts could indeed make mistakes. 'Remember the Arthur Allan Thomas case,' people said.

• • •

In March 1971, Arthur Allan Thomas was convicted of murder and sentenced to life imprisonment. His appeal was dismissed. In late 1971 his supporters petitioned the Governor-General. The retired Supreme Court judge who considered the petition concluded that no miscarriage of justice had occurred. However, following a second petition to the Governor-General, the case was referred to the Court of Appeal and a new trial was ordered. In April 1973, Thomas was again tried and convicted. The appeal was again dismissed. After a further petition to the Governor-General, the case was again referred to the Court of Appeal. The appeal was again dismissed. In July 1978, the Privy Council declined to consider the case. Later that year, following extensive public and media concern, and the publication of three books on the case, Prime Minister Rob Muldoon recommended to cabinet that they appoint Mr Adams-Smith QC to review the case.[11] In *My Way*, Muldoon wrote that, after receiving Adams-Smith's report:

We [cabinet) had the alternatives of either some further judicial inquiry which could only go over old ground, or a pardon. Without arguing the content of the Adams-Smith report, which could certainly be argued by those in possession of the facts, it was very clear to cabinet that the statements in the report, seen by the ordinary citizen, would cause him to say that Thomas had not been proved guilty 'beyond reasonable doubt'. It was on this basis that cabinet recommended to His Excellency, the Governor-General, that Thomas be pardoned.[12]

Shortly after the pardon, the Governor-General appointed a Royal Commission to inquire into the circumstances of Thomas's convictions.

'Mr Justice Taylor of New South Wales agreed to chair the Commission, as it was impossible for anyone connected with law enforcement or administration in New Zealand to take part,' Muldoon wrote. 'Mr Justice Taylor's conduct of the case, however, produced extreme opposition and resentment from counsel for the police – so much so that an application was made to the High Court to abort the Commission of Inquiry.'[13]

In *A Passion for Justice*, Peter Williams QC, senior counsel for Thomas, recalled: 'some politicians and certain judges regarded Thomas's crusade as an attack upon the whole New Zealand judicial system ... the vast majority of police saw the Thomas saga as an all-out attack on them.'[14]

• • •

The Thomas case was the only criminal conviction in recent New Zealand history to have been the subject of a commission of inquiry. An analysis of the constitutional and procedural issues raised by the Thomas inquiry would therefore have assisted the Attorney-General in his consideration of the calls for an inquiry into the Civic Crèche case. If nothing else, the Thomas case would have reminded Paul East that the justice system is sometimes unable to undo its own mistakes, and that, when people believe a miscarriage of justice has occurred, they will not let the matter rest, no matter how many times the courts uphold the guilty verdict. Curiously, Lowell Goddard made only two references to the Thomas inquiry in her briefing papers. One reference stated:

> The convention also exists that an inquiry may not be appropriate if there are civil or criminal proceedings relating to the matters before the Courts. In both the Erebus and Thomas Commissions, legal proceedings had ceased before the establishment of the inquiries. It should be noted that counsel for Peter Ellis has publicly indicated an intention to pursue an appeal to the Privy Council ...

With regard to the Erebus inquiry, Goddard's claim was untrue (claimants put their plans on hold, pending the outcome of the inquiry). With regard to the

Thomas inquiry, Goddard failed to mention that the legal proceedings had ceased because Thomas had been pardoned, and that cabinet could end Peter Ellis's legal proceedings by advising the Governor-General to pardon him.

Goddard's other reference to the Thomas inquiry was: 'There are possible flow on effects involving litigation brought to challenge the jurisdiction of an inquiry (this occurred in relation to both the Thomas and the Erebus inquiry) with the result that resolution of issues can be years off (with damaging effects to the children, parents and others concerned).' On this point, Goddard failed to mention that the legal challenge to the Thomas inquiry was unsuccessful, and that, despite being interrupted by 12 days of litigation, the Thomas commission completed its work 11 weeks ahead of schedule.[15]

Of all the lessons to be learnt from the Thomas case that Lowell Goddard failed to mention, the most important was this: if it wished to do so, there was no legal or constitutional reason why cabinet could not advise the Governor-General to pardon Peter Ellis and establish a commission of inquiry into the crèche case. The Governor-General could counsel against such action, and could do so vigorously if she felt that the integrity of the justice system was being impugned. But it is a cardinal rule of the New Zealand constitution that the Governor-General must act on the advice of ministers. Consequently, the issues before government in relation to the Civic Crèche case ultimately came down to one point: if cabinet had the political will to do so, it could address the problems raised, instead of burying them once again.

13.viii: The Christchurch City Council Appeals the Employment Court Decision

The Christchurch City Council's appeal of Chief Judge Goddard's Employment Court decision in favour of the crèche staff opened in the Court of Appeal on 21 August 1996. By then, Graham Panckhurst QC had been appointed to the High Court bench, so the crèche staff were represented by Hans van Schreven, with informal assistance from union secretary Peter Lawson. The city council was represented by Julian Miles QC, with assistance from Tom Weston. The appeal was heard by a five-judge bench comprising Justices Richardson, Henry, Thomas, Keith and Blanchard.

The appeal took place shortly after liberal Justice Cooke retired, and conservative Justice Richardson replaced him as president of the Court of Appeal. At a July 1996 law conference, Court of Appeal member Justice Thomas advised barristers to 'know their court':

If, for example, the preponderant mood of the court is to accept that the law must endeavour to do justice between the parties and should be applied in accordance with the needs and reasonable expectations of the community, then an appeal to the merits, principle, policy, and the fairness of the counsel's cause may be in order. If, on the other hand, counsel's assessment is that the court is conservative, a reiteration of earlier cases favouring a non-interventionist line, an argument stressing the dangers of activism, and an emphasis on the desirability of certainty in the law is likely to be more propitious.[16]

In their way, the issues before the Court of Appeal in the crèche employment proceedings were as much a legal, personal and political minefield as the issues before the Court of Appeal in the earlier criminal proceedings. To complicate matters, some of the employment issues had more to do with pre-existing tensions between the Employment Court and the Court of Appeal, than with the crèche case.

At the heart of the tensions was the 1991 Employment Contracts Act. According to the Act, parliament's aim was to 'promote an efficient labour market'. Some people thought the Act allowed employers to hire and fire workers more or less at will. They also thought the Employment Court would do little more than rule on whether the terms of a disgruntled worker's employment contract had been honoured. But Chief Employment Court Judge Tom Goddard took a different view. In 1996, he wrote:

> The characteristic that distinguishes the Employment Court from other Courts is that it is not only entitled but required to decide the cases that come before it (with certain exceptions) in accordance with equity and good conscience as opposed to doing so by the strict application of the rules of law ...[17]

Many disputes over the proper interpretation of the Employment Contracts Act were heard in the Court of Appeal. Back when Sir Robin Cooke was president, Justices Cooke and Richardson took opposing views in the landmark Brighouse case.[18] In legal circles, Richardson's displeasure at the outcome of the Brighouse case was legendary.

• • •

The essence of the Christchurch City Council's appeal was that Judge Goddard was wrong to conclude that the crèche staff had been unjustifiably dismissed, and had awarded them too much money. On the first issue, the argument went like this: City Manager John Gray was faced with a *fait accompli* on 2 September 1992. The closure of the crèche was beyond his control. Therefore the crèche staff were genuinely redundant. If the claimants disagreed, the onus was on them to prove it. The claimants had failed to prove that Gray's account of the meeting of 2 September was unreliable. Therefore, the staff's claim that they were unjustifiably dismissed had not been proved.

The problem with this argument is that Judge Goddard's assessment of the evidence relating to the meeting of 2 September was not a question of law but a question of fact, and the Employment Contracts Act allowed appeals only on questions of law.[19] (Broadly speaking, questions of law are concerned with legal principles, whereas questions of fact are concerned with the judge's evaluations of the witnesses and their evidence.) However, the question of whether there was any evidence at all to support the judge's findings was a question of law. If there was none, the Court of Appeal could reverse the verdict. Therefore, to succeed with their claim – that Judge Goddard was wrong in law to conclude that John Gray had dismissed the crèche staff on suspicion of misconduct, and not because they were genuinely redundant – the council's lawyers had to convince the Court of Appeal that there was no evidence from which Judge Goddard could reasonably have reached that conclusion.

• • •

In the light of Justice Richardson's conservative approach to the Employment Contracts Act, the prospect of having their appeal heard by a Richardson-led court was good news for the council's lawyers, and they tailored their approach accordingly.

'We decided that the linchpin of our case would be the minority decision in Brighouse,' Tom Weston told me.[20]

During the hearing, when Weston's senior Julian Miles QC referred frequently, and flatteringly, to the minority decision in Brighouse, his efforts did not go unnoticed by the bench.

'Now you know, Mr Miles, that I was party to the minority decision in Brighouse?' said Justice Richardson at one point.

'Thank you, Your Honour,' replied Miles, straight-faced. 'I'll ask my junior to note that.'

The council's legal team also suspected that Their Honours would be not impressed that Judge Goddard had issued an interim judgment, a supplementary judgment, a costs judgment and a further supplementary judgment, when one main judgment and a costs judgment should have sufficed. Nor would they be impressed with the amount of compensation awarded. So Miles made frequent, unflattering references to these matters too.

• • •

When Hans van Schreven came to present the case for the respondents it quickly became clear that he had a battle on his hands. Justice Richardson had studied the Employment Court file closely and appeared sympathetic to the council's case.

In response to questions from the bench, van Schreven acknowledged that Judge Goddard had no direct evidence that John Gray's account of the meeting of

2 September was unreliable. (As noted in Ch.13.vi, direct evidence on this point existed in Bede Cooper's brief of evidence, but, because Tom Weston had withheld that brief, Hans van Schreven did not know of its existence.) However, van Schreven argued that, while there was no direct evidence, the rest of the evidence presented to the Employment Court and traversed by Judge Goddard in his interim and supplementary judgments provided ample support for the judge's verdict [see Ch.13.vi]. Indeed, the only evidence supporting council's position was that given by John Gray and two of his staff, and, after seeing and hearing them give evidence and be cross-examined, Judge Goddard had concluded that their testimony was unreliable.

• • •

On 26 September 1996, Justice Richardson delivered the Court of Appeal judgment in the case of *Davidson & Others* v *Christchurch City Council*. He said that Judge Goddard erred in law in ruling that the crèche staff had been unjustifiably dismissed ('We can discern no basis in the evidence for a finding other than that the closure of the crèche led the Council to see it as a genuine redundancy situation'). Since the only support for this conclusion was in John Gray's evidence, Their Honours could have reached their verdict only by, on the one hand, discounting the evidence that supported Judge Goddard's verdict, and, on the other hand, accepting Gray's evidence as reliable.

In the light of this analysis, the Court of Appeal judgment appears to be fundamentally flawed. This is because the reliability or otherwise of the evidence is not a question of law, but a question of fact, and – as the Court of Appeal well knew – the Employment Contracts Act allowed appeals only on questions of law. Furthermore – as the Court of Appeal has often observed – the judge who has seen and heard the witnesses give evidence and be cross-examined is in the best position to make findings on the reliability of their evidence.

Having accepted John Gray's evidence as reliable, the Court of Appeal ruled that his only fault was a minor procedural one 'limited to the notification of redundancy on 3 September 1992 which was formally superseded the following morning by a suspension on pay of the workers'. As a result of their verdict, Their Honours slashed the compensation awarded to the 13 crèche staff from $863,000 to $83,500. They also expressed doubts about Judge Goddard's ruling requiring the council to pay the legal costs arising out of the arrests of the four women, but concluded that the Court of Appeal did not have the jurisdiction to interfere with the judge's decision on that point. Finally, Their Honours directed that each party pay their own costs.[21]

For some staff, the amount they were awarded did not meet the amount they owed in costs. When Jan Buckingham died of a stroke in November 2000, she still

13.viii: The Christchurch City Council Appeals the Employment Court Decision

owed around $8000 in legal aid repayments for the Employment Court case and appeal.

There is no right of appeal to the Privy Council on Employment Court matters. But the husband of one of the dismissed crèche workers assured the Christchurch *Press* next morning that the fight for a full inquiry would go on.[22]

CHAPTER 14

The Royal Prerogative of Mercy

14.i: The Safety Net

The royal prerogative of mercy has its origins in the ancient right of the sovereign to pardon anyone convicted of a crime. In New Zealand, the prerogative is delegated to the Governor-General, and exercised on ministerial advice. In a 1992 Court of Appeal judgment (*Burt* v *Governor-General*), Sir Robin Cooke observed that the prerogative was 'a recognised safety net for persons who may have been wrongly convicted ... a constitutional safeguard against mistakes'. In considering the problems created by wrongful convictions, Cooke cited the English 'IRA cases'.

'Recent cases in England where the Court of Appeal ... has quashed convictions on the ground that these were unsafe or unsatisfactory have been disturbingly frequent,' he noted. 'They have turned on police fabrication of evidence or failure by the prosecution or expert advisers of the prosecution to disclose relevant material; a third category of case is discovery of new scientific evidence.'[1]

Cooke expressed concern that abuses of that sort could damage the innocent and the guilty alike, and that the associated bad publicity could damage the justice system. However, he also said, repeatedly and emphatically, that miscarriages of justice were not a problem in New Zealand:

> If there were good reasons to believe that injustices as revealed by some English cases are occurring or likely to occur in New Zealand under our judicial review that could help prevent this. But we are not satisfied that there is good reason. The existing safeguards are considerable and there is no real evidence that they are not working ... Only the controversial *Thomas* case may be an arguable exception ... the current practice is that independent lawyers of standing are appointed to investigate petitions that may have substance. Nothing has been put before the Court to suggest that the practice does not operate satisfactorily. Examples of its operation are *Re Appelgren* ...[2]

When he made that observation in 1992, Justice Cooke presumably thought the long-running Appelgren case was over. But he spoke too soon.

The case began in 1985 when Ross Appelgren was convicted of a murder. His appeal was dismissed. In 1987, he escaped from prison and pleaded his innocence for four hours on talkback radio. Following his recapture, Appelgren discovered that the Crown had withheld evidence at his trial. His lawyer petitioned the Governor-General. The petition was initially declined, then reconsidered. The case was referred back to the Court of Appeal and a new trial was ordered. In May 1992, Appelgren was again convicted. The appeal was dismissed. But, by 1996, documented evidence of police and prosecution misconduct (including perjury, the withholding of further evidence and the offering of threats and inducements to witnesses) had emerged in the Appelgren case.[3]

Interestingly, in his 1992 review of the 'safety net', Justice Cooke made no mention of the Saifiti case. In 1970, Atenai Saifiti was convicted of assaulting a prison officer. His appeal failed. However, in response to public disquiet and prison unrest, the case was investigated by the Chief Ombusdman and a retired magistrate in 1972. On the basis of their report, Saifiti was pardoned.[4] Apart from the posthumous pardon granted to Mokomoko in 1992 for his 1866 murder conviction, only Thomas and Saifiti have received pardons since the introduction of the 1961 Crimes Act.[5]

In *Burt* v *Governor-General*, Sir Robin Cooke claimed that miscarriages of justice are extremely rare in New Zealand. But his failure to mention the Saifiti case, his view of the Thomas case as 'an arguable exception' (rather than a warning that the normal procedures for identifying and correcting miscarriages of justice could fail) and his use of the Appelgren case to support his confidence in the system, invites an alternative conclusion – that the New Zealand justice system has trouble recognising and correcting its own mistakes.

While the complacency and defensiveness of the people involved may be part of the problem, a close examination of the safety net reveals holes in its basic structure big enough to let most miscarriages of justice drop through unnoticed.

• • •

Normally, once an appeal has been heard and dismissed by the Court of Appeal, no further appeals are possible (if rehearings were possible, the argument goes, dissatisfied punters would want their cases reheard, over and over again, until they obtained the desired result).[6] Furthermore, with one exception in over 100 years, New Zealand criminal appeals to the Privy Council have been an expensive waste of time. This means that, once a New Zealander has been wrongly convicted, and the conviction has been upheld by the Court of Appeal, an appeal to the Governor-General under s. 406 of the Crimes Act (1961) is the only realistic option left. However, there are problems with this option:

1. The title of s. 406, 'Prerogative of mercy', is misleading (since the prerogative is a royal power and not a statutory one).
2. There is no information in the Crimes Act or anywhere else on how a pardon from the Governor-General may be obtained. Nonetheless, the title of s. 406 conveys the impression that the way to obtain a royal pardon is to lodge a petition under that section of the Crimes Act. In reality, nothing could be further from the truth. While the wording of s. 406 does not rule out the possibility, as far as I have been able to find out, no petition lodged under s. 406 has ever resulted in a pardon. In the Thomas case, three such petitions were lodged; none resulted in a pardon. Since the 1961 Crimes Act came into force, three pardons have been granted (to Saifiti, Thomas and Mokomoko). None of the three were granted as a result of a petition lodged under the Act.
3. Petitions to the Governor-General under s. 406 of the Crimes Act are passed directly to the Ministry of Justice for consideration. Since the essence of any such petition is that the justice system has failed, allowing officials of the justice system to assess the worth of a petition is arguably a breach of natural justice.
4. Procedures for the consideration of such petitions are informal and opaque. Sir Robin Cooke noted that 'independent lawyers of standing are appointed to investigate petitions that may have substance'. But there are no established procedures for determining whether a petition has 'substance', for selecting a suitable 'independent lawyer' or for evaluating the quality of that lawyer's advice.
5. According to s. 406(a) of the Crimes Act, the Governor-General may 'refer the question of the conviction or sentence to the Court of Appeal ... and the question so referred shall then be heard and determined by the Court ... as in the case of an appeal by that person against conviction or sentence or both'. In theory, such referrals make the Court of Appeal a key element in Sir Robin Cooke's 'constitutional safeguard against mistakes'. However, in successive judgments, the court has ruled that, no matter what the terms of the referral from the Governor-General, when the Court of Appeal hears a case for the second time, it will consider only new evidence, and overturn its earlier judgment only if that evidence indicates that a miscarriage of justice has occurred.[7] The 'new evidence' rule makes a nonsense of Cooke's claim that referrals from the Governor-General to the Court of Appeal are a 'safeguard against mistakes'. Indeed, the rule ensures that, not only does the Court of Appeal never have to correct its own mistakes, it never has to own up to having made any mistakes in the first place.

14.ii: Testing the Safety Net

In 1996, when Graham Panckhurst QC was appointed to the High Court bench, Peter Ellis's friends and family asked Dunedin barrister Judith Ablett-Kerr QC to take up the case. It was her reputation as a forceful, passionate and persistent advocate that caught their attention.

'She's like a Rottweiler,' long-time Ellis supporter Winston Wealleans told the *Listener*. 'She just locks on.'

In jury trials, Ablett-Kerr is famous for her relentless assaults on every obstacle in her path, and for her ability to seize on an ember of uncertainty and fan it into an inferno of doubt; and to keep on fanning it until she has every juror nodding in unselfconscious agreement with her cause.

In December 1997, Judith Ablett-Kerr petitioned the GovernorGeneral for a pardon for Ellis in respect of his remaining 13 convictions, or, alternatively, that they be 'returned to the Court of Appeal for its further consideration'. Shortly before the petition was filed, a documentary on TV3 startled the nation with its revelations about Detective Colin Eade and the Ellis trial jury.[8]

In the documentary, journalist Melanie Reid reported that Eade's superiors were concerned about his mental stability during the crèche investigation. He had propositioned the mother of the first child to formally disclose abuse and the mother had withdrawn her child from the case as a result. Eade also had affairs with two crèche mothers after the investigation was over. A few days later, TV3 added a social welfare officer to Eade's list of crèche-case conquests.

Among those interviewed for the documentary were Detective Eade, and the father of the child who retracted her allegations.

'Since the day she told us she lied, now over three years ago, she has been consistent in that stance and I have no reason not to believe her,' the father said.

'It does happen a lot with child complainants that to some extent or other they withdraw, or they try to withdraw from what's happened,' Eade commented.

'So has it happened in the crèche case?' Melanie Reid asked.

'Well I'm not sure how many, but I'd be surprised if not all of them have done it at some stage,' Eade said.

With regard to the Ellis jury, Reid reported that, at the time of the trial, the partner of a jury member worked in the same office as a complainant mother, and that, some years earlier, the foreman of the jury had officiated at the Crown Solicitor's wedding. However, Brent Stanaway said he had not seen the clergyman for more than 15 years, and had not thought it necessary to advise the judge of the earlier contact.

Next day, calls for an inquiry into the crèche case led radio and television news bulletins. The Solicitor-General said there would be an in-house investigation into the actions of the Crown Solicitor. The Police Commissioner said there would be an in-house investigation into the behaviour of Detective Eade. Police Association president Greg O'Connor said he was astounded at the public and political reaction to 'one very unbalanced television programme'.[9]

In reply to a parliamentary question, Minister of Justice Doug Graham admitted that the government had been receiving representations about the case since 1993, and advised that an enquiry could be reconsidered in the light of Ellis's application for a pardon.[10]

In February 1998, before any response to his application for a pardon had been received, Peter Ellis became eligible for parole. When he declined to appear before the Parole Board, the board adjourned its decision for 12 months and his lawyer issued a press release: 'Peter Ellis has maintained his innocence since he was first accused. He continues to maintain his innocence and whilst he is most anxious to regain his freedom and to return to family and friends he cannot accept that freedom if it is granted on the basis that he is a guilty man and his petition to overturn his convictions is still before the Governor-General.'[11]

In her petition to the Governor-General, Judith Ablett-Kerr raised five main areas of concern: that the crèche investigation was not objective; that the methods of obtaining evidence from the child complainants were flawed and had unacceptably high risks of contamination; that the complainant's retraction was of greater significance than the Court of Appeal had appreciated; that the jury was not impartial; and that the trial process was flawed. After the petition was filed, she added a further ground: that photographs of the crèche were not disclosed to the defence at the time of the trial.[12]

The Ministry of Justice officials who considered the petition noted that the applicant had not exhausted his legal options, and suggested that, in any event, a pardon seemed unwarranted. So the decision was made to refer the Ellis case back to the Court of Appeal under s. 406(a) of the Crimes Act on the grounds that there was 'evidence available that could lead the Court of Appeal to the conclusion that a miscarriage of justice might have occurred'. That evidence comprised: reports by psychologist Dr Barry Parsonson (on memory in children, interviewing of children, contamination and retraction); evidence of an association between a Crown witness and the partner of one of the jurors; and photographs that were not disclosed to the defence.[13]

• • •

In the Court of Appeal on 4 June 1998, Justices Richardson, Gault and Henry heard an application from Judith Ablett-Kerr to extend the scope of the reference under s. 406(a), and to obtain bail for her client. Section 406(a) states that cases referred by the Governor-General to the Court of Appeal should be 'heard and determined ... as in the case of an appeal by that person against conviction or sentence'. So it could be argued that the Court had the statutory power to reconsider the entire Ellis case. However, after reviewing a selection of legal precedents, Richardson concluded:

> Even if not compelled by the language of s. 406(a) we are satisfied that, conformably with legislative policy underlying the provision and with the course adopted in this country since *Morgan*, as a matter of practice the hearing and determination of references under s. 406(a) should be confined to matters raised in the reference.[14]

Richardson's comments reflect the Court of Appeal's commitment to honouring the policies behind the laws it is required to uphold. They also raise the question: what was the policy underlying the legislation allowing the Governor-General to refer criminal cases back to the Court of Appeal for reconsideration?

• • •

At a constitutional level, the history of the legislative policy underlying s. 406(a) of the Crimes Act is the history of the ongoing tensions between the right of parliament to make the laws, and the right of the courts to interpret them. At a social and personal level, it is a story of politicians passing laws to force the courts to recognise and correct miscarriages of justice; and of the courts passing judgments to thwart those laws.

The story begins in colonial times. In Wellington in 1889, Louis Chemis was convicted of murder and sentenced to hang. In response to public outrage at the verdict, the governor commuted his sentence to life imprisonment.

In 1893, the Criminal Code Act was passed. Its provision for a person convicted of a crime 'to apply to the Court of Appeal for a new trial on the ground that the verdict was against the weight of evidence' was prompted by parliamentary concern about the Chemis case. When the Upper House declared that the law could not be applied retrospectively, the Lower House introduced an amendment stating that 'Louis Chemis ... shall have the right to apply to the Court of Appeal for a new trial'.[15]

In the course of the Chemis debate, Sir Patrick Buckley (who became a Supreme Court Justice in 1895) said his duty to his profession prevented him from approving the Chemis amendment. Mr Rigg (a printer) said that a man's duty to his conscience and to his fellow man ought to be superior to his duty to any profession, and that if a man was innocent, and wrongly convicted, it was parliament's duty to see that justice was done. Mr Downie Stewart (a lawyer) said that constant agitation on behalf of convicted prisoners was detrimental to the administration of justice. Mr McGregor (a lawyer) said that legislative interference with a criminal conviction would create a dangerous precedent. Sir Robert Stout (who became Chief Justice in 1899) said that the case had already been decided by the court. Mr O'Regan (a radical lawyer and journalist) said that Sir Robert was bound by cast-iron precedents, and there were times when the law did not have the sanction of morality.[16]

The amendment was passed in 1895, and Chemis's lawyer applied to the Court of Appeal for a retrial. His application was declined, but public agitation about the case continued until Chemis was released in an amnesty to mark Queen Victoria's diamond jubilee in 1897.[17]

In 1901, the Court of Appeal considered another application for a retrial on the ground that the verdict was against the weight of evidence (*R v Styche*), and firmly quashed the application. For the next 45 years, the Court used *R v Styche* as a precedent in its rulings on all further applications for retrials on the same ground.[18]

However, retrial was not an issue in the Meikle case. Back in 1887, Southlander John Meikle was convicted of sheep stealing and sentenced to seven years in prison. Following his release, Meikle and his supporters campaigned to clear his name. In 1906, 'in order to have finality', the government asked the governor to appoint a Royal Commission to investigate the Meikle case. The commission was also asked to recommend a practicable way 'of placing on record his innocence, if in your opinion his innocence is established or may be presumed'.[19]

The commission found that evidence of Meikle's guilt was 'far from conclusive', and recommended that he should be 'treated as having been acquitted upon retrial'.[20] On that basis, the Meikle Acquittal Act was passed in 1908.

In 1909 the judiciary put an end to royal commissions usurping their role with a ruling that a commission could not lawfully inquire into a criminal matter.[21] By the time the Thomas commission sat in 1980, the law relating to commissions of inquiry had been broadened to cover criminal matters. But, for nearly four decades after the Meikle commission, public concerns about possible miscarriages of justice remained unaddressed.

• • •

In 1945, Attorney-General Rex Mason introduced the Criminal Appeal Bill. 'The Bill, I think, has its ultimate origin in the demand of the people for a means of rectifying mistakes that sometimes occur,' Mason told parliament. He said that similar legislation was introduced in England years earlier in response to a case 'where there was a miscarriage of justice, and where there was no means of putting it right, and where the officials of that day were not disposed to admit there was any possibility of mistake, but the pressure of public opinion was such that it was deemed proper to provide better facilities for appeal'.[22]

Section 17(a) of the 1945 legislation empowered the Governor-General to 'refer the whole case to the Court of Appeal, and the case shall then be heard and determined by the Court of Appeal'. In his introduction to that legislation, Rex Mason discussed *R v Styche* (1901), and voiced misgivings as to whether the Court of Appeal would honour the intention of the new law:

> It shows there [in *R v Styche*] that the Court had power to order a new trial if it considered the verdict was against the weight of evidence, but it construed that in such limited terms ... that there is little chance of reopening a verdict. I will confess that reading the case ... made me wonder whether the Courts might not construe the powers given by this Bill in the same restrictive way ...[23]

With reference to the 1893 Criminal Code Act, Mason said: 'Those who drafted the code originally had that same fear ... that precedent encrusts those provisions and limits them, and that they will then secure a far more limited application than is really intended.'

Mason's fears were well founded. In 1953, when the Court of Appeal considered a referral from the Governor-General under s. 17(a) of the Criminal Appeal Act, it did not apply the 1945 New Zealand statute; it applied a 1942 case-law precedent from Australia instead. In the Australian case, the judge ruled that matters already dealt with should not be reopened.[24]

• • •

In 1961, the New Zealand Crimes Act was subject to its first major revision since 1908. In the process, the Criminal Appeal Act (1945) was incorporated into the Crimes Act. As Justice Richardson pointed out in his ruling on Judith Ablett-Kerr's application, while s. 17(a) of the Criminal Appeal Act (1945) empowered the Governor-General to 'refer the whole case to the Court of Appeal', 'that was changed to its present narrower formulation in the 1961 statute: "refer the question of the conviction ... and the question so referred shall then be heard and determined"'.[25] But because the 1961 statute also requires 'the question so referred' to be heard and determined 'as in the case of an appeal', it could be argued that the legislative policy underlying the 1961 provision was the same as that underlying its 1945 predecessor (i.e. that, following a referral from the Governor-General, the whole case should be reviewed by the Court of Appeal).

Unfortunately, *Hansard* contains no mention of the legislative policy underlying the 'narrower formulation' in the 1961 statute. Nonetheless, the parliamentary debate is revealing. The 1961 Crimes Bill was introduced by Ralph Hanan, arguably New Zealand's most enlightened Minister of Justice ever.

Hanan told parliament that the death penalty had been retained in the new Bill, and added: 'I am opposed to capital punishment in any form.' Remarkably, by the time the Bill reached its third reading, Hanan had won the support of the House –

the death penalty was abolished. Under the circumstances, it is hardly surprising that the subtle change to s. 406(a) passed without comment. However, had Ralph Hanan realised that the change would be used by the Court of Appeal to justify its unwillingness to fully review alleged miscarriages of justice, he would probably have opposed it.

'The twin objects of any criminal code in a civilised country are to protect the person and property of every citizen while sheltering the innocent from being punished unjustly,' he told parliament. 'In framing this Bill a good many principles have been applied, but the over-riding policy has been never to impair, and wherever practicable to strengthen the rights of the accused person … The protection of the rights of every person accused of an offence is the only effective way to protect the rights of the ordinary man and woman against injustice or tyranny.'[26]

Once the 1961 Crimes Act had been passed, the Court of Appeal passed a new precedent-setting judgment: *R v Morgan* (1963) – the case quoted by Justice Richardson in his ruling that the Court of Appeal would consider only matters raised in the reference from the Governor-General on the Ellis case.[27]

• • •

Having declined Judith Ablett-Kerr's application to extend the scope of the reference under s. 406(a) of the Crimes Act, Justice Richardson then declined her application for bail for Peter Ellis.

CHAPTER 15

Doing Justice

15.i: New Evidence

The trouble with writing about a contemporary issue is that you can end up as a character in your own book. War correspondents know the feeling. One minute you're watching the action from a safe distance. Next minute you're a target.

• • •

Having failed to persuade the Court of Appeal to review the entire Ellis case, Judith Ablett-Kerr had few options left. She could petition the Governor-General a second time – for a pardon, for a commission of inquiry, or for wider terms of reference to the Court of Appeal. But the history of such petitions shows that the only way to overturn a conviction is to come up with new evidence. So, in late 1998, finding compelling new evidence – or, failing that, any new evidence that could provide a bit of much-needed traction – became a priority for Peter Ellis's counsel.

In pursuit of new evidence, Judith Ablett-Kerr's junior colleague Simon Barr asked me to meet with him on 17 September 1998. He said he had information on the Ellis case that was too sensitive to discuss on the phone. Over the previous 15 months I had met with Ablett-Kerr and Barr on three or four occasions. Each time I made comments along the lines of 'If you can get hold of document A, you might get to the bottom of puzzle B' or 'You're wasting your time going down track C, it's a dead end.' I also made it clear that my research interviews were confidential, and not for their use. This was because I had an agreement with everyone I interviewed. Among other things, it stated that 'all notes, tape recordings and documents will be treated as highly confidential. They will be exclusively for my own use. I will not make copies or give anyone else access to them.'

When I met Simon Barr, we agreed that whatever transpired would remain confidential. Then we traded gossip about the Ellis jury. Even if it were all true, nothing was said that could have ever amounted to grounds for an appeal.

About a month later, Judith Ablett-Kerr told me she wanted to use my comments about 'Juror C' – as reported to her by Simon Barr – in her second petition to the Governor-General. I said, 'I'm not giving you my permission.' She said she was going to use them anyway.

Ablett-Kerr submitted her second petition in November 1998, and made a bail application for her client the following month. Bail was refused, and the week commencing 31 May 1999 was set aside for Peter Ellis's second appeal hearing.[1]

In January 1999, retired High Court Judge Sir Thomas Thorp was asked to review the Ellis petition for the Ministry of Justice.[2] But before Sir Thomas had completed his report, Peter Ellis again became eligible for parole.

'I cannot accept any parole that you could offer me because the board can only release me as a guilty man,' he told the Parole Board. 'I am a human being and of course I very much want my freedom, but I simply cannot accept it, if it is to be given on the basis that I am a guilty man. I am not a guilty man. I am an innocent man.'

In its 17 March ruling, the Parole Board said it had taken into account 'the attitude of the inmate to the offending and any steps that had been taken to address the offending or to undertake programmes and courses designed to avoid future offending', and had concluded that this was a case of 'very serious offending against children' that 'has not been acknowledged or addressed'.[3]

The front-page headline in the Christchurch *Press* next day read: 'Innocence Stance Costs Ellis Parole.'[4]

• • •

The main thrust of Judith Ablett-Kerr's second petition was that the Court of Appeal was not an appropriate body to determine the claims of a miscarriage of justice in the Ellis case. She requested a 'Free pardon and a Royal Commission of Inquiry' or, alternatively, 'a Royal Commission of Inquiry into his case and for his whole case to be referred back to the Court of Appeal'.

After studying the petitions and related documents, Sir Thomas Thorp concluded that the greatest concerns were: 'the claims of defective interviewing techniques and of failure to assess or minimise the risk of "contamination" of the children's evidence'; and the claim that restrictions on the playing of children's videotapes at the Ellis trial deprived the jury of the 'evidence necessary for a proper assessment of the children's reliability'. He therefore recommended that the reference to the Court of Appeal be extended to include those points, and that no pardon be considered while the case was before the court.

Thorp also noted that the petitioner had made 'serious allegations' against a juror. 'I understand that your officers have asked the petitioner's counsel whether she can provide some evidentiary support for the new allegations,' he wrote.[5]

On 4 March, I received a letter from Val Sim, Chief Legal Counsel for the Ministry of Justice. 'The [Ellis] petition includes a statement by Simon Barr, which refers to a conversation between Mr Barr and yourself where you discussed an interview with [Juror C],' she wrote. 'Mrs Judith Ablett-Kerr QC has informed us that this interview was recorded on audiotape. It would greatly assist our inquiries if you were able to give us access to a copy of this tape.' I replied, tersely, that I was unable to assist.[6]

On 30 March Val Sim faxed a copy of my response to Judith Ablett-Kerr. Two days later, questions were asked in parliament about Sir Thomas Thorp's inability to demand the production of evidence in relation to the Ellis petition. On 29 April, the front-page banner headline in the *Dominion* read 'Leaked Letter Raises Questions on Ellis Trial Juror'. Judith Ablett-Kerr said that neither she nor her staff were responsible for the leak.[7]

Next day, the alleged tape was elevated to the status of The Holy Grail; The Secret Casket; The Answer to the Riddle of the Crèche Case. 'Ellis Lawyer Wanted Juror Tape Studied' (Christchurch *Press*); 'Ellis' Backers Angered by Tape Reports' (*Waikato Times*); 'Hand Tape Over: Supporters' (*Herald*); 'Author Should Hand Over Tape, Say Ellis Supporters' (*Dominion*).

Member of Parliament Rana Waitai issued a press release saying he was 'disgusted with the number of people who had allowed Peter Ellis to suffer for their own selfish ends', and that 'Lynley Hood should be forced to hand over her evidence', and that 'we have a writer who is prepared to hold onto critical evidence to make a profit, rather than helping an innocent man gain his freedom'.[8]

By then I was taking advice from Wellington media law experts, Sandra Moran and John Tizard. 'Say nothing,' they said. 'It's just hearsay. They can't act on hearsay.' So I stopped answering the phone. I made no comment.

On 13 May, the expanded terms of reference to the Court of Appeal arising from the second Ellis petition were published in the *New Zealand Gazette*. There were five headings: children's evidence; retraction; trial procedure; jury; and non-disclosure of material. Under the jury heading, three jurors were mentioned: Juror A ('who is said to have had a connection to a Crown witness through the juror's intimate partner'); Juror B ('who is said to have expressed the view in a public place that the applicant was guilty, before the case for the prosecution was complete'); and Juror C ('who is said to have told Ms Lynley Hood, an author proposing to write a book on the applicant's case, in an audiotaped interview: that he was sexually attracted to one of the child complainants at the applicant's trial; and, that he had counselling because of this attraction').[9]

On 20 May, Justice Gault issued a 'Minute of the Court'. It rescheduled the Ellis appeal for the week beginning 5 July, addressed various administrative issues and stated: 'there will be an order pursuant to s. 389(a) of the Crimes Act 1961 directed to Ms Lynley Hood for the production to this Court within seven days of the audiotaped interview she conducted with Juror C and any transcript of that audiotape'.[10]

The rarely used s. 389(a) of the Crimes Act gives the Court of Appeal the discretion 'if it thinks it necessary or expedient in the interests of justice' to 'order the production of any document exhibit, or other thing connected with the proceedings the production of which appears to the Court to be necessary for the determination of the case'. In a 1996 ruling, Justice Henry said: 'The discretion is not lightly to be exercised. It will normally require the establishment by the appellant of the likelihood of the existence of information which is cogent to the inquiry whether a miscarriage of justice has occurred ... The jurisdiction is not part of an investigatory procedure.' As far as I am aware, s. 389(a) has never previously been used against the media. Indeed, in the past the Court of Appeal has vigorously upheld the right of journalists to withhold confidential material on the ground that there is 'a legitimate public interest in protecting media sources from unnecessary revelation'.[11]

The order was served on me on 25 May. At that point, John Tizard advised the Court of Appeal that he would be applying on my behalf to have the order set aside, and I discussed the moral issues involved with Professor of Medical Ethics Grant Gillett.

'It's not as if Peter Ellis is on death row,' he said sagely. 'He's due for release next February anyway. So the most that could be achieved, if you had any evidence of real significance, would be to get him out a few months earlier. But, even if the allegation about the juror were true, I can't see that it has any significance at all. Individual jurors react to witnesses in all sorts of ways – it's integral to the way they reach their verdicts.'

At a hearing before Justices Gault, Henry and Tipping on 16 June, John Tizard submitted that the s. 389(a) order was misconceived. He argued that it was based on questionable presumptions (that I had interviewed Juror C, that a tape of the interview existed and that the tape contained evidence of jury bias). He also argued that the order had been issued without proper regard for some fundamental issues. These were: 'what privileges Ms Hood might have'; whether the court should be investigating the deliberations of the jury; what the allegations (if true) would prove; and whether the court should be conducting an investigation at all. The Crown agreed. Judith Ablett-Kerr did not. On the assumption that the tape existed, the court gave me two days to hand it over, and arranged for Sir Thomas Thorp to review it and report back on its contents.

'What'll they do if I don't hand it over?' I asked Sandra Moran and John Tizard when they phoned me with the news.

'Send you to jail,' they said emphatically, in unison.

I could see that having an independent person confirm that the juror *did not* say that he was sexually attracted to one of the child complainants had merit.

'Maybe I could just dub off the relevant comments,' I suggested.

'They want the whole tape.'

'There's more than one tape,' I said.

'They'll want the lot.'

Next day I talked to Dunedin barrister Steven O'Driscoll. 'You'll be adding fuel to the fire if you don't hand the tapes over,' he said. 'Everyone'll think you're hanging on to something sensational.'

I thought about handing over the tapes. I thought about the tapes being passed from hand to hand, being left in unlocked rooms overnight. I thought about the tapes being leaked to the media. I said I'd hand them over if I could deliver them to Sir Thomas Thorp myself. Steven phoned Sandra. She agreed to discuss security arrangements with Justice Gault.

On D-day I made a list ('warm clothes, toiletries, radio, money'). I bought two pairs of woollen socks, a set of thermal longjohns and an exercise book in which to write a children's story ('Grandma Goes To Jail'). I drafted a press release that began 'As has happened so often in the murky history of the Christchurch Civic Crèche case, at the first whiff of anything salacious and titillating, the authorities have reached for the sledgehammer without pausing to ask: Is this allegation true, and is it relevant?' Around 3.30pm, Sandra phoned. Justice Gault would deliver the tapes to Sir Thomas Thorp himself. That was his best offer. It had been a long 48 hours.

'Okay,' I said, defeated.

• • •

The 'Minute of the Court' of 28 June, issued by Justices Richardson, Gault, Henry, Thomas and Tipping was brief and to the point:

> The Court has now received the report requested from Sir Thomas Thorp which it has considered in conjunction with the transcript of the audio tapes. The Court is satisfied there is nothing disclosed in the audio tapes which would provide an evidential foundation for the referred ground of appeal relating to allegations that Juror C (a) was sexually attracted to one of the child complainants at the trial, or (b) had counselling because of this attraction. The Court therefore proposes to take no further action in this respect.[12]

15.ii: The Judith Ablett-Kerr QC Appeal

Judith Ablett-Kerr QC opened the case for Peter Ellis in the Court of Appeal on Monday 5 July 1999 before Justices Richardson, Gault, Henry, Thomas and Tipping. Simon France and Mary-Jane Thomas appeared for the Crown. It was Justice Tipping's first crèche case appeal. (Justice Gault had sat on the first Ellis appeal. Justices Richardson, Thomas and Henry had sat on the crèche workers' employment appeal.)

Prior to August 1996, the primary focus for any Court of Appeal hearing was the oral argument. However, when Justice Richardson became president, he restricted the time allocated for oral submissions, and shifted the focus to written submissions filed in advance. At a July 1996 law conference, Justice Thomas observed: 'A concise, well-constructed [written] submission will be received with appreciation. With that appreciation it will obtain a closer reading than a voluminous submission with much unnecessary and repetitive material which invites the reader to scan it rather than digest it.'

Justice Thomas also urged barristers to make concise oral submissions, to answer questions from the bench effectively and to address the question in issue. 'The style of advocacy which I most favour is an unadorned, tradesmanlike presentation of the argument,' he said. He added that, having read the submission in advance, the court may have formed a relatively firm view of the case. 'Counsel will know from the questions asked which way the wind is blowing,' he said. 'It may, of course, even be blowing in different directions.'[13]

In a Practice Note effective from 1 January 1998, Justice Richardson advised that the Court of Appeal would 'insist that time limits are strictly observed and that submissions are concise'. Of 'fresh evidence' he wrote: 'Leave is required before any further evidence is received … [a]ny applications and affidavit(s) must be filed three weeks before the date of hearing.' According to *Adams on Criminal Law*, in determining the admissibility of such evidence, 'the court will normally require that the evidence be fresh in the sense that it was not available at the trial, and that it be credible and cogent in the sense that if given along with the other evidence in the case the jury might reasonably have been led to return a different verdict. The overriding test however is the interests of justice.'

In the Practice Note, Justice Richardson also advised that the court required not less than three weeks' notice of 'grounds resting upon complaints about conduct or competency of defence counsel at the trial'. (That direction served to ensure that trial counsel would have the opportunity to give his or her side of the story when such complaints were made.)[14]

In responding to the expectations and requirements of the Court of Appeal, Tom Weston, barrister for the Christchurch City Council, told me that he relied on the maxim: 'Do not irritate the minds you seek to persuade.'

• • •

The grounds for the second Ellis appeal itemised on the reference from the Governor-General were: 'Grounds involving children's evidence' (which Judith Ablett-Kerr divided into 'contamination' and 'interviewing'); 'retraction'; 'trial procedure'; 'jury'; and 'nondisclosure'. In the reference, each ground was supported by several specific concerns. The wording of the reference was tailored to the Court of Appeal's requirement for new evidence ('since the applicant's appeal, material has become available or obtainable that shows …').

Judith Ablett-Kerr began by telling the Court of Appeal that it had made a mistake. 'No human being, no matter how clever or successful, is perfect. And no criminal justice system, no matter how well intentioned, is infallible,' she said. 'The fact is we all make mistakes. In the case of Peter Ellis the system failed and a miscarriage of justice has occurred.'

'That is your submission,' said Justice Richardson.

'That is my submission, sir,' agreed Ablett-Kerr.

Justice Richardson was not just stating the obvious. He was reminding Ellis's counsel that it was her place to make submissions, and the court's place to decide whether or not a miscarriage of justice had occurred.

Ablett-Kerr went on to argue that a miscarriage of justice had occurred primarily because the evidence of the child complainants was given a weight and confidence to which it was not entitled. 'It was given this unjustified credibility because of misconceptions about children's evidence and the need for care, and because of the failure of the system to recognise that this was a case where the evidence of children should have been treated at least with the greatest of caution, and at best by total exclusion,' she said. 'Because this was a case of mass allegation in a day-care centre.'

Before long, Judith Ablett-Kerr began raising issues that fell outside the ambit of the reference from the Governor-General, introducing evidence that had not been the subject of any prior application for admission and traversing the entire case from beginning to end. Her approach was of ongoing concern to the bench.

Early in the first session, Justice Richardson said: 'Before you go any further, it would help us if you could indicate a timetable … The case is set down for a maximum of four days. The assumption is that you will complete your submissions by the end of tomorrow.'

Judith Ablett-Kerr replied that preparing the case had not been easy. 'There are 190,000 pages of material we have had to look at,' she said. 'We cut them down to 500.'

'About ten times as long as the customary maximum,' observed Richardson.

Ablett-Kerr said that she'd done her best, and went on to comment on the strengths of the case.

'I think you're getting away from the question,' said Justice Thomas. 'You were asked: Can you assure us that you will complete the submission within the next two days?'

'I would like to think I could,' she said.

'You're going to have to,' said Justice Thomas.

Throughout the proceedings, on matters of timetabling, conciseness, relevance and admissibility, Their Honours sought to keep Ellis's counsel on course with the controlled exasperation of sheep dogs mustering a wayward and wilful ewe. 'I'm quite unable to make any intelligible notes because we're all over the place' (Justice Gault). 'I think you're throwing in matters which, with respect Mrs Ablett-Kerr, tend to cloud the water' (Justice Tipping). 'Are you inviting us to take into account material which is not admissible?' (Justice Henry). 'Would you just keep to the point' (Justice Thomas).

• • •

Judith Ablett-Kerr's principal argument was that, at the Ellis trial and first appeal, the extent of contamination of the children's evidence, particularly by their parents, had been underestimated and not properly investigated, and that 'there was a complete failure to identify the special risks that are now known to be associated with mass allegation crèche cases'. She also argued that: recent research had produced a better understanding of interviewing techniques and the risks of failing to follow prescribed guidelines; that rulings like Oral Judgment (No.14) denied defence counsel the opportunity to properly test the credibility of child complainants; and that the defence was hampered by the non-disclosure of crèche photographs and internal police documents.

In support of her arguments, Ablett-Kerr relied on evidence adduced at the Ellis trial and affidavits from psychologists Dr Parsonson, Dr Lamb and Professor Bruck. In addition, she relied on: the report of the Wood Royal Commission in New South Wales, the British 'Memorandum of Good Practice' for the conduct of children's interviews, other published research, police job sheets, statements and handwritten notes from parents, newspaper clippings, evidence from the depositions hearing, DSW interviewers' reports, children's books, Ms Dogwood's memoir (*A Mother's Story*), booklets made by Tess Hickory and her mother, the transcript of Dr Zelas's *Holmes* interview, letters written by Ellis's solicitor Chris Knight and various other documents. Because she had not sought leave to admit the additional material, the judges were unsure of its reliability, and had no idea how much of it was genuinely new and how much had been used – or was available but unused – at the time of the trial or the previous appeal.

• • •

In commenting on the proper approach to a referral from the Governor-General, Justice Richardson said: 'Clearly in terms of the Crimes Act, we view this as an appeal.' However, he also pointed out that, in terms of New Zealand and Australian case law [*Morgan* and *Gunn*], '... where there has already been an appeal that raises the same kind of issue, then it's not simply a matter of: clean slate, let's look at it again. It's really only if there's something special, different, new, that requires us to look at the matter in the light of what's new.'

Justice Tipping proposed a more flexible approach: 'Something "genuinely additional" is better than "new"', he suggested.

'*Morgan* and *Gunn* both use the expression "some new matter"', said Richardson.

To determine whether there was any cogent and credible fresh evidence in the material before them, Their Honours questioned Ellis's counsel closely on its status. Was it available at the time of the trial? If so, was it put before the jury? If not, why not? If there was some genuinely new material, how relevant and reliable was it? In the final analysis, was it of sufficient weight to convince the court that a miscarriage of justice had occurred?

Judith Ablett-Kerr admitted that her description of the spread of allegations during the crèche investigation (which was the primary focus of her presentation) was based on material available at the time of trial, and that much of that material had been put before the jury. However, she suggested that trial counsel had not used it as effectively as he might have done. She also held trial counsel responsible for the limited evidence of parental contamination put before the jury, and for the limited playing of children's videotaped interviews, and expressed concern about Rob Harrison's extensive cross-examination of witnesses at the depositions hearing, his choice of expert witness and his briefing of that expert.

Ablett-Kerr's belittling of trial counsel prompted Justice Richardson to remind her on more than one occasion that the conduct of the trial by defence counsel was not a ground for appeal. It also prompted Justice Tipping to invite her on more than one occasion to explain to the court the effect of the trial judge's rulings on defence counsel's conduct of the trial. But Ablett-Kerr did not take up the invitation.

At the end of the first day, Justice Richardson asked Judith Ablett-Kerr to provide the court with a summary of knowledge about interviewing techniques and the risks of contamination that was not available at the time of the trial or the previous appeal. When the court resumed next day, Ablett-Kerr conceded that the basic principles had been known for some time, but she said they were better known now. She also argued that the phenomenon of mass allegations in day-care centres had only recently been fully appreciated.

Justice Gault said that the issue of contamination had been raised 'emphatically and repeatedly' at the previous appeal. 'It was said that this was the very nature of the defence at the trial; suggestibility of the children, contamination of their evidence and unreliability of the interviewing techniques,' he recalled. In a similar vein, Justice Richardson pointed out the trial judge's references to hypervigilant parents, community hysteria and mass allegation cases overseas in his pre-trial rulings.

Junior counsel Greg King's submissions on the significance of Zelda Cypress's retraction, and on the questions of jury bias, spilled over into the third day. Then Simon France opened the case for the Crown. He argued that differences between family sexual abuse cases and mass allegation cases in day-care centres were matters of degree rather than kind, that the risks of contamination had been recognised and addressed at the Ellis trial and previous appeal and that the jury had been given a full picture of the case. 'What it didn't have was by [defence counsel's] choice,' he said. 'It was all available.'

Justice Tipping suggested that the problem with mass allegation cases was that 'the thing takes on a life of its own'. 'People quite naturally talk to each other,' he said. 'It's a bit like spontaneous combustion. Isn't that the suggested phenomenon that hitherto we haven't really recognised?'

'Doesn't it date back a long time?' said Justice Thomas. 'The Salem witch-hunt?'

The implication of that observation did not escape Justice Tipping. 'Maybe if it's been known for 300 years, Mrs Ablett-Kerr's on rather a sticky wicket,' he said.

In a case that had been leavened with irony from the outset, this was the ultimate irony. In July 1999, two judges of the highest court in the land toyed with the notion that the Christchurch Civic Crèche case had the characteristics of a classical witch-hunt, and concluded that, because the phenomenon of mass-allegation cases had been known about for a long time, that was reason to uphold, rather than overturn, the conviction of Peter Ellis.

• • •

In the Court of Appeal judgment issued on 14 October 1999, Their Honours criticised the conduct of the appeal by Ellis's counsel. With regard to the Ellis trial, they ruled that the judge had placed 'no undue restriction' on the defence. However, they did express concern about some of Dr Zelas's testimony. They also noted that expert opinion on the reliability of the children's evidence was sharply divided, and suggested that a commission of inquiry could better evaluate the competing claims.

The judgment concluded: 'we are not persuaded that any individual ground of appeal has been made out. Neither are we persuaded that their cumulative effect constitutes a miscarriage of justice. The appeal is therefore dismissed.'[15]

On 16 October 1999, a spokeswoman for the complainants told the Christchurch *Press* that the judgment had put Peter Ellis's guilt beyond all doubt. She said the children and their families 'had endured years of accusations and ridicule from the media and the community for having the courage to speak up', and added:

> Their honesty and courage stopped the abuse at the Civic Crèche. Now is the time for Ellis's victims to be allowed, at last, to lead as near normal lives as possible. It is to be hoped that they, and all victims of pedophiles, can have confidence that society will care for, listen to, and support children by condemning all forms of pedophilia.[16]

• • •

On 2 February 2000, Peter Ellis's seven years in prison came to an end. At a press conference he thanked his mother, his supporters, the crèche staff, the parents of crèche children who had stood by him and his fellow prisoners and their families. He announced that the fight to prove his innocence would go on.

'I do not intend to stop until my name is cleared and the truth is out for everyone's sake, including the children's,' he said.[17]

CHAPTER 16

'It is a Case that Simply Will Not Go Away'

FOLLOWING THE FAILURE of the second Ellis appeal in October 1999, and the Court of Appeal's observation that some matters raised by Ellis's counsel were better suited to a commission of inquiry, Judith Ablett-Kerr submitted her third application to the Governor-General on behalf of her client. She called for a free pardon and a Royal Commission of Inquiry into the Ellis case. Ellis supporters renewed the call following a change of government in November 1999, and at the time of Ellis's release in February 2000. On such occasions feminist lawyer Wendy Ball, spokesperson for the complainant parents [see Ch.5.iv], protested vigorously that no inquiry was needed.[1]

On 10 March 2000, Justice Minister Phil Goff announced that he had instructed former Chief Justice Sir Thomas Eichelbaum to investigate 'matters relevant to the assessment of the reliability of the children's evidence' in the Ellis case. Goff said he had opted for a Ministerial Inquiry, rather than a commission of inquiry, because the former was less expensive, less stressful for the complainant families, speedier, more flexible and more discreet.[2]

In his choice of inquiry head, Phil Goff could not have appointed a more authoritative jurist. Thomas Eichelbaum graduated in law from Victoria University of Wellington, New Zealand, in 1954. He was appointed Queen's Counsel in 1978, to the High Court bench in 1982 and Chief Justice in 1989. In the latter role he also presided in the Criminal Appeal Division of the Court of Appeal. As a barrister Eichelbaum appeared as counsel in a number of Commissions of Inquiry. Following his retirement in 1999 he served on two Ministerial Inquiries and chaired a Royal Commission.[3] During Sir Thomas's ten-year term as Chief Justice, the laws relating to child sexual abuse were changed, child sexual abuse convictions escalated, and controversy over the investigation and prosecution of the Christchurch Civic Crèche case raged nationwide.

In the normal course of events, judges are well equipped to conduct official inquiries, but any inquiry into one's own justice system is bound to heighten the many, often conflicting challenges. There is the need for closure (without which the justice system would cease to function), and the need to revisit a much considered case. There is the need to uphold the independence of the judiciary and the integrity of the justice system in the face of political and public attack, and the need to accept that a miscarriage of justice may have occurred. There is the need to sit in judgment on one's peers (but senior judges do that on a daily basis as part of the normal appeal process). There is the need to decide the matter without fear or favour, and the need to consider the effects of one's decision on the people and institutions involved (because no responsible judge can really apply the maxim: *fiat justicia, ruat coelum* [let justice be done though the heavens fall]). It was presumably with these challenges in mind that, in 1980, Prime Minister Rob Muldoon appointed an Australian judge to head the commission of inquiry into the controversial Arthur Allan Thomas case.

For his inquiry into the Ellis case, Sir Thomas Eichelbaum was instructed to investigate and report on: currently accepted best practice for the investigation of mass child abuse allegations; risks associated with failure to adhere to best practice; whether the investigation of events and the interviews of children in the Christchurch Civic Crèche case were conducted in accordance with best practice; whether any breaches of best practice in the interviews affected the reliability of the children's evidence; and 'whether there are any matters which give rise to doubts about the assessment of the children's evidence to an extent which would render the conviction of Peter Hugh McGregor Ellis unsafe and warrant the grant of a pardon'.[4]

The terms of reference required Sir Thomas to consider: reports from the Cleveland Inquiry, the Orkney Inquiry, the San Diego Grand Jury and the NSW Royal Commission; a NZ Law Commission Discussion Paper; the UK Memorandum of Good Practice and an associated research paper; and the Joint NZ Children and Young Persons Service & Police Operating Guidelines. Sir Thomas was also required to invite and consider written submissions from the Crown Law Office (on behalf of the Police, DSW and specialist interviewers), Peter Ellis, the complainant families and the Commissioner for Children (but not from the crèche staff); and to seek and evaluate the opinions of two 'internationally recognised experts'.

On 13 March 2001, Justice Minister Phil Goff announced Sir Thomas Eichelbaum's unequivocal conclusion: 'The case advanced on behalf of Mr Ellis fails to meet the test identified earlier, to satisfy the Inquiry that the convictions were unsafe, or that a particular conviction was unsafe. It fails by a distinct margin; I have not found this anything like a borderline judgment.'[5]

Phil Goff strongly endorsed Sir Thomas's conclusions. He said that issues concerning the reliability of the children's evidence had received extensive consideration in a very lengthy depositions hearing, a lengthy trial before 'one of New Zealand's foremost criminal trial judges', and two Court of Appeal hearings involving a total of seven judges. It had also been considered by 'a retired Judge with

16 years experience on the bench, 10 of them as Chief Justice' in conjunction with 'two pre-eminent international experts'.

'Neither the Courts which have considered the case nor the Inquiry have any doubts about the safety of Mr Ellis's convictions,' Goff said. 'Sir Thomas concludes that it must now be clear that the case has had the most thorough examination possible, and it should be allowed to rest. I agree entirely with Sir Thomas's conclusions. My advice is that Mr Ellis's application for a pardon should be declined.'[6]

In view of the duration and intensity of the crèche case debate, the assertion that it 'should be allowed to rest' requires careful scrutiny. While it is true that the case has been repeatedly reviewed by a succession of authoritative reviewers, arguments based on the number of reviews, the status of the reviewers and the (arguable) thoroughness of their reviews cannot resolve the controversy. Ultimately, whether the Eichelbaum report can bring closure to the crèche case debate must depend on the comprehensiveness of the investigation and the quality of the analysis in the Eichelbaum report itself.

• • •

Prior to establishing the Eichelbaum inquiry, Phil Goff indicated that he had read the judgment for the second Ellis appeal and the Thorp report on Ellis's second petition to the Governor-General.[7] Both documents advised that some matters raised by Ellis's counsel were better suited to a commission of inquiry. But the Eichelbaum inquiry's terms of reference covered only the matters identified by the Court of Appeal.

Sir Thomas Eichelbaum was required to review 'the investigation into the events at the Christchurch Civic Crèche case and interviews of the children' only in terms of the evidence given at depositions and trial. He was not authorised to make further enquiries or seek additional information to test the reliability of that evidence. The limited terms of reference also meant that many matters of public concern were not addressed. These included: whether the decision to prosecute the five crèche workers was soundly based; whether evidence was improperly admitted or improperly excluded in the court proceedings; whether Peter Ellis had a fair trial; whether the children's evidence was credible; and, given the layout and functioning of the crèche, whether the abuse could possibly have happened.[8]

Also, two important concerns raised in the Thorp report were not addressed in Eichelbaum's terms of reference. One was the 'sanitising' of the charges against Peter Ellis (so that allegations of brutal penetration became charges of indecent touching, and the violent and bloody abuse the children said they had suffered received no mention in the indictment). Thorp's other concern was the misleading effect of certain provisions of the 1989 Evidence Amendment Act. With regard to the provision for expert evidence (s. 23c), Thorp noted that, though Dr Zelas expressed no direct opinion on the credibility of individual complainants, her comments on the children's behaviour 'can hardly have appeared to the jury as otherwise than supportive of the children's credibility'. In Thorp's view, the supportive effect of Zelas's evidence was enhanced by her failure to identify any behaviour by any child that raised doubts about the credibility of their allegations.

'In cross-examination she was asked what characteristics were in her view inconsistent with abuse, and she said that "she hadn't thought about that", Thorp noted. In summary, he wrote:

> A whole series of [court] decisions has laboured over the practical difficulties of admitting expert evidence in terms of s. 23G without that evidence having the effect of taking over the jury's right to decide credibility. The present case exemplifies those difficulties. It also raises the question whether a provision which envisages expert evidence on whether a complainant's behaviour was 'consistent or inconsistent' with the behaviour of sexually abused children of the same age group has any purpose if the expert opinion is that no behaviour can be inconsistent.

Thorp also noted evidence of a 'sea change' in professional thinking about the risks of contamination of children's evidence since 1993, and observed:

> If indeed it is now accepted that very young children are in general more suggestible than their elders, it may also be appropriate to review 23H(c) which instructs judges: 'Not [to] instruct the jury on the need to scrutinise the evidence of young children generally with special care nor suggest to the jury that young children generally have tendencies to invent or distort.'[9]

In his interpretation of the terms of reference, Sir Thomas Eichelbaum further narrowed the scope of his inquiry. After acknowledging that the term 'investigation' could refer to 'any and all aspects of the Police investigation', he decided to focus on 'the obtaining of evidence from the children, including the part played by their parents and the parents of other crèche children'.[10]

In this regard, Sir Thomas Eichelbaum was on common ground with the trial judge, seven judges of the Court of Appeal and Sir Thomas Thorp. As was the case with the prosecutions of Arthur Allan Thomas (in New Zealand) and the IRA bombing suspects (in Britain), the judiciary found no merit in defence concerns that police misconduct may have affected the reliability of the evidence.

• • •

The requirement that Sir Thomas Eichelbaum consult 'at least two internationally recognised experts (if possible with experience in mass allegation child sexual abuse)' posed problems. Among other things, the requirement presumed the existence of a recognised body of reliable specialist knowledge on the subject, and the existence of at least two internationally recognised experts acceptable to all parties. It also presumed that, despite the passion and politics surrounding the issue, the chosen experts would evaluate the children's evidence with dispassionate objectivity.

Eichelbaum came to the view that any expert nominated by one party was likely to lack credibility in the eyes of the other, and any expert with previous involvement in the case was likely to have a predetermined view. On these grounds he eliminated two experts – Stephen Ceci and Maggie Bruck – whose work had helped overturn many American mass allegation cases. (In his report, Sir Thomas Thorp noted that Ceci had contributed to a television programme on the crèche case, and advised: 'His studies of the American "mass allegation crèche cases" suggest that his opinion could be of particular value. There seems no reason why the Ministry, or Crown Law if it preferred, could not seek his opinion.'[11] Bruck's previous contribution was an affidavit for the second Ellis appeal.) Eventually, after taking advice from 'counsel within the Ministry of Justice' and 'a USA Law professor', Eichelbaum appointed two psychologists – Professor Graham Davies of Leicester University in the United Kingdom and Dr Louise Sas of London, Ontario – as expert advisors to his inquiry.

Graham Davies' credentials included membership of the working party that drafted the UK 'Memorandum of Good Practice on Video Recorded Interviews with Child Witnesses', and leadership of the team that updated that document. He was generally regarded as mainstream in his field, though his work on child sexual abuse was almost entirely from a prosecution perspective and his views on recovered memory therapy were relatively uncritical.[12]

Louise Sas's credentials included extensive experience of working with child sexual abuse victims in the criminal justice system. Indeed, she and Wendy Ball (spokesperson for the complainant parents in the Civic Crèche case) were speakers at a workshop on that topic at the Second International Conference on Children Exposed to Family Violence in 1997. In addition, Sas's involvement in 'Project Guardian' and 'the Prescott case' would have qualified her as an expert 'with experience in mass allegation child sexual abuse' under the Eichelbaum Inquiry's terms of reference.[13]

According to Sas, Project Guardian was a child porn ring in London, Ontario (pop. 300,000) involving '60 young boys aged 8 to 17 and 80 adult male offenders'. In her report to the Eichelbaum Inquiry, she wrote:

> In the 'Project Guardian' case ... there was not one spontaneous disclosure! Not one child ever came forward to describe their abuse, despite the fact that for nearly fifteen years this sex ring operated in London. If it were not for the pornographic videos involving the children which were found in the river near our city, I doubt that there would have been an investigation at all!

Of the other mass allegation case, she wrote:

> The 'Prescott case' ... was the closest example of a multi-victim multi-offender ritualistic abuse case in Canada ... The case involved horrendous forms of sexual abuse of very young children who had disclosed when they were apprehended and placed in foster care ... The evidence involved bizarre settings for sexual abuse such as grave yards, stories of cruelty, forced ingestion of unknown materials and even witnessed animal killings.

When Sir Thomas Eichelbaum was selecting his experts, the text of a Canadian Broadcasting Corporation documentary series on Project Guardian, and investigative reports from a leading Canadian gay newspaper, were available on the internet. According to these sources there was no child porn ring. The videotapes found in the river featured teenage male prostitutes having sex with each other. Two men were charged with making the videos. The videos were not distributed to anyone else. So that should have been the end of the matter. But the police persuaded the young hustlers to name their clients and fellow hustlers. As a result, more than 60 men were arrested and hundreds of videotapes were seized. All but one of the arrested men were homosexual. Most of the men did not know each other. None of the seized videos contained child pornography, most contained no pornography at all. Despite intensive counselling and the availability of victims' compensation, most hustlers rejected the 'victim' label. They said they had solicited gay sex for fun and profit. Some complained that their business had fallen off following the arrests.[14]

Additional information of a confusing and contradictory nature on the mass allegation case in Prescott, Ontario (pop. 4500) was available to the Eichelbaum Inquiry on websites for CKLN radio, Believe the Children and the Ontario Centre for Religious Tolerance (OCRT). According to these sources, the investigation was called 'Project Jericho' after an infant named Joshua, who was believed to have been ceremonially murdered. However, as the ritual abuse expert interviewed on CKLN admitted, no evidence of Joshua's birth or death was ever found. There is no mention of any other tangible evidence being found either, even though up to 119 perpetrators (OCRT) and 234 victims (CKLN) were said to have been identified. Project Jericho appears to have been one of the largest ritual abuse investigations in North America. According to the OCRT, no investigative journalist has ever studied the case.[15]

• • •

In his report to the Eichelbaum Inquiry, Professor Davies said he was supplied with 'videotaped records of interviews with all children ... who gave evidence at trial and depositions'; 'transcripts of these interviews'; and 'transcripts of the examination and cross-examination of the evidence given by interviewers, parents and children at depositions and trial'. Dr Sas did not list the material supplied to her. Sir Thomas

Eichelbaum said he provided videotapes, depositions and 'relevant parts' of the trial record to the experts. This indicates that, in forming their opinions, the experts – and possibly also Sir Thomas – did not take into account all the trial evidence. To the defence, the trial evidence given by police, crèche staff, the owner of 404 Hereford Street, Ellis's tutor, the Marriage Guidance administrator and witnesses for the defence was crucial. Though marginalised at the Ellis trial – and unmentioned by Eichelbaum, Davies and Sas – it was central to the debate in the forum of public opinion. It was evidence that supported the argument that, because of the layout of the crèche and the way it functioned, the abuse could not have happened.

Another crucial block of evidence that Sir Thomas and his experts failed to mention (even though it was clearly relevant under the inquiry's terms of reference) was that relating to Zelda Cypress. Zelda was the oldest and most believable child witness. Her allegations were credible. As her baby sitter, Peter Ellis had the opportunity to offend. The jury returned guilty verdicts on all her charges. Two years after the trial, she retracted her allegations. Thereafter, she never wavered from her retraction.

• • •

Professor Davies and Dr Sas were asked to provide opinions on 'whether there are features of the investigation and/or interviews of the children (on the basis of the evidence at depositions and trial) which may have affected the reliability of the children's evidence, and if so, their likely impact'. In his report, Graham Davies noted that his contribution was limited, but assumed it was part of a larger inquiry. 'I perceive my role to be to provide independent advice and relevant information for others to draw their own conclusions, based on the wider evidence and circumstances of the case,' he wrote.

In his review of the children's interviews, Davies noted examples of leading and repeated questioning, negative stereotyping and other coercive techniques. But he considered the lapses to be minor, and the overall interviewing standard to be high. The risk that the children's evidence – especially as it related to unidentified people at unidentified places outside the crèche – could have been contaminated by 'cross-talk between families, against a background of persistent accusation against the suspect' concerned him far more. Of Kari Lacebark's fourth interview he said: 'There is nothing in this interview which convinced me that [Kari] visited Peter's house or was assaulted by a man called Joseph.' But he felt that cross-talk alone could not explain the similar accusations 'particularly in relation to incidents in the crèche toilets'.

Interestingly, though he considered the interviews to be well conducted and the crèche-based allegations to be credible, Davies recommended that reality checks be done to determine whether the alleged events could ever have happened. He wrote:

> [S]uch accusations ... need to be studied in the wider context of the investigation. For instance, do the toilet facilities at the crèche correspond in their layout and construction to those described by the children? Did the physical layout of the crèche afford sufficient privacy to ensure that abuse of the kind described by the children could have taken place? Where children specify that other children were present, does the evidence of these children corroborate their allegations? These are issues beyond my remit, but which the wider inquiry will wish to consider.[16]

In her report, Dr Sas focussed on 'multi-victim multi-offender (MVMO) cases'. She classified these as residential, sex ring, ritualistic and community-centred, and advised that 'the Ellis case most closely resembles the community-centred type' but 'there could also have been a "sex ring" of sorts involving at the very least pornography, and potentially sadistic even ritualised abuse'.[17]

When she compared the Civic Crèche investigation with her own 'Best Practice Model' for MVMO cases, she found that Civic Crèche parents were given potentially inflammatory advice, and that information sharing among parents, and between parents and children, was largely uncontrolled. She also noted flaws in the interviewing of the children, but considered that 'the investigative interviews as a whole were reasonably conducted, and in accordance with standard practice'.

In conclusion, Dr Sas acknowledged that 'there was some contamination ... by the over-involvement of parents in the investigation, and the sharing of information between complainant parents'. But she considered that the children's evidence was not seriously affected or unreliable as a result. 'The effect in my view was that there likely would have been more convictions if the issue of contamination by parents had not been raised so frequently,' she wrote.

• • •

Of the eight senior judges who had considered the Ellis case prior to the Eichelbaum inquiry (Justices Williamson, Cooke, Casey, Gault, Richardson, Henry, Thomas and Tipping), only Justice Williamson had viewed the children's videotaped interviews. When Justice Eichelbaum viewed the videotapes recorded with the six remaining children whose allegations had resulted in guilty verdicts (Kari, Lara, Eli, Tess, Bart, Molly), he found evidence of direct, suggestive, leading and repeated questions, over-long interviews, too many interviews and failure to advise a child that 'don't know' or 'can't remember' were acceptable answers. When he evaluated wider issues of contamination, he found that 'questioning and investigations by some parents exceeded what was desirable and had the potential to contaminate children's accounts'.

From his professional experience, Sir Thomas would have known that people of all ages can be pressured and manipulated into making false statements. From his personal experience he would probably have known that children are generally more suggestible and imaginative than adults. His review of the literature for the inquiry would have reinforced that knowledge. Nonetheless, when he considered the possibility that parental contamination and flawed interviewing techniques could have rendered the children's evidence unreliable, Sir Thomas Eichelbaum concluded that there was no cause for concern.

He described Kari's reluctant second interview as 'patient' and 'skilful'. He made no comment on the repeated and leading questioning in Kari's fourth interview (that preceded her disclosure of abuse by an unknown man at an unknown place). Of the story in Lara's second interview about Peter doing 'secret touching' in a big room with escalators and lots of people working at desks (on which no charges were laid), Sir Thomas commented: 'It seems obvious that this happened.' When Eli talked only of Peter's 'dunking games', Sir Thomas concluded that the boy was 'reluctant to disclose'. Of Bart's second interview, in which the lad talked about oral sex, eating excrement and repeated sodomy at Peter's house, Sir Thomas wrote: 'The allegation of [oral] sexual violation was elicited by leading, although the experts did not comment adversely. This apart I saw nothing objectionable in the way the interview was conducted.'

Unlike Professor Davies, who wanted reality checks done to determine whether the offences could ever have happened, Sir Thomas seemed prepared to believe what the children said. In response to Davies's scepticism towards Kari's allegation about an unknown man and an unknown place, Sir Thomas wrote:

> I was impressed with the strength of the evidence that Mr Ellis took children on visits to places away from the crèche. In particular, I thought that the body of evidence from which it could be inferred that he took children to the house at 404 Hereford Street, which contained various secret cavities, was convincing.

Sir Thomas found that the overall standard of interviewing compared favourably with the 'best practice' models advocated by Davies and Sas, and with comparable models from New Zealand and overseas. In all the models, interviewers are instructed to encourage the child to talk freely about the alleged abuse. Most models acknowledge that direct, leading, repeated and closed questions, anatomically correct dolls, body diagrams and social pressures can produce unreliable disclosures and are best avoided. But they also recommend the use of increasing levels of these coercive techniques if the child seems 'reluctant to disclose'.

At first glance this recommendation seems nonsensical. Why coerce a child into disclosing abuse when the reliability of the disclosure will be thrown into doubt by the coercion? However, in terms of the ideology on which the international child sexual abuse awareness campaign is based, the recommendation makes sense.

According to the ideology, child sexual abuse is an extremely widespread and well-hidden evil with serious long-term consequences: perpetrators rarely confess; physical evidence is hard to find; abused children rarely disclose. So, the argument goes, the best way to uncover and treat this terrible problem is to find the non-disclosing children, and make them disclose.

'Although research strongly supports the use of a free narrative technique in the beginning of an interview, professionals have to be realistic, and everyone recognises that some leading questions will need to be asked,' Dr Sas wrote. Professor Davies warned of the dangers of leading questions, but considered that they could be justified by the information elicited. The recommendation that children be told that 'don't know' and 'can't remember' were acceptable answers concerned Sir Thomas Eichelbaum. '[T]his would not be helpful in inducing reticent children to speak,' he wrote.

Through these and other comments, Eichelbaum, Davies and Sas signalled their acceptance of the ideology underpinning the international child sexual abuse awareness campaign. But, as discussed in Chapter 2.ii, that ideology is more a product of the sexual politics of our times, than of objective research.

Objective research tells us that child sexual abuse happens. But it also tells us that there is no epidemic. It tells us that many perpetrators confess. It tells us that most abused children suffer no long-term harm. It tells us that most abused children disclose voluntarily. It tells us that, if a child does not disclose, there is every likelihood that he or she has not been abused. When viewed in this light the 'best practice' models endorsed by Eichelbaum, Davies and Sas – that allow interviewers to coerce non-disclosing children into disclosing abuse – may seem in themselves to be forms of abuse.[18]

• • •

With regard to the ultimate question ('whether there are any matters which give rise to doubts about the assessment of the children's evidence to an extent which would render the convictions of Peter Hugh McGregor Ellis unsafe and warrant the grant of a pardon'), Sir Thomas Eichelbaum made several points. The first – that concerns about parental contamination and poor interviewing techniques had been repeatedly raised, and repeatedly rejected, in the course of successive court proceedings – was true. (However, it also begged the questions: Were the concerns ever adequately considered before being rejected? and, Was the fact that they had been rejected a valid reason in itself for rejecting them again?)

'A second preliminary point worth underlining is that the available legal processes have been exhausted,' Sir Thomas wrote. 'The Governor-General referred Mr Ellis's earlier Petition to the Court of Appeal, which, in theory, could have directed a new trial. However, given the lapse of time since the events, and the impossibility, from any point of view, of asking the children to testify again, a new trial has never been a potential outcome.'

But to say that the available legal processes were exhausted was an overstatement. In theory, a claimant may submit any number of petitions under s. 406 of the Crimes Act. However, there were problems with this option. One was that, if the petition was not rejected outright, the case would normally be referred back to the Court of Appeal (where, if no credible and cogent new evidence was presented, the appeal would almost certainly fail). Another was that no s. 406 petition has ever resulted in a pardon. Indeed, history suggests that, whatever the strengths of the legal issues involved, political expediency has been a crucial factor in pardons granted by the Governor-General on ministerial advice [see Chs 13.vii, 14.i & 14.ii].

In determining whether a pardon was warranted, Sir Thomas Eichelbaum considered 'the threshold standard required for the exercise of a pardon', and decided that 'the Inquiry must be brought to the point of being satisfied that on the information now available, the case against Mr Ellis was not proved beyond reasonable doubt'.

'My answer is no,' Eichelbaum concluded. 'I am satisfied as to the reliability of the children's evidence on which the convictions now remaining were based.'

In support of his conclusion, Sir Thomas claimed that 'doubtful allegations and charges' were weeded out in the course of successive court proceedings (though, in view of his willingness to regard the laundry chute at 404 Hereford Street a possible venue for abuse, Sir Thomas's ability to discriminate between doubtful and reliable allegations must be open to question). To further support his conclusion he said that the international experts shared his view that the children's evidence was reliable.

• • •

The Christchurch Civic Crèche case was the biggest, most complex and most controversial child molestation investigation in New Zealand history. After what Justice Minister Phil Goff called a 'comprehensive and detailed' inquiry, Sir Thomas Eichelbaum concluded, without reservation or qualification, that Peter Ellis's guilt had been proved beyond reasonable doubt.

But Sir Thomas Eichelbaum's inquiry was both narrow and flawed. His terms of reference failed to address many issues of public concern (such as the soundness of the decision to arrest the women, the sanitising of the charges against Peter Ellis, and the fairness of his trial). In his inquiry, Sir Thomas failed to carry out reality checks on the children's evidence. He failed to take seriously evidence showing that the children's statements had been obtained by pressure and manipulation. He failed to consider the role of the police. He failed to consider the likely effect on the jury of controversial evidence given by the Crown's expert witness. He failed to consider the effect of controversial laws relating to children's evidence on the investigation and prosecution of the case. He failed to mention (and apparently disregarded) the evidence of the child who retracted her allegations. In his conclusions, he failed to acknowledge that one of his own experts had serious reservations about some of the children's evidence.

To further complicate matters, both Sir Thomas Eichelbaum and Justice Minister Phil Goff failed to acknowledge (and presumably failed to realise) that, if the royal pardon is to serve its function as a constitutional safeguard against judicial mistakes, the fact that the judiciary refused to accept that it had made any mistakes in the Ellis case could never be a valid reason to deny Peter Ellis a pardon.

• • •

In Britain in the early '90s, nationwide concern over allegations of official misconduct in the investigation, prosecution and conviction of the IRA bombing suspects eventually led to the establishment of a full-scale commission of inquiry into the British criminal justice system. In New Zealand, the grounds for convening commissions of inquiry were discussed in the report of a 1966 Royal Commission on Tribunals of Inquiry:

> The history of inquiries ... shows that from time to time cases arise concerning rumoured instances of lapses in accepted standards of public administration and other matters causing public concern which cannot be dealt with by ordinary civil or criminal procedures but which require investigation in order to allay public anxiety.

New Zealand law allows commissions of inquiry to investigate and report on any question arising out of or concerning: the administration of the government; the working of any existing law; the necessity or expediency of any legislation; the conduct of any officer in the service of the Crown; or any other matter of public importance.[19]

For almost a decade, the Christchurch Civic Crèche case has been at the centre of a raging debate over the investigation and prosecution of child sexual abuse allegations nationwide. To many involved in the debate, Sir Thomas Eichelbaum's ringing endorsement of the conviction of Peter Ellis seemed like an attempt to bury the debate, instead of facing up to it. However, if the British experience in the IRA cases is any indication, the Eichelbaum Report will serve only to bring a commission of inquiry into the New Zealand criminal justice system that much closer.

References

Prologue (pages 19-22)

1. Lynley Hood, *Sylvia!* (Auckland: Penguin, 1988).
2. Lynley Hood, *Minnie Dean* (Auckland: Penguin, 1994).
3. Stanley Cohen, *Folk Devils and Moral Panics* (Oxford: Blackwell, 1987).
4. G. Ebrahim, 'Mass hysteria in school children', *Clinical Pediatrics*, 7 (1968). Peter Moss and Christopher McEverdy, 'An epidemic of overbreathing among schoolgirls', *British Medical Journal*, 2 (1966). Simon Wessely and Christopher Wardle, 'Mass sociogenic illness by proxy', *British Journal of Psychiatry*, 157 (1990). Rossanne Philen and others, 'Mass sociogenic illness by proxy', *Lancet* 2 (1989). Judith Mausner and Horace Gezon, 'Report on a phantom epidemic of gonorrhea', *American Journal of Epidemiology*, 85, (1967).
5. James Frazer, *The Golden Bough*, abr. repr. (New York: Criterion, 1959).

Chapter 1: What's the Problem?
(pages 23-37)

1. Jan Brunvand, *The Vanishing Hitchhiker* (New York: Norton, 1981).
2. Dorothy Bloch, *So the Witch Won't Eat Me* (London: Burnett, 1979). Bruno Bettelheim, *The Uses of Enchantment* (London: Penguin, 1991).
3. Stanley Cohen, *Folk Devils and Moral Panics* (Oxford: Blackwell, 1987).
4. Hugh Trevor-Roper, *The European Witch-Craze of the Sixteenth and Seventeenth Centuries* (London: Penguin, 1988).
5. Christina Larner, *Witchcraft and Religion* (Oxford: Blackwell, 1984). Rossell Robbins, *The Encyclopedia of Witchcraft and Demonology* (New York: Crown, 1974).
6. E. Williams, *Dictionary of English and European History* (Penguin: London, 1980). Thomas Bergin and Jennifer Speake, *The Encyclopedia of the Renaissance* (New York: Facts on File, 1987). Mary Daly, *Gyn/Ecology* (Boston: Beacon, 1990).
7. Mary Daly, *Gyn/Ecology* (Boston: Beacon, 1990).
8. Lynley Hood, *Minnie Dean* (Auckland: Penguin, 1994).
9. Dorothy Rabinowitz, 'Witch Hunt', *GH*, July 1990. In 1994 Kelly Michaels' conviction was overturned on appeal.
10. *R v Ellis* [1994] 12 CRNZ 172.
11. Bruce Ansley, 'Judgment in Christchurch', *NZ Listener*, 10 July 1993. *Davidson and Others v Christchurch City Council* [1995] 1 ERNZ 172.
12. Ian Hacking, *Rewriting the Soul* (Princeton: Princeton University Press, 1995).
13. Darrell Huff, *How to Lie with Statistics* (London: Gollancz, 1969).

Chapter 2: Sex, Sexism and the New Demonology
Introduction (pages 38-39)

1. Christina Larner, *Enemies of God* (London: Chatto & Windus, 1981). Erik Midelfort, *Witch Hunting in Southwestern Germany 1562-1684* (Stanford: Stanford University Press, 1972).

2.i: The Strands of the Seventies
(pages 39-48)

2. Pat Rosier, ed., *Broadsheet: Twenty Years of Broadsheet Magazine* (Auckland: New Women's Press, 1992).
3. Christine Dann, *Up From Under* (Wellington: Allen & Unwin/Port Nicholson Press, 1985).
4. E.g. the Council for the Single Mother and her Child, the Women's National Abortion Action Campaign, Women Against Rape, the Working Women's Alliance, the Women's Electoral Lobby, the Women's Studies Association and several women's health groups.
5. Letter, *Broadsheet*, May 1973.
6. *Broadsheet*, 1975-1985.

7. Juliet Thompson, 'Rape', *Broadsheet*, October 1975.
8. Gordon Allport, *The Nature of Prejudice* (New York: Anchor, 1958).
9. Theodor Adorno and others, *The Authoritarian Personality* (New York: Harper, 1950).
10. Heinrich Kramer and Jakob Sprenger, *Malleus Malificarum*, trans. by Montague Summers (London: Rodker, 1928).
11. Jan Emetchi and Pilar Michalka, 'Lesbianism Feminism', *Broadsheet*, March 1976. Heah Lee Lee, 'Rape', *Broadsheet*, December 1977.
12. Letters, *Broadsheet*, November 1977.
13. Jan Emetchi and Pilar Michalka, 'Lesbianism Feminism', *Broadsheet*, March 1976.
14. Sandra Coney, *Out of the Frying Pan* (Auckland: Penguin, 1988).
15. Virginia Myers, *Head and Shoulders* (Auckland: Penguin, 1984).
16. Miriam Saphira, 'Where Consciousness-raising Led Me', *Broadsheet*, July/August, 1982.
17. *Women in New Zealand* (Wellington: Dept of Statistics/Dept of Women's Affairs, 1990).
18. Tony Reid, 'Man with a Mission', *NZ Listener*, 15 April 1991.
19. Henry Kempe and others, 'The Battered-child Syndrome', *JAMA*, 181 (1962). Ray Helfer and Henry Kempe, *The Battered Child* (Chicago: University of Chicago Press, 1974).
20. C. Rycroft, 'Non-accidental Injuries', *New Society*, June 20, 1968. David Gil, *Violence Against Children* (Cambridge, Mass: Harvard University Press, 1970).
21. David Fergusson and others, *Child Abuse in New Zealand* (Wellington: Department of Social Welfare, 1972).
22. Ian Hacking, *Rewriting the Soul* (Princeton: Princeton University Press, 1995).
23. Ruth Kempe and Henry Kempe, *Child Abuse* (London: Fontana, 1978).
24. Debbie Nathan and Michael Snedeker, *Satan's Silence* (New York: BasicBooks, 1995).
25. Douglas Besharov, 'U.S. National Center on Child Abuse and Neglect', *Child Abuse and Neglect*, 1 (1977).
26. Katherine Faller, 'Problems in the U.S. Child Protection System', *Child Abuse and Neglect*, 9 (1985).

2.ii: The Knotted Web of the Eighties (pages 48–68)

1. Janet Malcolm, *In the Freud Archives* (New York: Vintage, 1985).
2. *All About Women in New Zealand* (Wellington: Statistics NZ, 1993).
3. Henry Kempe, 'Opening Address', *Child Abuse and Neglect*, 3 (1979).
4. 'Plunket Head at Child-abuse World Conference: Children Are Not Chattels', *The Press*, 27 September 1978. 'Much Work Still Needed in Study of Child Abuse', *The Press*, 14 March 1979.
5. 'Can You Help?' *NZ Woman's Weekly*, 17 September 1979.
6. *The Advertising Directory and Media Planner* (Wellington: Press Research Bureau, 1979).
7. 'Small Girls are Most at Risk from Friends, Family', *NZ Woman's Weekly*, 24 March 1980.
8. ibid.
9. Miriam Jackson, 'Incest: The Last Taboo', *Broadsheet*, November 1979.
10. 'Small Girls are Most at Risk from Friends, Family', *NZ Woman's Weekly*, 24 March 1980.
11. Miriam Saphira, *The Sexual Abuse of Children* (Auckland: Papers Inc., 1981).
12. ibid.
13. Edward Brecher, *The Sex Researchers* (New York: Signet, 1971).
14. ibid.
15. Alfred Kinsey and others, *Sexual Behaviour of the Human Female* (Philadelphia: Saunders, 1953).
16. Miriam Saphira, 'Researching Incest in the Community', 5th International Congress on Child Abuse and Neglect, Montreal, Canada, 1984.
17. Alfred Kinsey and others, *Sexual Behaviour of the Human Female* (Philadelphia: Saunders, 1953).
18. ibid.
19. Hilary Haines, 'Research in Focus', *Mental Health News*, August 1988.
20. Diana Russell, 'Incidence and Prevalence of Sexual Abuse of Female Children', *Child Abuse and Neglect*, 7 (1983).
21. Michelle Smith and Lawrence Pazder, *Michelle Remembers* (London: Joseph, 1980).

22. Mark Pendegrast, *Victims of Memory* (Hinesburg VT: Upper Access, 1995).
23. *The Primary Activation Method*, Institute of Primary Activation. [n.p.] [n.pub.] [1987(?)]
24. Elizabeth Loftus with Katherine Ketcham, *The Myth of Repressed Memory* (New York: St Martin's Press, 1994).
25. Miriam Saphira, *The Sexual Abuse of Children* (Auckland: Papers Inc., 1981).
26. Camille Guy, 'Feminism and Sexual Abuse', *Feminist Review*, 52 (1996).
27. Sue Dyson, 'Progression Against Aggression', *YWCA 'Rape and Sexual Violence to Women and Children' Conference Report* (Wellington: YWCA, 1983).
28. Lynda Morgan, 'Incest Survivors Group', *Child Abuse Prevention in New Zealand Revisited* (Auckland: Mental Health Foundation, 1987).
29. 'Incest Survivors Healing Each Other', *The Press*, 21 June 1984.
30. 'Sexual Abuse of Children', *The Press*, 10 November 1982. Suzanne Sgroi, ed., *Handbook of Clinical Intervention in Child Sexual Abuse* (Lexington MA: Lexington, 1981). Eileen Swan, 'Practical Steps for Dealing with Child Sexual Abuse', *Child Abuse Treatment and Prevention* (Auckland: Mental Health Foundation, 1985).
31. Roland Summit, 'The Child Sexual Abuse Accommodation Syndrome', *Child Abuse and Neglect*, 7 (1983).
32. Jeremy Laurance, 'Bentovim's Technique', *New Society*, 28 November 1986.
33. Eileen Vizard, 'Interviewing Young, Sexually Abused Children: Assessment Techniques', *Family Law*, 17 (1987).
34. Paul Mullen and others, 'Impact of Sexual and Physical Abuse on Women's Mental Health', *Lancet*, 1 (1988).
35. Randy Rockney and Thomas Lemke, 'Casualties from a junior-senior high school during the Persian Gulf War', *Developmental and Behavioural Pediatrics*, 13 (1992). Silvio Benaim and others, 'Hysterical epidemic in a classroom', *Psychological Medicine*, 3 (1973). M. Colligan and others, *Mass Psychogenic Illness* (Hillsdale NJ: Lawrence Erlbaum, 1983). Harold Merskey, *The Analysis of Hysteria* (London: Tindall, 1979).
36. Silvio Benaim and others, 'Hysterical epidemic in a classroom', *Psychological Medicine*, 3 (1973).
37. J. Shore and others, 'Evaluation of Mental Health Effects of Disaster', *American Journal of Public Health*, 76 (1986).
38. Caroll du Chateau, 'How the Mental Health Foundation is Trying to Drive Us Mad', *Metro*, October 1988.
39. John Hannafin (Telethon Trustee), interview, Radio NZ News, 26 June 1988. P. Spier, *Convicting and Sentencing of Offenders in New Zealand* (Wellington: Ministry of Justice, 1995).
40. F. Bondy, letter, *NZ Listener*, 23 July 1988.
41. Marilyn Waring, 1ZB News, 3.30pm, 14 June 1988. Caroll du Chateau, 'How the Mental Health Foundation is Trying to Drive Us Mad', *Metro*, October 1988.
42. Emily Flynn, 'Child Abuse: The Facts', *NZ Listener*, 13 August 1988. Caroll du Chateau, 'How the Mental Health Foundation is Trying to Drive Us Mad', *Metro*, October 1988.
43. Paul Mullen and others, 'Childhood Sexual Abuse and Mental Health in Adult Life', *British Journal of Psychiatry*, 163 (1993).
44. ibid.
45. Paul Mullen and others, 'The Long-Term Impact of the Physical, Emotional and Sexual Abuse of Children: A Community Study', *Child Abuse and Neglect*, 20 (1996).
46. National Center on Child Abuse and Neglect, *Study Findings: National Incidence and Severity of Child Abuse and Neglect*, Washington DC: US Dept of Health and Human Services, No. (OHDS) 81-3-325 (1981).
47. David Geddis and others, *A Private or Public Nightmare?* (Wellington: Advisory Committee on the Investigation, Detection and Prosecution of Offences Against Children, 1986). Police Commissioner, *Policy and Guidelines for the Investigation of Child Sexual Abuse and Serious Child Physical Abuse* (Wellington: Police National Headquarters, 1989). *Manual for the Medical Management of Child Sexual Abuse* (Auckland: Doctors for Sexual Abuse Care, 1991).

Chapter 3: *Crimen Exceptum*

Introduction (pages 69-70)

1. Christina Larner, *Witchcraft and Religion* (Oxford: Blackwell, 1984). Erik Midelfort, *Witch Hunting in Southwestern Germany 1562-1684* (Stanford: Stanford University Press, 1972).
2. Rossell Robbins, *The Encyclopedia of Witchcraft and Demonology* (New York: Crown, 1974).
3. Ellen Bass and Laura Davis, *The Courage to Heal* (New York: Harper & Row, 1988). Wendy Maltz, *The Sexual Healing Journey* (New York: HarperCollins, 1991).
4. Christina Larner, *Witchcraft and Religion* (Oxford: Blackwell, 1984).

3.i: The Rise of the Sexual Abuse Specialist (pages 70-88)

5. Domestic Purposes Benefit, Matrimonial Property Act, Equal Pay Act, Human Rights Act, Accident Compensation Act and National Superannuation reforms.
6. Evan Whitton, *Trial by Voodoo* (Milsons Pt NSW: Random House, 1994).
7. Wayne Innes, *Psychology in New Zealand* (Auckland: Social Analysis, 1976).
8. Robyn Dawes, *House of Cards: Psychology and Psychotherapy Built on Myth* (New York: Free Press, 1994).
9. Nigel Hawkes, 'Counselling Caution on a Cure-all for Life's Ills', *London Times*, 19 August 1997.
10. *Working Party of the Funding of Sexual Abuse Counselling Services: Phase One Report* (Wellington: Interdepartmental Working Party on the Funding of Sexual Abuse Services, 1989).
11. Constitution of the National Collective of Rape Crisis and Related Groups of Aotearoa Inc.
12. Ellen Bass and Laura Davis, *The Courage to Heal* (New York: Harper & Row, 1988).
13. Theodor Adorno and others, *The Authoritarian Personality* (New York: Harper, 1950).
14. Laura Brown, 'The Private Practice of Subversion, Psychology as Tikkun Olam', *American Psychologist*, 52 (1997).
15. Julie Sutherland, 'Department of Social Welfare Sexual Abuse Cases', *Child Abuse Treatment and Prevention* (Auckland: Mental Health Foundation, 1985).
16. ibid.
17. *Guidelines for the Investigation and Management of Child Sexual Abuse* (Wellington: National Advisory Committee on the Prevention of Child Abuse, 1986).
18. ibid.
19. ibid.
20. ibid.
21. Judge Ken Mason, 'Report on Inquiry into and Review of the Case of [Mary A]', 12 May 1989.
22. ibid.
23. ibid.
24. ibid.
25. ibid.
26. ibid.
27. Robin Wilson, Acting Director-General DSW, letter to Michael Cullen, Minister of Social Welfare, 20 November 1989.
28. Lotteries Welfare Services Distribution Committee, and the Departments of Justice, Health, Education, Labour and Social Welfare.
29. Archibald Blair, *Accident Compensation in New Zealand* (Wellington: Butterworths, 1978).
30. Grahame Aldous and John Alder, *Applications for Judicial Review* (London: Butterworths, 1985). Michael Supperstone and James Goudie, *Judicial Review* (London: Butterworths, 1992).
31. Accident Rehabilitation and Compensation Insurance Act 1992, s. 5 (10) (a). Lynda Angus, interview, ACC, 13 March 1997.
32. Lynda Angus, audiotaped interview, ACC, 26 November 1996.
33. ibid.
34. H v ACC (1980) ACC report, Nov–Dec 1980.
35. Susan Andrews, 'Accident Compensation', YWCA *'Rape and Sexual Assault of Women and Children'* Conference Report (Wellington: YWCA, 1983).
36. 'Survivors of Sexual Assault' (pamphlet) (Wellington: ACC, 1987).
37. Working Party on the Funding of Sexual Abuse Counselling Services: Phase One Report (Wellington: Interdepartmental

Working Party on the Funding of Sexual Abuse Services, July 1989).
38. ACC reports, 1985–1992.
39. *Working Party on the Funding of Sexual Abuse Counselling Services: Phase One Report* (Wellington: Interdepartmental Working Party on the Funding of Sexual Abuse Services, July 1989). 'Outrage as ACC Axes Payments', *Dominion*, 23 December 1988. *DSAC Newsletter*, February 1989.
40. Jeff Chapman, 'Accident Rehabilitation and Compensation Insurance Regulations: Counselling Services'. A submission to the Cabinet Committee on the Implementation of Social Assistance Reforms, 11 September 1992.
41. L. Briggs, National President NZAWS, letter to Michael Cullen, Minister of Social Welfare, 8 March 1990; J. Dugdale, Council Chairperson, NZCCP, letter to Helen Clark, Minister of Health and others, 4 December 1989; R. Hewland, Southern Regional Specialist Services Unit, DSW, letter to A. Dixon, Working Party on Funding Sexual Abuse Counselling, 12 December 1989.
42. Jeff Chapman, 'Accident Rehabilitation and Compensation Insurance Regulations: Counselling Services'. A submission to the Cabinet Committee on the Implementation of Social Assistance Reforms, 11 September 1992.

3.ii: *Crimen Exceptum* (pages 88–105)

1. *Guidelines for the Investigation and Management of Child Sexual Abuse* (Wellington: National Advisory Committee on the Prevention of Child Abuse, 1986).
2. Geoffrey Palmer, Minister of Justice, letter to Michael Cullen, Minister of Social Welfare, 7 November 1988.
3. Geoffrey Palmer, *Unbridled Power* (Auckland: Oxford University Press, 1979). Geoffrey Palmer, *New Zealand's Constitution in Crisis* (Dunedin: McIndoe, 1992).
4. Hansard, 13 December 1988.
5. Hansard, 7 November 1989.
6. Bernard Robertson, 'Expert Evidence in Child Sex Abuse Cases: A Comment', *NZ Law Journal*, May 1989. J. Gibson, 'Child Sexual Abuse', *NZ Law Journal*, August 1989. G. Vignaux and B. Robenson, 'Authorising Irrelevance? Evidence Act 1908, section 23G(2)(c)', *Family Law Bulletin* 67, 1990.
7. David Geddis and others, *A Private or Public Nightmare?* (Wellington: Advisory Committee on the Investigation, Detection and Prosecution of Offences Against Children, 1988).
8. Universal Declaration of Human Rights, United Nations, 1948.
9. The United Nations Covenant on Civil and Political Rights was agreed upon in 1966. After being ratified by the required 35 states it became international law in 1976.
10. Official Information Act, 1982. Summary Proeedings Act, 1957. *Commissioner of Police* v *Ombudsman*, 1 NZLR 397 [1988].
11. Keith Cronshaw, 'How Roger Almost Became a Victim', *Star*, 3 March 1989.
12. Evidence Amendment Act 1989, s. 23G(2)(a)(b)(c).
13. Evidence Amendment Act 1989, s. 23H(a)(b)(c).
14. David Geddis and others, *A Private or Public Nightmare?* (Wellington: Advisory Committee on the Investigation, Detection and Prosecution of Offences Against Children, 1988).
15. *R* v *Falwasser* [1992] unreported; *R* v *M* [1994] unreported; *R* v *E*, 7CRNZ351.
16. *R* v *Accused* [1992] 1 NZLR 385.
17. ibid.
18. Rossell Robbins, *The Encyclopedia of Witchcraft and Demonology* (New York: Crown, 1974).
19. 'The Position of Young Witnesses in Cases Involving a Sexual Offence', NZ Criminal Law Committee, 1977. 'Ought there to be an alternative procedure to calling child victims of sexual offences as witnesses in the trial of the accused person?' Background paper to the 1977 Criminal Law Reform Committee.
20. NZ Criminal Law Reform Committee, 'The Position of Young Witnesses in Cases Involving a Sexual Offence', 1977.
21. *R* v *Lewis*, 1 NZLR 409 [1991].
22. *R* v *Accused* (CA 449/91) 12 March 1992, unreported. *R* v *Neho* (CA 343/92), 27 November 1992,' unreported.
23. *R* v *B* [1987] 1 NZLR 362.
24. *R* v *Accused* [1989] 1 NZLR 715.
25. *R* v *Tait* [1992] 2 NZLR 666.

Chapter 4: Christchurch Possessed
4.i: The Place (pages 106-109)

1. Judith Devaliant, *Kate Sheppard* (Auckland: Penguin, 1992). Stevan Eldred-Grigg, *A New History of Canterbury* (Dunedin, McIndoe, 1982).
2. Ruth and Brian Manchester, *Notes Towards a History* (Wellington: NZ Association of Psychotherapists, 1996). Maurice Bevan-Brown, *The Sources of Love and Fear* (Christchurch: Raven, 1950).
3. Brian Harmer, 'Another Hung Jury', WSYWYG New Zealand News, 16 October 1995. Gay Oakes, *Decline into Darkness* (Auckland: HarperCollins, 1997).
4. Michelle Smith and Lawrence Pazder, *Michelle Remembers* (London: Joseph, 1980).
5. Debbie Nathan and Michael Snedeker, *Satan's Silence* (New York: BasicBooks, 1995).
6. Pamela Hudson, *Ritual Child Abuse* (Saratoga CA: R&E, 1991).

4.ii: The Fever (pages 110-120)

7. A. Jack, 'Child Health Clinics', in S. Havill and D. Mitchell (eds), *Issues in NZ Special Education* (Auckland: Hodder & Stoughton, 1972). There were no child psychiatric in-patient units in public hospitals, and child psychiatry was not covered by private health insurance.
8. 'To Cure the Child, Treat the Parent', *The Press*, 8 March 1974.
9. ibid.
10. *R v Accused* 11 CRNZ 189.
11. Confidential audiotaped interview, 25 April 1996.
12. Karen Zelas, *R v Ellis* [1993] p. 385: 'I have done no research in memory other than reading other people's research.' A search of medical, legal and current affairs databases revealed one book review, one letter to the editor and five articles by Karen Zelas: 'Toward prevention of child abuse in New Zealand', *Community Mental Health in NZ*, 1 (1) 1984; 'Community based treatment for intrafamilial child sexual abuse', *Community Mental Health in NZ*, 3 (2) 1987; 'Incest: A problem of major proportions', *Australian Patient Management*, 11 (8) 1987; 'Comments on the limits of s. 29$_A$ reports in custody hearings', *Butterworths Family Law Journal*, 1 (9), 1995; 'Sex and the doctor-patient relationship', *NZ Medical Journal*, 110 (1038) 1997.
13. Philip Jenkins, *Intimate Enemies* (Hawthorne NY: Gruyter, 1992).
14. Philip Jenkins, *Intimate Enemies* (Hawthorne NY: Gruyter, 1992). 'To Cure the Child, Treat the Parent', *The Press*, 8 March 1974.
15. 'Day-care Centres "Impossible Task"', *The Press*, 10 June 1974.
16. Director of Medical Services Address, Report of the 49th General Conference, Plunket Society, 1988.
17. Director of Medical Services, *Annual Report of the Council 1976-77* (Dunedin: Plunket Society, 1977).
18. 'Much Work Still Needed in Study of Child Abuse', *The Press*, 14 March 1979.
19. 'Where to Go for Help', *The Press*, 24 June 1984.
20. Miriam Saphira, 'Save the Children', *Broadsheet*, Auckland, Jan/Feb 1983.
21. 'Incest Survivors Healing Each Other', *The Press*, 21 June 1984. YWCA *'Rape and Sexual Violence to Women and Children' Conference Report*, Wellington, 1983. 'Too Close to Home', *Broadsheet*, July/Aug 1983.
22. Lynda Morgan, 'The Incest Survivors Group', *Broadsheet*, July/Aug 1983. 'Setting up an Incest Survivors Group', YWCA *'Rape and Sexual Violence to Women and Children' Conference Report*, Wellington, 1983.
23. 'Too Close to Home', *Broadsheet*, July/Aug 1983.
24. 'Lawyer Wants Reporting of all Child Abuse, Neglect', *The Press*, 20 May 1983.
25. Eileen Swan, 'Practical Steps for Dealing with Child Sexual Abuse', in Max Abbott (ed.), *Child Abuse Treatment and Prevention* (Auckland: Mental Health Foundation, 1985).
26. Confidential audiotaped interview, 4 December 1996.
27. Confidential audiotaped interview, 30 May 1996.
28. *Family Violence Conference Report 24th-27th September 1985* (Porirua: NZ Police College, 1985).
29. Les Ding, *Report of an Internal Inquiry into the Role and Function of Ward 24 Christchurch Hospital* (Christchurch: Canterbury Hospital

Board, 1989). Medical Council PPC report on complaints against Dr D. Espie, 10 July 1996.
30. Les Ding, *Report of an Internal Inquiry into the Role and Function of Ward 24 Christchurch Hospital* (Christchurch: Canterbury Hospital Board, 1989).
31. 'Too Close to Home', *Broadsheet*, July/Aug 1983.
32. Margaret Tennant, *Children's Health, the Nation's Wealth* (Wellington: BWB, 1994).
33. Dr D. Espie, Response to Medical Council PPC Complaints, 1995.
34. Confidential audiotaped interview, 4 September 1996.
35. Confidential audiotaped interview, 9 April 1996.
36. Confidential audiotaped interview, 4 December 1996.
37. *List of Participants*, 6th International Congress on Child Abuse and Neglect, Sydney, Australia, 11–14 August 1986.
38. *Programme*, 6th International Congress on Child Abuse and Neglect, Sydney, Australia, 11–14 August 1986.
39. David Finkelhor and others, *Nursery Crimes* (Newbury Park CA: Sage, 1988). Finkelhor was researching this book at the time of the Sydney conference.
40. Debbie Nathan and Michael Snedeker, *Satan's Silence* (New York: BasicBooks, 1995).
41. ibid.
42. Debbie Nathan and Michael Snedeker, *Satan's Silence* (New York: BasicBooks, 1995). 'Virginia McMartin Dead at 88: Grandmother Cleared in Molestation Case Dies', Associated Press, 19 December 1995.
43. Rt Hon Lord Justice Buder-Sloss DBE, *Report of the Inquiry into Child Abuse in Cleveland 1987* (London: HM Stationery Office, 1988)

4.iii: The Epidemic (pages 120-139)

1. 'Garden of Remembrance', *The Press*, 24 September 1987.
2. CPT members, audiotaped interviews, 9 April 1996, 12 June 1997, 26 February 1998.
3. Les Ding, *Report of an Internal Inquiry into the Role and Function of Ward 24 Christchurch Hospital* (Christchurch: Canterbury Hospital Board, June 1989). Dr William Watkins, Ward 24, Christchurch Hospital, 'Working Party's Submission on the Children and Young Person's Bill', personal submission, 11 February 1988.
4. Les Ding, *Report of an Internal Inquiry into the Role and Function of Ward 24 Christchurch Hospital* (Christchurch: Canterbury Hospital Board, June 1989).
5. 'Dramatic Increase in Child Abuse', *The Press*, 17 July 1987. 'Sixty Child Abuse Cases – Police', *The Press*, 18 July 1987. 'Incest Diversion a Likely Solution?', *The Press*, 1 August 1987. William Watkins, 'Children and Young Persons Bill: Personal Submission', Christchurch, 5 May 1987. 'Child Abuse Tragedy Feared', *The Press*, 30 December 1987.
6. Affidavit of Madeleine Harrison, 13 October 1995. *DSW* v *Mr & Mrs C* [1988]. Dianne Espie to Rob Harley, TVNZ *Assignment*, 26 April 1995. Notes taken at court hearing, *DSW* v *Mr & Mrs C* [1988].
7. Alan Fort, letter to Jim Gerard MP, undated [approx July 1989]. Mr B, letter to his lawyer, 5 July 1987.
8. Alan Fort, letter to Jim Gerard MP, undated [approx July 1989].
9. Dianne Espie, 'Response to PPC Complaints', 1995.
10. Paper IV, 'Medical Diagnosis and Examination', s. 5.2, *Guidelines for the Investigation and Management of Child Sexual Abuse*, National Advisory Committee on the Prevention of Child Abuse, 1986.
11. Grant Gillett, audiotaped interview, 17 February 1998.
12. Paper IV, 'Medical Diagnosis and Examination', s. 10.5, *Guidelines for the Investigation and Management of Child Sexual Abuse*, National Advisory Committee on the Prevention of Child Abuse, 1986.
13. S. Jean Emans and others, 'Genital findings in sexually abused, symptomatic and asymptomatic girls', *Paediatrics*, 79 (1987). (Emans's work challenging the 4mm rule was well known by the time it was published [personal communication, D. Nathan].) Astrid Heger and Bruce Woodling, 'The use of the colposcope in the diagnosis of sexual abuse in the pediatric age group', *Child Abuse*

and Neglect, 10 (1986). S. Ladson and others, *American Journal of Diseases of Children*, 141 (April 1987). Astrid Heger and S. Jean Emans, 'Introital Diameter as the Criterion for Sexual Abuse', *Pediatrics*, 85 (1990).

14. Anna C, Medical Report, Glenelg Health Camp, 22 June 1987. A. Berenson and others, 'Appearance of the hymen in newborns', *Pediatrics*, 1001 (1987). C. Jenny and others, 'Hymens in newborn female infants', *Pediatrics*, 80 (1987).
15. Herbert Kean, Report on the case of Anna C, undated [aprox 1995].
16. Dianne Espie, 'Response to PPC Complaints', 1995.
17. Anna C, statement, Medical Council PPC Complaint, 1995.
18. Trish Ross, social worker, DSW notes: TR: HL 5–13 July 1987.
19. Anna C, statement, Medical Council PPC Complaint, 1995.
20. Trish Ross, DSW, notes of visit to C home, 25/8/87.Transcript of evidence, *DSW v Mr & Mrs C*, 3 and 4 February 1988.
21. Anna C, DSW file.
22. Suzi Hall, DSW, memo re Anna C to Paul Muir, Senior Social Worker, Child Abuse Team, 8 January 1988. *DSW v Mr & Mrs C*, transcript of evidence, 3 and 4 February 1988.
23. *DSW v Mr & Mrs C*, 1988. Mr C, audiotaped interview, 16 June 1997.
24. DSW report, 7 July 1993. Anna C, statement, Complaint to Medical Council PPC, 1995.
25. START information leaflet for mothers, undated.
26. ibid.
27. ibid.
28. Keith Cronshaw, 'Child Abuse: Giving Evidence Another Ordeal', *Christchurch Star*, 14 November 1987.
29. ibid.
30. Ms E, Complaint to Jim Gerard MP, 1989.
31. 'Child Abuse Team Desperate for Funds', *Christchurch Star*, 27 August 1988.
32. Cate Brett, 'Review of Child Porn Ring Probe Ordered', *Christchurch Star*, 13 April 1989.
33. B. Walker and M. Steeman, 'Cult Groups Could Not Remain Hidden', *Christchurch Star*, 3 September 1991.
34. Theodor Adorno, *The Authoritarian Personality* (New York: Harper, 1950).
35. Cate Brett, 'The Nightmare of Child Abuse', *Christchurch Star*, 1 October 1988. Cate Brett, 'Group Identifies Child Abusers', *Christchurch Star*, 26 August 1988.
36. Cate Brett, 'Sex Abuse Inquiry Rejected', *Christchurch Star*, 29 March 1989.
37. Les Ding, *Report of an Internal Inquiry in the Role and Function of Ward 24 Christchurch Hospital* (Christchurch: Canterbury Hospital Board, June 1989).
38. Jim Gerard MP, letter to Michael Cullen, Minister of Social Welfare, 17 November 1988.
39. Madeleine Harrison (former Glenelg manager), letter to G. Phipps, 6 October 1995. Dianne Espie, letter to Medical Council, 12 August 1996.
40. *Frontline*, TV1, 13 April 1989.
41. Rosemary McLeod, 'A Public and Private Nightmare', *North & South*, July 1989.
42. ibid.
43. Paper III, Interviewing and Therapy, s. 3.3, *Guidelines for the Investigation and Management of Child Sexual Abuse*, National Advisory Committee on the Prevention of Child Abuse, Wellington, 1986.
44. Rosemary McLeod, 'A Public and Private Nightmare', *North & South*, July 1989.
45. *Frontline*, TV1, 13 April l989.
46. ibid.
47. ibid.
48. ibid.
49. ibid.
50. Rosemay McLeod, 'A Public and Private Nightmare', *North & South*, July 1989.
51. *Police v Mr & Mrs F*, 1989.
52. *DSW v Mr & Mrs G*, 1989.
53. ibid.
54. O. Udwin and others, 'Cognitive abilities and behavioural characteristics of children with idiopathic infantile hypercalcaemia', *Journal of Child Psychology and Psychiatry*, 28 (1987). H. Lenhoff and others, 'Williams Syndrome and the brain', *Scientific American*, December 1997. M. Davies and others, 'Adults with Williams Syndrome', *British Journal of Psychiatry*, 172 (1998).

55. *DSW* v *Mr & Mrs G*, 1989. Madeleine Harrison, 'Camp Manager's Report: Confidential', Glenelg Health Camp, 15 Sept 1987. (This report was not disclosed in the court proceedings.)
56. *DSW* v *Mr & Mrs G*, 1989.
57. Mr G, interview, 12 June 1997.
58. Child Protection Team Case Conference for Ben G Held at Ward 24 on 11/5/88 at 1.30 pm. (This document was not disclosed in the court proceedings.)
59. Mr and Mrs G, summons, 12 May 1998.
60. Police list of items removed from the home of Mr and Mrs G.
61. S.J. Hembrow (counsel for Mrs G), letter to Judge Ken Mason, 4 May 1989.
62. K.G. Hales (counsel for G children), letter to Registrar, District Court, Christchurch, 11 July 1988. C. Hood, DSW, letter to Housing Corp, Christchurch, 18 August 1988.
63. *DSW* v *Mr & Mrs G*, 1989.
64. Karen Zelas, report to Keith Hales, 24 July 1988.
65. Mr G, audiotaped interview, 12 June 1997.
66. *DSW* v *Mr & Mrs G*, 1989.
67. Cate Brett, 'The Tragic Case of Ben: Parents v Children v State', *Christchurch Star*, 28 March 1989.
68. Margaret Metherall, Brief of Evidence, *R* v *Mr H*, 1989.
69. '7 Years Jail on Child Sex Charges', *Christchurch Star*, 3 March 1989.
70. Cate Brett, 'Whichever Way You Look, He's a Loser', *Christchurch Star*, 28 March 1989.
71. Cate Brett, 'Abuse Victims Risk Return', *Christchurch Star*, 30 March 1989.
72. Rosemary McLeod, 'A Public and Private Nightmare', *North & South*, July 1989. Cate Brett, 'Sex Abuse Row: Innocents in a Sea of Fury', *Christchurch Star*, 24 April 1989.
73. George Balani interview with J. Bolger, Leader of the Opposition, ZB Network, 7 December 1989.

4.iv: The Ongoing Malaise (pages 139-150)

1. Tzvetan Todorov, *Facing the Extreme* (New York: Holt, 1996).
2. Lionel Penrose, *On the Objective Study of Crowd Behaviour* (London: Lewis, 1952).
3. Stanley Milgram, *Obedience to Authority* (New York: Harper & Row, 1974).
4. Tzvetan Todorov, *Facing the Extreme* (New York: Holt, 1996).
5. Judge Ken Mason, letter to Michael Cullen, Minister of Social Welfare 'Re: Mr and Mrs G', 12 May 1989. M. Steeman 'Recompense Urged for Families', *Christchurch Star*, 7 June 1989.
6. 'TV Item on Child Abuse Raises Ire', *The Press*, 15 April 1989. Cate Brett, 'Hospital Scapegoat, Says Child Specialist', *Christchurch Star*, 15 April 1989. 'Mistakes Small Price to Pay to Protect Children', *The Press*, 18 April 1989. Cate Brett, 'Child Abuse Expert Slams Frontline', *Christchurch Star*, 18 April 1989. Cate Brett, 'Frontline Impact Worries Prosecutor', *Christchurch Star*, 20 April 1989.
7. 'Doctors Fear Backlash from Reporting Child Abuse', *NZ Doctor*, 18 September 1989.
8. Cate Brett, 'Sex Abuse Row: Innocents in a Sea of Fury', *Christchurch Star*, 24 April 1989.
9. Cate Brett, 'Probe into Ward 24 Might be Widened', *Christchurch Star*, 22 April 1989.
10. Grant Gillett, audiotaped interview, 6 May 1988.
11. Judge Silvia Cartwright, *The Report of the Cervical Cancer Inquiry* (Committee of Inquiry into Allegations Concerning the Treatment of Cervical Cancer at National Women's Hospital and into Other Related Matters), Auckland, 1988.
12. Dr Les Ding, *Report of an Internal inquiry into the Role and Function of Ward 24 Christchurch Hospital* (Christchurch: Canterbury Hospital Board, 1989).
13. ibid.
14. Dr Brian Craig (acting director of Ward 24 during Dr Bill Watkins' 1989 study leave), audiotaped interview, 24 June 1997. Dr Les Ding, *Report of an Internal Inquiry into the Role and Function of Ward 24 Christchurch Hospital* (Christchurch: Canterbury Hospital Board, 1989). Ward 24 therapist, audiotaped interview, 28 August 1997.
15. Sydney Bloch and Paul Chodoff, *Psychiatric Ethics* (New York: Oxford, 1981).
16. Alan Goldman, *The Moral Foundations of Professional Ethics* (Totowa NJ: Rowman and Littlefield, 1980).

17. Sydney Bloch and Paul Chodoff, *Psychiatric Ethics* (New York: Oxford, 1981).
18. Royal Australian and New Zealand College of Psychiatrists Code of Ethics, August 1992.
19. Minister of Social Welfare, 'Sex Abuse Review – Judge Appointed', news release, 31 March 1989.
20. Cate Brett, 'Cullen Orders Case Reviews', *Christchurch Star*, 28 March 1989. Cate Brett, 'Cullen Seeks Court Leave', *Christchurch Star*, 15 April 1989. 'TV Item on Child Abuse Raises Ire', *The Press*, 15 April 1989. 'Welfare Sees No Need for Apology', *Dominion Sunday Times*, 2 April 1989. Cate Brett, 'Sex Abuse Inquiry Rejected', *Christchurch Star*, 29 March 1989.
21. Michael Cullen, 'Instrument of Direction (under Section 5 of the Department of Social Welfare Act 1971)', 11 April 1989.
22. Judge Ken Mason, 'Report of Inquiry into and Review of the Case of Mary A', 12 May 1989.
23. Judge Ken Mason, letter to Michael Cullen, 'Re: Mr and Mrs G', 12 May 1989.
24. Hansard, 27 April, 16 May 1989. Children, Young Persons and Their Families Act, 1989.
25. Judge Ken Mason, report to J. Grant, Director-General DSW, 13 November 1989.
26. Judge Ken Mason, letter to J. Gerard MP, 14 February 1990.
27. Judge Ken Mason, letter to Michael Cullen, Minister for Social Welfare, 8 October 1990.

Chapter 5: And a Little Child Shall Mislead Them

5.I: Enter The Devil (pages 151–165)

1. 'Doctors Fear Backlash from Reporting Child Abuse', *NZ Doctor*, 18 September 1989. P. Spier, *Convicting and Sentencing of Offenders in New Zealand* (Wellington: Ministry of Justice, November 1995).
2. Justice Holland, sentencing remarks, *R v Mr N*, 30 April 1991.
3. Sylvia Ashton-Warner, *I Passed this Way* (New York: Knopf, 1979).
4. 'Sex Offences Bring Jail', *The Press*, 1 May 1991. Barry Clarke, 'Sex-case School Wants Tougher Hiring Rules', *The Press*, 1 May 1991.
5. Confidential interview, 13 June 1998. Teacher's deposition, 30 January 1991. Confidential interview, 7 June 1998. Detective Ken Legat, deposition, 15 March 1991. M. McConnell, affidavit, 27 March 1991.
6. Chairman, School Board of Trustees, deposition, 14 February 1991.
7. Detective Ken Legat, deposition, 15 March 1991.
8. Report on Mr N, 30 November 1990.
9. Barry Clarke, 'Sex-case School Wants Tougher Hiring Rules', *The Press*, 1 May 1991.
10. Detective Ken Legat, deposition, 15 March 1991.
11. Report on Mr N, 30 November 1990.
12. Teacher's deposition, 30 January 1991.
13. Steven, deposition, 15 March 1991.
14. *R v Mr N*, Indictment.
15. Report on Mr N, 29 April 1991.
16. Amanda Cropp, 'When the Enemy Emerges from Within', *Dominion Sunday Times*, 15 December 1991.
17. Mr Larch, fax to Alistair Graham, Christchurch City Council, 18 December 1991.
18. Jenny Long, *Dominion Sunday Times*, 1 September 1991.
19. Philip Jenkins, *Intimate Enemies* (New York: De Gruyter, 1992). Jeffrey Victor, *Satanic Panic* (Chicago: Open Court, 1993).
20. Pamela Klein, transcript of address 'Interviewing the multi-personality child', NZCSA Conference, May 1990.
21. 'Ritual Action Group' information in the booklet *Reach Out* (Wellington: FVPCC, 1991).
22. *Free to Fly*, two cassettes and booklet (Wellington: National Radio, 1990).
23. Barry Clarke, 'Photos Back Claim of Child Sex Ring', *The Press*, 27 April 1991. 'Child Sex Ring Inquiry on Hold', *The Press*, 30 April 1991.
24. Colin Beyer, 'Chairman's Review', *Report for the Period Ending 30 June 1991* (Wellington: ACC, 1991).
25. John Ralston Saul, *The Doubter's Companion* (Toronto: Penguin, 1994).
26. 'Former Auditor-general Found Guilty on 10 Counts', *Otago Daily Times*, 1 March 1997.
27. *COSA Newsletter*, 1994–98, Auckland.
28. Martin Van Beynen, 'Sorry Lies and Satanic Abuse,' *The Press*, 13 May 1995.
29. ibid.
30. ibid.

31. FVPCC Newsletter, December 1992. Alan Samson, 'Ritual Abuse Story Grows Even Stranger', *Sunday Times*, 28 November 1993. ACC grants to FVPCC: 87/88 $150,000, 88/89 $500,000 [minutes of FVPCC Special Meeting 22/23 February 1989]; 89/90 $300,000, 90/91 $200,000, 91/92 $150,000 [letter ACC Research Analyst to the author]. The February 1989 minutes note that, in addition to the grants, ACC provided FVPCC with 'public affairs-media skills ... fax, toll calls, printing, courier costs and person time. Estimated value $70,000'.
32. Alan Samson, 'Crimes in Ritual Sex Abuse Unit Suspected', *Sunday Times*, 2 January 1994. 'Gresham Rejects Police Claims', *Dominion*, 3 January 1994. Alan Samson, 'Welfare Group Spent Lavishly', *Dominion*, 5 April 1994. Alan Samson, 'Ritual Sex, Baby Death Claim Linked to Welfare', *Sunday Times*, 28 November 1993. 'Ritual Abuse Story Grows Ever Stranger', *Sunday Times*, 28 November 1993.
33. Proceedings, *Family Violence: Prevention in the 1990s*. 1–6 September 1991, Christchurch (Wellington: FVPCC, 1991).
34. 'Ritual Sex Attacks', *Sunday Star*, 1 September 1991.
35. Jenny Long, 'Satanic Curses', *Sunday Times*, 1 September 1991. Martin Van Beynen, 'Floodgates to Open on Abuse', *The Press*, 4 September 1991. 'Satanic Sexual Torture More Than a Nightmare', *Evening Post*, 3 September 1991.
36. D. Newnham and C. Townsend, 'Pictures of Innocence', *Guardian*, 13 January 1996.
37. Lionel Penrose, *On the Objective Studies of Crowd Behaviour* (London: Lewis, 1952).
38. 'Child's Play', *60 Minutes*, TV3, 1 September 1991.
39. Melanie Reid, audiotaped interview, 14 December 1997.
40. 'Child's Play', *60 Minutes*, TV3, 1 September 1991.
41. Melanie Reid, audiotaped interview, 14 December 1997.
42. 'Child's Play', *60 Minutes*, TV3, 1 September 1991.
43. Melanie Reid, audiotaped interview, 14 December 1997.

5.ii: A Model for Early Childhood Education (pages 166–179)

1. Debbie Nathan and Michael Snedeker, *Satan's Silence* (New York: BasicBooks, 1995). Editorial, 'Justice for the Amiraults', *Wall St Journal*, 30 August 1995.
2. David Finkelhor and others, *Nursery Crimes* (Newbury Park CA: Sage, 1988).
3. J. Earl, 'The Dark Truth About the "Dark Tunnels of McMartin"', *Issues in Child Abuse Accusations*, 7 (1995).
4. David Finkelhor and others, *Nursery Crimes* (Newbury Park CA: Sage, 1988).
5. *Child Abuse and Neglect*, 15 (1991).
6. H. Cook, *Mind that Child* (Wellington: Blackberry, 1985).
7. ibid.
8. 'Day-Care Centre Plan for University Site', *The Press*, 16 December 1975. 'Modern New Child Care Centre', *The Press*, 19 December 1975. 'New Child Care Centre Opens Today', *The Press*, 9 November 1976. 'Child-Care Centre Opened', *The Press*, 11 November 1976. 'No Aid for Child Care', *The Press*, 16 September 1977.
9. 'Child-care Policy Lack Deplored', *The Press*, 13 October 1977.
10. Brochure for parents, Civic Child Care Centre, 1989.
11. Minutes of staff meetings, Civic Child Care Centre, 28 January and 25 February 1991.
12. Staff briefs of evidence, Civic Child Care Centre, *Davidson & Others v Christchurch City Council*. Ellis file, Christchurch City Council.
13. S. Hagley DSW, letter to John Gray, Christchurch City Council, 1 June 1991.
14. Supervisor's report, Civic Child Care Centre, 31 July 1986. Sharleen, audiotape interview, 5 March 1996. Kath Hollobon, Christchurch College of Education, letter to Administration Board Manager, Christchurch City Council, 24 April 1991.
15. David Close, audiotaped interview, 4 August 1997.
16. Pauline, audiotaped interview, 20 September 1995.
17. Susannah, audiotaped interview, 20 September 1995.
18. R. Davidson, conversation, 4 March 1996.

19. Bruce Ansley, 'Judgment in Christchurch', *NZ Listener*, 10 July 1993. Byron, audiotaped interview, 24 October 1996.
20. Ms Magnolia, statement, 26 October 1992.
21. Cate Brett, 'Beyond the Civic Crèche Case', *North & South*, September 1993. Bruce Ansley, 'Judgment in Christchurch', *NZ Listener*, 10 July 1993. Mr and Ms Sycamore, audiotaped interview, 6 March 1996.
22. Staff minutes, Civic Crèche, 1983–87; interviews with staff and parents.
23. Staff minutes, Civic Crèche, 14 February 1986.
24. Cate Brett, 'Beyond the Civic Crèche Case', *North & South*, September 1993.
25. Jan Buckingham, audiotaped interview, 8 November 1995. Sandi, audiotaped interview, 6 November 1995.
26. Mr and Ms Aspen, audiotaped interview, 5 March 1996.
27. Ministry of Education reference, 18 June 1990.
28. 'Members Mystified Over Plan to Quit Child Care', *The Press*, 10 April 1991. Management Committee files, Christchurch City Council and Civic Crèche, 1991.
29. Management Committee files, Christchurch City Council and Civic Crèche, 1991.
30. 'Members Mystified Over Plan to Quit Child Care', *The Press*, 10 April 1991.
31. Ms Rimu, audiotaped interview, 17 April 1997.
32. Susannah, audiotaped interview, 9 August 1995.
33. Ms Rimu, audiotaped interview, 17 April 1997.
34. Ms Sycamore, audiotaped interview, 6 March 1996.
35. Confidential audiotaped interview, 15 June 1998.

5.iii: Peter Ellis (pages 180–195)

1. Lesley Ellis, audiotaped interview, 28 October 1995. Peter Ellis, pre-sentencing report, 18 June 1993.
2. Peter Ellis, letter to Lynley Hood, 2 September 1998.
3. Minutes of staff meeting, Civic Child Care Centre, 18 August 1986.
4. John Jamieson, interview with Jenny Washington, Radio Rhema, 27 October 1992.
5. Supervisor's report, Civic Child Care Centre, 31 August 1986. Supervisor's report, Civic Child Care Centre, 30 September 1986.
6. Supervisor's report, Civic Child Care Centre, 15 September 1986.
7. Sandi, audiotaped interview, 4 November 1995.
8. Cate Brett, 'Beyond the Civic Crèche Case', *North & South*, September 1993.
9. Freda Briggs, 'South Australian Parents Want Protection Programs to be Offered in Schools and Preschools', *Australian Journal of Early Childhood*, February 1987.
10. Lucy Sullivan, 'Preventing Child Sexual Abuse: Whose Responsibility?', *Australian Journal of Early Childhood*, June 1990.
11. Unsigned and undated City Council memo, 'Peter Ellis: Employment at Civic Child Care', and in Police job sheet, Const Diane Smith, 14 April 1992.
12. This was confirmed by prison officers, and by people who visited and corresponded with Ellis following his imprisonment.
13. Davidson's discussion with the City Council personnel officer, notes, February 1991.
14. Sarah-Eve Farquhar, *A Few Good Men or a Few Too Many* (Palmerston North: Dept of Educational Psychology, Massey University, 1997).
15. Susannah, audiotaped interview, 20 September 1995.
16. Peter Ellis with Melanie Reid, videotaped interview, TV3, 1993.
17. ibid.
18. Sandi, audiotaped interview, 6 November 1995.
19. Supervisor's report, September 1988.
20. Ms Maple, audiotaped interview, 16 April 1997.
21. Peter Ellis with Melanie Reid, videotaped interview, TV3, 1993.
22. Ms Mahogany, audiotaped interview, 20 September 1995.
23. Mr Mahogany, audiotaped interview, 20 September 1995.
24. Mr and Ms Sycamore, audiotaped interview, 6 March 1996.
25. Ms Rimu, audiotaped interview, 17 April 1997.
26. Alistair Graham, Christchurch City Council, letter to Peter Ellis, 7 February 1989.
27. Peter Ellis, letter and conversation, September 1998.

28. Peter Ellis, letter to RJ, 30 November 1993.
29. Ms Rata, audiotaped interview, 17 September 1995.
30. Alison Mary, audiotaped interview, 20 September 1995.
31. Ms Rata, audiotaped interview, 17 September 1995.
32. ibid.
33. ibid.
34 Alison Mary, reference for Peter Ellis, 10 November 1991.

5.iv: The First Allegation (pages 195-207)

1. Wendy Ball, audiotaped interview, 17 November 1996.
2. Wendy Ball, 'Child Witnesses in Sexual Assault Cases: Issues of Credibility and Interviewing Practices', *Butterworths Family Law Journal*, September 1995; Wendy Ball, 'The Law of Evidence Relating to Child Victims of Sexual Abuse', *Waikato Law Review*, 3, (1995); Wendy Ball, 'The Last Decade: Issues for Children Testifying in the Criminal Justice System', *Second International Conference on Children Exposed to Family Violence* (London: Ontario, 1997). Wendy Ball, 'Comparison of Legal Processes: Australia and New Zealand: Mr Bubbles Case and *R v Peter Ellis*' (Christchurch Civic Crèche). 4th Annual Conference, AAT&D September 1995.
3. Roll Books, Civic Child Care Centre, 1989-90.
4. Gaye Davidson, audiotaped interview, 19 September 1995.
5. Suki, audiotaped interview, 8 March 1996.
6. Report, 1989. Confidential interview, August 1996. Mr and Ms Ash, notes and statements, August-December 1992.
7. Note on Peter Ellis's file, Christchurch City Council, 21 February 1991. Roll Book, Civic Child Care Centre, 1991.
8. Gaye Davidson, audiotaped interview, 19 September 1995.
9. ibid.
10. ibid.
11. Richard Kerr, 'The Lessons of Dr Browning', *Science*, 253 (1991).
12. Silvio Benaim and others, 'Hysterical Epidemic in a Classroom', *Psychological Medicine*, 3 (1973).
13. Rossanne Philen and others, 'Mass Sociogenic Illness by Proxy', *Lancet*, 9 December 1989. Simon Wessely and Christopher Wardle, 'Mass Sociogenic Illness by Proxy', *British Journal of Psychiatry*, 157 (1990).
14. Judith Mausner and Horace Gezon, 'Report on a Phantom Epidemic of Gonorrhea', *American Journal of Epidemiology*, 85 (1967).
15. Albert Hefez, 'The Role of the Press and the Medical Community in the Epidemic of "Mysterious Gas Poisoning" in the Jordan West Bank', *American Journal of Psychiatry*, 142 (1985). James Stewart, 'The West Bank Collective Hysteria Episode', *Skeptical Inquirer*, Winter 1991.
16. Karl Jaspers, *General Psychopathology*, 7th edn trans. by J. Hoenig and M. Hamilton (Manchester: Manchester University Press, 1962).
17. Ms Magnolia, statement, 26 October 1992.
18. Interview notes, August 1996.
19. X, audiotaped interview, 24 October 1996.
20. Roll Books, Civic Child Care Centre, 1989-1991. Ms Magnolia, statement, November 1991.
21. Details of source withheld to protect the anonymity of Ms Magnolia.
22. Ms Magnolia later claimed that her father died in April 1990, but his death was reported in April 1991 (details withheld to protect the anonymity of Ms Magnolia).
23. Minutes of staff meetings, Civic Child Care Centre, July and August 1991.
24. Discussion with Ellis, August 1996. Ms Magnolia, statement, November 1992.
25. Personal communication, 7 October 1992.
26. Richard Guilliatt, *Talk of the Devil* (Melbourne: Text, 1996). Morning Report, Radio NZ, 29 and 30 October 1991.
27. 'Tougher Porn Laws Sought', *The Press*, 5 November 1991.
28. William Birch, Minister of Labour, *Hansard*, 19 November 1991.
29. Gaye Davidson, audiotaped interview, 19 September 1995.
30. Barbara Newman, notes of meeting with Mr and Ms Magnolia, 20 November 1991. Audiotaped interview, 21 April 1997. Mr and Ms Magnolia, letter of complaint, 20 November 1991.

31. Ms Magnolia later claimed that the comment was made on 18 November, but in her original letter of 20 November she said that the comment was made 'on Sunday night', which was 17 November. Attendance Book, Civic Child Care Centre, 1991. Staff Register, Civic Child Care Centre, 1991.
32. Jan Buckingham, audiotaped interview, 8 November 1995.
33. Depositions evidence, *R v Ellis & Others*, 1992.

Chapter 6: A Complaint Has Been Made

6.I: The Scapegoat (pages 208–222)

1. James Frazer, *The Golden Bough, Part VI* (London: Macmillan, 1914).
2. Gordon Allport, *The Nature of Prejudice* (New York: Doubleday, 1948).
3. Sam Keen, *Faces of the Enemy* (San Francisco: HarperCollins, 1991).
4. Sharleen, audiotaped interview, 5 March 1996.
5. Sandi, audiotaped interview, November 1995.
6. Sharleen, audiotaped interview, 5 March 1996.
7. Sandi, audiotaped interview, 5 November 1995.
8. Jan Buckingham, audiotaped interview, 8 November 1995.
9. Chris Knight, audiotaped interview, 4 March 1996.
10. Christchurch City Council complaints procedures state: 'Notice must be given to the worker of the specific allegation of misconduct.'
11. Peter Lawson, Angela Counihan, audiotaped interview, 7 November 1995.
12. Peter Ellis, letter to Marshall Wright, 26 November 1991.
13. Sandi, audiotaped interview, 5 November 1995.
14. Debbie Gillespie, audiotaped interview, 6 December 1995.
15. Gaye Davidson, audiotaped interview, 19 September 1995.
16. Bruce Ansley, 'Judgment in Christchurch', *NZ Listener*, 10 July 1993. Education Review Office Report, Civic Child Care Centre, 25–29 November 1991.
17. Ms Arbutus, statement, 16 March 1992.
18. Ms Rata, audiotaped interview, 17 September 1995.
19. Handwritten report, November 1991.
20. Marshall Wright, handwritten notes, 25 November 1991.
21. Barbara Newman, memos, 25–26 November 1991.
22. Peter Lawson, fax to Chris Knight, 26 November 1991.
23. Chris Knight, letter to Mr and Ms Magnolia, 27 November 1991.
24. Colin Eade, police job sheet, 25 November 1991.
25. Melanie Reid, interview, *20/20*, 16 November 1997.
26. Barbara Newman, memo, 26 November 1991.
27. Gaye Davidson, audiotaped interview, 19 September 1995.
28. Barbara Newman, audiotaped interview, 21 April 1997.
29. Barbara Newman, memo, 27 November 1991.
30. ibid.
31. Barbara Newman, memo, 'Telephone call/discussion Colin Eade', 27 November 1991.
32. Barbara Newman, memo, 29 November 1991.
33. Alistair Graham, memo to Gaye Davidson, 28 November 1991.
34. Ms Jacaranda, audiotaped interview, 15 April 1997.
35. Management committee meeting, minutes, 20 November 1991.
36. Ms Gingko, audiotaped interview, 15 April 1997.
37. Ms Rowan, audiotaped interview, 17 April 1997; Mr Beech, audiotaped interview, 18 April 1997.
38. Mr Beech, audiotaped interview, 18 April 1997. Mr Larch, Ms Rowan, notes of meeting.
39. Mr Larch recorded this phrase, in quotation marks, in his notes of the meeting, and repeated it at a meeting with council staff next day. [Mr Larch, notes, 28 and 29 November 1991.]
40. Members of crèche management committee, audiotaped interviews, April 1997.
41. Ms Gingko, notes, 28 November 1991.
42. Ms Gingko, audiotaped interview, 15 April 1997.
43. Letter, *Sunday Times*, 18 July 1993.
44. Ms Linden, audiotaped interview, 4 March 1996. Mr and Ms Mahogany, audiotaped

interview, 20 September 1995.
45. Ms Cork, audiotaped interview, 2 November 1995.
46. Barbara Newman and Mr Larch, meeting notes, 29 November 1991.
47. Alistair Graham, audiotaped interview, 22 April 97.
48. Peter Lawson, audiotaped interview, 7 November 1995.
49. Rob Harrison, interview, 12 November 1996.
50. Confidential audiotaped interview, 1996.
51. Rob Harrison, interview, 12 November 1996.
52. 'New Group for Sex Abuse Victims', *Observer*, 2 December 1991.

6.ii: The Meeting Was Somewhat Volatile (pages 223-234)

1. Mr and Ms Sycamore, audiotaped interview, 6 March 1996.
2. Minutes of staff meeting, Civic Child Care Centre, 28 January 1991. Mr and Ms Ngaio, letter to Mayor of Christchurch, 1 May 1991; variations sent to: Leanne Dalzeil, Jim Anderton, Oscar Alpers, Rex Arbuckle, Morgan Fahey, Alex Clark. Attendance register, Civic Child Care Centre, May 1991.
3. Susannah, audiotaped interview, 20 September 1995.
4. *R v Ellis* [1993], trial transcript.
5. *Review of Sexual Abuse Investigation Policy and Evidential Interviewing Guidelines: Consultation with Service Providers* (Wellington: DSW, 5 March 1992).
6. Rob Dally's notes read: 'Sue Sidey: physical signs (rashes, abrasions); behavioural changes – reflected during play; interaction with other children/toys; verbal statements; oral sex with other children/toys; nightmares; clinginess; kids sworn to secrecy (gifts, lollies etc); "is there anyone at kindy you don't like?"'. Details of other aspects of Sidey's presentation are drawn from her own statements and recollections of her audience.
7. Ms Cedar, audiotaped interview, 13 November 1995.
8. Mr and Ms Sycamore, audiotaped interview, 6 March 1996.
9. ibid.
10. Ms Elm, audiotaped interview, 19 June 1996.
11. Ms Maple, audiotaped interview, 17 April 1997.
12. Mr and Ms Beech, audiotaped interview, 16 April 1997.
13. Ms Willow, audiotaped interview, 15 June 1998.
14. Mr and Ms Mahogany, audiotaped interview, 20 September 1995.
15. Ms Willow, audiotaped interview, 15 June 1998.
16. Ms Elm, audiotaped interview, 19 June 1996.
17. Rob Dally, notes of telephone conversation with Colin Eade, 13 December 1991.
18. 'Crèche for Inquiry', *The Press*, 3 December 1991. Transcript of news item, 91 FM, Christchurch, 4 December 1991.
19. Mr Larch, fax to Rob Dally, 4 December 1991.
20. Mr Larch, audiotaped interview, 18 October 1996.
21. Rob Dally, notes of telephone conversation with Sue Sidey, 4 December 1991.
22. Minutes, meeting on Civic Child Care Centre, 4 December 1991.
23. Martin Maguire, audiotaped interview, 22 April 1997.
24. Martin Maguire, memo, 'Civic Child Care Centre: Counselling Options', 4 December 1991.
25. Alistair Graham, notes of meeting with Martin Maguire and Mr Larch, 10 December 1991.
26. Mr and Ms Palm, letter to Mr Larch, 12 December 1991.
27. Ms Rimu, audiotaped interview, 17 April 1997.
28. Date of meeting recorded in M. Wright's chronology of events, other details recalled by Martin Maguire and Peter Ellis.
29. Mr Larch, letter to Alistair Graham, 18 December 1991.
30. Mr Larch, covering note to draft of letter to Alistair Graham, 13 December 1991.
31. DSW Specialist Services Report, 22 December 1991.
32. Ms Rimu, audiotaped interview, 17 April 1997.
33. Susannah, audiotaped interview, 20 September 1995. Alistair Mary, audiotaped interview, 20 September 1995.
34. Colin Eade, letter to Rob Dally, 20 December 1991.
35. ibid.

6.iii: Reinstatement Is Not an Option (pages 234–244)

1. Peter Lawson, audiotaped interview, 7 November 1995.
2. John Gray, audiotaped interview, 16 April 1997.
3. Peter Lawson, audiotaped interview, 7 November 1995.
4. Alistair Graham, audiotaped interview, 22 April 1997.
5. Martin Maguire, audiotaped interview, 22 April 1997.
6. ibid.
7. Rob Dally, letter to Peter Ellis, 23 January 1992.
8. Tony Couch, audiotaped interview, 17 October 1996.
9. ibid.
10. Ms Rata, audiotaped interview, 17 September 1995.
11. Ms Kowhai, audiotaped interview, 4 August 1995.
12. Jan Buckingham, audiotaped interview, 8 November 1995.
13. Sandi, audiotaped interview, 12 November 1995.
14. *Police* v *Ellis & Others* [1992], depositions evidence.
15. Lynda Morgan, *Katie's Yukky Problem* (Auckland: Papers Inc., 1986).
16. Jan Hindman, *A Very Touching Book* (Durkee: McClure-Hindman, 1983).
17. Mr and Ms Palm, letter to Mr Larch, Marshall Wright, 12 December 1991.
18. Ms Lime, letter to Marshall Wright and Rob Dally, 22 December 1991.
19. Tony Couch, audiotaped interview, 17 October 1996.
20. John Gray, audiotaped interview, 16 April 1997.
21. Peter Ellis, videotaped interview with Melanie Reid, TV3, 1993.
22. Maggie Bruck and Stephen Ceci, for the Committee of Concerned Social Scientists, Amicus Brief, *New Jersey* v *Michaels*, 1994.
23. Draft 'Sexual Abuse Guidelines, Evidential interview' (Wellington: DSW, 1992).

6.iv The Police Investigation Has Been Reactivated (pages 244–266)

1. Ms Mulberry, letter to Peter Ellis, 30 January 1992.
2. Ms Mulberry, letter to Gaye Davidson, 30 January 1992.
3. Civic Child Care Centre records.
4. Ms Hawthorn, audiotaped interview, 3 February 1997. Jan Buckingham, audiotaped interview, 8 November 1995.
5. Ms Lacebark, statement, 21 April 1992.
6. Jan Buckingham, audiotaped interview, 8 November 1995. Susannah, audiotaped interview, 20 September 1995.
7. NZ Childcare Association Christchurch tutors, letter to Childcare administration, Christchurch City Council, 3 February 1992.
8. Rob Dally and Marshall Wright, notes of meeting with Tony Couch. Chris Knight, notes of telephone conversation with Tony Couch after meeting, 10 February 1992.
9. Ms Rowan, audiotaped interview, 17 April 1997.
10. Barbara Newman, notes of meeting 26 November 1991 between Mr and Ms Magnolia, Alistair Graham, Marshall Wright, Barbara Newman. Civic Child Care Centre Attendance Register, Big End, November–December 1991.
11. Mr and Ms Magnolia, letter to 'Gaye and the staff of the Civic', 10 February 1992.
12. Civic Child Care Centre Management Committee, draft notice to parents (1), 17 February 1992.
13. NIWAR, Daily Climatological Record, Christchurch, 1992.
14. Civic Child Care Centre Management Committee, draft notice to parents (2), 19 February 1992.
15. Mr Larch, audiotaped interview, 17 October 1996.
16. Civic Child Care Centre Management Committee, handnotes on draft notice to parents (2), 19 February 1992.
17. Mr Larch, audiotaped interview, 17 October 1996.
18. Ms Palm, statement, 13 April 1992.
19. Ms Holly, depositions evidence.
20. J. Money, e-mail, 30 January 1999.

21. M. Rimm, 'Marketing Pornography on the Information Superhighway', *Georgetown Law Journal*, 83 (1995).
22. David Finkelhor and others, *Nursery Crimes* (Newbury Park: Sage, 1989). 'Ritual Abuse' (a Ritual Action Group handout), Wellington, 1991. Kate Sheppard Women's Bookshop, personal communication, January 1999.
23. Pamela Hudson, *Ritual Child Abuse* (Saratoga CA: R&E, June 1991).
24. Sandi, audiotaped interview, 12 November 1992.
25. 'Questions for the Management Committee', Civic Child Care Centre staff, 26 February 1992.
26. Susannah, audiotaped interview, 20 September 1995.
27. Mike Doolan, audiotaped interview, 10 October 1997.
28. One of the child complainants at the depositions hearing made no disclosure in her videotaped interview. The charge did not form part of the case against Ellis at his trial.
29. J. Williamson, Oral Judgment (No.1) 22 March 1993. J. Williamson, Oral Judgment (No. 2) 25 March 1993.
30. *R v Ellis* [1994], 12 CRNZ 172.
31. Mike Doolan, audiotaped interview, 10 October 1997.
32. ibid.
33. Peter Ellis, notes during his trial.
34. Mr Larch, Report of Meeting held at the Christchurch City Council on Wednesday 4 March at 8.30 am.
35. Council officer, Martin Maguire, who visited Ellis daily during this period, and the friends and relative who supported him throughout the case, insist that he was never suicidal. A 1994 psychologist's report on Eade stated that he attempted suicide at age 16, and that in May 1992 he presented with 'clear suicidal ideation'.
36. Jan Buckingham, audiotaped interview, 8 November 1995.
37. Ms Kowhai, audiotaped interview, 4 August 1995.
38. ibid.
39. Susannah, audiotaped interview, 20 September 1995.

Chapter 7: Parents in Terror of Abuse Discovery

7.i: There Seemed to be No Logic to It (pages 267–282)

1. Tony Couch, interview, 17 October 1996.
2. Chris Knight, fax to District Superintendent, Central Police Station, Christchurch, 10 March 1992.
3. Roger Carson, letter to Chris Knight, 11 March 1992. Colin Eade, letter to Chris Knight, 16 March 1992.
4. Specialist Services Unit Update, Specialist Services Christchurch, 9 June 1992.
5. Trial transcript, *R v P. Ellis* [1993].
6. Sir Maurice Casey, *Garrow & Casey's Principles of the Law of Evidence* (Wellington: Butterworths, 1996).
7. Stephen Ceci and Maggie Bruck, *Jeopardy in the Courtroom* (Washington DC: APA, 1995).
8. 'Evidential Video Interviews Guidelines' (Draft), DSW, 8 October 1990. [The draft guidelines in use in 1994 contain the same recommendation.]
9. Mike Doolan, audiotaped interview, 10 October 1997.
10. Sue Sidey, audiotaped interview, 28 June 1997.
11. 'Ritual Abuse', Ritual Action Group, Wellington, 1991. Pamela Hudson, *Ritual Child Abuse* (Saratoga CA: R&E, 1991).
12. Sue Sidey, audiotaped interview, 28 June 1997.
13. Rob Harrison, letter to Colin Eade, 5 May 1992.
14. *Manual for the Medical Management of Child Sexual Abuse* (Wellington: DSAC, 1991).
15. Ms Cork, audiotaped interview, 2 November 1995.
16. Ms Lacebark's notes record that some of Kari's informal disclosures prior to that interview were made after a visit to the QE II pool. Pamela Hudson, *Ritual Child Abuse* (Saratoga CA: R&E, 1991).
17. Rosemary Smart, audiotaped interview, 14 June 1997.
18. Rosemary Smart, 'Expertosis: Is it Catching?', *Australia and New Zealand Family Therapy*, 15 (1994).
19. Rosemary Smart, audiotaped interview, 14 June 1997.

20. Alistair Graham, audiotaped interview, 22 April 1997.
21. Martin Maguire, audiotaped interview, 22 April 1997.
22. Rosemary Smart, audiotaped interview, 14 June 1997.
23. Sandi, audiotaped interview, 12 November 1995.
24. John Gray and Mr Larch, letter to present and former crèche parents, 20 March 1992.
25. 'Press release from Mr Peter Lawson, Secretary of the Southern Local Government Officers Union', 23 March 1992.
26. Grandma Magnolia, letter to Peter Lawson, 23 March 1992.
27. Chris Knight, fax to Detective Inspector Carson, 23 March 1992.
28. TVNZ network news, 23 March 1992. Trial transcript, *R v Ellis*.
29. Detective Inspector Broad, letter to Chris Knight, 23 March 1992.
30. Chris Knight, audiotaped interview, 4 March 1996.

7.ii: Peter Was as Good as Hung
(pages 283–299)

1. A. Nixon (for Director-General), 'Report to the Minister of Social Welfare', 29 November 1989.
2. Sue Sidey, Specialist Services Report on Kari Lacebark, 16 June 1992.
3. Sally Latham, memo, Christchurch City Council, 26 March 1992.
4. Colin Eade, 'Peter Hugh McGregor Ellis: Request for Official Information', N.Z. Police Report to Howard Broad, 19 March 1992. 'Cult Groups Could Not Remain Hidden', *Christchurch Star*, 3 September 1991.
5. Roger Carson, audiotaped interview, 11 March 1999.
6. Colin Eade, Report: Christchurch Civic Child Care Centre, investigation of sexual abuse, 19 March 1992.
7. *20/20*, TV3, 16 November 1997.
8. Martin Van Beynen, 'Support Grows for Ellis Inquiry', *The Press*, 21 November 1997. 'Crèche Cop Cleared by Top-level Inquiry', *Sunday News*, 14 June 1998.
9. James Millar, *Detective Colin Eade: Christchurch Civic Crèche Inquiry* (Christchurch: NZ Police, 30 March 1998).
10. ibid.
11. Confidential audiotaped interview, 9 April 1996.
12. James Millar, *Detective Colin Eade: Christchurch Civic Crèche Inquiry* (Christchurch: NZ Police, 30 March 1998).
13. Roger Carson, audiotaped interview, 11 March 1999.
14. John Ell, audiotaped interview, 26 February 1998.
15. ibid.
16. Ell took three months' leave. Then he returned gradually to a senior position in a suburban police station, beginning by working half an hour a day, and gradually building up to full time work. Then he suffered another collapse. When we met in 1998, he was employed in a relatively unstressful area of police work.
17. Roger Carson, written instruction to Brian Pearce, 24 March 1992. Brian Pearce, *Holmes*, TV1, 14 June 1993.
18. John Ell, audiotaped interview, 26 February 1998.
19. Christchurch City Council, minutes of meeting re 31 March meeting for crèche parents, 26 March 1992.
20. Rob Harrison, interview, 26 November 1996.
21. Jan Buckingham, audiotaped interview, 8 November 1995.
22. Rob Harrison, interview, 26 November 1996.
23. ibid.
24. TV1 news, 31 March 1992.
25. Ms Cedar, audiotaped interview, 13 November 1995.
26. Mr and Ms Sycamore, audiotaped interview, 6 March 1996.
27. Mr and Ms Mahogany, audiotaped interview, 20 September 1995.
28. Alistair Graham and Martin Maguire, audiotaped interview, 22 April 1997.
29. Mr Larch, audiotaped interview, 18 October 1996.
30. Mr and Ms Aspen, audiotaped interview, 5 March 1996.
31. Alistair Graham and Martin Maguire, audiotaped interview, 22 April 1997.
32. Ms Rimu, audiotaped interview, 17 April 1997.

33. Mike Doolan, audiotaped interview, 10 October 1997.
34. Rob Harrison, interview, 25 May 1996.

Chapter 8: The Whole Crèche Thing Has Blown Up

8.I: Anyone Who Has Concerns Should Get in Touch (pages 300–322)

1. Mr and Ms Mahogany, audiotaped interview, 20 September 1995.
2. Ms Elm, audiotaped interview, 19 June 1996.
3. Ms Willow, audiotaped interview, 15 June 1998.
4. *The Feeling Safe Programme* (Wellington: Child Alert Trust, 1990).
5. Ruth Corrin, interview, 3 April 1999.
6. Mike Doolan, audiotaped interview, 10 October 1997.
7. Robin Wilson, audiotaped interview, 29 August 1997.
8. *Analysis of Child Molestation Issues*, San Diego County Grand Jury, San Diego CA, 1994.
9. Ms Cedar, audiotaped interview, 13 November 1995.
10. Ms Willow, audiotaped interview, 15 June 1998.
11. Maryanne Garry and others, 'Imagination inflation: Imagining a childhood event inflates confidence that it occurred', *Psychonomic Bulletin and Review*, 3 (1996).
12. Karen Dawson (Timothy Cork's therapist), letter to Ms Cork.
13. Ms Willow, audiotaped interview, 15 June 1998.
14. *Assignment*, TVNZ, 1995.
15. *Analysis of Child Molestation Issues*, San Diego County Grand Jury, San Diego CA, 1994.
16. Ms Laurel, statement, 4 May 1992.
17. Kee MacFarlane, *Sexual Abuse of Young Children* (New York: The Guildford Press, 1986).
18. Ms Cypress, statement, 8 June 1992.
19. 'Hazy Memories of Chats with Children', *New York Times*, 23 March 1999.
20. Ms Hickory, statement, 26 July 1992.
21. Ms Dogwood, depositions evidence, 2 December 1992.

8.II: A Sustained Campaign of State-Funded Contamination of the Evidence (pages 322–337)

1. Peter Ellis, videotaped interview with Melanie Reid, TV3, April 1993.
2. ibid.
3. Rob Harrison, interview, 26 November 1995.
4. Nigel Hampton, audiotaped interview, 13 October 1997.
5. M, audiotaped interview, 19 June 1996.
6. Rob Harrison, interview, 26 November 1995.
7. Rob Harrison, letter to Colin Eade, 5 May 1992.
8. Justices of the Peace Amendment Act, 1912.
9. Annual Report of the Legal Aid Board on operations of the Legal Aid Act 1969 for the year ended 31 March 1973. 'Aid Pay Delay Leaves Lawyers Short', *The Press*, 9 July 1991. 'Legal Aid Excesses', *The Press*, 9 July 1991.
10. 'The New Legal Aid Regime', *New Zealand Law Society Seminar*, February–March 1992.
11. Rob Harrison, letter to Secretary, Canterbury Legal Services Board, 8 June 1992.
12. Memo, 'Application to fix/increase total remuneration (applied to applications in civil aid and referrals in criminals by registrars after aid granted)', Canterbury District Legal Services Committee.
13. Rob Harrison, letter to Secretary, Canterbury District Legal Services Committee, 11 August 1992.
14. Chris Knight, audiotaped interview, 4 March 1996.
15. M, audiotaped interview, 19 June 1996.
16. Gen Crossen, Counselling Support Coordinator's Report, 25 May to 19 June 1992.
17. Gaye Davidson, audiotaped interview, 19 September 1995.
18. Martin Maguire, audiotaped interview, 22 April 1997.
19. Counselling Coordinator's Report, 25 May to December 1992, Civic Crèche Enquiry.
20. Mr and Ms Sycamore, audiotaped interview, 6 March 1996.
21. Ms Rimu, audiotaped interview, 17 April 1997.
22. Mr and Ms Aspen, audiotaped interview, 5 March 1996.
23. DSW files: Crèche Investigation Expenses from 8/5/92 to 15/8/92; Brief Progress Report

on Role of Prosecution Support Social Worker, 7/9/92; Cost of Crèche Inquiry, 5/5/93.
24. DSW, Crèche Investigation Expenses from 8/5/92 to 15/8/92.
25. Gaye Davidson, audiotaped interview, 19 September 1995.
26. 'Seeking Evil', *California Lawyer*, July 1994.
27. Janet Biswell, CYPS, letter to Martin Maguire, Christchurch City Council, 30 September 1992. Prosecution Support Social Worker Progress Report, 8/9/92–20/12/92.
28. Jan Gillanders, Brief Progress Report on Role of Prosecution Support Social Worker, 7 September 1992.
29. Mr and Ms Sycamore, audiotaped interview, 6 March 1996.
30. Ms Linden, audiotaped interview, 4 March 1996.
31. Grandma Magnolia, letter to Vicki Buck, Mayor of Christchurch, 25 June 1992.
32. Rob Dally, audiotaped interview, 5 August 1997.
33. Alistair Graham, audiotaped interview, 22 April 1997.
34. Gaye Davidson, audiotaped interview, 19 September 1995.
35. Mr Larch, memo to Crèche Management Committee, 7 July 1992.
36. Mr Larch, letter to John Gray, 10 July 1992.
37. Civic Child Care Centre staff, letter to John Gray, 14 July 1992.
38. Mr Larch, letter to John Gray, 10 July 1992.
39. Kathleen Coulborn Faller, *Understanding Child Sexual Maltreatment* (Newbury Park: Sage, 1990).
40. Shona, audiotaped interview, 13 November 1995.
41. Sigrid, audiotaped interview, 7 November 1995.
42. Sandi, audiotaped interview, 12 November 1995.
43. Alistair Graham, audiotaped interview, 22 April l997.
44. Rosemary Smart, audiotaped interview, 14 June 1997.
45. Ms Linden, audiotaped interview, 4 March 1996.
46. Bruce, audiotaped interview, 6 March 1996.
47. Ms Magnolia, list of bizarre allegations, 1992.

8.iii: Concerns of Abuse by Other Crèche Staff (Totally Confidential) (pages 338–352)

1. Letter 'To whom it may concern', August 1989.
2. Ms Dogwood, statement, 16 October 1992. Mr Dogwood, statement, 25 June 1992.
3. Ms Dogwood, statement, 12 August 1992.
4. 'Joy Bander', *A Mother's Story* (Auckland: Howling at the Moon, 1997).
5. Sequence from parents' notes, statements and evidence.
6. John Ell, audiotaped interview, 26 February 1998.
7. Minutes of meeting, 12 August 1992.
8. Brian Pearce, audiotaped interview, 14 October 1997. Minutes of meeting, 12 August 1992.
9. Brian Pearce, audiotaped interview, 14 October 1997.
10. Karen Zelas, letter to John Ell, 28 August 1992.
11. Grace Todd, telephone conversation, 5 March 1998.
12. Interim Judgment of the Chief Judge, *Davidson & Others v Christchurch City Council*, [1995] 1 ERNZ 172.
13. ibid.
14. Judgment, Court of Appeal, *Christchurch City Council v Davidson & Others*, [1996] 2 ERNZ 1.
15. Janet Biswell, audiotaped interview, 25 February 1998.
16. John Ell, audiotaped interview, 26 February 1998.
17. Janet Biswell, audiotaped interview, 25 February 1998.
18. Bede Cooper and Grace Todd, audiotaped interview, 23 February 1998.
19. Brief of Evidence of John Gray, *Davidson & Others v Christchurch City Council*.
20. Bede Cooper and Grace Todd, audiotaped interview, 23 February 1998.
21. Michael Deaker, audiotaped interview, 15 July 1997.
22. E-mail, Peter Lawson, 29 May 1998.
23. John Ell, audiotaped interview, 26 February 1998.
24. Michael Deaker, audiotaped interview, 15 July 1997.
25. John Ell, audiotaped interview, 26 February 1998.

Chapter 9: They Were All Under Suspicion

9.i: It Was Like a Police State Thing Closing In (pages 353-366)

1. J. Gray, CV.
2. Peter Lawson, audiotaped interview, 7 November 1995.
3. Sigrid, audiotaped interview, 7 November 1995.
4. Susannah, audiotaped interview, 20 September 1995.
5. John Gray, confidential memorandum to mayor and councillors, 3 September 1992.
6. 'Anger Over Crèche Closing', *The Press*, 4 September 1992.
7. Police press release, 'Re: Cancellation of Civic Child Care Licence', 4 September 1992.
8. 'Staff in Tears Over Crèche Decision,' *The Press*, 5 September 1992.
9. Peter Lawson, audiotaped interview, 7 November 1995. Press release, 7 September 1992. John Gray, memorandum to staff of the Civic Child Care Centre, 7 September 1992.
10. Evidence of council staff in *Davidson & Others v Christchurch City Council*, C48/93.
11. John Gray, confidential memorandum to Cultural and Services Committee and council staff, 7 September 1992.
12. Mr Beech, audiotaped interview, 5 February 1997. Bede Cooper, Ministry of Education, notes of telephone conversation with Det. Sgt. Hardie, 22 September 1992.
13. Ms Hawthorn, audiotaped interview, 5 February 1997.
14. Tim Langley, Superintendent of Methodist Mission, press release, 11 September 1997.
15. Ms Maple, audiotaped interview, 18 April 1997.
16. Shona, audiotaped interview, 13 November 1995.
17. Sharleen, brief of evidence, *Davidson & Others v Christchurch City Council*, C48/93.
18. Peter Lawson, audiotaped interview, 7 November 1995.
19. Byron, audiotaped interview, 20 October 1996.
20. Ms Magnolia, statement, 14 September 1992.
21. Supervisor Crèche X, audiotaped interview, 28 August 1997.
22. Administrator Crèche X, notes September 1992.
23. Administrator Crèche X, notes September 1992; audiotaped interview, 13 June 1997.
24. Bruce, audiotaped interview, 6 March 1996.
25. Bede Cooper, notes of telephone conversation with Det. Sgt. Hardie, 22 September 1992.
26. Ms Kowhai, audiotaped interview, 4 August 1995.
27. Ms Macrocarpa, audiotaped interview, 3 March 1996.
28. Mr Macrocarpa, audiotaped interview, 3 March 1996.
29. Bernard, documentation 1992-95, audiotaped interview, 6 March 1996.
30. Jan Buckingham, audiotaped interview, 8 November 1995.
31. Peter Lawson, fax to Brian Pearce, 25 September 1992. Howard Broad, fax to Peter Lawson, 28 September 1992.
32. Peter Lawson, press release, 29 September 1992.
33. Susannah, audiotaped interview, 20 September 1995.

9.ii: Four Child Care Workers Arrested (pages 366-382)

1. Jan Buckingham, audiotaped interview, 8 November 1995.
2. Search warrant issued 30 September 1992. Identical search warrants were issued on all the crèche workers' homes.
3. Sigrid and Winston, audiotaped interview, 7 November 1995.
4. Shona, audiotaped interview, 13 November 1995.
5. Susannah, audiotaped interview, 20 September 1995.
6. Debbie Gillespie, audiotaped interview, 6 December 1995.
7. Nancy and Murray Gillespie, audiotaped interview, 15 November 1995.
8. Susannah, audiotaped interview, 20 September 1995.
9. Marie and Roger Keys, audiotaped interview, 8 November 1995.
10. Gaye Davidson, audiotaped interview, 19 September 1995.
11. Susannah, audiotaped interview, 20 September 1995.
12. Shona, audiotaped interview, 13 November 1995.

13. Nancy and Murray Gillespie, audiotaped interview, 15 November 1995.
14. Sigrid and Winston, audiotaped interview, 7 November 1995.
15. Jan Buckingham, audiotaped interview, 8 November 1995.
16. Ms Willow, audiotaped interview, 15 June 1998.
17. Ms Maple, audiotaped interview, 18 April 1997.
18. Ms Linden, audiotaped interview, 4 March 1996.
19. Ms Jacaranda, audiotaped interview, 15 April 1997.
20. Sharleen, audiotaped interview, 5 March 1996.
21. Sandi, audiotaped interview, 9 November 1995.
22. Ms Cedar, audiotaped interview, 13 November 1995.
23. Lesley Ellis, audiotaped interview, 28 October 1995.
24. Debbie Nathan and Michael Snedeker, *Satan's Silence* (New York: BasicBooks, 1995).

Chapter 10: Depositions
(pages 383–401)

1. Confidential audiotaped interview.
2. 'Mother Wanted Abuse Expert's Aid', *The Press*, 4 December 1992.
3. 'Children "Put Under Trapdoor", Former Crèche Staff Face Child Sex Abuse Charges', *The Press*, 3 November 1992.
4. Nancy and Murray Gillespie, audiotaped interview, 15 November 1995.
5. Jan Buckingham, audiotaped interview, 8 November 1995.
6. Gaye Davidson, audiotaped interview, 19 September 1995.
7. *End Ritual Abuse Newsletter*, June 1994.
8. Debbie Gillespie, audiotaped interview, 6 December 1995.
9. Bruce, audiotaped interview, 6 March 1996.
10. Alison Mary, audiotaped interview, 20 September 1995.
11. Prosecution Support Social Worker Progress Report, 8 September–20 December 1992. Family Violence Prevention Coordinating Committee, *Newsletter* 8, 1992.
12. Alistair Graham and Martin Maguire, audiotaped interview, 22 April 1997.
13. '500 Sexual Abuse Claims in a Week', *The Press*, 9 November 1992.
14. Ms Hawthorn, audiotaped interview, 5 February 1997.
15. Gerald Nation, evidence-in-chief, *Davidson & Others v Christchurch City Council*, Employment Court, March 1995.
16. Keith Le Page, evidence-in-chief, *R v Ellis*, 1993.
17. Gerald Nation, evidence-in-chief, *Davidson & Others v Christchurch City Council*, Employment Court, March 1995.
18. Ms Rata, audiotaped interview, 17 September 1995.
19. Rossell Robbins, *The Encyclopedia of Witchcraft and Demonology* (New York: Crown, 1974).
20. Sir Maurice Casey, *Garrow & Casey's Principles of the Law of Evidence* (Wellington: Butterworths, 1996).
21. ibid.
22. Gaye Davidson, audiotaped interview, 19 September 1995.
23. *W v Attorney-General* [1992] 8 CRNZ 427.
24. 'Crèche Workers Sent for Trial', *The Press*, 12 February 1993.
25. Rob Harrison, interview, 11 November 1996.

Chapter 11: Pre-Trial Manoeuvres
(pages 402–420)

1. *Prosecution Guidelines as at 09.03.92*, Crown Law Office, Wellington.
2. Where the evidence indicates that an offence occurred a number of times over a period, the Crown may lay a representative charge. However, no representative charges were laid in the crèche case. Each charge referred to one offence, albeit between widely spaced dates.
3. Crimes Act 1961, s. 329.
4. *Tuckerman v R* [1986] unreported.
5. Crimes Act 1961, s. 340.
6. Draft indictment, *R v Ellis and Others*, 5 March 1993.
7. *20/20*, TV3, 7 March 1993.
8. Melanie Reid, videotaped interviews with Peter Ellis, TV3, 1993.

9. Jan Gillanders, 'Prosecution Support Social Worker's Progress Report: 1–31 March 199.
10. 'Mothers of Abuse Victims to Air Feelings on Radio', *The Press*, 11 March 1993. 'Prevention of Child Abuse', *The Press*, 11 March 1993.
11. 'Requiem Mass for "Man of Compassion and Humility"', *The Press*, 20 February 1996.
12. 'Crèche Case Applications Begin', *The Press*, 19 March 1993.
13. Justice Williamson, Oral Judgment (No. 1), 22 March 1993.
14. ibid.
15. Justice Williamson, Oral Judgment (No. 2), 25 March 1993.
16. Justice Williamson, Oral Judgment (No. 3), 6 April 1993.
17. Martin Van Beynen, 'Child Care Trio Vow to Rebuild', *The Press*, 7 April 1993. 'Women Talk of Compo', 'Guilty Until Proven Innocent', *Dominion*, 7 April 1993.
18. Martin Van Beynen, 'Crèche Parents Call for Inquiry', *The Press*, 8 April 1993. Matt Conway, 'Court Gag on Crèche Four', *Sunday News*, 11 April 1993.
19. Martin Van Beynen, 'Crèche Inquiry Bill Likely to Top $1m', *The Press*, 10 April 1993. Martin Van Beynen, 'Mid-year Grievance Hearing Expected', *The Press*, 12 April l993. George Balani, 'What More is There to Say', *Sunday News*, 11 April 1993.
20. 'Crèche Case Media Breaches Alleged,' *The Press*, 16 April 1993. 'Civic Duty to Knock Over Crèche Accused', *The Press*, 24 April 1993.
21. Justice Williamson, Oral Judgment (No. 4), 20 April l993.
22. ibid.
23. ibid.
24. Justice Williamson, *R v Holdem* [1987] 3CRNZ, 103.
25. Justice Williamson, Oral Judgment (No. 4), 20 April l993.
26. Justice Williamson, *R v Ellis*, summing up, 3 June 1993.
27. Sharleen, audiotaped interview, 5 March 1996.
28. *NZ Truth*, 23 April 1993.
29. Justice Williamson, Oral Judgment (No. 5), 21 April 1993.
30. ibid.
31. Justice Williamson, Oral Judgments (No. 5) & (No. 6), 21 and 23 Apri11993.

Chapter 12: The Trial

12.i: The Beginning (pages 421–449)

1. Melanie Reid, TV3, videotaped interviews with Peter Ellis, May 1993.
2. *Rondel* v *Worsley* [1969] 1 AC 191.
3. Bruce Robertson (ed.), *Adams on Criminal Law* (Wellington: Brookers, 1998).
4. Justice Williamson, Oral Judgment (No. 5), 21 April 1993.
5. In the final indictment (but not in the draft indictments), Ellis was charged under s. 66 of the Crimes Act in relation to both the multi-perpetrator charges.
6. Confidential audiotaped interview, 9 April 1996.
7. ibid.
8. Justice Williamson, Direction to the Jury (No. 2), 5 May 1993.
9. Melanie Reid, TV3, videotaped interview with Peter Ellis, May 1993.
10. Sue Sidey, audiotaped interview, 28 June 1997.
11. 'JoyBander', *A Mother's Story* (Auckland: Howling at the Moon, 1997).
12. Justice Williamson, Oral Judgment (No. 5), 21 April 1993.
13. Justice Williamson, Direction to the Jury (No. 3), 6 May 1993.
14. Justice Williamson, Oral Judgment (No. 5), 21 April 1993.
15. Justice Williamson, Oral Judgment (No.16), 31 May 1993.
16. The 'recent complaint' rule, which allows evidence that the alleged victim of a sexual offence made a verbal complaint soon after the offence was alleged to have occurred.
17. Justice Williamson, Oral Judgment (No. 8), 5 May 1993.
18. Details of judgment withheld to protect the identity of Ms Dogwood.
19. Ms Dogwood, letter to Colin Eade, Rob Nicholl, John Ell and the Specialist Services Unit DSW, August 1992.
20. Justice Williamson, Oral Judgment (No. 9), 7 May 1993.
21. Justice Williamson, Oral Judgment (No. 5), 21 April 1993.

22. Sir Maurice Casey, *Garrow & Casey's Principles of the Law of Evidence* (Wellington: Butterworths, 1996).
23. Melanie Reid, TV3, videotaped interview with Peter Ellis, May 1993.
24. Justice Williamson, Oral Judgment (No. 11), 13 May 1993.
25. Melanie Reid, TV3, videotaped interview with Peter Ellis, May 1993.
26. Ms Rata, audiotaped interview, 17 September 1995.
27. Justice Williamson, Oral Judgment (No. 14), 26 May 1993.
28. Justice Williamson, Oral Judgment (No. 15), 27 May 1993.

12.ii: The End
(pages 449-469)

1. Preliminary Paper 37 – Vol 2, Warren Young and others, *Juries in Criminal Trials, Part 2*, Law Commission, November 1999. Sir Maurice Casey, *Garrow & Caseys Principles of the Law of Evidence* (Wellington: Butterworths, 1996).
2. Crèche grandparent, letter to Justice Williamson, 14 June 1993.
3. Ms Gingko, audiotaped interview, 15 April 1997.
4. L, telephone conversation, 12 May 1998.
5. Ms Mahogany, audiotaped interview, 20 September 1995.
6. Mr Mahogany, audiotaped interview, 20 September 1995.
7. Keith Le Page, letter to Paul East, 1 March 1995.
8. Ms Rimu, audiotaped interview, 17 April 1997.
9. Justice Joshua Strange Williams, *The Supreme Court Act Amendment Bill*, pamphlet, [n.p.] 1894.
10. 'Crèche Case Jury Still Out', *The Press*, 5 June 1993. Bruce Ansley, 'Judgment in Christchurch', *NZ Listener*, 19 July 1993.
11. *R v CS* [1993] 11 CRNZ 45.

Chapter 13: The Aftermath
13.i: The Tide Turns (pages 470-473)

1. Civic Child Care Inquiry Organisation, letter to Hon. Doug Graham, 24 May 1993.
2. Letters from members of the public to the Minister of Justice released under the Official Information Act.
3. Paul Holmes interview with Det. Insp. Brian Pearce, *Holmes*, TV1, 14 June 1993.
4. Letters from members of the public to the Minister of Justice released under the Official Information Act.
5. Attorney-General, letter to Civic Child Care Inquiry Organisation, 22 July 1993.
6. Minister of Justice, letter to Civic Child Care Inquiry Organisation, 6 July 1993.
7. Minister of Social Welfare, letter to Civic Child Care Inquiry Organisation, 6 July 1993.
8. Minister of Police, letter to Civic Child Care Inquiry Organisation, 1 July 1993.
9. Bruce Ansley, 'Judgment in Christchurch', *NZ Listener*, 10 July 1993. Cate Brett, 'Beyond the Civic Crèche Case', *North & South*, July 1993.
10. Gerald Nation, letter to Minister of Justice, 7 July 1993.
11. Gerald Nation, letter to Minister of Justice, 26 October 1994.

13.ii: The Women's Costs Application
(pages 473-476)

12. Costs in Criminal Cases Act, 1967. Justice Williamson, Costs Application Davidson & Others, unreported, 15 December 1993.
13. Memorandum of Counsel for Applicants, Costs Application Davidson & Others, 1993.
14. ibid.
15. Gerald Nation, interview, 4 August 1995.
16. Justice Williamson, Costs Application Davidson & Others, unreported, 15 December 1993.
17. 'Crèche Case Costs Move Rejected', *The Press*, 16 December 1993.
18. Gerald Nation, interview, 4 August 1995.

13.iii: The Nigel Hampton QC Appeal
(pages 476-478)

19. I.M. Richardson, President, CA, 'Criminal Appeals', Practice Notes, 1 January 1998.
20. Nigel Hampton, interview, 13 October 1997.
21. Rob Harrison, interview, 25 May 1996.
22. ibid.

13.iv: The Graham Panckhurst QC Appeal (pages 478-490)

23. Graham Panckhurst, interview, 17 November 1995.
24. ibid.
25. R v *Lewis*, 1 NZLR 409 [1991].
26. R v *Accused* (CA 449/91), judgment 12 March 1992, unreported.
27. R v *Tait* [1992] 2 NZLR 666.
28. Crown Book: the record kept by the registrar of the sequence of events in court (the verbatim transcript of evidence is recorded separately by a typist).

13.v: Graham Panckhurst QC Considers his Options (pages 490-494)

1. Graham Panckhurst, letter to Brent Stanaway, 12 September 1994.
2. *Nadan* v *R* [1926] AC 482.
3. Legal Services Act 1991, s. 4b.
4. Graham Panckhurst, letter to The Hon. Paul East, Attorney General, 22 February 1995.
5. R v *Ellis* [1994] 12 CRNZ 172.
6. John McGrath, letter to Graham Panckhurst, 15 March 1995.
7. John Upton, report to Lowell Goddard, 13 March 1995.
8. John McGrath, letter to Graham Panckhurst, 15 March 1995.

13.vi: *Davidson and Others* v *Christchurch City Council* (pages 494-504)

9. Peter Lawson, letter to John Gray, 28 September 1995.
10. Torn Weston, letter to Peter Lawson, 12 October 1995.
11. Peter Lawson, audiotaped interview, 7 November 1995.
12. *Hale & Son Ltd* v *Caretakers IUW* [1991] 1 NZLR 151.
13. Employment Contracts Act 1991.
14. Opening for the Applicants, *Davidson & Others* v *Christchurch City Council*. C 48/93.
15. ibid.
16. Supplementary Judgment, *Davidson & Others* v *Christchurch City Council* [1995] 1 ERNZ 532.
17. Opening submission of the Respondent, *Davidson & Others* v *Christchurch City Council*. C 48/93.
18. Tom Weston, audiotaped interview, 17 June 1998.
19. ibid.
20. Jo Appleyard, file note, 11 March 1995.
21. Bede Cooper, fax to Jan Breakwell, 7 March 1995. Jan Breakwell, interview, 15 June 1998.
22. Bede Cooper, Brief of Evidence (Appleyard version).
23. Bede Cooper, Brief of Evidence (McAteer version).
24. Jo Appleyard, file note, 11 March 1995.
25. Tom Weston, audiotaped interview, 17 June 1998.
26. Interim Judgment, *Davidson & Others* v *Christchurch City Council* [1995] 1 ERNZ 172.
27. 'Crèche Staff Win $1m Grievance Payout', *The Press*, 17 March 1995.
28. Supplementary Judgment of the Chief Judge, *Davidson & Others* v *Christchurch City Council* [1995] 1 ERNZ 532.
29. ibid.

13.vii: More Calls for an Inquiry (pages 504-509)

1. Member of the public, letter to Paul East, 14 June 1995.
2. 'Police Inquiry into Crèche Defended', *The Press*, 23 March 1995. 'Crèche Case Parents Don't Want Inquiry', *Christchurch Star*, 29 March 1995. Sandra Coney, 'Well-orchestrated Crèche Campaign', *Sunday Star Times*, 2 April 1995.
3. Lowell Goddard, briefing papers for Attorney-General (29 March 1995) and Cabinet Strategy Committee (31 March 1995).
4. Graham Panckhurst, letter to Paul East, 15 March 1995.
5. Keith Le Page, letter and enclosures to Attorney-General, 1 March 1995.
6. Gerald Nation to Paul East, 25 October 1994.
7. Lowell Goddard, briefing papers for Attorney-General (29 March 1995) and Cabinet Strategy Committee (31 March 1995).
8. Lowell Goddard, 'Christchurch Civic Crèche: Call for an Inquiry', memorandum to Attorney-General, 29 March 1995.
9. Paul East, press release, 8 June 1995.
10. Graham Panckhurst, letter to Paul East, 21 June 1995.

11. The Honorable R.L. Taylor, the Right Honorable J.B. Gordon and the Most Reverend A.H. Johnston, *Report of the Royal Commission to Inquire into the Circumstances of the Convictions of Arthur Allan Thomas for the Murders of David Harvey Crewe and Jeanette Lenore Crewe*, 1980.
12. Robert Muldoon, *My Way* (Wellington: Reed, 1981).
13. ibid.
14. Peter Williams QC, *A Passion for Justice* (Christchurch: Shoal Bay Press, 1997).
15. Royal Commission on Thomas Case [1980] 1 NZLR 602. The Honorable R.L. Taylor, the Right Honorable J.B. Gordon and the Most Reverend A.H. Johnston, *Report of the Royal Commission to Inquire into the Circumstances of the Convictions of Arthur Allan Thomas for the Murders of David Harvey Crewe and Jeanette Lenore Crewe*, 1980.

13.viii: The Christchurch City Council Appeals the Employment Court Decision (pages 509-513)

16. Hon Justice E.W. Thomas, 'Advocacy in the Court of Appeal Having Particular Regard to the New Procedures', presented at NZ Bar Association Conference, July 1996, published in *Employment Law Conference* (Wellington: NZ Law Society, 1998).
17. Tom Goddard, 'Decision-making in the Employment Court', *New Zealand Law Journal*, November 1996.
18. *Brighouse Ltd v Bilderbeck* [1994] 2 ERNZ 243.
19. Employment Contracts Act 1991, s. 135.
20. Tom Weston, audiotaped interview, 17 June 1998.
21. *Christchurch City Council v Davidson & Others* [1997] 1 NZLR 275.
22. 'Court Slashes Award to Crèche Staff', *The Press*, 27 September 1996.

Chapter 14: The Royal Prerogative of Mercy

14.i: The Safety Net (Pages 514-516)

1. *Burt v Governor-General* [1992] 3 NZLR 672.
2. ibid.
3. Keith Davies, 'Blinded Justice', *Metro*, July 1996.
4. Sir Guy Powles and Mr L.G.H. Sinclair, 'Report on the Atenai Saifiti Case', *Appendices of the Journals of the House of Representatives*, A.6A (Wellington: Government Printer, 1972).
5. The Tauranga-Moana Maori Trust Board Act 1981, and The Te Runanga O Ngati Awa Act 1988, restored the reputations of members of the tribes and granted pardons in respect of matters arising from the colonial land wars. These were statutory, rather than royal, pardons.
6. See discussion of s. 406 Crimes Act 1961 in *R v Ellis* [1999].
7. *R v Morgan* [1963] NZLR 593.

14.ii: Testing the Safety Net (pages 517-522)

8. 'The Case in Question', *20/20* Special, TV3, 16 November 1997.
9. Alan Samson, 'Ellis Inquiry May Look at Actions of Crown Lawyer', *Dominion*, 18 November 1997. Martin Van Beynen, 'Support Grows for Ellis Inquiry', *The Press*, 21 November 1997. 'Police Defend Investigation', *The Press*, 21 November 1997.
10. Doug Graham, reply to question for written answer, 25 November 1997.
11. Ablett Kerr QC, press release, undated.
12. Order in Council, 'Reference to the Court of Appeal on the Question of the Convictions of Peter Hugh McGregor Ellis for Sexual Offences against Children', *NZ Gazette*, 7 May 1998.
13. ibid.
14. *R v Morgan* [1963] NZLR 593. *Ellis v R* [1998] 3 NZLR 555.
15. *Hansard*, 15, 19, 20 October 1894.
16. *Hansard*, Criminal Code Act Amendment debates, 1894-95.
17. Criminal Code Amendment Act, 20 August 1895. *Chemis v R* [1895] NZLR 393. Ellen Ellis, 'Annie Chemis' in *Dictionary of NZ Biography*, Volume 3 (Auckland/Wellington: Auckland University Press/Department of Internal Affairs, 1996).
18. *R v Styche* [1901] NZLR 744.
19. *Hansard*, Meikle Case debates, 1906-1908.
20. *Hansard*, Meikle Acquittal Bill, 22 October 1907.

21. *R v Styche* [1901] NZLR 744.
22. *Hansard*, Criminal Appeal Bill, 1 August 1945.
23. ibid.
24. In *Re O'Connor & Aitken* [1953] NZLR 776. *R v Gunn* (No. 1) [1942] 43 SR (NSW) 23.
25. *Ellis v R* [1998] 3 NZLR 555.
26. *Hansard*, Crimes Bill debate, 1961.
27. *R v Morgan* [1963] NZLR 593.

Chapter 15: Doing Justice

15.I: New Evidence (Pages 523–527)

1. Justice Henry, *R v Ellis*, unreported, CA120/98, 18 December 1998.
2. Sir Thomas Thorp, 'Opinion for The Secretary of Justice re Petitions for the Exercise of the Royal Prerogative of Mercy by Peter Hugh McGregor Ellis', March 1999.
3. Decision of the National Parole Board, Peter Hugh McGregor Ellis, 17 March 1999.
4. 'Innocence Stance Costs Ellis Parole', *The Press*, 18 March 1999.
5. Sir Thomas Thorp, 'Opinion for The Secretary of Justice re Petitions for the Exercise of the Royal Prerogative of Mercy by Peter Hugh McGregor Ellis', March 1999.
6. Val Sim, letter to Lynley Hood, 2 March 1999. Lynley Hood, letter to Val Sim, 16 March 1999.
7. Alan Samson, 'Leaked Letter Raises Questions on Ellis Trial Juror', *Dominion*, 29 April 1999. 'Hand Tape Over: Supporters', *NZ Herald*, 30 April 1999.
8. Rana Waitai 'Ellis Jailed Because of Selfish People Said Waitai', press release, 29 April 1999.
9. 'Reference to the Court of Appeal of the Questions of the Convictions of Peter Hugh McGregor Ellis for Sexual Offences Against Children (No. 2), *NZ Gazette*, 13 May 1999.
10. J. Gault, Minute of the Court, *R v Ellis*, CA120/98, 20 May 1999.
11. Justice Henry, *R v D*, unreported, Auckland, 17 April 1996, CA 371/95. *European Pacific v TVNZ* [1994] 3 NZLR 43.
12. Minute of the Court, *Ellis v R*, 28 June 1999, CA120/98.

15.II: The Judith Ablett-Kerr QC Appeal (pages 528–533)

13. Hon Justice E.W. Thomas, 'Advocacy in the Court of Appeal Having Particular Regard to the New Procedures', NZ Bar Association Conference, July 1996, published in *Employment Law Conference* (Wellington: NZ Law Society, 1998).
14. Justice Richardson, 'Practice Note: Criminal Appeals (effective as from 1 January 1998).'
15. *R v Ellis* [2000] 1 NZLR 513.
16. 'Ellis's Guilt "Beyond Doubt"', *The Press*, 16 October 1999.
17. Martin van Beynen, 'Ellis May Get Inquiry', *The Press*, 3 February 1999.

Chapter 16: 'It is a Case that Simply Will Not Go Away' (Pages 534–545)

1. Martin van Beynen, 'Ellis Supporters Vow to Fight On', *The Press*, 15 October 1999. 'Ellis Free: Inquiry Promised', *NZ Herald*, 3 February 2000.
2. Minister of Justice, media release, 'Ministerial Inquiry to be Held into Ellis Case', 10 March 2000.
3. Sir Thomas Eichelbaum, CV.
4. Terms of Reference, Ministerial Inquiry into the Peter Ellis case, March 2000.
5. Phil Goff, Minister of Justice, press release on Ellis Inquiry, 13 March 2001.
6. Phil Goff, Minister of Justice, letter to Hugo Judd, Official Secretary, His Excellency the Governor-General, 8 March 2001.
7. Ministry of Justice, 'The Peter Ellis case', Media statement, 2 February 2000.
8. Terms of Reference, Ministerial Inquiry into the Peter Ellis case, March 2000.
9. Sir Thomas Thorp, 'Opinion for the Secretary for Justice re Petition for the Exercise of the Royal Prerogative of Mercy by Peter Hugh McGregor Ellis,' Auckland, March 1999.
10. Sir Thomas Eichelbaum, 'The Peter Ellis Case: Report of the Ministerial Inquiry, for the Honorable Phil Goff', February 2001.
11. Sir Thomas Thorp, 'Opinion for the Secretary of Justice rePetitions for the Exercise of the Royal Prerogative of Mercy by Peter Hugh McGregor Ellis', March 1999.

12. Professor Graham Davies, CV. B. Andrews and others, 'Characteristics, context and consequences of memory recovery among adults in therapy', *British Journal of Psychiatry*, 175, (1999).
13. Dr Louise Sas, CV. Workshop 4: The Last Decade: Issues for Children Testifying in the Criminal Justice System. Second International Conference on Children Exposed to Family Violence, London, Ontario, 4-7 June 1997.
14. http://www.radio.cbc.ca/programs/ideas/shows/trials.html; http://www.xtra.ca/site/toronto2/news/head3.shtm
15. http://www.ritualabuse.net/MCF/clcln-hm.htn [CKLN]; http:/Inemasys.com/rahome/tesources/ra_cases2.shtml [Believe the Children]; http://www.ags.uci.edu/dehill/witchhunt/
16. Professor Graham Davies, 'Comments on the investigation and interviewing of children in the Ellis case', 4 January 2001.
17. Dr Louise Sas, 'Ministerial Inquiry, "Ellis Matter"', 23 February 2001.
18. Paul Mullen and others, 'The long-term impact of the physical, emotional and sexual abuse of children,' *Child Abuse and Neglect*, 20 (1996). A. Bradley and J. Wood, 'How do children tell?' *Child Abuse and Neglect*, 20 (1996).
19. Commissions of Inquiry Act, 1908.

Index

ABBREVIATIONS
ACC Accident Compensation Commission/
 Corporation
ACIDPOAC Advisory Committee on the
 Investigation, Detection and Prosecution of
 Offences Against Children
CA Court of Appeal
Cvc Civic Child Care Centre/Civic Crèche
DC District Court
DSW Department of Social Welfare
EC Employment Court
DG Debbie Gillespie
FC Family Court
GD Gaye Davidson
GP General Practitioner
HC High Court
JB Jan Buckingham
MK Marie Keys
MP Member of Parliament
PE Peter Ellis
NACPCA National Advisory Committee on the
 Prevention of Child Abuse
RAG Ritual Action Group
SLGOU Southern Local Government Officers
 Union

'A' family case: 78–82, 88, 89, 147, 148
Ablett-Kerr, Judith [QC]: 1st petition 517, 518,
 521, 522; 2nd petition 523–26; CA 528–33;
 3rd petition 534
ACC: background 83–88; claims 102, 128, 160–62,
 179, 201, 306, 307, 314, 394, 485; legislation
 204, 205, 236; publications 63, 64; cited 281,
 302, 328, 332, 396

Adams on Criminal Law: 423, 528
Adams-Smith, Mr [QC]: 507
Advisory Committee on the Investigation,
 Detection and Prosecution of Offences
 Against Children [ACIDPOAC]: 55, 63, 91,
 93, 118, 145 (*see also* Geddis, O'Reilly, Zelas,
 NACPCA, *Guidelines for the Investigation and
 Management of Child Sexual Abuse, Public or
 Private Nightmare*)
Alder [Cvc family]: *Jodie* 400, 404
Alexander, Bev [lawyer]: 408
Allen, Trish [therapist]: 125, 376
Akiki case [USA]: 331
American Psychologist: 73, 75
Amirault case [USA]: 166, 381
Anderson, Judge [DC]: depositions 385–400; cited
 257, 273, 322, 407, 413
Angus, Lynda [ACC staff]: 85
Appelgren case: 514–15
Appleyard, Jo [lawyer]: 494, 502
Arbutus [Cvc family]: *parents*: support for crèche
 177; management committee 213, 215–16,
 217–18, 220; networking 223, 235, 247; Ms A
 propositioned by Eade 290; Mandy withdrawn
 from case 339; *Mandy*: disclosure 243–44;
 effects of disclosure 245, 268; PE arrest
 294–96; cited 249, 263, 276, 283
Arendt, Hannah [author]: 140
Ash [Cvc family]: *parents* 174, 197, 199; *Mikey*
 196, 197, 340, 393
Ashton-Warner, Sylvia [author]: 20, 34, 152
Aspen [Cvc family]: *parents* 176–77, 330
Attorney-General (*see* East, Hanan, Mason, Palmer)
Authoritarian Personality, The: 41, 75, 130
Avonside Drive house [urban commune]: 175, 201

'B' case: 122
Balani, George [journalist]: 139, 412
Ball, Wendy [lawyer]: 195-96, 198, 199, 236, 534, 538
Balsa [Cvc family]: *Judy*: depositions 391; pre-trial applications 412, 419-20, 484; trial 428, 429, 434, 435, 447
Banks, John [Minister of Police 1990-93]: 471, 472
Barr, Simon [lawyer]: 523-25
Bartlett, Patricia [anti-porn activist]: 45, 57, 471
Beech [Cvc family]: **parents**: 191, 220, 226, 355; **Tania**: 226
Belinda [DG's former partner, Cvc staff]: 239, 391-92, 417-18, 448, 455
Bentovim, Arnon [UK psychiatrist]: 58-60, 118-19, 120
Bernard [video store owner]: 201, 364-65
Bill of Rights Act [1990]: 96, 398, 416
Birch [Cvc family]: **parents** 288
Biswell, Janet [DSW manager]: 348, 350
Blair, Judge [ACC Appeal Authority]: 83, 86
Blanchard, Justice [CA]: 509
Bodin, Jean [16th century French jurist]: 26, 69
Bolger, Jim [Leader of the Opposition 1986-90, Prime Minister 1990-97]: 139, 288
Breaking the Circle of Satanic Ritual Abuse: 331
Breakwell, Jan [lawyer]: 502
Brett, Cate [journalist]: 137, 138, 142, 147, 165, 176
Brighouse case: 510, 511
Broad, Howard [police]: 282, 289, 365
Broadhurst, Heather [therapist]: 126, 131, 143, 165 (*see also* START)
Broadleaf [Cvc family]: **parents** 310; **Mia** 310, 332, 384, 391, 404
Broadsheet: 40, 42, 43, 44, 51, 64
Bruce [owner of 404 Hereford St]: child visitors 182, 183; police searches 337, 362-63; depositions 391, 392-93; pre-trial 414-15; trial 447-48, 463, 480
Bruck, Maggie [USA psychologist]: 99, 269, 312, 530, 538
Brunvand, Jan [author]: 24
Bubbles, Mr, case [Australia]: 196, 226
Buckingham, Jan [Cvc staff]: PE suspension 206, 210, 211, 212; police investigation 245, 246, 247, 264-65, 287, 341, 365; JB arrest 366-71 *pass.*, 378, 379; depositions 393-401 *pass.*,

425; JB pre-trial applications, discharge 402-12 *pass.*; PE pre-trial applications 417-18; trial 435, 448, 456; costs 473-75 *pass.*; EC 497, 504, 512-13; cited 27, 176, 187
Buckley, Sir Patrick [19th century MP, judge]: 519
Bull, Carolyn [lawyer]: 293
Burt v *Governor-General*: 514-16
Byron [Crèche X staff]: 358-61, 393

'C' family case: 123-26
Canterbury Hospital Board: 118, 121, 139, 141-43, 279 (*see also* Ding, Watkins, Zelas, Child and Family Guidance Centre, Ward 24)
Campbell Centre [therapy]: 279, 306 (*see also* Smart)
Campbell, Helen [therapist]: 331
Carson, Roger [police]: phantom paedophile ring 130, 165; Cvc case 268, 282, 289, 291-92
Cartwright, Judge Silvia [DC]: 102, 138-39, 143, 505
Caseley: Ann [therapist] 205; Terry [paediatrician] 126, 134, 143
Casey, Justice Sir Maurice [CA]: 269, 476, 477, 481, 483, 488, 541
Cathedral Square Community Crèche: 169
Caton, Anne [DSW manager]: 163, 412
Ceci, Stephen [USA psychologist]: 99, 269, 538
Cedar [Cvc family]: **parents** 225, 297, 304; **Opal** 304
Chambers, Heather (*see* Broadhurst)
Champion, Patricia [psychologist]: 133, 143
Chapman, Jeff [ACC general manager]: 87, 161, 162
Chappell, Michael [police]: 391, 448
charges faced: at start of depositions 383; at end of depositions 402; at start of trial 425-29
Chemis case: 519-20
Child Abuse and Neglect: 47, 113, 169, 274
child abuse, physical (*see* Kempe, statistical claims)
Child Abuse Prevention and Treatment Act [USA]: 47
Child and Family Guidance Centre: **history**: 113-14, 116, 117, 118, 121, 126; **cases**: 'D' 127; 'F' 132; 'G' 135; 'H' 138; 'N' 153; Cvc 224; **inquiries**: Ding 142, 143, 145; Mason 148, 149 (*see also* Child Health Clinic, Dick, Watkins, Zelas)
Child Care Centre Regulations [1960]: 169

Child Health Clinic: 50, 110–11, 113 (*see also* Child and Family Guidance Centre)
child protection movement [1970–90] (*see* Geddis, Kempe, Zelas)
Child Protection Team: *Christchurch*: 120–21, 131, 144–45; *cases*: 'A' 78; 'F' 133; 'G' 136; *cited* 76, 89, 148, 292
Child Sexual Abuse Accommodation Syndrome: 58–59, 98, 119 (*see also* Summit)
child sexual abuse – background (*see* feminism, statistical claims)
child sexual abuse cases: preschools (*see* Akiki, Amirault, Bubbles, Civic Crèche, McMartin, Michaels); other (*see* 'A', 'B', 'C', 'D', 'F', 'G', 'H', 'N', Cleveland, Orkney, Prescott, Project Guardian)
Child Sexual Abuse Study: Role of Expert Witnesses in Criminal Trials: 91
Children, Young Persons, and Their Families Bill/Act [1989]: 89–90, 148, 365, 398
children's interviewers [DSW] (*see* Crawford, Morgan, Sidey)
children's interviews [DSW]: *summary*: 27, 256–58, 332, 385; *played to jury*: 426–27, 435; *basis for guilty verdicts* [in order in which videotapes played to the jury]: Cypress 313–14, Sumach 321; Laurel 308–10; Hickory 315–17; Dogwood 338–39; Lacebark 258–61, 277–79, 284–87; Palm 270
Christchurch [history, geography, people]: 106–08
Christchurch City Council: complaint procedures 186–87; councillor (*see* Close); office staff (*see* Dally, Graham [Alistair], Gray, Latham, Maguire, Mitchell, Wright); Cvc ownership 169–70, 177; Cvc appointments 185–86; Cvc management 217
Christchurch College of Education: 172–73, 176
Christchurch Star: 97, 128, 130, 134, 137, 142, 289
Christchurch Technical Institute: 169, 170
Civic Child Care Inquiry Organisation: 470, 505
Civic Crèche case: *summary of case*: 27–30; *summaries of evidence*: 398–90, 413–13, 479–81; *principal events*: 1st complaint 202–06; 1st parents' meeting 223–26; investigation closed 233–34; PE dismissed 236–37; 1st disclosure 243–44; investigation reopened 249–51; PE arrested 294–96; 2nd parents' meeting 297–98; crèche closed 353; women arrested 366–72; depositions 383–401;

women discharged 404, 411; PE trial 421–69; women's costs application 473–75; Hampton appeal 476–78; Panckhurst appeal 478–91; EC case 494–504; EC appeal 509–13; Ablett-Kerr appeal 528–332; PE released 533; Eichelbaum inquiry 534–45
Civic Crèche families: *1st complaint* (*see* Magnolia); *1st disclosure* (*see* Arbutus); *complainants in court proceedings*: depositions only (*see* Alder, Broadleaf, Deodar, Juniper, Linden, Matai); depositions and trial (*see* Balsa, Cypress [retraction], Dogwood, Fir, Hickory, Holly, Lacebark, Laurel, Ngaio, Palm, Pine, Sumach, Yew); *non-complainant prosecution witnesses*: (*see* Magnolia [depositions only], Kapok, Kowhai); *defence witnesses* (*see* Beech, Linden, Mahogany, Sycamore); *management committee* (*see* Arbutus, Beech, Gingko, Jacaranda, Larch, Maple, Rowan); *other* (*see* Ash, Aspen, Birch, Cedar, Cork, Elm, Hawthorn, Hazelnut, Laburnum, Lime, Macrocarpa, Mulberry, Rata, Rimu, Tamarack, Walnut, Willow)
Civic Crèche [history, policies, programme]: 29, 158, 170–73, 174–79, 213–14
Civic Crèche staff: 172–73 (*see also* Belinda, Buckingham, Byron, Davidson, Gillespie, Kapok, Keys, Little, Reinfeld, Sandi, Sharleen, Shona, Sigrid, Solvig, Suki, Susannah, Sylvia)
Close, David [hospital board member, city councillor]: 141, 173–74
Clark, Helen [Minister of Health 1989–90]: 139
Cleveland case [UK]: 120, 126, 131, 142, 144, 410, 470, 505, 535
Collins, Judy [therapist]: 126
Commissioner for Children: Hassall 373, 374; McClay 535
conspiracy theories: 108–10
contamination of evidence: 303–07
Cooke, Justice Sir Robin [CA]: judgments 99, 100, 103, 111; Hampton appeal 476–78; Panckhurst appeal 481–90 *pass*.; *Burt v Governor-General* 514–16; cited 509, 510, 541
Coney, Sandra [author]: 43, 505
Cooper, Bede [Ministry of Education manager]: Cvc closure 346–52 *pass*.; EC 499, 501–03; cited 363, 512
Corbett, Hildegard [therapist]: 313

Cork [Cvc family]: *parent*: 219, 227, 277; *Timothy*: 277, 306–07
Corrin, Ruth [author]: 301
COSA [Casualties of Sexual Allegations]: 161
Costs in Criminal Cases Act [1967]: 473
Couch, Tony [lawyer]: 237, 242–43, 247, 267
Counihan, Angela [SLGOU]: 206, 212, 229
Courage to Heal, The: 63, 65, 74–75, 99, 160, 330
Court of Appeal: A.A. Thomas case 507; Ablett-Kerr 523–32; Eichelbaum inquiry 535–36, 537–38, 543–44; Hampton 476–78; Panckhurst 478–93; women's EC appeal 509–13; royal pardon 514–22 *pass.*; cited 257–58, 347, 399–400, 403, 409, 410, 411, 415, 422, 495; (*see also* Blanchard, Casey, Cooke, Gault, Henry, Keith, McMullin, Richardson, Thomas, Tipping)
courtroom rules and procedures [traditional]: 93–96, 422–23, 465
Crane, Sara [therapist]: 230, 281, 331
Crawford, Cathy [DSW interviewer]: 303, 385, 397–89, 413, 434, 440
Crèche X: 358–61, 393, 497
crimen exceptum: 69, 70, 93, 100, 105, 161
Crimes Amendment Bill/Act (No.3) [1989]: 92, 103
Crimes Bill/Act [1961]: *s. 344A*: 409–411, 415; *s. 347*: 411–16 *pass.*; *s. 385*: 477, 479; *s. 389*: 526–27 *pass.*; *s. 406*: 515–22 *pass.*, 544; cited 95, 402, 403
Criminal Appeal Act [1945]: 520, 521
Criminal Code Act [1893]: 519, 521
Criminal Law Reform Committee: 101–02
Cropp, Amanda [journalist]: 158
Crossen, Gen [social worker]: 303, 328–33, 342, 343
Crown Law Office: 138, 145, 535, 538 (*see also* France, Goddard, McGrath, Thomas)
Crown Prosecutors: 157–58, 384–91, 422–23 (*see also* Lange, Saunders, Stanaway)
CTV: 392
Cullen, Michael [Minister of Social Welfare 1987–90] 'A' case 78–82 *pass.*; Geddis proposals 89–91; Christchurch cases 131–38 *pass.*, 141, 147–49; cited 63, 87, 285
Cypress [Cvc family]: *parents*: PE babysitting 182; trial 437–38, 447, 460; TV3 545; cited 339; *Zelda*: disclosure 310–14; trial 427–28, 429, 432–33, 435, 436, 452, 463; verdict 467; Panckhurst appeal 479, 480; retraction 485–87, 490; Eichelbaum inquiry 540; cited 183, 238, 246, 314, 323, 337, 532

'D' family case: 127–29
Dally, Rob [city council administrator]: PE suspension 220, 229–30, PE dismissal 247, 263, 293, 334; Cvc closure 350; EC 500, 501
Daly, Rose [journalist]: 222, 297, 323
Daniel and his Therapist: 63, 330
Davidson, Gaye [Cvc supervisor 1987–92]: as supervisor 174–77 *pass.*, 183, 246; supervision of PE 185–94 *pass.*, 231, 245–46; alleged 'earlier disclosures' 196–99; 1st complaint 204–06; PE suspension 210–17; parental criticism 248; police investigation 250, 287, 329, 330; GD job under threat 334–35; Cvc closure 353, 358; GD arrest 368–71; depositions 383–401; indictment 425; pre-trial applications 402–11; PE trial 459, 460; GD calls for inquiry 468, 470–73; costs application 473–75; EC 495, 497; EC appeal 511–12; cited 350, 365
Davies, Graham [UK psychologist]: 538, 539–41, 542, 543
Davies, Sonja [MP, day-care pioneer]: 169, 373
Dawson, Karen [therapist]: 306–07
De Cleene, Trevor [lawyer, MP]: 99
De la Démonomanie des Sorciers: 26
Deaker, Michael [Ministry of Education manager]: 346, 351–52, 354, 499, 500, 502
Dean, Minnie [19th-century childcare worker]: 20, 23, 26, 34, 169
defence counsel: 422–23 (*see also* Ablett-Kerr, Alexander, Barr, Hampton, Harrison, Knight, McNulty, Panckhurst)
Dennison, Karen [nurse]: 132, 133
Deodar [Cvc family]: *parents*: 378; *Fran* 378, 404
Department of Social Welfare [DSW]: *general*: abuse reports 46, 121; CYPF Act [1989] 90, 148; Geddis influence 76–78; interview procedures 27, 29, 34, 97, 103, 198, 243, 268, 271–72; Mason inquiry 148; on CPT 120; RAG 161–64 *pass.*, 394; re Cvc 173; Saphira influence 51–52, 56, 76; use of experts 396; *other cases*: 'A' 79–82, 147; 'C' 125–26; 'F' 133; 'G' 136, 141, 148; *Cvc case*: admin 216, 222, 229, 230, 250, 290, 293, 298, 299, 302–03, 326, 331–32, 347; interviewing 202, 213, 215,

218, 219, 223, 224, 249, 270, 305–06, 307, 381, 385, 390, 464, 530, 535; response to calls for inquiry 505, 506 (*see also* Biswell, Caton, Crawford, Cullen, Doolan, Ellen, Gillanders, Good, Morgan, Ross, Saphira, Shipley, Sidey, Watson, Wilson)
Dialectic of Sex, The: 43
Dick, Sue [therapist]: 126, 127, 224
Ding, Les [psychiatrist]: 142–47
Disabled Persons Community Welfare Act: 87, 88
District Legal Services Subcommittee [DLSS]: 326, 396
Dogwood [Cvc family]: ***parents***: 32, 197, 321–22, 373, 396–97, 439–40, 447, 497, 530; ***Bart***: interviews 321–22, 338–42, 379; flow-on effect of disclosures 344–46, 361, 362, 380, 396–97, 400, 443; pre-trial applications 410, 412, 413–15, 416, 420; Crown trial opening 425–28 *pass.*; trial evidence 432, 434–35, 436, 441, 447–48 *pass.*, 455, 456, 459; Crown summing up 462–63; verdicts 467; women's costs application 475; Panckhurst appeal 479–81 *pass.*, 484, 489; Eichelbaum inquiry 541–42; cited 330, 361 (*see also* GD, JB, MK arrests)
DNA testing: 99–100
Doctors for Sexual Abuse Care [DSAC]: 63, 138, 204, 236, 275–76, 302
Dominion: 411, 525
Dominion Sunday Times: 78, 80, 88, 158, 471
Donnelly, Jill [therapist]:135
Don't Make Me Go Back Mommy: 331
Doolan, Mike [DSW manager]: 257–58, 271, 299, 302
Doublett, Simone [ACC claimant]: 161–62
Doubter's Companion, The: 161
Douglas, Roger [MP]: 92
Downie Stewart [19th century lawyer, MP]: 519
DSAC (*see* Doctors for Sexual Abuse Care)
DSW (*see* Department of Social Welfare)
Dunedin Multidisciplinary Health and Development Research Unit: 67

'E', Dr [GP in 'A' family case]: 78
East, Paul: Attorney-General [1990–97] 458, 470, 472, 473, 491–92, 504–08 *pass.*; Minister of State Services 504
Eade, Colin [police]: initiates investigation 181, 196, 215–18 *pass.*, 220; 1st parents meeting 224, 225–26, 227; investigation continues 230–31; investigation closed 233–34; investigation escalates 239, 243–82 *pass.*; PE arrested 289–97; investigation escalates further 304–39 *pass.*, 362, 363; Crèche X 360; depositions 383, 388, 393, 396; trial 423, 436, 439, 448; TV3 517; cited 29–30, 33–34
Eason, Moira [therapist]: 135
Education (Early Childhood Centres) Regulations [1990]: 346
Education, Ministry of (*see* Cooper, Deaker, Todd)
Education Review Office [ERO]: 213, 217, 249
Eichelbaum, Justice Sir Thomas [rtd]: 534–45
Ell, John [police]: Ding inquiry 143; Cvc case 291–93, 297, 298, 301–03 *pass.*, 320, 342–52 *pass.*
Ellen, Donna [DSW social worker]: 332
Ellis, Lesley [Peter Ellis's mother]: 180, 206, 379–80, 384, 386
Ellis, Peter: background 180–95 (*see also* Ablett-Kerr, Eichelbaum, Civic Crèche case/families/staff, Hampton, Harrison, Knight, Panckhurst)
Elm [Cvc family]: ***parents***: 226, 300; ***Nina***: 227, 300
Employment Contracts Act [1991]: 510, 511, 512
End Ritual Abuse [ERA]: 33, 109, 196, 386
Erebus Commission: 508–09
Erikson, Fran [social worker]: 126
Espie, Dianne, Dr [GP]: 117, 120, 121–26, 145
Evidence Amendment Bill/Act (No.3) [1989]: 92, 96, 103, 396, 466, 469, 482, 505, 536–37
Evidence (Videotaping of Child Complainants) Regulations: 103
Expert witnesses: 95–96, 395–6

'F' Dr [psychiatrist in 'A' family case]: 80
'F' family case: 132–34, 141–42, 143
Faces of the Enemy: 209
Faller, Katherine Coulburn [author]: 335
Family Court: 71, 73–74, 76, 88–89, 118, 125, 126, 133–34, 137, 396
Family Law Bulletin: 92
Family Violence Conference 1985: 55
Family Violence Prevention Coordinating Committee [FVPCC]: 63, 161, 162, 394
Fantham, Peter [registrar, Christchurch HC]: 163, 407, 485
Farquhar, Sarah-Eve [author]: 188

Feeling Safe: 63, 301
feminism: politics of rape 40-44; politics of child sexual abuse 48-62, 63-68
Fir [Cvc family]: **Abigail**: 428, 429, 435, 436, 447, 467
Folk Devils and Moral Panics: 21
folklore: 23-24
Fort, Alan [Glenelg staff]: 122, 131
France, Simon [lawyer]: 528, 532
Frances, Jocelyn [RAG]: 162-63
Frankfurter, Justice Felix [USA]: 71
Free to Fly: 160, 199
Freud, Sigmund: 48
Finkelhor, David [USA sociologist]: 119-20, 166-69, 199, 254, 335
Frontline [TVNZ]: 131, 132-33, 138-39, 141-47, 148

'G' family case: 134-38, 141, 143, 145, 147-48, 224
Gabites, Laurie [police]: 159, 160, 163
Garry, Maryanne [psychologist]: 306
Gault, Justice Thomas [CA]: 476, 477, 481-82, 483, 518, 525-26, 527, 528, 530, 532, 541
Geddis, David [paediatrician]: background 50, 55, 113, 118; NACPCA 76-77, 89-90; ACIDPOAC 90-105 *pass.*, 118; cited 148
General Practitioners (*see* Gray, Lyttle, Metherall, Thornley)
Gerard, Jim [MP]: 131, 149
Gibson, Catherine [Ministry of Education manager]: 352
Gillanders, Jan [DSW social worker]: 303, 328-33, 342, 343, 394, 397, 405
Gillespie, Debbie [Cvc staff]: 192, 209, 211, 212, 239, 246, 287, 357; arrest 365, 368, 369-72, 374, 375, 376, 378, 379; depositions 383-401, pre-trial to discharge 402-05, 417, 455, 459-60, 473-75, 497
Gillespie, Mr & Mrs [Debbie's parents]: 369, 370-71, 384, 385, 391
Gillett, Grant [medical ethicist]: 123, 142-43, 526
Gingko [Cvc family]: **parents**: 217-18, 219
Glenelg Children's Health Camp: 116, 117-18, 121-25, 131, 135, 142, 145, 148, 230
Glover, Rupert [lawyer]: 505
Goddard, Lowell [lawyer]: 492, 505-06, 508-09
Goddard, Judge Tom [EC]: 347, 492-503, 509, 510, 511-12
Goff, Phil [lawyer, Minister of Justice 1999-]: 534, 535-36, 544-45

Golden Bough, The: 21, 208
Good, Raewyn [DSW staff, RAG]: 162-63, 307
Good Housekeeping/GH [magazine]: 26
Goodman, Gail [USA psychologist]: 63, 98, 99, 120
Governor [17th-century Massachusetts]: 100
Governor [19th-century NZ]: 519, 520
Governor-General: 507-09 *pass.*, 514-16 *pass.*; 519-24 *pass.*, 529, 531, 544
Graham, Alistair [City Council administrator]: impressions of PE 185, 191, 192; Cvc case 158, 206, 216-17, 220, 229, 234-35, 249, 250, 263, 280, 298, 334, 336, 394
Graham, Doug [lawyer, Minister of Justice 1990-99]: 325, 470, 472, 473, 518
Gray, Dr [GP]: 391
Gray, John [Christchurch City Manager]: Cvc investigation 220-25 *pass.*, 229-30 *pass.*, 234, 243, 281, 293, 298; social workers appointed 303; Smart report 336; Cvc closure 347-48 *pass.*; EC 494-504; EC appeal 510-11
Green, Judge [DC]: 380
Guardian [UK]: 164
Guidelines for the Investigation and Management of Child Sexual Abuse [Geddis report I]: 77, 90, 118, 120, 122, 123, 124, 132, 145 (*see also* ACIDPOAC)

'H' family case: 138, 149
Haden, Frank [journalist]: 471
Haines, Hilary [psychologist]: 44, 51, 53, 55
Hales, Keith [lawyer]: 136
Hampton, Nigel [QC]: 323-24, 326, 381, 407-08, 473, 476-78
Hanan, Ralph [lawyer, Minister of Justice & Attorney-General 1960-69]: 521-22
Handbook of Clinical Intervention in Child Sexual Abuse: 56, 57
Hardie, Bob [police]: 342, 343, 344-45, 348, 359-62, 363, 377, 478
Harrison, Madeleine [Glenelg manager]: 121-22, 135
Harrison, Rob [lawyer]: background 221-22; PE arrest 296-97, 299; as counsel for PE 275, 322-27, 358, 378, 381-82; depositions 385-401, pre-trial 405-20; trial 284, 340, 421-69; Hampton appeal 477, 478, 481; Panckhurst appeal 481, 483-84, 485, 487, 490; Upton 493; Ablett-Kerr 531

Hassall, Ian [paediatrician, Commissioner for Children]: 373, 374
Hawkins, [police]: 342
Hawthorn [Cvc family]: **parents**: 219, 246, 356, 394
Haye, Lynne [psychologist]: 161-62
Hazelnut [Cvc family]: **Ruby** 404
Health, Department of: 110, 120
Heath, Greg [police]: 333, 337, 338, 363, 370, 375, 396, 447, 448
Heger, Astrid [USA paediatrician]: 63, 119-20, 203-04, 205, 275
Help Foundation: 56, 57, 78, 80, 86, 115, 224
Henry, Justice [CA]: 509, 518, 526, 527, 530, 541
Herald: 181, 525
Hereford St [404] and 'Peter's house' [alleged]: 181, 182-83, 315, 337-38, 340-43 *pass.*, 362-65 *pass.*, 371, 378, 379, 391-96 *pass.*, 414, 425, 427, 439, 447, 453, 454-55, 457, 462, 480, 489, 542, 544 (*see also* Bruce)
Hickory [Cvc family]: **parents**: 219, 314-15, 438; **Tess**: 314-20, 332-33, 337, 412, 413, 428, 432, 434, 435, 436, 438, 441-42, 447, 452, 462, 467, 479-81, 481, 530, 540, 541
Historical Essays Concerning Witchcraft: 100
Holland, Justice [HC]: 138, 152
Holly [Cvc family]: **parents** 238-39, 252-53, 264; **Yelena** 238, 239, 246-47, 249, 252-53, 264, 268, 276, 277, 279, 283, 294, 304, 305, 310, 313, 412, 428-29, 432, 435, 436, 463, 468
Holmes [TVNZ]: 142, 283-84, 292, 311, 412, 446-47, 471, 530
Homosexual Law Reform Act/Bill 1986: 130, 181
How to Lie with Statistics: 37
Hudson, Pamela [author]: 109, 253, 273-74, 276, 278, 330, 342
Hyde, Brent [police]: 129-30, 160, 165

Incest Survivors Group: 56, 57, 114-15, 303 (*see also* Lynda Morgan)
Indecent Publications Tribunal: 394
inquiry, calls for: 78, 131, 138-39, 142-43, 147-49, 412, 468-69, 470-73, 504-07, 508-09, 534
International Congress on Child Abuse and Neglect: 47, 49, 113; sixth 118-20
International Covenant of Civil and Political Rights: 94, 96
Internet: 'Believe the Children' 28; porn 164, 253-54; Canadian cases 538-39
Interpol: 394

'Invasion from Mars' panic: 61, 164
IRA cases [UK]: 398, 514, 537, 545

Jacaranda [Cvc family]: **parents** 217, 374
Jackson, Miriam [psychologist] 44, 50-52 (*see also* Saphira)
Jamieson, John [police]: 181
Jaspers, Karl [psychiatrist, philosopher]: 200
Jenkins, Neville [police]: 344, 357, 362, 363-64, 368, 370, 376, 396, 397, 442, 443-44
Jeopardy in the Courtroom: 269
Joint NZ Children and Young Persons Service and Police Operating Guidelines: 535
Journal of Experimental Psychology: 312
judges (*see* Anderson, Blair, Blanchard, Buckley, Cartwright, Casey, Cooke, Eichelbaum, Frankfurter, Gault, Goddard, Green, Henry, Holland, Kean, Keith, McAloon, McMullin, Mahon, Mahony, Mason, Noble, Richardson, Roper, Taylor, Thomas, Thorp, Tipping, Williamson)
Jung, Karl [psychoanalyst]: 25, 42
Juniper [Cvc family]: **grandparent** 198-99; **parents** 196-99; **Kane** 195, 196-99, 314, 393, 404
jury, Ellis trial: 70, 86, 523, 524, 525, 526
Justice, Department of: 44, 55, 56, 279, 327

Kapok [Cvc family/staff]: **parents** 391, 392, 447, 453
Katie's Yukky Problem: 63, 184-85, 225, 240, 310, 330
Kean, Herbert [physician UK]: 124
Kean, Judge [FC]: 126, 137, 145
Keith, Justice Sir Kenneth [CA]: 509
Kempe, Henry [paediatrician USA]: 45, 46-47, 49-50, 56, 76, 112, 113, 115
Keys, Marie [Cvc staff]: 27, 31, 187, 246, 287, 341, 342, 365, 368-69, 370-72, 378, 379, depositions 383-401; pre-trial applications and discharge 402-12, 425; PE trial 435, 459, 460-61; costs application 473-75
Keys, Roger [MK's husband]: 371, 386
King, Greg [lawyer]: 532
Kinsey, Alfred [sexologist USA]: 52-53, 65
Klein, Pamela [therapist USA]: 63, 159-60
Knight, Chris [lawyer]: 211-12, 214-15, 220-21, 236-37, 267-68, 282, 289, 294-95, 296, 323-24, 326-27, 358, 530

Kohanga Reo [preschool]: 174, 192, 194
Kowhai [Cvc family/PE's former partner]: *parent* 183, 206, 238-39, 265, 359, 363, 392, 447, 480; ***Gary & Ethan*** 238

Laburnum [Cvc family]: ***parents*** 227, 230
Lamb [psychologist UK]: 530
Lacebark [Cvc family]: ***grandparent***: 246; ***parents***: 246-47, 249-53, 251-52, 261, 277, 287, 310, 359; ***Kari*** 253, 256, 258-264, 268, 276-79 *pass.*, 283-87 *pass.*, 294, 305, 314-19 *pass.*, 323, 332-33, 337, 340-42 *pass.*, 345-46, 359, 360, 361, 371, 378, 379-80, 412, 414, 425, 428, 432, 435, 436-42 *pass.*, 447, 452, 460, 467-68, 479-81, 540, 542
Laing, R.D. [psychiatrist UK]: 72
Lange, Chris [lawyer]: 290, 291, 342, 343, 346, 348-49, 350, 371, 377, 380, 384, 388, 399, 402, 457, 481, 487
Lange, David [lawyer, Prime Minister 1984-88]: 92
Larch [Cvc family]: ***parents***: 158, 220, 224, 229-30, 230-31, 232, 241, 247-48, 249, 250-51, 256, 263-64, 281, 288, 293, 297, 298, 334, 356, 498
Latham, Sally [city council administrator]: 186, 187
Laurel [Cvc family]: ***parents*** 307-08, 390, 397, 438; ***Eli*** 307-10, 313, 323, 379, 384, 391, 397, 428, 429, 432, 433, 435, 436, 438, 441, 442, 443, 447, 452, 456, 467, 479, 481, 541, 542
Law Commission: 535
Law Reform (Miscellaneous Provisions) Bill [1988]: 91-92
Lawson, Peter [SLGOU]: PE 211-12, 214, 220, 228, 232, 234, 236, 237, 242, 281-82, 289; Cvc closure 351, 353-55, 357, 365-66, 412; EC 494-99 *pass.*; EC appeal 509
lawyers (*see* Ablett-Kerr, Adams-Smith, Alexander, Appleyard, Ball, Barr, Bodin, Breakwell, Bull, Couch, De Cleene, Downie Stewart, East, France, Glover, Goddard, Goff, Graham, Hales, Hampton, Hanan, Harrison, King, Knight, Lange [Chris], Lange [David], McArthur, McAteer, McGeehan, McGrath, McGregor, McNulty, Miles, Mitchell [Isabel], Mitchell [Peter], Moran, Nation, O'Driscoll, O'Regan, O'Reilly, Palmer, Panckhurst, Pengelly, Rowan, Saunders, Stanaway, Taffs,

Taylor, Thomas, Till, Tizard, Upton, van Schreven, Weston, Williams)
Le Page, Keith [psychiatrist]: 311, 395, 410, 450, 458-59, 461, 466, 473, 505
leaders and followers: 39
Lee, Graeme [MP]: 471
legal aid: 221, 325-27, 396, 473-74, 513
Legal Services Act 1991: 325, 491
Legat, Ken [Police]: 153-57, 158, 369, 375, 391, 394, 396, 397, 440, 448
Lesbian Nation: 43
Lime [Cvc family]: ***parents*** 228, 241-42; ***Clayton*** 241-42
Linden [Cvc family]: ***parents*** 219, 332-33, 337, 339, 373, 438; ***Amy*** 314, 316, 317, 319, 332-33, 337, 404
Listener: 65, 175, 472, 517
Little, Liz [Cvc supervisor -1983]: 174-75
Locke, Ali [therapist]: 205
Loftus, Elizabeth [psychologist]: 54-55
Lyttle, Dr [GP]: 391, 396

McAloon, Judge [FC]: 126
McArthur, Ian [police lawyer]: 350
McAteer, Neil [lawyer]: 502
McAuley, Karen [police]: 359-60, 369, 376, 396
McDonald's [fast food]: 276, 308, 319
MacFarlane, Kee [USA therapist]: 119-20, 308
McGeehan, R.A. [lawyer]: 93
McGrath, John [Solicitor-General]: 422, 473, 492, 493, 517
McGregor, Mr [19th-century lawyer, MP]: 519
McLeod, Rosemary [journalist]: 139
McLoughlin, David [journalist]: 280
McMartin case [USA]: 63, 119-20, 151, 166, 204, 254, 255, 375, 308
McMeeking, Ian [police]: 342
McMullin, Justice [CA]: 104
McNulty, Siobhan [lawyer]: 408, 436, 447, 457-58

'M' [psychologist]: 323-24, 326-28, 395
Macrocarpa [Cvc family]: ***parents*** 356, 363-65, 371, 399
Magnolia [Cvc family]: ***grandparents*** 126-27, 202, 246, 281-82, 333-34; ***aunt*** 288; ***parents*** 32, 126-27, 130, 151, 175, 177, 196, 199-225 *pass.*, 227-33 *pass.*, 235, 246-56 *pass.*, 261, 264, 265, 268, 269, 271, 288, 297, 304, 311, 314, 330, 333, 338, 339, 342, 358-61, 364-65,

390–91, 416, 438–39; *Geoffrey* 151, 196, 202–07, 210–11, 213, 215, 233, 235, 238, 239, 248, 306, 314, 333, 338, 342, 358–61
Maguire, Martin [city council administrator]: 229, 230, 232, 235, 236, 263, 280, 293, 298, 329, 334, 336, 350, 394, 499, 500, 501
Mahogany [Cvc family]: *parents* 190, 219, 227, 298, 300, 457–58; *Leo* 227
Mahon, Judge [FC]: 133–34
Mahony, Judge [FC]: 163
Malleus Malificarum: 41, 51
Manual for the Medical Management of Child Sexual Abuse: 275
Maple [Cvc family]: *parents* 226, 356, 373
Marriage Guidance [MG]: 73–74, 107, 170, 391, 443, 444, 540
Marshall, Brent [police]: 369, 396,
Mary, Alison [NZCA]: 192–93, 195, 233, 393
Mason, Judge Ken [rtd]: 78, 79, 80, 81, 82, 139, 147–50
Mason, Rex [Attorney-General & Minister of Justice 1940–49]: 520–21
mass hysteria: 60–63 (*see also* mass psychogenic illness, moral panic, scapegoating)
mass psychogenic illness [and mass psychogenic illness by proxy]: 21, 199–201
Matai [Cvc family]: *Ryan* 387–89, 400, 404
Matrimonial Property Act: 40
Megan's Secret: 63, 330
Meikle case: 520
Members of Parliament: 65, 78, 130, 131, 180, 223 (*see also* Banks, Bolger, Buckley, Clark, Cullen, Davies, De Cleene, Douglas, Downie Stewart, East, Gerard, Goff, Graham, Lange, Lee, McGregor, Mason, Muldoon, O'Regan, Palmer, Rigg, Shipley, Waitai, Waring)
Memorandum of Good Practice [UK]: 530, 535
Mental Health Foundation [MHF]: report 63; conference 114–15, 117; cited 51–52, 53, 55, 55
Metherall, Margaret [GP]: 138, 158, 276, 278, 441–42
Methodist Central Mission: 355, 356–57
Metro: 64, 65
Michaels, Kelly, case [USA]: 26–27
Michelle Remembers: 54, 56, 109, 129
Miles, Julian [QC]: 509, 511
Milgram, Stanley [author]: 140–41
Millar, Jim [police]: 290–92

Minister of Education: 470
Minister of Justice (*see* Graham, Goff, Hanan, Mason, Palmer)
Minster of Police (*see* Banks)
Minister of Social Welfare (*see* Cullen, Shipley)
Ministry of Education: 153, 288, (*see also* Cooper, Deaker, Todd)
Ministry of Justice: 96, 101, 516, 518, 538
Ministry of Women's Affairs: 87
Mitchell, Isabel [lawyer]: 133, 143
Mitchell, Peter [city council lawyer]: 229, 350, 499, 500, 501
Mitchell, Roy [police]: 342
Mokomoko case: 515, 516
Money, John [sexologist]: 253, 264
Moral Foundations of Professional Ethics: 145–46
moral panic: 21, 24, 26, 27 (*see also* mass hysteria, mass psychogenic illness, scapegoating)
Moran, Sandra [lawyer]: 525, 526, 527
Morgan, Lynda [DSW interviewer]: 57, 63, 114–15, 116, 117, 120, 136, 184, 225, 240, 303, 312–13, 314, 320–21, 322, 330, 385, 435, 440
MS [magazine]: 49
Mulberry [Cvc family]: *parents* 227–28, 231, 245–46, 261; *Derwent* 231
Muldoon, Rob [Prime Minister]: 77, 507–08, 535

'N', Mr, case: 152–59
Nation, Gerald [lawyer]: 248, 357, 368, 369–72, 377, 378, 380–82; depositions 383–401; pre-trial applications 404–11; 440, 473–75, 498–99, 505–06
National Advisory Committee on the Prevention of Child Abuse [NACPCA]: 55, 63, 76–77, 89, 90, 103 (*see also* ACIDPOAC)
Nature of Prejudice, The: 40, 41, 209
National Collective of Rape Crisis and Related Groups of Aotearoa (*see* Rape Crisis)
National Study of the Incidence and Severity of Child Abuse and Neglect [USA]: 67
natural justice: 84
New Zealand Association of Psychotherapists: 86, 112, 236, 279
New Zealand Child Abuse Prevention Society seminar: 55–56
New Zealand Childcare Association [NZCA]: 170, 185, 192–95, 198, 233, 247, 397, 443 (*see also* Mary, Rata)
New Zealand Doctor: 142, 151

New Zealand Gazette: 525
New Zealand Law Journal: 92
New Zealand Woman's Weekly: 50, 51, 64
Newman, Barbara [city council administrator]: 204, 206, 215–17, 218, 220, 229, 293
Ney, Philip [psychiatrist]: 116–17, 118
Ngaio [Cvc family]: *parents* 223–24, 225, 227, 230, 252, 261, 307, 310; *Derek* 223, 233, 251, 252, 253, 258, 268, 270, 272–73, 276, 283, 310, 313, 412, 428–29, 432, 435, 426, 468
Nicholl, Rob [police]: 342, 367–68, 379–80, 396
Noble, Judge: 296
North & South: 88, 139, 175, 176, 472
Nursery Crimes: 167–69, 199, 254, 335

Obedience to Authority: 140–41
O'Driscoll, Steven [lawyer]: 527
Official Information Act: 267, 290, 356, 365
On the Objective Study of Crowd Behaviour: 140
Orkney case [UK]: 470, 505, 535
O'Regan, Mr [19th-century lawyer, journalist]: 520
O'Reilly, Laurie [lawyer]: 116, 118, 120, 145 [*see also* ACIDPOAC]
Otago Women's Mental Health Surveys: 60, 65–66

PAIN [Parents Against Injustice]: 131, 138, 142, 147, 149, 150
Palm [Cvc family]: *parents* 228, 231, 241, 247–48, 252–53, 261, 268, 269–70, 307, 310; *Lara* 251, 252–53, 258, 268, 269–71, 272, 276, 283, 287, 294, 310, 313, 323, 393, 412, 429, 432, 435, 436, 452, 460, 463, 468, 479, 480
Palmer, Sir Geoffrey [lawyer, Attorney-General, Minister of Justice 1984–89]: 91–92, 96
Panckhurst, Graham [QC]: 257, 347, 478–95, 496, 497, 499, 505, 507, 509, 517
Paparua Prison: 31, 32, 149, 472, 485
Parsonson, Barry [psychologist]: 518, 530
Parole Board: 518, 524
Pearce, Brian [police]: 244, 292, 293, 297, 342–43, 344–46, 347, 348, 350–52, 365, 471
Pengelly, Jill [lawyer]: 125, 127
Penrose, L.S. [author]: 140, 164
Pine [Cvc family]: *parents* 430; *Frances* 428, 429–31, 431, 435
Pithers, David [UK psychologist]: 133
Plunket Society [Royal New Zealand Society for the Health of Women and Children]: 50, 107, 113, 120

police: 77, 78, 79, 91, 120, 121, 125, 129–30, 133, 136, 137, 146, 151, 152, 153, 162 (*see also* Banks, Broad, Carson, Chappell, Eade, Ell, Gabites, Hardie, Hawkins, Heath, Hyde, inquiry, Jamieson, Jenkins, Legat, McAuley, McMeeking, Marshall, Millar, Mitchell, Nicholl, Pearce, Scott, Smith, Stokes)
Police Association: 290, 518
Policy and Guidelines for the Investigation of Child Sexual Abuse and Serious Physical Abuse [police]: 90
Post Traumatic Stress Disorder [PTSD]: 62, 66
Prescott case [Canada]: 538–39
Press, Christchurch: 57, 111, 112, 113, 114, 115, 121, 158, 161, 163, 222, 228, 246, 281, 325, 355, 372, 401, 405, 411–12, 475, 503, 504, 513, 524, 525, 533
Primary Activation Therapy: 54–55
Principles of the Law of Evidence: 268–69, 441
Private or Public Nightmare, A [Geddis Report II]: 91, 92, 93, 99, 131, 124, 145
Privy Council: 491, 492, 493, 504, 507, 508, 513, 515
Project Guardian [Canada]: 538–39
Prosecution Guidelines [Crown Law Office]: 402
psychiatrists (*see* Bentovim, Bevan-Brown, Ding, Dr 'F', Laing, Ney, Summit, Szasz, Tylden, Watkins, Zelas)
Psychological Medicine: 61
psychologists (*see* Bruck, Ceci, Champion, Davies, Garry, Goodman, Haines, Haye, Jackson/Saphira, Lamb, Le Page, Loftus, 'M', Parsonson, Pithers, Sas, Sidey, Silva, Watson)
Public Finance Act: 90

R v Morgan: 522
R v Styche: 520, 521
Rape Crisis: 40, 44, 49, 74, 76, 236
Rata [Cvc family, NZCA]: *parents*: 192–95, 213, 237–38, 397, 444
Ravenswood, Chris [RAG]: 163
Raymond Donnelly and Co: 291, 407, 478 (*see also* Lange [Chris], Panckhurst, Stanaway, Saunders, Williamson)
Reid, Melanie [journalist]: 164–65, 189, 290, 322, 405, 422, 432, 441, 442–43, 517
religious conservatism: 40, 44–45, 48, 55, 169, 352, 471
Reinfeld, Dora [Cvc supervisor 1983–86]: 174, 175–76, 181–82, 183–86 *pass.*

Richardson, Justice Sir Ivor [CA]: 509, 510, 511, 512, 518–19, 521, 522, 527, 528, 529–30, 531–32, 541
Rigg, Mr [19th-century MP]: 519
right to a fair trial, erosion of: 88–105
Rimu [Cvc family]: *parents*: 178, 191, 233, 298, 330, 460; ***Nadia***: 233
Ritual Action Group [RAG]: 159–66 *pass.*, 199, 203, 254, 273, 307, 394
Ritual Child Abuse: 69, 109, 253, 254–56, 273–74, 330
Rolleston Prison: 32
Ross, Trish [DSW social worker]: 124, 125
Roper, Justice Sir Clinton: 103
Rowan [Cvc family]: *parents* 219, 248
Rowan, John [lawyer]: 505
Royal Australian and New Zealand College of Psychiatrists: 111, 146, 236, 458
Royal Commission on Social Policy: 63
Royal Commission on Tribunals of Inquiry: 545
Russell, Diana [USA sociologist]: 53–54, 56, 63

Saifiti case: 515, 516
St Albans Medical Centre: 128
San Diego Grand Jury Report: 303, 307, 535
Sandi [Cvc staff]: 176, 184, 189, 209–10, 212, 239, 256, 280, 335–36, 358, 374, 376–77, 378, 379, 380, 397, 403, 435
Saphira, Miriam [psychologist]: 51–53, 55, 56, 57, 60, 63, 74, 102, 114, 116, 120, 163, 303, 405
Sas, Louise [Canadian psychologist]: 538, 539–41, 542, 543
Saunders, David [lawyer]: 120, 143, 291
scapegoating: 21, 22, 24, 41, 151–52, 208–09, 421
Scott, Donna [police]: 153, 154, 158
Second International Conference on Children Exposed to Family Violence: 538
Sexual Abuse of Children, The: 51–52, 53, 56
Sexual Abuse of Young Children: 308
Sexual Behaviour in the Human Female: 52
Sharleen [Cvc staff]: 209–10, 265, 357, 374–76, 391, 392, 417–18, 435, 448, 455, 456, 480, 494
Shaw, Colleen [therapist]: 132
Shipley, Jenny [Minister of Social Welfare 1990–93]: 470, 472
Shona [Cvc staff]: 335–36, 357, 368–69, 497
Sidey, Sue: background 147, 154; Cvc case 224–34 *pass.*, 240, 243–44, 247, 249, 256–65 *pass.*, 268–78 *pass.*, 281, 284–87 *pass.*, 293, 298, 303, 305, 308–10, 315–20, 340–43 *pass.*, 385, 432, 436, 440, 462, 463
Sigrid [Cvc staff]: 335, 354, 367–68, 369–70, 374
Silva, Phil [psychologist]: 67
Sim, Val [lawyer]: 525
Smart, Rosemary [therapist]: 279–81, 293, 334–36, 345, 350–51, 374
Smith, Diane [police]: 264, 279, 396
Social Welfare Department (*see* Department of Social Welfare)
social workers: 36, 47, 77–79 (*see* Crossen, DSW, Gillanders, Ross)
Society for the Promotion of Community Standards: 45, 55, 57
Solicitor-General (*see* McGrath)
Solvig [Cvc staff]: 186
somatoform disorder: 62, 63
soul: 36
Sources of Love and Fear, The: 107
Southern Local Government Officers Union (*see* Counihan, Lawson)
Southland Times: 412
Springbok Tour: 74, 175, 197, 370
Stanaway, Brent [lawyer]: 187–88, 273, 291, 310, 314, 377, 402–20, 422–63, 474, 478, 481, 483–84, 487, 490, 491–96, 505, 517
Stapp, Ann-Marie [RAG]: 162, 163
START [Sexual Abuse Therapy and Rehabilitation Team]: 63, 86, 126–27, 128, 131, 134, 138, 143, 145, 148, 165, 201, 230, 281
State Sector Act: 90
statistical claims: child physical abuse 45–46, 47–48; child sexual abuse 51–54, 56–60, 64–68
Stogre Power, Diane [RAG]: 160
Stokes, Neville [police]: 289, 377
Stout, Sir Robert [19th-century MP, judge]: 519–20
Suki [Cvc staff]: 196–97, 199, 209, 236, 379, 394
Sumach [Cvc family]: *parents* 321; ***Molly*** 183, 192, 321, 323, 427, 428, 432, 435, 436, 467, 479, 541
Summary Proceedings Amendment Act/Bill [No.2] 1989: 92, 95, 96, 103
Summers, Sir Montague [author]: 26
Summit, Roland [USA psychiatrist]: 58, 59, 60, 98, 119, 120, 168, 199
Sunday News: 290, 412
Sunday Star: 163
Sunday Times: 163

Susannah [Cvc staff]: 174–75, 178, 188, 189, 192, 195, 212, 223, 233, 247, 256, 265–66, 288, 354, 357, 365, 366, 368–69, 372, 379–80, 435, 456, 459
Swan, Eileen [therapist]: 57–58, 115
Sycamore [Cvc family]: **parents** 175, 178, 191, 223, 225, 226, 298, 329, 332, 384; **Kezia** 191; **Glenda** 332
Sylvia [Cvc staff]: 374
Szasz, Thomas [USA psychiatrist]: 61, 72

Taffs, Douglas [lawyer]: 97
Tamarack [Cvc family]: **Ali** 251
Taylor, Justice [Australia]: 508
Taylor, Neville [lawyer]: 353
Telethon: [1977] 73; [1988] 64–65, 78, 102
THAW [The Health Alternatives for Women]: 170, 236
therapy [counselling]: 36, 54–55, 68–69, 71–76, 82–83 (see also ACC, DSW, Allen, Broadhurst, Chambers, Campbell, Caseley, Collins, Corbett, Crane, Dawson, Dick, Donnelly, Eason, Klein, Locke, MacFarlane, Ravenswood, Smart, Shaw, Swan)
Thomas, Arthur Allan, case: 507–09, 515, 516, 535, 537
Thomas, Justice [CA]: 111, 509–10, 527, 528, 530, 532, 541
Thomas, Mary-Jane [lawyer]: 528
Thompson, Mervyn [white middle-class male]: 102
Thornley, Amama [GP]: 313, 391, 441
Thorp, Justice Sir Thomas [rtd]: 524, 526, 527, 536–37, 538
Till, Nicholas [lawyer]: 485–86
Tipping, Justice [CA]: 526, 527, 528, 530, 531–32, 541
Tizard, John [lawyer]: 525, 526
Todd, Grace [Ministry of Education]: 346, 348, 349, 350, 351
Todorov, Tzvetan [author]: 141, 145
Too Close for Comfort: 63
Trevor-Roper, Hugh [author]: 25–26
Truth: 50, 51, 56, 70, 159, 418
TVNZ/TV1: 88, 142, 281, 282, 283, 471–72
TV3: 164–66, 222, 290, 297, 322, 366, 392, 405, 422, 517
Tylden, Elizabeth [psychiatrist UK]: 133, 142

United Women's Coventions: 40
Understanding Child Sexual Maltreatment: 335
Universal Declaration of Human Rights: 94
Upton, John [QC]: 492–93

van Beynen, Martin [journalist]: 161
van Schreven, Hans [lawyer]: 494, 509, 511–12
Vanishing Hitchhiker, The: 24
Very Touching Book, A: 184–85, 225, 240, 310

Waikato Times: 525
Waitai, Rana [MP]: 525
Walnut [Cvc family]: **grandparent** 288; **Audrey** 251, 288
Ward 24 cases: 89, 116–17, 121, 126, 129, 131–37, 138, 139–40, 142, 143–47, 148
Waring, Marilyn [MP]: 65
Watkins, Bill [psychiatrist]: 113–14, 118, 121, 133, 134, 136, 143, 144, 145, 147
Watson, John [psychologist DSW]: 138, 143, 147, 331
Wealleans, Winston [spouse of Cvc staff member]: 367–68, 369, 374, 517
Weston, Tom [lawyer]: 347, 494–95, 498, 499, 501, 502–03, 509, 511, 512, 529
What's Wrong With Bottoms: 63, 311
Whitman, Mitchell [therapist USA]: 163
Williams, Peter [QC]: 508
Williams Syndrome: 134–35, 223–24
Williamson, Justice Neil [HC]: 28, 257, 273, 393, 400, pre-trial rulings 407–20; trial 423–69; 474–75, 476, 478, 481, 482–84, 487–88, 489–90, 541
Willow [Cvc family]: **parents** 226–27, 300, 304–05, 306, 373
Wilson, Robin [DSW manager]: 82, 302–03
Winnicott, D.W. [psychoanalyst]: 112, 113, 137
witch-hunts [16th and 17th century]: 20–22, 24–26, 30, 31, 38, 41, 69–70, 100, 109, 200, 398, 532
Women Against Pornography: 55, 56
Women's Refuge: 40, 76, 127
Wood Royal Commission [Australia]: 530, 535
Wright, Marshall [City Council administrator]: 214, 229, 232, 234, 236, 242, 247, 263, 499, 500
Wynn Williams and Co: 357, 381, 473–74, 498–99 (see also Nation)

Yew [Cvc family]: *parents* 320, 438–39; *Julian* 320, 340, 342, 361, 369, 371, 378, 379, 414–15, 428, 429, 432, 435, 436, 447, 452, 462, 467

Zelas, Karen [psychiatrist]: *background* 50, 90, 110–16, 118, 120; *other cases*: 'C', 125–26; 'F' 133, 'G' 137; Frontline 142, 143, 145, 147, 151–52; *Cvc case*: investigation 224, 271–72, 273, 283–84, 291, 298, 311, 340, 342, 345–46, 375–76, 388, 395, 395–96, 398; pre-trial applications 407, 410, 413, 419; trial 423–24, 429–30, 440, 444–47, 458, 459, 461, 464; Panckhurst appeal 481, 484, 487, 489; Ablett-Kerr appeal 530, 532, 537 [*see also* ACIDPOAC]